The Correspondence of Henry Oldenburg

Volume VII

1670-1671

The
Correspondence
of
Henry Oldenburg

Edited and Translated by
A. RUPERT HALL & MARIE BOAS HALL

Volume VII
1670-1671

The University of Wisconsin Press

Madison, Milwaukee, and London 1970

Published by
The University of Wisconsin Press
Box 1379, Madison, Wisconsin 53701
The University of Wisconsin Press, Ltd.
27–29 Whitfield Street, London, W. 1
Copyright © 1970 by the
Regents of the University of Wisconsin
All rights reserved
Printed in the Netherlands by
Koninklijke Drukkerij G. J. Thieme N.V., Nijmegen
ISBN 0–299–05630–9
Library of Congress Catalog Card Number 65–11201

Contents

THE CORRESPONDENCE

List of Plates

Preface

Now that our work has reached its seventh volume it needs very little by way of preface except a statement of our grateful indebtedness to colleagues who have patiently answered our queries in many and varied fields. This has been particularly necessary in view of the richness of scientific and technical content of the letters here printed. We are most especially grateful to Dr. D. T. Whiteside of Trinity College, Cambridge, for sharing his generous and expert knowledge of seventeenth-century mathematics, to which both the notes and the Introduction owe a very great deal. If we have made imperfect use of the store of knowledge he has placed at our disposal, the fault is ours, not his.

Dr. J. E. Hofmann greatly assisted us by providing detailed information about Leibniz manuscripts and helping us to obtain a microfilm of the Leibniz-Oldenburg correspondence in the Königliche Bibliothek in Hanover; Dr. Gerda Untermöhlen of the Leibniz-Forschungsbibliothek was also most helpful in this regard. These letters have been published more than once before, but never with translation into a modern language or with commentary. We have gladly availed ourselves of the texts printed by Gerhardt in 1899 and the slightly fuller texts of such letters as have been more recently published in the *Sämtliche Schriften* (to which we have not specifically referred in the headings, since only Gerhardt published the complete Leibniz-Oldenburg correspondence), but we have in all cases taken our texts from the original manuscripts.

Professor Harcourt Brown, whose investigations into seventeenth-century intellectual relations have in many particulars preceded our own, generously shared their results with us and furnished offprints of numerous articles of great value. We are indebted for a like kindness to Professor J. W. Olmsted, whose writings clarified many points for us. We should like to thank, among many others, Mr. E. J. Freeman of the Wellcome Historical Medical Library, Dr. E. H. de Jong of the Academisch Historisch Museum der Rijksuniversiteit in Leiden, Professor Kathleen Coburn of Victoria

College, Toronto, Father Pierre Costabel, Professor B. W. Downs, Dr. Ethel Seaton, Professor Stillman Drake, Mr. R. G. Davies of the Zoology Department of Imperial College, Dr. A. I. Sabra, Dr. E. S. de Beer, and Mrs. Diane Van Helden. We particularly thank our Secretary, Mrs. K. H. Fraser, for her patient typing of this unwieldy material. As always, our main debt must be to the President and Council of the Royal Society and to their Librarian, Mr. I. Kaye, and his assistants.

A. RUPERT HALL
MARIE BOAS HALL

Imperial College
November 1968

Abbreviated Titles

Adelmann
  Howard B. Adelmann, *Marcello Malpighi and the Evolution of Embryology*. 5 vols. Ithaca, N.Y., 1966.

Birch, *Boyle*
  Thomas Birch (ed.), *The Life and Works of the Honourable Robert Boyle*, 2nd ed. 6 vols. London, 1772.

Birch, *History*
  Thomas Birch, *The History of the Royal Society*. 4 vols. London, 1756–57.

B.M.
  British Museum.

BN
  Bibliothèque Nationale, Paris (Lat. = Fonds Latin; Fr. = Fonds Français; N.a.L. = Nouvelles acquisitions Latines; N.a.f. = Nouvelles acquisitions françaises).

Bologna
  Biblioteca Universitaria di Bologna.

Boncompagni
  Bullettino di Bibliografia et di Storia delle Scienze Matematiche e Fisiche, pubblicato di B. Boncompagni, Vol. XVII. Rome, 1884.

Brown
  Harcourt Brown, *Scientific Organizations in Seventeenth Century France*. Baltimore, 1934.

Brown, *Fogel*
  Harcourt Brown, "Martin Fogel e l'idea accademica lincea," in Reale Accademia Nazionale dei Lincei, *Rendiconti della Classe di Scienze morali, storiche e filologiche*, Ser. VI, Vol. XI, fasc. 11–12. Rome, 1936.

Browne, *Travels*
   Edward Browne, *A Brief Account of Some Travels . . . in Europe*, 2nd ed. London,
   1685.

Christ Church Evelyn Letters
   The John Evelyn Papers are at present deposited in the library of Christ Church
   College, Oxford.

C.S.P.D.
   Calendar of State Papers Domestic.

CUL MS. Add.
   Cambridge University Library, Additional Manuscript.

Gerhardt
   C. J. Gerhardt (ed.), *Der Briefwechsel von Gottfried Wilhelm Leibniz mit Mathema-*
   tikern, I. Berlin, 1899.

Grew, *Musaeum*
   Nehemiah Grew, *Musaeum Regalis Societatis. Or A Catalogue & Description of*
   the Natural and Artificial Rarities belonging to the Royal Society and preserved at
   Gresham College. London, 1681.

Hannover MSS.
   Leibniz briefe 695 in the Königliche Bibliothek, Hannover, Germany.

Laurenziana
   R. Biblioteca Mediceo-Laurenziana, Florence, collezione Ashburnham-Libri,
   Catal. Ashb. 1866.

Leiden
   The Library at the Rijksuniversiteit, Leiden.

MHS (1878)
   Massachusetts Historical Society, *Proceedings*, XVI (1878).

Newton, *Correspondence*
   H. W. Turnbull *et al.* (eds.), *The Correspondence of Isaac Newton.* Cambridge,
   1959——.

Notes and Records
   Notes and Records of the Royal Society.

Observatoire
Volumes VI to XII of the bound correspondence of Hevelius, preserved in the library of the Observatoire de Paris. These letters are numbered, not foliated.

Œuvres Complètes
Christiaan Huygens, *Œuvres Complètes*. The Hague, 1888–1950.

Olmsted
J. W. Olmsted, "The Voyage of Jean Richer to Acadia in 1670," *Proc. Am. Phil. Soc.*, CIV (1960), 612–34.

Parkinson
John Parkinson, *Theatrum Botanicum: The Theater of Plants. Or, an Herball of Large Extent*. London, 1640.

Phil. Trans.
Henry Oldenburg (ed.), *Philosophical Transactions: giving some Accompt of the present Undertakings, Studies and Labours of the Ingenious in many considerable parts of the World*. London and Oxford, 1665–77.

Pizzoli
Ugo Pizzoli, *Marcello Malpighi e l'opere sua*. Milan, 1897.

P.R.O.
Public Record Office, London.

Ray, *Further Correspondence*
R. W. T. Gunther (ed.), *Further Correspondence of John Ray*. London, 1928.

Rigaud
[Stephen Jordan Rigaud], *Correspondence of Scientific Men of the Seventeenth Century... in the Collection of ... the Earl of Macclesfield*. 2 vols. Oxford, 1851.

Sämtliche Schriften
Paul Ritter (ed.), *Sämtliche Schriften und Briefe.* . . . Zweite Reihe, Erste Band (Philosophischen Briefwechsel I). Darmstadt, 1926.

Sprat, *History*
Thomas Sprat, *The History of the Royal Society of London, for the Improving of Natural Knowledge* [1667], 3rd ed. London, 1722.

Turnbull, *Gregory*
H. W. Turnbull, *James Gregory Tercentenary Memorial Volume*. London, 1939.

Winthrop Papers
  Papers of the Winthrop family, preserved by the Massachusetts Historical
  Society, Boston, Mass.

Introduction

The correspondence in this seventh volume extends from the spring of 1670 to that of 1671. It was a period of busy activity for Oldenburg: the Royal Society was working vigorously, and besides the literary services for Robert Boyle that had already occupied him for several years Oldenburg was engaged in translating on his own account. Nothing appeared of his Latin version of the *Philosophical Transactions*, perhaps because he was forestalled by that published at Hamburg, though this contained many faults; but his English editions of Steno's *Prodromus*, Charas's *New Experiments upon Vipers*, and Bernier's *Voyages* came successfully from the press. Whether or not Oldenburg's personal circumstances were improved by these ventures, or otherwise, we cannot tell; there is an almost complete lack of personal news in this period.

Oldenburg's foreign correspondence at this time was on balance more significant than the domestic, for his English provincial correspondents embraced a large, bucolic group. The letters of Newburgh, Nelson, Reed, Cotton, and the aged Beale are chiefly interesting as giving a picture of a limited intellectual environment, where even a University trained medical man, lawyer, or clergyman was a rare figure; Adam Martindale figures briefly as a slightly more enterprising rural virtuoso than most. But it was difficult to comprehend the Royal Society's aims in the depths of the countryside, unless one had exceptional drive and ability, connections, and patronage. The provincial correspondents who stand out in this volume had these advantages. The young Flamsteed continued to rise in stature, though inexperience still tinged his growing self-confidence; and through the help of such friends as the Towneleys and Jonas Moore he soon became, in effect, a member of the London scientific circle. It must have been of immense value to him to have such a correspondent as Oldenburg who, besides lending him books, could give him up-to-date information about the work of foreign astronomers and a great deal of useful data. Oldenburg also made him known to the world at large by publishing his predictions in the *Philosophical Transactions*, carefully correcting his bad Latin and hasty English. Flamsteed thus received far more aid in his devotion to science than any provincial of the previous generation, like Henry Power, and one can trace here the emergence of the future Astronomer Royal. Another young scientist of almost equal ability was Martin Lister (Letter 1503), at this time practising medicine at York, a former member of John Ray's circle at Cambridge and so well acquainted with Willughby and Skippon also. Although Lister may be criticized for being conservative and credulous on occasion, he was an extremely keen and observant naturalist, with a detailed knowledge of the flora and fauna of the North. In his letters (as well as in those of his older colleagues) one sees very clearly the difference between the new natural history aiming at exact description and taxonomy, and the traditional country "lore" (largely superstition and fable) represented earlier by Fairfax and here by Israel Tonge. A spider could well serve as a touchstone of this new approach. Willughby, Ray, and Lister (all correspondents in this volume) were forging a new school of natural history.

Lister, like so many of the naturalists of this period, was professionally a physician to whom (as to Malpighi also) the cares of practice could be onerous at times. Other physicians took to chemistry as their science; more distinguished than the obscure practitioners named by Peter Nelson in Letter 1575 was Robert Wittie (first mentioned in Volume VI, Letter 1440), who is of some interest as the pioneer of the English taste for spas, which was to make Bath, Tunbridge Wells, and other towns such great resorts of fashion during the next century and a half. Wittie was confident that the proper analysis of spa waters would provide "an increase of materia medica for the benefit of the inhabitants" of England. Letter 1660 from Robert Selbie portrays, by contrast, a chemical empiric of the type so much distrusted by learned physicians.

Most of the English correspondents show, at some point or other, concern at criticism of the Royal Society commonly associated with the pen of that mysterious character, Henry Stubbe. It is unfortunately impossible to tell how widespread knowledge of and contempt for Stubbe's writings and ravings really were, for the correspondents may have been reacting to news of these things that Oldenburg himself conveyed: Willughby, for example, in Letter 1479 expresses aristocratic disdain in response to a lost letter that must have closely resembled Oldenburg's report to Evelyn (Letter 1482) a week later. It does not appear that anyone took Stubbe himself and his menaces very seriously (except perhaps Glanvill, who was personally attacked); what was deplored was the countenance given to him by dignitaries of the University of Oxford (Letter 1539) and presumably of the College of Physicians—despite the presence of an active and most distinguished group of the latter within the Royal Society itself. There is certainly no sign that criticism had any effects. In a letter to Lady Anne Conway (14 March 1670/1), Henry More, the Cambridge philosopher who had also incurred Stubbe's wrath, made his own contempt very plain:

> At my returne I found a letter of Mr Glanvills here, which signify'd to me how grossly and vehemently Stubbes rayled at me in the coffy houses in Oxford ... all men universally excuse me from medling with such an unworthy person, and it never so much as came into my thoughts to answer him ... [1]

Among foreign correspondents the outstanding newcomer was Leibniz (Letter 1486), as yet a very young man who regarded jurisprudence as his main interest. Leibniz had published one small tract on a mathematical topic already, but he made no claims to mathematical excellence, and his philosophical writing was of a highly speculative, not to say metaphysical character. One can guess already that the official English empirical line would have little appeal to him, but as a beginner he was glad to seek the Royal Society's patronage.

Oldenburg's mind was also recalled to his native Germany by a letter from an old correspondent, P. J. Sachs, and the arrival of the *Miscellanea curiosa*, a new periodical differing in character and content from the well-established *Journal des Sçavans* and *Philosophical Transactions*. Oldenburg does not seem to have admired it greatly, and indeed (despite the continental complaints of the English writing only in English) Germanic Latinity was to become increasingly old-fashioned.

Italy appears in this volume as a great center of interest, with Malpighi dominating the scene. Montanari, also at Bologna, was a new correspondent; a more important one was the English diplomatist at Venice, John Dodington, through whose good offices (and his masters') Oldenburg was enabled to correspond far more freely with Italy than ever before. In Letter 1473 Dodington gave an amusing picture of the complete and complacent ineptitude of the Finch ménage in Florence, to which Oldenburg had so often appealed vainly in the past. Giovanni Alphonso Borelli and the Italian botanist Boccone also appear cursorily as correspondents, as does, once again, Travagino. For the first time Oldenburg had good firsthand news of

[1] Marjorie Hope Nicolson, *Conway Letters* (London, 1930), p. 327.

the Italian scientific scene, and was able to collect not only news of Italian books, but copies of many of them.

Another new focus of communication, after many vain endeavors, was Scandinavia. After the election as Fellow of the Royal Society of the elderly Swedish scholar, Georg Stiernhelm, the "father of Swedish poetry" (Letter 1463), and the visits of the young aspirants Foss and Helmfeld, relations were at last opened with Erasmus Bartholin at Copenhagen and Olaus Rudbeck at Stockholm. A first fruit was the arrival in England of the former's book on the double refraction of Iceland spar, sent through the young Hamburg physician, Paisen, who was lamentably to die prematurely in October 1670. More was to come from Scandinavia (and even Iceland) in subsequent years, Oldenburg's correspondence profiting, as it had in Italy, from strong diplomatic representation in Copenhagen. It does not seem to have been realized in the past what a valuable service the Crown did the Royal Society when it put its diplomatic communications at the Society's disposal.[1]

Of the older northern correspondents, Hevelius was frequently in touch with London as his *Machina coelestis* neared completion; in Letter 1637 he shows that human nature has not altered much in three hundred years! It is interesting that, at this time, the problem of variable stars attracted much attention, astronomers being reasonably confident by now that appearances and disappearances were not merely due to the imperfect record of observations though, as Montanari's experience related here seems to indicate, human errors could complicate the business. Meanwhile, it is worth noting that in Flamsteed, England had produced an astronomer not too timid to criticize the sage of Danzig. From Hamburg, besides matters of botany, Vogel's letters raise a question of interest to historians of science: what was the *Life of Galileo* in discussion between him and Oldenburg? None was in print, except that in the second volume of Thomas Salusbury's *Mathematical Collections and Translations*, a book virtually destroyed in the fire of London. It is likely enough that Oldenburg had access to the unique copy of Vol. II, Part II, of this work, containig the *Life*, which was the property of John Collins and survived into modern times.

Relations with France remained much as before, Vernon's letters giving the best picture of the French scientific scene. For much of this period Huygens was convalescing in Holland, and though it is likely that Justel wrote frequently, few traces of his correspondence remain. J. B. Duhamel

---

[1] For a general discussion, see Ethel Seaton, *The Literary Relations of England and Scandinavia in the Seventeenth Century* (Oxford, 1935).

exchanged a few letters with Oldenburg after his visit to England; it is difficult to believe that he was in any real sense Secretary of the Académie Royale des Sciences since, as he remarked, he went to the King's Library very little. In fact the Académie had very little organization at this period; but as an individual Duhamel did at least ship a number of useful books to England. Huet, now at the Court, was an eager if anatomically ill-informed correspondent, but for some mysterious reason letters both to and from him took an inordinate amount of time to reach their destination.

The hunger of the English for foreign books, and in particular of John Collins for mathematical works, both printed and manuscript, is a notable feature of the correspondence in this volume; it is a pity that Collins's bibliography was not more accurate. He became a most important coadjutor of Oldenburg, indeed in all subjects mathematical his mentor, virtually dictating the letters received by Sluse, for example. Although not generating any original ideas of importance, these two men between them served as intermediaries between the continental mathematicians and the rising generation of younger English ones—James Gregory, Isaac Barrow, and Isaac Newton. (Collins, of course, maintained his own private correspondence with all of these, much of it published by Rigaud, and with a few European figures, notably at this time the Jesuit Bertet at Lyons, who supplied some information about books. But for the continent he relied chiefly upon Oldenburg.) A decade earlier, when John Wallis (during much of this period ill with malaria) and his associates like Christopher Wren had been the main representatives of mathematical knowledge in England—then a backward region in such knowledge—Wallis himself and his friend Sir Kenelm Digby had maintained contact with the great French school of mathematicians (Descartes, Fermat, Roberval, Pascal, Frénicle), while John Pell in Holland had been another link with the Germanic end of Europe as well as France. After a long time in which little had passed either way communications were resumed, initially with France through Justel, then directly with Sluse, and (most important in the long run) with Leibniz. And in the period of the present volume, thanks to Oldenburg and Collins and the long stay in Italy of the Scottish mathematician James Gregory, the English learned of the recent activities of the Italian mathematicians also.

In the fairly lengthy mathematical discussions in this volume two themes dominate: the solution of algebraic equations of high powers, and the basic problems of the calculus. In the first case the issues in question are: can complicated equations be reduced by following regular fixed rules to

simpler forms more readily capable of solution; and can mechanical sche-
mata be drawn up representing the general pattern of sets of equations,
serving in turn to solve a particular equation when it is put into its proper
place in the pattern? Of even greater interest were the procedures developed for obtaining the roots of equations from the intersection of loci (a
plane locus being a circle, a *solid locus* a conic section, and a *linear locus* any
other curve), techniques long familiar to Sluse and Huygens, which were
to be exploited by Barrow in his two sets of published lectures, and further
explored by Newton in papers unprinted at this time, but not without
private circulation.[1]

For example, in Letter 1489 Sluse (here commenting upon Barrow) has
to resolve the quartic equation

$$(I^2 - R^2)(x - b)^2 + I^2 c^2 = R^2 \left(a - \frac{ab}{x}\right)^2;$$

this he constructs as the meet of two hyperbolas

$$\text{(i) locus } (P): \frac{ab}{x} = y;$$

$$\text{(ii) } (DP): (I^2 - R^2)(x - b)^2 + I^2 c^2 = R^2 (a - y)^2.$$

Again, rather more obviously, in Letter 1548 he solves the canonical case
of Alhazen's Problem (finding the points of reflection on a circle) by locat-
ing the intersections of the circle ($x^2 + y^2 = d^2$) and an hyperbola

$$\left(y^2 + \frac{a^2 + bc}{ae} xy + \frac{d^2}{2a} x = \frac{d^2}{e} y + \tfrac{1}{2} d^2\right),$$

once more concealing the analysis upon which the synthetic construction
described in the letter was based. And finally in Letter 1643 Sluse solves
for *y* in the equation

$$y^4 + 2qy^3 + (d^2 + q^2)y^2 = bd^2,$$

and constructs the geometrical solution by the intersection of a circle and
a parabola. This problem leads him to discuss the relationship between the
roots of an equation and maximum and minimum values, determined by
the method of tangents he had already described in his *Mesolabum*.

Hints of the calculus abound in this mathematical correspondence,
though developed wholly in the absence of general concepts, to which the
nearest approach is found in a passage quoted from Isaac Barrow (Letter

[1] On Newton's mathematical writings of this period, see D. T. Whiteside, *The Mathematical Papers of Isaac Newton*, Vol. II, 1667–1670 (Cambridge, 1968).

1590); but Sluse also sees profoundly when he remarks (Letter 1548): "To conclude with one word: *monachos*, tangent, maxima and minima, are one and the same thing." Indeed, Sluse claimed mastery of methods of differentiation more general than those published by Barrow, but these he did not yet communicate to Oldenburg; for an example of a particular differentiation one may refer to Letter 1507, where it is (to quote D. T. Whiteside's words) "Sluse's concern to give a hint to the knowing that he has mastered the mathematical theory of the primary rainbow, *without* giving anything away to anyone who has not mastered it." But, as before, Sluse here suppresses his own analysis of the problem.

These mathematical exchanges were, it will be obvious, solely for the benefit of the knowing, of whom there were very few and Oldenburg not one of them, for which he can hardly be blamed. That the letters of Sluse, in particular, were greatly influential is certain, for they were made available to both Barrow and Newton. Huygens' renewed interest in Alhazen's Problem evidently rekindled that of both Barrow and Sluse in the same topic;[1] Barrow, in his *Lectiones opticae*, published the observation on refraction in the water drop sent by Sluse to Oldenburg in 1667 (Vol. III, p. 596), which in turn stimulated Sluse to write Letter 1507. This was a small world in which several men pursued closely similar lines, often reaching identical results independently and almost simultaneously. In this volume Barrow appears as by far the most able and ingenious English member of the group. The mathematical issues are extraordinarily rich, and much skill in analysis lay behind the rather stilted geometrical form of the letters passing between them.

In experimental optics, of course, the great event of this time was the arrival in England of Bartholin's discovery of double refraction; otherwise the physical sciences had little to report, except astronomy. Here the return of Saturn to the appearance of 1655 (at the other end of the diameter of its orbit), the date at which Huygens had framed his theory of the ring, provided an opportunity for a verification of that theory. The motions of the moon and of Jupiter's satellites still attracted attention, and both presented continuing difficulties. The improvement of telescopes was, as ever, of critical importance, but the benefits to be gained by increasing the focal lengths of objectives were running to a limit with Burattini's 140-foot lens.

In biology the bulk of the correspondence relates to the studies of insects made by Willughby and Lister, of particular interest being Lister's efforts to understand how ants could produce an acid which turned blue

[1] Sluse and Huygens had previously exchanged letters on the same problem.

colors red. In botany there was a long and rambling debate about the rising and falling of the sap in plants, a problem illustrating very clearly the ineffectiveness of unco-ordinated information; here Willughby, Lister, Tonge, and Beale were on much of a level of insight. John Winthrop continued to transmit natural curiosities from New England, and there were always discussions on agriculture and cider. The protracted and acrimonious correspondence in which Regnier De Graaf was involved at last draws to a close without reflecting much to the credit of English physiology, which at this moment had little else to offer as a recompense for its churlishness towards De Graaf. There is less, also, of that ubiquitous seventeenth-century preoccupation with anatomical and medical abnormality, perhaps reflecting the decrease in the number of country virtuosi and the rise of a new generation of biologists like Lister and Ray. The scientific content of this volume is, on the whole, very high.

The Correspondence

1455
Oldenburg to Willughby
3 May 1670

From the memorandum in Royal Society MS. W 3, no. 34

Answ. May 3d. 70. desired to try ye success of all kind of grafting, and to observe, whether Lunations be really considerable.[1]

To send what's observable in ye change of ye Cartrage, I sent him.[2]

Will send him shortly ye Therm[ometer] and soon after ye Barometer. as also Dr Tongs directions of ye duel between spider and toad.[3]

NOTES

Reply to Willughby's Letter 1453 (Vol. VI), received on 18 April.
1 That is, whether the success of the graft varies with the phase of the moon.
2 With Letter 1399 (Vol. VI).
3 See Vol. VI, Letters 1423, 1453.

1456
Oldenburg to Wittie
5 May 1670

From the copy in Royal Society MS. O 2, no. 27

London May 5. 1670

Sir

I have received your Box, and ye discourse upon the mineral substances and liquors, contained therein, and I took the freedom to produce all before the Royall Society at their last meeting,[1] where also was read so much of your paper as concerned the same. They were so well pleased with your ingenuity and labors, yt they enjoined mee to let you know, yt those specimina of Extracts and spirits, made by you of ye Scarborow Spa, were very acceptable to them, and yt they much wish, ye like care and pains were taken by other ingenious persons, yt have opportunityes, about other Medicinal waters in all ye parts of England, as a thing yt would much conduce to ye perfecting of the naturall History of this Island, and to the encrease of ye Materia Medica for ye benefit of ye inhabitants. I doubt not, Sr, but you will still go on in your researches, wch are very commendable, and will extend ym to as many other minerall waters, as are to be found in your, & ye circumjacent quarters, and communicate further, wt you shall from time to time meet wth, worth knowing. And I assure you I shall not hide from ye curious and learned your discoveryes, nor be silent of ye praises due to your merit, being Sir

yr humble and faithful Servant

H. Oldenburg

To Dr Wittie

NOTES

Reply to Letter 1440 (Vol. VI).
1 On 28 April 1670.

1457
Justel to Oldenburg

7 May 1670

From the original in Royal Society MS. I 1, no. 68

le 17 May 1670 [N.S.]

Je me donnerai l'honneur de vous ecrire le plus souvent que ie pourrai.[1] Vous auriez toutes les semaines de mes nouvelles si j'avois de quoy vous entretenir comme ie le souhaitterois bien.

Il ne vous manque qu'un Journal que ie vous envoye par la personne dont ie vous ai parlé. Vous m'obligeres de la vouloir aider et dela conseiller. Nous choisirons quelques pasquinades raisonnables pour vous les envoyer.

On travaille a debrouiller les memoires de Monsieur Thevenot[2] qui estoit aux Indes sils s'impriment vous en aures aussitost.

Monsieur goldolfin[3] vous doit donner un pacquet que ie vous ai envoyé et Mr. Vernon vous fera tenir les regles du mouvement.[4] J'aurai celles de Monsieur Mariotte qu'il m'a promises pour vous.[5] Mr. Vernon vous rendra raison dela reponse de Mr. Mercator.[6] Je vous envoye le traittè dela reunion du Christianisme.[7]

le voyage de Madame allarme bien du monde.[8] l'Empereur ne craint plus rien du costé dela Croatie, le Comte de Serin etant a Vienne l'envoyé du grand seigneur s'en va dans dix ou douze iours.[9] la diete de Pologne s'est rompue et le Roy est fort embarassé. la fin de cet esté nous apprendra des nouvelles.

Monsieur Huggens est toujours malade. On ne croit pas qu'il en puisse rechaper. il y a un nommé Emskirke qui pretend avoir trouvé un passage par le Nort pour aller a la Chine.[10] il dit qu'il va iusques au 80 degrè et qu'il descend puis apres iusques au 33. il a apporté dela peleterie de ce pays la. le Roy le fait lieutenant general de toutes les descouvertes qu'il fera. on ne luy donne point de l'argent. Plusieurs personnes se sont associées avec luy. Vous laves veu en Angleterre.

Je vous envoye la description dune machine qui est utile, á ce que l'on dit; vous en aves, peut estre, oui parler.

la Machine de Dunkirke consiste en deux grands basteaux ou pontons plats de 70. pieds de long et de douze de large, chacun desquels soit fortement ioincts ensemble par les deux bouts, en laissant une espace de cinq pieds au milieu, ou doit estre une roue de 42 pieds de diametre, ayant autour de sa circonference six cuilliers a distance egale de trois pieds de large, quatre de long et deux de profondeur. ceste roue par le moyen d'une vis se hausse et se baisse entre ces deux pontons, selon la profondeur que l'on desire, et par un seul tour vuidera, à ce que l'ingenieur asseure, douze pieds de sable en superficie sur un pied de profondeur, et la vidange s'en fera par le moyen d'une grande cuillier en forme de pesle, laquelle recevant ce sable le iette dans les batteaux qui seront destines pour le recevoir.[11] la roue tournera par le moyen dedeux chevaux, qui marcheront sur une petite platteforme establie sur le ponton. Voila Monsieur tout ce que i'en ai sceu.

ADDRESS

A Monsieur
    Monsieur de grubendol
        á Londres

TRANSLATION

17 May 1670 [N.S.]

I shall give myself the honor of writing to you as often as I can.[1] You would have news from me every week if I had sufficient material to entertain you with, as I should very much like.

You lack only one *Journal*, which I am sending you by the person of whom I spoke to you. You will oblige me by kindly helping and advising him. We shall pick out some passable lampoons to send to you. The memoirs of the Mr. Thevenot who was in the Indies are being sorted out;[2] if they are printed you shall have them immediately.

Mr. Godolphin[3] should give you a packet which I have sent you, and Mr. Vernon will see that you have the laws of motion.[4] I shall have those of Mr. Mariotte, which he has promised me for you.[5] Mr. Vernon will give you the explanation demanded by Mr. Mercator's reply.[6] I send you the treatise on the reunification of Christianity.[7]

Madame's journey alarms many people.[8] The Emperor no longer fears anything from the Croatian side. Count Serenye, who is at Vienna as the envoy of the Sultan, will leave in ten or twelve days.[9] The Diet of Poland has broken up and the King is much embarassed. The end of the summer will bring us news.

Mr. Huygens is still ill. It is believed here that he will not recover. There is a man named Emskirk who claims to have discovered a northern passage to China.[10] He says that it goes up to 80 degrees and then descends to 33. He has brought some furs from that country. The King appoints him lieutenant-general of all the discoveries he shall make, but he gets no money. Several people have associated themselves with him. You have seen him in England.

I am sending you the description of a useful machine (as it is said); you have perhaps heard of it.

The Dunkirk Machine consists of two large hulls or flat pontoons, seventy feet long and twelve wide, each being firmly joined to the other at the two ends, leaving a space five feet wide between, where there is a wheel forty-two feet in diameter which carries on its circumference six buckets, at equally spaced intervals, each three feet wide, four long, and two feet deep. By means of a screw this wheel can be raised and lowered between the two pontoons to suit the depth as one wishes, and with a single revolution (the engineer affirms) will remove twelve cubic feet of sand; the sand will be removed from it by means of a great bucket shaped like a scoop which receives the sand and throws it into boats provided for the purpose.[11] The wheel will be turned by two horses walking on a small platform built on the pontoon. That, Sir, is all I could learn of it.

ADDRESS

　　Mr. Grubendol
　　　London

NOTES

1 Since this is almost a unique letter from Justel in this period, it is impossible to explain the personal allusions in it.
2 Jean Thevenot; see Vol. V, Letter 1014, note 4. The publication of his *Relation d'un Voyage fait au Levant*, begun at Paris in 1664, ended with the completion of the third part in 1684. There was a reprint of the whole in five volumes (1689) and an English translation.
3 Sidney Godolphin (1645–1712), the future statesman, then a page at the Court of Charles II, was first sent to Paris in March/April 1669 to inquire after the health of Henrietta Maria, Charles's mother. In May 1670 he was again sent to France to assist in escorting "Madame" to London (see note 8).
4 No extant letter from Vernon deals with this.
5 See Vol. VI, Letter 1398 and note 7.
6 Presumably this refers to Mercator's paper in *Phil. Trans.*, no. 57 (25 March 1670), 1168–75; see Vol. VI, Letter 1376, note 2. See further, Letter 1513.
7 We have not identified this.
8 "Madame" was Henrietta Anne (1644–70), Duchess of Orléans and fifth daughter of Charles I; she was about to negotiate the Treaty of Dover between Charles II and Louis XIV (signed 1 June 1670, N.S.). She died a month later.
9 According to a contemporary newsletter, "Count Peter Serini" (Serenye seems to be the modern form of this name) married a daughter to Prince Ragotzki and went over to the Emperor.
10 This was possibly Sir Laurence van Heemskerk, well known to Pepys, who had taken service with Charles II; he built and commanded a ship of his own invention, and was involved in a court-martial in the Spring of 1668/9. Possibly the scheme mentioned here was based upon the explorations of Jacob van Heemskerk (1567–1607), who had commanded Barent's expedition to Spitzbergen and Novaya Zemlya in the years 1596–97 and brought back the survivors; they certainly reached 80° N. latitude. There was a large and distinguished family of this name in Holland during the seventeenth century.
11 Presumably the meaning is that the silt falling from the top of the scoop-wheel as it turns falls into a hopper, and thence down a chute into the barges.

1458
Oldenburg to Vernon
9 May 1670

Mentioned in Vernon's reply, Letter 1484, as enclosing a letter from Gregory.

1459
Oldenburg to Winthrop

9 May 1670

From the original in the Winthrop Papers XVI, 39
Printed in MHS (1878), pp. 245-46

London May 9th 1670.

Sir,

I have lately, viz. March 26. 70,[1] written so large, that I shall doe litle else by this opportunity of Dr Pells son,[2] than to referr you to yt letter, and to the Books, I sent you together wth thesame. Only I shall here mention, that, since yt time, here is come abroad a new Hypothesis of the Fluxe and Refluxe of the Sea, devised by one Mr Hyrne,[3] supposing, yt ye Earth, besides ye Diurnal and Annual motion, hath another, directly from North to South, for ye space of 6 hours and some odd minuts, and then again from South to North for ye same time; and yt in this Motion ye Earth does not always move to thesame points, but farther, when we have Spring-tides, yn at other times; And yt ye motion of ye Earth in each vibration from the Spring-tide to ye neap-tide decreaseth, as yt of a Pendulum will doe; and from thence again increases in yesame proportion it decreased, till the Tydes be at ye highest.

From this Hypothesis he pretends to solve all the phaenom[ena] of ye diurnal and menstrual Tydes, adscribing the Annual to meer casualties. Hence he will give a reason, why ye spring tides are all the world over at yesame time, on the same side of the Æquater; and why a place hath the greater tydes, ye farther it is distant from the Æquater, etc.

It would be worth knowing, whether, according to this supposition, it be high water on yr American shore all over, at yesame time it is high water all over the European shore. He affirms particularly, yt in the Bay of Mexico there is but a very litle or no rise and fall of ye water, and pretends to salve this phaenomenon also by his Theory.

Sir, you will doe us and Philosophy a good piece of service to acquaint us wth what particulars you know of the matter of fact in America, and of what you can learne from observing and credible navigators all over that part of the world. This gentleman is very confident of the truth of this Hypothesis, taking the liberty to say in writing, yt he hath been for many years as fully satisfyed in his judgement concerning the Cause of this Phaenomenon, as of any in Nature.

This must be examined by good Observations, and a general and faith-full History of ye Tydes: To wch that you would contribute your and yr friends symbols,[4] is the errant of this letter from Sir

> yr very afft and faithfull servant
> *H. Oldenburg*

The books sent March 26. were; 1, Mr Boyles Continuation of Experiments concerning ye Spring and Weight of the Air. 2. Dr Holders Philosophy of speech. 3. Dr Thrustons Diatriba de respirationis usu primario. [4.] All the Transactions of A. 1669.

ADDRESS

> To his honored Friend
> John Winthrop Esquire
> Governour of Conecticutt
>   in
>   New England.
> To be inquired for at Boston.
> By a friend.

NOTES

Second reply to Letter 1293 (Vol. VI).
1 Vol. VI, Letter 1433.
2 John Pell (1643–1702), son of the mathematician of the same name, was appointed his own heir by his uncle Thomas Pell, a gentleman of the bedchamber to Charles I, who went to America in 1635 and acquired large tracts of land in Westchester County, New York (then and still known as Pelham Manor), and Connecticut. On the death of his uncle in 1669 the younger John went to claim his inheritance, which he did in December 1670, becoming the ancestor of a large colonial family. At the request of Lord Brereton, Winthrop was to meet Pell at Boston, Massachusetts, in September.
3 See Vol. VI, Letter 1432, note 1.
4 "contributions."

1460
Oldenburg to Justel
12 May 1670

Letter 1457 was endorsed by Oldenburg as received on 12 May, and answered the same day.

1461
Oldenburg to Flamsteed
13 May 1670

From the memorandum in Royal Society MS. F 1, no. 60

Answ. May 13. 70. Sent him Transact. of March and April.[1] refer'd Telescope till his coming to London

NOTES

Reply to Letter 1446 (Vol. VI) which arrived on 11 May; it is referred to in Flamsteed's reply, Letter 1466.

1 Nos. 57 (25 March) and 58 (25 April).

1462
Jean Baptiste Duhamel to Oldenburg
14 May 1670

From the original in Royal Society MS. H 1, no. 109

de Paris
ce 24 de May 1670 [N.S.]

Monsieur

Comme Mr Michalest[1] envoye un gros pacquet à Mr Martin, Je l'ay prié d'y mettre les livres, que ie Vous addresse. Il ya 3 livres pour Monsieur Colins, un de Mr frenicle;[2] bachet de la théorie des planetes[3] et le triangle Arithmétique de Monsieur Pascal;[4] Je n'ay encore pû trouver les petits traitez de Mr Payen qui ne sont que des feuilles volantes,[5] ny d'autres livres du mémoire: quoyque ie m'en sois bien informé; ces trois livres coustent 4 livres 5 sols monnoye de france, ie feray mon possible pour en découvrir encore d'autres. outre ces trois livres il y a le Medecin des pauvres; le cours de Médicine en français,[6] et un petit livre de Mr de Cordemois,[7] qui sont pour Vous; Je vous aurois envoyé plusieurs exemplaires de La Lettre de Mr de Cordemois, mais ie nay trouvé que celuyla De relie ce sera quand il vous plaira; enfin il y a deux de mes livres, dont il y en a un que ie Vous prie davoir agréable, lautre est pour Monsieur boyle,[8] ie prends la liberté de luy en écrire. Il y a quelques fautes qui se sont glissés dans limpression, qui ne sont pas dans l'errata, parcequelle nostent pas le sens Vous aurez la bonté de les excuser et beaucoup dautres qui y sont par ma faute, comme cela est presque inevitable. Mon dessein, comme ie me suis donné lhonneur de vous ecrire,[9] est de donner a Nos philosophes le goust de la belle philosophie, et d'expliquer le plus nettement que ie puis les plus belles experiences qui se sont faites de Nostre temps, et qui sont dispersées dans un grand nombre de livres. Je Vous prie Monsieur de ne le lire pas avec toute la severité, que demandent ces sortes d'ouvrages, ce n'est pas que Je ne vous aye grande obligation si Vous avez la bonté de me mander a Vostre Loisir, vostre sentiment dans la verité, et la candour qui Vous sont si naturelles. Vous ne blamerez pas comme Je crois la maniere de traitez les questions en doubtant le plus souvent, car ie scais que Vous n'aimez pas ceux qui sont si forts dogmatistes et qui ne doubtent de rien.

Jay fait mon possible pour trouver un livre du p. fabry; Mais il n'y en a

point, et on ma dit, qu'il ne veut pas qu'on les debite que tous ensemble; il
est retourné a Rome; si ien peut découvrir ie ne manqueray pas de Vous en
envoyer. Jay mis dans les 3 derniers chapitres du mien, ce que iay trouvé
de plus considerable dans celuy du P. Fabry; qui en sont gros et fort long.[10]

comme le pacquet en quoi l'on envoye par mer n'arrivera pas aussitost,
que cette lettre, Je Vous prie d'avoir la bonté d'en avertir Monsieur boyle.
Je suis avec respect Monsieur

Vostre tres humble et tres obeissant serviteur
du hamel p. de St. l.[11]

Je vous prie que quand Vous me ferez l'honneur de méscrire d'envoyer
Vos lettres a Monsieur de St hilaire,[12] car ie les reçois bien plustost, et il ny
a point de port.

ADDRESS
A Monsieur
Monsieur grubendol
Londres

TRANSLATION

Paris
24 May 1670 [N.S.]

Sir

As Mr. Michallet[1] is sending a large package to Mr. Martin, I have requested him
to add to it the books which I intend for you. There are three books for Mr.
Collins: one by Mr. Frénicle,[2] Bachet on planetary theory,[3] and Mr. Pascal's
Triangle arithmétique;[4] I have not yet been able to get hold of the little treatises of
Mr. Payen which are only fugitive sheets,[5] nor of the other books on the list,
although I have a good deal of information about them. These three books cost
four pounds, five shillings in French money. I shall still do my best to find the
others. Besides these three books there are *Le medicin des pauvres*, the *Cours de medicine* in French,[6] and a little book by Mr. de Cordemoy,[7] which are for you. I would
have sent you more copies of Mr. de Cordemoy's letter, but I only found this one
bound up. This will be when you wish. Finally, there are two of my books of which
I hope you will keep one for yourself, the other is for Mr. Boyle;[8] I take the liberty
of writing to him of it. There are some errors which slipped by in the printing
which are not among the errata because they do not confuse the meaning. You
will be good enough to forgive these and many others which are my fault, as is

nearly inevitable. My plan, as I did myself the honor to write to you,[9] is to give our philosophers a taste for the best philosophy and to set out as succinctly as possible the finest experiments of our time, which are dispersed in a large number of books. I beg you, Sir, not to read it with the strictness which this sort of book calls for; which is not to say that I should not be greatly obliged to you if you are good enough to send me at leisure your opinion with that truthfulness and candor so natural to you. You will not, as I think, blame me for my manner of treating the questions, that is to say by doubting most commonly, for I know that you do not care for those who are very dogmatic and doubt nothing.

I have done everything I could to find a book by Père Fabri, but there are no copies and I have been told that he wishes people to buy only complete sets. He has returned to Rome; if I can discover any I shall not fail to send them to you. I have put what I have found most useful in the work of Père Fabri into the last three chapters of my own book; his are very large and long.[10]

As the package which is being sent by sea will not arrive as soon as this letter, I beg you to be so good as to advise Mr. Boyle about it. I am with respect, Sir,

> Your very humble and obedient servant,
> *Duhamel*, Prior of St. Lambert[11]

I beg you when you do me the honor to write me to send your letters to Mr. de St. Hilaire,[12] for I receive them sooner and there is no charge to pay.

ADDRESS

> Mr. Grubendol
> London

NOTES

Jean Baptiste Duhamel (1624–1706) studied at Caen and Paris; he took orders and was appointed a King's almoner (1656). He was nominated Secretary of the Académie Royale des Sciences in 1666, but his office was long performed by the Abbé Gallois while Duhamel accompanied Colbert de Croissy to the peace negotiations at Aix-la-Chapelle in 1668 and afterwards to England (see Letter 1135 and note 8). He returned to France via Holland (see Letter 1223 and note 3). He wrote much, including a history of the Académie des Sciences.

1 Etienne Michallet, printer-in-ordinary to Louis XIV, who printed some of Duhamel's books.

2 No separate volume was ever published under the name of Frénicle de Bessy. It is just possible that the work intended here was his "Traité des triangles rectangles en nombres," though the first printing of this was (apparently) in the Académie des Sciences' *Recueil de . . . traitez de mathématique* (Paris, 1676). However, Frénicle in 1654 drew up a list of his works which were ready for the printer; these include a French translation of Galileo's *Dialogue*, a treatise on aliquot parts, a *Traité des combinaisons* and a "theorie des planètes." The latter of these is mentioned by Claude Mylon (who had seen it) in a letter to Huygens of 1657 (*Œuvres Complètes*, II, 9), and

there is some evidence that others were known to contemporaries, either in manuscript or (as kindly suggested to us by P. Costabel) in printed form, not formally published.

3 Claude Gaspar Bachet (1581–1638) edited an edition of Diophantus (1621) and published *Problemes plaisans et delectables* (Lyons, 1612–many subsequent editions); he also wrote on scholarly subjects but not, it seems, on astronomy. There appears to be a mistake here; the word "bachet" is plainly written, but perhaps Duhamel was confused and Frénicle's tratise (see note 2 above) is really intended.

4 Blaise Pascal, *Traité du Triangle Arithmétique* . . . (Paris, 1665).

5 See Vol. III, pp. 287–89.

6 The first (published anonymously at Paris in 1669) was in fact by Paul Dubé; the second is probably *Nouveau cours de medecine* (also published anonymously at Paris in 1669), a Cartesian work perhaps by Louis Henri de Rivière.

7 G. de Cordemoy [under the pseudonym Desfournelles] *Copie d'une lettre écrite à un sçavant religieux de la Compagnie de Jesus* (Paris, 1669). An English version of this defense of Descartes appeared in 1670.

8 Possibly *De corporum affectionibus tum manifestis tum occultis, libri duo, seu promotae per experimenta philosophiae specimen* (Paris, 1670), of which there is a notice in *Phil. Trans.*, no. 65 (14 November 1670), 2105–2007 (*sic!*).

9 This letter has not been found.

10 See below, Letter 1471 and note 2.

11 "Prieur de St. Lambert"; the date of Duhamel's appointment as prior is uncertain, as is the whereabouts of his house. It is probable that he was prior of St. Lambert des Levées near Saumur (P. Costabel).

12 It seems from a later allusion he was in the French Embassy to London.

1463

Stiernhelm to Oldenburg

17 May 1670

From the original in Royal Society MS. S 1, no. 112

Nobilissimo atque Clarissimo Viro Domino
Henrico Oldenborgio, Societatis Regiae Secretario
et Sodali dignissimo Georg Stiernhielm S.P.D.

Quanta mentem meam perfuderint laetitia Literae Tuae, Vir Nobilissime, verbis condigne exprimere nequeo, intelligens voti me mei, ardentissimique desiderij compotem, in augustissimum Societatis Regiae Collegium, summa omnium voluntate, et consensu, cooptatum: Quo quid mihi sane optatius in vita ac honorificentius obtingere potuerit non video. Lycea, Academice, Athenea, vetera et nova, magno mihi in honore semper et merito habita sunt: Sed quae istorum cum hoc Collegio comparatio? Magna fuerunt, fateor, omnique laude dignissima; quippe matres et magistrae omnium artium et scientiarum, vitae communi proficuarum, simul atque morum et virtutum, quorum cultu mortalium vita misera, beata atque immortalis efficitur. Multos et magnos haec Collegia pepererunt Viros, quorum famam fatis exemptam, nulla abolere potest mortalitas. Cuncta vero haec Collegia, universam eorundem professionem, omnes eorum magistros et alumnos continet et comprehendit, suoque in sinu fovet unum hoc Collegium Societatis Regiae Anglicanum. Huic Syderum Choro alterius instar Apollinis praesidet supremus moderator et arbiter Rex ipse; adsident Regum Filij, Principes, Duces, Magnates, Terrarum Rectores, Comites, Barones, ingenti Succenturiati hominum Nobilissimorum atque omnium Ordinum doctrina et sapientia Clarissimorum virorum caterva. Horum omnium finis ac scopus unus, conquirere, atque in symbolam conferre quidquid in rerum Naturae usquam arte, ingenio, experientia indagari potest, quod vitae communi et Societati humanae utile, atque conducibile sit; unde aliquando certum aliquod et indubium, Philosophiae non verbosae et inanis, sed solidae et generi humano frugiferae, Systema confici possit. Huic caetui tam bonae mentis, tam excelsi conditij, atque salubris instituti, quis se non exoptet dignum adscribi? quis se adscriptum et infertum non serio triumphet? Mihi jam seni, et cum corpusculo meo colluctanti hunc honorem unanimi omnium consensu delatum ex animo gaudeo, ingens me reputans exactae in Literis vitae, exantlatorumque laborum praemium adeptum. De quo Tibi, Vir Nobilissime, totique Collegio, quibus verbis gratias agam non reperio: unum hoc unice promittens, sedulam me daturum operam, ut quidquid ad sanctissimam illam Collegij augustissimi intentionem, decus, et gloriam promovendam pertinere intellcxcro, dum vitali hac fruor aura, enixe ac pro virili accuraturum, ne tanti in me collati beneficij Collegio ulla unquam subitura sit poenitendi causa. Vale Vir Nobilissime, meque Tui amantem redamare perge. Dabam Stockholmi die 17. Maij, Ao 1670.

P.S.   De ijs quos referunt casu subter glaciem in aquas demersos, et postmodum extractos, vitalibus auris restitutos, post multam disquisitionem, unum tandem reperi, hodie etiamnum visum, Hortulanum Serenissimae Reginae in Drottningsholm,[1] annos natum 64. nomine Erich Biörnsson, qui Ao. 1646. die 26. Martij alij cuidam demerso opem laturus, ipse glacie fracta, in aquam incidit, profundam, ut post compertum est, orgyas

18. Incidit circa horum vespertinam sextam; mane ulterius diei hora nona extractus, nullo tum apparente vitae vestigio, in hypocaustum delatus satis calidum, lectoque repositus, stragulis insuper calefactis refocillatus est, ubi post unam alteramve horam, postquam modicum aquae evomuisset, liberius respirare, ac post paucos dies omnibus vitae munijs defungi coepit, nisi quod una aure aquis gelidis obturata, surdaster adhuc hodie maneat. Notoria res est, vir ipse toti Aulae notissimus; Cujus etiam effigiem in rei memoriam depictam, in suis aedibus ostentare non dedignantur Illustrissimi quidam Senatores, inter quos fuit etiam permagnus Dominus Achatius Axelsson, Mareschallus olim Regni Suethiae.[2] Haec non solum ex ore ipsius hominis qui haec passus est, sed etiam ex ore Illustrissimorum Dominorum, Comitis Magni Gabrielis De la Gardie R.S. Cancellarij,[3] item Comitis Gabrielis Oxenstierna, R.S. Mareschalli,[4] Gustavi Soop,[5] Senatoris, et plurim, eodem plane tenore narrata, accepi, ut nullum sit dubium de veritate rei. Nec tales casus apud Nos tam insoliti sunt aut miri, ut de rei veritate cuiquam dubium movere mereantur.

TRANSLATION

Georg Stiernhelm presents many greetings to the very noble and famous Henry Oldenburg, most worthy Fellow and Secretary of the Royal Society

I cannot find fit words to express the joy with which your letter filled my mind, noble Sir, understanding from it the granting of my prayers and ardent desires by my unanimous election into the most august body of the Royal Society. I cannot imagine obtaining anything more desirable and honorific in this life. I have always held in esteem Lycea, Academies, and Athenaea both old and new, as is just, but which of them can be compared with this assembly? They were great, I admit, and worthy of every praise, for they were the mothers and mistresses of al the arts and sciences and of the conveniences of daily life, as well as of morality and virtue, by the cultivation of which the wretchedness of human life is rendered blessed and immortal. Many great men were brought forth by these assemblies, whose fame, superior to fate, no mortality can diminish. But this one English assembly contains and embraces all these assemblies, all their professions, all their masters and pupils, and cherishes them in its bosom. Like a second Apollo the King himself presides as supreme moderator and governor of this band of stars, among whom are to be found the sons of kings, princes, dukes, magnates, landowners, counts, barons, great patrons of noble men, and a host of men of all orders distinguished for their learning and wisdom. Of all these the sole aim and object is to examine and to record everything in nature, wherever it may be, that can be investigated by art, intelligence, and experiment, and that may be useful and profitable to human life, whence may be constructed at some time what is certain and beyond cavil, that is, a system of philosophy not empty and wordy but solid and fruitful to mankind. Who would not desire to be enrolled in a group having so good a purpose, so high a foundation, so sound an object? Who, having been enrolled and introduced, would not rejoice in earnest? I delight in this honor brought by the unanimous voice of all to one who is now aged and enfeebled of body, thinking myself richly rewarded for a life passed in scholarship and the labors I have undergone. I can find no words to repay my thanks for this to you, noble Sir, and to the whole assembly, promising only this, that so long as I breathe I will earnestly and with all my might devote myself to whatever I shall understand to conduce to the promotion of the exalted purpose, honor, and glory of this august assembly, lest the very great favors done me should be the cause of any future regret arising. Farewell, noble Sir, and continue to love one who loves you. Stockholm, 17 May 1670

P.S. Of those men who, they say, were plunged into the water by a fall under the ice, and afterwards were pulled out and restored to life, I at length after much inquiring found one, and saw him today. He is the gardener of H.R.H. the Queen at Drottningsholm,[1] aged 64, by name Erich Biörnsson, who on 26 March 1646, in lending a hand to another man who had fallen in himself, broke the ice and plunged into water which was afterwards found to be eighteen fathoms deep. He fell in about six o'clock in the evening and was rescued about nine o'clock next morning, showing no signs of life. He was taken to a pretty warmly heated room and put to bed, where he was revived with warm coverings; there, within an hour or two, after he had brought up some water, he began to breathe more freely, and after a few days all the normal vital functions returned to him, except that one ear was deafened by the cold water and he remains hard of hearing to this day. The event is notorious and the man himself very well known to all the Court. Certain most illustrious senators, including even the very great Mr. Achates Axelsson, former Marshal of the Kingdom of Sweden,[2] have not been too proud to show in their houses the picture of him painted in memory of the event. I gathered these details not only from the very mouth of the man who suffered the experience, but from the illustrious lords Count Magnus Gabriel de la Gardie,[3] Chancellor to the King of Sweden, Count Gabriel Oxenstjerna,[4] Marshal to the King, Gustav Soop,[5] a Senator, and many others all telling the same tale, so that there can be no doubt of the truth of the event. And such falls are not so unusual or so extraordinary among us that any one need be caused to doubt its truth.

NOTES

Reply to Letter 1339 (Vol. VI).

1 Drottningsholm Castle, Stockholm, was to be—if it was not already—famous for its gardens.

2 We could not identify this man—the family name is both distinguished and common.

3 Magnus Gabriel de la Gardie, Count of Avenburg (1622–86), a general, became Chancellor of the Kingdom and Prime Minister to Charles XI.

4 Gabriel Thureson, Count Oxenstjerna (1641–1707), a nephew of the great Axel Oxenstjerna, fell into disgrace later by becoming a Catholic.

5 Not identified.

1464
Oldenburg to Willughby
17 May 1670

From the memorandum in Royal Society MS. W 3, no. 34

I wrote again May 17th, and told, I had sent by ye care of Le Hunt ye wood wth cartridges:[1] I added Dr Tongs communication of ye combat of spider and Toad, and of ye seedling beeches etc.[2]

NOTES

Reply to Letter 1453 (Vol. VI).

1 These were a second set of larval insects in rotten wood, brought in by Dr. King on 5 May (from Northamptonshire), of which it was ordered that a sample should be sent to Willughby.

2 Evidently this sentence refers to a letter from Tonge now lost. For Tonge's full "relation," see Letter 1467.

1465
E. Browne to Oldenburg

30 May 1670

From the original in Royal Society MS. B 1, no. 152
Printed in Birch, *History*, II, 437–39

May 30. 1670.

Sr

At Kottenberg eight Bohemian miles from Prague are about thirty Silvermines. the hills about the towne are not very high, some of the deepest mines are sixty and some seventy fathom deepe; they have worked here seven hundred yeares, I went into that mine which was first digged but was afterwards left for a long time, but now they dig there again, it is called the Cotna. A Monke walking over the hill in which this mine is, founde a silvertree sticking to his garment, which gave the occasion as they still report of searching after silver in these partes and of digging this first mine. The largest mines are at some distance from the towne Northward where they have also their melting furnaces, the river Elbe being nigh to helpe them in their workes. That mine into which I descended by Ladders nigh to the towne is nineteen fathomes deepe. the cheif veyne of Ore runneth South, & is about a foot in bredth. the Ore contayneth Silver and Copper, so as out of an hundred pounde weight of Ore they ordinarily get an ounce or an ounce and halfe of silver and nine or ten ounces of Copper. a blew earth which they meet with in digging is the most certain signe they have that they are nigh to some veyne of Ore, not long since two men died in this mine having made a fire in it a little before. Some of the Ore of this mine is here at your service.

Nigh to Freyberg in Misnia are divers remarkable silvermines. Some are at an English miles distance others at two, and some are nearer to the towne.

The mine upon the high hill is considerable for its depth, it being deepe above seventy fathom of that country as I was informed, each of which fathoms containeth twelve of their ells and three of their Ells make almost two of our yardes; a depth exceeding any mine I have observed elsewhere.

In another mine called the Himmelfürst or prince of heaven was found ore not long since so rich as in a hundred pounds weight to containe a hundred and thirty marke of silver or sixty five poundes in an hundred, but there was not much of it and when the veynes are richest they are observed to be thinnest of a finger or two fingers breadth, but the ordinary ore holdeth but an ounce or an ounce and half in an hundred pound weight or not so much for if it holdeth but half an ounce they worke it having many helpes to open the body of the Ore whereby it may be melted, as a sort of Silver ore containing lead in it, and the brimstone ore which is founde here, and lead, also the drosse of the metall taken out of the pan and burned two or three times in an open furnace.

The Virgula divina[1] is used here.

The greatest inconvenience to them is the dust in the mines which doth spoyle their lunges and fret their skins.

They have divers sorts of ore which contayne either Silver and Copper, silver and lead or all three, but they worke the ore onely for silver.

Brimstone ore is also digged out of some of these mines, it is hard and stony that which hath red spots is the best, they use a particular furnace to melt the brimstone from its ore the richest of which yieldeth three pounds of brimstone out of an hundred pound of Ore, which as it melteth runneth out of the furnace into water, and is once again melted and purified, some of the brimstone ore containeth silver in it and some copper, and some in a small proportion both.

After that the brimstone is melted from its ore the remainder serveth either to the melting of silver ore or to the making of vitriol.

To the former thus, a proportion of it is cast into the melting furnace with the silver ore to this ende (to use the miners expression) to make the silver ore, which is to harde, fluid.

To the latter, viz. to the making of vitriol thus. they take the ore out of which the brimstone hath been already melted and burne it once again or let it continue burning sometime in the open ayre, then putting it into a large fat or vessell they poure water upon it and after some time let it out and boyle it to a convenient heighth, then poure it into long troughs in which are set up many crosse sticks the purest crystallised vitriol adheareth to the sticks that in powder to the sides and bottome of the trough.

Your humble servant

Edward Brown

NOTES

This letter was read at the meeting of 26 May, when some silver ore from Kottenberg (now Kutna Horá in Czechoslovakia) and minerals from Freiberg (near Dresden) were presented to the Society by Edward Browne. The former mines are described in Browne's *Travels*, p. 162, and the latter at pp. 169–70.

1 "divining rod."

1466
Flamsteed to Oldenburg
30 May 1670

From the original in Royal Society MS. F 1, no. 61

Derby May 30 1670

Sr

Yours of May ye 13 I reaceaved on Friday last[1] with the Phi. Trans. inclosed, from my kinsman[2] for yr civill respects to whom I am as much obliged as ye daily favors to my selfe; which whilst yu cumulate upon mee, you onely make mee so much more in yr debt & unabler to make yu satisfaction: You mention in yr letters one of yrs of Aprill ye 5th, which never came to my hands.[3] My kinsman tells mee yt you intimated, it would be convenient I should performe my praedictions sooner yt yu might communicate them to forreigners who are delighted wth ye heavens, & would willingly waite for such appearances. I accept ye intimations, for commands; and therefore I have set upon ye calculations of ye appearances of ye next yeare, which I find will be more frequent then in this, & ye burden is like to fall heavier on mee; by reason of a sometimes intervening distemper: which yet I hope to beare the better by how much I find the phaenomena will be of more importance: I intend to fit the calculation to London, which I suppose will make them more acceptable.   and if yu thinke it may be convenient, or for ye advancement of our Countries reputation amongst strangers; I shall accordeing to my poore abilities, performe them in Latine.   which will make them more generally understood & usefull: I can shcw in what places & how far (supposing ye Certainty of our tables) ye occultations may be visible: which I intend to doe. I desire yr advice how to publish them, and that yu would please to let me know as soone as yu can what yu may thinke most convenient to be added or varied in my methods, & whether it be better to explaine them in a preface to ye praedictions, or to leave it till I can produce my Comment on ye Mercurius sub sole of Hevelius[4] in which I doe it largely : pray at yr spare houres deigne mee 2 or 3 lines in answer to this which with thanks for yr repects & favors to him is from Sr

Your servant to command
John Flamsteed

P.S. On May 23 last past: I observed the occultation of Antares: when Arcturus was 44° 06' high in ye West, ye Starre was one minute distant from ye limbe of the moon, who presently after, (to wit when Arcturus was elevated 43°–52') seized upon the star, which seemed to goe under the moone, about the lenght of the orientalle foot, (or to Ricciolus of Grimaldi)[5] beneath it: by the altitudes I find the time of ye first phases at 12h-29⅓', of ye subingresse 12h 31$\frac{1}{10}$' pm but my instruments not being too good I dare not be confident but desire yu to let me know what others have observed at London or elsewhere.

Sr this letter was intended to be sent the day it was directed but by a crosse accident failed: since when I have some hopes of seeing London wthin a forthnight when I intend to present my services to yu by word of mouth & confer of the things I mention there wth more liberty.[6] So yt yu need not put yrselfe to ye trouble of answering this My services, pray to Mr Collins when you see him. Yrs

J. F.

ADDRESS

    To Henry Oldenburge
    Esqe At his house in
    the middle of ye Pellmell
    in St Jameses feilds
      Westminster these
        present

NOTES

Reply to Letter 1461.
1 27 May.
2 Named Wilson.
3 Letter 1439 (Vol. VI).
4 Correctly, *Mercurius in sole visus* (Danzig, 1662). In his autobiography, Flamsteed wrote: "The following years, till 1669, I employed my spare hours in calculating the places of the planets, observed by Hevelius, and related in his *Mercurius sub sole visus*, from the Caroline Tables [of Streete]: whereby I found they agreed not so well with the heavens, as I presumed they had . . . " Francis Baily, *An Account of the Revd. John Flamsteed* (London, 1835). Nothing separate was printed, but Flamsteed makes many criticisms of Hevelius in subsequent letters.
5 The system of naming features of the moon after distinguished persons (mainly astronomers,) which is still in use, was devised by Francesco Maria Grimaldi (1618–63) and published in G. B. Riccioli's *Almagestum novum* (Bologna, 1651). "Riccioli" is on the center line of the moon near the eastern rim (Lat. 0°, Long. −70); see, con-

veniently, Edward Sherburne, *The Sphere of Manilius* (London, 1675), pp. 176–78, with map. "Oriental foot" is presumably "eastern limb."

6 Flamsteed(according to the autobiography) went to London in June 1670—not Easter as is stated elsewhere—where he met Oldenburg, Sir Jonas Moore (who became his patron), and others. He was back in Derby by mid-July, when his correspondence resumes, having (apparently) passed through Cambridge, where he met Barrow and Newton. He enrolled as an undergraduate at Jesus College, but not until December after his return home. He did not matriculate.

1467

Tonge to Oldenburg

6 June 1670

From the copy in Royal Society MS. T, no. 35

June 6. 1670

Worthy Sr

I thank you for your last Transactions,[1] wch I received not before. The Reflections I have to make on it and our subject I must reserve to another time. I will here give you such account as I have yet gained of our Duallists.

After I had sometime attended, but not found by my observation, any such large feild—or garden—spiders, as I judged to be overmatches for a well growne Toade, I repaired to the place of the related combat, where I hoped by view of the lists, and relation of Eye and other witnesses to get an accurate accompt of the character and kind of the Spider Victor, and of the time and Season of the year, wherein such might commonly be found; wch particulars of inquiry, I thought most materiall. But my successe hath not hitherto answered my labor and expectation in these points. And I am forced for ye present to leave ye farther enquiry after them to an Eyewitnesse of that memorated combat, made here in this neighbourhood, whom I have employed to find out, and take some of those spiders, wch hee described to mee as of force and courage to attack and overcome a toad, and in ye interim having observed very many small Toads to crawle about this season, I designe myselfe to gather and preserve some of them, and reserve them in glasses, to try if I can find any spider, that will seize on one of them, as I assure my selfe those of ye right fighting-kind will do.

The Duell I enquired after, was not at Hottorne, as I sometime supposed by mistake, but at Marden[2] a small village, some 5. miles from this place, at ye white Lyon formerly a taverne, now an Alehouse. Inquiring of my hoast of ye white lyon an intelligent person and somtimes an able clothier, Hee could give mee no accompt of ye combat I had heard of, fought at his garden pale, and certifyed mee, yt all the spectators thereof, whom I enquired after, saving his cousen, Elias Rolfe, were dead. To him therefore I addressed my selfe, and did not only write downe there on the place from his mouth all such particulars of ye duell, as he did perfectly remember, & ye best description of ye season, and spider, as hee could make, but drew him out with mee, and hee and I did diligently search both the place of ye fight and the adjacent garden, and all ye likely places neare there unto; for such spiders as he described, but found none such as wee desired; to his care therefore I have committed ye farther enquiry after yt particular. The persons hee affirmed to be eye witnesses of ye Tragedy, as well as himselfe, was his father, ye Vintner, who then kept ye taverne there, his mother, ye servants of ye house, and one or two other persons, then accidentally present. After I had made ye best inquiry I could after ye aforesaid persons, and sought in vain for ye spiders; and before I acquainted my host of ye said white lyon at Marden wth my designe, I demanded of him if he had ever heard his Kinsman ye Vintner his Predecessour in yt house, or any other relate any particulars of a fight betwixt a spider and a toad. To wch he answered yt heretofore hee had used clothing, and did constantly frequent a market towne called Mavell in Sussex,[3] about 16 miles distant from Marden, then and now ye place of his habitation, and yt he was credibly informed about 20. years agoe, yt there happened then in an alley of a garden at ye Oake, now ye house of John Marden, a butcher in Mavell aforesaid, a famous combat betwixt a spider and a toad, and hee assured mee, yt one William Whetley a butcher and many other persons, who of his knowledge were yet living in Mavell, would attest upon Oath ye truth of it, and satisfy mee better than hee could concerning the time of ye day and yeare, & ye kind of ye spider, and event of ye fight, wch hee described unto mee according to his best remembrance being very cautious, as I perceived least he should relate any circumstance that might bee contradicted by those persons hee referred mee unto.

Hee positively affirmed, yt ye spider was of ye bignesse of ye end of a child's little finger or bigger; yt she was ye aggressour, but whether ye Toad dyed or not upon ye place, he was not positive, but only said, yt, to ye best of his remembrance, he did dy presently. In my returne homewards from Marden, not far from yt village I encountred one captain Butcher a

Gentleman of a pretty estate, lying there round about his dwelling house, an Industrious & Ingenious Gentleman whose courtesy having induced him to invite mee to a glasse of Cider at his house, and his curiosity to enquire what occasion had drawne mee so far from home, whence by ye acquaintance hee had with mee, he knew I did not often nor easily depart: I acquainted him, it was to enquire after and record a famous duell, wch happened in his neighborhood at Marden in ye time of ye late warre, and wn I had signifyed ye names of ye combatants according to his desire, hee presently affirmed, another combat of ye same kind to have been viewed by an ingenious friend of his, from whom hee promised ye particular description of ye Spiders, season &c. That wch he particularly remembered of ye fight, and manner of it, as related by his learned freind, did perfectly agree wth ye 2 other relations of ye Mavel and Marden duell, wch was this only, yt ye occasion of ye spectators observing these black, and not otherwise easily noted Duellists, was ye squeaking noise of ye Toad, for they all agree, yt ye spider is still ye couragious aggressor, & ye toad a cowardly fugitive. Secondly ye Relations allsoe consent in ye manner of ye Spiders assault & fight, wch is yt she skips upon his back, & fastens her teeth in his neck in ye place where his head is joined to his body, & there bites or pinches him in such a manner, as causes him to squeake through feare or paine. Thirdly, yt ye spider, wn the Toad squeakes speedily dismounts, and attends ye issue, but goes not from him, wch is also her custome in fighting wth great flyes, bees, wasps, &c possibly taught by instinct in that manner to avoid the convulsive twitches of her dying Enimyes, wch in some of them might otherwise prove mortall unto ye victor. I think allso yt wee may set downe ye fourth particular, as agreed on all hands namely yt the toad dyed on ye place, & yt ye spider left not ye lists, till she perceived her enimy to be dead, and stirre no more. For my host of ye white lyon, though hee assert it not positively, yet beleives it was so in yc Mavell duell. To these I have (besides ye better knowne relation of Erasmus in his Colloquyes, as I remember,)[4] now at length, & what I mentioned of Van Helmont,[5] to be added, wch adds some very remarkable particulars to our other relations. Namely yt ye narrow leaved *plantaine*, wch I take to bee our *Ribwort*, is of that force as to cure the toad at once both of his wound & feare, so yt this excellent plant according to his relation is an effectuall antidote not only against the spider poyson, but ye toads cowardize. Now if I may have liberty to argue with Van Helmont, according to his owne principles, it might seeme, yt *Ribwort* were a better Antidote against ye poyson of ye plague, wch seizing ye head kills so suddenly after ye manner of yt of a spider, yn any Amulet (for

I love not yt horrible barbarous Paracelsicall choakeing word Zenexton, fit for no mouth by a Mountebanke, nor any eares but those his silly amuzed Auditors;) even than his highly cryed up Butlers toad, prepared this month.[6] For how should yt defend another against ye most subtile and furious of all poysons by its irradiations wn dead, wch in its life and vigor could not defend it selfe. Besides if those Relations of Erasmus, and Van Helmont be true wch I see no just ground to deny; God himselfe seems to mee by his providence to have ordered these combats for yt very end (though not yt alone, nor perhaps not to yt principally so various and infinite doth his wisdome appeare in every ye most contemptible of his creatures) to informe us off and direct us to a no lesse powerfull than ready and familiar Antidote, against ye most violent sudden & deadly poysons, in wch also his bounteous goodnes reaching & providing for ye toad (one of ye most vile and to us odious creatures) in him for us, is yet more manifest. Pardon this extravagance to my profession. To conclude this relation; Wee have strong presumptions yt ye summer months are ye proper time for this combat, from all relations. My Marden spectator affirms ye spider he saw to have a whitish list[7] downe her back, and before the combat to be all white from ye extremity of her taile: that is to mee a Symptome or accident of breeding time.

Mavell-relator, who allows not that colour, intimates to us, yt it may be sooner or later, than their sitting time; after wch (if I mistake not) some cast their skins. But herein I must request M. Willoughby's information, of whom I long since was informed, that he is curious in such observations.

P.S. june 6. 1670 After ye enclosed accompt, I this day observed some particulars about spiders, not impertinent to be here recorded. Some spiders I found abroad, who caryed their Eggs about with them in a large white bag allmost as big as themselves; some yt were not only white on their tayles, but all over their bodyes: And one pretty large one, on whom there appeared no whitnesse at all. This last I enclosed in a walnut shell, but not so close, as to exclude all ye Air at some cranyes, by wch I observed after a while many very small live spiders of ye same colour and shape of their dam to issue, and looking in upon ye mother spider, I found, she had strangely shrivelled and contracted her selfe in ye bottom of ye wallnut shell, where she lay. This gives mee occasion to inquire whether this be not ye season of their breeding, laying and hatching, in wch some are more forwards than others as it happens in most Animals. And if so, whether yt wch was white all over her body were not a breeder, as ye other was manifestly a hatcher. And concerning this last, that poured out her young from my Wallnut shell, I enquire first, whether there be not some Antipathy betwixt wallnuts, even ye shells, and a spider? 2. Whether these young ones, yt issued so nimbly thence were borne by their dam wthin her body, as it is certain, Adders are in time of danger by theirs, or were somewhere adhaerent to her, as ye apes are said to hang on theirs. I looked earnestly on ye spider before I put it up, both on ye ground, and whilst my com pan ion held her by ye Leg, and yet I perceived none of her brood about her, neither could I easily, had I perceiv[8] any such thing, because of their all-most imperceivable smallnesse, and samenesse of colour with their dam.

To this accident I will adde another, wch befell me this day also and wch possibly may not be inacceptable to M. Willoughby. I took a toad ye largest I could get, in ye Afternoon, according to Helmonts direction, and hanging him neare ye chimney by ye Legs, and set under him not a platter of wax, wch was not at hand, but of white Earthen ware, where into hee hath this evening about sun set voided Earth and water, whereas according to Hellmonts Experiment hee should not have voided any thing at all, till ye 3d day, and then have dyed shortly after: And whether Helmonts toad either did vomit ye Earth hee found ye 3d day in his waxen platter, or he supposed it to be so; It is apparent, yt ye Earth, wch proceeds from mine is indeed his dung, there being yet neare as much of it hanging on his body, as is fallen into ye platter. Upon this observation, I also propound to ye Ingenious these inquiryes, whether to adde ye body of ye powdered toad, or ye wax-platter, be adviseable according to Helmonts direction, or it were better to make trochiskes,[9] as he prescribes of ye dung and pisse only, as having greater power in lesser bulke. The ground of my Inquiry is this: I have found by experience, yt a toads pisse is so hot, yt it will scorche a glove whereon it falls, as a live coale would doe if laid thereon. So yt it is worth inquiry, whether in case many toads were hung up after such manner as mine is, and did void much dung and urin, trocheskes, made of those Excrements only, would not be of more force yn those in wch their Skin, bones &c reduced to powder, were also incorporated. On ye contrary trocheskes made of ye whole body and Excrements, should also be experimented for these reasons: toads this month, and ye latter end of ye last, have some of them a kind of white milky substance, wch may be of the same nature of their pisse, wch started out of ye head of one whilst I endeavoured to bore it through ye head wth a sharpe stick. Other Authors ascribe much to ye body, though van Helmont contradicts them. A Gentl. of my acquaintance, a practitioner in Chirurgery, hath often related unto mee, as frequently experimented by him, yt great toads dryed besides ye knowne virtue they have of staying bleeding, have from some Narcotique faculty a power of suspending the merriest good fellows jollity in ye midst of his cups, if they be privily and unawares conveyed into his pockets. To this accords also ye observation of ye fresh thighbone of a toad, curing ye tooth-Ach, untill it hath been over-dryed, and thereby looses its virtue. Lastly ye wonderfull powder of ye Ashes of calcined Toads to help incontinencie of Urin, even where ye neck of ye bladder is torne, makes for Van Helmont, if wee may not say, yt here ye excrements, urine, and all are operative, because ye calcination is required to be of live-toads, and that ye dry of ye thigh-bone takes away its Narcotique Virtue. And why may not I, all these premises considered, enquire of ye Virtuosi, whether wee may not attribute something of ye admired power, Helmont ascribes to his toads against ye plague, to yt Narcotique power they are endued with, arresting ye furious emotions of bloud and waste of spirits, thence arising, and bringing death so suddenly in ye plague, in ye same manner, as they say involuntary motions of humors in ye Gums and bladder, and those mad friskes of mirth in ye veynes, bloud or other spirits, agitated with bot liquor to extravagancy. Q. Whether ye Insects wch V. Helmont relateth to have been found in his wax-dish, and vomited by ye toad were not ye Insects, whereon ye Toad feeds; for Dr Tong found in ye Excrements of a toad, he suspended (as above related) ye sheaths of ye wings of certain beetles of yt Chrysoprasous, gold and green, colour, wch Van Helmont attributes to ye Muscae ambulantes,[10] vomited by his toad?

Elias Rolfe, son of John Rolfe of Marden in ye county of Kent, aged about 30. years, relates, yt about 20. years agoe wn he was about ye age of 10. or 11. and lived wth his sd father at ye white Lyon in Marden aforesaid, he ye sd Elias being in ye brewhouse wth Anne Hunt servant unto his said father, and Francis Stephens of Marden, he and they heard a strange squeaking noise, and going forth to fetch some billets from ye wood pile hee perceived, yt ye noise, they had heard in the brewhouse, was made by a toad in fight with a spider. The manner of their fight was like yt of 2 fighting cocks, somtimes approaching and sometimes retiring. The manner by wch ye toad did labor to defend himselfe, was by spitting wch he cast from him a foot or 2, and ye spider avoided it by leaping up on high, so yt somtimes she would leap above a foot right up from ye ground. This skirmish continued for ye space of an houre & more, till at last ye spider got upon ye toad & killed him. This spider was a large one of ye bignesse of a childs fingers end, and white bag'd, had a white dun list down her sad coloured back.

NOTES

This copy is endorsed by Oldenburg "Dr Tong of ye combat of a Toad and spider."
1 Probably no. 58 (25 April 1670), containing Letters 1431 and 1453 (Vol. VI).
2 Marden is in Kent, nearly eight miles from Maidstone. Tonge was presumably writing from Sissinghurst.
3 Mayfield.
4 See Erasmus, *The Colloquies* (trans. H. M.; London, 1671) under "Friendship," where a natural "disaccord" between spiders and toads is alluded to, and the toad is said to "cure himself by biting of plantaine leaf" (p. 512).
5 J. B. van Helmont, who held some extremely revolting and silly ideas about the use of toads in making a cure for plague, also relates a tarradiddle about a fighting spider and toad, in which the latter used plantain as a medicine (see *Oriatrike or, Physick Refined*, trans. J. C. [London, 1662], p. 1151).
6 See Van Helmont, *Oriatrike*, p. 1147 ff. Paracelsus' word seems to signify an antidote or panacea.
7 "stripe."
8 "nor could I easily have perceived."
9 A medicated pastille.
10 "walking flies."

1468
Willughby to Oldenburg
7 June 1670

From the original in Royal Society MS. W 3, no. 35

Middleton June 7th

Sr

a t my returne From London I Found one From you here and have received another since in answer to your First. I must confesse my selfe yet a Haeretick, in deniing that the moone has anie influence upon our selves or the Animalls and Vegetables. wee are conversant with having bene defeated in all the attempts I have made to discover it. as by diligently observing the times of Parturition. examining the Braines of Rabbits &c For a long time togather. this or another year (if I live) I purpose carefully to try those observations you mention and diverse other of P. Lauremb.[1] but mee thinks the doctors that Have the oversight of Bedlam might sooner discover whither Lunaticks deserve that name or not. all that I

can gather From a Few I have observed Here in the countrie is that Fits
of the Epilepsia or Phrensie usually seise the patients within 7 daies of the
Full or new moone that is indifferently at all times.

as soone as ever I can get out of a great manie troublesome businesses
that doe now rob mee of most of my time I will againe thoroughly examine
Dr Wrens noble Theorie.[2]　you have corrected an errour I was in that
your Cartrages came from N. England.[3]

I was very sorry I was not so happy to Find you at home, and shall bee
very Fond of your cartrages when I receive them which I expected to have
done last weeke but did not.　that single one you sent mee before is not
yet changed, though set in a very advantagious place. I must acknowledge
my own Dulness in not being able to expound Dr Tongs ingenious riddles
you sent mee in your last and doubt wee must bee Forced to seeke For an
Aenigmaticall sence in the storie of the spider combat. I have described
above 40 sorts of spiders and never yet met with anie of that Bulke I
suppose it must bee the losse of Blood and not poyson that makes ye
spider appear lanker after the battle for ye receptacles of poyson if there bee
anie, must needs bee very small, and ly nearer the little Hooks in Her Head
with which shee strikes. I perceive you have received all mine and am sorry
that this and all the rest should bee so emptie.

your Faithfull Freind and servant
Fra: Willughby

if you please you may give Dr King my thanks for the cartrages[4]

ADDRESS

　　For Mr Henry Oldenburg
　　Secritery to the royall
　　Society in the pallmall
　　　London

POSTMARK　IV　10

NOTES

　　Reply to Letters 1455 and 1464.
1　Petrus Laurenberg (1585–1639), botanist and physician.
2　Compare Letter 1190 (Vol. V).
3　The first set of "cartridges"—originally dispatched with Letter 1399 (Vol. VI)—were
　　in fact produced by Croone (see Vol. VI, Letter 1371).
4　This refers to the second sample, mentioned in Letter 1464.

1469
Oldenburg to Vernon
10 June 1670

Mentioned in Vernon's reply, Letter 1484, as enclosing a letter from Wallis.

1470
Malpighi to Oldenburg
17 June 1670

From the original in Royal Society MS. Malpighi Letters, I, no. 6

Eruditissimo et Praeclarissimo Viro
Dno. Henrico Oldemburg Regiae Societatis Anglicanae Secretario
Marcellus Malpighius S.P.

Avide celebratissimi Highmori epistolam, tua humanitate transmissam, perlegi, tibique pro tanto munere grates rependo.[1] Laetor apud vos bonarum artium incrementa novis Sociorum inventis quotidie vigere, sed taedet hujusmodi laboribus nobis sero perfrui concessum.

Libellum de paralaxi Doctissimi Mengoli hic adjunctum reperies, alter autem de sono nondum luce fruitur.[2] Quid moliantur Florentini Professores, caeterique famosiores Itali ignoro.

Audio Clarissimi Borelli secundum librum de vi precussionis, in quo curiosa quaedam physica pertractantur, laborare sub praelo, quo expedito promissam Aetnae incendij historiam evulgabit.[3] Librorum fasciculum mari transvehendum quamprimum recipies a Dno. Verbequio,[4] vel saltem a Dno. Francisco Teriesi Florentino Mercatore, ad cujus manus primo devenient. Bombycinam historiam vestra munificentia excusam adhuc desidero. Ruri moror, et inchoatas observationes quoquo modo prosequi enitor, mentis enim tenuitatem infensa corporis valetudo sic hebetat, ut quidquam speciosi elaborare desperem. Vale, et me tui addictissimum devinctissimumque reputa.

Dabam in Suburbano Bononiensi die 27. Junij 1670 [N.S.].

ADDRESS

Eruditissimo et Praeclarissimo Viro Domino Henrico
Oldenburg Regiae Societatis Anglicanae
                Secretario
Londini

TRANSLATION

Marcello Malpighi greets the very learned and famous Mr. Henry Oldenburg,
Secretary of the English Royal Society

I have eagerly read the epistle from the worthy Highmore sent to me by your
kindness, and I return you thanks for so considerable a gift.[1] I rejoice because the
new inventions of your Fellows daily stimulate the improvement of useful arts,
but regret that there is so great a delay in our enjoyment of these labors.

You will find here attached the learned Mengoli's little book on parallax, but
the other on sound has not yet come forth.[2] I do not know what the Florentine
professors and other more distinguished Italians are working on.

I hear that the famous Borelli's second volume on the force of percussion is
now in the press. In this he deals with some odd questions in physics and when it is
out of the way he will publish his promised account of the eruption of Etna.[3]

You may soon receive the package of books transported by sea from Mr. Ver-
becke,[4] or at any rate from Mr. Francisco Teriesi, a Florentine merchant into
whose hands it was first entrusted. I am still waiting for the account of the silk
worm, printed by your generosity. I am living in the country and strive to make
scattered observations as best I can, for the ill condition of my body has so dulled
my poor brain that I despair of perfecting any more majestic task. Farewell, and
believe me most devoted and obliged to yourself.

From the suburbs of Bologna, 27 June 1670 [N.S.]

ADDRESS

To the very learned and famous
Mr. Henry Oldenburg, Secretary
   of the English Royal Society
            London

NOTES

Reply to Letter 1368 (Vol. VI).
1 Nathaniel Highmore, *De hysterica et hypochondriaca passione responsio epistolaris ad Dr.
Willis* (London, 1670).
2 Pietro Mengoli, *Refrattione e parallasse solare* (Bologna, 1670); *Speculazioni di musica*
(Bologna, 1670).

3 Borelli's chief work on mechanics in press at this time was *De motionibus naturalibus a gravitate pendentibus liber* (Reggio, 1670) but he was also preparing "Responsio ad censuras ... Honorati Fabri contra librum ... de vi percussionis," appended to *Historia et meteorologia incendii Aetnaei anni 1669* (Reggio Julio, 1670).
4 See Vol. VI, Letter 1450.

1471
Duhamel to Oldenburg
18 June 1670

From the original in Royal Society MS. H 1, no. 110

de Paris ce 28 du juin 1670 [N.S.]

Monsieur

Je ne sçais si Vous avez receu le pacquet que ie vous aj envoyé, et qui est adressé a Monsieur Martin;[1] Je crains qu'il ne soit pas encore arrivé, à cause des destours qu'il a fallu prendre par Rouens et par la Mer. Je vous en envoye un autre de quelques livres Nouvaux du p. fabry, que Vous m'avez tesmoignes souhaiter; un gros tome des premieres qualitez; une nouvelle géometrie, et un autre traité de physique en forme de dialogues;[2] Je ne vous en dis rien; car ie ne pretends pas prévenir vostre iugement. pour Nostre petit livre ie vous le recommande comme a une personne qui peut luy donner le prix.[3] Il se debiste assez bien icy, et quelques professeurs le trouvent assez passable. Mon dessein n'ajant esté que de leur donner envie de s'appliquer a la belle philosphie. Il y a quelques fautes, mais celles n'empeschent pas le sens, et elles sont presque inevitables dans les livres latins. Je laisse a Vostre prudence d'en parler, ou de n'en parler pas dans vos transactions, pourveu qu'il ne soit pas desagreable a Vostre Societé; jen suis satisfait.

Je vais fort rarement a la biblioteque du Roy:[4] ie croy que Nous aurons bientost un iournal ou lon parlera de lusage de la balance de Monsieur de Roberval;[5] le laboratoire est achevé ou lon travaille fortement; on continue lobservatoire. on ma dit qu'il y avoit un nouveau livre d'Astronomie imprimé a Lyon, et composé par un nommè Monsieur Masson.[6] Je vois souvent Monsieur vernon, qui est fort honneste homme, et tres capable, il m'a promis de Vous faire tenir ce pacquet a la premiere occasion;

quand les livres de Monsieur boyle seront imprimes, ie priraj Monsieur de st. hilaire de me les envoyer. on m'avoit dit que lon traduisoit en latin Vos transactions,[7] si on les imprime ie Vous supplie Monsieur de me le faire sçavoir. Je suis avec respect Monsieur

Vostre tres humble et tres obeissant serviteur

j. b. du hamel

ADDRESS

 A Monsieur
 Monsieur de grubendol
  a Londres

TRANSLATION

Paris, 28 June 1670 [N.S.

Sir,

I do not know whether you have received the package I sent to you, addressed to Mr. Martin;[1] I fear that it has not yet arrived because of the detours it has had to follow going by Rouen and the sea. I am sending you another containing some new books of Père Fabri, which you told me you would welcome: a fat tome on the primary qualities; a new geometry; and another treatise on physics in dialogue form.[2] I say nothing to you about them for I do not wish to prejudice your judgment. As for my little book I commend it to you as to a person who can give it a tribute of praise.[3] It is selling pretty well, and some teachers find it pretty good, my purpose having been only to give them some desire to apply themselves to sound philosophy. There are some slips but they don't spoil the sense and they are almost inevitable in Latin books. I leave it to your good sense whether to speak of it in your *Transactions* or not; provided that it [the book] be not disliked by your Society, I shall be satisfied.

I go very rarely to the King's Library;[4] I believe that we shall soon have a *Journal* in which the use of Mr. Roberval's balance will be discussed.[5] The laboratory is finished and they are hard at work. The Observatory is being continued. I have been told of a new book on astronomy by one Mr. Masson printed at Lyons.[6] I often see Mr. Vernon, who is a very decent fellow, and very able; he has promised me to let you have this package at the first opportunity. When Mr. Boyle's books are printed I shall beg Mr. de St. Hilaire to send them to me. I have been told that your *Transactions* are being translated into Latin;[7] if they are being printed I beg you, Sir, to let me know. I am with respect, Sir,

Your very humble and most obedient servant,

J. B. Duhamel

ADDRESS

To Mr. Grubendol
London

NOTES

1 See Letter 1462.
2 Honoré Fabri was engaged on a great survey of knowledge; he had published at Paris in 1666 *Tractatus duo, quorum prior est de plantis et de generatione animalium, posterior de homine*; Oldenburg regarded these as the logical conclusion to the later work *Physica, id est scientia rerum corporearum in decem tractatus distributa* (Lyons, 1669–71)— see his notice of the latter in *Phil. Trans.*, no. 68 (20 February 1670/1), 2082–83. This work was extended subsequently by Fabri into five volumes. He was also author of *Synopsis geometrica* (Lyons, 1669) and *Dialogi physici, quorum primus est de lumine, secundus et tertius de vi percussionis et motu, quartus de humoris elevatione per canaliculum, quintus et sextus de variis selectis* (Lyons, 1669), of which there are notices in *Phil. Trans.*, no. 67 (16 January 1670/1), 2055–59.
3 See Letter 1462, note 8.
4 Despite Fontenelle's authority for the selection of Duhamel as Secretary to the Académie des Sciences by Colbert in 1666—the Académie met in the King's Library— this statement makes it obvious that he did not consider himself as such in effect, while Vernon, for example, considered Gallois to be the official Secretary (see Vol. VI, pp. 6, 504).
5 See Vol. VI, Letter 1409, note 1. Nothing further appeared in the *Journal des Sçavans*.
6 We could not trace this book or its putative author.
7 See Vol. III, p. 66, note 3, and Vol. IV, index, s.v. *Philosophical Transactions*; also below, Letter 1638.

1472
De Graaf to Oldenburg
19 June 1670
From the original in Royal Society MS. G, no. 7

Gratissimum mihi fuit doctissime Oldenburgi quod intellexerim ex transactionibus vestris,[1] quas una cum clarissimi Domini Clarkii epistola ad me mittere dignatus es, sententiam meam de Testibus, gliris Testiculo ad vos misso tam praeclaros invenisse patronos, ut non nisi exiguae quaedam difficultates de seminis generatione remanserint, iis solummodo, qui, refutatis modo sive exturbatis e testibus glandulis cum sui generis parenchymate, concipere non possunt quomodo diversae istae materiae ab invicem separantur, ac propterea medium quoddam excogitarunt, ut eius beneficio materia semini conficiendo idonea a sanguine separaretur: dicunt enim materiam mucosam, qua vascula seminaria, ut aiunt, obducuntur vel membranas tenuissimas, quas inter vascula seminaria n nonnullis animalibus excurrere statui, ad medii vicem obeundam maxime necessariam concipi posse; quibus conceptibus, quandoquidem doctissime Oldenburgi id ita a me desideres, reponsum volo: me vascula illa ita separare posse ut nihil mucosi conspiceatur, atque falli illos qui existimant materiam in liquore, quo testiculus ad vos missus innatat, circa fundum repertam esse materiam mucosam qua vascula mea naturaliter obducuntur; quandoquidem nihil aliud est quam semen e vasculis seminariis agitatione vitri disruptis effusim, nam si vascula conserventur integra, qualia erant dum illa ad vos mitterem, nihil simile reperies: sed concesso quod haec vascula semper et in omnibus animalibus exterius mucosa aliqua materia obducantur, quis mortalium clare explicabit, qua ratione illa medii vicem obire potest? Quod ad alteram sententiam quae statuit membranas tenuissimas inter vascula seminaria excurrentes medii vicem obire, respondemus non necesse est ut requiramus ad tenuissimas illas membranas, quae in nonnullorum animalium testibus visus acie non deteguntur; quandoquidem tale cribrum sive medium habeamus, quod in omnium animalium testibus cuique ad oculum demonstramus, tunicas videlicet vasculorum seminariorum quae longe facilius medii vicem obire possunt quam membranulae tenuissimae inter vascula seminaria excurrentes, quae adhuc aliud vasculorum genus, a nemine hactenus in testibus detectum, desiderarent, per quae seminalis materia ex medio illo ad vascula seminaria veheretur, quae vascula secundum meam opinionem superflua sunt; nam demonstrare possimus [*see Plate I, Fig. 1*] per arterias *A* ad vascula seminaria *BB.* quae in amplexu suo undique detinent sanguinem arteriosum propelli, et in eorum cavitatem partem ponerando semini idoneam deponi, reliquam vero partem in venarum *C.* extremitates ibidem copiose existentes propulsam ad cor redire: atque sic circulari sanguinem spermaticum (si fas sit ita loqui) per vasculorum seminariorum tunicas, quemadmodum meseraicus per tunicas intestinorum. in eodem medio vasa lymphatica lympham suam haurire posse nemini Anatomicorum absurdum videbitur. sed ne ea quae in tractatu nostro pag 80 et alibi pluribus proposuimus hic repetamus, dicemus solummodo nos non posse concipere quare a nobis edoceri volunt *quomodo diversae istae materiae ab arteriis separatae sine aliquo medio separari possint,*[2] quandoquidem in tractatu nostro medium iam depictum assignaverimus. Ad ea quae

C. D. Clarkius in ultima sua epistola de motu seminis per vesiculas tanto fastu proponit nihil aliud respondemus quam quod in praeterita mea epistola[3] de caruncula aperta, et in tractatu meo pag. 88. de caruncula clausa loquar quae si recte consideraverit doctissimus ille vir animadvertet potius se deceptum, quam me proprio meo experimento refutatum; dicit enim C. D. Clarkius quod in angulo communionis *A* [*see Plate I, Fig. 2*]. ita construantur ista vasa, ut semen prius extremum superius vesicularum seminalium *B.* petere debeat, quam per foramen *D.* in urethram exire non aliter ac si vas deferens *E.* incurvato ductu usque ad supremum vesicularum *B.* assenderet, et motus seminis secundum puncta . . . . contigere deberet.

Ego vero constant erassero vasa deferentia *E* [*see Plate I, Fig. 3*]. angusto exitu *I I.* in principio sive collo vesicularum seminalium *FF.* terminari ita ut semen affluens, si caruncula clausa sit (ut ordinario extra veneris actum existit) in vesiculis *OO.* excipiatur. in veneris actu vero dum caruncula aperta est, vel vesiculae *OO.* sunt distente, tunc semen quod per vasa deferentia *EE.* in collum vesicularum *FF* affluit equibene in urethram propelli potest ac debet quam quod e vesiculis *OO* prodit ita ut omne semen non supremum vesicularum seminalium *BB* petere debeat quam per foramen *D* in urethram exire possit.

Pluribus ad longissimam clarissimi medici Clarkii epistolam responderem, nisi desiderio illius satisfacturus, disputationibus nostris finem imponere mallem, speram fore ut clarissimus ille vir imposterum curiosiora quae in Anatomia vestratibus occurrent, mihi sit communicaturus, ego pariter eodem officii genere *C.* illo viro nunquam deero postquam ea ipsi non ingrata [fuere] intellexero.

Salutas pariter meo nomine D. Kingh cuius experimenta circa testes mihi vehementer placuere, et adhuc magis mihi placuisset illius figura si meo modo testiculum in spiritu vini dissolutum exhibuisset.[4] admodum desideramus hic cognoscere experimenta, quibus probat pancreas et alias glandulas non nisi ex vasculis constare, quod nostratibus fere impossibile videtur. Amicissime Oldenburgi cur tardius ad te scripserim est latore huius intelliges,[5] qui mihi plus temporis non concedit quam ut dicam quod sim

> Tuus humillissimus atque
> observantissimus famulus
> *R De Graaf*

raptim delphis 29 Junii 1670 [N.S.]

D. fossius mihi dixit, te aliquid per gallum quemdam ad me misisse, sed nihil hactenus accepi[6]

ADDRESS
   A Monsieur
   Monsieur Oldenburg
      A Londres

TRANSLATION

It was most welcome to me, learned Oldenburg, when from your *Transactions*[1] (which you were so good as to send to me along with the famous Mr. Clarke' letter) I learned that my views concerning the testes had found such distinguished supporters among you after the testis of the dormouse had been sent to you; so that only trifling problems concerning the generation of the semen remained for those alone who, now that little glands have been banished or expelled from the testes together with a special sort of parenchyma, cannot imagine how those different materials can be separated one from another; and accordingly they invent a certain intermediate substance, so that by this device the materials suitable for making the semen may be separated from the blood. For they say that the mucous matter with which, as they put it, the seminal vessels are enveloped, or the very thin membranes which I have established as running between the seminal vessels in several animals, can be conceived as particularly necessary for bringing about the alteration of this intermediate substance.

Since you wish it of me, learned Oldenburg, I am willing to make my reply to these ideas: that I can so separate those vessels that no mucous matter can be seen, and that they are mistaken who suppose the matter observed at the bottom of the fluid containing the testis sent to you to be the mucous matter with which, in the natural state, my vessels are enveloped. For this is nothing but the semen which has escaped from the seminal vessels disrupted by the shaking of the glass container. If the vessels had remained entire (as they were when I sent them to you) you would find nothing of the kind. Yet, admitting that always, and in all animals, these vessels are enveloped with a certain mucous substance, what mortal man will clearly tell us how that can effect the change in the intermediate substance? As for the alternative view, postulating that the very thin membranes running between the seminal vessels bring about the change in the intermediate substance, I reply that it is needless to ask this of those thin membranes (which the sharpest sight fails to discern in the testes of some animals), since we do have such a sieve or intermediary, which can be made plain to anyone's eye in the testis of any animal, that is to say the tunics of the seminal vessels which can far more easily effect the alteration of the intermediate substance than the very little, thin membranes running between the seminal vessels, which demand still another class of vessel (detected by no one in the testis as yet), through which the seminal matter is to be carried from that intermediary to the seminal vessels, such [imaginary] vessels being to my mind superfluous. For we can show [*see Plate I, Fig. 1*] that the arterial blood is propelled through the arteries *A* to the seminal vessels *BB* which everywhere retain it in their grasp; that within their cavities one part [of the blood] which is fit for appropriating to the semen is held back while the rest, propelled to the extremities of the veins *C* and copiously evident there, returns to the heart. And thus the spermatic blood (if one may so term it) is circulated through the tunics of the seminal vessels just as the mesenteric is through the tunics of the intestines. No anatomist will think it absurd that, in the same medium, the lymphatic vessels can attract their lymph. But in order not to repeat here what I have suggested in my treatise on page 80 and in many other places, I shall only say that I cannot imagine why anyone should wish to learn from me "how those different materials can be separated from the arteries without any means of separation,"[2] since in my treatise I had chosen the means [intermediary] now described. I have no other reply to what Mr. Clarke has put forward in his last letter with so much scorn about the motion of the semen through the vesicles than what I wrote in my former letter[3] about the open caruncle, and in my treatise (page 88) about the closed caruncle. If he had taken these into careful consideration that learned man would have seen that it is rather the case that he is mistaken than that I am refuted by my own experiment. For Mr. Clarke says that at the point of union *A* [*see Plate I, Fig. 2*] those vessels are so constructed that the semen ought to reach the very top of the seminal vesicles *B* before issuing through the hole *D* into the urethra, exactly as if the vas deferens *E* ascended by a curvature of the duct to the top of the vesicles *B*, and the movement of the semen ought to occur along the line of dots . . . .

But I steadfastly affirm that the vasa deferentia *E* [*see Plate I, Fig. 3*] are terminated at a narrow exit *II* at the beginning or neck of the seminal vesicles *FF* so that when the caruncle is closed (as is the normal state without sexual activity) the flow of semen may be received into the vesicles *OO*. But in the sexual act when the caruncle is open, or when the vesicles *OO* are distended, then the semen that flowed through the vasa deferentia *EE* into the neck of the vesicles *FF* can just as well be propelled into the urethra and should be so, as that it should come from the vesicles *OO*. So that the whole of the semen should no more seek the top of the seminal vesicles *BB* than pass through the hole *D* into the urethra.

I could say much more in answer to the famous Dr. Clarke's letter but that I prefer to satisfy his wish that we should put an end to our disputations. I hope that this distinguished person will in the future communicate to me whatever unusual points in anatomy crop up among you, and I will never fail in the same service to him when I shall know it is agreeable to him.

Likewise, greet Mr. King from me; his experiments on the testes have pleased me greatly and his figure would have pleased me still more if he had shown the testis dissolved after my fashion in alcohol.[4] We long to know the experiments by which he proves that the pancreas and other glands are made up of nothing but vessels, which seems almost impossible to us. Friend Oldenburg, the bearer of this will tell you why I have written to you so tardily;[5] he leaves me no more time than to say that I am

Your most humble and obedient servant,

R. De Graaf

In haste. Delft, 29 June 1670 [N.S.]

Mr. Foss told me that you had sent something to me by a certain Frenchman, but I have received nothing as yet.[6]

ADDRESS
    To Mr. Oldenburg
        London

NOTES

Reply to Letter 1348 (Vol. VI), sent by Oldenburg to De Graaf at an unknown date. The translation (and perhaps the discussion) is perplexed by an apparent failure to distinguish between the questions: "Is there a medium [intermediate substance] between blood and semen?" and "Is there a *medium* [intermediary agent, or means] preparing semen from blood?"

1 *Phil. Trans.*, no. 52 (17 October 1669), 1403–7 and plate. Oldenburg there quotes from De Graaf's Letter 1244 (Vol. VI).
2 See Vol. VI, pp. 381 and 387. De Graaf's treatise was *De virorum organis generationi inservientibus* (Leiden, 1668).
3 Vol. VI (Letter 1244), p. 123.
4 *Phil. Trans.*, no. 52 (17 October 1669) contains in the plate Edmund King's figure of the structure of the human testis; King was by now fully convinced that "all Glands (so called) are nothing else but Vessels (and their Liquors) variously wrought . . . "
5 We have no other record of this traveler.
6 See Vol. VI, Letter 1413; and for Foss, see Vol. VI, Letter 1421, and below Letter 1510.

1473
Dodington to Oldenburg

24 June 1670

From the original in Royal Society MS. D 1, no. 16

Venice July 4. 1670 [N.S.]

Sr

I have but too long omitted writing to you, not that I am not a lover of scribbling but I have forborn, that I might not trouble you with impertinent leters. Now I write, that you may not have hard thoughts of me touching the Leters you committed to my care, And the Memorandums you honoured me withall.

Those Packetts wch you address'd to yr friend at Paris, were very faythfully delivered as I doubt not but you have heard long since.

At Florence I enquired for Sgr Magalotti, & Sigr Falconieri, the former of wch is now at Padoa, in employment there, as the latter is in Sicily. the Schoole of the Florentine Philosophers being broken up and no manner of Philosophicall experiments advanced since a late book printed there de vacuo:[1] of wch I wonder that his Ma: Resident[2] & Dr Baynes both fellowes of the R. Society, have given you no earlyer accompt.

In yr memorandums I finde 2. lines written in Sr Rob. Murryes hand viz. *To endeavour to get a Copy of a Greek Chymical Book in the D. of Florence's Library recommended formerly to Sr John Fynch for his Maties use.* There is also an Asterisme in the Margent, so that I considered it as a necessary thing, and accordingly address'd my selfe to finde it out and set the matter in motion. But my labour hath binn fruitlesse. First, the Gr. duke was newly dead,[3] and the Library not to be seen. Secondly our stay was very short there, being 3 dayes only. Thirdly when I applyed myselfe to Sr John Fynch in this matter, wth great hopes of some Light from him & doctor Baynes: I was answered alla Fiorentina,[4] wth two Convulsions in their faces & three shruggs of their shoulders. Both averred to me, they never heard a word of it, nor know of any such book, so I came away re infecta,[5] wch doth not a little mortify me, because I much desire to observe the commands, of that most Honourable Person who recommended this Province to me, & I pray give him this acct of it.

Your leter to Sigr Malpighi at Bologna was carefully delivered as you may see by the inclosed wch I send you. 'My stay at that place was one night only so that I had not time for any long discourse wth yt excellent person, whom since I was to see so little, I wish I had not seen at all. Yr other leters to Rome[7] I sent by a friend, who hath delivered them as he since assureth me.

That to Sr Francisco Travagino[8] I have stil by me wth a resolution to delliver the next weeke, by wch time my Lords Ambrs. Entrance and Audience will be over, and I shall have an hower of Leasure to discharge yr comands wth some content to my selfe, which is a double advantage to me. Nor will I be wanting to give you exact accompts not only of the things mention'd in yr noate, but of wt else occurs worthy yr knowledge, and if hitherto, I have binn tardie you may be pleased to impute it to the continual hurry and motion wee have binne in, ever since wee left London, until this week. But Sr not to interrupt yr other thoughts, I will conclude this wth assuring you, I wish all good successe to yr Endeavours in re literaria, and to my selfe ye honor of serving the ends of the R.S. or yr selfe and so I rest Sr

yr must humble faythfull servant
John dodington

Mr. Henry Oldenburg

NOTES

1 Reply to Letter 1364 (Vol. VI).
  We have not identified this, unless it is an obscure allusion to the *Saggi*.
2 Sir John Finch.
3 He died on 13 May 1670.
4 "in the Florentine way."
5 "with my task undone."
6 Letters 1368 (Vol. VI) and 1470.
7 See Letter 1367 (the only one we know of).
8 Letter 1369.

1474
———— to Oldenburg
25 June 1670

From *Phil. Trans.*, no. 65 (14 November 1670), 2092

... a Carthusian of Dyon,[1] having from time to time for divers years taken particular notice of what might occur remarkable in the Constellations of Cygnus and Cassiopea, did on the 10th of December A. 1669. discover a Star of the Third magnitude, beneath the Head of Cygnus, scituated in the Section of the two straight lines, one of which goeth from Lyra to the nearest of the Quadrangle in the Dolphin, and the other from the Eagle to the Star, which is on top of the upper wing of Cygnus.[2]

NOTES

Oldenburg gave the date of this letter as 5 July [N.S.] and described it as a letter from Paris about a new star.

1 Dijon, France.

2 The name of the observer is given as Antelme in Letter 1484; Anthelme Voituret (*c.* 1618–83) became a Carthusian at Dijon in 1641; his interest in astronomy bore fruit in a number of publications, especially a list of star positions (1679). The nova is now assigned to the constellation of Vulpecula (1950 position, RA 19h. 46 min.; dec. $+ 27°$ 11 min.). It never exceeded the third magnitude. See further, Letter 1509.

1475
Hevelius to Oldenburg

25 June 1670

From the original in Royal Society MS. H 2, no. 21

Illustri Viro
Domino Henrico Oldenburg
Illustrissimo Regiae Societatis Secretario
J. Hevelius Salutem

Miraberis sane diuturnum meum silentium, quod tam longo temporis intervallo, postquam lentes pro longissimo illo Telescopio accepi, ne verbulum quidem ad literas Tuas longe mihi gratissimas reposuerim. Causa autem nulla alia fuit, quam quod prius Tubum pro lentibus illis construere, deinde etiam vires illius Tubospicilli explorare voluerim. At vero negotium illud ob artificum supinam negligentiam, postmodum etiam ob hyemis summam frigiditatem, verisque intemperiem, ac modo ob defectum obiectorum cum Planetae fere omnes sub radijs lateant Solis, tum quod noctes apud nos lucidissimae sint, de die in diem hucusque procrastinatum est; sic ut necdum aliquid singulare per Tubum illum, ob dictas causas animadvertere potuerim. Nihilominus tamen nolui diutius responsionem meam differre, ne plane immemor beneficiorum esse videar. Gratias itaque et Tibi et domino Hoockio, praevia officiosissima salutatione, multo habeo, et ago maximas pro multifarijs in me collatis beneficijs; quod non solum haud gravatus fueris mei caussa libros meos divendere, sed etiam lentes egregia opera domini Hookij pro Telescopio 50 fere pedum longo, cum Exellentissimo Microscopio mihi transmittere. Microscopium quantum dijudicare possum, optime exspectationi meae satisfacit; de Telescopio nolo etiam vel quicquam dubitare; quando vero ad Astra illum adhibuero, certius quid de eo Vobis referre potero; inprimis cum Illustris Viri Domini Burattini[1] similes lentes pro Telescopio 62 pedum construendo ad idem obiectum direxero, quas primo tempore mihi dono mittet: prout etiam iam quasdam ab ipso possideo, sedecim viginti, et triginta pedum, quas profecto praeclarissimas esse inveni. Quid autem in specie unusquisque Tubus praestiterit, proximo autumno, deo danti, Vobis aperiam. Sperassem Elaboratorem lentium transmissarum cum 40 lb. sterling fore optime contentum, eo non solum attento, quod mihi, qui olim etiam istis rebus haud parum operam dedi, satis videatur, sed quod etiam aequiori pretio quam 'dominus Rivius eas expoliri promiserat, [1a] tum quod longe brevior lens sit, quam esse debebat: quippe 60 pedum aequare debuerat, cum vix 50 sit pedum: adhaec cum nudas solummodo lentes absque Tubo transmiserit; sed quicquid sit, si Vobis videatur aequum dabitis ipsi adhuc 5 lb sterling. Dioptrum Telescopicum a Clarissimo domino Hoockio promissum avidissime exspecto. Idcirco quam humanissime Vos rogo, ut prima die illum construere curetis; quicquid constiterit, poterit de residua pecunia, quam possides, defalciri, rem ut mihi facietis gratissimam, sic operam daturus, ut nunquam non benevolum Vestrum erga me affectum, quibuscunque modis demereri non nequeam. Quid praeterea in Illustri Societate Nostra, vel Parisiensi peractum et observatum sit, lubens cognoscerem, inprimis Ephemerides Eruditorum a Numeri 49[2] ad haec usque tempora haberem Utinam eas, ut ut reliqua praeclarissima opera Anglice alioquin edita, in commodum totius Literati Orbis, in quem scripta sunt, Latine redderetis; omnes, crede, Literarum Cultores valde Vobis obstringeretis; quantum in Te est, Vir Clarissime, fac ut rem adeo utilissimam ac perquam necessariam suo loco pro viribus promoveas. Nuper die 22 Junij St. n. circa Solstitiam, inquisivi rursus declinationem Magnetis, quam anno 1642, ante viginti octo annos pariter summa industria hic Dantisci observaveram, simul eo tempore etiam mecum sed Regiomonti Clarissimus Linnemannus Professor olim Matheseos;[3] ambo invenimus acum Magnetis eo tempore occasum versus ad 3° 5′ a Septentrione deflectere. Num vero res longe aliter sese habet; quippe declinatio quam studiosissime investigatum ivi, ad 7° 20′ eandem plagam versus omnino vergit; sic ut 28 annorum spatio ad 4° 15′ aucta fuerit. Anno 1635 cum deprehendi tantummodo fere graduum,[4] et anno 1628, si recte memini unius propemodum gradus, nempe ad occasum. Quam declinationem tamen initio huius Seculi, vel exeunte priore ortum versus, et quidem ad 8° 30′ extitisse, Clarissimus Petrus Crügerus Praeceptor olim meus[5] plurimum venerandus constanter asseverabat, imo etiam ea declinatione orientali in describendis Sciatericis semper usus est, prout ex opusculo eius quod de Sciatericis conscripsit luculenter videre est.[6] Ex quibus colligere datur Magnetem olim hic Dantisci ortum versus ad 8°30′ declinasse (sed a quo, et quo anno id observatum sit, id mihi non adeo certo constat) nunc vero anno 1670 occidentem versus ad 7° 20′ excurrere. Deinde ex nostris recentioribus observationibus haud obscure etiam liquet, declinationem hanc Magnetis hic Dantisci, singulis fere Septenis annis, vel accuratius loquendo annis scilicet 6 et 7 mensibus ad integrum gradum, atque sic uno anno 9′ 6″ excrescere. Sed quod satis superque Vestratium observationes Lymhousij prope Londinum habitae, primo a Clarissimo Burrusio[7] anno 1580, deinde a Clarissimo Gontero[8] anno 1622, et denique a Clarissimo Gellebrando[9] anno 1634, confirmare videntur. Primus namque declinationem deprehendit 11° 16′, secundus 5° 36 30″, tertius vero 4° 3′ 30″. Ex duabus prioribus observationibus annorum scilicet 1580 et 1622, provenit motus progressionis anuus 10′ 37″; ex observationibus vero annorum 1622 et 1634, idem motus annuus saltem fit 9′ 25″. Unde mihi subolet motum hunc annuum hoc tempore quasi decrescere; praesertim cum ex meis observationibus annorum videlicet 1642 et 1670 habitis liquidum sit, hunc motum tantummodo nunc esse 9′ 6″. De reliquo autem certissimum est, variationem declinationis Magnetis etiam in uno eodemque dari loco, ut nemo amplius hac de re dubitare possit. Quousque autem haec deflexio progredietur, et quo loco, quave in distantia a vero Meridiano ipsi declinationis lateant limites, observationes sequentium annorum docebunt: inprimis, num haec libratio, et variatio omni tempore, et ubivis locorum futura sit eadem, et sibi omnino constans? adhaec utrum fiet retrograda? an vero, et quandiu mansura sit stationaria: quae omnia ut recte suo tempore, per totum orbem Terrarum detegantur animitus opto. Forte ex his observationibus profundiores contemplationes originem trahent. Ego, in ea fere sum opinione, ex motu Terrae hanc oriri Magnetis diversitatem. Sine dubio, quemadmodum in Luna, certa aliqua datur libratio, sic etiam suo modo in Terra, ex motu illo annuo diurnoque dari posse certam aliquam Librationem, haud apud me est absonum. Variationem atque declinationem enim hanc Magnetis in ipso Magnete, vel in aetheris corporibus latere, neutiquam mihi imaginari possum, nec alias adhuc rationes perspicio, ob quas id ipsum evenire possit, nisi ipsam causam in Globum Terrenum, et in Variationem lineae meridianae rejiciamus. Sed hanc subtillissimam quaestionem sublimioribus Ingenijs disquirendum relinquo. Quid Vos vero hactenus in eadem materia deprehendistis, quaeso communices, praesertim quanta hoc tempore Londini sit Magnetis deviatio, et quorsum vergat; ego, si divinare liceat ex superioribus observationibus tam Vestris, quam Nostris ausim dicere, hoc anno, eandem declinationem quae anno 1634, 4° 3′ 30″ extitit ad orientem, nunc esse hoc anno ad occidentem, et quidem ad 1° 30′ circiter. Num autem probe divinem, vel quantum a vero aberrem, ex Vestris observationibus modo habitis accurate patebit.[10] Caeterum accepi hisce diebus ab homine aliquo ad littus maris Balthici habitanti frustulum succini, quod molle est, instar cerae aliquanto durioris, adeo ut sigillum meum illi infixerim; colorem prae se fert flavam, quali succinum plerumque gaudet; perspicuum est, et flagrat, pari modo ut reliquum succinum, sed odor eius aliquanti est vehementior, ac si certum aliquod bitumen glutinosum esset; nihilominus ex ipso mari hoc anno eiectum, ac in littore inter reliqua frusta succini repertum est. Referebat eo tempore frater eius, homo alias fide dignissimus, se habuisse frustulum succini, quod altera parte molle, altera vero (in qua musca latuit) durissi-mum fuerat. Haec eo fine commemero, cum sciam Illustrissimam Societa-tem, harum rerum esse avidissimam, Cui meo nomine obsequiosa nostra officia, promptissimaque studia, cum voto omnimodae felicitatis debite offeras, etiam atque etiam Te rogo. Vale, et me amore Tuo porro honorate. Dabam Gedani Anno 1670 die 5 Julij st. n.

ADDRESS
 A Monsieur
 Monsieur Grubendol
  A
  Londres
 Franco Antwerpen

TRANSLATION, partly from *Phil. Trans.*, no. 64 (10 October 1670), 2059–61

[J. Hevelius greets the illustrious Mr. Henry Oldenburg, most illustrious Secretary of the Royal Society

You will surely have marveled at my long silence, since in so long a period of time after I had received the lenses for the very long telescope I made no least word of reply to your very welcome letter. However, the cause was no other than my wish to build a tube for those lenses in the first place, and then to test the power of this telescope. But indeed this business has been put off from day to day to this very time by the negligent slackness of the workers, and afterwards by the extreme cold of the winter and an unseasonable spring, until now when our nights are exceedingly bright and there is a lack of objects because almost all the planets are hidden in the sun's rays; so that I could perceive nothing remarkable through that tube, for the reasons stated. Nevertheless, I was reluctant to delay my reply still further lest I should seem wholly neglectful of acts of kindness. Accordingly, I am most grateful to you and to Mr. Hooke (after a very dutiful greeting) and return my thanks for manifold kindnesses towards myself, because not only were you so good as to sell my books on my behalf but also to convey to me, along with a splendid microscope, the lenses for a fifty-foot telescope which were the notable provision of Mr. Hooke. So far as I can judge of the microscope it satisfies my expectations very well; I am reluctant to seem doubtful concerning the telescope too, and as soon as I can direct it to a star I shall be able to tell you something about it more certainly. Especially as I shall direct the similar lenses of the illustrious Mr. Burattini[1] (for a telescope of 62 feet which is to be constructed) to the same object; he is sending them to me as a gift at the first opportunity. I already possess some of his lenses of sixteen, twenty, and thirty feet, which I have found to be absolutely outstanding. Next autumn, God willing, I shall disclose to you the results furnished by each telescope. I had hoped that the maker of the lenses sent me would have been quite content with £40 sterling, not only because it seemed to me quite enough (having devoted no little labor to these things in the past), but because he had promised to polish them for a better price than Mr. Reeve;[1a] yet the lens is much shorter [in focal length] than it ought to be, that is barely 50 feet, whereas it should be of 60 feet. Moreover, he sent only the bare lenses without a tube. However that may be, if it seems fair to you, you may pay him another £5. I eagerly await the telescopic sight promised by the famous Mr. Hooke. Accordingly I beg you to be so kind as to see to its construction as soon as possible; the maker of it can be satisfied from the remaining money that you have. You will do something most welcome to me, so that I shall strive never to fail to deserve in every way your kind regard for me. I would gladly learn what further things are done or observed in our illustrious Society and in that of Paris, and in particular I would like the *Transactions* of the learned from No. 49[2] to the present time.]

Would to God, that those [and other] Excellent Books that are publish't in English, were, for the benefit of the whole Learned World, made Latin: All Learned men would be exceedingly obliged to you for it. I am perswaded, Sir, you will do your part in taking care, that so useful and so necessary work may not be left undone.

Lately, on the 22th. of June (st. n.) about the time of the Solstice, I was searching after the present Declination of the Magnet, which 28 years ago (vid. A. 1642) I had likewise observed here [at Danzig] with great care; as about the same time at Konigsberg Monsieur Linnemannus the then Professor of the Mathematicks there,[3] had observed also. We both found the Magnetick Needle at that time to decline from the North 3° 5′ West-ward. But now it is far otherwise; for it declines at present, as I have very carefully observed, 7° 20′ to the same Quarter; so that in the space of twenty eight years, that declination is increased 4° 15′. [In the year 1635 as I understood it was only about ———,[4] and] In the year 1628, if I remember aright, I found it near 1. degree West-ward: Which declination was affirmed by the Learned Petrus Crugerus (once my worthy Praeceptor)[5] to have been, about the beginning of this Age, or the end of the next foregoing, 8° 30′ East-ward; the same Crugerus also making use of that Oriental Declination in describing all his Dyals, as may be seen in the Tract he hath written of the same.[6] [From which it may be gathered that the magnet here at Danzig formerly declined 8° 30′ eastward], though it be not certainly known, by whom, and in what year that Observation was made. [And now in the year 1670 it actually points 7° 20′ toward the west].

Further, It appears by our more recent Observations, that this Declination of the Load-stone doth here, at Dantzick, almost every seventh year, or, to speak more precisely, every six year and seven months, increase to one whole degree and so each year, to 9′ 0″. Which is sufficiently confirmed by the Observations made at Lime-house near London, by those three famous English men [first by Borough[7] in 1580, then by Gunter[8] in 1622 and lastly by Gellibrand[9] in 1634. For the first found the declination to be 11° 16′, the second 5° 36′ 30″, and the third 4° 3′ 30″. From the two earlier observations, of 1580 and 1622, the annual shift amounts to 10′ 37″; from those of 1622 and 1634 the same annual shift becomes at least 9′ 25″. Whence I draw a notion that at this time the annual shift is decreasing, especially as it is obvious from my observations of 1642 and 1670, that this shift is now only 9′ 6″.]

Lastly, It being now certain, that the Needles Declination varieth in one and the same place [so that no one can have doubts of this any longer]; the accurate Observations of the subsequent years will shew, How far this Deflexion will proceed, and where, and in what distance from the true Meridian, the very bounds of this Declination really are; especially, whether this Libration and Variation will be the same, and regular at all times and in all places; [whether it will become retrograde;] or whether, and how long, it will remain Stationary. All which particulars that they may be accurately discovered, is a thing very much desired. Possibly considerable speculations and researches may arise from such Observations. As for me, I am almost of the opinion, that this Magnetical Diversity comes from the Motion of the Earth. Doubtless, as there is a certain Libration in the Moon, so 'tis not absurd to me, to hold a kind of Libration in the Earth, from the Annual and Diurnal motion of the same. For that the cause of this Declination and Variation of the Load-stone is inherent in the Stone it self, or to be ascribed to Æthereal Corpuscles, is not imaginable by me; nor can I yet devise any cause of those Appearances, except we impute them to the Globe of the Earth, and the Variation of the Meridian. But this subtile Question I leave to deeper Wits to discusse. What you in England have [hitherto learned] in this matter, I should be very glad to be informed of [, particularly what is the present magnetic declination in London, and in which direction; for my part, if I may guess from the above observations (both yours and ours) I make bold to say, that the declination which was 4° 3′ 30″ eastwards in 1634 has now become westward, about 1° 30′. It will appear from the observations you make now, accurately, whether I have guessed rightly or how much I err from the truth.[10]

Furthermore,] I lately received from one, that liveth on the side of the Baltick Sea, a piece of Amber, which is so soft, [like a rather hard wax] that I printed my Seal on it. It is yellowish, as most Amber is; transparent, and burning as other Amber; but its scent stronger, as if it were a kind of glutinous Bitumen; and yet it hath been cast up from the Sea this year, and was found [on the shore] among other pieces. His Brother, a very credible person, related at the same time, that he had been master of a small piece of Amber, soft on one side, and very hard on the other, wherein lay buried a Fly. [This I note because I know that the very illustrious Society hankers after this kind of thing. I beg you again and again to offer it, on my behalf, my most humble services and ready zeal, with a wish for every kind of success, in due fashion. Farewell, and continue to honor me with your affection. Danzig, 5 July 1670, N.S.

ADDRESS

To Mr. Grubendol
  London
Postfree to Antwerp

NOTES

Reply to Letter 1262 (Vol. VI). The passages in square brackets have been translated by the editors.

1 Titus Livius Burattini (1617–81) was an Italian astronomer living in Poland, often mentioned previously in Hevelius' correspondence.

1a Compare Vol. IV, pp. 581–82.

2 Dated 19 July 1669.

3 Albrecht Linnemann (or Linemann, 1603–53) taught mathematics at Königsberg from about 1630, and also in Holland. He was a prolific writer on practical mathematics.

4 The number is omitted from the original.

5 Petrus Crüger (1580–1639) taught mathematics at Danzig from 1606 onward and received the title of professor in the year of his death. He wrote much on astronomy —mainly in German.

6 Among Crüger's many publications we have found no separate work on dialing listed, though he did publish a *Doctrinam astronomiae sphaericam* (Danzig, 1635).

7 William Borough (1537–98), of Limehouse, was a master pilot who became Comptroller of the Navy. His work on variation is described in *A Discourse of the Variation of the Cumpas* (London, 1581).

8 Edmund Gunter (1581–1626), a well-known applied mathematician, was Gresham Professor of Astronomy after 1619. His geomagnetic observations at Limehouse in 1622 are detailed in his *Description and Use of the Sector, Cross-staff and other Instruments* (London, 1623).

9 Henry Gellibrand (1597–1636) succeeded Gunter at Gresham College. In *A Discourse Mathematicall on the Variation of the Magneticall Needle* (London, 1635), he related observations made at Deptford and elsewhere in 1633 and 1634, confirming John Marr's earlier observation that the magnetic declination had lessened since 1622. This led Henry Bond to predict zero variation at London for 1657.

10 In his reply (Letter 1520) Oldenburg gave the variation as 2° 18′ West.

1476
Oldenburg to Newburgh
28 June 1670

Mentioned in Newburgh's reply, Letter 1481.

1477
Oldenburg to Willughby
28 June 1670

From the memorandum in Royal Society MS. W 3, no. 35

Answ. june 28. 70.
recommended Dr Wrens motion, the Moons influence upon animals and vegetables; the flying spiders. and given notice of Grube,[1] Charas;[2] and Cordemoy's Moses Cartazanas.[3] of stub.[4]

NOTES

Reply to Letter 1468. The first three points recorded have all occurred in the previous correspondence.

1 No doubt the book was Hermann Grube's *Commentarius de modo simplicium medicamentorum facultates cognoscendi* (Copenhagen and Frankfurt, 1669), reviewed in *Phil. Trans.*, no. 60 (20 June 1670), 1085–86.

2 Presumably *New Experiments upon Vipers* (London, 1670); see Vol. VI, Letter 1410.

3 Oldenburg was clearly writing in haste and confused Cordemoy's defense of Descartes (see Letter 1462, note 7) with Johann Amerpoel, *Cartesius Mosaizans* (Leeuwarden, 1669), an attempt to reconcile Cartesian philosophy with "Mosaic history" which is reviewed in *Phil. Trans.*, no. 59 (23 May 1670), 1053–54.

4 We cannot tell which of Stubbe's books against Glanvill and the Royal Society Oldenburg may have mentioned here, as the exact moments of their appearance are uncertain; see Vol. VI, Letter 1248, note 5, and below, Letter 1482 and its note 2.

1478
Wittie to Oldenburg
4 July 1670
From the original in Royal Society MS. W 3, no. 47

Worthy Sir,

According to my promise, I have sent the black sediment that falls to the Bottome upon the change of the water with Gall, after it has stood some howres; It never came neer the fire, but as it comes out of the well I strain it from all sabulous mixture, & put in the gall very grosse, & so strain it againe after it is coloured. In the paper signed ♂ you have the same powder calcined. Now this I conceive to be the Iron, the calcined powder being like the scoria ♂tis.[1] I have also inclosed a piece of the Earth, that falling from the Cliffe about 6 score paces from the well, turnes into this hard substance, & is doubtles an Iron stone, wch being put into a Smiths forge flowes like metal, & out of wch a Gentleman well skill'd in that Art, & imployed in the Iron mines in Darbyshire said that he could extract Iron. Sir, I have also sent you a little of the Nitre wch I take of the mineralls of this water; according to the processe I mentioned in my papers sent before, signed wth the letter B.[2]

Honoured Sir, I must now return you my humble thanks for your obliging letter; wch before I did expresse to Mr Martyn with desire to impart it to your selfe, being not willing to interrupt your weighty affaires wth bare complements. I must also ever acknowledge my deep obligations to those noble Gentlemen of the Royall Society for their candour & condescention to take notice of my weake endeavours; whom I wish I were able or worthy to serve in any thing. I have some notions wch ere long I shall make publick in defence of this water, wch has been blasted by an angry Brother of our Faculty;[3] wherein I have occasion (through him) to speake concerning the petrifying well at Knaresbrough, called the dropping well, & the causes of Petrification in Springs &c. Not worthy indeed to be looked on by such piercing eyes: Yet as to the things that relate to the water I am certain I have truth on my side, & as to other things that fall in to be discoursed of by the way, I shall in modesty offer my reasons. Sir, I leave those papers to be disposed of as you please, wch if they may be serviceable to the publick,

I am content they be exposed as in your letter you expressed.[4] This from Honoured Sir,

Your most humble & faithfull servant

R. Wittie

York
Monday July 4th 70

ADDRESS

   For the much Honoured
   Henry Oldenburg Esq
     these
      London

NOTES

Reply to Letter 1456, read at the meeting of 21 July, when the specimens were presented.
1 "scoria Martis": crude iron oxide.
2 See Letter 1440 (Vol. VI, p. 607).
3 Nathaniel Highmore; see Vol. VI, Letter 1440 and note 7.
4 Presumably in his actual letter (though not in the copy, Letter 1456) Oldenburg had expressed his intention of printing Letter 1440 in his *Philosophical Transactions*.

1479

Willughby to Oldenburg

4 July 1670

From the original in Royal Society MS. W 3, no. 36

Middleton July 4th

Sr

The same post that brought mee yours, brought Mr Wray an account From Dr Hulse of the Flying of Spiders.[1] which about the same time was both observed by Him and mr Lister, whose letter upon that subiect mr Wray formerly sent you, and you printed.[2] mr Le-Hunt must bee called to account for your rarer Cartridges.[3] which I have not yet received, and I doubt may bee spoyled before they come to my hands. manie thanks for your accounts of the severall new bookes. I doubt not but Stubs has now exhausted Himselfe quite of His Venome. and may bee as safely dealt with as Redis Viper after severall bitings or Dr Tongues spiders after the combate. Hee must by all meanes bee soundly chastised. for the ignorant Hectors doe every where with a great deal of insolence challenge us to answer him. there is an errour in your last Transactions but one, which I hope would have been corrected in your last, but I find is not.[4] it is in our account of the bleeding of Trees, where the word morning is mistaken for noone our sence beeing, that a sunshinie morning, after a Frostie night, makes the Trees bleed afresh soone after sun rise but this renewed bleeding usually ceases before no one about 10 or 11 a clock; which mr Lister now confirmes in a letter to Mr Wray observing 1. that in ye monthes november, december, Jan. Feb. and part of March, that Sycamore never bled but after a Frost. which yet it did for above 40 times in that time beginning after a frost and then ceasing againe. 2. the frost did not alwaies set a bleeding the wounds it found, though sometimes it did, as for example the 17. december, but upon its going away or much relenting the wounds either made in that instant of time or manie months before never failed to bleed more or lesse 3. particularly upon the breaking up of the two great and long frosts, the first of which Happened 3d Jan: the other about ye 12, 13. 14 Feb. all the wounds ran wonderfully so that such times may bee looked upon as the proper seasons for gathering great Quantities of Sappe though perhaps it may be thought more spirituous when gathered after the Aequinoxe: so farre mr Lister

> your faithful Freind and servant
> *F: Willughby*

ADDRESS

    For mr Henry Oldenburg
    Secretary to the royall
    Society in the pallmall
       London

POSTMARK IV 6

NOTES

Reply to Letter 1477.
1 Edward Hulse (1636–1711), M.A. Cantab. 1660, M.D. Leiden 1668, was, like his friend John Ray, ejected from a College Fellowship because of refusal to conform to

the religious tests, in 1662. He was F.C.P. 1677 and became physician to the Prince of Orange. The "account" sent to Ray is published in *Phil. Trans.*, no. 65 (14 November 1670), 2103–4.

2 Lister's observation of the darting of spiders was actually forwarded to Oldenburg by Philip Skippon(see Vol. V, Letter 1113) and printed in *Phil. Trans.*, no. 50 (16 August 1669), 1011–16.

3 See Letter 1464 and note 1.

4 See *Phil. Trans.*, no. 58 (25 April 1670), 1200, which has "commonly ceaseth before morning" for "commonly ceases before Noone" (Vol. VI, p. 635).

1480

Oldenburg to Sluse

4 July 1670

This second letter is mentioned by Sluse in a postscript to Letter 1489 as received on 26 July 1670.

1481

Newburgh to Oldenburg

July 1670

From the original in Royal Society MS. N 1, no. 4

Sr

I must acknowledge myself very much obliged by yr complements particularly the last wch yrs of June 28 brought me.

I wish I could keep pace wt yu either by ye diligence or Importance of my Returns. But wt is wanting in either of these Respects I will indeavor to make up by my Thankfullnes wch may possibly be more happily exprest hereaft then my present penury will admit. In the interim I must run further into yr debt & so generous & obliging a person I am Confident will not be displeased yt I make bold so to do. You acquaint me that there is an ingenious piece translated out of French about Vipers[1] if yu please to procure it for me I shall thankfully repay wt it costs wn I know it. You may send it any other Saturday by Mr Mathews who lies at ye Redlyon in red Crosse street, directing it is to be left for me to Mr Robert Bishop an Apothecary in Brid[port]. In yr printed Transactions there is mention made of a Book in ye same language concerning silkworms,[2] if yu can procure it for me it will be very welcome if it come in company wth the other. I shall also be thankfully sensible of yr kindnes if yu please to let me know whether ye Instructions of our (now) King[3] or any of his ph[ilosophical] lessons concerning planting mulberries wch I think yu hint at in the same pages be purcheaseble if so I shd be glad to make such a purchase. I am now in my 2d year of keeping silkworms & am mightily confirmd yt it is unspeakeably much ye shame of ye English nation yt we do not set ourselves about ye work. But I dayly perceive too manifest ye Chriticism (or rather censure) of ye great Erasmus wch he bestows upon ye English [*illegible*] Angli ingeniosi utinam non desidiosi.[4] As for ye Responses [?] of ye sworn Enemy of ye R.S. whom you speak of[5] I think for ye greatest part of it they deserve no other answr then a discreet person wd give to a Billingsgate scold. Though to deal freely wth yu concerning somethings I doubt it may be sd—pudet haec opprobria nobis Et dici potuisse et non potuisse refelli.[6] I shall wn leisure befriends me better, wth yt friendly freedom wch I know I may use towards yu, acquaint yu more particularly wt I mean. And tis no wonder if among so many idle stones one or other hit. Yu know whose rule it is. Calumniare fortiter aliquid haerebit.[7] But wt is sd concerning persons may comfort in this case so honorable a Corporation Nam vitijs nemo caret optimus ille in minoris urgetur[8] & if by his freedom from mistakes he had defind any part of yt Philosophy he takes he might seeme ye more Excuseable. No doubt ye greatest losse will in ye end be his own & theirs whose malice or ignorance makes ym Credulous hearers or readers of all his slanders; & who for a few [*illegible*] reject, a great many usefull Truths. To such I think ye answr of ye Rose in ye Emblem to ye filthy Gnat yt passd scornfully by her may suffice Sus non tibi spiro.[9] And I hope if it be truly sd Marcet Virtus sine adversario,[10] the society will receive no damage by this or other adversaries affronts. Virtus repulsae nescia sordidae Intaminatis fulget honoribus.[11] Sr I hope with yt honorable Assembly, Tu cujus pars magna mihi minimam accreditesses;[12] but not wth the least affection, Sir,

yr humble servt
John Newburgh

I have desired the friend who brings ye letter to pay yu 7s 6d for wch I am yr servants debtor in one kind & much more yt in another.

Pray pardon the rudeness of this hasty scribble wch perhaps may cost yu more trouble ye reading the [*illegible*]

ADDRESS

To my honored Freind
Henry Oldenburg Esq
At his hous on ye Pel Mel
       these present

NOTES

This letter is endorsed as received on 9 July 1670.

1 See Letter 1477, note 2, for this translation of the book by Moise Charas.

2 In *Phil. Trans.*, no. 5 (3 July 1665), 87–91, is an account of Christophle Isnard's *Memoires et Instructions pour le plant des meuriers blancs, nourriture des vers a soye et l'art de filer, mouliner et aprester les soyons dans Paris* (Paris, 1665).

3 The hortatory letters of James I and Charles II are mentioned at the end of Oldenburg's account just noted; James I had first commanded the planting of mulberry trees in 1607 as a measure of encouragement to the silk industry.

4 "Would that the ingenious English were not also idle." We have not traced these exact words, but in a letter to William Gonell (28 April 1514) Erasmus wrote: "Tanta est apud Britannos laboris fuga, tantus amor ocii, ut ne tum quid excitentur, cum spes dolosi affulserit nummi" ("So readily do the British avoid labor, so great is their love of ease, that they are not stimulated even by the glitter of deceitful coin", from P. S. Allen, *Erasmi epistolae*, I, Ep. 292, Oxford, 1906–12. We owe this reference to Fr. James McConica, C.S.B.

5 Presumably Stubbe.

6 "It shames us both that these scandalous things could be said, and that they could not be rebutted" (Ovid *Metamorphoses* i.758).

7 "Slander with a will; something will stick" (Bacon, *De augmentis scientiarum*, Pt. VIII, sect. 2; the original has *audacter*).

8 "For no one is without faults; he is best whose faults are least" (a recollection of Horace *Satires* i.3.68).

9 "Swine, I do not blow [= bloom] for you." An emblem, or device, consisted of a motto linked to a symbolic illustration with a few lines of explanation of the meaning, usually allegorical and moral. The words might be Latin or vernacular or a combination of the two, in verse or prose. A picture of the pig and sweet marjoram (not gnat and rose) with the motto "Non tibi spiro" appeared as No. 93 in Joachim Camerarius, *Symbolorum et emblematum ex re herbaria* (Nuremberg, 1590) and again on the title page of Sir Philip Sidney's *The Countesse of Pembroke's Arcadia* (London, 1593). (We are indebted here to Dr. Barbara E. Rooke and the publishers of *The Collected Coleridge*, Messrs. Routledge & Kegan Paul and the Bollingen Foundation.)

10 "Virtue withers without an antagonist" (Seneca *De providentia*, sec. 2).

11 "Virtue, admitting no dishonoring defeat, shines forth with unstained luster" (Horace *Odes* iii. 2, 17).

12 "You who are a great figure in it will confer credit on me, the least."

1482
Oldenburg to Evelyn
8 July 1670

From the original in the Christ Church Evelyn Letters, no. 1062

Sir,

What accompanies these, was brought to my house from Mr Glanvil for you.[1] I hope, we shall shortly see the picture, he hath drawn of Stub, who hath now given his 4th onset, and therein would make the royal Soc. ye Common Ennemy of Universities, Religion, Monarchy, Physitians, Apothecaries, Tradesmen, and what not;[2] and a worse mischief to England, than ye Dutch Warr, the Plague and the Fire; and therefore by all good men to be destroyed; wth threatnings, yt if they submit not to the Universities and the Colledge of Physitians, he will yet handle them worse, and attack their other writings, among wch he threatens you also, and saith that he will handle you as he hath done Henshaw;[3] and such like stuff, made up of meere malice, and containing nothing but calumnies, untruths, prevarications, grosse mistakes; for wch he must be soundly lashed to undeceive the Vulgar. You will be amazed, to see the vileness of this 4th book and of ye soule of its Author.

Yrs
Henr. Oldenburg.

London july 8. 1670.

After I had written this, I was desired by Mr Boyle to intreat some of our Philosophical friends, among whom he nam'd you expressly, yt they would oblige him by sending him a few Glow-worms, put up wth some grass in a glas-viol, and loosly stopped. Sr If you can meet wth any, I pray, remember us, and send ym out to my house, if you please, and you will doe M. Boyle a particular pleasure; who, though weak enough in his health, doth yet delight in carrying on Experiments.

ADDRESS
 To his honored friend
  John Evelyn Esq
   these

NOTES

1 There is no record of the enclosure, which was presumably a letter.

2 Stubbe's three earlier tracts against the Royal Society were *A Censure upon ... the History of the Royal Society; Legends no Histories*; and *The Plus Ultra of Mr. Joseph Glanvill reduced to a Non-Plus* (see Vol. VI, Letter 1248, note 5). The fourth was *Campanella Revived, or an Enquiry into the History of the Royal Society, whether the Virtuosi there do not pursue the Projects of Campanella for the reducing England into Popery* (London, 1670), of which various portions are dated 16 May 1670, 2 June 1670, and 14 June 1670. Glanvill's retort, expected by Oldenburg, appeared in his *A Praefatory Answer to Mr. Henry Stubbe* (London, 1671), which was in the main a reply to Stubbe's criticisms of himself in *The Plus Ultra ... reduced to a Non-Plus*, but a "Postscript" further extends Glanvill's ridicule to *Legends no Histories* and *Campanella Revived*. This "Postscript" contains a letter from Stubbe to Dr. Christopher Merret dated 16 August 1670; the whole *Praefatory Answer* had appeared before 30 November 1670, when Stubbe dated his answer to part of it.

3 Thomas Henshaw, F.R.S. (1618–1700), an original member of the Royal Society's Council, had contributed to Thomas Sprat's *History of the Royal Society* (pp. 263–83) an account of the making of saltpeter and gunpowder which was lengthily (but carpingly) criticized by Stubbe in *Legends no Histories*. In *Campanella Revived* (sig. A3) Stubbe spoke of criticisms "which Mr Evelyn's discourse of Forrest-Trees may invite me unto; the Second Edition whereof wants not its defects; and if I should trouble myself to examine his account of the Birch-Tree, it will appear as ridiculous as the History of Salt-Peter: and 'tis to me a Miracle, that neither He, nor all his Correspondents should inform us better of so obvious a thing . . ."

1483
Oldenburg to Willughby
9 July 1670

Oldenburg endorsed Willughby's Letter 1479 of 4 July as having been received on the sixth, and answered on the ninth.

1484
Vernon to Oldenburg
9 July 1670
From the original in Royal Society MS. V, no. 13

Paris July 19. 1670. [N.S.]

Sr.

Two of yours I have received the first of May 9th, the other of June 10th in the first came enclosed the Letter from Mr Gregorie & in the Latter that from Dr Wallis. Both of wch were extreame Welcome to mee & For wch I owed you almost certaine acknowledgement of thankes, butt I could not returne them till now. For a most important concerne wch I have had for an accident happend to a Friend of mine hath soe wholly ingrosst my time that I have not had vacancie for civilities. for omissions of wch I scarce know how to excuse. butt your goodnesse & experience in such necessarie diversion makes mee imagine your Pardon not difficult. butt since such a Parenthesis hath happend in our correspondence it could scarce have come in a conjuncture more suited for it. what have wee of newes, since my last unto you wch is of eminent Consideration: The Royall Academie this Summer time gave themselves a Relaxation & most wt is done there is the shewing of Plants, & making some experiments & observations upon them. the last subiect of moment they considerd in Philosophy was concerning the nature of gravity & what is the cause of weight.[1] into wch speculation they could not dive very deepe for they found it very intricate & something neere a Principle. severall opinions were propounded whether it were a Pressure of other Bodies wch fill the universe & the impulse of other springs upon the heavy body moving downewards. whether It were an inhaerent Principle & a compactednesse of the Parts of the Heavy body. butt they did not determine any thing in the case. of wch it was very hard to bring demonstrations to confirme their conjectures. they likewise examined the motion of Projected Bodies of wch I believe you will see some effects.[2] they have receaved a new member into their Academie one Monsr Borell one of a sharp witt & well verst in Chymistry & have given him a Pension of 1200 livres per annum.[3] The Herball of Monsr Marchand & Duclos goes on Apace butt It had received an impediment because Monsieur Robert one of those who graves the

Plantes had kept his Bed for three Moneths, by Reason a Coach had run over his legges.[4] butt now hee begins to worke againe & things will goe forward Apace. Monsieur labbé Beaugrands enlargement of Ferrarius his Lexicon geographicum is neere finisht & will shortly come forth.[5] Those of Portroyall are about a French Dictionary wch it is supposed will bee better then any yet extant, & are come as farre as the letter T.[6] Monsieur Pelisson is about Writing a History of these Moderne Revolutions Butt I cannot tell you when hee will publish it.[7] Monsieur Picart is very forward wth his booke about the measure of the earth & many of the Plates are already graved by one la bossiere I believe it will bee finisht by the end of Summer.[8] Sigre Cassinis Tables of the Circumioviales are not yet done.

That wch now causeth most discourse is the new Starre by the Beake of Cygnus, first discoverd by a Chartreuse of Dijon called the Pere Antelme who sent the newes of it to Monsieur Labbe Mareotte one of the Royall Academie, who hath communicated it to the rest.[9] They all agree it is a new Starre. Though Monsieur Boulliau opposeth It & saith it is in Bayerus,[10] butt they demonstrate another Starre wch they suppose gave the aequivocation to Monsieur de Bulliau. For wthout any more Criticall notes to distinguish this from that, this Starre at its first appearance was very bright & as big as the starres of the third magnitude since it is growne lesse & lesse & now is very small wch noe other starre about Cygnus at present is observed to doe.

The measures then whereby you may find it are these

		Deg.	min.	secds.
The bright starre ad Rostrum Cygni its	Ascentio Recta is	289.	22.	
	Declinatio Boreal	27.	19.	20.
This new Starres	Ascentio Recta is	293.	33.	
	Declinatio Boreal	26.	33.	20.
	Longitudo	1.	55. Aquarij	
	Latitudo	47.	28.	10.
its distance from that ad Rostrum Cygni towards jaculum is		3.	47.	

This is ample enough for your present satisfaction touching this matter now I will proceed to tell you what other Treatises are now forming & like to bee published amongst us. Monsieur Bernier will Print his Voyages of the East Indies.[11] Barbin who hath the Coppy tells mee It will bee done & Printed wthin a Moneth.

Tavernier likewise intends to Publish his Voyages. & Monsieur Le Premier President intends to Correct & Polish them for him.[12] for hee is butt a Jeweller[13] & noe schollar & therefore will have need of some beautifications. All that Monsr. Bulliau tells mee he hath done of now is that hee hath found out another way to demonstrate the quadrature of the Parabola & made another Hypothesis. For the Phaenomena of Saturne. Padre Riccioli, Sigre Cassini tells mee, hath made a new volume of Chronologie.[14] I have sent you from Monsieur duhamel a Pacquet wch I consigned to Mr Gee my lady Northumberlands steward of wch hee will give you an Account.[15] wherein are some late Pieces of Padre Fabri printed by Molin at Lions. those wch are yet arrived at Paris are only Summula Theologia, Synopsis geometrice, Physicall Dialogues, Euphyander ceu Vir ingeniosus.[16] Some more Pieces of his are shortly expected of wch when they arrive I shall give you an account. Monsieur Auzout is still at Rome & extreamly satisfied wth Mr Barrowes Optiques wch Monsr Justel sent him.

Mr Huygens, Thankes bee to God, I thinke I may say is now Recoverd. I walkt wth him on Saturday last above an hour in the garden ioynd to the house where the Royal Academie assembleth, & where hee lodgeth. Hee is weake still & very thin, butt yet still hee is a man, & not a Ghost as hee was before. for I never saw any thing like him except it were the Lower figure in Bishop Chicheleyes tomb at Canterburie, wch was the bishops shape when hee was quite emaciated & whitherd away.[17] For my part I wonderd every time I saw him how such a shadow of Death could live. yet hee hath, & will now againe I hope turne from a shadow to substance, for hee recruites reasonably fast, & reassumes humane nature. Hee askt mee if I had heard any newes from Doctor Wallis I had not then, but since Abbé Fromentin hath given mee his Letter.[18] I shall give him the Perusall of it wch I know will bee a content gratefull to his expectation in this Garden wee were sometime considering a new Clock made wth a Pendulum whose first motion is receivd from water. the devize an[d] Fancy to move a Pendulum by water was Monsr Peraults.[19] Abbé Fromentin extreamely extolls your civility & in generall of the whole royall society. You doe well to engadge Persons of soe great desert.[20] Pray my Respects to Mr Boyle, my affections to Mr Hooke, and all my Friends. Sr I am

Your most affte Friend & Servant,
Francis Vernon

NOTES

1 There is an account of the Academy's discussions of gravity from August 1669 onwards, in which Huygens, Roberval, Frenicle, Perrault, Mariotte, and Buot participated, in J. B. Duhamel, *Regia scientiarum academiae historia* (Paris, 1698), pp. 80–87; see also *Œuvres Complètes*, XIX, 618–45.

2 Possibly Vernon alludes to Huygens' investigations during 1668 and 1669 of the motions of bodies in resisting media; see *Œuvres Complètes*, XIX, 102–57.

3 This was Jacques Borelly (d. 1689); see Vol. V, Letter 1159 and note 7.

4 This was the work published by the Académie in 1676 as *Mémoires pour servir à l'histoire des plantes*; see Vol. IV, p. 480, note 1. Nicolas Robert (1610–84) was the celebrated flower painter. For Léon Marchand (d.*c.* 1682), see Vol. IV, p. 259, note 5.

5 Michel Antoine Baudrand's edition of Philippus Ferrarius' *Lexicon geographicum* was published at Paris in 1670. There were numerous earlier editions, including several published at London.

6 We have not been able to confirm this.

7 Paul Pellisson [-Fontanier] (1624–93) wrote an unpublished account of the siege of Dôle (1668) and other works, but none concerned with "revolutions." He was a renegade Protestant who became an official historiographer.

8 [Jean Picard], *Mesure de la terre* (Paris, 1671); compare Letter 1370 (Vol. VI). The plates were engraved by Sébastien Le Clerc (1637–1714); there was no "La Bossière."

9 Compare Letter 1474 and note 2. Oldenburg summarized this note and printed the data in *Phil. Trans.*, no. 65 (14 November 1670), 2092.

10 Johann Bayer, *Uranometria* (Augsburg, 1603).

11 François Bernier, *Historie de la derniere revolution des Etats du Gran Mogol*, was published by Claude Barbin at Paris in 1670. Later editions are entitled *Voyages* . . .

12 Jean Baptiste Tavernier (?1605–89) returned to Paris from a lifetime of travel in Europe, the Near East, and the Orient in 1668. At some point (possibly at Geneva in 1670) he engaged the French Protestant author, Samuel Chappuzeau (1625–*c.* 1701), to put his notes into literary form. Because Chappuzeau proved dilatory, about 1672 Tavernier invoked the aid of his friend Guillaume de Lamoignon (1617–77), Premier President since 1658 of the Parlement de Paris; he in turn brought Louis XIV's interest in Tavernier's travels to Chappuzeau's notice, so that he set to work. (See, for Chappuzeau's account, Pierre Bayle, *Dictionnaire historique et critique*, s.v. Tavernier, note C.) Tavernier's experiences appeared successively in *Nouvelle relation de l'intérieur du serrail du Grand Seigneur* (Paris, 1675); *Les six Voyages* (Paris, 1676); and *Receuil de plusieurs Relations et Traitez* (Paris, 1679).

13 Actually, he traded in jewels among the princes of the East.

14 G. B. Riccioli, *Chronologiae reformatae* (3 vols.; Bologna, 1669).

15 Elizabeth, the younger Dowager Countess of Northumberland, had married in 1662 Josceline Percy (1644–70), the tenth Earl, who died during their Italian travels on 21 May.

16 Honoré Fabri, *Summula theologica* (Lyons, 1669); *Synopsis geometrica, cui accessere tria opuscula* (Lyons, 1669); *Dialogi physici* (2nd enlarged edition, Lyons, 1669); *Euphyander, seu vir ingeniosus: opusculum* (Lyons, 1669).

17 Henry Chichele (1362?–1443), Archbishop of Canterbury; his tomb, erected in his lifetime, shows him both as an archbishop in his robes and, after death, as a skeleton in a shroud.

18 The Abbé Formentin (1631–1701), who spelled his name thus, was also well known to John Locke. He was a Canon of Orléans and Vicar-General of the diocese.

19 See [Claude] Perrault, *Recueil de Plusieurs Machines de Nouvelle Invention* (Paris, 1700), p. 25.
20 We have found no other trace of a correspondence.

1485
Oldenburg to Vogel
9 July 1670

Mentioned in Letters 1490 and 1498.

1486
Gottfried Wilhelm Leibniz to Oldenburg
13 July 1670

From the copy in Royal Society Letter Book IV, 51-53
Printed in Gerhardt, pp. 39-40, and in *Sämtliche Schriften*, pp. 59-60

A Letter from Dr Leibnitzius to M. Oldenburg

Vir Amplissime,

Ignosce quod ignotus scribo ad non ignotum; cui enim Regiam Societatem non ignoranti ignotus esse possis? Et quem Societas latere possit, qui aliqua verae Eruditionis cura ducitur, verae inquam, quae paulatim vestris potissimum auspicijs a Criticorum ambulacris in arcem naturae se recipit. Est, fateor, gens gente in accipiendis his igniculis languidior; sed scis, alium alijs constantius semel haustos tenere. Nostris certe non desunt experimenta praeclara, sed, prout nunc est Reip. status, pro cujusque promptitudine aut invidia recondita vel aperta, quod in Societates coitum non est, nec ita facile inter tot in una Resp. Respublicas coiri potest.[1]

Me quidem, cujus alioquin potissima opera, instituto vitae meae congrua in Juris prudentia ad eas rationes prope demonstratorias revocanda, quae Philosopho utcunque severo satisfacere possint, consumitur; a natura exactius pervestiganda non pauca alia prohibuerunt: videor tamen mihi nonnulla observasse, quae fortasse conferre poterunt aliquid ad accensum a vobis verae Philosophiae lumen. Nam de veris Motus rationibus Elementa quaedam condidi, ex solis terminorum definitionibus Geometrica methodo demonstrata, in quibus causam connexionis, flexionis, duritiaeve in corporibus, hactenus, quod sciam, a nullo explicatam aperuisse mihi videor,[2] atque illud etiam ostendisse, Regulas illas, quas de motu incomparabiles viri Hugenius Wrennusque constituerunt, non primas, non absolutas, non liquidas esse, sed per accidens, ob certum globi Terr-aq-aera statum, evenire (non minus quam gravitatem;) non axiomata, non theoremata demonstrabilia, sed experientias, phaenomena, observationes, at faelices, at praeclaras, (ultra quas hactenus nemo processerit) esse; in medio tamen quiescente, vel aliter moto, alia omnia eventura. Nam et separatas meditationes habeo, quibus ex unica quadam hypothesi certi motus universalis in globi nostro Terraquaero, (quem et Copernicus, et Tycho admittere possit) omnium motuum, quos in corporibus miramur, insueta hactenus claritate reddi ratio potest Gravitatis, Levitatis, Paradoxorum omnium hydrostaticorum, Mechanicorum, motus projectorum, Reflexionum, Refractionum; Sed et, quod mireris, trium Chymicorum, quae vocant, principiorum, a confusione vulgari ad accuratas definitiones reductorum, omniumque solutionum, reactionum, praecipitationum, idque non atomis quibusdam, non ramentis, non abstractis, sed familiari quadam, et pene mechanica ratione. Edidi etiam ante quadriennium dissertatiunculam de Arte Combinatoria, in qua nova non pauca, quaedam etiam forte profutura, observata sunt, sed quod per aetatem, adolescentiam vix ingressam, tunc illaboratior fuerit edita, resumere aliquando cogito. Caeteroquin apud nos avide expectatur, quid Eruditi, et Vos inprimis, de Hugeniano Longitudinum, opc pcnduli, Iuvento sentiant, cujus mentio in Ephemeridibus Gallicanis:[3] satisne vobis perfectum videatur; tum quae fuerit ratio quive exitus tentaminis Gallici de dulcescentia aquae marinae procuranda. A Clarissimo Hezenthalero[4] habeo, quae de perfecta quadam ad usum Philosophiae lingua condenda celeberrimus vester Wilkinsius deliberet. Idem significavit, Jungij Phoranomica lucem, quam merentur, vobis obstetricantibus, visura. Quod linguam Universalem attinet, scio, Virum aliquem Illustrem sumptuosis itineribus plaerarumque orbis linguarum radices collegisse et comparasse, condendae linguae matricis causa. Sed et Athanasius Kircherus mihi scripsit, Ferdinandi III Caesaris auspicijs multum ea in re a se, sed nondum pleno successu, laboratum compluraque eo

in negotio observata a Se in turrim Babel, mox edendam, translata esse.[5]
Sed nolo Te a negotijs immortalis vestrae Societatis, cui nihil decedere
generis humani interest, diutius avocare. Vale, faveque Vir Amplissime,

Nominis Tui Cultori
Gottfredo Guilielmo Leibnitio
J. U. Doctori et Consilio Moguntino[6]

Moguntiae
Aug. 23. 1670 [N.S.]

TRANSLATION

Worthy Sir,

Pardon the fact that I, an unknown person, write to one who is not unknown;
for tow hat man who has heard of the Royal Society can you be unknown? And
who has not heard of the Society, if he is in any way drawn to an interest in true
learning, the true learning I mean which under your guidance particularly is
withdrawing from the groves of the critics into the fastnesses of nature. Some
nations, I admit, are less keen than others to cherish these sparks, but you know
that some are more persevering than others when once aroused. Remarkable experiments are not wanting among us, but, such is the state of politics [in Germany]
now, on account of the open eagerness of one and the hidden envy of another,
that there can be no uniting into societies, nor is it easy for so many states to be combined into one nation.[1]

As for myself whose chief efforts are in any case, following the scheme of my
life, devoted to bringing jurisprudence back to such more or less demonstrable
principles as may satisfy any rigorous philosopher, various other things restrain me
from a more exact inquiry into nature. Yet I seem (to myself) to have observed
some things which might perhaps contribute something to your fanning of the
true philosophic blaze. For I have put together certain elements to do with the
true theory of motion (demonstrated in the geometrical way from the definitions
of terms only), in which I seem to myself to have disclosed the cause of the cohesion, bending, and hardness of bodies hitherto accounted for by none, so far as I
know;[2] as also to have shown that those rules of motion established by the incom-
parable Huygens and Wren are neither primary nor absolute nor evident, but arise
by accident from a certain state of the terraquaerial globe, no less than gravity;
that they are neither axioms nor demonstrable theorems but facts of experience,
phenomena, observations, although happy and outstanding ones (beyond what
any one has previously attained). For in a quiescent medium, or one otherwise
moved, all things would happen differently. And I have other ideas by the aid of

which, adopting a certain unique hypothesis of a particular universal motion in our terraquaerial globe that both Copernicus and Tycho can accept, I can give the theory of all the motions in bodies that puzzle us, with a hitherto unusual clarity—that is, of gravity, levity, of all hydrostatical paradoxes, of mechanics, the motion of projectiles, of reflections and refractions; and also (you will be astonished) of the three chemical principles, so called, when reduced from the ordinary state of muddle to precise definitions, and so of all solutions, reactions, precipitations; and that not by means of certain atoms nor fragments nor abstractions but by means of a familiar and almost mechanical way of reasoning. More than four years ago I also published a little essay, *De arte combinatoria*, in which no small number of novelties was remarked upon, some of them useful too, perhaps, but because of my youth (for I was barely entered on adolescence) the essay was published in an imperfect form, and I plan to take it up again some day.

For the rest, we are here eagerly awaiting the opinion of the learned, and especially of yourselves, concerning Huygens' discovery of the longitude by means of the pendulum clock, of which mention is made in the French *Journal* [*des Sçavans*],[3] does it seem to you sufficiently perfected? Then what is the method, and the outcome, of the French attempts at obtaining sweetened sea water? From the famous Hesenthaler[4] I learn what your celebrated Wilkins has in hand towards creating a perfect language for philosophical purposes. The same person informed me that we should see Jungius' *Phoranomica* brought to light, as they deserve to be, with yourselves as the godparents. As regards the universal language, I know that a certain illustrious man has traveled far and wide collecting and comparing the roots of many of the world's languages, in order to reconstruct the mother language. And Athanasius Kircher wrote to me that under the patronage of the Emperor Ferdinand III he had labored much on this task himself, but not with complete success, and that he had inserted many points which had occurred to him in this context in his *Tower of Babel*, soon to be published.[5] But I don't wish to distract you any longer from the business of your immortal Society, which should not for humanity's sake be neglected. Farewell, worthy Sir, and cherish

This admirer of your fame,
Gottfried Wilhelm Leibniz
Doctor of Laws and Councilor at Mainz[6]

Mainz, 23 August 1670 [N.S.]

NOTES

The copy of this letter in the Letter Book (the original, as with several other letters from Leibniz, is now lost) bears the date 23 August N.S., but Oldenburg's reply attributing the letter to 13/23 July was itself composed on 10 August (though again wrongly dated in the Letter Book).

Leibniz (1646–1716) was at this time still in the first stages of his career, as councilor and legal adviser to the Elector of Mainz, Johann Philipp von Schönborn. At the University of Leipzig he had studied philosophy under Jakob Thomasius, to which he subsequently added civil law; but he proceeded to Doctor of Laws at Altdorf because Leipzig refused to grant a dispensation for his insufficient age. He had by this time print-ed a number of academic exercises at Leipzig (as was requisite), followed by *De arte combinatoria* (Leipzig, 1666), though in mathematics Leibniz was largely self-taught. In traveling he met the Baron von Boineburg, who introduced him into the service of the Elector of Mainz (1667). Shortly before the date of the present letter Leibniz had also begun to form acquaintances with learned men in Paris, particularly Pierre de Carcavy. He was to leave Mainz for Paris in March 1672, remaining there four years apart from a visit to England lasting from January to March, 1673, when he met Oldenburg and other Fellows of the Royal Society, to which he was himself elected in April.

1 We have rendered the rather puzzling construction of this sentence freely.
2 For this treatment of motion by Leibniz, see below Letter 1644.
3 This must refer to an extract of a letter from Huygens to Jean Chapelain of 26 Janu-ary 1664/5, published in the *Journal des Sçavans* for 23 February 1665 [N.S.], and re-printed in *Œuvres Complètes*, V, 223. An English account was printed in *Phil. Trans.*, no. 1 (6 March 1664/5), 13–14.
4 Hesenthaler (1621–81) was Professor of Politics and Rhetoric in the University of Tübingen, according to Gerhardt, who does not give his full name.
5 Athanasius Kircher's letter to Leibniz on this point is published in *Sämtliche Schriften*, pp. 48–49; his book was *Turris Babel* (Amsterdam, 1679).
6 "J. U. D." is the abbreviation for "Juris Utriusque Doctor," that is, "Doctor of both [Civil and Canon] Laws."

1487
Oldenburg to Dodington
15 July 1670
From the draft in Royal Society MS. O 2, no. 29

An Answer to Mr Dodington's Letter of July 4.1670 [N.S.]

Sr

You manifest by yours of July ye 4th 1670 (wch I received the 9th of the same our style) so great care and generosity in matters committed to your trust, that I cannot but hasten to returne you our hearty and thank-full acknowledgement for it. Sr. R. Moray, to whom I gave the account, you ordered mee concerning the chymicall book at Florence, joyns wth mee in those thanks, being satisfyed with your enquiry after that MS,

though you found it not. I received together with your letter an answer of
Signr Malpighi to mine,[1] and therein a very obliging intimation of some
Phil. Books as of Signr Borelli's second book de *Vi Percussionis*,[2] and of
S. Mengoli's Treatise *de Sono*,[3] both under the presse at present; which
when finished, wee hope you will further oblige us in transmitting to us a
copy of each by sea as you have done in conveying ye printed sheets of
Mengolus *Degli Refrattioni del Sole* over land.[3] I am alltogether persuaded,
that Signr Travagino at Venice will receive and entertaine you wth as
much humanity, as ye rest, to whom I took the freedom to addresse you,
have done, and I am very desirous to be informed from that learned and
experimenting person, what progresse he hath made in his important
Philosophical worke, which, as hee formerly signifyed to us, was designed
by him for ye publick, and of which hee hath allready printed a synopsis,
transmitted to us severall yeares agoe.[4]

Sr, you are still like yourselfe in engaging that you will not faile to give
us exact accounts, not only of the particulars mentioned in my note, but of
what else shall occur worthy our knowledge. You may, if you please,
acquaint the Philosophers you converse with in those parts, that ye R.S.
still persists in prosecuting experimentall studyes, and doubts not, but
those excellent persons, with whom Italy abounds, will jointly pursue the
same, as the most certaine way to encrease solid and usefull knowledge.
You may adde, that severall good books of Mathematicks and Physicks
have been lately published by divers members of the R.S. Viz the 2d part
of Mr Boyles usefulnesse of experimental Philosophy, as also his Introduction into the History of particular qualityes, and his Tract of cosmical
qualityes, which depend from the constitution of the universe, and another
of the temperature of subterraneous and submarine Regions.[5] Item, ye
2d part of Dr Wallis's work de *Motu et Mechanica*, which is *de centro Gravitatis ejusque Calculo*.[6] Item Dr Barrows *Lectiones Geometricae*.[7] Item Dr Lower
de *Catharris*.[8] These 3 last in Latine, but those of Mr Boyle in English, yet
to be turned into Latin as soon as may be.[9]

This being all I can give you notice of at present, and enough, I think,
to interrupt your publick affaires, I shall conclude remaining Sr

Your very humble and faithful servant
H. Oldenburg

London
July 15. 1670.

NOTES

Reply to Letter 1473.

1 Letter 1470.
2 See Letter 1470, note 3.
3 See Letter 1470, note 2.
4 The sending of the *Synopsis* is mentioned in Letter 591 (Vol. III, p. 300), but the print itself has not been traced. See also Letter 1519.
5 *Some Considerations touching the Usefulnesse of Experimental Naturall Philosophy . . . the Second Tome* (Oxford, 1671); *Tracts . . . about the Cosmicall Qualities of Things* [etc.] (Oxford, 1671).
6 *Mechanica, sive de motu tractatus geometricus; pars secunda* (London, 1670).
7 *Lectiones geometricae* (London, 1670). See Vol. VI, Letter 1283, note 4, and the review in *Phil. Trans.*, no. 75 (18 September 1671), 2260–63.
8 Lower's *Dissertatio de origine catharri* was attached to the third edition of his *De corde* (Amsterdam, 1671). See *Phil. Trans.*, no. 73 (17 July 1671), 2211–12.
9 No extant translation of the *Usefulnesse* appeared at this time, the first recorded Latin version being that of Lindau, 1692; of the *Cosmicall Qualities* a Latin translation (with which Daniel Georg Morhof was associated) appeared at Amsterdam and Hamburg in 1671, followed by another, London, 1672. It is not clear whether the two texts are different, but Morhof's verses are omitted from the London book. It is known that Boyle received a manuscript Latin translation of *Cosmicall Qualities* from Oldenburg in the summer of 1671 (Royal Society MS. Boyle Letters III, no. 41).

1488

Oldenburg to Malpighi

15 July 1670

From the original in Bologna MS. 2085, VII, ff. 14–15
Draft in Royal Society MS. O 2, no. 29
Printed in Pizzoli, pp. 55–56

Clarissimo Viro
Dn. Marcello Malpighio, Med. et Phil. Bononiensi
Henricus Oldenburg Salutem

Aegre sane ferimus, Vir Celeberrime, Historiae tuae Bombycinae, quam omnes Docti, quibuscum mihi conversari datur, apprime laudant, Exemplaria a nobis transmissa etiamnum desidari. Asseverat interim Bibliopola, navim, cui ipsa commiserat, Livorniam certo certius jam ante aliquot menses appulisse. Navarcham appellant Johannem Noble, ipsaque Navis

Famae insignibus decoratur. Mercatoribus Anglicis, Livorniae degentibus, Thomae Death scilicet et Ephraimo Skinner vocatis, cura incumbit, ut fasciculus Tibi destinatus ad Dominum Passerinum curetur.[1]

Prodiit nuper in lingua Belgica Doctoris Swammerdami Historiae Insectorum Pars prima,[2] in qua honorificam Tuae de Bombycibus Dissertationis mentionem facit, agnoscitque Te unicum esse, qui de vera Bombycum mutationis ratione et modo quicquam solidi scripserit. Speramus, Authorem ipsum operam daturum, ut hic ipsius partus, lingua Doctorum, quarumvis gentium Philosophis quantocyus exponatur.

Mengoli doctissimi Tractatulum de Parallaxi[3] nunc versant Astronomi Londinenses, vobisque de eo munere gratias maximas reponunt; alio tempore suam de eo scripto sententiam exposituri. Ejusdem de Sono librum, quem etiamnum ineditum scribis, avidi exspectamus; simul et gaudemus, Clarissimi Borelli secundum de Vi Percussionis librum sub praelo jam sudare, promissamque Aetnaei incendii historiam propediem evulgandam esse.[4] At singularis inprimis gaudio perfundimur, Temet ipsum, quod scribis, in consectandis observationibus inchoatis, valetudine adversa nequicquam reclamante, cordatum perserverare. Felicissimum Tibi successum, vegetamque et perennem valetudinem ex animo comprecamur.

Nobilis Boylius noster Alteram de Physicae Experimentalis Utilitate partem, nec non varia Opuscula Philosophica, puta, Qualitatum particularium Historiam, Qualitates Cosmicas, atque ab Universi Fabrica et Constitutione dependentes, ut et Regionum Subterranearum et Submarinarum Temperiem, spectantia, nuper in lucem emisit, sermone quidem vernaculo, at brevi in Latinum vertendo. Praeterea de Catharris quaedam non vulgaria commentatus est Doctor Lowerus. Inque Mathematicis Eximii Viri, D. Wallisius, et D. Barrovius, ille quidem de Centro Gravitatis ejusque Calculo. hic vero Lectiones Geomctricas insigniores publici juris Latina lingua fecere.[5] Haec sunt, Vir Clarissime, quae hac vice scire Te volui. Vale et nos porro ama. Dabam Londini die 15. julii 1670.

ADDRESS

Celeberrimo Viro
Domino Marcello Malpighio
Philosopho et Medico Bononiensi,
Fautori plurimum colendo
　　　　　Bononiae

TRANSLATION

Henry Oldenburg greets the famous Marcello Malpighi, physician and philosopher of Bologna

We are certainly very displeased that the copies of your account of the silk-worm that we sent you are still missing; it is a book that all learned men with whom I have chanced to speak praise to the skies. Meanwhile, the bookseller assures me that the vessel to which he committed them has assuredly reached Livorno several months ago; the master was John Noble and his boat was adorned with the insignia of *Fame*. The responsibility of sending the package addressed to you to Signor Passarini¹ rested with two English merchants living at Livorno called Thomas Death and Ephraim Skinner.

There has lately appeared in the Dutch language the *Historia insectorum, pars prima* of Dr. Swammerdam,² in which he makes a laudatory mention of your *De bombyce* and admits that you are the sole author who has given a solid account of the true manner of the silkworm's metamorphosis. We hope that the author himself will take care to have this offspring of his exposed to the philosophers of all peoples as soon as possible, in the language of learning.

The London astronomers are now considering the learned Mengoli's little tract on parallax³ and return you their best thanks for the gift of it. At another occasion their opinion of that paper shall be set out. We are eagerly awaiting his book on sound, which you say is still unpublished; and we are glad that the famous Borelli's second volume *De vi percussionis* is now in press, as also that the promised account of the eruption of Etna is soon to be published.⁴ But we particularly rejoice that you persevere wholeheartedly in making scattered observations (as you write) despite your poor health. We wish you a happy success with all our heart, and a brisk, continuing good health.

Our noble Boyle has recently published another part of his *Usefulnesse of Experimental* [*Naturall*] *Philosophy* and a group of minor scientific works, that is, concerning the *History of Particular Qualities, Cosmical Qualities*, arising from the fabric and constitution of the universe, and *The Temperature of Subterranean and Submarine Regions*; these are in the vernacular, soon to be turned into Latin. Dr. Lower has made some uncommon observations *De catharris*. In mathematics, those distinguished persons Mr. Wallis and Mr. Barrow have lately made public in Latin *De centro gravitatis ejusque calculo* and some noteworthy *Lectiones geometricae*, respectively.⁵ This is what I wished to write to you at the present moment, famous Sir. Farewell, and continue to love us.

London, 15 July 1670

ADDRESS

To the famous Mr. Marcello Malpighi
Philosopher and Physician of Bologna
Our very dear Patron
        Bologna

NOTES

Reply to Letters 1450 (Vol. VI) and 1470.
1 See Vol. VI, Letter 1265.
2 Jan Swammerdam, *Historia insectorum generalis, ofte algemeene verhandeling van de bloede-loose dierkens* (Utrecht, 1669).
3 See Letter 1470, note 2.
4 See Letter 1470, note 3.
5 For these works see Letter 1487, notes 5 through 8.

1489
Sluse to Oldenburg
15/16 July 1670

From the original in Royal Society MS. S 1, no. 63
Printed in Boncompagni, pp. 642–45

Nobilissimo et Clarissimo Viro
D. Henrico Oldenburg Reg. Societatis Secretario
Renatus Franciscus Slusius S.

Nisi mihi saepe perspecta esset tua singularis humanitas, Vir Clarissime, negligentiae a te accusari vereor ob diuturnum silentium meum. Verum benigne, ut soles, illud imputabis tum occupationibus plurimis (neque enim ex felicium illorum numero sum, quibus arbitrium sui temporis relictum est) tum vel maxime valetudini, quam parum prosperam ab ultimis frigoribus mihi semper infensis expertus sum. Eo enim adductus fui ut peiora timerem, nisi quod acidularum nostrarum beneficio, quas ab aliquot septimanis haurio, meliora sperare iam coepi. Pro ijs itaque quae ad me misisti, praeter gratiarum actiones, nihil respondere possum, cum a similibus studijs feriari me oportuerit. Cum tamen ante aliquot dies, ad me liberalitate tua pervenissent Virorum Clarissimorum opera, Wallisius nempe pars prima de motu et Barrovus praelectiones opticae una cum acutissimi Gregorij exercitationibus, temperare mihi non potui quin illa statim pervoluerem;[1] ac vel levi inspectione, doctissimis auctoribus suis digna mihi visa sunt, adoe in illis omnia ex veris fundamentis, ordine et ἀκρίβεια geometrica deducta inveni. In praelectionibus aliquot Problemata occurrerunt de quibus olim cogitaveram, et quorum solutionem, bona tua cum venia, hic adscribam, Clarissime Collinsio, si tanti videbitur, communicandam; omne enim punctum tulisse me credam, si ipsi non displiceat. Primum pag. 38 in casu quo solidum est facile solvitur per duas hyperbolas.[2]

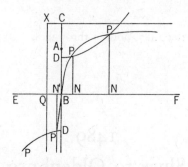

Sit enim recta positione data *EF*, unum punctum *A*, aliud *X*; et ex illis demissae in *EF* normalis *AB*, *XQ*. perficatur rectangulum *XQBC*, et per punctum *B*, circa asymptotes *XQ XC*, fiat Hyperbola *BPP*. Tum (data ratione refractionis quam Clarissimus auctor perpetuo ponit ut *I* ad *R*) fiat ut *Iq* minus *Rq*, ad *Rq*, ita *ABq*. ad *DBq*.[3] et vertice *D*, semiaxe transverso *BD*, describatur alia Hyperbola *DPP*, in qua ratio axis transversi ad rectum sit eadem quae *Iq*. ad *Iq–Rq*. Haec enim, si occurrat priori, vel tanget in uno vel secabit in duobus punctis *P*, ex quibus demissae normales ad *EF* dabunt puncta *N* quaesita. Sectio huic ultimae hyperbolae opposita, secat quoque priorem hyperbolam in alio puncto *P*, a quo demissa normalis in *EB*, dat quoque punctum *N* pro alio casu, nimirum cum iunctis *XN AN*, producitur *XN* usque dum concurrat cum *AB* producta; pars enim ipsius *XN* producta, futura est ad *AN* in ratione *I* ad *R*.

Problema Lemmaticum pag: 40[4] sub Vietae postulato 1º in Supplemento Geometriae[5] continetur; cum in Problemate rectus angulus datus supponatur, in postulate quilibet. Postulatum autem me olim soluisse memini per duas parabolas, per parabolam et hyperbolam, per circulum et parabolam vel hyperbolam, sed omnium facillime per duas hyperbolas. Ijsdem itaque modis solvi posset Problema, sed aliam solutionem per circulum et

Hyperbolam, quae statim mihi occurrit adscribam. Sit itaque angulus rectus *FPX* datus; punctum datum *Y*; ex quo cadat in *FP* normalis *YB*, perfectoque rectangulo *YBPD*, circa asymptotes *YB*, *YD*, describatur Hyperbola

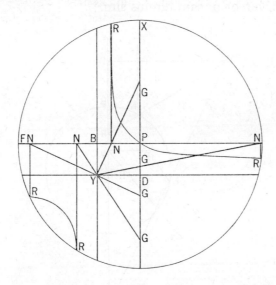

transiens per punctum *P*. Tum centro *P*, intervallo lineae datae *T*, fiat circulus secans hyperbolam in *R* puncto, ex quo cadat in *FP* normalis *RN*; iuncta enim *YN*, occurrens *PX*, in *G*, dabit *NG*, aequalem *T*. Idem circulus sectionem quoque oppositam vel tangere vel secare potest uti et priorem, in duobus punctis, ut patet ex schemate, in quo *T* adeo magnam assumpti ut quatuor solutiones complecteretur.

Aliud Problema est pag: 52[6] cuius quatuor solutiones (cum occurrant) modo facillimo per hyperbolam et circulum exhibentur. Evidens enim nihil aliud hoc Problemate quaeri, nisi ut, dato circulo ex centro *C* [*see figure, p. 76*], eiusque diametro *BCP*, ac puncto *X* extra illam, ducatur recta *XNR*, occurrens diametro in *R*, circulo in *N*, ita ut rectae *NR*, *RC* sint aequales. ita autem id effici potest. Cadat in *CB* productam, si opus fuerit, normalis *XD*. tum fiat ut *CD* ad *CB*, ita dimidia *CB* ad *CV*: et ut *XD* ad *DC*, ita *CV* ad *CG* normalem: iunctaque *GV*, erigatur normalis *VE*, quae possit dimidium quadrati *CB*.[7] Tum circa Asymptotes *VG*, *VD* describatur Hyperbola transiens per punctum *E*. Illa satisfaciet proposito, siquidem circulo occurrat vel in uno vel duobus punctis ut *N*. Idem quoque efficeret ipsius opposita in diversis casibus, quos fusius persequi, esset patientia tua abuti, et sufficit indicasse.

Celebre quoque Problema quod δυσμήχανον et inter omnia difficillimum vocat Clarissimus Barrovius pag. 64. olim construxi per sectiones oppositas datum circulum intersecantes: quarum una in speculo convexo punctum quaesitum ostendit, altera in concavo: sed constructio paullo operosior est, et vereor ne iam nimius sim.[8]

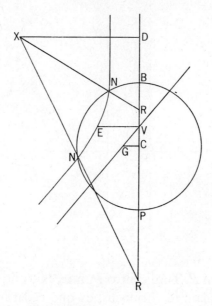

Quod nullum hactenus ex libris, quos a me petiisti, miserim, id quaeso ne meae sed Bibliopolarum nostrorum incuriae adscribas, a quibus nullum obtinere potui. Itaque cum hoc Vere Lugdunum Galliae proficisceretur amicus quidam meus, ipsi in mandatis dedi, ut quoscunque reperire posset, secum referre ni gravaretur. quod et se praestitisse redux mihi nuper affirmavit, sed se unicum tantum nactum esse. quis autem ille sit, ignoro, neque enim sarcinas adhuc recepit, et ipse rerum similium non valde peritus, tituli oblitus est. Scripsi etiam ea de re ad Clarissimum Riccium,[9] qui se aliquot ex illis transmissurum promisit, cum occasionem, quae raro occurrit, nanciscetur. addet tamen plerosque ex illis, operam non mereri. Ab ipso etiam petieram, an nihil eorum, quae in exercitatione sua[10] promiserat, publico daturus esset; sed respondit se alijs studijs occupatum vix nunc Geometricis vacare posse.

Literas ad Clarissimum Wallisium apertas hic habes, quae vix quidquam praeter gratiarum actionem continent. Tacquetum ea de re non vidi; uti nec Stephani Angeli ac Borelli libros de vi percussionis.[11] Prioris quidem opera facile habiturus sum, sed de horum libris, plane despero cum in Nundinis Francofurtensibus non comparuerint. Adderem aliquid de curvis Clarissimi Barrovij, quarum specimen in eius praelectionibus vidi, sed tempus est ut prolixitati meae tandem finem imponam. Vale itaque Vir Clarissime meque ex asse tuum, quo soles affectu prosequi perge. Dabam Leodij 25 Julij Gregor: MDCLXX.

P.S. Scripseram haec cum allatae sunt ad me literae tuae 4 Julij, quae mihi ruborem incusserunt quod tamdiu prioribus responsum differe debuissem. Rursus itaque tibi ac D. Collinsio gratias ago maximas, avideque expecto, quae liberalitate iam nimia, ad me misistis. Tangentes curvarum ipsius non examinavi, quod Methodus mea solas Geometricas, quas ad aequationem aliquam reducuntur, comprehendat; nondum autem videre licuit an hae tales essent necne.

Inventio Griembergeri de focis sectionum, nullo negotio deducitur ex mea.[12] Nam in ellipsi exempli gratia, cum rectangulum *DIE* aequale sit rectangulo sub dimidijs *EB* vel *XV*, et *VD*; erit illius quadruplum, aequale rectangulo *XVD*. est autem illud quadruplum una cum quadrato *II*,

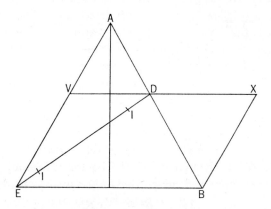

aequale quadrato *DE*, seu rectangulo *XVD* cum quadrato *DB*; Igitur *II* aequatur *DB*. Basilij Valentini opera in linguam latinam versa fuisse audivj, verum ubi edita sint, ignoro.[13] neque valde sollicitus fui, quod illa possiderem manuscripta gallice si non eleganter, utcumque tamen versa. inquiram tamen, eiusque te brevi certiorem reddam. Cedro dignum est quidquid ab Illustri Boylio venit. sed utinam Latina lingua, tam ipse quam D Clarkius scribere in animum inducerent; magnam profecto a multis, a me saltem gratiam inirent. Nuper huc reperi Librum D. Du Hamel de affectionibus corporum, in quo obiter vidi, quoties accuratissimis Illustris illius Viri experimentis utatur. Iterum Vale, 26 Jul: raptim, festinante Tabellario.

TRANSLATION

René François Sluse greets the very noble and famous Mr. Henry Oldenburg, Secretary of the Royal Society

If I had not often observed your singular kindness, famous Sir, I should fear to be accused of negligence by you, on account of my long silence. So, as is your way, be so good as to attribute it partly to multiplicity of business (for I am not of that happy band whose time is at their own disposal) and partly to the great weakness of my health, which I have found little improved by the recent freezing weather, always bad for me. I was brought to the point where I should have feared worse things had I not begun to hope for better, thanks to our spa [waters] which I have been taking for a few weeks. So that beyond returning thanks I can make no reply to what you sent me, as I have to rest from such studies. Yet as, by your generosity, the works of some distinguished persons reached me a few days ago, that is, Wallis's *De motu*, Part I, and Barrow's *Lectiones opticae*, together with the *Exercitationes* of the very acute Gregory, I could not bring myself not to start looking through them straightaway;[1] even after cursory examination they seemed to me worthy of their learned authors, so completely did I find everything in them deduced from true premises, in an orderly manner and with geometrical acuity. A few problems occur in the *Lectiones* upon which I had once had some thoughts, the solution of which, with your leave, I here transcribe for communication to the famous Collins, if they seem to merit that; for I shall think myself to have carried every point, if they do not displease him. Firstly, page 38, in the case where the problem is solid it is easily solved by two hyperbolas.[2] For [*see figure, p. 74*] let the given straight line lie along *EF*, one point being *A* and the other *X*, and the rectangle *XQBC* is completed by dropping the normals *AB*, *XQ* on *EF*. With asymptotes *XQ*, *XC*, let the hyperbola *BPP* be drawn through *B*. Then—the ratio of the refractions being given which the author invariably states as *I* to *R*—let

$$AB^2 : DB^2 = I^2 - R^2 : R^2.[3]$$

With vertex *D*, transverse semiaxis *BD*, let the hyperbola *DPP* be described, in which the ratio of the transverse diameter to the latus rectum is as $I^2 : I^2 - R^2$. For this, if it meets the former hyperbola, will either touch it at one or cut it at two points *P*, *P*, normals dropped from which upon *EF* will give the points *N* that are sought. The opposite branch of this last hyperbola also cuts the first at another point *P*, from which a third normal dropped upon *EB* also gives a point *N'* for the other case, for in fact when *XN'* and *AN'* are joined and *XN'* produced to meet *AB* produced, the produced part of *XN'* will be to *AN'* as *I* to *R*.

The problem serving as a Lemma (p. 40)[4] is embraced in Viète's first postulate to his *Supplementum geometriae*[5] save that in the problem a given right angle is proposed, in the postulate any angle. Yet I remember that I once resolved the postulate by means of two parabolas, by a parabola and a hyperbola, by a circle and a parabola or a hyperbola, but most easily by two hyperbolas. So the problem might be constructed by these same methods, but I will write out another solution by means of a circle and a hyperbola that occurs to me just now. Thus [*see figure, p. 75*], let FPX be the given right angle, Y the given point from which let fall the normal YB upon FP and when the rectangle $YBPD$ has been completed let a hyperbola be described passing through the point P and having YB, YD as its asymptotes. Then with center P, radius T (the length of the given line), let a circle be drawn cutting the hyperbola at R, from which point let fall the normal RN upon FP. Join YN meeting PX at G and NG will be equal to T. The same circle may touch or cut the opposite branch [of the hyperbola] as it does the first one, at two points, as may be seen from the figure where T is chosen large enough to embrace the four solutions.

Another problem is that on page 52[6] whose four solutions (when they occur) are readily displayed by an hyperbola and circle. For it is evident that in this problem no more is required than: through a given point X [*see figure, p. 76*] exterior to a circle (whose center C and diameter BCP are also given) to draw such a straight line XNR meeting the diameter in R and the circle in N that the lengths NR and RC are equal. It may be done thus. Let fall the normal XD on CB (or, if need be, on CB produced). Then make $\dfrac{CB}{2} : CV = CD : CB$; and make

$XD : DC = CV : CG$ (the normal), join GV, and raise the normal $VE = \sqrt{\dfrac{CB^2}{2}}$.[7]

Then, with asymtotes VG, VD describe a hyperbola passing through E. This satisfies the requirement, since it meets the circle in one or two points N. In other cases the opposite branch may do the same; to pursue them in detail would be to exhaust your patience, and the hint is enough.

I have in the past also constructed the celebrated problem which Barrow calls (p. 64) "hard to effect and most difficult of all" be means of both branches [of an hyperbola] intersecting a given circle, one of which reveals the desired point on a convex mirror, the other on a concave mirror, but the construction is a little more laborious and I fear I run on too much already.[8]

I beg you not to attribute the fact that I have so far sent you none of the books you asked for to my negligence, but to that of our booksellers, from whom I could get nothing. Accordingly, as a friend of mine was traveling to Lyons this spring I commanded him to find what he could of them, and bring them back with him if it was not too much trouble. He has recently upon his return assured me that he did this, but could obtain only one [book]. Which it is I do not know, for he has not yet received his baggage and being little skilled in such things himself he has forgotten the title. I also wrote about this business to the famous Ricci,[9] who promised to send a few of them himself when an opportunity should arise, but that rarely happens. But he adds that many of them are not worth the trouble. I have asked him whether nothing was to be published of those things that he promised in his essay,[10] but he replied that he was engaged in other studies and could now hardly spare time for geometry.

You have here an unsealed letter to the famous Wallis which contains hardly anything but a word of thanks. I have not seen what Tacquet writes on that point, as also neither Stefano degli Angeli's nor Borelli's books on the force of percussion.[11] I shall indeed easily get the writings of the former, but I am quite in despair over the books of the two latter since they did not appear at the Frankfurt Fair. I should add something about the famous Barrow's curves, of which I saw an example in his lectures, but it is time for me to bring an end to my longwindedness at last. So farewell famous Sir and continue to count me wholly yours, on whom you customarily bestow kindness.

Liège, 25 July 1670, N.S.

P.S.   I had written these lines when your letter of 4 July was brought to me, which caused me to blush because I had been bound so long to defer my reply to your former letter. So I again offer my best thanks to you and to Mr. Collins and I eagerly await what you with a generosity already excessive have sent me. I have not looked into the tangents to his curves, because my method only comprehends geometrical curves which may be expressed by some equation; it has not yet been possible to see whether these are such, or not.

Grienberger's discovery about the foci of conic sections is deducible from mine without any bother.[12] For in the ellipse, for example [*see figure, p. 77*], as the rectangle DIE is equal to that formed by the halves of EB (or XV) and VD, its quadruple is equal to the rectangle $XV.VD$. But this quadruple together with I^2 is equal to DE^2, or $(XV.VD+BD^2)$. Therefore $I^2 = BD$.

I had heard that the works of Basil Valentine had been turned into Latin but I do not know where they were published.[13] Nor was I very eager to know, because I own manuscript copies of them in French, if not elegantly translated, still translated at any rate. But I will inquire and let you know shortly. Whatever comes from the illustrious Boyle is worthy of immortality. But would that he, like Mr. Clarke, would make a resolution to write in Latin; they would earn great thanks from many, surely; from me at least. I lately came across Mr. Duhamel's book *De affectionibus corporum* here, in which I saw , in passing, how many times he had made use of the experiments of that illustrious person [Boyle]. Farewell again, 26 July, [N.S.]. In haste, the post urges me.

NOTES

Reply to Letters 1434 (Vol. VI) and 1480. For a detailed commentary on the mathematical points involved we are much indebted to Dr. D. T. Whiteside, who points out that a copy of this letter was made by Collins and sent to Barrow, who showed it to Newton (CUL MS. Add. 3971.1, ff. 17–18).

1 For the dispatch of these books see Vol. VI, Letters 1424 and 1434.
2 The problem Lecture V, p. 38 is: "Given a point A, illuminating a given straight

line *EF* [which is the interface between two refracting media], to find the incident [ray] which passes through a second given point [*X*]." Without affecting the argument, Sluse puts *X* on the same side of *EF* as *A*, *XN* being an extension of the refracted ray *Nα*.

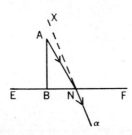

3 To satisfy the conditions this should read "let $\dfrac{AB}{DB} = \dfrac{R}{I}$," and correspondingly below (D. T. W.).

4 "Given a right angle *XPF* and a point *Y*, draw through *Y* a straight line intercepting the sides of the angle so that the intercept [*NG*] may have a given length *T*." This is the form to which Barrow had reduced the problem on refraction just stated. By coincidence, Sluse's construction is "exactly that of Barrow's *Lectiones geometricae*, VI, § III, in effect" (D. T. W.).

5 First published at Paris in 1593, but no doubt Sluse refers to the version with Schooten's commentaries in the *Opera mathematica Fr. Vietae*, pp. 240–57 (D. T. W.).

6 "Given a reflecting circle *BNP* whose center is *C*, and a straight line *CB* in a given position, assign a ray parallel to this line whose reflection passes through a given point." This is a particular case of Alhazen's Problem. Referring to Sluse's figure (p. 76), if *CN* be produced to *T* and *NQ* be the ray *XN* reflected at *N*, it is obvious that *NQ* is parallel to *CR*, solving Barrow's problem.

7 This is the required sense, though not clearly indicated in the Latin (D. T. W.)

8 This is the Problem of Alhazen propounded in his *Optics* (early eleventh century); in its original, general form it was: given two points (such as an illuminated object and the eye) and a spherical, cylindrical, or conical mirror which may be convex or concave, in a given position, to find the point on the mirror at which the object is reflected into the eye. The simplest special case is that of the sphere (that is, a circle and the two points all in one plane).

9 Michelangelo Ricci (1619–82). See J. E. Hofmann in *Centaurus*, IX (1963), 139–93.

10 *Exercitatio geometrica de maximis et minimis* (Rome, 1665; reprinted London, 1668).

11 See Vol. VI, p. 599. André Tacquet, *Opera mathematica* (Antwerp, 1669); Stefano degli Angeli, *Terze considerationi sopra una lettera del . . . Signor Gio. Alfonso Borelli* (Venice, 1668); G. A. Borelli, *De vi percussionis* (Bologna, 1667).

12 See Letter 1424 (Vol. VI, p. 570). In Sluse's figure *EAB* is a right circular cone, *ED* the major axis of any elliptical section with *I, I* its foci, *BE* and *VD* are drawn parallel to the base. His result follows from the fact that the major axis $= \sqrt{\overline{VD. \ EB + BD^2}}$ and the minor axis $\sqrt{\overline{VD. EB}}$.

13 Collins in Letter 1424 asked about a Latin edition from Giessen, which does not seem to exist. Various writings by, or attributed to, "Basil Valentine" were available already in Latin, as indeed in French and English also. Possibly Collins had heard of Theodor Kerckring's *Commentarius in currum triumphalem antimonii . . .* (Amsterdam, 1671).

1490
Paisen to Oldenburg
Mid-July 1670

From the original in Royal Society MS. P, no. 67

Vir Clarissime,

Cum proima hebdomade D. Fogelio Communi Amico nostro scrip-seris,[1] miror, te nullam mentionem fecisse Fasciculi, quem ante tres menses per Samuelem Free Anglum,[2] ut jusseras, ad Te deferri curavi. Continebat ille praeter Libros, quos Ego mittebam, Exemplaria duo Dissertationis Clarissimi Erasmi Bartholini de Crystallo Norvegiae nuper invento dysdiaclastico,[3] quorum Alterum ab Auctore Tibi, alterum D. Wallisio destinatum una cum frusto Lapidis, quod ad Experimenta facienda sufficeret.[4] Pro quo munere, (nam et mihi donavit), hactenus Clarissimi Auctori gratias non egi, tuas literas exspectans, quo conjunctim, unaque opera id fieret. Quare, si Fasciculum dictum accepisti, quaeso, proxima occasione literas ad Bartholinum mittas;[5] sin minus, per tuos de fasciculo inquires apud Mercatorum Londinensem, quem ex ista Scheda a Samuele Free mihi tradita cognosces.

Nobilissimi D. Boyle adversam valetudinem gravissime fero, melioremque precor. Summopere mihi gratum accidit, quod scripta ejus ipso superstite eduntur, dummodo caveat, ne nimium labore illo lassetur.

Ego, quam possum diligentissime pergo in perficiendo Opere Phytoscopico Jungii nostri p.m., de quo ultimis meis ad Te scripsi.[6] Si Deus vitam, et sanitatem concesserit, spero proxima aestate inprimi typis posse.

Nescio an videris Epistolam a Curiosorum Germaniae Collegio editam, qua non tantum aperierunt propositum singulo semestri spatio Ephemerides illarum rerum, quae inter ipsos in Medicina, et Physicis peractae sunt, publicandi, sed etiam insuper omnes et singulos invitarunt, ut si quae vel invenerint nova, vel experiundo conati fuerint, communicent, promittentes, illos bona fide relata, et communicata suis Ephemeridibus inserturos.[7] Epistolae annexae erant quaedam a Clarissimo Bartholino, Segero,[8] alijsque communicata[e].

Quem in D. Fogelij nostri literis desideras librum,[9] Ego Tibi proxima occasione mittam, ubi certiorem viam mihi indicaveris, qua curetur. Ad

cetera Fogelius ipse proxime respondebit, qui Te interim salvere jubet.
Vale, Vir Clarissime, mihique multum amare, et favere perge

T.
M. Paisen

ADDRESS
  A Monsieur
  Monsieur Grubendol
       a
            Londres
franco Envers

TRANSLATION

Famous Sir,

As you have written last week to our common friend Mr. Vogel[1] I am surprised that you do not mention the package which, upon your instructions, I took care to have transported to you by the Englishman, Samuel Free.[2] Besides the books I sent you it contained two copies of the famous Mr. Erasmus Bartholin's dissertation "On the recently discovered double-refracting Norwegian Crystal,"[3] of which one is intended by the author for yourself and the other for Mr. Wallis, together with a piece of the crystal which should be enough for making experiments.[4] For which gift—since he made the same to myself—I have not yet returned thanks to that celebrated author, expecting your letter which, with mine, would kill two birds with one stone. Accordingly, if you have received this package, I beg you to write to Bartholin at the first opportunity;[5] if you have not, inquire about the package at the London merchant's who received it, as you know from the receipt given me by Samuel Free.

I am grieved to hear of the noble Mr. Boyle's poor health, and pray for its improvement. It would be most welcome to me if he might survive to publish his own remaining writings, so long as he takes care not to exhaust himself by excessive efforts.

For my part, I continue as diligently as I can to perfect the *Phytoscopium* of our Jungius (of pious memory) about which I wrote to you in my last.[6] If God give me life and health I hope to be able to have it printed next summer.

I do not know whether you have seen the letter published by the College of Investigators of Germany, in which they not only propose publishing a semi-annual journal of those things they perform in medicine and physic, but invite all and sundry to communicate any new discovery or attempted experiment promising that those which are reported and communicated in good faith will be inserted in their journal.[7] The enclosed letters were some communicated by Bartholin, Seger, and others.[8]

The book you asked for in your letter to our Mr. Vogel[9] I shall send you at the next opportunity when you shall have indicated a safer way by which it may be entrusted. For the rest, Vogel himself will reply soon and meanwhile wishes you good health. Farewell, famous Sir, and continue to love and cherish in many things your

M. Paisen

ADDRESS
    To Mr. Grubendol
        London
postfree to Antwerp

NOTES

1 Oldenburg endorsed this letter as received on 6 August; when writing, Paisen was aware of Oldenburg's letter whose date is given in Vogel's reply (Letter 1498) as 9 July.

2 See Vol. VI, Letter 1454, in which Samuel Free is not specifically named. An English merchant of this name living at Hamburg is known to have petitioned for the right to import timber into England in June 1669 (*C.S.P.D.*, 1668–69, p. 358).

3 Paisen has made a slip; the correct title is *Erasmi Bartholini experimenta chrystalli Islandici dis-diaclastici* (Copenhagen, 1669).

4 Apparently on receipt of this letter Oldenburg at once sought his package, for he collected it on 8 August (Birch, *History*, II, 448), although Bartholin's book was not generally known until September (Turnbull, *Gregory*, p. 107). The volume was presented to the Royal Society on 27 October, and Wallis received his copy about the same time.

5 Oldenburg's first letter of acknowledgement to Bartholin (of unknown date) was lost; he wrote a second time on 15 November (Letter 1552).

6 Vol. VI, Letter 1454.

7 Vol. I of the *Miscellanea curiosa medico-physica academiae naturae curiosorum . . .* , edited by P. J. Sachs, was published at Leipzig in 1670. It was intended to be (and was) an annual volume. The "Epistola invitoria ad celeberrimos Europae medicos" is printed on pp. 1–8 of this first volume.

8 The first "Observatio" in this first volume is on a false conception, by Thomas Bartholin. The third "Observatio" (and others) came from Georg Seger (1629–78), a student of Bartholin's, who was physician to the King of Poland, and physician-in-ordinary at Torun.

9 Possibly J. J. Becher's *Actorum laboratorii chymici Monacensis, seu physicae subterraneae libri duo* (Frankfurt, 1669), mentioned in Letter 1498.

1491
André de Monceaux to Oldenburg
16 July 1670
From the copy in Royal Society MS. M 1, no. 62

Extraict d'une Lettre de
Monsieur De Monceaux
A Monsieur Oldenburg Secretaire
De la Societe royalle

... La vertu quelque fois n'est pas moins Interessée que lAmour, l'un et lautre monsieur veullent recevoir de temps en temps des gages qui respondent pour Ceux qu'Ils unissent d'une secrette Intelligence; La Vostre devroit m'en demender qui vous servissent de caution pour l'avance qu'il vous a pleu me faire de lhonneur de Vostre amitié[1] et comme Je n'ay rien a present qui merite de vous estre sitost envoyé, que dailleurs Je ne veux pas vous donner le loizir de vous deffier de mes forces ny de vous repentir de m'avoir si legerement fait part de vostre estime Je vous envoye pour vous dedomager de vos pretentions sur moy une relation de l'Indolstan,[2] ou vous trouverés des Evenemens si singuliers que vous avouerés que Je ne pouvois vous faire un present plus agreable, et que monsieur bernier[3] qui la Escrite est un tres galant homme Et (sil m'est permis de me servir de ce terme) de la paste dont Il devoit a souhaiter que tous ceux qui Voyagent fussent pestris: Nous voyageons ordinairement par Inquietude plustost que par Curiosité, a dessein de voir les Villes plustost que d'en Connoistre leur peuples, et ne soiournons Jamais assez en un endroit pour en approfondir le gouvernement, la politique, les Interests, et les meurs de ses habitans. Monsieur Bernier apres avoir profitè plusieurs années de l'entretien du fameux Gassendi, l'avoir veu expirer entre ses bras, avoit succedé a ses connoissances, et herité de ses opinions et de ses descouvertes, sembarqua pour l'Egypte; demeura plus d'un an au Caire, et prit l'occasion des Vaisseaux Indienne qui trafiquent dans les ports de la mer rouge pour passer a Surat, et apres douze ans de seiour a la cour du Mogol est enfin venu chercher son repos en son pais, par une secrette obligation de rendre compte a sa patrie de ses scavantes descouvertes et respandre dans son sein tous les thresors quil avoit ramassé dans l'orient.

Je ne vous diray rien monsieur de ses avantures que vous apprendrés des relations qui succederont a Cellecy, qu'il abandonne a l'avidité des curieux Impatiens qui preferent leur satisfaction a son repos et Le persecutent desia pour en avoir la suitte. Je ne vous diray rien des hazards qu'il a courus pour s'estre trouvé dans le voizinage de la Meke; ny de la prudente conduitte qui luy a fait meriter lEstime de son genereux Faze el Kam[4] qui depuis est devenu premier ministre de ce grand Empire, a qui il donna l'Intelligence des principalles langues de lEurope apres luy avoir traduit en Persien La philosophie entier de Gassendi Et dont il na peu obtenir son congé qu'apres luy avoir fait venir un nombre choisy de nos meilleurs livres Pour le consoller par leur entretien et la perte quil faizoit en sa presence. J'ay au moins a vous asseurer monsieur que Jamais voyageur n'est party de chés luy avec plus de capacité pour observer les choses n'a escris avec plus de connoissance de cause plus de Candeur et de sincerité que Je l'ay connu a Constantinople et en quelques villes de Grece d'une Conduitte si singuliere, que Je me la proposois pour Modelle dans le dessein ou Je'stois pour lors de pousser ma curiosité Jusques aux terres ou se leve le soleil; que Jay souvent noyé en la douceur de son entretien les amertumes quil m'auroit fallu boire tout seul dans des routtes aussy penibles et aussy desagreables que celles de la'zie.

Vous me fairés plaizir monsieur de me mander le sentiment de vostre illustre societé sur cet ouvrage son approbation au reste fait bien des Jalous parmy les scavans qui nont tous autre ambition que de luy plaire. Je vous avoueray mesme que si Je croyois la pouvoir meriter Je ne m'opposerois pas si opiniastrement que Je fais a la publication de mes memoires et des observations que Jay faites en Levant,[6] Je souffrerois que mes amis les Enterrassent du Cabinet ou pour le peu de cas que J'en fais elles courent risque de Tenir prizon perpetuelle, amoins d'un autre costé que le Roy mon maistre par l'ordre duquel J'ay entrepris Mes Voyages ne me commanda d'authorité de leur rendre la liberté et de leur laisser promener a leur tour par le monde; Vous m'obligerés cependant monsieur d'asseurer ces grands hommes qui composent auiourdhuy la plus scavante Compagnie de la terre de la Veneration que Jay pour les Oracles qui partent de leur bouche que Je prefere leur Lycée a Celuy d'Athenes et que de tous leurs admirateurs il n'y en a point qui prenne plus de part a leur gloire que

De Monceaux

De Paris ce 26me Juillet 1670 [N.S.]

TRANSLATION, from F. Bernier, *The History of the Late Revolution of the Empire of the Great Mogul* (London, 1671), sigs. A2–A5

An Extract of a Letter
Written to Mr. H. O.
FROM
Monsr de Monceaux the Younger,
Giving a Character of the Book
here Englished, and its Author

Vertue sometimes is no less interessed [*sic*] than Affection: Both, Sir, are glad to receive from time to time pledges mutually answering for those that have united themselves in a close correspondence. Yours indeed should demand of me such, as might be a security to you for the advance, you have been pleased to make me of your Friendship.[1] But since at present I have nothing worth presenting you with; and yet am unwilling to give you any leisure to be diffident of my realness, or to repent for having so easily given me a share in your esteem, I here send you a *Relation* of *Indostan*,[2] in which you will find such considerable Occurences, as will make you confess I could not convey to you a more acceptable Present, and that Monsieur Bernier,[3] who hath written it, is a very Gallant man, and of a mould, I wish all Travellers were made of. We ordinarily travel more out of Unsetledness than Curiosity, with a designe to see Towns and Countries rather than to know their Inhabitants and Productions; and we stay not long enough in a place, to inform our selves well of the Government, Policy, Interests and Manners of its People. Monsieur Bernier, after he had benefited himself for the space of many years by the converse of the famous Gassendi; seen him expire in his Arms, succeeded him in his Knowledge, and inherited his Opinions and Discoveries, embarqued for Ægypt, stay'd above a whole year at Cairo, and then took the occasion of some Indian Vessels that trade in the Ports of the Red Sea, to pass to Suratte; and after Twelve years abode at the Court of the Great Mogul, is at last come to seek his rest in his native Countrey, there to give an Accompt of his Observations and Discoveries, and to poure out into the bosome of France, what he had amassed in India.

Sir, I shall say nothing to you of his Adventures which you will find in the Relations that are to follow hereafter, which he abandons to the greediness of the Curious, who prefer their satisfaction to his quiet, and do already persecute him to have the sequel of this History. Neither shall I mention to you the hazards he did run, by being in the neighbourhood of Mecca; nor of his prudent conduct, which made him merit the esteem of his generous Fazelkan,[4] who since is become the first Minister of that Great Empire, whom he taught the principal Languages of Europe, after he had translated for him [into Persian] the whole Philosophy of Gassendi in Latin,[5] and whose leave he could not obtain to go home, till he had got for him a select number of our best European Books, thereby to supply the loss he should suffer of his Person. This, at least, I can assure you of, that never a Traveller went from home more capable to observe, nor hath written with more knowledge, candour and integrity; that I knew him at Constantinople, and in some towns of Greece, of so excellent a conduct, that I proposed him to my self for a Pattern in the designe I then had to carry my curiosity as far as the place where the Sun riseth; that I have often drowned in the sweetness of his entertainment the bitternesses, which else I must have swallowed all alone in such irksome and unpleasant passages, as are those of Asia.

Sir, you will do me a pleasure to let me know the sentiment, your Illustrious Society hath of this Piece. Their Approbation begets much emulation among the Intelligent, who all have no other Ambition than to please them. I my self must avow to you, that if I thought I could merit so much, I should not so stifly oppose as I do, the publication of the Observations and Notes I have made in the Levant.[6] I should suffer my Friends to take them out of my Cabinet, where, from the slight value I have for them, they are like to lie imprisoned, except the King my Master, by whose order I undertook those Voyages, should absolutely command me to set them at liberty, and to let them make their course in the world. Mean time Sir, you would oblige me to assure those Great Men, who this day compose the most knowing Company on Earth, of the Veneration I have for the Oracles that come from their Mouth, and that I prefer their Lyceum before that of Athens; and lastly, that of all their Admirers there is none, that hath a greater Concern for their Glory, than

De Monceaux

Paris, Julij 16, 1670. [N.S.]

NOTES

André de Monceaux, the son of one of Louis XIV's councilors, was well known to Huygens from being his neighbor in Paris. In Letter 1537 Huygens, introducing him to Oldenburg, writes of him as a former traveler in the Levant who had collected many architectural drawings. During his visit to England he was elected F.R.S., on 15 December 1670. He died not long afterwards.

1 Nothing of this survives.
2 François Bernier, *Histoire de la derniere revolution des Etats du Gran Mogol* (Paris, 1670). The English translation of this book, from which we take the English of this letter, was by Oldenburg.
3 François Bernier (1620–88) studied at Paris and entered the household of the philosopher Pierre Gassendi (1592–1655) and followed his courses at the Collège Royale. After some diplomatic travel (1648–50) he rejoined Gassendi; following the philosopher's death he embarked on the travels described in the letter. He published, besides accounts of his experiences, an *Abrégé de la philosophie de Mr. Gassendi* (Paris, 1675).
4 "Perfect Lord." It seems that Mohi ud-din Mohammed Aurangzeb (1618–1707), the last of the great Mogul emperors of India, is intended here, for he is the hero of

Bernier's history, which is concerned with Aurangzeb's fight for the succession after
the collapse of his father, Shah Jehan (d. 1666), in 1657.
5 These two words are not in the French.
6 We could not find that Monceaux published anything.

1492
Oldenburg to Wallis
c. 18 July 1670

This letter was received by Wallis on the morning of Wednesday, 20 July, delivered
by a Dr. Upsall in the suite of the Landgrave, then traveling incognito as the Count of
Schaumburg, who had arrived in Oxford the previous evening. It begged Wallis to
look after the distinguished visitor, hinted darkly at his identity, and enclosed various
papers. It is mentioned in Wallis's Letter 1494. For identifications, see Letter 1494.

1493
Willughby to Oldenburg
19 July 1670

From the original in Royal Society MS. W 3, no. 37

Middleton July 19th

Sr

Mr Listers meaning[1] most certainly was, that though the trees bled for
above 40 times after Frostie nights, yet they did not allwaies bleed at the
old wounds, but that sometimes they bled at the old and at new wounds
never Failed to bleed. I should bee beholden to you at your leisure to give
mee some account of mr Hookes later Invention for the easie drawing up
of Water out of deep pits.[2] I remain allwaies

your Faithfull servant
Fr : Willughby

ADDRESS
    for mr Henrie
    Oldenburg secre-
    tary to the
    royall society at
    His house in the
    Pal Mal
            London

                                        POSTMARK IV 22

NOTES

1 See Letter 1479.
2 On 5 May 1670 Christopher Wren had at a meeting of the Society "produced a new
  contrivance of his for a more convenient winding up of weights by ropes, and serving
  for wells, mines and cranes, and thought applicable to clocks" (Birch, *History*, II,
  435). Hooke was then directed to try this with clocks, though there is no record that
  he did so. Willughby was evidently confused.

1494
Wallis to Oldenburg
22 July 1670
From the original in Royal Society MS. W 1, no. 111

                                        Oxford July 22. 1670.

    Sir,

I was just going to blame you for your last letter,[1] when upon a further
view thereof I find it will (at lest in part) return upon myself. You intimate
therein, but so obscurely that I did not understand it, that the Landgrave
himself was coming hither.[2] But your words being onely, that the bearer
was of *the suite of this prince now intending to see Oxford*; & himself onely acknowledging his relation to that Prince, but that his business here was to
wait on a young Count whom he called the *Count of Schawmburg*; I apprehended no other sense of your words but that *the suite* (not *the Prince*) was
now intending to see Oxford; of whom I took this *Count of Schawmburg* to

have been one. Nor was I delivered from that mistake till they were just going away. Otherwise, he should not have been so meanly attended at his own lodgings as by myself onely. 'Tis true, that they brought a letter from Sr Charles Coterel[3] to ye Vice-chancellor,[4] signifying his condition. But it was so late ere they delivered that Letter, as that hee was thereby hindered from giving such Academical Reception as would otherwise have been due to a Prince of his quality. They came hither late on Tuesday night; & the next morning your letter (with the inclosed papers for which I thank you) were delivered mee by Dr Upsall[5] (if I mistake not the name:) whom I received with the Ordinary civility due to strangers: & (the rather because of your recommendation) understanding that hee did here attend a Count who came to see the place (though I knew not of what quality) I offered with him to attend that Count at his lodgings, and wait on him to such places as hee had a desire to see. He signified, that the Count was then somewhat indisposed, & did not intend to goe forth that morning, nor would till about two hours after be in a condition to be attended. But (his indisposition, it seems, being pretty well over) when I came at the time appointed, I found them not within, (being gone, as it afterward appeared, to see the Schooles, the Library, the Theater &c.) I left word that I had been there, & would again attend the Count after Dinner. At which time, I waited on his Highness from there to Christchurch; where (missing of Dr Locky,[6] who speaks French, but was then not at home) I went with them to the Deans lodgings,[7] who having treated them with a Glass of wine &c, did him self wait on them to shew his Highness their Church, their Library, their Hall &c: and then at ye College Gate left them to my further conduct. Thence, having taken a short view of the Colleges of Oriel, Corpus Christi, & Merton, wee went by Coach to the Physick Garden: where Bobart (the Gardiner)[8] having in Dutch[9] given him an account of the Garden and some of his rarities there, wc went cross the way to Magdalene College: where it being then Prayer time, his Highness went into the Chapel (attended with his Company) & stayd there all the time, to see the manner of the Service, (Singing, Organs, &c;) which Ended; the President, Dr Piers,[10] (to whom I had intimated what I knew concerning the quality of ye Person,) treated him (in French) at his lodgings, with a Glass of Wine, Cidar, &c, & then shewd him their Library, Walks, Hall, &c, & conducted him to his Coach. His Highness being then weary, & not willing to see more Colleges, I onely shewed him the outsides of University College, All-Souls Colledge, & St. Mary's Church, (as wee passed by,) returning to his lodgings at the Bear. Understanding there, that the Vice-Chancellor (with all his Bedles)

had been there whilst his Highness was absent to wait on him: I then waited
on him to the Vice-chancellor's lodgings: who there received him (with
the attendance of his Bedles,) excused himself (by reason of the late reception of Sr Charles Coterels letter that afternoon) that he had not waited on
him sooner: discoursed with him some time in French (which language his
Highness chose rather to speak than Latine, though he speaks this allso,)
treated him with a Glass of Wine &c, shewed him their Library, & walks,
& then attended him to his Coach; being desired by his Highness (as since
I understand) not to take notice of his quality: of which I was all this while
ignorant. Having then waited on him to his Inne, I there took my leave of
him: Yet afterwards waited on him again, to shew him a little curiosity of
my own (of wch there had before been mention made, by some of his
attendants who had seen it at my house,) and some of Mr. Birds Stained
Marble.[11] That night, & on Thursday morning (when I waited on him
again before he went out of Town) I began to discern my Error. And therefore, before he went, I thought myself obliged to make an Apology; That,
thought it were not civil for mee to be too inquisitive into what hee pleased
to conceal: yet (by the Title of *Serenissimus* which I once discerned to fall
unawares from one of his Attendance) I could not but beleeve him to be of
a much higher quality than at first I apprehended, or did so much as suspect: beseeching his pardon as well in my own name as of the University:
that hee had not been received with that Honor & Respect which his Quality, had it been known, would have required: & that what ever neglects or
mistakes had been [made] he would impute onely to our perfect ignorance
of his condition; of which had wee been aware, his reception would have
been much otherwise, & more sutable to his quality: But it being so late
before I did so much as suspect it, it was now impossible (his Highness
being just ready to take Coach for Salisbury) to make any other amends,
than by professing our Ignorance & craving his Pardon. Which hee did
not seem to take amisse. And it was then owned, that hee was indeed such
a Person as I apprehended, (the Count of Schawmburg being allso one of
his Titles) but being willing to passe Incognito, it would rather be a favour
to conceal his quality. After which he presently took Coach & went away
towards Salisbury; when I had taken my leave of him at the Coach side.
Had wee had timely notice of it, the University would doubtless have received him after another fashion, & somewhat answerable to his quality,
as they did the Prince of Tuscany the last year. (At lest it should not have
been my fault if they had not.) Or had ye Vice-chancellors letter been delivered him the same night they came to Town, or betimes the next morn-

ing: there had been time to have called a Convocation & given him therein some Academical Reception, & conferred some Degrees on those of his attendance, (if himself should not do us the Honour to accept of any:) For though wee do not, in ordinary course, grant Degrees without respect had to Time & Exercises: Yet wee are not so tyed up but that on such occasions our Honorary Degrees are conferred without such considerations.

Sr, Having given you this Narrative, I have nothing further to adde, but to desire that you will, as there shal be occasion, make the best apology for any neglect of ours, & that ye fairest constructions may be put upon them: & to thank you for the honour you have given mee, in affording the opportunity of waiting on so Eminent a Prince. Resting,

Yours, to serve you,
John Wallis

ADDRESS
These
For Mr Henry Oldenburg
in the Palmal near
St. James's
London

NOTES

1 That is, Letter 1492 which is lost.
2 There is no record of a visit by a German nobleman to Oxford at this time, and perhaps the reasons for this lack are sufficiently given in Wallis's letter. Nor is there any mention elsewhere of the visitor's real identity. In *C.S.P.D.*, 1670, p. 362, a letter writer reports the departure from Dover of the Comte de Schomberg, with a retinue of 23 persons, on 2 August; this can hardly have been the celebrated general. Wallis's visitor *could* have been Anton Egon Furstenberg (1656–1716), whose father was a Prince of the Empire.
3 Sir Charles Cotterell (1612?–1702), Master of Ceremonies at Whitehall.
4 Peter Mews (1619–1706), President of St. John's.
5 Not identified.
6 Thomas Lockey (*c*. 1602–79), Bodley's librarian from 1660 to 1665.
7 Dr. John Fell (1625–86).
8 Jacob Bobart (d. 1679) of Brunswick, Germany, Keeper of the Physic Garden at Oxford.
9 That is, German.
10 Thomas Peirse (*c*. 1632–91), President of Magdalene from 1661 to 1672.
11 On 27 January 1675/6, at a meeting of the Royal Society, Oldenburg showed a piece of marble stained to show a picture, the work of Prince Rupert, "a great improvement on what had been done at Oxford by a certain stonecutter there." This was no doubt Bird.

1495
Oldenburg to Newburgh
22 July 1670
From the memorandum in Royal Society MS. N 1, no. 4

Rec. july 9. 70; sent papers and received 7½ sh.
Answ. july 22. 70. and sent him Book of vipers for 3 sh. and lent him Book of Silkworms of Isnard for 2. months, and offred copies of more papers of Agriculture. Promised to inquire for our kings or K. James instruction concerning silkworms

NOTE

Reply to Letter 1481. When Newburgh acknowledged its receipt in Letter 1504 he dated it as 28 July; however there is no valid reason to reject Oldenburg's date.

1496
Oldenburg to Rudbeck
23 July 1670
From the copy in Royal Society MS. O 2, no. 30

Clarissimo Viro
Domino Rudbeckio, Philosopho Medico Upsaliensi
H. Oldenburg S.R. Secr. Salutem

Quamvis semel atque iterum,[1] data occasione ad Te scripserim, Vir Celeberrime, Teque ad studiorum Philosophicorum consociationem invitaverim, cum tamen ex silentio verear ne literae illae nostrae, ut saepe sit, interciderint, commodumque se offerat in sueciam abituriens serenissimi Regis nostri mandatarius, Generosus Dominus Woordenus,[2] visum omnino fuit, praegressas literas in compendium hic redigere, utque Argumentis sequentibus pro humanitate et eruditione tua respondeas, sollicitare.

Pars est instituti Societatis Regiae Historiam condere Naturalem, genuinam et summa fide elaborandam, cui solidum demum et ferax Philosophiae Systema superstruatur. Agnoscis facile, quorumvis totius universi Virorum Illustrium operas in hanc rem esse jungendas, mutuisque commercijs tantum opus conficiendum. Complures aliarum gentium Philosophos in eam curam jam accendimus. Credimus etiam, multa occurrere in Suecia, tum de Aere, tum de Terra, et Fossilibus inprimis, tum de aquis, observatu dignissima. In votis est, ut quae Tu, Vir Eximie, alijque Viri docti circa res istas naturales in regno vestro observastis, vel imposterum observaturi estis, fideliter edoceamur. Quae nostra Tellus suppeditat, libentissime vicissim, siquidem id vobis allubescat, impertiemur.

Narravit Nobis Ornatissimus Dominus Edwardus Chamberlain,[3] Occupatum Te fuisse, cum in Suecia nuper ageret, in extruendo Ponte non vulgari, nec non in alia quadam machina singularis artificij, conficienda. Salutem ille plurimam Tibi scribit, impenseque, una mecum, rogat, ut quousque opera illa expediveris, nos edocere velis. Egregij quidam libri hic nuper a nonnullis R. Soc. Assectis in lucem prodiere, puta, Wallisij nostri de Motu et Mechanica pars prima et 2da; quas brevi excipiet pars tertia: Adhaec Barrovij Lectiones Opticae, et Geometricae: Nec non Loweri Tractatus de Motu Cordis et Sanguinis Editio altera cum appendice de Catharris. Non dubito, quin harum lator generosissimus, hosce aliosque libros oris vestris sit illaturus, nobisque vicissim librorum in Suecia, a Viris Illustribus de re Philosophica editorum, Catologum transmissurus.

Rogaveram in meis ad Te novissimis, ut mihi Historiam partus Caesarei Uxoris Tuae, in quo Temet felicissimo successu operatum fuisse intelleximus, perscriberes. In gemino nunc, quod jam ante petij, nec Te desiderio nostro facturum satis, diffido.[4] Vale et rem Philosophicam augere et ornare perge. Dabam Londini die 23. Julij 1670.

TRANSLATION

Henry Oldenburg, Secretary of the Royal Society, greets the famous Mr. Rudbeck, philosopher and physician of Uppsala

Although I have once and again written to you,[1] celebrated Sir, when opportunity served, inviting you to a fellowship in philosophical studies, as I fear from your silence that my letters must have perished, and as H. M. Resident (Mr. Werden)[2] on his departure for Sweden offered his services, it seemed altogether wise here to abbreviate the preceding letters and to beg you to reply to the following points out of your kindness and learning.

It is part of the design of the Royal Society to compile a trustworthy natural history to be executed in the most reliable manner, upon which a solid and fruitful natural philosophy may be erected. You will readily agree that the efforts of all distinguished men, over the whole globe, should be combined for this purpose, and that so great a work should be prepared by their mutual exchanges. We have already inspired several philosophers of other countries to this task. We also believe that in Sweden there are many things very worthy of note, in the air, in the earth (fossils particularly), and in the waters. It is desired that you, excellent Sir, and other learned men shall faithfully teach us what you observe of such natural phenomena in your country, or what you shall observe in the future. In return we shall gladly impart to you what our country renders us, if that will please you.

The most polished Mr. Edward Chamberlayne,[3] who was lately visiting Sweden, has reported to us that you were engaged in building an extraordinary bridge, and in making some other machine of unusual ingenuity. He sends you many greetings, and along with myself earnestly begs you to please to tell us how far you have proceeded with those tasks.

Some remarkable books have been published here lately by some members of the Royal Society, for example, Wallis's *De motu et mechanica*, Parts I and II, to which Part III will soon succeed; Barrow's *Lectiones opticae et geometricae*; and the second edition of Lower's *De corde* with an appendix *De catharris*. No doubt the wellborn bearer of this letter will import these and other books to your country, and in return transmit to us a catalogue of the books published in Sweden by distinguished writers on philosophical topics.

I had asked in my last letter to you that you should write for me the narrative of your wife's Caesarean delivery, in which we understand that you performed the operation yourself with a most fortunate outcome. I am doubtful whether you will have satisfied our importunity already, and I now ask a second time what I sought for before.[4] Farewell, and continue to adorn and improve philosophy. London, 23 July 1670

NOTES

1 See Vol. V, Letter 1069 (8 January 1668/9) and Vol. VI, Letter 1338 (9 December 1669).

2 John Werden or Worden (1640–1716) was traveling to Sweden as Envoy Extraordinary from Charles II.

3 See Vol. VI, Letter 1338, note 2.

4 We are not confident of the meaning of this sentence. We can now add that the obstetric operation about which Oldenburg inquired, permitting the birth of Rudbeck's eldest son (Johannes Caesar!) in 1656, consisted in the removal of a tumor or polypus. It was not a Caesarean section. Four normal births occurred later. No account of the operation was in print at this time, and there are few recorded allusions to it.

1497
Oldenburg to De Graaf
26 July 1670

Oldenburg has endorsed Letter 1472 from De Graaf to the effect that he received it on 22 June and answered it on 26 July.

1498
Vogel to Oldenburg
28 July 1670

From the original in Royal Society MS. F 1, no. 29

Viro Nobilissimo
HENRICO OLDENBURGIO
S.P.D.
Martinus Fogelius.

Ne illis quidem, quas 9 Julii ad me perscripsisti, literis mihi constat, utrum meas superiore Decembre ad te datas acceperis.[1] Quin potius & has, quibus idem sciscitabar, interceptas fuisse suspicor, quod nihil plane ad eas respondeas. Scripseram autem 9 Aprilis una cum D. Paisenio,[2] & praecipue de his, quae de Toxico Hispanorum (Yerva de Balestero) inquirenda habeo.[3] scilicet

1 an paretur per totam Hispaniam eodem modo.
2 ex qua vel ex quibus Herbis; & quo tempore anni.
3 figura Herbae ad quam Iconem Matthioli,[4] Lobelii,[5] alique Botanici accedat.
4 Plantae aliquot intra chartas explicatae & exsiccatae ad nos mittantur.
5 an Balearidum incolis sit cognitum.
6 annon Cornu unum et alterum Toxico plenum ad nos transmitti possit.
7 an per Vedegambre Hispani solum Elleborum album ubique intelligant, an solum Nigrum, an utrumque.

8 quodnam Antidoton cujus vim inpingat.

Quamvis autem jam accuratiorem hujus Toxici cognitionem partim in Hispania, partim hic acquisiverim, quam ullus forsan hactenus habuit; certior tamen & tua opera de his reddi etiam atque etiam optarem. Grisleus forsan vester,[6] & in Majorica Vincentius Mutus[7] mihi gratum poterunt praestare officium, publice a me praedicandum.

Clarissimo Morisono[8] est quidam in iisdem reposueram, quae nolo repetere.

Quod ad Schedas Phoranomicae, misimus, quas inprimis desiderabas. Siferus spe Professionis Mathematicae hactenus turbatus, minus promovendae Phoranomicae vacare potuit.

D. Paisenius mittit tibi Becheri Physicam Subterraneam,[9] quam cum his literis tibi pro ea, qua est humanitate, affere non recusavit Nobilissimus & Amplissimus Morhofius,[10] Professor Chiloniensi, & I.U.D., qui & Experimenta quaedam Becherii repetiit, & recte instituta deprehendit. Sed secundum librum inprimis desideramus.[11]

Basilium Valentinum recudere constituit noster Bibliopola,[12] sed lingua Germanica. Huic autem minime de alio idem destinante constabat. habet jam aliquot ejus opuscula, & si a vobis esse sperare unum et alterum poterit, gratissimum facietis, si quamprimum transmittetis. Non incipiet autem praelo ea committere ante exactam hiemem.

Nolo Eruditionem singularem et Virtutes D. Mohrhofii tibi commendare, quas tum publica Viri Dignitas, tum Monumenta ejus satis commendant. Vale Vir Doctissime, & me ama.

Dabam Hamburgi 28 Jul 1670.

ADDRESS

A Monsr
Monsr Henry Oldenbourg,
Secretaire de la Societe Royale
　　　　a
　　　　　Londres
　　　　　　au pelle mele
avec un pacquet

TRANSLATION

Martin Vogel sends many greetings to the very noble Henry Oldenburg

From your letter written to me on 9 July I am doubtful whether you have received mine of last December.[1] I rather suspect, by what I can learn from yours, that it was lost on the way since you obviously make no reply to it. However, I had written on 9 April together with Mr. Paisen,[2] particularly about my inquiries relating to the Spanish poison (white Hellebore),[3] that is,

1 Whether it is prepared in the same way throughout Spain?
2 From what or which plants, and at what time of year?
3 What illustration in Mattioli,[4] De l'Obel[5] or other botanist approximates to the form of the plant?
4 A few plants pressed between paper and dried to be sent to us.
5 Is it known to the inhabitants of the Balearic Islands?
6 Could a horn or two filled with the poison be sent to us?
7 Whether by *Verdegambre* the Spaniards mean white Hellebore only, or the black, or both?
8 What antidote opposes its virulence?

Although I have already acquired a more accurate knowledge of this poison than any one has had before, perhaps, partly in Spain and partly here, I would like still more information and your assistance to this end. Perhaps your countryman, Mr. Grisley,[6] and Vicente Mut[7] in Majorca could oblige me by their services, of which I would make public acknowledgment.

I made something of an answer to the famous Morison,[8] which I do not wish to repeat.

As for the sheets of *Phoranomica*, we have sent what you particularly requested. Sivers, who has been distracted by his prospects in the teaching of mathematics up to now, has had the less leisure for pressing on with *Phoranomica*.

Mr. Paisen sends you Becher's *Physica subterranea*,[9] which our most noble and excellent Morhof,[10] with his usual kindness, has not refused to bring to you along with these letters; he is a professor at Kiel and Doctor of Civil and Canon Law, who has repeated some of Becher's experiments and believes them to be properly performed. But we particularly wish for the second book.[11]

Our bookseller has decided to reprint Basil Valentine,[12] but in the German tongue. He knew nothing of anyone else's having the same intention. He has already a few of his works and if one or two more could be hoped for from you it would be most welcome if you could send them as soon as possible. But he will not send them to press before the end of the winter.

I have no need to commend the extraordinary learning and merits of Mr. Morhof to you, for he is sufficiently commended by his known standing and his accomplishments. Farewell, learned Sir, and love me.

Hamburg, 28 July 1670.

ADDRESS

> To Mr. Henry Oldenburg
> Secretary of the Royal Society
> London
> in the Pall Mall
>
> with a package

NOTES

1 Letter 1330 of 27 November (Vol. VI), which Oldenburg did receive.
2 Letter 1444 (Vol. VI); there is no surviving separate letter from Paisen of a nearby date.
3 See Vol. VI, pp. 346 and 620, also note 10, p. 348, and note 6, p. 621.
4 P. A. Mattioli, *Dioscoride libri cinque della historia et materia medicinale* (Venice, 1544, and many subsequent and enlarged editions).
5 Matthias de l'Obel, *Plantarum seu stirpium historia* (Antwerp, 1576), is the best known work of this botanist.
6 See Vol. V, Letter 1124.
7 See Vol. VI, Letter 1444, note 12.
8 See Vol. VI, Letters 1341 and 1373.
9 See Letter 1490, note 9.
10 Daniel Georg Morhof (1639–91); see Letter 1542.
11 Despite its title, the *Physica subterranea* contains only one book; a supplement (*Experimentum chymicum novum*) was published, also at Frankfurt, in 1671.
12 The bookseller was presumably Gottfried Schulz (see Vol. VI, Letter 1444), to whom we could trace no edition of "Basil Valentine." However, there was a collected *Chymische Schriften* of "Basil" published by Nauman and Wolff (Hamburg, 1677), subsequently reprinted.

1499
Oldenburg to Wallis
28 July 1670

From the endorsement on Royal Society MS. W 1, no. 111

D r Wallis to be thanked for his Book. Answ. july 28. 1670.

NOTE

Reply to Letter 1494; it is mentioned in Letter 1500 as containing the letter from Sluse to Wallis also mentioned in Letter 1489 (p. 76).

1500

Wallis to Oldenburg

4 August 1670

From the original in Royal Society MS. W 1, no. 112

Oxford Aug. 4. 1670.

Sir,

I have yours of July 28. with that from M. Slusius inclosed. To whom I desire, when you next write, to return my thanks for it, & for the Theoreme therein contained: which is very ingenious. There being nothing in it which requires an answere I forbear to give him a letter merely of complements. The two books for beyond sea,[1] I therefore ordered you, because you desired them the last time: but you did not tell mee for whom: I suppose they may bee for Hugens & Slusius. Before you send them; be pleased with your pen to make these additions.

pag. 560. lin. 28. after $\dfrac{h^2}{h^2-n^2}L$ adde $+ \dfrac{n^2}{h^2-n^2}T$.

pag. 561. lin. 5 after $\dfrac{h^2}{n^2-h^2}L$ adde $+ \dfrac{n^2}{n^2-h^2}T$.

pag. 565. lin. 11 after conjugatus, adde sin curvam tangat; perinde est ad utrumvis casum referas: quippe tum Hyperbolae degenerant in Opposita Triangula, quorum communis Vertex est O, punctum contactus; evanescente Axe transverso.
pag. 556. lin. 24. after Genetricis, adde, aut etiam hyperbolam hanc ubivis tangat.[2]

I should have ordered more copies to my friends in the Society, but that the Book-seller complained the last time that I thereby prevented those from buying who were most likely so to do; which in a book of so slow a sale as Mathematick bookes usually are, is a considerable prejudice to him; & therefore I hope my friends will not take it as any disrespect.

I find, (by a letter from Mr Collins,) that Mr Pits, the Book-seller, is not satisfied in the price the Counsel of the Society hath put on the books for wch their members have subscribed.[3] I could wish (though I am not concerned in it) that they had satisfied him. For I know the printing of it hath been very troublesome & very chargeable, beyond what other books are of the same bulk: & ye number of the Impression but smal, & the sale (as of other mathematick books, especially those more intricate, & not for every ones understanding,) but slow. (And, if I may say it, this is so closely penned as that if they have not bulk inough, they will at lest have matter inough for their mony; the same matter being inough to have filled large volumes). And, considering how few are willing to undertake ye printing of books that are a little out of the common road; I would not have those discouraged that are. I adde no more, but that I am

Yours to serve you
Joh. Wallis

ADDRESS
>   These
> For Mr Henry Oldenburg
> in the Palmal near
>   St James's
>   London

NOTES

Reply to Letter 1499.
1 Presumably copies of *Mechanica, sive de motu, pars secunda*.
2 "conjugate . . . unless it touches the curve; it matters not to which case you refer; in fact then the hyperbole degenerate into opposed triangles having a common vertex at O, the point of contact, the transverse axis vanishing . . . or even touches the hyperbola anywhere."
3 Compare Wallis to Collins, 4 August 1670 (Rigaud, II, 524): "I am sorry those of the Society have no better satisfied Mr. Pitts in the price of the book, which I am very sensible was both troublesome and chargeable to print." Moses Pitt (*fl.* 1654–96) was a bookseller and publisher dogged by ill-success; in 1689–91 he was imprisoned for debt. On 26 July 1670 the Council of the Society discussed Pitt's proposal to sell the two volumes for fifteen shillings and sixpence. "Whe[re]upon the council declared, that since he did not think fit to abate any thing of that price, and to take fourteen shillings for both the volumes, he was at liberty to sell them as he could; but that then the subscribers, who had agreed to pay such a rate, as should be set by the council, were also left at liberty to buy or not buy at his rate" (Birch, *History*, II, 446–47).

1501

Oldenburg to Willughby

5 August 1670

From the memorandum in Royal Society MS. W 3, no. 37

Answ. Aug. 5. 70. of ye grubs turnd to Bees, Dr King.[1] Dr Wrens Invention of drawing weights out of deep pits.[2] Of Dr Tongs relation of duel,[3] not seen yet by himself, but receiv'd from others, wth several Queries about Spiders and Toades. Hope, he received Thermometers.

NOTES

Reply to Willughby's Letter 1493.

1 On 14 July (according to Birch, *History*, II, 443–44), various papers were registered, including Dr. Edmund King's "Observations on insects lodging themselves in old willows"; it is printed in *Phil. Trans.*, no. 65 (14 November 1670), 2098–99 and describes various "cartrages" containing maggots, which later produced bees.
2 See Letter 1493, note 2.
3 See Letter 1467.

1502

Oldenburg to Wallis

6 August 1670

Letter 1500 bears an endorsement stating it was answered on this date.

1503
Martin Lister to Oldenburg
9 August 1670
From the original in Royal Society MS. L 5, no. 20

Sr

This last Post I received a Letter from Mr John Wray: wherin he told me, yt, being questioned about it, he had given in to you a Note, concerning ye first Observer of ye darting of Spiders, & yt he beleeves you would print it.[1] if you are not yet fully satisfied about it, I have this further to tell you: yt Mr Wray knew nothing of my knowing it, noe more than I knew, yt either he or or any body else knew it, untill such time as I occasionly sent him (in order to ye making good a philosophical correspondence wch he & I had been some yeares engaged in) a Catalogue of our English Spiders: upon wch subject, ye next Letter he put this amongst other questions to me, wither I had observed the darting of spiders: to wch I answered in ye affirmative, relating to him many other circumstances unknown to him afore & than he desired of me, to draw up my notes & suffer him to present ym to ye R.S., wch I did & you was pleased after to print ym. This Sr, is ye truth of ye busnesse; wch Mr Wray will not deny & his letters will sufficiently evidence: yt ye observation is as well mine, as his, from whom Mr Wray had first notice of it & yt I was not in ye least beholden to him for it: but yt I writ it to Mr Wray, not as a thing alltogether unknown to him, but to confirme & enlarge it by ye addition of my owne observations. Sr. I presume from your Civilitie (wch I did well understand yt moment I had ye happinesse to kisse your hands wth Mr Skippon at your house in London) & prudence, yt if such Note be printed (& it may already be for ought I know, it being soe remote a corner where I live, Yt I have not yet seen June Booke)[2] noe unhandsome reflection will be made upon me or anything detracting from my credit in suffering my notes to be published. This Letter I ventur to send to you by Mr Martin your printer at ye Bell: but if you please to send me how I may direct a Letter to you & to entertain a correspondance wth me, I happen upon something now & than wch may not be unwelcome to you & I am at present not altogether unfurnished of such matters I am

Your humble servant
Martin Lister

Carlton in Craven
August 9th 1670

For me at Carleton in Craven
To be left at Ferry briggs[3]
for Bradford post.

ADDRESS
 These
For Mr Oldenburgh
To be left wth Mr Martin
Bookseller at ye Bell neer
 Temple-Barr
   London

POSTMARK AU 12

NOTES

Martin Lister (?1638–1712) has already appeared in the correspondence as a friend and companion of Skippon and Ray, whom he met at Montpellier in the winter of 1665–66, and as a modestly anonymous writer on snail shells and spiders. In 1669, upon his marriage, he purchased Carlton Hall near Skipton in the western part of Yorkshire; soon after writing this letter he moved to York where he practised medicine until 1683. From 1671 onwards he was a constant correspondent, many of his letters being printed *in extenso* in the *Philosophical Transactions*. He was elected F.R.S. on 2 November 1671. His main scientific interests were spiders and shells.

1 See Letter 1479 and notes 1 and 2. Oldenburg published both the account sent by Ray and the next sentence of Lister's present letter in *Phil. Trans.*, no. 65 (14 November 1670), 2103–4. The friendship between Lister and Ray survived this dispute, though in later years when they drifted apart Ray thought Lister still held it against him that he had espoused Hulse's priority.

2 I.e., the *Philosophical Transactions* for June.

3 Now Ferrybridge, on the Great North Road south of York; evidently the mail for the West Riding was left there by the post on his way to York.

1504
Newburgh to Oldenburg
9 August 1670

From the original in Royal Society MS. N 1, no. 5

Sr

I have recd the books wch accompanied yr kind Letter of ye 28th past I must very heartily thank yu both for ye procurement of ye one & loan of ye other wch I shall carefully use & return according to yr appointment. The remaining papers Concerning Husbandry I hope I may ye next term Inspect in London & shall then intreat yr Amanuensis to transcribe wt I best like. In ye interim I shall request yu if anything new relating to yt or like matters of usefull Practice occur yu wd oblige me by yr imparting ym. I hope ye smarting of our stubbed & stubborn Adversary[1] will have a good effect upon ye Society to wch he presumes to shew his teeth, but pretty harmlessly while he cannot bite.

God sends shrewd Cows short hornes, as we say in our Country proverb. If ye rest of ye World were as credulous of his Calumnies as he could wish, while our Royall patron & founder ownes us he will bark to as litle purpose as bawling Currs by night at ye Moon. But there is an higher then ye highest on Earth from whom so good a designe as ye Service of Mankind by profitable & beneficiall Experiments may expect patronage beyond ye term of ye present Age; wch is hoped by

Yr affect freind and servt
John Newburgh

Worth Fr
Aug 9—70

The friend who brings yu this[2] will pay yu ye 3s–6d yu laid out for me wth many thanks

ADDRESS
    To Henry Oldenburgh
    Esq At his hous in
    ye Pelmel
    These present
            London

NOTES

Reply to Letter 1495; we cannot explain the discrepancy between the dates given by Oldenburg and Newburgh.
1 Stubbe.
2 Oldenburg has endorsed the letter "Rec. Aug. 23. 70. by Mr Quarles."

1505
Oldenburg to Johann Christian von Boineburg
10 August 1670

From the copy in Royal Society MS. O 2, no. 31

Illustrissime et Generosissime Domine Baro

Multum debeo Generositati tuae, quod opella mea in compellando Serenissimo Principe Ruperto uti dignatus es. Ipse manu mea tradidi epistolam, et significavit Princeps, se jam ante, literas tuas accepisse, et responsum liquidum reddidisse; velle tamen supcriarum summam repetere, et prima quaque occasione ad Te transmittere.

Hobbius noster nil quicquam, post nuperam librorum ipsius Syllogen, (Amstelodami, ni fallor, impressam) edidit.[1] jam octuagenario major, desidiam et quietem amplectitur, et vegetas juniorum Antagonistarum occursiones declinat. Quid Boylius, Wallisius, Barrovius, aliique nonnulli de Regia Societate Philosophi nuper emiserint, in literis ad consultissimum Dominum Leibnitium hic insertis indicavi,[2] ijs simul generatim indigitatis, quibus dicta Societas ipsa nunc occupatur. Utinam Germaniae nostrae, tam litionum quam scientiarum, Proceres Symbolas suas ad instaurandam augendamque Philosophiam cordatius quam hactenus factum conferrent, et hoc ipso Angliae, Galliae, et ipsius Italiae Exemplum in versandis experimentis alacriter imitarentur. Non est unius alteriusve gentis opus, quod molimur. Omnium Regionum, Principum et Philosophorum opes, operae et studia coeant necessum est, ut hoc interpretandae Naturae pensum, ea qua est cura et industria expediatur. Tu Vir Illustrissime, Provinciae tuae nequaquam deeris, opinor, quin et hortaberis Serenissimum Electorem vestrum, ut caepta haec Philosophica, ad scientias utiles et solidas promovendas comparata, auspicijs et juvamentis suis splendidissimis, pro singulari suo in illa studia favore et benevolentia provehere et exornare non desinat. Valeat Illustrissimus Dominus atque imperatis suis porro honestare dignetur

Generositatis suae observantissimum Cultorem

H. Oldenburg S.R. Secr.

Londini d. 10. Aug. 1670

ADDRESS

Illustrissimo et Generosissimo Domino,
Domino Johanni Christiano, Libero Baroni a Boïneburg etc
Domino et Fautori suo colendissimo

Mogu[ntiae]

TRANSLATION

Most illustrious and wellborn Freiherr,

I am much indebted to your excellency because you have thought fit to employ me in addressing His Royal Highness, Prince Rupert. I delivered the letter to him by my own hand, and the Prince informed me that he had already received your letter and had returned a plain reply; but he would repeat the gist of it and send it to you at the first possible opportunity.

Our fellow-countryman Hobbes has published nothing since the recent collection of his works printed at Amsterdam,[1] unless I am mistaken. He is already more than eighty years old and seeks quiet and repose; and refuses to be drawn by the lively sallies of younger antagonists. What Boyle, Wallis, Barrow, and not a few other philosophers in the Royal Society have issued recently I have set forth in a letter to the very wise Mr. Leibniz, here enclosed,[2] indicating in a general way the present concerns of the Royal Society. Would that those who excel in litigation and in the sciences in our Germany would make their contributions towards the restoration and perfection of philosophy with a better will than they have shown hitherto, and would eagerly imitate in this the example of England, France, and Italy herself in turning to experiments. What we are about is no task for one nation or another singly. It is needful that the resources, labors, and zeal of all regions, princes, and philosophers be united, so that this task of comprehending nature may be pressed forward by their care and industry. I think that you, illustrious Sir, will never be found wanting in your responsibility to exhort His Serene Highness the Elector, so that when this philosophical [co-operation] has once been initiated, with the intention of promoting the solid and useful sciences, he will not fail to assist and perfect it by his august support and endowments, out of his singular goodwill and kindness towards such studies. May your most illustrious lordship fare well, and further dignify by his commands,

> Your excellency's most devoted adherent,
> *H. Oldenburg*, Secretary of the Royal Society

London, 10 August 1670

ADDRESS

> To the most illustrious and highborn Lord,
> Johann Christian, Freiherr von Boineburg,
> His Lord and most affectionate Patron,
> Mainz

NOTES

Johann Christian von Boineburg (1622–72) was a diplomat, first in the service of the Landgrave of Hesse Cassel and, at this time, in the service of the Elector of Mainz; he was also a Councilor of Mainz. Originally a Protestant, he had been for some years now a Catholic convert. He was a lifelong scholar, book collector, and patron of learning, with a wide correspondence; he seems to have been responsible for putting Leibniz in touch with English and French scholars and scientists. We do not know what his business with Prince Rupert was, but it is known that the Prince spent some time at Mainz in the late 1650's.

1 *Opera philosophica, quae Latine scripsit omnia* (Amsterdam, 1668). Hobbes had, of course, as Oldenburg knew very well, published *Quadratura circuli* in 1669, but perhaps he thought that Boineburg would not be interested in Hobbes's mathematical vagaries.

2 Letter 1506.

1506
Oldenburg to Leibniz
10 August 1670

From the original in the Hannover MSS., ff. 1–2
Printed in Gerhardt, pp. 41–43

Amplissimo et Consultissimo Viro
Domino Gothofredo Guilielmo Leibnitzio J. U. D. etc.
Henr. Oldenburg S.P.D.

Obtinere a me non potui, Vir Consultissime, ut Literas tuas 13/23 julij novissimi Moguntia ad me datas silentio praeterirem. Spirant quippe humanitatem non vulgarem; quin et eximiam in provehenda re Philosophica voluntatem testantur. Hujusmodi nova non leviter eos afficiunt juvantque, qui in votis omnino habent, ut omnium gentium viri sagaces et industrii velint studia et exercitia sua ad augendam ornandamque solidam et feracem Philosophiam consociare. Anglia nostra eo inprimis annititur; molitur idem Gallia, et ipsa Italia: nec Germaniam opinamur post principia latere. Tu, Vir Amplissime, insigniorem pro aetate tua in rebus physicis tum affectum tum progressum significas, eaque de veris Motus Rationibus epistola tua subinnuis, quae Salivam mihi et aliis movent, unicam illam tuam, de qua loqueris, certi motus Universalis in Globo nostro Terraquaereo Hypothesin cognoscendi; ex qua scilicet omnium, quos in corporibus est deprehendere, motuum ratio, insueta hactenus claritate, reddatur. Virum sane philosophum Te praestabis, si tanti momenti negotium confeceris, remque feceris Societati Regiae gratissimam, si Hypothesis illius summam et rationes exponere non graveris. Idem jam fecit de suis Motus Regulis Hugenius,[1] aliis ipsum in eodem argumento explicando imitantibus; quorum nomina aeque ac meletemata, Cedro digna, nunquam intermoritura in Societatis Regiae Archivis, suum cuique tribuere summopere satagentibus, perennitatem consequuntur: Quod idem tuis eveniet meditationibus et inventis, siquidem in iis edisserendis et communicandis cordatum et facilem Te mihi praebueris.

Quam de Arte Combinatoria Dissertationem edidisse Te scribis, ea ad oras nostras necdum pervenit. Eam tanto magis videre opto, quod in ea Te nova non pauca, quaedam etiam profutura observasse, subindicas. Quae hactenus de Arte illa varii scripserunt, vanam potius loquendi de variis amplitudinem, quam judiciose disserendi et nova solida ac profutura excogitandi rationem docuerunt.

Societas nostra in consectandis perpetim Experimentis laborat; unde Sylva suo tempore confertissima succrescet, amplissimam Naturae Historiam complectens, solido et feraci Physices Systemati condendo posteritati forte suffecturam. Quidam ejus Socii de variis varia nuper in lucem emiserunt. Nosti jam, quae Dominus Boylius per aliquot annos feliciter edidit, quorum postrema sunt de Formarum et Qualitatum Origine:[2] de Argumento illo, Num detur absoluta, sive perfecta Quies in corporibus etiam solidissimis?[3] De Qualitatibus Systematicis sive Cosmicis: De Suspicionibus Cosmicis: de Regionum Sub-terranearum juxta ac Sub-marinarum Temperie, Deque Maris Fundo: quibus accessit Ejusdem Introductio in Historiam de Qualitalibus particularibus.[4] Insuper Dominus Wallisius imprimi nuper curavit duas partes priores Mechanicae, sive Tractatus sui Geometrici de Motu, in quarum prima, de Motu praemittit Generalia, agitque de Gravium descensu, et Motuum Declivitate: speciatim vero de Libra doctrinam tradit: In secunda vero de Centro Gravitatis, ejusque Calculo in figuris quamplurimis Curvi-lineis, atque ex his oriundis Solidis, et Superficiebus curvis. Tertiam et ultimam partem habebimus, quam primum per Praeli difficultates licebit.[5] Adhaec D. Barrovius, priori haud impar Author, Lectiones edidit tum Opticas tum Geometricas, a subacti judicii Lectoribus magni aestimatas.[6] In Anatomicis prodiere Dr Lowerus de Motu Cordis et Sanguinis, ubi Experimenta istius generis egregia inseruntur:[7] nec non Doctoris Thrustoni de Respirationis Usu primario Diatriba.[8]

Non ita pridem ad manus meas e Germania pervenerunt chartae quaedam impressae, quarum Titulus; Inventum Novum Artis et Naturae Connubium, In copulatione Levitatis cum Gravitate, per Artificium Siphonis, Machinae Aquaticae, et Antliae, exhibitum a Georgio Christophoro Wernero, Memmingensi; excusum Augustae Anno 1670. Ait Author, Machinam hanc, non modo in minori, sed et majori forma descriptam, in aedibus ipsius, ad quorumvis conditionis hominum servitia prostare. Scire percuperem, num dicta Machina per Germaniam longe lateque innotuerit, et a viris harum rerum callentioribus laudem impetraverit. Multum me Tibi diviceris, Vir Spectatissime, si Memmingae, ubi Inventi Author degit, vel Augustae Vindelicorum, ubi excusus est Libellus, rei et successus veritatem sollicite inquiras, meque de re tota, et de ipsius inprimis artificii ratione perfecte edoceas.[9]

Hugenianum Longitudinis, Penduli beneficio, Inventum adhuc in suspenso est. Existimant nonnulli, duo adhuc istius Automati complemento deesse; unum est, quod necdum perpetuo retineatur in situ perpendiculari; alterum, quod multum incommodi ab irregulari motu Aeris ingeratur. Spes tamen est, remedium, defectibus hisce curandis aptum, non adeo esse difficile inventu: quin degit inter nos Vir quidam Mathematicus, qui actu se invenisse remedium illud affirmat, cumque opportunum fuerit, se propalaturum pollicetur. Haec sunt quae Tuis regerenda hac vice suppetebant. Tu interim, Vir Doctissime, rem philosophicam ornare et augere perge. Dabam Londini die 10 Augusti 1670.

P.S. Literas tuas Domino Hobbio inscriptas rus, ubi nunc degit, transmisi.[10] Si quid responsi dederit, sine mora ad te curabitur.

TRANSLATION

Henry Oldenburg presents many greetings to the very worthy and wise Mr. Gottfried Wilhelm Leibniz, Doctor of Laws, etc.

I could not persuade myself, learned Sir, to pass over in silence your very recent letter to me, dated at Mainz 13/23 July. It breathes no ordinary goodwill, not to say manifests an outstanding desire for the advancement of philosophy. Anything new of this kind both influences and strengthens those who have it much to heart that the wise and industrious of all nations should combine their studies and efforts towards the increase and perfection of a solid and fertile philosophy. Our England especially strives for this; so do France and Italy too, and Germany we think will not lag behind the leaders. You display, excellent Sir, an interest and a degree of advancement in the physical sciences remarkable for your years, and your hints in your letter at the true causes of motion whet my appetite (and that of others) to know that hypothesis of a certain universal motion in our terraquaerial globe, from which is to be deduced with unprecedented clarity the reason for all the movements detected in bodies. You will prove yourself to be a true philosopher if you bring a project of such importance to completion, and you will perform an act most welcome to the Royal Society if you will take the trouble to explain the gist and the foundations of that hypothesis. Huygens has already done this for his laws of motion,[1] following others who have unraveled this business; the names and researches of these, worthy of immortality, will be assured undying fame by their preservation in the archives of the Royal Society, where each is certain of his due. The same may befall your own reflections and discoveries if you will but prove yourself ready and sensible by communicating and explaining them.

The dissertation *De arte combinatoria*, of whose publication you write, has not yet reached us here. I am the more eager to see it because you suggest that in it you have observed not a few novelties and some things of use. The various authors who have hitherto written of that art teach rather an empty prolixity of talking about various things than a way of speaking judiciously and discerning by re-flection solid, useful novelties.

Our Society labors perpetually in pursuit of the experimental method, whence in due time will arise a most rich treasury [of observations], constituting a very complete natural history, which will perhaps enable posterity to establish a solid and fruitful system of physical science. Certain of its Fellows have lately published various things on various topics. You are already aware of what Mr. Boyle has been publishing for several years with happy success, of which the latest are *On the Origine of Forms and Qualities*,[2] and on the question, whether there is an absolute or perfect rest in bodies, even the most solid ones?[3] *Of the Systematicall or Cosmicall Qualities of Things*; *Of Cosmicall Suspitions*; *Of the Temperature of the Subterraneal Regions* and of the *Submarine Regions*, and *Relations about the Bottom of the Sea*, to which is added (by the same author) *An Introduction to the History of Particular Qualities*.[4] Moreover Mr. Wallis has lately had printed the two first parts of *Mechanica, sive de motu tractatus geometricus*, in the former of which he deals first with the general rules of motion and then with the descent of heavy bodies and the declivity of motion, and particularly with the theory of the balance; in the second part are: on the center of gravity and the calculation of it in several curvilinear [plane] figures, and in the solids produced by these, and in curved surfaces. The third and last part we shall have as soon as the difficulties of its impression permit.[5] Further, Mr. Barrow (an author scarcely inferior to the last) has issued *Lectiones opticae* and *geometricae* greatly valued by readers of acute judgment.[6] In the field of anatomy Dr. Lower's *De corde, item de motu & colore sanguinis*, including some re-markable experiments upon that subject, has appeared[7] and also Dr. Thruston's *De respirationis usu primario diatriba*.[8]

Not long ago there came to my hands from Germany some printed sheets bearing the title: "A new discovery of the marriage of Art and Nature in the union of lightness and heaviness in a syphonic machine, an aquatic mechanism, and a pump, displayed by Georg Christoph Werner of Memmingen, printed in August, 1670." The author states that this machine, built full scale at his own house and not merely as a model, serves the needs of men of every class. I should very much like to know whether it has been known through the length and breadth of Germany, and whether it has won praise from those who are skilled in these mat-ters. You will very much oblige me, worthy Sir, if you will inquire carefully about the thing and the truth of its success at Memmingen, where the author lives, or at Augsburg where his pamphlet was printed, and inform me of the whole business, and especially explain completely the working of the machine itself.[9]

Huygens' discovery of the longitude by means of a pendulum [chronometer] is still in doubt. Many think that two complements to this clock are still lacking: one is, that it cannot yet be held always in a perpendicular position, and the other is that much disturbance arises from the irregular movement of the air. Yet it is hoped that a remedy appropriate for rectifying these defects is not so difficult to find but that there lives amongst us a certain mathematician who alleges that he has himself found that remedy, and promises to reveal it at an opportune moment. These are the matters on hand at this moment by way of a reply to your letter. Meanwhile, learned Sir, continue your improvements to philosophy.

London, 10 August 1670

P.S.　I have sent your letter to Mr. Hobbes into the country, where he now lives.[10] If he makes any answer I will send it on to you without delay.

NOTES

Reply to Letter 1486. The original is plainly dated 10 August 1670, although the copy in Royal Society Letter Book IV, 82–85, is dated 25 September 1670.

1　Presumably this is a reference to Huygens' paper in the *Journal des Sçavans* for 18 March 1669, N.S.

2　The Latin translation was first published at Oxford in 1669 and then at Amsterdam in 1671.

3　"A Discourse about the Absolute rest in Bodies" came out with the second edition of *Certain Physiological Essays* (London, 1669), but no Latin version of it is recorded before 1677 (Geneva).

4　See Letter 1487, notes 5 and 9.

5　It is reviewed in *Phil. Trans.*, no. 76 (22 October 1671), 2286–87.

6　See Vol. VI, Letter 1283, note 4.

7　See Vol. VI, Letter 1242, note 7.

8　See Vol. VI, Letter 1368, note 1.

9　We have not found out anything else about Werner; but see below, p. 170. The printed sheets do not exist now.

10　This letter (of the same date as Letter 1486) is printed in the *Sämtliche Schriften*, pp. 56–59.

1507
Sluse to Oldenburg
10 August 1670

From the original in Royal Society MS. S 1, no. 65
Printed in Boncompagni, pp. 646–48

Nobilissimo et Clarissimo Viro
Domino Henrico Oldemburg S.R. Secretario
Renatus Franciscus Slusius Salutem

Cum nuper ad te scripsi, Vir Clarissime, nondum in evolvendis Lectionibus Opticis eo perveneram, ubi celeberrimus auctor mei meminisse dignatus est,[1] alioqui te rogare non omisissem (quod nunc enixe facio) ut plurimas eius humanitati meo nomine gratias ageres. Caeterum quoniam de literarum quas ipsi communicasti,[2] sensu subdubitare visus est, quae etiam brevitate sua fortasse obscuritatem aliquam involvunt, existimavi simul totius rei seriem ad te perscribendam, ut si tanti iudicaveris, ipsi communices, eiusque censurae subjicias. Ac primum, arcum spatii in globo illuminati totidem esse graduum quot est angulus Iridis, animadverteram ex ipsa Cartesii figura cum eam olim examinarem.[3] Considera quaeso hic

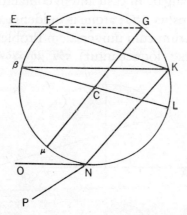

adiunctam, additis duntaxat, linea $K\beta$ parallela FG, et $GC\mu$, βCL diametris. Evidens est arcus βG, KN, esse aequales: ablati itaque a duobus semicirculis $G\beta\mu$, $GN\mu$, relinquunt excessus aequales; hoc est arcum $\beta\mu$ (sive GL) aequalem duobus arcubus μN, GK. unde ablato communi GK, remanet arcus KL aequalis arcui μN. Arcum autem μN esse mensuram anguli *ONP*, patet ex ipso Cartesio illum invenire docente, subducendo duplum arcus *FK* (sive arcum *FKN*) ex aggregato arcus *FG* et semicirculi (sive ex arcu *FKµ*).

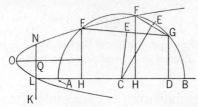

Hac occasione solvendum mihi proposueram sequens Problema. In semicirculo *AGB* cuius centrum *C*, a dato punctum *G*, inflectere rectam *GF*, ita ut duae normales *FH* ad *AB*, et *CE* ad *FG*, habeant inter se rationem datam. Quod quidem variis modis construi posse animadverti, sed effectionem simplicissimam, per parabolam nempe cum circulo dato, hic adscribam.

Data sit ratio *b* ad *r*, et cadat ex *G* in *AB* normalis *GD*. Tum fiat ut *DC* ad *CA*, ita haec ad *CL* in directum; erectaque normali *LN*, quae sit ad *DG*, ut *bb* ad *2rr*, sumatur *LK*, quae sit ad *DC* in eadem ratione *bb* ad *2rr*. Demum bisecta *LN* in *Q*, et erecta *QO* tertia proportionali ipsarum *KL*, *LQ*; vertice *O*, axe *OQ*, latere recto *KL* describatur parabola *ONF*, quae utique transibit per *N* et *L*, ut patet; et quae, si non occurrat circulo, Problema impossibile ostendit: si vero secet in duobus punctis, dat duplicem solutionem, unicam vero si tangat. In casu autem contactus evidens est maximam haberi longitudinem ipsius *DG*; atque is quidem ex hac etiam constructione inveniri potest: Verum cum universalem Problemata determinandi, seu (ut veteres Geometrae loquebantur) τόν μοναχὸν inveniendi,[4] regulam

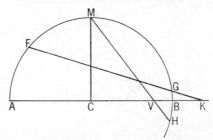

haberem, eam ad aliam constructionem magis facilem applicui, ut simul aliquid aliud, quod infra indicabo, reperire possem. Producta itaque *FG* usquedum concurrerit cum *AC* producta in *K*, quaesivi longitudinem ipsius *CK* in casu του μοναχου. Reperi autem (quod et alias observaveram) licet problema solidum sit, tamen eius μοναχον haberi per locum planum:

quod mihi ansam dedit ad te scribendi Cartesii tabulis opus non esse, cum arcus ille sive Iridis semiangulus, absque illis et quidem per locum planum haberi posset: non considerata etiam, de qua prius egeram, partis in globo illuminatae mensura. Erigatur enim in centro normalis *CM*, et inflectatur *MV* ad diametrum, ita ut *MV VC*, sint in ratione *b* ad *r*. Dico *CK* posse triplum *CV*, uti et *KF* triplum *VM*. Atque hinc posita ratione *b* ad *r* ut 4 ad 3, brevi calculo invenitur arcus *BG* 21 grad: si autem supponeretur ratio Cartesii 250 ad 187, prodiret idem arcus 20° 46′ circiter.[5]

Aliud, quod me quaesivisse supra dixi, erat, in qua ratione *b* ad *r* accidat, ut producta *MV* ad circumferentiam in *H* (quando nimirum *V* cadit inter *B* et *C*) et ducta *FGK* μοναχόν determinante, arcus *GB*, *BH* sint aequales [*see lower figure, p. 116*]. Analysis autem me docuit tunc *b* ad *r* esse ut $\sqrt{\sqrt{108}-8}$ ad unitatem: atque ita in qualibet minori ratione, arcum *BH* vel nullum esse, vel excedi ab arcu *GB*, in qualibet maiori illum superare.[6] Ex his, opinor, planius videbit Vir Clarissimus quid voluerim, omniaque, ni fallor, inventis suis quamvis alio modo deducta congruere agnoscet. Pluribus itaque non insistam, nec corollaria prosequar quae inde derivari possunt, cum in accuratis illis Lectionibus nihil non praestitum sit. addam tantum me maximopere laetatum cum Problema quod ante plures annos mihi propositum solveram, nimirum, radios ad punctum determinatum tendentes, in alio puncto citra vel ultra per superficies sphaericas accurate congregare: Cum inquam hoc Problema a Viro Clarissimo eodem plane medio atque a me solutum reperi.[7] Sed horum satis.

Basilii Valentini opera latine versa, quamvis in Catalogo Nundinarum Francofurtensium saepius promissa, nondum tamen prodiisse intellexi.

Librum, de quo nuper scripseram, Lugduno accepi: est autem Antonii Lalovere Soceitatis Jesu de Cycloide cum aliquot appendiculis,[8] quem prima occasione ad te transmittam. Vale interim Vir Nobilissime meque tuorum in numero semper habe.

Dabam Leodii XX Augusti Gregor. MDCLXX.

TRANSLATION

René François Sluse greets the very noble and famous Henry Oldenburg, Secretary of the Royal Society

When I wrote to you recently, famous Sir, I had not yet progressed so far in examining the *Lectiones opticae* as the place where its celebrated author finds me worthy of mention,[1] otherwise I would not have failed to ask you (as now I earnestly do) to render him many thanks in my name for his kid_ness. Moreover, since he seems to have some doubts about the meaning of the letter you showed him,[2] which perhaps because of its brevity contained some obscurity, I have thought fit to write out the sequence of the whole thing for you so that if you think it of sufficient moment, you may communicate it to him [Barrow] and subject it to his judgment. And firstly, the arc of the illuminated area upon a sphere will embrace as many degrees as are in the angle of the rainbow, as I noticed from Descartes's own figure when I examined it some time ago.[3] Consider that annexed here, please, which adds only the line $K\beta$ parallel to FG, and the diameters $GC\mu$, βCL [*see figure, p. 115*] It is obvious that the arcs βG, KN are equal; so, subtracting these from the two semicircles $G\beta\mu$, $GN\mu$, there remain equal excess quantities; this is the arc $\beta\mu$ (or GL) equal to the two arcs μN, GK. Whence subtracting the common arc GK, there remains the arc KL equal to the arc μN. However, that arc μN is the measure of the angle ONP appears from Descartes's own instructions how to find it, by subtracting twice the arc FK (or arc FKN) from the sum of the arc FG and the semicircle (that is, from the arc $FK\mu$).

This gave me occasion to propose the following problem to myself: in the semicircle AGB, whose center is C, so to inflect a straight line GF from the given point G that the two perpendiculars FH on AB, and CE on FG, have a given ratio to each other [*see upper figure, p. 116*]. I observed that this could be solved in a number of ways, but the most simple means, by a parabola and the given circle, I set out here.

Let the given ratio be as b to r, and let the normal GD fall from G upon AB. Then make $DC:CA = CA:CL$, in the same straight line, and, erecting the normal LN, so that $LN:DG = b^2:2r^2$, draw LK such that $LK:DC = b^2:2r^2$. Finally, having bisected LN at Q, and drawn [the normal] QO as a third proportional between KL and LQ, the parabola ONF is described, having vertex O, axis OQ and *latus rectum* KL, which passes through N and L, as is obvious, on either side. If this parabola does not intersect the circle it shows that the problem is impossible of solution; if it cuts it at two points it gives two solutions, and a unique one if it is a tangent. However, in the case of contact it is evident that the maximum length of DG is obtained, which is thus given by this same construction. Indeed, as I possessed the universal rule for determining problems or (as the ancient geometers put it) finding the maximum or minimum value,[4] I applied it to another, easier construction so that I could at the same time discover something else, which I will indicate later. So, having produced FG until it meets AC produced at K, I sought for the minimal length of CK [*see lower figure, p. 116*]. Yet I observed (as I have done in other instances) that although the problem is a solid one, yet its maximum or minimum value could be gained from a plane locus, which gave me cause to write to you that there was no need for Descartes's tables, as that arc, or the radius of the rainbow, could be obtained without them and indeed from a plane locus. But we have not yet considered the measurement of the illuminated area of the globe, with which I was dealing at first. Let the normal CM be drawn from the center C and MV be so inclined to the diameter that $MV : VC = b : r$. I say that CK^2 becomes three times CV^2, and KF^2 three times MV^2. And so, assuming that $b : r = 4 : 3$ by a short computation the arc BG is found to be 21°; or if Descartes's ratio of 250 : 187 is assumed, the same arc becomes 20° 46′ roughly.[5]

The other thing I was after, as I said before, was to find out what the ratio of $b : r$ must be so that when MV is produced to the circumference at H (when that is to say V falls between B and C) and FGK is drawn determining the least value, then the arcs GB, BH are equal [*see lower figure, p. 116*]. Analysis had taught me that in this case $b : r = \sqrt{\sqrt{108} - 8} : 1$, and so in any lesser ratio whenever either the arc BH becomes zero or it is exceeded by the arc GB; in any greater ratio it exceeds GB.[6] From all this, I think, that distinguished person [Barrow] will see more clearly what I was driving at, and if I mistake not will acknowledge that although all these are derived by a different method they agree with what he has discovered. I pass over many other points and neglect the corollaries that can be derived thence, because nothing is omitted from those very accurate lectures. I will only add that I was delighted adove all because [I found] a problem that I had formulated and solved many years before, that is, given rays [of light] directed towards a fixed point, to collect them accurately in another point (either nearer than the first or beyond it) by means of spherical [refracting] surfaces—because, I say, I found that this problem had been solved by this famous person and by myself, by quite the same means.[7] But enough of these topics.

The works of Basil Valentine turned into Latin have not yet appeared, I understand, although they have often been promised in the catalogue of the Nuremburg Fair.

I have received from Lyons the book about which I wrote recently, but it is Antoine de la Loubère, S.J.'s *De cycloide* with a few little appendices.[8] I will send it to you at the first opportunity. Meanwhile, farewell, noble Sir, and always count me as one of your own.

Liège, 20 August 1670, N.S.

NOTES

1 See Isaac Barrow, *Lectiones XVIII . . . in quibus opticorum phaenomenon genuinae rationes investigantur* . . . (London, 1669), p. 84: "From this it appears (as a friend advised by the very distinguished Mr. Sluse pointed out to me) that the Cartesian determination of the angular breadth of the rainbow can be effected without the compilation of tables" [*editors' translation*]. The "friend" was Oldenburg, drawing attention to Sluse's letter of 14 November 1667 (Vol. III, p. 596). As Dr. Whiteside points out, Sluse was perhaps put out by this (probably unauthorized) divulgence of an observation which permits an analytical approach to the theory of the rainbow; he now goes on to make his command of this theory obvious, without giving away the analysis, with which Dr. Whiteside has most courteously furnished us.

2 Descartes's problem (*Discours de la Méthode . . . Les Meteores*, Discours Huictiesme; pp. 380–83 in the edition of Paris, 1668) was to find the limits of the primary and

secondary rainbows, in angular measure from the observer's eye. He solved it by considering the angles at which light impinging on a water drop can emerge from it after
refraction and reflection. In the figure, *EF* is the incident ray, *NP* the emergent, and
∠ *ONP* is the angle to be determined, which is the angular width of the primary bow.

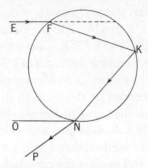

Descartes tabulated values of ∠ *ONP* for different points of incidence *F*, finding that
the greatest diameter for the primary bow is about $41\frac{3}{4}°$, and the least diameter for the
secondary bow just over $51\frac{1}{2}°$. Sluse suggested that the angle could be found from a
simple experiment on a glass globe full of water, but Barrow (p. 85) was doubtful
whether complete accuracy could result from this.

3 This is the figure in note 2 above.

4 We are again indebted to Dr. Whiteside for the following: the term *monachos* (unique)
was first used mathematically by Pappos to signify a least ratio. After Commandino's
publication of Pappos in 1588 it was taken to denote the reduction of two meets of a
curve and straight line to one, for example, or the condition of tangency, and the case
where the two roots of an equation are equal. "*Monachos*, tangent, maximum and minimum value, these are one and the same" writes Sluse in his next letter (p. 255). It will
appear that the ratio *b/r* mentioned here is that of the refractive indices of two media.

5 This ratio of the refractive indices of air and water is given in the *Meteores*; see note 2
above. Note that Sluse here conceals the analytical process (equivalent to differentiation) by which he has found the least value of *CK*; and that the width of the rainbow
is twice arc *BG*, that is about 41° 31′, as Descartes said.

6 By deriving two expressions for the length *MH* and equating them, it appears that
$$6\sqrt{3}r^2 = 8r^2 + b^2, \text{ whence } \frac{b^2}{r^2} = 6\sqrt{3} - 8 = \sqrt{108} - 8 \text{ [D. T. W.]}.$$

7 Such problems are treated by Barrow in Lectio XIV.

8 We could discover nothing later than the already mentioned *Veterum geometria
promota in septem de cycloide libris et in duabus adjectis appendiculis* (Toulouse, 1660); La
Loubère died in 1664. It seems likely that it was in these appendices that Emmanuel
Maignan was attacked (see Vol. IV, p. 343); certainly Maignan replied to them in
his appendices to *Philosophia sacra* (there are four in the edition of Lyons, 1672). La
Loubère held that geometry was an essential foundation to physics. Maignan
rejected this claim ("Ita ego facile putarem . . . non esse res Physicas subiiciendas
legibus quibuslibet Geometricis . . ."). See Ramon Cenal, S.J., "La filosofia de Emmanuel Maignan," *Revista de Filosofia*, Año XIII (1954), 15–68. Compare Rigaud, I,
177.

1508
Gustavus Helmfeld to Oldenburg
17 August 1670

From the original in Royal Society MS. H 3, no. 1

Nobilissime Domine, Amice plurimum colende.

Quanquam jamdudum officij mei ratio postulasset parvo quodam epistolio Te status mei certiorem facere, debitasque pro tot ac tantis beneficijs quibus me Londini praesentem cumulasti reddere gratias. Nolui tamen prius literis Te adire quam ipse de subsistendi loco certus essem, ne saepius interpellando Te in publicum bonum peccarem cui omnes Tuae curae atque operae sunt consecratae. Tuo igitur, quod admiror revocato consilio animus mihi sedet per destinatum Galliae tempus Lutetiae commorari, praesertim cum Tuae literae commendatitiae,[1] quibus multum debeo, literarum mihi aditum fecerint ad Dominum Justellum. Vir hic certe videtur esse valde humanus pariter ac profunde doctus adeo ut ejus suavissima conversatio multum mihi promittat utilitatis. Tu interim Vir Clarissime nobiscum es et juvat vivere cum ijs in quorum memoria Tu semper vivis et qui mecum Tuas virtutes continue admirantur. Si lubet, si vacat responso me dignari, mandata Tua expecto au fauxbourg St. Germain a la rue de Tournon chez Monsr. Landanet vis a vis l'hostel des Ambassadeurs extraordinaires, et qua possum promptitudine exequor, prae primis cum me Tua benevolentia ita obligatum feceris, ut quam diu vixero non possim non esse Tui

Nobilissime Domine, Tuarumque virtutum
cultor maximus atque admirator
Gustavus Helmfeld

Lutetiae die $\frac{17}{27}$ Augusti Anno 1670

ADDRESS
A Monsieur
Monsieur Grubendol
a
Londres

TRANSLATION

Most noble Sir, very dear friend,

Although I have been in duty bound for a long time to let you know how I am, and to return you due thanks for the many and great kindnesses you heaped upon me when I was in London, yet I was reluctant to approach you by letter until I was certain of remaining in one place, lest by disturbing you too often I should offend against the common weal, to which all your labors and concerns are devoted. So, having recalled your advice (which pleased me very much) I have made up my mind to stay at Paris in France for the appointed period, especially as your letter of recommendation,[1] for which I am greatly indebted, has opened a literary path for me with Mr. Justel. This man certainly seems to be unusually obliging and also deeply learned, so that I promise myself great advantages from an acquaintance with him. Meanwhile, Sir, you are of the company too, and it rejoices me to live with men in whose memory you are still vivid, and admire your virtues as I do. If you please and have leisure to honor me with a reply, I shall expect your commands at Mr. Landanet's house in the rue de Tournon opposite the residence of the Ambassadors Extraordinary, in the Faubourg St. Germain, and I will execute them as soon as possible, the more so because you have made me so obliged to you by your kindness that, so long as I live, I must remain, most noble Sir, full of devotion and admiration for your virtues,

Yours,
Gustavus Helmfeld

Paris, 17/27 August 1670

ADDRESS
    To Mr. Grubendol
        London

NOTES

Gustavus Helmfeld (1651–74)—already mentioned in Vol. VI, Letter 1223—was the son of Simon Grundel-Helmfeld (1617–77), a Swedish general; at the age of eleven, it is said, he knew ten languages. He had published at the age of seventeen *Ratio status barbarorum, duabus orationibus* (Leiden, 1668). He made an extensive tour of Europe, and was admitted as a Fellow of the Royal Society on 21 April 1670, presumably during his stay in London to which reference is made in the letter.

1 No trace of this has been found.

1509
Hevelius to Oldenburg
17 August 1670

From the original in Royal Society MS. H 2, no. 22
Partly printed in *Phil. Trans.*, no. 65 (14 November 1670), 2087–91

Illustri Viro
Domino Henrico Oldenburg
Societatis Regiae Secretario
Johannes Hevelius Salutem

Etiamsi non dubitem ultimas meas die 5 Julij scriptas Tibi[1] optime esse traditas, nihilominus tamen hisce Te rursus invisere volui, quo Vos de observatione quadam notatu digna certiores facerem, mentemque simul meam ea de re Vobis exponerem: de nova videlicet illa fixa circa Cygnum nuper deprehensa;[2] non quidem de illa, quae in pectore eius iam anno 1600 illuxit, et anno 1660 rursus evanuit, ac denuo anno 1666 Mense Sept. instar stellulae Septimae magnitudinis emicuit, de qua eo tempore, si recte memini fusius Vobis perscripseram, sed de fixa prorsus diversa tertiae magnitudinis fere, circa et infra caput Cygni inter quasdam informes conspicua, cuius longitudo 1° 52′ 26″ Aquarii et Latitudo 47° 25′ 22″ Bor. modo existit, ut observationes die 25 Julij a me habitae luculenter ostendunt. Novam autem stellam hanc ipsam omnino esse, et in coelo ad annum 1660 penitus inconspicuam fuisse, non est quod quisquam dubitet. Nam, uti scis, a plurimis iam annis, et Planetarum et Fixarum observationibus maxime (quod praecissime dixerim) operam dedi; sic ut non solum omnes illas a Tychone olim observatas, globorum adscriptas sed et reliquas hactenus neglectas, nudo tamen oculo bene conspicuas, tam quartae, quintae et sextae magnitudinis in quibusvis Asterismis accurate notarem, inque catalogum referrem: quo imposterum eo facilius si qua nova prodiret fixa deprehenderetur. Accidit igitur, ut anno iam 1659, 1660, et 1661 plerasque stellas illas omnes in Asterismo Cygni apparentes summa diligentia debitis Organis dimensus fuerim, atque ita omnes illas, etiam circa collum et caput deprehensibiles, notavi, earumque distantias a diversis fixis cepi; nullam autem stellam tertiae magnitudinis eo loco, ubi iam dicta nova notatur, tum deprehendi; quam tamen optime, si adfuisset, conspexissem. Nam, cum (sub nota *6* et *7*) in delineatione nostra,[3] supra scilicet cuspidem alae Borealis Aquilae, et

quidem multo minores, tum (*b*) duarum informium, caput Cygni praece-
dentium, inferiorem, tum ipsum caput sexta magnit., nec non *c, d, n, m, l, k*,
stellas sextae et quintae magnitudinis probe ac distincte viderim, quidni
etiam hanc ad duos tresve gradus ab his remotam, et quidem tertiae magnitudinis observassem? Sic ut primo hinc certus sim anno 1660 et 1661 hanc
stellam nondum extitisse visibilem. Deinde clare etiam patet ex Bayeri
Uranometria, hunc modo dictam novam stellam nec anno 1603 apparuisse,
et per consequens neque Tychoni, multo minus Hipparcho. Siquidem et
Bayerus fixam tantae magnitudinis deprehendisset, cum haud procul ab illa
aliam (sub numero *δ*) in meo schemate, sextae magnitudinis depinxerit:

prout in Asterismo eius Cygni videre est. At inquies, forte ea ipsa est, quam Tu novam dicis; quippe cum Bayerus congruis Organis stellas illas haud observaverit, fieri facile potuit, ut a vero eius loco ad gradum vel paullo plus aberraverit. Sed, crede id factum non est; quandoquidem stella illa parvula (*δ*) adhuc eodem loco, ubi Bayerus fere eam deposuit, commoratur, nec maior est sextae magnitudinis ut eodem tempore ei videbatur. Distat enim, ut ipsemet nuper deprehendi ab ore Pegasi 32° 39′ 0″, et a dextro genu Pegasi 39° 32′ 45″; hinc provenit eius longitudo 0° 6′ 28″ Aquarii et latit. 46° 11′ 14″ Bor. ad annum scilicet currentem 1670 complet. Iulium. At nova (*a*) elongatus ab ore Pegasi 32° 31′ 35″, et a dextro genu Pegasi 38° 18′ 50″, ex quibus distantijs Longitudo 1° 52′ 26″ Aquarii et Latitudo 47° 25′ 22″ Boreal. elicitur. Adeo ut haec nova plane sit diversa ab illae sextae magnitudinis a Bayero notata; (quanquam ambae nondum ad duos gradus ab invicem removentur) atque ex dictis manifestum sit hanc novam nec anno 1603, nex anno 1660 inter ceteras emicuisse stellas. Quo autem Astrophili eo distinctius tam stellam illam tam locum eius cognoscant volui totum Cygnum, cum adhaerentibus Stellis, nec non omnibus illis minoribus globo hactenus nondum adscriptis, ac a me per distantias varias sedulo observatis delineatum dare, ac Illustrissimae Societati quantocyus transmittere; ut simul constet, quot incognitis fixis Asterismos omnes, divina ope hucusque iam ditaverim ac exornaverim. Ego, solo Cygno 35 addidi: quippe Tycho non nisi 18 in suo catalogo exhibet, quibus Keplerus 8 addidit; sic ut Constellatio Cygni in globo nostro modo 60 fere stellis Fixis luceat.[4] De caetero bene imposterum attentendum erit, an saepius dicta stella (*a*) in eadem magnitudine sit permansura, an vero ratione magnitudinis luminisque diversam aliquam induerit faciem? Cum primitus a me observabatur, quoad magnitudinem et splendorem, ei in pectore Aquilae[5] aequabatur, nisi quod aliquanto obtusioris fuerit luminis; quoad situm, respectu reliquarum Stellarum, in linea recta cum illa in ancone alae Superioris Cygni, et illa in humero Aquilae[6] nec non cum lucida Lyrae et illa in rhombo Delphini mediarum borealiori[7] consistebat: triangulum vero aequilaterum cum illa in capite et rostro Cygni constituebat.[8] Altera vero illa nova in pectore Cygni,[9] quae rursus anno 1666 illuxit, sensim crescere videtur, quanquam necdum maior est Stellis Sextae magnitudinis ac minor adhuc illis tribus *m*, *l*, et *k* in collo a me observatis. At illa in collo Ceti,[10] nunc maxime splendet; quippe secundae fere magnitudinis, tum insignis claritatis videtur. Ultimo, cum hesterna die 26 Augusti, optimam occasionem nactus fuerim, coelo admodum annuente Telescopium illud 50 pedum longum, quod non ita pridem mihi transmisistis ad sidera adhibui, et quidem primo ad Lunam, inveni quod officio suo adeo satisfaciat, ut merito habeam, cur Vobis maximas agam gratias; ad Saturnum, ut ut Luna fuerit praesens, satis superque vires etiam suas extendit; siquidem faciem eius nitidissime ac clarissime detegebat: quali autem mihi apparenti, adiecta delineatio commonstrabit. Videbis [*see figure, p. 124*] Saturnum hoc tempore, alta scilicet Aquila 29° 32' o", in distantia ab extrema alae Pegasi 33° 48' o", et ab ore eius 24° 51' 40", in 4° 11' Piscium in 1° 53' Latit. Austr., in ipsa nempe oppositione Solis existente Saturno, plane alia facie quam anno [   ]¹¹ Clarissimo Hugenio, tum Vobis anno 1666,¹² tum Parisiensibus anno 1669¹³ apparere. Siquidem annulus qui Saturnum circundat, multo nunc arctior, compressiorque animadversus, quam illo tempore; quasi obliquiori, respectu terrae modo incedat via. Non dubito, si Vestrates illum nuper observarunt, quin eadem forma ijs quoque apparuerit: nam summa diligentia illum adumbravi. Illustrissimus dominus Burattinus nuper mihi diversas lentes pro longioribus Telescopijs dono misit, inter quas unam 70 pedum elegantissime et supra modum nitidissime elaboratam ac expolitam, in diametro 8 poll. inveni; sed cum talem longissimum tubum ad manus nondum habeam, illius vires explorare hac vice nequivi, faciam autem id Deo volente, prima occasione: Nullus dubito quin exspectationi meae suo tempore respondeat. Nam reliquae lentes breviores, utpote 20 et 30 pedum clarissime ac mire distincte obiecta omnia detegunt, tam terrestria quam aetherae; nisi quod ratione longitudinis suae, non adeo obiecta, ut illa lens 50 pedum, quemadmodum etiam fieri haud potest, amplificent, atque augeant, ut nemo non facile concesserit.

Quod superest, ne obliviscavis earum rerum, quarum in nuperis literis mentionem feci. Vale, et Illustrissimae Societati Nostrae, praevia salutatione debita, paratissima mea officia studiaque [deferas]¹⁴ etiam atque etiam rogo. Dabam Gedani Anno 1670, die 27 Augusti st.n.

ADDRESS
A Monsieur
Monsieur Grubendol
    A
    Londres
Franco Antwerpen

TRANSLATION

Johannes Hevelius greets the illustrious Mr. Henry Oldenburg, Secretary of
the Royal Society

Although I have no doubt that my last of 5 July [N.S.][1] was quite safely delivered
to you, still I wished to address you again in this letter in order to inform you of
a certain noteworthy observation and to express my opinion of it. I speak of that
new fixed star lately detected near Cygnus;[2] not that in its breast which was already
shining in 1600 and vanished again in 1660 only to spring to life once more as a
little seventh-magnitude star in September 1666—of this, if I remember rightly,
I wrote to you at greater length at the time—but that very different star of the
third magnitude near and below the head of Cygnus, conspicuous between certain
blurred ones, of which the longitude is now 1° 52' 26" in Aquarius and the latitude
47° 25' 22" north, as is clear from my observations of 25 July [N.S.]. That this is
an absolutely new star, quite invisible in the sky during 1660, is something no one
can doubt. For, as you know, I have made observation of both the planets and
the fixed stars my chief business for many years now, and I might say in the most
exact manner, so that I might accurately record and catalogue in each system of
stars not only all those formerly observed by Tycho Brahe which are marked on
globes, but the rest which have been neglected up to now although clearly apparent to the naked eye, being of the fourth, fifth, and sixth magnitudes. In this way
it will in the future be more easily found out if a new star shall appear. Thus it
happened that in the years 1659, 1660, and 1661 I took measurements of almost
all the stars visible in the constellation of Cygnus with great care and using proper
instruments, and noted all those discernible about the head and neck, taking their
distances from various fixed stars. At that time, however, I found no star of the
third magnitude in that place where as I have said the nova is recorded, which,
had it been there, I should have plainly seen. For as I saw clearly and distinctly (in
my sketch [*see figure, p. 124*], nos. *6* and *7*)[3] much smaller stars above the point of
the northern wing of Aquila, as also (*b*) the lesser of two blurred stars preceding
the head of Cygnus and the head-star itself of the sixth magnitude, not to say (*c, d,
n, m, l, k*) stars of the fifth and sixth magnitudes, why should I not also have observed this of the third magnitude at two or three degrees distance? So that in the
first place I am confident from this that this star did not yet appear visibly in 1660
and 1661. It is again obvious too, from Bayer's *Uranometria*, that this new star had
not yet appeared in 1603, and consequently not to Tycho, much less to Hipparchos.
For Bayer would have detected a star of such magnitude, as he depicted another
(no. *8* in my sketch) not far from this one, of the sixth magnitude, which may be
seen in his constellation of Cygnus. But you may say, perhaps, that this is the
one you call new, since it might easily happen that Bayer should err from the
true place by a degree or a little more because he did not observe those stars with

proper instruments. But, believe me, it is not so; that little star (𝛿) is still in the same place, almost, where Bayer put it and is no brighter than the sixth magnitude, as when he saw it. For its distance from the mouth of Pegasus (as I lately measured it myself) is 32° 39′ 0″ and from Pegasus' right knee 39° 32′ 45″; hence its longitude is 0° 6′ 28″ in Aquarius and its latitude 46° 11′ 14″ north, that is, in the present Julian year of 1670. But the nova (a) is distant from Pegasus' mouth 32° 31′ 35″ and from the right knee 38° 18′ 50″, from which distances the longitude works out as 1° 52′ 26″ in Aquarius and the latitude 47° 25′ 22″ north. Thus the nova is plainly a different star from the sixth magnitude star noted by Bayer (although the two are not two degrees apart), and from all this it becomes evident that in 1603 and in 1660 this nova did not shine among the other stars.

In order that lovers of astronomy might learn to know this star and its place the more distinctly it was my intention to make a drawing of the whole of Cygnus and the adjacent stars, including all those lesser stars that are not yet marked on the globe which I have observed carefully by taking various distances; and to transmit this as soon as possible to the illustrious Society that it might at once appear how much I had enriched astronomers and perfected their art already (by divine aid) with these unrecognized fixed stars. I have added thirty-five to Cygnus alone, for Tycho shows only eighteen in his catalogue to which Kepler added eight; but the constellation Cygnus on our globe now shines with nearly sixty stars.[4] Moreover, it will have to be carefully observed in the future, whether that star (a) will more often remain of that same magnitude, or whether it assumes some different appearance by way of magnitude and brightness? When I first observed it, it was equal as to magnitude and brilliance with that in the breast of Aquila[5] except that its light was a little duller; as to position with respect to the rest of the stars, it was in a straight line with that in the bend of Cygnus' upper wing, and that in the shoulder of Aquila,[6] as also with the bright star in Lyra, and that in the rhombus of Delphinus which is the more northerly of the middle ones.[7] Indeed it formed an equilateral triangle with those in the head and beak of Cygnus.[8]

That other nova, in the breast of Cygnus,[9] which shone again in 1666, seems to grow gradually although it is yet no greater than the sixth magnitude and as yet less than those three stars I have observed in the neck (*m, l,* and *k*). But that in the neck of Cetus[10] is now of the highest brilliance, since it may be seen as almost of the second magnitude and of remarkable whiteness.

Lastly, I was offered yesterday (26 August [N.S.]) a very good opportunity of directing to the stars that fifty-foot telescope you sent me not long ago, the sky being very favorable, and choosing first the moon, I found it did its duty so well that I have good reason to thank you most warmly; then turning to Saturn, although the moon was in the sky, again its powers extended far enough and beyond, for it revealed the planet's aspect most clearly and brightly, appearing to me as the attached sketch depicts it. You will see [*see figure, p. 124*] that Saturn at this time (with Aquila at altitude 29° 32′ 0″), distant from the tip of Pegasus' wing 33° 48′ 0″

and from his mouth 24° 51′ 40″, in 4° 11′ of Pisces and 1° 53′ south latitude, being in opposition to the sun, has an appearance quite different from that which he revealed to the famous Huygens in [1655],[11] to yourselves in 1666,[12] and to the Parisians in 1669,[13] for the ring surrounding Saturn is seen to be much narrower and more compressed than it was then, as though it advances along a path more oblique to the Earth. If your astronomers observed it at that time, I have no doubt it showed the same aspect to them, for I have drawn it with the greatest care.

The very illustrious Mr. Burattini recently sent me as a gift a variety of lenses for very long telescopes, among which I found one of seventy feet [focal length], eight inches in diameter, most elegantly and brilliantly polished and finished beyond compare, but as I have no tube of such a length at hand I cannot at the present time explore its powers as with God's aid I shall do at the first chance. No doubt it will in due time fulfill my expectations. For the other, shorter lenses, of twenty and thirty feet, display everything with a wonderful clarity and sharpness, both terrestrial and celestial objects. But because of the difference in length they do not magnify and enlarge objects so much as that lens of fifty feet, as they hardly could do, which anyone will allow.

As for the rest, do not forget the points I mentioned in my recent letter. Farewell, and after a due greeting please, I beg you, offer[14] my most ready service and zeal to our Society.

Danzig, 27 August, N.S.

ADDRESS

> To Mr. Grubendol
> > London
> Postfree to Antwerp

NOTES

1 Letter 1475.
2 See Letter 1474, and Letter 1484, p. 61.
3 The figure, which we reproduce, is now in Letter Book IV, between pages 56 and 57.
4 Hevelius sent with this letter a Latin list of the stars in Cygnus as he saw them; it was printed in *Phil. Trans.*, no. 65 (14 November 1670), 2090–91. We have omitted this here as it adds nothing.
5 β Aquilae.
6 δ Cygni and γ Aquilae.
7 Vega and α Delphini. The two straight lines drawn between these four stars intersect approximately on the nova.
8 The former of these is φ and the latter β Cygni.
9 First noticed in 1600, its position in 1950 was RA 20h 16′, dec. + 37° 52′. See Vol. III, p. 257.
10 Mira (o Ceti), first noticed in 1596 and catalogued by Bayer, varies in brightness from magnitude 1.7 to 9.6 in a period varying widely, whose mean is rather less than a year. See further, Vol. IV, p. 194, note 2.

11 The date is omitted from the letter; *Systema Saturnium* was published in 1659.
12 See Vol. III, p. 91.
13 This undoubtedly refers to an observation of Huygens and Picard on 27 August
     1668; see *Phil. Trans.*, no. 45 (25 March 1669), 900, taken from *Journal des Sçavans*
     for 11 February 1669 [N.S.], pp. 518–21.
14 This word was inserted by Oldenburg.

1510

Foss to Oldenburg

18 August 1670

From the original in Royal Society MS. F 1, no. 56

Vir Nobilissime, Clarissime,

Pudet diurturni silentij, quo hisce temporibus usus sum, cujus quidem
jam dudum evitassem culpam si quidquam Tua Claritate dignum
offendissem; ut nihil loquor de officio, quod tot in me merita jure suo
efflagitant: verum ut aliqualem curae meae commissorum habeas rationem,
paucis me expediam: Literas Nobilissimo Domino Thevenoto, nec non
Excellentissimis Dominis Travagino et Yerburij[1] adscriptas de manu in
manus tradidi; de charactere quo caetera mihi incongruo, tantis me exhibuit
Viris gratias quas possum ago maximas.[2] Epistolam fidei Domini de la
Massay[3] concreditam necdum acceperat Dominus de Graeff, qua de injuria
valde conquestus est, praeprimis ob adjunctam humani corporis particulam,
quam avide exoptaverat, ratus eam liti, quae ipsi cum Domino Clarckio
intercedit, decidendae multum conferre posse, interea vasa mulierum
generationi destinata publici juris propediem futura meditatur. Quae apud
Dominum Kerckringium[4] in sceletopoia, [de] cadaverum praeservatione,
et multis aliis non ubique obviis vidi, quaeque de perfectione foetus a
prima conceptu audivi momenta; tanti, meo quidem judicio, sunt ponderis,
ut eis delineandis non sufficiam; quo eo magis supersedeo labore, quod
ipsum vobis nunc adesse credam, vel brevi adfuturum. De caetero reliquos
in Hollandia aequos Societatis vestrae admiratores, Tuae claritatis nomine,
prout in mandatis habui, salutavi, apud quos nihil, quod quidem orbi non
patefecerint, detexi, utut tanta ingenia nunquam minus otiosa sint, quam
cum otiosa, adeoque litteratorum de se conceptam spem vix aut ne vix

quidem frustratura. Dominus Rusius,[5] qui Androtomiam apud Amstelodamenses profitetur, methodum praeservandi cadavera habet egregiam, licet
operosa sit multique temporis indiga, qua via dicit se cadavera reddere
sicca et dura, exteriore quidem figura et pulchritudine manente integra, et
ab omni corruptione eximere posse [*see Plate III*]: quod ego vidi, erat
cubitus, cum musculis omnibus invicem separatis, in demonstrationis
anatomicae usum praeservatus: habet sub manibus integrum cadaver, de
quo docti egregia sibi pollicentur. Memini me accepisse tum a Tua claritate,
tum etiam ab aliis magnae notae viris in Anglia viam haud difficilem inter
vos versari, quod non tantum rei dexteritas et successus, sed et facilitas sine
magno temporis dispendio commendat:[6] optarem sane, nisi labor et in-
vestigatio locum omnem praeripuisset vobis, ut publico concederetur, uni-
versalioris enim videtur utilitatis, quin multis iisdemque variis inserviret
rebus; Praeter ea nihil deprehendi, nec licuit prae brevitate temporis
ulterius progredi. In Mathematicis parum occurrebat, quin potius omnium
oculos conversos vidi in Excellentissimum Vestrum Dominum Smeth-
wieck, ut attente observent, quid sua recens inventa praestare queant.[7] Et
quoniam placuit Tuae Claritati mihi inter alia injungere quoque Medica,[8]
ex eo genere hoc unicum tacito praeterlabi pede non possum; quod, utut
ex novellis unicuique satis superque sit perspectum, Ego tamen, novitate
rei et multitudine promissorum persuasus, penitiore indagine dignum
judicavi; quam in rem haec paucula observare, quasi per transennam, licuit.
Sed ab ovo; habitat Amstelodami vidua quaedam nomine vulgari, Annetje
Roest, quae egregium idemque unicum habet medicamen, quod in majorem
rei gratiam antipodagricum simul vocat et Hydroticum, ut sileam reliquos,
quibus Panacaeae instar dominari fertur, morbis: est formae liquidae instar
olei; datur ad quantitatem granorum decem pro dosi in Spiritus Vini
optime rectificati cochleare 1. quo cum illico unitur, et visum penitus
effugit: operatur praeprimis diuretice et diaphoretice, et aliquando per
salivationem, (quam aegri irrorationem gratam potius vocant; eam etiam
ob causam multi Antimonij, alij Cupri vel Vitrioli, nonnulli Mercurij colligunt praesentiam): Sed via et modo naturae non minus amico quam
grato: Chimiae bonitatem, metallo autem originem debet: primam autem
ejus inventionem acceptam refert Domino de Rosy, nunc defuncto, olim
autem Medicinam quondam Clevae exercenti, postea eandem in Univer-
sitate, quae Franequerae est,[9] publice profitenti, a quo dicta vidua, promis-
sis matrimonij praeviis, testamenti loco hoc obtinuit. Verum, his omissis,
devenio ad ea, quorum oculare exhibere possum testimonium; brevissimo
sex vel septem hebdomadarum spatio tres sexagenarii majores, (virum

unum, foeminas autem duas) hydrope ascite tumidos inexspectatae sanitati restituit: talem in his edidit operationem; post quintam exhibitionem (quae decimamsextam vel vigesimam pro integro curriculo vix excedit) alvus, quae in his suo plerumque caret beneficio, vinculis, ut ita loquar, laxabatur, modo quidem consueto, interdum bis, interdum semel de die: sudores a primo die aderant; urinae paulo post liberius fluere incipiebant, singulis quidem vicibus in pauca quantitate, sed quae reiterationibus saepius repetitis compensabatur, et tanto quidem cum impetu, ut cohiberi nullo modo possent; id quod eo tantum contingere die observavi, quo remedium erat assumtum: sitis remittebat: venter detumescebat; noctes somnis debitae, et omnia sanis haud dissimilia. Alia, praeter modo nominatos, foemina, spe non exigua exinde hausta, ipsius se commiserat cura, sed quae recidivo hydrope laborabat; omnia tarde procedebant usque ad meum abitum, sed quid evenerit necdum audivi; Ego ipsi quidem vereor, utpote viribus nimium quantum destitutae: Semel in hydropico sene infelicem obtinuit successum, cujus rei causa substantia alicujus visceris corrupta adscribitur: nec mirum si votis interdum decidat, non enim est universale quid, ne quidem Panacaea, huic tamen, si quae datur; valde vicinum remedium. Quantum ad Arthritidem, de ea nihil inconcussi habeo, excepto, quod dolores in viro clerico ab inveterata Arthritide excitatos post secundam exhibitionem mirum quantum mitigaverit, ipsique qui pedes et manus ante biduum vix movere poterat, liberam incedendi potestatem conciliaverit; uberiorem hujus rei notitiam mihi denegavit iter, quod eo ipso tempore suscipere cogebar. Vitium prolixitatis deprecor: rei novitas et quantum mihi videtur, magnitudo brevioribus comprehendi non potuit: vereor ne Tuae Claritati risum potius quam Consensum extorqueat, id quod multis contigit usque quo rem manibus quasi palpitarent. Si finis respondebit initus nullus dubito, quin validus inventus sit malleus, quo monstro morborum multicipiti contundantur colla. Dominum Stephanum Angeli Tuae Claritatis verbis compellandi nulla hucusque data mihi est occasio; in Patria enim ferias Academicas celebrat;[10] quae etiam in causa sunt, cur unusquisque a munere publico quiescat, adeo que nihil agatur nihil tractetur quod Tuae Claritati nuntiem. Reliquas Italiae propediem visitaturus urbes jussa Tuae Claritatis ea, qua par est, promptitudine exequi conabor, et si quid occurrat, quod tenuitas ingenii comprehendere valeat, quodque Tuae Claritati sit dignum, officii mei non ero immemor. Ex Patria de liquore illo antinephritico a Domino Bartholino nihil certi habeo, nec id hucusque permisit itineris et vitae saltatoriae ratio; ut primum quidquam scivero, meis partibus non deero. Ne molestum ducat

Tua Claritas meam ad quaevis officia promptitudinem offere Nobilissimo
Domino Boyl, cujus tam in me beneficia, quam in literatum orbem merita
incertus sum adoremne an admirer. Interea valeas, Tua Claritas, nec inique
feras suscipere, susceptumque fovere et amare Tuae Claritati

addictissimum et multo nomine obstrictum
Laurentium Fossium

Dabam Patavij d. 28 Aug.
Anno 1670. aeris Gregorianis

ADDRESS
A Monsieur
Monsieur Oldenburg
Secretaire de la Societé royale
treshumblement
a Londres

TRANSLATION

Noble and famous Sir,

I am ashamed at the long silence I have maintained up to now, the blame for
which I could have avoided if I had come across anything worthy of your excellency; I say nothing of the duty which so many obligations impose on me as of
right. Truly, I can in few words give you some account of the commissions entrusted to my care: the letters addressed to Mr. Thevenot and to those excellent
gentlemen Travagino and Yerbury[1] I delivered with my own hand, and I repay
you with my best thanks for the character you gave me in the eyes of such men,
too flattering to me indeed.[2] Mr. de Graaf had not yet received the letter confided
to Mr. de la Massay;[3] he lamented this misfortune very much, especially on account of the human anatomical specimen annexed to it, which he eagerly longed
for, having a firm conviction that this would do much to settle the dispute that
had broken out between himself and Mr. Clarke; moreover he was thinking of
publishing in the near future on the female organs of generation. What I saw in
Mr. Kerckring's dissecting room[4] about the preservation of bodies and many
other out-of-the-way matters, and what important things I heard about the
development of the fetus from conception onwards—all these were of such great
importance, in my opinion, that I am incapable of describing them, and I rather
decline that labor because I believe he is now among you himself or will soon be
so. For the rest, I have greeted in your name the rest of the Society's well-wishers
as you instructed me to do, among whom I discovered that there was nothing that

they concealed from the world; such great minds are never less idle than when at leisure and thus they cannot but fulfill the expectations of the learned. Mr. Ruysch, the professor of anatomy at Amsterdam,[5] has a remarkable way of preserving bodies, although it is tedious and takes much time; by this method, he says, he can make the bodies hard and dry while preserving their external form and beauty unchanged and free them from all [risk of] putrefaction [*see Plate III*]. What I saw was an elbow with its muscles separated out one from another preserved as an aid to the demonstration of anatomy; he has in hand [the preparation of] a whole body, of which the learned have formed great expectations. I remember that I learned from you, famous Sir, as also from other men of distinction, that there was generally known in England a method that recommended itself not only by its skill and success, but by its ease and saving of time;[6] I wish very much that it might be made public, lest he should deprive you English of all credit for the labor and research, for it seems to be of a wider use, and to serve many of the same or different purposes. Besides these things I have learned nothing, nor did the shortness of the time allow me to do more. There was little doing in mathematics, except that I observed all eyes to be turned towards your excellent Mr. Smethwick, so that they may attentively observe what his recent invention will offer.[7] And since it pleased your excellency to enjoin medical topics upon me, among others,[8] I cannot slip silently over this one instance of that kind which I judged worthy of more thorough investigation, although it may perhaps be an innovation all too well examined by others, for I was convinced by the novelty of the thing and the multitude of its promised benefits. These few points I was able to observe, as it were, in passing.

But to begin at the beginning: there lives at Amsterdam a certain widow named in the vernacular Annetje Roest, who possesses a remarkable and unique medicament which, for the greater glory of the thing, she calls an anti-gout and anti-dropsy—I pass over the other names by which, like a panacea, it is said to master diseases. It is in the form of a fluid, like an oil; the dose administered is ten grains in one spoonful of well rectified alcohol, in which it dissolves and seems quite to disappear. It works partly diuretically and partly by sweating and somewhat by salivation (which the sick like to call a pleasant dewfall; on this ground many infer the presence of antimony, some speak of copper or vitriol, others of mercury), but in a fashion and with an action no less friendly than pleasant in nature. Its value comes from chemistry, its origin from a metal. She says that she received the first discovery of it from Mr. de Rosy, now dead, once in medical practice at Cleves and afterwards a public Professor of Medicine at the University of Franeker,[9] from whom the widow (who had become engaged to marry him) obtained it as a bequest. In truth, passing over all this, I come to those things of which I was an eyewitness: in the short space of six or seven weeks she has restored to unlooked-for health three sexagenarians (one man and two women) swollen with dropsy of the abdomen. On them it wrought these effects: after the fifth dose was taken (their number hardly exceeding sixteen or twenty for the whole course) the bonds upon their bowels (of which they had for the most part lost the benefit) were, so to speak, relaxed, resuming their usual habit once or twice a day; they sweated from the first day; a short time after the urine began to flow more freely, indeed in small quantities at each occasion but made up for by frequent repetitions, and with such force that it could not possibly be held back. This, I observed, happened only on the days when the remedy was administered. Their thirsts abated, their bellies diminished, their nights were spent in sleep, and all else was equally healthy. Another woman besides those mentioned, drawing no little hope from this and suffering from a recurrent dropsy, submitted herself to the cure of it; everything went slowly until my departure and I have not yet heard what happened. I am in truth fearful for her, as being exceedingly weak. It failed once in an old dropsical man, the cause being ascribed to the corrupted substance of some internal organ, and it is not surprising if it defrauds one's hopes sometimes for it is not a universal remedy, nor indeed a panacea, yet it comes extremely near to being this, if such a thing there be.

As for arthritis, I have nothing certain about it, except how wonderfully it mitigated the pains provoked in a clerical gentleman by a chronic arthritis after the second dose, granting a free power of walking to one who could scarcely move his hands and feet two days before. The journey that I thought of undertaking at that time prevented my having a fuller account of this affair. I deplore this vice of prolixity; the novelty and importance of the thing, as it seemed to me, could not be contained in fewer words. I fear it may arouse your excellency's laughter rather than win your agreement, as happens with many things until one (as it were) experiences them directly. If the end is proportionate to the beginning, I doubt not but that this is a true discovery of a weapon for bruising the neck of the many-headed monster of disease. So far I have had no opportunity of addressing your excellency's words to Mr. Stefano degli Angeli, for he is celebrating the university holidays in his native city,[10] which also explains why everyone rests from public business, so that there is nothing done or discussed which I can relate to your excellency. I shall try to obey your command to visit the remaining cities of Italy at an early date with due promptitude, and if anything occurs which my poor brain can fathom and which is worthy of your excellency, I shall not be unmindful of my duty. I have nothing definite from Mr. Bartholin at home about that anti-nephritic fluid, nor has my itinerant and restless way of life permitted it as yet. As soon as I know anything I shall not fail for my part. If it is not too much trouble, worthy Sir, offer my readiness for any service to the very noble Mr. Boyle, whose benevolence towards myself and merits in the learned world I cannot tell whether I adore or admire. Meanwhile, farewell, excellent Sir, recognize as friend, cherish, and love

Your most devoted and for many reasons obliged,
Laurens Foss

Padua, 28 August 1670, N.S.

ADDRESS

> To Mr. Oldenburg
> Secretary of the Royal Society
>   most humbly
>   London

NOTES

For the writer of this letter, see Vol. VI, Letter 1412.

1 See Vol. VI, Letter 1396, note 3.
2 These were obviously letters of introduction, of which Oldenburg kept no copies.
3 See Letter 1413 (Vol. VI), and Letter 1472 (p. 40, above).
4 For Theodor Kerckring, see Vol. VI, Letter 1451. He came to England only in 1678.
5 Frederik Ruysch (1638–1731) achieved great fame as a preparer of anatomical specimens, collected in his famous museum, of which the first catalogue was published in 1691. He was trained in medicine at Leiden, and went to Amsterdam as Professor of Anatomy in 1666. He developed great skill in the technique of injecting wax into the vascular parts of specimens, and was very proud of his preserving fluids. One of these, of which the secret was solemnly revealed to the French Académie des Sciences after his death, consisted simply of a distillate of alcohol containing spices.
6 For early English interest in this art, see Vol. I, p. 322, note 3.
7 On Francis Smethwick's lenses, see Vol. IV, p. 225, note 2. He is not mentioned in this context in the early part of 1670, however.
8 For the instructions—roughly speaking—supplied to Foss, see Vol. VI, Letter 1372.
9 David Anguilla Rosaeus or Rosée was appointed an extraordinary professor at Franeker on 16 March 1648 and dismissed a year later for "frivolous behavior." He lectured on various subjects including surveying but not, apparently, medicine.
10 Stefano degli Angeli (1623–97), Professor of Mathematics at Padua, was a native of Venice.

1511

Willughby to Oldenburg

19 August 1670

From the original in Royal Society MS. W 3, no. 39
Partly printed in *Phil. Trans.*, no. 65 (14 November 1670), 2100

Astrop[1] August 19th

Sr

Yours of August ye 5th was sent after mee Hither where before I received it, I had the good luck to Find a great manie of your Cartrages in a rotten Willow. and by the shape of ye Maggot was most confident, they would produce insects of ye bee tribe. and this I should most certainly have foretold to you had I ever received those you sent by mr Le-Hunt. but having onely that one you sent mee before, I was so Fond and choice of it that I durst not open it. I thinke now I have Found out the whole mysterie, and if you please to send mee Dr Kings account and one of your bees, I will adde if Hee Have omitted anie thing and shall be glad to be instructed in any thing that has escaped mee. I desire one of the bees, because all mine beeing of a late Hatch, and none of them yet turned into nymphas, (which is the word of art for ye Aurelia of a bee) I fear I shall not see their last metamorphosis this yeare. in a garden near ye Willow I found where they got their leaves for their Cartrages which are not Willow but Rose: &c I will proceed no Further for I fear of telling you a story that you know better allreadie. I thinke it deserves very wel to bee putt into your Transactions with a good Cut of ye Cartrages.[2] their boroughs in ye wood the Theca, nympha, Bee &c.

I find ye word morning corrected in the errata, but I should bee still more beholden to you, if you would enter a line or two in some transaction that the renewed bleeding allwaies ceases before noone.[3] for I feare that amendment in the errata will not bee taken notice of and there is nothing else considerable in that relation but this I leave to your own prudence, whither it bee Fit to bee done or not. manie thanks for your account of Dr Wrens Invention[4] though I doe not yet fully master it.

There are divers Spiders that carrie their eggs in balls under their bellies. others that Having made them up in a sphaericall Ball envelop them afterwards a good distance round about with a loose web of which there is one very common sort that allwaies stands sentinel a loof of to secure them From Danger I am confident there are no Viviparous spiders perhaps the old one, inclosed in the wallnut shel might have met with some bruise and then ye young ones might bee Hatched after Her Death and Creep out of Her. I have made no observation of ye whitenesse beeing a signe of Praegnancy but the big bellies discover themselves in them as in all other creatures. mr Lister can discover the instruments of generation in both sexes. and I agree with him that the males Have all of them Knobbed antennae ——o the Females slender antennae which I am sure holds in manie if not all Crabs. the great production of spiders is in July and August which makes the air so Full of webs in September I suspect ye Wallnut tree is not very pleasing to spiders and shall observe further. Besides those a forementioned spiders that make up their Eggs in balls there are others that fixe them in Flat Circles upon leaves. when I come Home I will examine Van Helmont, but the Doctor is best able Himselfe to make medicall inferences From his own ingenious observations.[5] those parts of Insects were doubtlesse eaten by ye Toad. but I suspect the Virulent Pisse might bee eiaculated From some Tubercles in Her bodie. I thinke mr Lister Has observed something to that purpose. I am ever,

your Faithfull servant
F: W:

I am just now returning towards Middleton.
Stubs has been with us Here and threatens to enter a . . . . [*crossed out*]

ADDRESS
> For mr Henrie Oldenburg
> secretarie to the royall society
> at His House in the Pall Mall
>   London

POSTMARK AU 29

I the leafe out of which a long peice II and a round peice
III were bitten IIII the cartrage V the theca

NOTES

Reply to Letter 1501.
1 The Willughby family seat was at Middleton Hall, near Coleshill in Warwickshire; he had presumably gone to Astrop (a small village in Northamptonshire near the Oxfordshire border, east of Banbury) for its mineral springs, discovered in 1664.
2 See the figure set at the end of this letter which Oldenburg cut out of Willughby's letter and had pasted in Letter Book IV, between pages 46 and 47. He also altered Willughby's numbers, since he eventually published these drawings with an extra one in the *Philosophical Transactions*, illustrating extracts from this letter and Letter 1518.
3 See Letter 1479 and note 4; the correction "before noon" is noted in *Phil. Trans.*, no. 60 (20 June 1670), 1086, and no further one was made.
4 See Letter 1493, note 2.
5 See Letters 1464 and 1467.

1512
Oldenburg to Lister
25 August 1670

Lister's Letter 1503 is endorsed as received on 15 August 1670 and answered ten days later.

1513
Vernon to Oldenburg
25 August 1670

From the original in Royal Society MS. V, no. 14

Paris 7 bre 4th [N.S.]

Sr

It is not wthout some little guiltinesses of neglect that I have omitted soe long to write unto you.[1] butt while the Duke of Buckingham was in towne[2] it was wholly impossible to doe it, for there did arise soe many suddain turnes & changes of businesses whilst hee was here, that It was altogether inconsistent to mind that, & my Friends to. butt now hee is gone I have gott a release from the one & I crave pardon of the other

The booke of Dr Wallis wch you sent mee by Dr Williams[3] I received at his arrivall as I believe Monsieur Justel hath given you advice of before now. & I Returne my thankes to Dr Wallis in this Letter wch I desire you to send forward[4]

Thursday 28 Augt. Monsieur Huygens went away for holland. I saw him two or three dayes before butt could not that day by Reason of multiplicity of other businesse. hee remembred his respects most kindly to all of the Royall Society. Hee intends to come hither againe next summer. butt I believe hee must never use that application to Mathematiques hee had formerly although before hee went hee began to Chirp at them.

Monsieur de Bulliau since hee hath received his Letters from Hevelius is convinct of the reality of the new starre in Cygnus although at first hee opposed it Contrary to the Judgement of Sigre Cassini & Monsieur Picart, who Immediately received it for new whilst Monsieur de Bulliau maintained it was antiently putt downe in Bayerus. butt the Neerenesse of another wch is there designed it seemes deceived him. & then hee began to observe it late, his first observations not having beene till July when much of it's greatnesse was diminisht. Hee saith that Hevelius exceedingly Commends to him the glasses of a Telescope hee received from Engld of 51. foot long, wch he affirmes to bee the best hee ever yet used. & that now hee is going to try one wch Sigre Burattini had made for him of 62 foot long the successe of wch hee expects wth great passion.

His Demonstration of Dr Wallis his Arithmetica infinitorum & his new Hypothesis for salving the Phoenomenas about Saturnes Armilla hee is now fitting for the presse, & hee saith the treatise will prove bigger & more bulky then hee expected.[5]

Sigre Cassini extreamely admires Mr Barrows Optiques, wch I sent him & soe did Monsieur Picart who had Read it before. & all that have seen it say it a very pretty piece, & full of Curiosity.

As to Sigre Cassini's Resentment of what Mr Mercator had written concerning his finding the excentricities, it was Nothing Violent.[6] hee said indeed that Mr Mercator went about to attribute the beauty of the Invention to the Bishop of Sarisburies Treatise of Astronomie wth whom hee did not care to Contest. Neither did hee envie any Honour to the Bishop of Sarisburie since hee knew hee deserved more then could be given him, and whether the Bishop or hee had the glory of the invention, it troubled not him: or whether the Principles of it were laid downe in that treatise. What hee knew, hee said, was this, that hee had meditated on that particular [more] then any body else, & if severall wayes brought to the same end, as long as his was as sure as any, that was all hee aimed at. For Ambition did not soe possesse him as that hee could not suffer other people to practise about the same propositions, about wch hee himself was imploid, & to make laudable discoveries in them. Soe that if any body thought that hee was discomposed, because Mr Mercator had intimated that the whole glory of the Invention belonged not to him It was an evident Mistake. For hee could admitt not only of Rivals in that art hee profest, butt of Superiours, & of the Bishop of Salisbury for the great perspicacity hee discoverd in his writings as soone as of any other since hee did not count it a disparagement to give place to a Person of soe great an elevation of witt.

This time of Vacation the Royall Academie doe noe great matters they are still Conversant upon the subject of Motion. & in Chymistry about rarefaction.

There is little of novelty lately come forth. Monsieur Berniers Historicall Narration Monsieur Justel hath sent you. & I have Consigned it to Mr James Potter who is gone to Engld wth the Duke & from him you will heare newes of it. Monsieur Nicol the Jansenist hath lately putt out a treatise sur l'Education du Prince[7] wch because of the politenesse of the Phrase & choysenesse of the matter is well received. Abbe Beaugrands Lexicon Geographicum (by whose care, Ferrarius is much enlarged)[8] is at last come forth, & I believe will not bee unwelcome to the World. This [is] all I shall trouble you wth now, butt I hope shortly to have leisure more large about mee & now the Duke is Gone whose presence gave a traverse biasse to my former course of businesse, I doe not at all Question it. in the meane time Pray my humble Respects to Mr Boyle. My services to Mr Hooke & all my Friends of your society. I rest

Yours wth all affection
Francis Vernon

NOTES

1 Vernon's last letter was dated 9 July (Letter 1484).
2 In July 1670 Charles II had sent the second Duke of Buckingham (1628–87) to France to negotiate a revision of the Treaty of Dover. Negotiations were only completed at the end of the year.
3 This is presumably not the same Dr. Williams who was mentioned in Vol. VI, Letter 1423, note 7.
4 This is naturally no longer with the letter.
5 Boulliaud's *Opus novum ad arithmeticam infinitorum libris sex comprehensum* was not

published until 1682. He seems not to have completed the work on Saturn's rings.
6 See Letter 1457 and its note 6; this is presumably the "explanation" promised there
   by Justel.
7 Pierre Nicole, *De l'Education d'un prince* (Paris, 1670).
8 See Letter 1484, note 5.

1514
Winthrop to Oldenburg

26 August 1670

From the original in Royal Society MS. W 3, no. 23

Boston in New-England
Aug: 26: 1670

Sr

I have received yours of Mar: 26: last together wth those new bookes, and
the Phylosophicall transactions of the last yeare, for wch I returne my
humble thankes, esteeming them all very highly, and so doe such other
persons heere, who know the worth of them, to whom I am communicating
them as I have such former, wch came to my hands, to their great delight
& satisfaction: I have indeavoured about that stellar fish according to
those particulars of inquiry directed in your letter, but can yet meet wth
none (though I have asked of many fishermen, both before it was sent
away, and since I had your letter) who have to their remembrance seene
the like: but am in hope shortly to speake wth that very person a fisherman,
who brought it from sea, he is master of a Vessell, & is now out at sea
upon a fishing voyage, but he is shortly expected. I have now sent a few
more such things as these parts affoard: they are in 2 round boxes and an
other small long box.[1] they are put aboard a ship of wch Capt: ———
Peirce is master: and are directed to Mr Adam Winthrop for the Royall
Society;[2] they are marked on one of the tops as in the marg Be pleased to
present my humble duty to the President & Royall Society to whose commands I am alwaies obliged & ready to obey: For that perticular you are
pleased to intimate about a naturall history of this country: although I am
often observing and collecting and have some fragments of what hath

come to hand yet I thinke it may be too soone to undertake that worke, there having beene but little tyme of experience since our beginnings heere and the remote Inland partes little discovered, matters reported by Indians many tymes uncertaine and need good examination & further inquiry: but a little tyme may give more advantage for some beginning, at least of such an adventure: there is yet no certainty, of what is underground, there are some appearances upon the surface in some places of lead & other mine-ralls, but there have yet none wrought upon but Ironston, wch hath beene also mostly of that sort wch is called the Bog mine, wch is found only in low grounds not deepe nor of any great thicknesse; the hinderances, and difficulties of further discoveries of subterraneall productions were men-tioned formerly in other letters.[3] some other things I expect hither shortly, wch are intended for the Repository of the Royall Society, wch I directed to be brought hither before I came from Connecticutt, wch I hope may be sent by some other ship and then you may also expect other letters from

your affectionate servant
J Winthrop

Be pleased to present my humble service to Sr. Robert Moray, and acquaint him that I am very mindfull of his commands by your letter about the Silkepodds, but the season is not yet, they are not yet ripe, and when they are ripe they must be withered awhile before they can be putt up.

I am not unmindfull about those cranburies for your selfe, but the season is not yet for them (as I am informed) nor for their transportation I hope to have a fitt oportunity, in the sutable tyme, and if I should be gone hence before I intend to leave order wth some freind for the pro-curing & shipping of them.

I should be glad to be informed whether you had a letter of the yeare 1668: wherin was a large letter to Mr Haake[4] they were sent wth a pecquet to mr Henry Ashurst[5] (as I remember) but I have not heard whether re-ceived by mr Haake or your selfe.

In the biggest of those boxes now sent there are two skinnes of those snakes wch they call heere rattle snakes; from the rattle yt is upon the taile they have that denomination: they are stuffed wth somthing to the pro-portion of their bignesse, when they were alive: they are not of the largest size, I had formerly sent over much bigger, but they came not to you. I could at this tyme procure no other: one of them hath its rattles whole upon the other I doubt have some broken off, except it be very young. But it is as the Indian brought it: Its said their age is knowne by the number of those partitions upon the rattle, and that every yeare is added another of those fibers to the rest the snake usually makes a noise, by shaking that rattle upon its taile when it seeth any come towards it, and at other tymes. and by that meanes is often warning of the danger, before one cometh neer them but somtymes they are asleepe, or lye still wch is dangerous to such as walke in the woods, & to horse & other cattle.[6]

There is also some of the roote of that herbe wch is called the Virginia snakeweed,[7] of wch there is both of that wch grow in Virginia and of the like sort wch groweth in the more Westerly parts of New England & Long Island. but I have seene nor heard of any in these Easterly parts it is used as a certaine meanes of cure to those who are bitten by that snake the cure is by chewing a little of it, and swallowing some of the Juice of it, and applying some, of that wch was chewed, to the place:

There is in the other round box some eares of Indian corne of such a kind yt it wilbe ripe heere as soone as the other sort though planted much later, this grew in the same ground after turnep seed had been ripe & gathered the same spring yt it was planted, it may be likely to ripen in England If planted in Aprill In that manner they traie[8] their corne to hang up, & so it will keepe long, although hung abroad It is putt up so that their manner of tracing may be seene one halfe of the traice was cutt of before it was put up. the planter desirous to reserve some to be planted again having but little of the seed of that kind: In the same box is also in a bag some nuts like wallnutts wch are usually called butternutts, & by some oylenutts.[9] the Indians make an oyle of them: there are also hazell nutts wch being of the naturall growth of this country, & not of plants or nutts brought out of England, are put in to fill up the box.

In the long box are some of the dwarfe oakes, wch were gathered Early at the beginning of the budding of the acornes, that they might not fall of as the riper acornes doe they were prepared to be sent before I had intelligence of the former received & being ready put up I thought fitt to send them; and in the same box are a few branches of ye butternut tree.

There is also a small long fish taken here in the salt water I know no name for it nor have seene of them before, It is in a paper wth in a peice of a caule There is also a fish wch they call an Horn fish, but I thinke it is not of these seas, but brought from about Jamaica, or some part of the West Indies:

In one of the round boxes is also a small stone like chrystall wch An Indian (from whom I had it) affirmed fell wth thunder & they call them thunderstones, & the Indians all agree to their relation of them that such fall downe wth thunder.

ADDRESS

> For my worthy freind
> Mr Henry Oldenburg
> Secretary to the
>   Royall Society
>   In
>   London

NOTES

Reply to Letter 1433 (Vol. VI). This present letter reached Oldenburg on 27 October 1670, according to his endorsement.

1 These were produced at a meeting of the Royal Society on 27 October 1670.
2 Adam Winthrop (1647–1700) had come to England in the winter of 1669/70, after graduating from Harvard College, and was soon to settle as a merchant in Bristol. He was John Winthrop's nephew. John Winthrop's initials, I°W, appear in the margin of the original near this point.
3 Winthrop was himself directly involved in ironworking ventures in Massachusetts and at New Haven; on his mission to Europe in 1641 he had been made particularly responsible for gaining knowledge of the smelting of this metal. The first successful furnace was that at Saugus, Massachusetts.
4 There exists a copy in the Winthrop Papers (V, no. 163) of a letter to Haak possibly written in July 1668. There is no reference to it in any other extant letter to Oldenburg.
5 Henry Ashurst (1614?–80) was a London merchant notable for his charity; he was active in the Society for the Propagation of the Gospel.
6 For the rattlesnake skins in the Royal Society repository, see Grew, *Musaeum*, pp. 50–51.
7 *Aristolochia serpentaria* is still called the Virginia snakeroot. Winthrop's specimens are mentioned in Grew, *Musaeum*, p. 227.
8 The word should no doubt be "traice," as in the next sentence, signifying "plait." This word, related to "tress," seems to be local to the English West Country, and is (or was) also applied to plaiting a trace or string of onions.
9 The butternut tree is *Juglans cinerea*, of the walnut family.

1515

Oldenburg to Newburgh

27 August 1670

An endorsement on Letter 1504 indicates that it was delivered by a Mr. Quarles on 23 August and answered on 27 August.

1516

Richard to Oldenburg

28 August 1670

From the original in Royal Society MS. R, no. 35

Monsieur

Celui qui vous rendra cette lettre est un fort honneste homme, illustre en sa profession, qui est d'enseigner l'Italien et l'Espagnol, et dont le nom est cognu par quelques livres qu'il a faits il s'appelle Monsr Juliani.[1] J'ay prit la liberté de le charger de ce billet pour vous par ce que ie scay que vous estes le patron de tous les illustres en quelque genre d'estude que ce soit; et parce, aussi, que i'ay esté bien aise de trouver une occasion de vous asseurer que ie vous considere tousiours infiniement.

    Je n'ay point receu de response a la derniere lettre[2] que ie vous ay escritte, (il y a environ six ou sept mois de cela), ou ie repondois a quelques questions que vous m'avies faittes et vous rendois conte d'une remarque que i'avois faitte dans les rognons d'une porcille. Depuis ce temps la, Mrs de l'academie Royale De Paris ont remarqué la mesme chose dans un ours et dans un autre animal. Il n'y a rien de nouveau en ce pays icy qui merite de vous estre mandé, si ce n'est un petit prodige qui arriva il y a quelque temps, dans la riviere de charente. ou deux gros poissons, que nous appellons des buffars,[3] de 32 pieds de long et seise de large, monterent neuf ou dix lieues, et furent tues vers Taillebourg.[4] Sil arriye, desormais que vous me veuilles faire la grace de m'escrire, il n'est plus besoin de se servir de l'addresse de Monsr Bouhereau parce qu'a present ie suis establi a la Rochelle.

Je souhaiterois de tout mon coeur trouver quelque occasion de vous tesmoigner combien ie suis, Monsieur

> Vostre tres humble &
> tres obeissant serviteur
> *Elie Richard*

A La Rochelle le 7 de Septembre 1670 [N.S.]

ADDRESS
> A Monsieur
> Monsieur Oldenbourg secretaire
> De la Societe Royalle, In palmal street
> A Londres

TRANSLATION

Sir,

He who will deliver this letter to you is a very cultivated man, notable in his profession, which is the teaching of Italian and Spanish; his name is known from several books he has written, and is Mr. Julliani.[1] I have taken the liberty of burdening him with this letter for you because I know that you are a patron of all distinguished men in every branch of learning, and because I was, as well, very glad to find an opportunity for assuring you that I always esteem you infinitely.

I never received any reply to the last letter[2] I wrote to you (about six or seven months since) in which I replied to several questions you had put to me and gave you an account of an observation I had made in the kidneys of a porpoise. Since then the gentlemen of the Royal Academy at Paris have observed the same thing in a bear and in another animal. There is nothing new in this country which deserves to be passed on to you, unless it is a minor prodigy which took place some time ago in the Charente River, where two of the large fish which we call "buffars,"[3] thirty-two feet long and sixteen wide came nine or ten leagues up river and were killed near Taillebourg.[4] If you should in the future happen to want to honor me with a letter, it is not necessary to use Mr. Bouhereau's address because I am now settled in La Rochelle.

I hope, with all my heart, to be able to find some opportunity to testify to you how much, Sir, I am

> Your very humble and
> very obedient servant,
> *Elie Richard*

La Rochelle, 7 September 1670 [N.S.]

ADDRESS
To Mr. Oldenburg, Secretary
of the Royal Society, In Pall Mall
London

NOTES

1 This visitor is known only by his publications: the *Nomenclature du sieur Julliani*
(Paris, 1659), and *Les proverbes divertissans du sieur Julliani* (Paris, 1659), both reprinted
more than once.
2 Vol. VI, Letter 1358.
3 We could find this word in no dictionary.
4 Taillebourg (Charente-Inf.) is a small town on the river near Saint-Savinien.

1517
Oldenburg to Helmfeld
29 August 1670

Oldenburg endorsed the envelope of Helmfeld's Letter 1508 as having been received
on 26 August and answered on 29 August.

1518
Willughby to Oldenburg
2 September 1670

From the original in Royal Society MS. W 3, no. 40
Printed in *Phil. Trans.*, no. 65 (14 November 1670), 2100–2102

Middleton 7ber 2d 1670

Sr

at my comming home I found the Barometer and both the Thermometers which were brought very safe.[1] manie thanks for your trouble
about them. I will make bold to deferre the paying for them till I come to

London which I intend shortly. I found allso your long expected Cartrages, and some of the bees Hatched, so that now wee want nothing to compleat their History. I will trouble you onely with those particulars, that I find not mentioned in Dr Kings Paper, to whome wee owe the first sight of these cases, and knowledge of their Productions.[2] and whose observations concerning them our own experience has since confirmed.

Mr Snel an ingenious gentleman brought of them to the Wels at Astrop.[3] who directing mee to the place where hee got them, I found great plentie in the Trunke of a dead Willow. Beginning to unfold some of them, Mr Wray immediately judged them to bee made up of peices of rose leaves, and called to mind, that this very spring a worthie freind of his, mr Francis Jessoppe,[4] Brought him a rose-leafe, out of which himselfe saw a bee bite such a peice, and Fly away with it in her mouth: whereupon searching the Rose Trees thereabouts, wee found a great manie leaves with such peices bitten out of them, as these cartrages are made up of; some of which I sent you inclosed in my last. the Holes or Cuniculi never crosse the graine of the wood, excepting where the bee comes in, and where they open one into another.

From the place of entrance they are wrought both upwards and downwards: so that sometimes the Bee maggot lys under her food and sometimes above it. One end of the cartrage, Viz: that, which is next the entrance, is allwaies a little concave; the other end, which is furthest from the entrance, a little convexe, and is received into the concave of the next beyond it. The sides of the Cartrages are made up of oblong peices of leaves pasted together; the ends, of round: And wherever they doe not ly close one to another, the intermediate space is Fild up with a multitude of these round peices, laid one upon another. the cartrages containe a pap or batter of the consistencie of a gellie or something thicker of a middle colour between sirup of Violets and the conserve of red roses; Of an acid tast and unpleasant smel: in each of these at ye concave end there lys one bee maggot, which feeds upon the forementioned matter till it grows to its ful bignesse, and then makes, and encloses her selfe in, a Huske or theca, of a darke red colour and ovall figure; in which shee is changed into a bee. The remainder of Her food you may find dried into powder at the convexe end; and Her excrements at the concave without the Theca. The bees I found in your boxe, (which are the only ones I have yet seen) were of a shorter and thicker figure then the common Honie bee, more Hairier &c. but the surest marke to distinguish them, is, that the forcipes or teeth of these are bigger broader and stronger in shape, like those of a Wasp or Hornet; From which shee allso sufficiently differs in having a tongue like a bee which they want. they made their way out along the channel thorough all the intermediate cartrages and not thorough the solid wood: of the corruption of the matter within the cases, when the Bee maggots or nymphae happen to miscarry are bred little Hexapods, which produce beetles; 2ly maggots, which produce flys; 3ly mites. &c. from what has been observed concerning this bee and by a great manie more parallel instances, wee may answer a Quaerie of some authors that have written of bees: whither it bee the old bee or the bee maggot that covers the Cells before the change? that it is the maggot and not the old one. for here the old bee when shee has left provision enought, with an Egge closes up the cartrage; and Has no more to doe; the maggot a great while after making the Theca, which is analogous to the cover of the Cells. I am Sr

> your Faithfull servant
> *Fran: Willughby*

ADDRESS

    For Mr Henrie
    Oldenburg secretarie
    to the Royall society
    at his house in the
    Pal Mal
        London

                                POSTMARK SE 7

NOTES

1 See Letter 1501.
2 Actually—as Oldenburg pointed out in his reply—Croone was the first; see Vol. VI, Letter 1371.
3 For Astrop, see Letter 1511, note 1; we cannot identify Mr. Snell, who may have been a member of the Wiltshire family of this name.
4 Francis Jessop (1638–91) came from Yorkshire and was apparently a friend of Ray's of some years' standing.

1519
Travagino to Oldenburg

7 September 1670

From the original in Royal Society MS. T, no. 12

Nobilissimo atque Doctissimo Viro
D. Henrico Oldenburg
Regiae Societatis apud Anglos
Secretario
Franciscus Travagino Salutem

Accepi nudius tertius abs Clarissimo atque Illustrissimo Domino Legati vestri Secretario[1] quas ipsi litteras ad me commiseras ad 15. Januarii. Utinam citius ipsas reddidisset vel certe posterioribus tuis litteris (quibus est iam responsum)[2] Ipse aliquid annuisses ex quo hominem istiusmodi, suapte virtute commendabilem, etiam a Te mihi commendatum resciscerem; utique ipsum prolixius excepissem, ac si omnibus quae ex Te atque ex tua commendatione merebatur officijs essem pro virili prosecutus, ut eorum quae ab amico et hospite iure expectantur, nihil unquam a me esset desideratum; verum, uti scis, et Tu siluisti, et quemadmodum ex Ipso audies, cum nuper tantum, atque, ut ita dicam, in ipso solum istinc discedendi articulo, mihi litterarum eiusmodi copiam fecerit, habebis excusatum si minus prolixe quam uterque voluisset meruissetque, fuerit exceptus. Quin et tanto adhuc Tibi excusatiores videbimus, quod eodem tempore, praeter tumultuariam eius istinc discedendi festinationem,[3] ita ego quoque (sic fatis volentibus) ob nescio quam litem domesticam, districtus habebar iri tribus foris, ut nec mei quidem mihi copia relinqueretur; quod utique tanto piguit magis quod etiam ex praecipiti ac tumultuaria hac Viri quam delibavi conversatione ipsum probavi meritissimum qui votis omnibus mihi fruendus quam prolixissime expectatur. Salutabit Ipse Te meo nomine ac referet, quam Tibi vere et ex animo vivam addictus: quin et caetera quae de me atque a me scire Te velle significas. Vale Vir Celeberrime.

Dabam Ven. 17 Septembris 1670 [N.S.]

ADDRESS

Nobilissimo ac Celeberrimo Viro Domino
Henrico Oldenburg, Regiae Societatis
apud Anglos Secretario
Londini

TRANSLATION

Francisco Travagino greets the very noble and learned Mr. Henry Oldenburg,
Secretary of the Royal Society of England

The day before yesterday I received from the worthy gentleman who is secretary to your ambassador[1] the letter you had entrusted to him on 15 January. Would that he had delivered it more quickly, or that at least in your previous letter (to which I have already replied)[2] you had hinted something from which I might have learned of this man, made worthy of commendation by his own merits and moreover commended by you. For I would assuredly have entertained him longer, and if I had showered upon him all the courtesies merited by yourself and your commendation (as is expected by right of friendship and hospitality) to the limit of my powers, nothing more could have been desired of me; but in truth, as you know, you kept silent and since (as you may hear from the man himself) it was only in the very act of departing hence, so to speak, that he gave me the copy of that letter, you will excuse me if I entertained him more briefly than either of us intended and he deserved. That I may seem the more forgivable, besides the hurry and bustle of his departing hence,[3] because of some domestic upset or other (for so luck would have it) I was called out three times, so that I had no further leisure; which, to be sure, annoyed me the more because even in the hurry and bustle, by the little taste I had of this man's conversation I found him to be very worthy, one who might be expected at a fuller opportunity to prove as delightful as one could wish. He will give you my greetings and assure you that I live in true and heartfelt devotion to you; be sure to let me know what else you wish to learn from me, and by my means. Farewell, famous Sir.
Venice, 17 September 1670 [N.S.]

ADDRESS

To the very noble and celebrated
Mr. Henry Oldenburg, Secretary
of the Royal Society of England
London

NOTES

Reply to Letter 1369 (Vol. VI).
1 John Dodington.
2 See Vol. VI, Letter 1396.
3 Whatever was meant—Dodington may have been going on some trip—he certainly remained in Venice for some years to come; see Vol. VI, Letter 1364, note.

1520
Oldenburg to Hevelius
8 September 1670
From the original in Observatoire X, no. 36

Illustri Viro
Domino Johanni Hevelio, Gedan. Consuli Amplissimo
H. Oldenburg Salutem

Diuturnum silentium tuum,[1] Vir Celeberrime, adeo anxios nos habuit, ut de secunda valetudine tua admodum dubitare inciperemus. Laetabundi tandem literas tuas, 5. Julij datas, accepimus; quibus respondendis cum post aliquas exinde septimanas me accingeram, Ecce, aderant alterae tuae 27. Augusti exaratae. Priores quod attinet, maximam ejus partem (tota quippe ipsam non spectabat) Regiae Societati, tum temporis nondum ferianti, publice praelegi;[2] Ejusdemque Jussu singulares pro Jucundissimis communicatis gratias hisce Tibi reponere debui. De posterioribus vero commemorare apud Ipsum nil quicquam hactenus licuit, cum Ea per aliquot hebdomadas, pro hujus tempestatis more, caetus suos agitare intermiserit, quos cum ante Octobris mensem non sit instauratura, eo usque mihi rerum iis traditarum communicatio fuerit differenda.[3] Interim lubentissime intelleximus, tum Microscopium, tum Telescopium, hinc Tibi transmissa, exspectationem tuam non lusisse; quin magnopere gaudemus, tum quod novam circa et infra Cygni caput stellam detexisti, tum quod dicti Telescopii ope praesentem Saturni phasim luculenter observasti. Latere Te non putem eandem 3ae magnitudinis stellam in Gallia d.20. Decemb. 1669. a Gallo quodam Carthusiano, omnium quod sciam primo, Divione detectam fuisse, qui nuntium ea de re ad Abbatem Mariotum Parisios transmisit, unde istius rei notitia, literis 5 Julij ad me datis,[4] in Angliam pervenit: ubi hactenus illud Phaenomenon (qua culpa, nescio) in Nostratium Observationem non incurrit. De ejus novitate Astronomi Parisienses etiamnum disceptant, Bullialdo affirmante, eam ipsam in Bayeri Tabulis jam extare; caeteris, puto, omnibus contrarium asserentibus, atque ut sententiam suam tueantur hanc rationem ineuntibus. Dicunt scilicet, Ejus, quam Bullialdus apud Bayerum indigitat, ad Cygni rostrum,

Ascensionem rectam esse	289°.	22′.	0″.
Declinationem Borealem	27°.	19 .	20 .
At hujus Novae Ascensionem rectam esse	293°.	33 .	0 .
Declinationem Borealem	26 .	33 .	20 .
Longitudinem	1 .	55 .	Aquarii
Latitudinem	47 .	28 .	10 .

Ejusdem distantia ab illa, quae est ad ⎫
rostrum Cygni, versus Iaculum, esse ⎭   3 .   47 .   0 .

Quae observatio quomodo cum Tua conveniat, facile Tibi fuerit dignoscere.[5] Alius quidam in Gallia Philosophus positum dictae Stellae sic mihi describit;

"Stellam novam videri est in Sectione duarum linearum, quarum una ducitur a Lyra ad proximam Rhombo Delphini; altera, ab Aquila ad illam in ancone Alae superioris Cygni; adeoque Triangulum facit quasi aequilaterum cum illa in Rostro et Oculo Cygni."[6]

Quod vides tuae Observationi, apprime congruere.

Spero, Hookium nostrum, quamprimum ipsi vacaverit, huic etiam Observationi invigilaturum, eo inprimis fine, ut innotescat, novane haec stella eandem sit magnitudinem servatura, an minus. Idem nunc observare instituit Declinationis Magneticae Variationem. Vereor interim, ne Aedificationis Londinensis cura, quae Ipsi cum aliis incumbit, eum ab hac et aliis Observationibus Philosophicis peragendis divertat; simul et obstet, quo minus in aliis, quae amicis suis fuerat pollicitus, fidem datam tempore praestituto liberet.

Caeterum, Vir quidam Londinensis,[7] Rei magneticae perquam callens, Theoriam quandam, necdum evulgatam, excogitavit, qua Phaenomena haec variantia Magnetis rite se explicaturum confidit. Secundum eam audacter statuit, Variationem Magnetis Londinensem, quae antehac per multos annos Ortum versus contingere observata fuit, hoc tempore Occasum versus, et quidem hoc ipso anno, hic Londini 2. grad. 18 minuta, eandem plagam versus, deflectere, observato fere istiusmodi motu progressionis annuo, qualem tu nuper in prioribus tuis literis indicaveras.

Gratulamur Tibi de dono, quo Illustrissimum Burattinum Te locupletasse scribis; nec ulli dubitamus, quin vires illius Lentis, quae pro 70. pedum longitudine elaborata fuit, quamprimum eas habueris exploratas, nobis sis communicaturus.

Perplacebant ea, Societati Regiae, quae de variis rarioribusque Succini frustulis perscripseras. Utinam sine nimio incommodo portiunculam aliquam succini illius, sigillo cedentis, et odore bituminoso pollentis, nec non illius, quod altera parte molle, altera durissimum fuisse scribis, comparare Tibi et Nobis possis. Id quidem egregie Gazo-phylacium nostrum Physicum exornaret, nosque porro Generositati tuae magis magisque devinciret.

Clarissimus Wallisius priores duas partes Tractatus sui Geometrici de Motu in publicum emisit, ubi de generalibus regulis motus, de Descensu Gravium, de Libra, de Centro Gravitatis ejusque Calculo, multa perdocte et Latine edisserit. Dr Barrovius, paulo post, Lectiones suas Opticas et Geometricas, Cantabrigiae habitas, magna quoque cum laude edidit; in quarum prioribus Opticorum Phaenomenum genuinae rationes investigantur et exponantur; in posterioribus vero, Generalia praesertim Curvarum Linearum Symptomata Latine sermone declarantur. Nobilissimus Boylius dehinc in Lucem porro dedit Tractatulos quosdam Physicos Anglice adornatos, qui Historiam Qualitatum Particularium, nec non Qualitates Cosmicas (hoc est, a Constitutione Universi dependentes) ut et Regionum Subterranearum atque Submarinarum Temperiem, Marisque Fundum spectant. Siquidem jusseris, ut horum Exemplaria Tibi transmittam, lubentissime, quamprimum id indicaveris, parabo.

Quem progressum feceris in Machina tua Caelesti concinnanda scire perquam avemus. Perspecta nobis est non minus indus[tria—*torn*] tua, quam Astronomicae perficiendae cupido. Hinc nihil apud Te, Vir Amplissime, urgemus; sed omnia fausta et felicia assiduis tuis conatibus ex animo comprecamur. Vale, et me Tibi perpetua Addictissimum crede. Dabam Londini d. 8. Septemb. 1670

ADDRESS
   Illustri Viro Domino
   Johanni Hevelio Consuli
   et Astronomo Dantiscano
   Celeberrimo.
                  Dantzick.

TRANSLATION

H. Oldenburg greets Mr. Johannes Hevelius, very worthy Senator of Danzig

Your long silence made us so anxious,[1] famous Sir, that we had begun to entertain serious doubts of your good health. At length we received with great
satisfaction your letter of 5 July [N.S.], and I was a few weeks later gathering
myself together in order to frame a reply to it, when, lo and behold! your further
letter of 27 August [N.S.] came to hand. As for the former, I read the great part
of it (for the whole was not relevant) to the Royal Society which had not then
begun its vacation,[2] and by order of the same I was to return you particular thanks
for these most agreeable communications. It has not yet been possible to draw its
attention to anything in the later letter as the Society has, according to its custom at
this season, intermitted its meetings for a few weeks, not resuming them until
October and so putting off my imparting of things delivered to me until then.[3]

Meanwhile we have learned with great pleasure that both the microscope and
the telescope sent to you from here have come up to your expectations; and we are
also delighted that you have discerned that new star near and below the head of
Cygnus, and further by means of that telescope mentioned just now have observed
so excellently the present aspect of Saturn. You cannot be ignorant, I think, of the
fact that the same third-magnitude star was, so far as I know, first of all observed
by a certain French Carthusian at Dijon in France on the twentieth of December
1669; he sent word of it to the Abbé Mariotte in Paris, whence news of it reached
me here in England in a letter dated 5 July.[4] Since that time that phenomenon has
not come under the observation of our astronomers—where the fault lies I cannot
tell. The Parisian astronomers are still debating whether it is a nova, Bouliaud
asserting that it is in Bayer's plates, while all the rest, I believe, hold to the contrary view and defend it by this argument. For they say, that star which Bouliaud
instances in Bayer, in the beak of Cygnus, has RA 289° 22′ 0″, north declination
27° 19′ 20″. But this new star has RA 293° 33′ 0″, north declination 26° 33′ 20″;
longitude 1° 55′ in Aquarius and latitude 47° 28′ 10″. Its distance towards Sagitta
from that in the beak of Cygnus is 3° 47′. You will easily perceive how this observation agrees with your own.[5] Another French philosopher describes the place
of that star to me thus:

"The nova is to be seen at the intersection of two lines, one being drawn from
Lyra to the nearest star of the rhombus of Delphinus, the other from Aquila to that
in the bend of the upper wing of Cygnus; and so it forms a triangle, almost equilateral, with the stars in the beak and the eye of Cygnus."[6]

Which you see agrees closely with your observation.

I hope that as soon as he has leisure our Hooke will look out for that observation especially, in order to discover whether that new star will maintain the

same brightness, or a less one. He has now decided to observe the magnetic declination. Meanwhile I fear lest the responsibility for the rebuilding of London that falls upon him as well as others may divert him from carrying out this and other philosophical observations, and may also prevent him from fulfilling at the appointed time the promises he has made to his friends.

Moreover, a certain Londoner[7] who is very much given to the study of magnetism has worked a theory of some sort, not published yet, by which he is confident these phenomena of the variation of the compass will be properly explained. Upon this basis he has boldly asserted that the magnetic variation at London, observed to lie towards the east for many years previously, would turn towards the west at this time and be here at London in this very year 2° 18′ in that direction, following almost the same kind of progressive annual change that you indicated in the former of your letters.

I congratulate you on the present the very illustrious Burattini has made you, as you write, and have no doubt but that you will communicate to us the powers of that lens which was worked for a length of 70 feet as soon as you have investigated them.

What you have written about various rare fragments of amber pleased the Royal Society very much. Would that you could without too much trouble get hold of some little portion—both for yourself and for us—of that piece yielding to a seal, and having a bituminous smell, as well as of that other piece which (you say) was part soft, part extremely hard; it would exceedingly adorn our natural history collections and render us yet more obliged to your excellency.

The famous Wallis has published very learnedly and in Latin the first two parts of his *Tractatus geometricus de motu*, in which he has set out many things relating to the general rules of motion, the descent of heavy bodies, the balance, and the center of gravity and its calculation. A little more recently Dr. Barrow printed, with applause, his optical and geometrical lectures, delivered at Cambridge. In the former of these he investigates and explains the true causes of the phenomenon of optics, and in the latter he declares the general characteristics of curves in particular, employing the Latin tongue. Next, the very noble Boyle issued some further physical papers composed in English, which are concerned with the history of particular qualities and the cosmic qualities (that is to say, those arising from the structure of the universe), the temperature of the submarine and subterranean regions, and the bottom of the sea. If you should command me to send you copies of them I will provide them as soon as you have sent me word, very gladly.

We are most anxious to know what progress you have made in composing your *Machina coelestis*. Your industry is no less obvious to us than your desire to improve astronomy. So we do not in any way hurry you on, worthy Sir, but we offer a wholehearted prayer that all fortune and success may attend your constant endeavors. Farewell, and believe me always most devoted to you.

London, 8 September 1670

ADDRESS

> To the illustrious Mr. Johannes Hevelius
> Most celebrated Senator and Astronomer
> of Danzig
>
> Danzig

NOTES

Reply to Letters 1475 and 1509.
1 Letter 1128 (Vol. V) from Hevelius was dated 11 March 1668/9.
2 Letter 1475 was read on 21 July 1670.
3 Letter 1509 was read on 27 October.
4 See Letter 1474.
5 The figures are taken by Oldenburg from Letter 1484. We have given the more usual name for the constellation known as the Arrow (*Sagitta*) or Dart (*Tela* or *Jaculum*).
6 This letter has not been traced.
7 This was Henry Bond; see Vol. V, p. 95, note 1.

1521

Oldenburg to Willughby

10 September 1670

From the memorandum in Royal Society MS. W 3, no. 40

Rec. Sept. 8. 70
Answerd Sept. 10.
Croon ye first.[1]

Not told us, how they get those pieces in wth their bodies. Webs not only made by spiders, because you find ym, when there are no spiders, in ye midst of Winter, in uliginous[2] fields towards an evening, overspread on a sudden wth ym. and in glasses, wherein he[3] had distilled, and in [*illegible*] upon a sudden raised, from vapors.

NOTES

Reply to Letter 1518.
1 See Letter 1518, note 2.
2 Marshy.
3 If this word is correct—the memo is a mere scribble—there is no clue to the identity of the person.

1522

Oldenburg to Edward Bernard

13 September 1670

From the original in Bodleian Library MS. Smith 45, f. 75

Sir,

I could not but let you know, yt, I think myself obliged to you for having me in yr thought, of wch you lately gave me ye assurance by a letter deliver'd to me by ye Son of Olaus Wormius, whom I shall be ready to serve in what I may.[1] As to our Noble friend, Mr Boyle, I think (and am very glad I have ground to doe so) he is recover'd as to ye maine, though some weaknesse remains yet upon him, and chiefly upon his arms and hands; wch, I hope, time and good care will also remove.

Concerning the Dutch Mathematicians, you mention, I know of nothing, yt Wassenaer (who indeed is much commended to me for his great skill in Algebra, as not at all inferior to yt of Des-Cartes) hath published.[2] Van Hudde is at present so taken up wth his place and office in the Magistracy, yt he hath laid by his Opticks.[3] Kinkhusen is dead, but hath left us, you know, 3 tracts Mathematical in Low Dutch, viz. 1. an Introduction (wch Mr Newton at Cambridge is now reviewing and augmenting, to have it publisht in English wth his additions;) 2. Conic Sections; and 3. a Tract of Geometrical Problems solved by Algebra, wherein I understand he treates somewt of ye method *de maximis et minimis*.[4]

When I see those persons, whom you salute in yr letter, I shall not faile to discharge yr commission. Dr Wallis I have not yet seen; and believe he is gone into Kent. I remaine Sir

Yr affectionat servant
Oldenburg

London Septemb. 13. 1670.

NOTES

Edward Bernard (1638–96) of St. John's College, Oxford, was already known as an Oriental scholar (Vol. IV, p. 141); early in 1669 he had visited Leiden to consult MSS. there (see Vol. V, pp. 235, 342, 472), accompanied by John Wallis the younger. In 1673 he succeeded Wren in the Savilian Chair of Astronomy, and began work on the MSS. of ancient mathematicians and astronomers. He was also for a time tutor to Charles II's sons by the Duchess of Grafton. He published little of any scientific importance.

1   This letter of introduction has not survived. Olaus Wormius (1588–1654), the cele-
    brated scholar and physician of Copenhagen, had eighteen children; this son may
    have been Matthias (1636–1707), who certainly visited England.

2   For Jacob van Wassenaer (b. *c.* 1607), see Vol. V, p. 231, note 6. He published nothing
    of any magnitude.

3   Johannes Hudde (1628–1704) was many times burgermeister of Amsterdam. The
    date of birth given in Vol. III, p. 434, is erroneous.

4   This information about Gerard Kinckhuysen was derived from Pell and Collins.
    Nothing about his life seems to have been recorded. The title of the works mentioned
    here are (1) *Algebra, ofte stel-Konst* (Haarlem, 1661); (2) *De Grondt der meet-Konst*
    (Haarlem, 1660); (3) *Geometria ofte meet-Konst* (Haarlem, 1663). On the translation of
    the first of these into English, see Vol. V, p. xxv; the translation was put into New-
    ton's hands for a "review" of the book between August 1669 and January 1670.
    Nothing was ever published.

1523
Von Boineburg to Oldenburg
14 September 1670
From the original in Royal Society MS. B 2, no. 5

Nobilissime domine

Summa me voluptate perfudit epistola tua, qua me vicissim dignari
voluisti. Iam iterum dego [?] maiorem in modum, quandoquidem a
Serenissimo principe Ruperto inde ab anni 1666 initio nil plane responsi
accepi, ut habes pusillas literulas ipsi adsis semel coram tradere, simulque
rogare velis, ut respondeat tandem. Clarissimo Leibnizio tuas[1] tradam,
faxoque, ut per omnia Tibi satisfaciat. Proxime plura. Interim oro praecor-
que summopere, apud principem Rupertum mei cum effectu, memor quidem perseveres [?] et responsionem exsculpas, quam tamdiu debet, ad tot
meas. Quas quod se accepisse fatetur, gaudeo. periter enim quin sic,
quas ipsis indideram, acceperit, ambigi non potest. Ideo vel ideo responsu-
rum, confido. Neque enim [*illegible*] humanitatem dedidicerit, memineas,
quam sincere ipsi servire studuerim in omni fortuna. Sane et liquidum
hoc nomine et reale et benignissimum mihi ab ipso responsum neque ultra

cunctabundum, omnino polliceor. Tibi vero, vir optime, sum ad omnia, grato animo,

obligatissimus
I C Baro a Boineburg

Francofurti XIV. Sept. 70.

TRANSLATION

Most noble Sir,

The letter with which you chose to honor me in return filled me with the greatest pleasure. Having received no reply from His Highness Prince Rupert since the beginning of the year 1666, I now live more cheerfully again, because you have my paltry little notes to hand to him [when] once you are in his presence and are willing to beg him to answer them. I shall deliver your letter to the celebrated Leibniz[1] and have him satisfy you on every point. More in [my] next. Meanwhile I beg and beseech you most earnestly to continue urging recollection of myself upon Prince Rupert, with good results, and to extract that reply to so many of mine that he has owed for so long. I am glad that he admits receiving them. For then it cannot be doubted that he equally well had notice of what I reported in them. On that account, I am sure, a reply will be made. And should he be forgetful of [*illegible*] kindness, you may remind him how sincerely I strove to serve him through all contingencies. Truly and certainly, I promise [myself], his answer to me will for this reason be both royal and benign, and without further delay. To you, excellent Sir, I am in all things your grateful

and most obliged
J. C. Freiherr von Boineburg

Frankfurt, 14 September 1670

NOTES

Reply to Letter 1505. It is very badly written and many readings are uncertain.
1 Letter 1506.

1524
Leibniz to Oldenburg
18 September 1670

From the copy in Royal Society Letter Book IV, 85–91
Printed in Gerhardt, pp. 43–47

. . . .

Meditationes meas de primis abstractisque Motus rationibus conceperam superiore anno sualbaci in ipso acidularum usu, cum Clarissimus
Mauritius,[1] Iuris Consultus Chiloniensis, Vir varie eruditus, ostendisset
mihi in Transactionibus philosophicis; quarum aliquas secum habebat,
ingeniosissimorum Virorum Hugenij Wrennique, cogitata de rationibus
motuum.[2] Ea cum primum vidi, dixi, mihi ea Phaenomena vera videri, sed
primas abstractasque Motuum rationes longe alias necessario esse; Phaenomena autem haec sane admiratione digna, si modo accurata experientia
comprobata sunt, oriri ex statu Mundi; in vacuo, aut medio quiescente,
omnia longe alia esse; prorsus ut gravitas motusque in gravibus acceleratio,
non innata corporum vi, sed externis insensibilibusque causis contingunt.
Continuo igitur sumto calamo, et scribendi impetu simul, coepi exarare,
quae dudum ea de re conceperam; demonstrationibus figurisque illustrandi
spatium non fuit. Bidui triduive spatio elaborata monstravi Mauritio; is
cum esse sibi vobiscum usum literarum diceret,[3] missurum se vobis pollicetur. Resumo, expolio, atque inde ei mitto; accepit sed mox extinctae
conjugis domestico infortunio afflictus, rem, opinor, ex animo dimisit,
certe vobis, ut video, non misit. Cum vero supersit mihi exemplum, ex
Nundinis Francofurtensibus, si qua occasio suppetit, ad vos mittam. Summa interim huc redit: Longe alias esse Motus veras Regulas, quam apparent.
Nam pleraque moveri insensibiliter, quae quiescere videntur; pleraque
quae videntur unum corpus, non esse nisi congeriem plurium; sensus
nostros nunquam mendaces, plerumque tamen dissimulatores esse: Corporis vere quiescentis nullam resistentiam ac reactionem esse posse; imo
nullam Massam, quantumcunque magnam, plane quiescentem, esse revera
unum ens unumve corpus, sed constitutum in statu, ut sic dicam, materiae
primae levissimo cuicunque rei impulsu disjici posse. Non esse consenta-
neum primis motuum regulis, ut absolute anguli incidentiae et reflexionis
sint aequales; alias longe eius rei causas subesse; multa alia id genus

Theoremata in Phaenomenorum potius numero habenda, quorum de principijs causisque ita apparendi inquirendum sit, tantum abest ut ipsa sint pro principijs agnoscenda. Sed ut ad rem propius accedam: in ratione eorum, quae apparent, ex liquidissimis notionibus Corporis, Magnitudine, figura, et mobilitate, reddenda, nihil me torsit magis quam partium in toto, aut plurium totorum inter se cohaesio, cujus species sunt, durities, mollities, tenacitas, flexitas, fragilitas, friabilitas pleraeque aliae tactus qualitates, quas vulgo secundas vocant. Agnoscebam facile, necessariam esse aliquam in rebus cohaesionem ad Oeconomiam rerum; sed unde ea fieret, exputare mecum non poteram. Plaerique Philosophi tanti momenti rem ne tetigerunt quidem; ipse Cartesius cum varia corpuscula et ex eorum collisu ramenta facta supponit, non reddit rationem cur ista corpuscula consistant, nec ad quemlibet impulsum divellantur.⁴ Breviter, qui fit, quod manus meas ad quemlibet conatum a corpore avelli non potest? cur ventus nobis capita non aufert instar pileorum? cur lapis in terram projectus non eam totam aquae instar ad centrum usque perforat? Ridicula haec quaesita sunt, sed difficilia explicata. Plebs nos insanos putaret, si talia quaerentes audiret, et quaerenda sunt tamen. Nec densitas ad rationem resistentiae reddendam sufficit. Cum enim densitas vulgo definiatur, multum materiae in parvo spatio: quiescentis autem nulla sit actio (omnis enim actio corporis est motus) quid poterit summa densitas massae quiescentis ad perforationem impediendam. Gassendus videtur vidisse difficultatem; igitur, ut atomos suas connecteret, hamos atque uncos commentus est; sed ubi jam ipsarum atomarum, ipsorum hamorum consistentia et durities explicanda est, confugiendum est ipsi ad Voluntatem Creatoris. perpetuo igitur ad continendas atomos miraculo opus est. Cartesius qui nihil insecabile admittit, sed gradus quosdam duritiei ac tenacitatis in rebus statuit, causam tamen, quod ego sciam, reddit nullam. Ipse Hobbius consistentiam seu cohaesionem in rebus velut quiddam ἄρρητον assumpsit: unde page 240. edit. Londinensis Elementorum de Corpore,⁵ statuit, fluidum durumque aeque esse homogenea atque ipsum vacuum: Et pag. 271. definit durum, ac recte quidem, quod sit corpus, cujus pars moveri non potest sensibiliter nisi moto toto; et addit, ex molli fieri durum tali partium subtili motu, ut partes simul omnes impingenti resistant, sed qualis sit ille motus; neque ipse, neque quisquam alius hactenus explicuit.

Nihil attinet recensere, quae ego hujus rei explicandae causa sim commentus: ad extremum visus mihi sum in rationem quandam facilem et universalem incidisse. Nimirum, rectissime Aristoteles contigua definit, quorum termini sunt simul, et continua quorum termini sunt unum. Quorum

igitur termini unum sunt, ea connexa ac sibi cohaerentia sunt, quamdiu per-
durat terminorum unitas. Sed quomodo effici potest ut duorum corporum
termini sint unum, et quomodo rursus ex uno eoque indivisibili (termini
enim rerum indivisibiles sunt) possunt fieri duo, ad res tum connectendas,
tum dissolvendas? Haec pendent ex subtilissima contemplatione de natura
puncti seu indivisibilium, ex qua pleraque miracula in rebus naturalibus
oriuntur. Statuo igitur: Quaecunque ita moventur ut unum in alterius
locum subire conetur, ea durante conatu inter se cohaerent. Conatus enim,
ut rectissime observante Hobbio, est initium motus, seu id in motu, quod
in linea punctum. Si igitur unum conatur intrare in locum alterius, alterum-
que (ne detur penetratio dimensionum) ex eo expellere, sequitur ut primo
momento temporis jam sit in primo puncto loci, quem intrat, extremo puncto suo ingressum; sed eodem primo momento alterum, expellendum, nondum est egressum: duo igitur puncta seu extremitates corporis, expellentis
et impulsi, se penetrant (datur enim punctorum, non corporum, penetratio)
et proinde unum sunt. Admirabilis profecto est natura punctorum; quanquam enim punctum non sit divisibile in partes positas extra partes,
est tamen divisibile in partes antea non positas extra partes, seu in partes
antea se penetrantes.[6] Angulus enim nihil aliud est, quam puncti sectio, et
doctrina de Angulis non est alia quam doctrina de quantitatibus puncti:
sed, ut in viam redeam, si quod totum ita moveatur, ut pars una alteram
expellat loco suo et in eum subeat, eo ipso cohaerebunt eae partes, non
absolute quidem, sed dum ingruat fortior motus. Finge columnam moveri
linea recta in longitudinem, cohaerebunt sibi partes ejus in longitudinem;
sed neque in latitudinem neque in profunditatem. Unde siquid ingruat vel
occurrat fortiore motu secundum longitudinem, id secare poterit columnam
secundum longitudinem in duas partes, et abripere secum quam tangit,
reliquam praetervehi sinet. At siquid ingruet in latitudinem vel profunditatem, id si debiliore motu ingruit, simul abripietur, motu tamen totius
imminuto; sin aequali, faciet cessare connexionem columnae, et utrumque
quiescet reductum in arenam sine calce, (corpora enim quiescentia nihil
aliud sunt quam mera puncta sine unione, sine lineis, sine superficiebus
nisi spatij cui insunt;) sin fortiore, non avellet partem columnae quam
quiescenti abstulisset, differentia celeritatum, sed auferet totum, unde reliquum columnae non perget (ut prius cum in longitudinem divideretur,)
sed sequetur. Obscuriuscula haec sunt nec nisi figuris illustrabilia; certissi-
ma tamen, et, siquis rem attente expendat, necessaria. Nec possibilis est
alia ratio solida connexionis in rebus, nisi entibus incorporalibus evocatis
perpetuoque extra ordinem concursu alligatis. Caeterum ex his, primo

adspectu parvis, multa ac magna deduci queunt. Primo enim demonstrare possum, dari aliquod spatium vacuum corporibus; deinde, dari tempus vacuum motibus; seu, ut clarius loquar, impossibile esse ut omnia sint plena; impossibile item, ut datus aliquis motus rectus sit semper generatus ab alio motu in omnem retro aeternitatem, nec posse mundum, ut nunc est, Entibus incorporalibus carere aut caruisse; quae una propositio, concessa etiam possibilitate processus in infinitum (cujus impugnatione potissimum pugnari vulgo pro Deo solet) a me, ut spero, clare demonstrata nulli Euclideae certitudine cedet, et ubi primum se detexit, majore me gaudio imbuit, quam si quadraturam circuli, aut perennem motum invenissem. Conabor aliquando me distincte explicare, ac demonstrationis de tanta re, a qua felicitas generis humani pendet, judicem constituere R. Societatem. Tempus est, ut ad eam rem accedam, quam Tu, Vir Amplissime, potissimum a me postulare videris, id est, Expositionem Hypotheseos, cujus in prioribus literis[7] mentionem feceram, quae ex universali quodam motu in Globo nostro supposito, rationem Phaenomenorum in corporibus plerorumque reddat. Hanc ergo breviter ruditerque sic accipi, et si indigna est oculis vestris, quod vereor, tentamentis hominis imbellicitatem suam fatentis, et jussu potissimum Tuo ad hanc audaciam excitati, ignosce, eandemque ijs veniam a tot magnis viris, in R. Societate congregatis, impetra. Ego mihi hoc saltem assecutus in ea videor, ut, paucis mutatis, sectis plaerisque omnibus quadrare possit. Theoriam ipsam de Motus rationibus abstractis majoris facio, non sua, non hypotheseos ei superstructae causa, sed quod me in mentium non existentiam tantum, sed et naturam intimiorem, a corporea distinctam (quod cordatissimi quique et severissimi Philosophorum hactenus desperavere,) mira quadam Claritate duxit: sed de his alio tempore aut loco.

Hypothesis consistit in circulatione aetheris cum luce seu sole circa terram, circulationi Terrae contraria, ex qua gravitatem et elaterem, et magnetis verticitatem, et ex his, omnes rerum antipathias et Sympathias, et Solutiones et praecipitationes, et fermentationes, et reactiones derivo; usque adeo ut credam admirandos omnes et extraordinarios naturae effectus huic aetheris motui deberi; nec jam amplius stupendam esse musculorum, arcus, pulveris pyrij, venenorum vim, cum non particularis rei, quam nos agentem credimus, virtute, sed ipsius systematis laborantis nisu actiones tam vehementes exerceantur. Quae res mihi spem fecit, posse rem quandam, aere exhaustam, aethere distentam, ac proinde aere aequalis spatij leviorem parari, cujus applicatione in ipsum aerem homines attollantur: de quibus alijsque maximi momenti consequentijs hypotheseos meae, fusius in ipsa dixi.

Hoc ipso momento, quo haec scribo, literas ab amico accipio de Wernero Memingensi. Is suis ipse manibus machinas ejus contrectavit, expertusque est, tantam in ijs vim esse, ut, etsi puer, rotam motricem levissimo negotio circumagat, aliae tamen machinae partes (author vocat die stieffelen) ne a fortissimo quidem viro sisti possint: Sed rationem inventi ab authore celari; nunc ab Electore Bavariae evocatum in Swacensibus[8] fodinis ab aquarum importunitate liberandis specimen dare; ex cujus exitu poterit de re liquidius judicari. Ubi plura didicero perscribam.[9] Dab. Moguntiae d. 28 Sept. 1670.

TRANSLATION

. . . .

I formed my ideas of the basic and abstract principles of motion last year when I was at Swabach to take the waters there, when the famous Mauritius,[1] jurisconsult at Kiel and a man learned in several ways, showed me in the *Philosophical Transactions* (of which he had some with him) the thoughts of the very ingenious Huygens and Wren about the principles of motion.[2] When first I saw these, I said that those phenomena seemed to me true, but that basic and abstract principles of motion of a very different character were necessary; however, these phenomena were indeed worthy of admiration, if only they were proved by accurate trials; but they arose from the state of the universe, for in a vacuum or a motionless medium everything would be quite otherwise, because gravity and the acceleration of motion in heavy bodies do not depend upon an innate force of bodies but on external, imperceptible causes. Accordingly I at once took up my pen and having the urge to write I began straightaway to indite my thoughts on this subject. There was no leisure for illustrating them with demonstrations and figures. When the paper was finished after two or three days I showed it to Mauritius; he, remarking that he had a correspondence with you,[3] promised to send it to you. I took it back, polished it, and then sent it to him again; he received it but soon after a domestic calamity, the death of his wife, banished the thing from his mind, I believe, for certainly he did not send it to you, as I see. As I still have a copy I will send it to you from the Frankfurt Fair, if an opportunity arises. Meanwhile, this is a précis of it:

The true laws of motion are very different from the apparent ones. For many things that seem to be at rest move imperceptibly; many things that seem to be a single body are a collection of many; our senses are never deceitful, yet they often mislead us. No resistance nor reaction can arise from a body truly at rest; no mass, however great, which is quite at rest, is truly a single entity or body but is so made up of primary matter (if I may so call it) that it may be disturbed by the least impulse from any source. It is not in accord with the primary laws of motion that the angles of incidence and reflection should be absolutely equal; the causes of this effect are very different. Many other theorems of that kind are rather to be included in the class of the phenomena, the principles and reasons for the appearance of which are to be inquired into, so far are they from being acknowledged as principles themselves. But to come to the heart of the matter. In stating the theory of the appearances of things from very precise notions of Body, Magnitude, Figure, and Mobility, nothing gives me more trouble than the cohesion of parts to make a whole, or of several whole bodies between themselves: the various species of cohesion are hardness, softness, tenacity, flexibility, fragility, friability, and many other of those tactile qualities commonly called secondary. I readily admit that some cohesion in things is necessary for the economy of things [*sic*], but I could not excogitate its source. Several philosophers have not even touched upon so important a question: Descartes himself, when he postulates a variety of corpuscles and the fragments arising from their collision, gives no reason why these particles should stick together, nor why they should be split apart towards any impulse.[4] In brief, who says why it is that my hands cannot be dispatched from my body for any purpose? Why does not the wind carry off our heads like balloons? Why does not a stone hurled to the Earth penetrate it to its center, as though it were made of water? These questions, ridiculous as they are, are difficult to answer. People would think us mad if they should hear of such things being investigated, yet investigated they should be. Nor does density suffice to explain resistance. For as density is commonly defined as much matter in a small space, yet no action arises from a body at rest (for all physical action results from motion), what can the highest density of a mass at rest oppose to penetration? Gassendi seems to have seen this difficulty; accordingly, in order to join his atoms together, he has contrived hooks and barbs; but when the solidity and rigidity of these hooks and barbs upon the atoms is to be explained, he takes refuge in the will of the Creator. And so for holding the atoms together one must resort to a perpetual miracle. Descartes, allowing of no atoms, postulates certain degrees of hardness and softness in things without giving any reason for them, so far as I know. Hobbes himself assumed the existence of a consistency or cohesion in things to be a kind of irrational [fact]; whence on page 240 of the London edition of the *De corpore*[5] he postulates that the fluid and the hard are equally homogeneous, and so also the vacuum itself. And on page 271 he defines as *hard*, rightly indeed, a body the parts of which are incapable of perceptible motion without motion of the whole; and he adds that the *soft* is converted into the *hard* by such a subtle motion of the parts that all of the parts at once resist an impinging body. But what kind of motion this is neither he nor anyone else hitherto has explained.

It is pointless to relate here what I have devised in order to explain this business; in the end, as it seemed to me, I had hit upon a certain plausible and universal theory. Undoubtedly Aristotle was quite correct in defining as contiguous things whose boundaries are together, and as continous those whose boundaries are one. Those things whose boundaries are one are, accordingly, united and coherent so long as the unity of the boundaries lasts. But how can it be so arranged that the boundaries of two bodies are one, and how again can two be made out of one (and that single thing indivisible, for the boundaries of things are indivisible) in order to join things together, and then separate them? These matters are dependent upon a very subtle consideration of the nature of the point, or of indivisibles, from which spring many miraculous ideas about the nature of things. And so I postulate: Whatever things so move that one seeks to enter into the place of another, these cohere, so long as that endeavor lasts. For this endeavor (as Hobbes very rightly observed) is the beginning of motion, or stands in the same relation to motion as a point to a line. And so if one seeks to enter the place of another and this other to move out of it (for there can be no interpenetration of dimensions), it follows that in the first instant of the time the entering body is already at the first point of the place it enters, with *its* first point, while at the same instant the other, which is to move away, has not yet left it; thus the two points or extremities of the body impelling and the body being impelled penetrate one another (for it is admitted that points, but not bodies, may interpenetrate) and hence become one. Truly wonderful is the nature of points, for although the point is not divisible into separable parts (parts placed outside parts), still it is divisible into parts not formerly separated one from another, or into parts that were previously interpenetrating.[6] For an angle is nothing but the division of a point and the theory of angles is nothing but the theory of the magnitudes of a point. But to return to my theme: if a whole body be so moved that one part expels another from its place and succeeds it there, those parts cohere, not indeed absolutely but until a stronger motion impinges. Imagine a column moved longitudinally in a straight line; its parts will cohere along its length, but not along its breadth or depth. Whence, if it meets or is impinged upon by a stronger motion along its length, this can break the column into two parts longitudinally, and take along with itself what it touches, permitting the rest to be carried along [as before]. But if it is assailed along the line of its breadth or depth, and the impinging motion is weaker, it is thrust off all together with the motion of the whole unaffected; if it is equal, it disrupts the connection of the column and both come to a halt, reduced to sand without lime (for bodies at rest are nothing but mere points without union, lines, or surfaces apart from the intervals within them); if it is stronger it does not drive away that part of the column it would have removed from a resting body, with a difference in speed, but carries away the whole whence the remainder of the column does not continue (as it did before, when split longitudinally) but follows on. This business is pretty obscure and not capable of illustration without the aid of figures; yet it is very certain, and to anyone who ponders it attentively, necessary. Nor is any other sound theory of the connection between things possible, unless some incorporeal entities are evoked and they are bound together in some perpetual praeternatural

arrangement. Moreover from these ideas, trivial at first glance, many and considerable matters may be deduced. For in the first place I can demonstrate that
there must be some space void of bodies; next, that there must be some time void
of motion; or, to speak more plainly, that it is impossible that all things be full and
impossible too that any given rectilinear motion be always generated by some other
motion through all past eternity, nor can the universe (as it is today) lack or have
lacked incorporeal beings. Granted also that it is possible for a process to continue
infinitely (yet it is by combating this view that, in general, people fight most vehe-
mently on God's behalf), this one proposition which I have, I hope, clearly
demonstrated, yields nothing to Euclid in certainty and when I first discovered it,
it filled me with a greater joy than if I had discovered how to square the circle or
make a perpetual motion. I will try sometime to explain myself distinctly, and
appoint the Royal Society judge of the demonstration of this great matter, upon
which the happiness of mankind depends.

It is time for me to come to that point which you seem most particularly,
worthy Sir, to ask of me, namely an account of the hypothesis mentioned in my
former letter,[7] which derives the theory of very many phenomena in bodies from
a certain universal motion supposed to be in our globe. Accordingly, read it here
in a brief and crude form, and if it is unworthy of your eyes, as I fear it is, pardon
the efforts of a man acknowledging his own incapacity who was mainly spurred
on by your own injunction to this audacity; and I beg the same forgiveness from
those many great men assembled in the Royal Society. To myself I seem at least
to have attained in that business this much, that with a few changes and many
excisions it can be made perfect in every respect. I frame that theory of the abstract
principles of the greater motion not for its own sake nor for the sake of the hypotheses founded upon it, but because I have with wonderful clarity introduced into
[people's] minds not only existence but the inmost nature too, distinct from body
(which the most prudent and rigorous philosophers have all despaired of hitherto):
but [more] of these things at another time and place.

The hypothesis supposes that there is a circulation of ether with light or by
itself about the Earth, contrary to the rotation of the Earth; from this I derive
gravity and expansion [of the air?], and the orientation of the compass, and from
these all the sympathies and antipathies of things; solutions, precipitations, fermentations, and reactions, to the extent that I believe all marvelous and extraordinary effects in nature to be attributable to the motion of this ether. And I do
not now regard as wonderful any more that power of muscles, bows, gunpowder,
and poisons since it does not arise from any virtue in the particles of the substance
that we believe to be active, but rather such violent forces are exerted by the pressure of this driving system. This causes me to hope that some special thing may
be made, empty of air and swelled out by the ether, so as to be lighter than an
equal volume of air, by the application of which men may be lifted up into the
very air itself; of these matters and other consequences of great moment following
from my hypothesis, I have spoken more fully in [relating] it.

At this very moment, as I am writing, I receive by a friend a letter concerning Werner at Memmingen. He has examined his machines with his own hands, and discovered by trial that so great is their force that if, say, a boy spins a movable wheel with only the least effort, other parts of the machine (what the inventor calls the barrels) cannot be held still even by the strongest of men. But the theory of the invention is concealed by the inventor, who is now summoned by the Elector of Bavaria to the mines of Swabia[8] to furnish a specimen [trial] by freeing [them] from the nuisance of water. From the outcome the thing can be more plainly judged. When I have more to tell you I will write.[9]

Mainz, 28 September 1670

NOTES

Reply to Letter 1506; personal remarks were obviously deleted when the letter was transcribed into the Letter Book.

1 Erich Mauritius (1631–91), a legal scholar, had been since its foundation (1665) Professor of Law at Kiel University. He was later a correspondent of Oldenburg's.
2 See *Phil. Trans.*, nos. 43 (11 January 1668/9), 867–68 and 46 (12 April 1669), 925–28; see further Vol. V, pp. 319 ff. and 375, note 5.
3 Probably the sense is "you English"; at any rate, though we cannot name Mauritius' correspondent, it seems fairly obvious that at this moment he was not in correspondence with Oldenburg.
4 "a quolibet impulsu" ("by any impulse") would seem to make better sense.
5 Thomas Hobbes, *Elementorum philosophiae; sectio prima de corpore* (London, 1655).
6 The English is not a literal rendering of the Latin, which is very obscure. Leibniz seems to say that although the geometrical point is, by definition, without parts—that is, parts that could be separated, so dividing the point—still the point could be thought of as containing interpenetrating parts, incapable of separation.
7 See Letter 1486, p. 67.
8 Presuming that the Latin should read "Swavensibus"; Memmingen is just east of this region. Swabach is just south of Nuremberg.
9 As will appear from Oldenburg's reply, Letter 1568, this copy omits a closing passage in which Leibniz discussed his scheme for a perpetual motion.

1525
Oldenburg to Huygens

20 September 1670

From *Œuvres Complètes*, VII, 38–40
Original in the Huygens Collection at Leiden

A Londres le 20 Septembre 1670.

Monsieur,

Ayant sceu, que vous aviez si bien recouvert vostre santé, que d'estre en estat de visiter vostre pais,[1] i'ay voulu embrasser cete occasion d'un estudiant Polonois,[2] qui va repasser en Holland, que de vous tesmoigner la joye, que i'ay parmi quantité d'autres, de vostre reconvalescence, souhaitant de tout mon coeur, qu'elle s'affermisse de plus en plus pour vostre contentement propre, et pour le bien des belles sciences. Vous trouverez cellecy accompagnee d'un present de Monsieur Wallis, asscavoir de la seconde partie de son *Tractatus Geometricus de motu*, qu'il m'a desiré de vous envoyer. Je ne doubte pas que vous n'ayez vû les Leçons Geometriques de Monsieur Barrow, dont i'envoiay à Monsieur Justel un Exemplaire au mois de Juillet dernier,[3] qu'il aura sans doubte fait voir aux personnes capables d'en juger; ou vous trouverez quelque chose, dans la Leçon XI, qui vous touche.[4]

Vous aurez sceu, sans doubte, que Monsieur Hevelius a observé la nouvelle Estoile aupres du bec du Cygne, aussi bien que le Chartreux de Dyon;[5] comme aussi qu'il a fait l'observation de la phase presente de Saturne, par le moyen du Telescope, que ie luy avois envoyé d'icy, de 50 pieds. Monsieur Hook l'a faite de mesme le 16. de ce mois (celle de Hevelius ayant esté faite le 26. Aoust) laquelle ne s'accorde pas mal avec l'autre. Je croy, que l'une et l'autre s'inprimera dans les Transactions d'Octobre, que ie vous envoieray, pour en Juger.[6] A present ie vous envoie avec ledit livre de Monsieur Wallis, les Experiences Nouvelles de Monsieur Boyle touchant la Respiration, dont on inprimera la suite devant la fin du mois courant.[7] Le mesme a aussi publié, depuis peu, plusieurs petit Traités joints ensemble dans un mesme livre, touchant l'Histoire des Qualitez particulieres, les Qualitez Cosmiques (qui dependent de la Constitution de l'Univers) la temperature des Regions soubterraines et soubmarines, et le Fonds de la mer; tout en Anglois. Et un autre de la Societé Royale, appellé Monsieur

Wray, a fait inprimer le *Catalogus Plantarum Angliae*⁸ *in quo praeter Synonyma necessaria, facultates quoque summatim traduntur, una cum Observationibus et Experimentis Novis Medicis et Physicis.* C'est tout ce [que] i'ay à vous mander de nouvelles Philosophiques de ce pais-cy: Esperant que, quand vostre santé le permettra, vous nous ferez scavoir ce qui se passe de telles matieres au pais ou vous estez astheur; ce quoy faisant vous obligerez particuliere-ment Monsieur

> Vostre treshumble et tresobeissant serviteur
> *H. Oldenburg*

Je vous prie, quand vous me faitez l'honeur de m'escrire par la poste, d'addresser vos lettres pour moy, de cete maniere;
  A Monsieur
Monsieur Grubendol à Londres

Rien que cela, et tout me sera rendu plus surement, que si vous vous serviez de mon nom propre.

ADDRESS
    A Monsieur
Monsieur Christian Hugens de Zulichem
        A la Haye

Avec un pacquet. Par amy.

TRANSLATION

London, 20 September 1670
  Sir,

Having learned that you had so far recovered your health as to be in a fit state to visit your own country,¹ I wanted to seize the opportunity afforded by a Polish student² who is going to cross into Holland to demonstrate to you the joy which I share with many others in your convalescence, hoping with all my heart that it will be more and more perfected, both for your own sake and for the benefit of true learning.

You will find this accompanied by a present from Mr. Wallis, namely the second part of his *Mechanica sive de motu,* which he wished me to send to you. No doubt you have seen Mr. Barrow's *Lectiones geometricae,* of which I sent a copy to Mr. Justel last July,³ which no doubt he showed to those capable of judging its worth; there, in Lecture XI, you will find something which concerns yourself.⁴

You doubtless will know that Mr. Hevelius observed the new star in the beak of Cygnus, as well as the Carthusian of Dijon,[5] and that he has also observed the present phase of Saturn with the fifty-foot telescope which I sent him from here. Mr. Hooke did the same on the sixteenth of this month (that of Mr. Hevelius having been made on 26 August), and these [observations] do not agree badly. I think that both will be printed in the *Transactions* for October, which I shall send you so that you may judge.[6] Now I send you with the book of Mr. Wallis already mentioned the "New Pneumatical Experiments about Respiration" of Mr. Boyle, of which the continuation will be printed before the end of the present month.[7] The latter has also published recently several little *Tracts* joined together in the same book concerning *The History of Particular Qualities, The Cosmicall Qualities of Things* (which depend upon the constitution of the universe), *The Temperature of the Subterraneall Regions* and *of the Submarine Regions,* and *The Bottom of the Sea,* all in English. And another Fellow of the Royal Society, named Mr. Ray, has had printed the *Catalogus plantarum angliae*[8] in which there is besides "the most necessary *Synonyma* of the Plants here enumerated, a summary Description of their principal Vertues; enterlaced with the mention of many new Observations and Experiments, Medical and Physiological."

This is all I have to relate to you in the way of philosophical news from this country; hoping that, when your health permits, you will let us know what is happening as regards such matters in the country where you now are, a thing which will particularly oblige, Sir,

Your very humble and obedient servant,
H. Oldenburg

I beg you, when you do me the honor to write to me by the post, to address your letters in this way:

A Monsieur
Monsieur Grubendol à Londres

Nothing else, and everything will reach me more surely than if you make use of my own name.

ADDRESS
To Mr. Christiaan Huygens of Zulichem
At the Hague

With a packet. By a friend.

NOTES

1 See Letter 1513, p.140.
2 His name is not recorded.
3 See Letter 1513, p.140.

4 Barrow refers to Huygens' *De circuli magnitudine inventa* (The Hague, 1654).
5 See Letters 1509 and 1474.
6 It was actually inserted in *Phil. Trans.*, no. 65 (14 November 1670), 2093.
7 Boyle's "New Pneumatical Experiments about Respiration" were published in *Phil. Trans.*, no. 62 (8 August 1670), 2011–31 and continued in no. 63 (12 September 1670), 2035–56.
8 Published at London, 1670; there is a brief notice of it in *Phil. Trans.*, no. 63 (12 September 1670), 2058, from which we have taken the last part of this sentence in Oldenburg's English.

1526
Magalotti to Oldenburg
23 September 1670

From the original in Royal Society MS. M 1, no. 50

firenze li 3 octob 1670 [N.S.]

Io non saprei come piu nobilmente contracambiar la vostra generosita nell'obbligarmi che con l'amicizia del Cavaliere che vi rendera la presente.[1] Gli e amicissimo mio, e voi potrere facilmente riconoscere dalla sua conversazione con quanta ragione se gli deva stima ed affecto. Durevere fatica a immaginarvi cosa che sia bella, e che non sia oggetto della sua curiosita, e della sua intelligenza; conquesto parmi d'aver detto assai, e confido che riconoscereve prosissimo che non ho detto troppo. Quello ch'egli vorrebbe in primo luogo e conoscer voi, perche Egli e gia informato che voi solo valere per molti, & che molti, ansi tutti si possono arrivare a conoscere per mezzo vostro. Pero fatevi pur da un capo del catalogo dei suggetti della Societa reale, e fateglieli conoscer tuti ch'ei non vuol'altro. Io gli ho dato lettere per il S. Boyle, per il Sig Slingsby, e per il Cav. Morland.[2] Volontierissime gliel averei dare per il Sig Ashmol,[3] perche appresso di lui ci e'un'ampia conserva di memorie e di cognizioni, che al genio di questo Cavaliere riuscianno stimabilissime; ma la mia malattia mi lascio cosi poco campo di coltivar l'amicizia, alla quale mi onoraste d'introdurmi di questo Sigr, che ho dubitato di potergli facilmente essergli uscire delle memoria, non avendo io altro titolo commendabile per rimanervi in capo a si lungo tempo, che quello d'amico, e servitor vostre. Spero nondimeno, ch' [Egli] non tralascereve di farglielo cononcscere, acciocche non gli manchi per questo conto la sodisfazione di veder cose intorno alla antiche memorie d'Inghilterra, ch'ei non potrebbe cosi facilmente veder altrove. Del resto tutto quello che e libri, librerie, manoscritti, machine, conserve di curiosita naturali tutto fa per lui, L'amicizia del Sr Hook di grazia non resti nell'ultimo luogo; in somma considerarelo come un uomo che viaggia unicamente per conoscer persone di lettere, e per approfitarsi in quelle scienze che egli por [?] di gia possiede. Voi intanto riconoscere nella mia confidenza quanto io speri della continuazione della vostra bonta, e crediate a questa istessa misura ferma, e immutabile la professione che fo di essere

Vostre Devotissimo Obbedientissimo Servitore
L Magalotti

TRANSLATION

Florence, 3 October 1670 [N.S.]

I did not know how more nobly to repay your generosity in obliging me than with the friendship of the gentleman who will deliver this present letter.[1] He is a great friend of mine, and you will easily gather from his conversation with what good reason he merits esteem and affection. You will find it difficult to imagine anything fine that is not an object of his curiosity and intelligence; with this, it seems to me, I have said enough, and I am sure that you will very soon recognize that I have not said too much. What he will desire in the first place is to know yourself, for he is already aware that you alone rate above many, and that one may become acquainted with many persons, indeed all persons, through yourself. However, be so kind as to make him a summary of the list of members of the Royal Society and introduce him to those he will not see elsewhere. I have given him letters for Mr. Boyle, for Mr. Slingsby, and for Sir Samuel Morland.[2] I would very willingly have given him one for Mr. Ashmole,[3] because within him there is an ample store of memories and knowledge which would suit most estimably with the disposition of this gentleman, but my illness leaves me so little opportunity for cultivating the friendship with which you honored me by introducing me to that gentleman that I have fears of being easily able to escape his recollection, as I have no good grounds for remaining after so long a time anything but your friend and servant. Nevertheless I hope that you will not fail to make him known, so that he will not for this reason lose the satisfaction of seeing things relating to the ancient memorials of England, which he could not so easily see elsewhere. For the rest, everything to do with books, bookshops, manuscripts, machines, cabinets of natural curiosities—all please him. The friendship of Mr. Hooke should not be left to the last, if you please; in short, consider him as a man who travels solely in order to become acquainted with men of letters and to advance himself in those sciences that he already is familiar with. Meanwhile you will recognize in my confidence how much I hope from the continuation of your goodwill, and will in the same measure believe in the firmness and immutability of my profession of being

Your most obedient and devoted servant,
L. Magalotti

NOTES

1 According to a letter of Thomas Platt to Oldenburg (27 July 1672), a Dr. Francini was "the same person that Mr. Magalotti writt to you about 3 yeares since, that had thoughts of goeing for England to improve himselfe there in ye study of Physick . . ." We could discover nothing else.
2 There is no other record of such letter. For Henry Slingsby (*c.* 1621–88 or 1690), Master of the Mint, see Vol. II, p. 317, note 3; for Sir Samuel Morland (1625–95), see Vol. IV, p. 392, note 4.
3 Elias Ashmole (1617–92); see Vol. V, p. 495, note. This is the only known contact between Ashmole and Magalotti.

1527
Oldenburg to Von Boineburg
24 September 1670

Von Boineburg's Letter 1523 is endorsed by Oldenburg as having been answered on 24 September, with instructions about the Grubendol address.

1528

Oldenburg to Sluse

24 September 1670

From the draft in Royal Society MS. O 2, no. 33
and the copy in Letter Book IV, 74–82

Reverendo admodum et Clarissimo Viro
Domino Renato Francisco Slusio, Canonico Leodiensi
H. Oldenburg Salutem

Ex animo gratulamur tam Orbi literato, quam Tibimet ipsi de valetudine recuperata, eamque indies firmiorem perennemque exoptamus. Mens sane, ex silentio tuo praeter solitum diuturniori non parum anxia, valetudinem tuam afflictam verebatur; uti jam de ea restituta (binis tuis literis, 25. julij et 20. Augusti ad me datis, id nunciantibus) impense gaudet. In earum priori, inter alia, solutionem tuam difficiliorum quorundam Problematum, In Opticis Barrovianis occurrentium; in posteriori tuam Arcus Angulive Iridis absque Tabulis inveniendi rationem, qua motae cuidam a Barrovio difficultati respondetur, accepimus. Idem Barrovius, S.S. Theologiae aeque ac Mathematum Doctor, nuper in Sacellanorum Regiorum ordinem cooptatus,[1] Mathesi vacare deinceps haud ita jugiter poterit, quamvis quae praeter jam edita, hactenus in studiis Mathematicis est commentatus, impertiri publico eum non detrectaturum putem.[2] Ex difficilioribus opticorum ejusdem Problematibus, illud *De Loco Imaginis in Speculo Sphaerico Concavo aut convexo*, a Clarissimo Hugenio, antequam cum novissimo morbo satis periculoso, at jam fere averruncato, conflictaretur, Opticis Barrovii Praelectionibus adhuc ineditis, fuit solutum, quam solutionem ipse, ceu novae suae Artis Typographicae Specimen, ad Societatem Regiam transmisit;[3] cujus Apographum, cum Tibi ingratum haud fore credam, communicare non dubitabo:

Problema Alhaseni

Dato Speculo cavo aut convexo, itemque oculo et puncto rei visae, invenire punctum reflexionis.

Esto Speculum ex Sphaera, qua Centrum habeat etc. Vid. ipsum Autographum in Libro 3. Epistolarum Societatis Regiae p. 82.[4]

Hisce ita praelibatis, celare Te non possimus, meditari Ingeniosos quosdam Anglos vernaculi cujusdam Tractatus Perspectivae, Catoptrices et Dioptrices impressionem, cum tale quid, quod mereatur laudem, sermone Anglico nondum extet.[5] Dominus Barrovius non renuit suas de *Perspectiva* Praelectiones dummodo sint Anonymae, in eam rem conferre.[6] Iis jungere cupientes *Dioptricen*, Catoptricenque, Consilium et sententiam quoque tuam de melioris circa Argumenta illa nota Authoribus ambimus. Quid videtur de Perspectiva et Catoptrice Tacqueti?[7] Quid de Centuria (siquidem tota illa prodiit) Opticorum Problematum Eschinardi?[8] Quid de hoc Themate scripsit Manzinus?[9] Schombergeri Problematum Opticorum Centuriam[10] quod attinet, ea nomine tenus duntaxat apud nos innotuit: Quod idem de Wentzeli Iamitzeri Compendio Optico, quod sub Syntagmatis Opticae Titulo extare dicitur,[11] conquerimur. Dominus de Beaune, in stricto quodam Scriptorum Mathematicorum Galliae Catalogo, Gallicae Irlonis cujusdam Grammaticae annexo, Opticam scripsisse perhibetur;[12] nobisque in eam Parisiis inquirentibus, rarissima esse ejus Exemplaria rescribitur. Arduam nimis esse Barrovii Opticorum Versionem, et vulge captu forte superiorem opinamur. Hinc est, quod infrunitis hisce quaestiunculis molestiam Tibi facessimus, quas pro humanitate tua facile Te excusaturum arbitramur.

Ornatissimus Dominus Collins per nautam Belgam Johnsonum ante aliquot Septimanas Tibi transmisit Secundam partem Doctoris Wallisii Tractatus Geometrici de Motu, ubi de Calculo Centri Gravitatis; nec non Barrovii Lectiones Geometricas: super quibus doctas tuas pro candore solito Observationes nobis pollicemur; quas quidem Societati Regiae exhibere, ejusdem monumentis publicis cum honorifica nominis Tui praefatione inserere nulli dubitabimus.[13] Animadversiones tuae in ultimam Barrovii de Aequationibus Praelectionem nobis erunt gratissimae: Et cum doctissimus Riccius Geometricis amplius se vacare non posse scribat,[14] enixe Tu rogandus es, ut Theorematis Mesolabii tui pag. 116, quod Determinationum doctrinam, quartum nempe Caput Miscellaneorum tuorum *de Maximis et Minimis*, complet, Applicationem evulgare ne digneris.

Idem Dominus Collins observat Gerhardum Kinkhusium tres de Algebra Tractatulos sermone Belgico edidisse, Introductionem scilicet, Sectiones Conicas, et Problemata Geometrica per Algebram soluta, ubi nonnulla circa *Methodum* de *Maximis et Minimis* tractatur.[15] Centuria Problematum, eorumque Determinationes, antehac ab Honorato Fabri promissae, nuper Lugduni Gallorum typis sunt editae.[16] At idem notat, non exspectari illud in horum Authorum alterutro, quod docti de subacto tuo Ingenio sibi pollicentur. Est quidam inter Nostrates Vir perdoctus, sed in edendis suis difficilior,[17] qui apud sibi familiares asseruit, Posse se exactissime, quavis Aequatione proposita, ostendere, quod esse debeat ipsissimum Homogeneum Comparationis,[18] ut Radicum quodvis par vel quaevis paria (puta, binae, quaternae, senae &c) suam possiblitatem acquirant amittantve: Deinde, posse se ex illa Limitum doctrina, sine magno labore, Columnas complere, omnes istas Radicum tum Negativarum tum Affirmativarum series continuentes. Hujus rei specimen (ut infra videbis) Tibi transmittimus in Aequationibus Cubicis, ad mentem nostram eo melius explicandam. Dicti Viri Methodus non erat per Depressionem, ut in exemplo infra memorato, sed scandendo,[19] quali utebatur in Limitibus suis, limitando praecise Aequationes Quadraticas primo; dein Cubicas, tum Biquadraticas etc; tum vero, Columnarum istarum adminiculo Radices constituendo lineas ordinatas vel respectivis Homogeneis, vel Homogeneorum illorum radicibus applicatas juxta gradum primi termini Aequationis, invenire genium Curvarum, cujusque generis Aequationibus idonearum, per Ordinatarum istarum summitates transeuntium.

Descriptio quarundam Barrovii Curvarum per puncta, Seriei numerorum rationalium beneficio, ex hujus Problematis dependet solutione:

In Serie continuorum Proportionalium, data vel assumpta ad libitam summa vel Differentia Extremorum, invenire terminos dictae seriei rationales; si numerus terminorum in dicta serie sint tria, tum reapse id nil aliud est, quam invenire Ordinatas Circuli vel Hyperbolae aequilaterae rationales.

In *Circulo*, Diameter est summa Extremorum; ibique Problema huc redit: Dividere scilicet Quadratum Radii in duo Quadrata: Quod Problema Diophanti etiam solutum est in Herigonio[20] etc. atque ab illa solutione Series posset derivari.

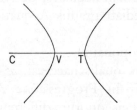

In *Hyperbola* aequilatera, si *VT*, transversus Axis, sit Unitas, tunc, si portio Axis ab *V* versus *C* sit aliquis terminorum Seriei sequentis, Ordinatae erunt rationales; $\dfrac{1}{3} \dfrac{4}{5} \dfrac{9}{7} \dfrac{16}{9} \dfrac{25}{11}$

Ex. gr. $1\frac{1}{3} \times \frac{1}{3} = \frac{4}{9} \sqrt{} = \frac{2}{3}$

etiam $1\frac{4}{5} \times \frac{4}{5} = \frac{36}{25} \sqrt{} = \frac{6}{5} = 1\frac{1}{5}$

Atque fractiones tolli possunt, factum ex earum Denominatoribus constituendo. Hoc Problema operam meretur et laborem Commentatoris in Diophantum.[21]

Quaestio est considerata digna, Possitne Radices Aequationum in Numeris inveniri ejusmodi Canonum sive Tabularum ope, quales jam nobis suppetunt, aliarumve quae in eum finem construi queant. Quae id videntur probabile reddere, a Domino Collins ita suggeruntur;

Dominus Isaacus Newton, Matheseos in Academia Cantabrigiensi Professor,[22] affirmat, Aequatione nonnisi ex duobus terminis composita praeter Homogeneum Comparationis, quamlibet istiusmodi Aequationem converti in Seriem infinitam posse, summamque tot Aequationis illius terminorum, quot requiruntur, Tabularum ope colligi.[23] Hujus Specimen (paulo infra subjiciendum) Tibi transmittimus in Problematis de Censu Annuo solutione, quod in sublimem evadit Aequationem, creberrimi apud Aedificatores et Emptores (hic Londini imprimis) usus.

Haec Methodus una cum illa, cujus mentionem facit Du Laurentius in Praefatione[24] (quod forte non ita observant Lectores) rem extra dubium ponit. Pollicebatur idem in Tractatu proximo (quem Viri mors nobis negavit) Methodum, qua cujuslibet Aequationis terminos omnes intermedios auferre licet, et quidem duos tresve per ea quae hucusque reperta sunt; Quod si sic fuerit, non videtur esse aliud, quam Artificium, unam numerorum Seriem, cujus ultimae differentiae sunt aequales, ex alia, cujus ultimae differentiae sunt etiam aequales, derivandi, habito ad justos respectu, ut scilicet intermediati gradus Aequationis introduci vel destrui possint.

Ut rem paulo aliter proponamus,

Pone, ad Aequationem, qualis haec est, $a^5 \pm Ba = N$ a nobis assumi seriem Radicum quae sit in Progressione Arithmetica, constituatque seriem ex N sive Homogeneis, quorum differentiae quintae erunt aequales; quidam asserere videtur,[25] si nude series illa Homogeneorum proponeretur, ut inveniatur quaenam Aequationes isti seriei communes forent, inveniri diversas Aequationes ipsi communes posse, istarumque Aequationum quamlibet habere, vel saltem habere posse (prout constitui poterit Aequatio) unam Radicum seriem in Progressione Arithmetica, proindeque radicum cujusque Aequationis differentias esse Proportionales inter se.

Problema de Censu Annuo, solutum a Domino Newtone,[26] hoc est;

Ad investigandum, quanto pretio faenoris compositi (N per centum) Annus census B fuit acquisitus pro spatio 31. annorum, pretio A. Regula est

$$\frac{6 \text{ Log. } \left(\frac{31B}{A}\right)}{100 - 50 \text{ Log. } \left(\frac{31B}{A}\right)} = \text{Log. } \frac{100 + N}{100}$$

E.g. si 1200 lb. nunc solvantur pro 100 lb. per annum, pro 31. annorum spatio, Logarithmus $\frac{31B}{A}$ est $= 0{,}41218$, proindeque per regulam, $\frac{2{,}47308}{79{,}39100}$ vel $0{,}03111$ est Logarithmus $\frac{100 + N}{100}$; unde $\frac{100 + N}{100} = 1{,}0743$ et $N = 7{,}43$; adeo ut proventus annus emptus fuerit 7,43 lb. per centum.

Haec Regula non est exacta, quia pauci tantum termini Seriei hic adhibentur; adeo exacta tamen est, ut nunquam fallat ultra $\lfloor$ 01 ad summum, quando pretium non superat 16 lbs per centum (quod excedit quorumvis locorum usum:) Et si pretium supergrediatur 16 vel 18 per centum, vel, quod idem est A $\sqsupset$ 6B, tunc haec Regula $\frac{A + B}{A} = \frac{100 + N}{100}$ non fallet ultra $\lfloor$ 1:[27] Explorare poteris harum Regularum veritatem Aequatione $x^{32} = \frac{A + B}{A} x^{31} - \frac{B}{A}$ ponendo $\frac{100 + N}{100} = x$, atque Logarithmica arte operando.

Complures Aequationes particulares solvi per Tabulas posse, extra dubium est. Praedictus Laurentius ostendit modum ejusmodi Aequationes solvendi, quales solvi possint per Media Proportionalia, Canonis Logarithmorum Canonisque Sinuum ope: At alia hinc nasci quaestio potest, viz: Possintne Illae, vel saltem nonnullae illarum, quae solvuntur beneficio Unius Canonis, solvi etiam adminiculo Canonis alterius. E.g. Si Problema juberet Dividere sphaeram in *ratione data*: Hoc ipsum Problema Hugenius in Tractatu suo de Magnitudine Circuli[28] expedit Anguli Trisectione; cum reapse Problema sit idem, ac Dividere quamvis Parabolam in ratione data, ope Diametri ejus: Id quod Lalovera in Elementis suis Tetragonismicis[29] praestat Duorum Mediorum Inventione: Et Ferguson in Labyrintho suo

Algebrae[30] vult, eandem Regulam generalem inservire ambobus Casibus Aequationum Cubicarum: quocum facere videtur Laurentius, qui Characterem Trisectionis mera Ignorantiae nota insignit.

In libello, cui Titulus *Invention Nouvelle* Alberti Gerardi Amstelodami edito A. 1629,[31] invenire est Methodum inveniendi radices Aequationum Cubicarum ope Tangentium Naturalium: Et Doctor *Pellius* subinde innuit, velle se Tractatum adornare de Canonis sinuum usu in Aequationibus solvendis: Sed ille talem requirit Canonem, in quo quilibet gradus cujusvis Arcus in 1000 partes dividitur. At non ausim ea me spe lactare, nos vel ejusmodi Canonis vel dicti Viri Tractatus compotes fore.

Ipse pag. 173. Algebrae suae[32] mirum Problema in medium adfert ad naturales Sinuum et Tangentium Canones spectans. Affirmat, A. 1638. quendam in Hollandia Stampionem[33] proposuisse sibi Aequationem sexti gradus, in qua Terminorum nulli deerant, seque omnes Radices illius deprompsisse Canonum Logarithmicorum adminiculo.

Atque generatim quoad Tabulas observare est,

1. Numeros ad Progressionem Arithmeticam pertinentes habere eorum differentias ultimas aequales; ut in Tabulis Quadratorum, Cuborum, Numerorum figuratorum etc.

2. Vel inaequales, ut in Tabulis Sinuum, Tangentium, Logarithmorum etc. Tamen admittendo eas aequales quousque res fert eas adhibendi, puta usque ad 10, 12, vel 15. loca figurarum, uti usuvenit in Logarithmis Numerorum 2000, 2001, 2002, 2003, 2004, 2005, 2006 (qua de re vide Briggii Arithmeticam Logarithmicam)[34] quod in tali casu, si Logarithmus proponeretur excedens Logarithmum 2000, sed minor Logarithmo 2001, quamque Numerus correspondens requireret, quod, inquam, ope Methodi et Tabulae in cap. 13 dicti Briggii numerus correspondens facile inveniri possit verus usque ad 13 vel 14 loca figurarum. Atque hoc nil aliud est, quam Aequationis quinti gradus resolutio; inventio scilicet istius Radicis, quae proprie pertinet ad dictam Aequationem tam sublimiter elevatam, vel talis Involutionis. Verum istius Aequationis Inventio, ad hoc redit Problema, viz:

Serie Numerorum quorum differentiae quintae sunt aequales, proposita, invenire Aequationem, communem isti seriei, vel saltem isti seriei prout refertur ad Progressionem Arithmeticam, ad quam pertinet.

At quidam affirmant, Aequationes una plures illi esse communes: sed necdum ipsorum ea de re speculationes accepimus.

Verum, annon exspectare licebit, res istas elucidatum iri in Reinaldini Geometra promoto,[35] vel etiam in Fermati in Diophantum Commentariis? Quousque Tractatus isti sint expiditi, scire averemus.

Ex sequenti Tabula et Exemplo apparet, Supposita affecta Aequatione Cubica, uni Seriei Radicum Arithmetice Proportionalium (puta 1. 2. 3. etc) accommodata, reliquas duas Radices, ei respondentes, Arithmetice proportionales non fore. At series Coefficientium in terminis mediis Aequationum Quadraticarum, duas illas minores Series continentium, omnino erunt tales, i.e. Arithmetice proportionales. Atque etiam, ex numeris absolutis in Quadraticis istis Aequationibus, differentiae secundae aequales erunt, uti fuissent, si in iis omnibus idem fuisset Coefficiens termini medii, atque una Series, ut 1. 2. 3. etc.

Nota etiam, si in ulla ejusmodi Serie Aequationum (uti hic in Cubicis) una Series Radicum sit Arithmetice proportionalis, tunc Seriem Aggregatorum reliquarum omnium serierum (quae sunt Coefficientes terminorum secundorum in Aequationibus subordinatis, uti hic in Quadraticis) etiam esse Arithmetice proportionalem, sed decrescentem, si primae istae creverint, et contra crescentem, si illa decreverint. Proindeque si Series proposita sit Aequationum Quadraticarum, quarum una Series proposita sit Aequationum Quadraticarum, quarum una Series sit Arithmetice proportionalis, reliquae similiter tales erunt. Series quippe Aggregatorum alia non est quam series Radicum.

Differentiae			N		a	a	a
			+40	1	4,	10,	
		+16					
	−18		+56	2	2,7251	10,2749	
6		−2					
	−12		+54	3	1,7575	10,2425	
6		−14					
	−6		+40	4	1,	10,	
6		−20					
	±0		+20	5	0,4194	9,5826	
6		−20					
	+6		±0	6	0,	9,	
6		−14					
	+12		−14	7	0,2425	8,2425	
6		−2					
	+18		−16	8	0,2749	7,2749	
6		+16					
	+24		±0	9	0,	6,	

Differentiae		N	[Radices Quaesitae]		
			a	a	a
6	$+40$				
	$+30$	$+40$	10	1,	4,
6	$+70$				
	$+36$	$+110$	11	————	
6	$+106$				
	$+42$	$+216$	12	————	
6	$+148$				
	$+48$	$+364$	13	————	
6	$+196$				
	$+54$	$+560$	14	————	
6	$+250$				
	$+60$	$+810$	15	Impossible	
6	$+310$				
	$+66$	$+1120$	16	————	
	$+376$				
		$+1496$	17	————	

Aequationes Quadraticae continentes
duas posteriores series Radicum   Differentiae

$a^2 - 14a = -40$		
	12	
$a^2 - 13a = -28$		2
	10	
$a^2 - 12a = -18$		2
	8	
$a^2 - 11a = -10$		2
	6	
$a^2 - 10a = -4$		2
	4	
$a^2 - 9a = \pm 0$		2
	2	
$a^2 - 8a = +2$		2
	0	
$a^2 - 7a = +2$		2
	2	
$a^2 - 6a = \pm 0$		2
	4	

Aequationes Quadraticae continentes   Differentiae
duas posteriores series Radicum

$a^2 - 5a = -4$	2
6	
$a^2 - 4a = -10$	2
8	
$a^2 - 3a = -18$	2
10	
$a^2 - 2a = -28$	2
12	
$a^2 - 1a = -40$	2
14	
$a^2 \pm 0a = -54$	2
16	
$a^2 - -1a = -70$	2
18	
$a^2 - -2a = -88$	

[Aequatio data $a^3 - 15a^2 + 54a = N$][37]

Ex quo superiora expediveram, accepimus literas a Jacobo Gregorio,[38] in quibus narrat, duxisse se Tangentem ad Spiralem Arcuum rectificatricem (qua de re ad Te scripsimus,)[39] diversasque invenisse Methodos dandi sinus cujusvis Arcus satis accuratos, nec non cujuslibet Logarithmi numeros; adjectis aliis nonnullis Mathesin spectantibus, quae quando acceperimus, lubentes Tibi impertiemur.[40] Vale et huic prolixatati ignosce. Dabam Londini d. 24 Septemb. 1670.

TRANSLATION

H. Oldenburg greets the very reverend and famous Mr. René François de Sluse, Canon of Liège

I congratulate both the world of learning and you yourself wholeheartedly upon the recovery of your health, and we wish it to be with each day stronger and long lasting. Your unusually long silence filled our minds with no little anxiety and we feared that you must be ill; so that the news of your restored health (conveyed in your two letters to me of 25 July and 20 August) gave great pleasure. In the former of these we received among other things your solution of some difficult problems occurring in Barrow's *Optics*, and in the latter your way of finding the arc or angle of a rainbow without tables, in response to a certain difficulty raised by Barrow. The same Barrow, who, being a Doctor of Theology as well as of Mathematics, has lately been appointed one of the chaplains to the King,[1] will hardly have such regular leisure for mathematics as before, though I think he will not be deterred from giving to the public his mathematical studies completed up to now, in addition to those published already.[2]

Among the more difficult mathematical problems in optics, that concerning the place of the image on a concave or convex spherical mirror was solved (at a time when Barrow's optical lectures were still unpublished) by the famous Huygens, before he was very recently attacked by a pretty serious illness of which he is now almost cured; this solution he has himself transmitted to the Royal Society as a specimen of his new art of printing.[3] I shall not hesitate to communicate a transcript of this to you since I believe it cannot be unwelcome to you:

"Alhazen's Problem

"Given a concave or convex mirror, given also [the position of] the eye and a point of the object seen, to find the point of the reflection.

"Let the mirror consist of a sphere, whose center is . . . "
See the copy of this in Vol. III of the letters of Royal Society, p. 82.[4]

After this appetizer we cannot hide from you the fact that some ingenious Englishmen have been thinking about publishing a vernacular treatise on perspective, catoptrics, and dioptrics, as nothing of the sort worthy of esteem exists in English at present.[5] Mr. Barrow does not deny the contribution of his lectures on perspective, so long as they remain anonymous.[6] Being eager to add dioptrics and catoptrics to these we solicit your opinion and advice concerning the best authors on this notable topic. What do you know of the perspective and catoptrics of Tacquet?[7] What of the hundred optical problems of Eschinardi, if he produced so many?[8] What did Manzini write on this subject?[9] As for Schoenberger's *Problematum opticorum centuria*,[10] this is known to us by name only, and we regret that the same is true of the optical compendium of Wenzel Jamnitzer which is said to exist under the title *Syntagmata optica*.[11] In a certain brief list of French writers on mathematics attached to the French *Grammar* of one Irlon, Mr. de Beaune is said to have written an *Optics*;[12] but in reply to our inquiries in Paris we were told that copies of it are extremely rare. A translation of Barrow's *Optics* is too difficult and we think it over most people's heads. Hence it is that we trouble you with these tiresome little queries, for which we think your kindness will easily find excuses.

The very worthy Mr. Collins sent you a few weeks ago by the Dutch seaman Johnson the second part of Dr. Wallis's *De motu, tractatus geometricus*, wherein [he treats] of the calculation of the center of gravity, as also Barrow's *Lectiones geometricae*, on which we promise ourselves your learned observations, made with your usual frankness. We expect to present these to the Royal Society and to insert

them with an honorable reference to yourself in the public records of the same.[13]
Your animadversions upon Barrow's last lecture about equations will be very
welcome to us. And as the learned Ricci writes that he has no more leisure for
geometry,[14] you are to be asked most earnestly to be so good as to publish the
application of the theorem in your *Mesolabe*, page 116, which completes the theory
of determinations, that is, the fourth chapter of your *Miscellanies* on maxima and
minima.

The same Mr. Collins remarks that Gerard Kinckhuysen has published three
little treatises on algebra in Dutch, that is, an introduction, on conic sections, and
on the solution of geometrical problems by algebra, in which there is some
material on maxima and minima.[15] The hundred problems and their solutions
formerly promised by Honoré Fabri have recently come from the press at Lyons.[16]
But the same Collins observed that what the learned world anticipates from your
experienced genius is not to be expected of either of these authors. There is a
certain very learned man among us here, with a disinclination to publish,[17] who
has asserted amid his friends that he can very exactly show in any equation propounded to him what its *homogeneum comparationis* must be,[18] so that any pair or
pairs of roots (say the second, fourth, sixth, etc.) may gain or lose their possibility.
Then he can from that theory of limits without great labor fill up columns continuing the series of those roots both negative and positive. As you will see below,
we are sending you a specimen of this in cubic equations that our meaning may be
better understood. The method of this person was not by depression, as in the
example noted below, but *scandendo*,[19] and the same in his limits, limiting precisely
first quadratic equations, then cubics, then biquadratics, etc; then, by aid of those
columns, making the roots ordinates, applied either to the respective *homogenea* or
to the roots of those *homogenea* according to the degree of the first term of the
equation, to find the nature of curves proper to equations of each kind passing
through the tops of those ordinates.

The describing of some of Mr. Barrow's curves by points, by aid of a series of
rational numbers, depends on the solution of this problem: In a series of continual
proportionals giving or assuming at pleasure the sum or the difference of the
extremes, to find the rational terms of this series. If there are three terms in the
given series then in effect the problem is none other than finding the rational
ordinates of a circle or equilateral hyperbola.

In the circle, the diameter is the sum of the extremes, and here the problem
reduces to dividing the square of the radius into two squares. Of this Diophantine
problem the solution is given by Hérigone,[20] etc., and from that the series can be
derived.

In the equilateral hyperbola, if *VT* [*see figure, p. 179*], the transverse axis, be
unity then if the portion of the axis from *V* towards *C* be any one of the terms of

the following series the ordinates will be rational: $\dfrac{1}{3}, \dfrac{4}{5}, \dfrac{9}{7}, \dfrac{16}{9}, \dfrac{25}{11}$.

For example, $\frac{4}{3} \cdot \frac{1}{3} = \frac{4}{9}$ [of which the] square root is $\frac{2}{3}$;

again, $\frac{9}{5} \cdot \frac{4}{5} = \frac{36}{25}$ "" "" "" "" "" $\frac{6}{5} = 1\frac{1}{5}$.

And the fractions may be removed by forming the product of the denominators. This problem would be worthy of the attention and labor of a commentator upon Diophantos.[21]

The question is worth considering: Can the roots of equations be found in numbers by the aid of canons or tables of this kind such as we have already or by means of others which can be constructed for that purpose? The considerations making this probable are thus proposed by Mr. Collins:

Mr. Isaac Newton, Professor of Mathematics in the University of Cambridge,[22] asserts that if an equation consists of two terms only besides the *homogeneum comparationis* he can convert any equation of this kind into an infinite series and that the sum of so many terms of that equation as may be required [can] be obtained by means of tables.[23] We send you an example of this (to be annexed below) in the solution of a problem concerning annuities, which results in an equation of high degree, of common and daily use amongst builders and purchasers (here at London especially).

This method, together with that mentioned by Dulaurens in his preface[24]—though possibly readers may not notice it as such—puts the matter out of doubt. The same person promised [to publish] in his next treatise (which the man's death robbed us of) a method by which all the intermediate terms of an equation can be removed, and even [to remove] two or three by those [methods] that are already known. If it were so, then it seems to be nothing but a device for deriving one series of numbers (of which the final differences are equal) from another (whose final differences also are equal), respecting always the proper rules, so that the intermediate terms of an equation may be inserted or suppressed.

To make the same point a little differently: Let us suppose that to an equation such as this, $a^5 + Ba = N$, a series of roots may be assumed which shall be in arithmetical progression and form a series from N or the *homogenea*, of which the fifth differences shall be equal. A certain person seems to assert,[25] that if merely that series of *homogenea* were propounded in order to discover what equations are common to that series, it is possible to discover different equations common to it, and for any one of those equations to have a single series of roots in arithmetical progression (or at least to be able to have it according to the form of the equation); and hence the differences of the roots of any equation are proportional one to another.

The problem about annuities, solved by Mr. Newton,[26] is this: It is desired to know at what rate of compound interest (N per cent) an annuity B was acquired for the period of 31 years, the price being A. The rule is

$$\frac{6 \log \frac{31B}{A}}{100 - 50 \log \frac{31B}{A}} = \log \frac{100 + N}{100}$$

For example, if £1200 is paid out now for [an annuity of] £100 per annum for thirty-one years, the logarithm of $\frac{31B}{A}$ is 0.41218; and so by the rule $\frac{2.47308}{79.39100} =$ 0.03111 is the logarithm of $\left(\frac{100 + N}{100}\right)$, whence $\left(\frac{100 + N}{100}\right) = 1.0743$, and $N =$ 7.43. Thus the annual yield purchased was £7.43 per cent.

This rule is not exact because only a few terms of the series are employed here, yet it is so exact that it never errs beyond £0.01 at the most, when the price does not exceed £16 per cent (which is greater than the rate of interest anywhere). And if the price were to exceed 16 or 18 per cent, or, which is the same thing, $A < 6B$, then this rule $\frac{A + B}{A} = \frac{100 + N}{100}$ does not err beyond £0.1.[27] You may try the truth of these rules by the equation $x^{32} = \frac{A + B}{A} x^{31} - \frac{B}{A}$ making $x = \frac{100 + N}{100}$ and working by logarithms.

It is beyond question that several particular equations may be solved by tables. The aforementioned Dulaurens teaches a way of this kind for solving such equations as may be solved by mean proportionals, by the use of tables of logarithms and tables of sines. But this prompts another question, namely: Can those, or at any rate some of those that are solved by means of one table also be solved by employing another? For example, if the problem requires one to divide a sphere in a given ratio, this very problem is dealt with by Huygens in his treatise *De magnitudine circuli*[28] by trisection of an angle, when actually this is the same problem as: "Divide any parabola in a given ratio by means of its diameter," which La Loubère shows how to do (in his *Elementa tetragonismica*)[29] by finding two means [proportionals]; and Ferguson in his *Labyrinthus algebrae*[30] claims to have rendered this same rule universal for both types of cubic equation, with which Dulaurens seems to operate in distinguishing the trisection with a simple mark of ignorance.

In a little book whose title is *Invention nouvelle*[31] (published at Amsterdam in 1629) Albert Girard [discovered] the method of finding the roots of cubic equations by means of [the tables of] natural tangents; and Dr. Pell has from time to time hinted his intention to complete a treatise upon the employment of tables of sines in solving equations. But he requires a table in which each degree of any arc is divided into 1000 parts. But I have not dared to deceive myself with the hope that we shall see such a table or Dr. Pell's treatise.

The same person on page 173 of his *Algebra*[32] brings forward a remarkable problem concerning the tables of natural sines and tangents. He asserts that in the year 1638 one Stampioen in Holland[33] propounded to him an equation of the sixth degree, including all terms, and that he elicited all its roots by means of tables of logarithms.

And generally as regards tables it should be noted that:

1. The numbers belonging to an arithmetical progression have their last differences equal, as in the tables of squares, cubes, figured numbers, etc.; or

2. unequal, as in the tables of sines, tangents, logarithms, etc. Yet by taking these to be equal so far as they need be stated, say up to 10, 12, or 15 places, as happens with the logarithms of the numbers 2000, 2001, 2002, 2003, 2004, 2005, 2006 (for which see Briggs's *Arithmetica logarithmica*),[34] in such a case, if the logarithm proposed should exceed log 2000 but be less than log 2001, and the corresponding number be sought, then I say the number corresponding may easily be found by [the method shown in] Briggs's Chapter XIII, true to thirteen or fourteen places. And this is nothing but the solution of an equation of the fifth degree, that is to say the finding of that root which properly belongs to this equation raised to so high a degree, or of such an involution. Indeed the finding of that equation reduces the problem to this:

A series of numbers being proposed whose fifth differences are equal, find the equation common to that series or at any rate common to that series in so far as it is referred to that arithmetical progression to which it belongs.

But certain people say that many equations may be common to that one [series]: but we have as yet not accepted any of their speculations on this question.

Truly, may we expect any elucidation of these things in Renaldini's *Geometra promotus*[35] or even in Fermat's commentaries on Diophantos? We desire to know how far those treatises are advanced.

From the following table and example it appears that, supposing an adfected cubic equation to be accommodated to a single series of roots in arithmetical proportion, say, 1, 2, 3 . . . , the remaining two roots corresponding to it will not be in arithmetical proportion. But the series of the coefficients of the middle terms of quadratic equations containing those two lesser series will certainly be such, that is, arithmetically proportional. And further the second differences [taken] from the absolute numbers in those quadratic equations will be equal, as they would have been if the coefficient of the middle term in all of them had been the same, and a single series as 1, 2, 3, etc.

Observe also that if in any series of equations of this kind (as here in cubic equations) one series of roots is arithmetically proportional, then the series of the aggregates of all the rest of the series—which are the coefficients of the second terms in the subordinate equations, which in this example are quadratics—are also in arithmetic proportion, but decreasing if those primary ones increased, and increasing if they decreased. Hence if the proposed series be of quadratic equations of which one series is arithmetically proportional, the remainder will be so likewise. For the series of the aggregates is none other than the series of the roots.

[*Here follows the Table printed on p. 183*][36]

After completing the above we received a letter from James Gregory[38] in which he tells us that he has drawn a tangent to the *spiralis arcuum rectificatrix* (about which we wrote to you)[39] and discovered various methods for giving the sine of any arc and the number of any logarithm, which are pretty accurate. He adds several other matters relating to mathematics which, when we have received them, we will gladly impart to you.[40] Farewell and forgive this prolixity.
London, 24 September 1670

NOTES

Reply to Letters 1489 and 1507.
This letter was based partly on an English draft by Collins (misdated October), published in Rigaud, I, 147–50, and partly on Collins' "Narrative about Aequations," of which copies were also sent to Gregory, Barrow, and others. Presumably this version into Latin was made by Oldenburg; in translating this back into English we have followed Collins' own words as closely as possible. An English version of parts of the "Narrative" is to be found in Turnbull, *Gregory*, pp. 110–17, 142–46.

1 Barrow took his degree of D.D. in July 1670 and was Chaplain-in-Waiting during August; see Turnbull, *Gregory*, p. 109.
2 For interest in Barrow's unpublished mathematical works, see Rigaud, I, 137–38.
3 See Vol. VI, Letter 1213. There is a fascimile of this leaf in *Œuvres Complètes*, VI, facing p. 462. Huygens' construction deals only with a special case of Alhazen's problem; see Letter 1489, note 8.
4 Oldenburg here directs the amanuensis to complete his fair copy for Sluse from the transcript of Huygens' construction entered in the Letter Book. This Oldenburg was to publish later in *Phil. Trans.*, no. 97 (6 October 1673), 6119. Its English is as follows:

"Given a concave or convex mirror, and also the positions of the eye and the object, to find the point of reflection:

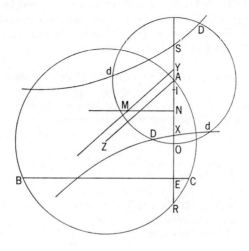

Let the mirror be [the surface of] a sphere whose center is A, with the eye at B and the object at C. The plane containing A, B, and C intersects the sphere in the circle Dd, in which the points of reflection occur. Let a circle be described through A, B, and C, whose center is Z, meeting AE (normal to BC) produced at R. Make $AN = \dfrac{AO^2}{AR}$, then MN parallel to BC forms one asymptote [of an hyperbola]. Again, $AI = \dfrac{AO^2}{4AE}$, and taking $IY = IN$, MY is drawn parallel to AZ, constituting the second asymptote. Lastly, taking IX, IS both equal to $\sqrt{\dfrac{AO^2}{2} + AI^2}$, the points S and X will lie upon an hyperbola, or its opposite branch, Dd, having the asymptotes already found. Their intersections with the circle DO give the required points of reflection. This construction holds whenever the problem is to be solved by a solid locus, except in one case where a parabola is to be drawn in place of the hyperbola, that is, when AE is a tangent to the circle A, B, C."

This construction treats only of the spherical mirror.

5 According to Collins' letter to Gregory of 29 September 1670 (Turnbull, *Gregory*, p. 107), "Mr. Martin the Bookseller and Mr. Faithorne the Graver" were the chief actors; the first idea was to translate Tacquet and Eschinardi (see notes 7 and 8 below).

6 For Barrow's lectures on perspective, see Turnbull, *Gregory*, p. 107; he sent the MS. of them—together with that of his Apollonios—to Collins on 11 October 1670 (Rigaud, II, 75).

7 *Opticae libri III* and *Catoptricae libri III* form the third and fourth parts of André Tacquet's *Opera mathematica* (Antwerp, 1669).

8 Francesco Eschinardi, *Dialogus opticus* (Rome, 1666, 1668) contains altogether two hundred problems.

9 Carlo Antonio Manzini, *L'Occhiale all'Occhio, Dioptrica practica* (Bologna, 1660).

10 Georg Schoenberger (1596–1645), a Jesuit born at Innsbruck, was author of *Centuria emblematum opticorum* (Friburg, 1626).

11 Wenzel Jamnitzer, *Perspectiva corporum regularium* ([Nuremberg], 1568) is not concerned with optics; we could not find Collins' title.

12 On Florimond de Beaune, see Vol. IV, p. 343. It seems likely that the grammar intended is that of Claude Irson, *Nouvelle Methode pour apprendre facilement les principes et la pureté de la langue française* (Paris, 1656, etc.), which, it is said, contains a list "des auteurs les plus célèbres de notre langue." Compare Rigaud, I, 162.

13 "in their Journal" was Collins' phrase.

14 See Letter 1489, p. 80.

15 See Letter 1522, note 4. According to Collins, Kinckhuysen used Hudde's method of maxima and minima (Turnbull, *Gregory*, p. 144).

16 Presumably the work here mentioned is the *Synopsis geometrica* noted in Letter 1484, note 16, which contains *De maximis et minimis centuria*.

17 This was John Pell, to whom Collins often referred in other letters using similar language.

18 The *homogeneum comparationis* is, says Collins, the "known number" N to which an expression is made equal, that is, $f(x) = N$.

19 "Ascending"; Collins (in English) uses this Latin term. For an identical passage in a letter from Collins to Newton of 19 July 1670, see Newton, *Correspondence*, I, 37.

20 Pierre Hérigone, *Cursus mathematicus* (Paris, 1634–37).

21 The English text in Rigaud ends here.

22 [Newton had succeeded Barrow as Lucasian Professor of Mathematics in the summer of 1669.

23 Collins knew of this facility of Newton's at least as early as July 1670 (see note 19 above), though the exact date of the communication cannot be ascertained. Collins wrote of it to Gregory on 24 December 1670 (Newton, *Correspondence*, I, 55). The third occurrence of the word "equation" in this sentence is a slip for "series."

24 François Dulaurens, *Specimina mathematica* (Paris, 1667). See Vol. IV, *passim*.

25 This was Collins himself; compare the identical passage in the letter to Newton mentioned in note 19.

26 The solution was sent to Collins by Newton in his letter of 6 February 1669/70; see Newton, *Correspondence*, I, 24.

27 Newton had said twopence or threepence, and two shillings.

28 See Letter 1525, note 4.

29 Antoine de la Loubère, *Elementa tetragonismica seu demonstratio quadraturae circuli et hyperbolae ex datis ipsorum centris gravitatis* (Toulouse, 1651).

30 Johan Jacob Ferguson, *Labyrinthus algebrae* (The Hague, 1667); Oldenburg prepared an unpublished translation of this book; see Vol. V, p. xxv.

31 Albert Girard, *Invention Nouvelle en Algèbre* (Amsterdam, 1629).

32 J. H. Rahn, *Introduction to Algebra . . . alter'd and augmented by Dr. J. P[ell]*, trans. T. Branker (London, 1668).

33 See Vol. V, p. 231, note 6. Compare similar remarks by Collins in Turnbull, *Gregory*, p. 142, and Rigaud, II, 472–73.

34 Henry Briggs, *Arithmetica logarithmica* (London, 1624).

35 Carlo Renaldini or Rinaldini (1615–98) was a former member of the Accademia del Cimento. The work intended here is presumably *Artis analyticae mathematum pars secunda: tractatus de algebra, de resolutione & compositione mathematica & geometram promotum complectens* (Padua, 1669).

36 The same table is found in Turnbull, *Gregory*, p. 116, accompanying Collins' letter of 1 November 1670.

37 We take this line from the source just stated.

38 Dated 5 September and addressed to Collins; see Turnbull, *Gregory*, pp. 102–4.

39 Literally "the rectifying spiral of arcs" but always referred to by Collins and Gregory under its Latin appellation; the problem of drawing a tangent to this curve was proposed by Collins to Gregory in a letter of 4 December 1669 (Turnbull, *Gregory*, pp. 75–76); for the posing of this question to Sluse, see Vol. VI, Letters 1424 and 1434.

40 Gregory's results were communicated on 23 November 1670. See Turnbull, *Gregory*, pp. 118–37.

1529
Oldenburg to Grisley
29 September 1670
From the memorandum in Royal Society MS. F 1, no. 27

D. 29. Sept. 1670. Scripsi ad Dn. Grisley Olyssipone degentem, et in Botanica versatum de Toxico illo Hispanicae, hic memorato.

TRANSLATION

29 September 1670. I wrote to Mr. Grisley, who lives at Lisbon and is skilled in botany, about the Spanish arrow-poison mentioned here.

NOTE

This memorandum is written on the back of Letter 1444 (Vol. VI), from Vogel. For Gabriel Grisley, see Vol. V, p. 432, note.

1530
Sachs to Oldenburg
1 October 1670
From the original in Royal Society MS. S 1, no. 33

Amplissime et Excellentissime
Oldenburgi

Si caecutiente oculo ad Illustrissimae Societatis Regiae Solem accedentes titubemus, et a recto tramite aliquantulum aberremus; veniam dabis, Vir Amplissime; licet etenim sub Augustae Aquilae Patrocinio vivamus non Aquilina tamen acie sumus instructi. Solis benigni radij dum se blande diffundunt, omnibus vitam largiuntur, eandemque conservant: ijdem tamen si violentiores sint, omnia quoque exurunt et consumunt.

Quod Germana Curiosa Societas Amplitudini Tuae audet Exemplar Ephemeridum Medicarum Germanicarum[1] temerariae quodam ausu offere, benevolum sibi exoptat Solis aspectum, non timet Icarium casum.

Causam nostrae fiduciae brevibus declarabo. Ne soli laboriosi Germani videantur otiosi in communi omnium Nationum fervore, praecipue illustrissimae Societatis Regiae Anglicae inimitabili quidem exemplo incitati, vestigia quaedam legere tentarunt, licet maxime impari gressu. Dum etenim Ephemerides quoque colligunt, Medicas saltem et Physicas, sane non eum in finem factum fuisse Aequi videbunt Rerum Aestimatores, quasi cum aliarum Nationum Collegijs in arenam descendere, ijsque palmam facere dubiam velint; absit hic; absit! optime nostrae tenuitatis memores herbam alijs lubentur porrigimus. Quis enim Maxima a nobis expectaret, qui saltem Medici sumus molestae Praxeos negotijs irretiti; cujus Collegij Germanici Membra sparsim divisa, nec in uno corpore cohaerentia: qui adminiculis necessarijs et nervo rerum gerendarum destituti, quo Exterae Nationes innumeris parasangis nos antecellunt: qui in angulis latentes plerique degimus ad quos raro, nec nisi multis cum impensis Exterorum Scripta perveniunt? Non invidemus Angliae raram istam Felicitatem, siquidem faecundissimus Ipsius Oceanus, quasi communis Parens, diffundit utilissimos et faecundantes per totum Orbem rivulos: Itaque ut isti rivuli eo citius ad omnes Germaniae angulos derivari possint, institutum nostrum erit, ut Physica et Medica rarissima, nova Inventa. Experimenta indubia, in Transactionibus Anglicis Anglice conscripta, hinc inde excerpta in nostris Miscellaneis exhibeantur: praeprimis vero si quid rari aut Curiosi in Germania reliquisque Europae regnis, in Anatomicis, Botanicis, in Curationibus Morborum contigerit, colligatur, et postmodum pro facilitandis et felicitandis saepe difficillimorum Morborum Curis, cum utilitate et jucunditate communicetur.

Primum Laborem de mutuandis quibusdam ex Anglico opere non speramus Illustrissimae Societati Regiae futurum ingratum, cum eo ipso Regij Collegij Membrorum fama etiam in Germania latissime propagetur, et Eruditi Galli quaedam Ephemeridibus Galliosis, tanquam pretiosissimas gemmas insperserint: reliqua Germanorum Medicorum Miscellanea Medica non penitus inutilia fore speramus, licet non omnia unius sint ponderis, ea ratione ut in sylvis humiles frutices[2] adstant annosis et pulchrissimis Quercubus.

Haec nostra est fiducia, ut AMPLITUDINI TUAE, quam cum Illustri Societate Regia tota deveneratur Europa, Primitias nostri laboris offerre ausi simus, quod si vero qualescunque hos nostros Labores singulis annis continuandos, aliquibus favoris radijs ab Illustri Societate et ab Amplitudine Tua videremus irradiatos: imo si ab Eadem quibusdam rarioribus observatis Medicis exemplo Italorum et Belgarum, qui partim communicationem promiserunt, partim cum Riva[3] ex Roma, cum Regner de Graff ex Hollandia praestiterunt,[4] pro communi Posteritatis commodo nostras opellas viderimus condecoratas; de summa hac felicitate nobis gratularemur, et perpetui inter alios Regiae Societatis Praecones licet dignitate minimi, affectu tamen et veneratione omnibus pares essemus futuri.

Vale, Seculi nostri Ornamentum, Amplissime OLDENBURGI, et quem Nativitatis Sors Germanum fecit Germanis favere perge. Quod si Responsorijs me dignari velit, illi Hamburgum ad Dn. Godefr. Scholz Bibliopolam Hamburgensem dirigi possent, qui easdem Vratislaviam transmittet.

> Nobilissimi Amplitudinis Tui
> Cultor addictissimus
> *Philippus Jacobus Sachs a*
> *Lewenheimb*. Ph. et Med. D.
> Academiae Curiosus.

Vratislaviae Silesiorum
ipsis Kalend. Octobr.1670

ADDRESS
> Viro
> Nobilissimo, Amplissimo, Excellentissimo
> Domino Henrico Oldenburgio
> Illustrissimae Societatis Regiae Anglicanae Secretario,
> Domino et Patrono Magno
> > Londinum in Angliam

TRANSLATION

Excellent and worthy Mr. Oldenburg,

If, blinded by its sun-like brilliance, we stumble in approaching the illustrious Royal Society and wander a little from the straight and narrow path, you will forgive us, worthy Sir, for though we live under the protection of the Imperial Eagle we are not blessed with the eagle's sight. As the benign rays of the sun gently pour down they bring life to everything and preserve it, but if they were more powerful they would burn and consume everything. When the German

Academy of Investigators dares to offer your excellency a copy of the *Miscellanea curiosa*,[1] not without a certain rash temerity, we promise ourselves the grateful warmth of the sun rather than fear the fate of Icarus.

I will declare the reason for our confidence in few words. Lest only the German workers should appear indolent amid the common enthusiasm of all nations, stirred by the inimitable example of the illustrious English Royal Society in particular, they are endeavoring to follow the same track, though with uncertain steps. For while they too gather together at least a medico-physical journal, this was certainly not done so that they shall seem to impartial judges of things as it were to descend into the arena with colleagues from other nations and compete with them; far be it from that! Being mindful of our frailty we cheerfully yield the field to others. For who would expect the very greatest things from us, who are at best physicians ensnared in the toilsome cares of practice, widely scattered members of a German College wanting cohesion into one body; who are lacking in all necessary aids and means for carrying on the business in which foreign nations outpace us by many leagues, and to whom living as we do in remote corners for the most part the writings of foreigners reach but rarely and at great cost? We do not envy England that rare felicity, since her prolific Ocean, like a father to all, extends in useful and fertile streams over the whole Earth; and so, in order that those streams may be directed the more swiftly into all corners of Germany, it will be our purpose to display the rarities of medicine, the new discoveries, the proven experiments, recorded in the English *Transactions* in that tongue, excerpted thence into our *Miscellanea* here. And particularly if anything unusual in matters of anatomy, botany, or the cure of diseases shall have happened within Germany or the other kingdoms of Europe, it will be assembled and afterwards published, usefully and agreeably, in order to facilitate and render more successful the cure of the more recalcitrant diseases.

We have no doubt that our first efforts in borrowing certain things from the work of the English will be welcome to the illustrious Royal Society, since in that way the fame of the Fellows of that Royal Academy is spread farther abroad, even in Germany, and the learned in France have scattered certain of them [already] like precious stones in the *Journal des Sçavans*. We hope that the remainder of the *Miscellanea medica* of the German physicians will not be quite useless, though not all are of the same importance; in the same way humble bushes[2] grow in forests amid the aged and magnificent oaks.

This is our faith, and so we are emboldened to offer to your excellency (whom the whole of Europe admires, together with the Royal Society) the first fruits of our labors, that if these labors of ours (such as they are) are continued through successive years, we may see them enlightened by some favorable rays from yourself and the illustrious Society; and if we may see our little publication adorned by yourself for the common good of posterity with certain more unusual medical observations like those of the Italians and the Netherlanders, who have in part given promise of communication and in part performed it, with [contributions from] Riva[3] in Rome and Regnier de Graaf in Holland,[4] we should congratulate ourselves upon this very great happiness, and would be perpetual exalters of the Royal Society; though the least among others in respect of dignity, yet in goodwill and veneration second to none.

Farewell, worthy Oldenburg, ornament of this age, and as fate made you German by birth continue to look kindly upon Germany. If you wish to honor me with a reply, it may be addressed to Hamburg, to Mr. Gottfried Schulz, Bookseller, Hamburg; he will transmit the letter to Breslau.

> Your noble excellency's most devoted admirer,
> *Philipp Jacob Sachs von Lewenheimb.* Ph.D., M.D.
> Member of the Academia Curiosorum

Breslau in Silesia
1 October 1670

ADDRESS

> To the very noble, worthy, and excellent
> Mr. Henry Oldenburg
> Secretary of the most illustrious English Royal Society
> Lord and great patron
>   London, England

NOTES

So far as we know Sachs had not written to Oldenburg since 12 January 1664/5 (Vol. II, p. 342). For Sachs's connection with the Academia Curiosorum, see Vol. VI, Letter 1267, note 5.

1 The first annual volume of the *Miscellanea curiosa medico-physica academiae naturae curiosorum, sive ephemeridum medico-physicarum Germanicarum curiosorum* appeared at Leipzig in 1670. It is reviewed in *Phil. Trans.*, no. 68 (20 February 1670/1), 2077–82.
2 Possibly there is a pun here, for this word also carries the sense of "blockheads."
3 Giovanni Guglielmo Riva (1627–77) was an anatomist and surgeon of the Ospedale di Santa Maria delle Consolazione in Rome. He founded a museum and a medical society.
4 Riva has three contributions (Observations 18, 39, and 117, all concerning surgical practice) and De Graaf two (Observations 127 and 128, both pathological) in Vol. I of the *Miscellanea curiosa.*

1531
Huygens to Oldenburg
5 October 1670

From the original in Royal Society MS. H 1, no. 69
Printed in *Œuvres Complètes*, VII, 40–41

A la Haye ce 15 Oct. 1670 [N.S.]

Monsieur

Cellecy vous sera rendue par Mr. Morhovius[1] et luy servira d'introduction aupres de vous, si vous l'agreez. Il est Professeur dans l'Academie de Kiel en Holstein, scavant dans les belles lettres, bon Poete, et amateur de la Philosophie telle que la pratique Vostre Illustre Soc. R. et, a ce que j'ay peu comprendre, son voiage en Angleterre n'est a autre fin que d'apprendre a connoistre des personnes qui font tant parler d'eux dans le monde.

Vous avez sceu Monsieur ma maladie peu moins que mortelle,[2] et n'aurez pas estè estonnè de n'avoir rien receu de ma part pendant un si long temps. J'ay creu que pour changer d'air et pour me reposer de toute sorte d'affaires, je ne pouvois mieux faire que d'aller faire quelque sejour dans le pais Natal ce qui en effect m'a bien reussi, et il ne s'en faut guere que je n'aye repris mes premieres forces. Je sens mesme quelque tentation d'accompagner mon pere dans le voiage qu'il va faire en vos quartiers avec M. le Prince d'Orange,[3] mais dans la saison ou nous sommes j'apprehende que la fatigue seroit trop grande pour un reconvalescent comme moy. Cependant je vous prie de ne me point laisser ignorer ce qui se fait de nouveau parmy vos Messieurs de la Societe, et de m'envoier les Transactions, dont les dernieres que j'ay veus sont celles ou vous avez inserè mon petit traitè des Parelies.[4] Je vous en suis obligè, par ce que cela fera qu'il sera examinè par plus de personnes. Je vis, devant que partir de Paris, la seconde partie du livre de Mr. Wallis de Motu, mais n'osay en aucune maniere en entreprendre, la lecture, le voyant rempli des calculs tres longs et difficiles. Il vint accompagnè d'un autre traitè de Geometrie d'un de vos Messieurs,[5] dont jeus bien de la peine aussi a m'abstenir, mais j'avois estè trop mal traitè par ma maladie pour oser contrevenir aux defenses des Medecins.

Je vous baise les mains et suis de tout mon coeur Monsieur

Vostre treshumble serviteur
Hugens de Zulichem

ADDRESS

    A Monsieur
Monsieur Oldenburg
Secretaire de la Societè Royale
au Pal mail
              A
                   Londres

TRANSLATION

                           The Hague, 15 October 1670 [N.S.]
Sir,

This will be delivered to you by Mr. Morhof[1] and will serve as his introduction to you, with your permission. He is a professor in the Academy of Kiel in Holstein, learned in literary matters, a good poet, and a lover of the kind of philosophy practised by your illustrious Royal Society; indeed, from what I understand, his journey into England has as aim only to make the acquaintance of the people who are so much talked of in the world.

You will have learned, Sir, of my illness, so little short of fatal,[2] and will not have been surprised at having received nothing from me for so long a time. I thought that for a change of air and a rest from all kinds of business I could not do better than to make a stay in my native country; this has, indeed, succeeded, and I have very nearly recovered my original strength. I am even rather tempted to accompany my father in the journey he is to take into your parts with the Prince of Orange,[3] but I fear lest at this time of year the consequent fatigue might be too great for a convalescent like myself. However, I beg you not to leave me in ignorance of anything new occurring among the Fellows of your Society, and to send me the *Transactions*; the last of these I have seen is [the number] in which you inserted my little treatise on parhelia.[4] I am very much obliged to you for that, because this will ensure its scrutiny by more people. Before I left Paris I saw the second part of Mr. Wallis's *De motu*, but did not dare to attempt to read it at all, seeing it was filled with very long and difficult calculations. It came accompanied by another treatise on geometry by one of your Fellows,[5] which I refrained [from reading] with great difficulty, but I had been too badly treated by my illness to venture to go against the prohibitions of the physicians.

    I kiss your hands and am, Sir, with all my heart,

                               Your very humble servant,
                               Huygens of Zulichem

ADDRESS

    To Mr. Oldenburg
Secretary of the Royal Society
in Pall Mall
          London

NOTES

1 See Letter 1542.
2 See Vol. VI, Letter 1398.
3 Constantijn Huygens the elder (1596–1687) arrived in London with the Prince of Orange on 31 October 1670; the Prince (who was now twenty years old) ended his visit, during which he received honorary degrees from the two English Universities, on 13 January 1670/1, but the elder Huygens remained until the following October.
4 See Vol. VI, Letter 1398, note 14.
5 Presumably Barrow's *Lectiones geometricae*.

1532
Winthrop to Oldenburg
11 October 1670
From the original in Royal Society MS. W 3, no. 25

Boston octob: 11: 1670

Sr

Since my former of Aug: 26. last[1] wch was sent by Capt: Peirce his ship, whereby also some few things for the Repository of the Royall Society, as 2 Ratlesnake skins, Eares of Indian corne wch will ripen in a shorter tyme then the other sorts, & severall other particulars mentioned in that letter: I have now putt up in a box a kind of shell fish, wch I thinke are not knowne in Europe (but if common in some places there its but to lay them aside and excuse my ignorance thereof) they are very common in most parts of this coast in the harbours and creekes of the sea in summer tyme: the body of them is like an horses foot and thence the English of these parts call them Horsfoot, they have a long sharp taile, of a strong horny, or boney substance:[2] there is also in the same box a smal box wherein is a trifle, yet being rare to be seene I have adventured to put it wth other such seeming noveltie, It is the nest of a very small bird, wch we call an humming bird from the huming noise it maketh whiles it flieth from flower to flowre sucking hony like a bee. There are also 2 of the Eggs of that bird in the Nest, if they be not broken by some accident, they were whole when putt up, the nest, as may be seene is so artificially covered wth the mosse like the mosse of the bowe on wch its fastened, that its hard to be discerned from it, especially at some distance: there is in the same box an other small box in wch is as very a trifle, as the former, but I hope to be excused, it seeming to me to be a very novelty: It is a fly wth feathers, or something like feathers on the wings. I cannot remember that I have seene an other of the like: there is also in that box an other small box wherin are some round bullets and other peices of earth or clay of several formes, and small shells, all wch were taken from the inward parts of an hill, wch was this last summer removed miraculously out of its place (the bottom being turned uppermost) of wch I have written (as much as I could know of it) to the Right Honorble the Lord Brereton:[3] I have also ordered to be put up into a vessell or caske, as much as I could for this season procure, of the silke downe of those silke podds, for Sr Robert Moray, according to his commands mentioned in your letter:[4] the downe is in 2 baggs wthin the cask, it is not cleered from all the seeds, that it might appeare to be the right kind of the silke pods downe, but may be cleered from those seeds wth the same labour yt must be bestowed to pull it & make it fine & soft, being prested together in the bagge & thereby be extended to fill a large receptacle there are also some of the podds tied together wch opend may yeild a good quantity more of that downe, & it was intended that all should have beene sent over in the Podd but they being laid to dry & wither, that silke doune did worke it self quite out of the podds and therfore is put into baggs. I have not beene unmindfull of cranberies for your selfe, but have taken order to have some brought to Boston and put up carefully & to be put aboard wth the aforementioned things, when the ship is ready to sett forth. Mr Fairewether is the first ship its thought wilbe ready of those later ships, and by him it is intended they be sent: I am necessitated to be going up to Connecticutt before the hard wether come, and severall occasions hastning my returne thither, but shall leave order for the shipping of those things, and these letters, and another pacquett to or by an other ship and am now hastned to subscribe that I am really

your most faithfull servant
John Winthrop

ADDRESS

    For my Worthy freind mr

    Henry Oldenburge

    Secretary to the Royall

      Society:

          In

            London

NOTES

This letter was endorsed by Oldenburg as received on 6 March 1670/71, with a further note, "At Mr Parsons in Canon-street at ye signe of ye gilded half moon about ye midle, in London-stone. About 1. a clock To call for a smal boxe, left there by Mr Fairewater, Master of a New-England ship."

1 Letter 1514.
2 *Xiphosura polyphemus*, the horseshoe crab. It is not mentioned by Grew, *Musaeum*.
3 Winthrop's letter (of the same date as this) is printed in Birch, *History*, II, 473–74.
4 See the last paragraph of Letter 1433 (Vol. VI).

1533
Oldenburg to Williamson
11 October 1670
From the original in P.R.O. MS. S.P. 78/130, no. 172

Sir,

These particulars came by the last, I had from Paris;

1. "On mande que ceux de Hamburg veulent restablir la fontaine salée d'Olderlo,[1] qui a esté autrefois ruinée par ceux de Luneburg. Ils raffinent depuis un mois ou deux le sel dela mer, come on fait en Hollande. S'ils reussissent, on se passera de nostre sel de France.

2. "Le Chevalier de Bouillon s'est battu contre un nommé Rochecourbon.[2] Le premier en est mort.

3. "Monsr Pelisson,[3] dont le nom et le merite vous sont conus, a changé de religion. Ceux qui sont à la Cour, ont dela peine à resister aux caresses et aux advantages, qu'ils en esperent. Ceux qui demeureront seront a l'es-preuve.

4. "On ne songe nulle part au Duc de Loraine, et sans l'ombrage qu'on prend dela France, on ne s'interesseroit point du tout dans la perte de ses Estats, parce que sa conduite est pitoyable.[4]

5. "Le Comte de Vaudement a mandé à Monsr de Crequi que Bitik[5] luy avoit esté donné par contract de mariage, que neanmoins si le roy le vouloit avoir, qu'il n'estoit pas besoin qu'il y envoiât son armee, et qu'il estoit prest de luy en faire ouvrir les portes.

6. "On songe à faire des troupes en hyver."

This from

Yr humble servant
Oldenburg

London Octob. 11. 70.

ADDRESS

For Joseph Williampson Esq,
These

TRANSLATION

.   .   .   .

1. "They say that in Hamburg they plan to revive the salt springs of Oldesloe,[1] formerly ruined by men from Lüneburg. For the last month or two they have been refining sea-salt, as they do in Holland. If they are successful they will do without our French salt.

2. "The Chevalier de Bouillon has fought with one Rochecorbon[2] and the former is dead.

3. "Mr Pellisson,[3] whose name and worth are known to you, has changed his religion. Those at Court can hardly resist the favors and the advantages which they expect from it. Those who remain will be put to the test.

4. "No one anywhere thinks anything of the Duke of Lorraine and without the umbrage taken against France no one would be in the slightest interested in the loss of his lands, because his conduct is miserable.[4]

5. "The Count of Vaudemont has told Mr. de Créqui that Bitik[5] was given him in his marriage contract, that nevertheless if the King wanted to have it it was not worth his while to send his army, and that he was ready to have it open its gates.

6. "There are plans for raising an army in the winter."

.   .   .   .

NOTES

This letter was presumably from Justel but there is no direct trace of his correspondence at this period.

1 Now Bad Oldesloe, a spa and a railway junction on the line from Hamburg to Lübeck.

2 This duel does not seem to have caused any very great stir. The Chevalier de Bouillon presumably was related to the great Turenne.

3 Paul Pellisson (see Letter 1484, note 7) was indeed recently converted at this time.

4 Charles IV, duc de Lorraine and comte de Vaudemont (1604–75), had become Duke in 1624 by the abdication of his father, and had indeed had a stormy reign. He had married three times; presumably the reference below concerns his first marriage to his cousin Nicole. He was finally expelled from his domain by François de Marines de Créqui de Blanchefort, Marshal of France (*c.* 1624–87), in September 1670.
5 We cannot explain Bitik unless Bitburg or Bibrich in Luxemburg is meant.

1534
? Justel to Oldenburg
19 October 1670

From *Phil. Trans.*, no 65 (14 November 1670), 2083–84

An Extract of a Letter, written to the Publisher out of France, Octob. 29, 1670. [N.S.]

A Friend of mine, a professed Physitian, hath assured me, that at Montpelier, a German hath discover'd the vessels, which convey the Chyle to the Breasts of Nursing Women; and shew'd, that they do issue out of the Ductus of Monsieur Pecquet.[1] This is a discovery of a thing, the *being* of which hath been believed long since, though not made out. Another person[2] hath assured me, that there is certainly another passage of the Urine to the Bladder than by the Ureters; an Experiment having been lately made, whereby the Ureters of a Dog were so carefully tyed up, that nothing could pass that way, and yet the Urinary Bladder was found full of Water.

NOTES

When Oldenburg produced this letter at the Society's meeting on 27 October he said that it came from Paris. The original is lost.
1 There is a contribution on this subject from Johann Ferdinand Hertodt, physician of Brno, in the first volume of the *Miscellanea curiosa* (see Letter 1530).
2 This was Huet; see Letter 1535, long delayed in the post.

1535

Huet to Oldenburg

20 October 1670

From the original in Royal Society MS. H 1, no. 98

Monsieur

Depuis que j'ay receu le livre de Mr. Wallis, *de motu*, dont vous m'avez regalé, j'ay esté partagé en tant d'occupations differentes, et j'ay mené une vie si agitée et si tumulteuse, que je n'ay presque n'en fait de ce que je voulois, et que je devois faire. estant allé a Caen pour mes affaires, i'y fus attaqué d'une perilleuse maladie, qui me tourmenta long tems, & dont je n'estois pas encore delivré, Lors que je fus rappellé icy pour un employ dont Mr. Justel vous a informé.[1] Cette nouvelle occupation a troublé les autres, et m'a jetté dans un genre de vie fort esloigné de celuy que j'ay mené jusqu'a present. Il ne m'a pourtant pas osté Le souvenir de vostre present, Monsieur, ny la reconnoissance que je vous dois, & je vous en rends enfin, quoy qu'un peu tard, de tres humbles graces. Je vous avois supplié par ma Lettre precedente de me mander le sentiment de vostre Academie touchant l'augmentation ou diminution des corps humides dans la plaine oula nouvelle Lune. Je vous fais encore la mesme priere. et de m'apprendre si je pourrois esperer la communication des Balances qui examinent le magnetisme de la terre, & la traitté qui mesure les Spheres de l'oeil.[2] Pendant mon sejour a Caen j'ay voulu rechercher le conduit de l'Urine dans les animaux, et pour cela ayant fait boire beaucoup d'eau a un chien, je fis lier ses deux Ureteres, et fis vuider sa vessie. apres deux heures je trouvay la vessie vuide, et les Ureteres n'estoient point gonflez au dessus de la Ligature; cela m'ayant surpris, je crus que la cause pouvoist venir du refroidissement des parties interieures, qui avoient esté exposées à l'air pendant tout ce tems, car j'avois fait faire la section en croix, a la maniere ordinaire. Pour eviter cet inconvenient, je reiteray l'experience sur un autre chien. Je fis faire de petits ouvertures aux deux costez, suffisantes pour trouver et lier les ureteres, et pour exprimer et faire sortir l'Urine de la vessie en la pressant avec la main. Cela fait, je fis recoudre les ouvertures, et ayant en suitte fait boire beaucoup d'eau au chien, je le laissay pendant prés de trois heures en la posture la mois violente que pouvoient souffrir ses Liens. Puis ayant fait rouvrir les deux trous, et la vessie ayant esté pressée avec la main, il en sortit de l'Urine en quantité assez raisonnable. et les Ureteres me parurent un peu gonflez au dessus de la ligature. Cette opera-tion fut faite avec beaucoup d'exactitude, mais neantmoins comme elle est de consequence pour la decouverte du chemin de l'Urine, je l'aurois reiterée plusieurs fois, si je n'avois pas eté obligé de revenir avec precipi-tation. Je ne suis pas presentement en estat de le pouvoir faire. Mais je vous exhorte Monsieur d'obliger quelques uns de vos meilleurs anatomistes de donner quelques soins a cette recherche. Mr. Hauton pretend que son eau dessalée est entierement salubre.[3] Il le prouve premierement par l'ex-perience qu'il en a faite sur des hommes et sur des bestes. Secondement par raison, qui est que la terre qu'il mesle avec l'eau distillée, emousse la pointe des esprits volatils de sel, et donne, pour ainsi dire, des fourreaux a ces pointes, et leur oste leur force, et leur acreté maligne. En quittant Caen, et faisant transporter icy ma Bibliotheque, mes meubles, et ma famille, j'ay resigné l'Academie, qui s'assembloit chez moy depuis huis ans, et que j'avois, pour ainsi dire, fondée et etablie, a Un de ceux qui la composent,[4] & L'on y continuera les experiences Philosophiques a la maniere accoustu-mée. Ainsi Monsieur je vous demande pour elle la continuation de vostre liaison et de vostre correspondance. & pour moy la conservation de vostre bienveillance, & la permission de me dire Monsieur

Vostre tres humble & tres obeissant serviteur
Huet

A St. Germain le 30 8bre 1670. [N.S.]

Trouvez bon, s'il vous plaist, que j'assure Monsieur le Chevalier Wroth de mon obeissance. L'addresse est toujours chez Mr. Cramoisy, Libraire, rue St. Jacques, A Paris.

TRANSLATION, partly from *Phil. Trans.*, no. 67 (16 January 1670/1), 2049–50

[Sir,

Since I received Mr. Wallis's book *De motu*, of which you made me a present, I have been torn between so many different concerns and have led such an agitated and tumultuous life that I have done almost nothing that I wished to do or ought to do. Having gone to Caen on business I was attacked by a dangerous illness which tormented me for a long time and from which I had not yet recovered when I was recalled here to an employment about which Mr. Justel will have told you.[1] This new business has disturbed the others and has plunged me into a kind of life very remote from that which I have led up to now. Yet it has not deprived me of the remembrance of your present, Sir, nor of the gratitude I owe you, and I now send you at last, though belatedly, my very humble thanks.

I begged you in my last letter to let me know the opinion of your Society about the increase or diminution of humid bodies with the full or new moon. I again make the same request, as also that you will let me know if I may hope for information about the balances for examining terrestrial magnetism and the treatise which measures the eye ball.[2]]

Having been, [during my stay at Caen] employed in searching after the Passage of the Urine in Animals, I made, for that purpose, a Dog drink a good quantity of water, and thereupon caused his Ureters to be well tyed about, and emptied his bladder. After two hours I found the Bladder empty, and the Ureters were not tumid above the Ligature. Being surprised thereat, I believed, that the cause might be the too much cooling of the inward parts, that had been exposed to the Air; the Section having been made Cross-wise, after the ordinary manner. To avoid this inconvenience, I thus reiterated the Experiment upon another Dog: I caused a small opening to be made on each side, sufficient to find and to tye the Ureters, and to squeese the Urine out of the Bladder, by pressing it with ones hand. This done, I made these Openings to be sow'd up again; and then having made the Dog drink good store of water, I left him for near three hours in the least violent posture that his Ligatures would permit. Afterwards having open'd both the holes, and the Bladder being pressed with the hand, there issued out of it a pretty quantity of Urine, and the Ureters seemed to be a little swelled above the Ligature. This Operation was made with great exactness; but yet as it is of importance for discovering the way of the Urine, I would have repeated it often, if I had not been obliged hastily to come away from the place where I then was, I am not now at leisure to try it again; but I exhort you, Sir, to engage some of your best Anatomists, among other researches to employ themselves in this Inquiry.

Monsieur Hauton maintains, that his distill'd Sea-water . . . is altogether salubrious.[3] He proveth it first from Experience, it having been given to Men and Beasts without any ill effect at all upon them. Secondly, from Reason, grounded on this, that that peculiar Earth . . . being mixed with the distilled Water, blunts the points of the Volatil Spirits of the Salt, and serveth them for sheaths, if I may so speak, taking away their force and maligne sharpness.

[On leaving Caen, and having my library, furniture, and domestics all brought hither, I resigned the Academy which during eight years had met in my house and which I had, so to speak, founded and established, to one of its members,[4] and they will continue philosophical experiments in their habitual manner. Hence,

Sir, I ask you on their behalf for the continuation of your connection and your correspondence with it. For myself I ask the continuation of your goodwill, and the permission to call myself, Sir,

Your very humble and obedient servant,
Huet]

St. Germain, October 30. 1670. [N.S.]

[Please be so good as to assure Sir John Wroth of my respects. My address is still "Chez Mr. Cramoisy, Libraire, rue St. Jacques, A Paris."]

NOTES

The part of the translation in square brackets is by the editors. The rest is Oldenburg's. The last letter from Huet was Letter 1393 (Vol. VI).

1 Huet had been chosen to assist Bossuet as tutor to the Dauphin.
2 See Vol. VI, p. 488.
3 See Vol. VI, pp. 113, 487–88.
4 This was evidently André Graindorge (1616–76; compare Brown, p. 226), who is to be distinguished from the monk Jacques, no doubt of the same family, several times referred to in Vol. V. André Graindorge, who had taken his M.D. at Montpellier and practised medicine at Narbonne, soon after his arrival in Caen (which cannot have been much before 1660, and was perhaps later) suggested to Huet the formation of a scientific academy to parallel the literary group already existing in the city. Graindorge was a follower of Gassendi and author of several works on natural philosophy and medicine.

1536
Hevelius to Oldenburg
21 October 1670

From the original in Royal Society MS. H 2, no. 23
Partially printed in *Phil. Trans.*, no. 66 (12 December 1670), 2023–28

Illustri Viro
Domino Henrico Oldenburg
Regiae Societatis Secretario
J. Hevelius Salutem

Non potui responsum Tuum ad meas ultimas 27 Augusti [N.S.][1] exspectare, quin rursus ad Vos scriberem, deque recentioribus quibusdam phaenomenis et observationibus hic a me feliciter habitis certiores redderem: cumprimis cum videam meas quales quales animadversiones Caelestes, Illustrissimae Nostrae Societati Regiae hactenus non omnino displicuisse. Primo; die 29 Sept. styl. n. mane Eclipsin Lunae caelo perquam sereno ab initio usque ad finem ex voto observavi, cuius observationis

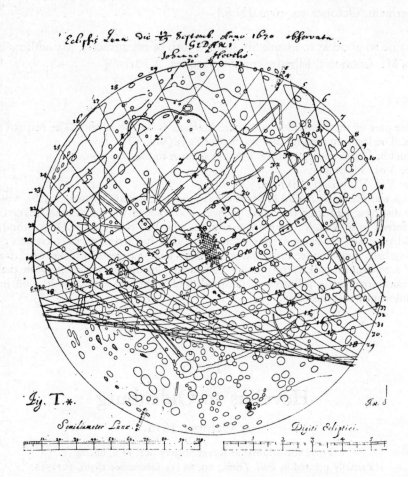

typum hic simul transmitto. Videbitis initium incidisse hora 2 2′, quan-quam vix omnino accurate illud ipsum observari potuit, ob umbram terrae dilutissimam. Siquidem durante Eclipsi, tota umbra adeo erat tenuis et diluta, ut omnes praecipuas maculas per eam Tubo meo viginti pedum, etiam brevioribus optime conspicere potuerim. Maxima obscuratio incidit hor. 3.50′, finis vero hor. 5 21′. Tota itaque duratio extitit hor. 2 59′, et quantitas vix amplius 9 digit. Quibus vero Tabulis, huius Eclipseos observatio accuratius respondeat, Vos judicabitis. Iuxta Rudolphinas hic

Gedani incidit

initium Hor	2	37'	5"
max. obscuratio	4	2	50
Finis	5	28	35
Tota duratio	2	51	30
Quantitas	9	4	0 digit
secundum vel Riccioli Tabulas² initium Hor.	2	14	47
maxima obscuratio	3	55	37
Finis	5	36	27
Tota duratio	3	21	40
Quantitas digit	11	43	0

Circa medium huius Eclipsis hor. 3 40' stellulam quandam incognitum, ac solo tubo conspicuam, a Luna circa Lacum nigrum Maiorem³ tectam, clarissime conspexi; sed exire eam non deprehendi. Deinde finita Eclipsi, iucundissimum quoque observata erat, bina luminaria simul supra horizontem. Nam priusquam Luna occideret, Sol oriebatur: caetera notatu digna ex ipsa observatione, eiusque typo deprehendebitis [*see figure, p. 210*].

Secundo, die 11. Octob. st. n. incidit mane post Solis ortum hora circiter octava hic Gedani Coniunctio ♀ et ☽, quam calculus Rudolphinus pariter, eodem fere tempore, indigitavit; quo videlicet Luna parte sua inferiori Venerem occultare ad 23" nimirum debebat; ad quod rarissimum spectaculum observandum me tubo 20. ped. accinxeram; et etiamsi aer non omnino esset defaecatus, atque rariusculae nubes hinc inde obvolitarent, Sole pariter iam orto, nihilominus et Lunam et Venerem clarissime conspeximus, ad horam usque decimam, imo diutius potuissemus, si opus fuisset; sed Luna ut ut Tabulae dictae occultationem illam penitus confirmabant, nequaquam tamen Venus ab ea, illo tempore tecta fuit, sed aberat circa veram scilicet coniunctionem a limbo lunae inferiori ad 4 vel minimum 3 minut. sic ut nulla eo tempore occultatio, sed tantum arctus extiterit transitus. Volupe profecto erat illud iucundissimum spectaculum de die, Soleque splendente adeo distincte ac dilucide contemplari: Luna namque erat tenuissima ad Coniunctionem propendens, et admodum corniculata: Venus vero propemodum plena, et corpore valde diminuto. Si aer non adeo extitisset vaporosus frequentius et accuratius distantias Veneris et Lunae a Jove, vel ab alijs quibusdam Fixis cepissem; nunc vero non nisi eas, quas mitto observare licuit. Hora 7 46', ea ipsa die tres parelij apparuerunt. Quid Vos hac de re deprehendistis hisce de rebus, prima occasione exspecto.

Tertio, Nova illa Stella sub capite Cygni,[4] quae initio tertiae videbitur
magnitudinis, mirum in modum Mense Septemb. decrevit, adeo ut 14.
Octob. nulla ratione amplius Sextante observari potuerit, licet omnem
adhibuerim diligentiam. Nam vix ac ne vix quidem nudo oculo animadverti
potuit; sic ut ab hac die illam amplius non viderim, ut ut singulis diebus
Caelo serenissimo omnes oculorum meorum nervos ad illam intenderim.
Altera vera nova in collo Ceti[5] ad medietatem usque mensis Octobris
Mandibulae Ceti[6] aequalis fere extitit magnitudine, et claritate eam propemodum vicit: adeo ut hoc anno secundae extiterit magnitudinis; ac maior
quam praecedentibus annis, excepto anno 1660, quo etiam maior Mandibulae Ceti deprehensa a me est, alijs temporibus non memini illam stellas
tertiae magnitudinis superasse. Certam igitur est, non eandem semper prae
se ferre magnitudinem, nec claritatem, ut ut in maximo suo existat incremento; hesterna vero die multum decreverat. Lentem illam pro tubo 70
ped. Domini Burattini, nondum explorare hactenus licuit; promisit quoque
aliam 140 ped. quas quamprimum accepero vires illarum simul explorabo,
Vosque deinde de omnibus et singulis certiores reddam. Succinum quod
sigillo cedit, inter rarissima merito habetur, quae unquam apud nos reperiuntur: quippe dum vixi, si illa bina excipias, ne unquam quidem vel minimum frustulum vidi, ut ut tale a multis annis sollicite quasiverim; nihilominus tamen ut Illustrissimae Societati promptitudinem meam declarem,
mittam Illi ex binis illis frustulis, quae penes me sunt alterum, proxime
verno tempore navis quadam: non video enim, qua occasione terra illud
transmitti debeat, ut faciem, figuram atque insignia impressa omnino
retineat. An unquam frustulum altere parte molle, altera durissimum possim
impetrare, valde dubito: quandoquidem rarum admodum est contingens
tale unquam reperire vel obtinere. Tractatus illos, quorum mentionem
fecisti, Clarissimorum videlicet Virorum Wallisij, Barrovij, Boylij, gratissimum utique mihi erit, ut prima occasione illos omnes habere possem, nec
non Ephemerides Eruditorum Vestratium de quibus iam toties Te
admonui; si igitur sine nimio tuo incommodo fieri poterit, rogo ut simul
primo vere illos libros omnes, nummis illis qui adhuc penes te sunt, coemas,
mihique transmittas; facies rem mihi multo gratissimam, inprimis si adiun-
xeris Instrumentum illud pro capiendis minoribus distantijs, tam quae
interea de rebus Mathematicis insuper prodierint. Dominus Christophorus
Cock, nuper per literas a me petijt adhuc 10 lib. Sterling. ratione lentium
transmissurum, cui etiam hisce adiunctis (quas ipsi tradas rogo) simul
respondi,[7] ijs fere verbis, quibus in prioribus ad Te datis feci; solvas itaque
ipsi adhuc 5 lib. sterling: quod cum factum fuerit, profecto carius ab ipso

emptae sunt ea lentes pro Telescopio 50 ped. quam si eas una cum Tubo a domino Rivio mihi comparassem;[8] acquiescat igitur 45 lib. sterling. Misit mihi dictus dominus Cock magnitudinem lentis cuiusdam pro tubo 100 ped.; sed tum adeo care coemenda vitra mihi amplius non sit consultum, tum aliam lentem pro tubo 140 ped. propediem exspectam, non video, quod ea pro 100 ped. opus habeam; Velim tamen scire quid in effectu praestiterit, si dabitur occasio eam examinandi. Commoratus apud Vos modo Iuvenis quidam nomini Samuel Skütt,[9] natione Suecus, qui cum sit modestus, ac Rei Astronomicae perquam deditus, Tibi illum de meliori modo commendo; forte illius opera imposterum uti potero in conficiendo et suppetando Fixarum catalogo; hinc fere constitui illum suo tempore evocare Dantiscum, inprimis si laudabiliter se gesserit, studiaque suscepta diligenter excoluerit. In Machina mea Coelesti alacriter et constanter, quantum occupationes unquam permittunt, pergo; deus O.M. voto Vestro annuat, quo ea omnia, quae menti concepi, etiam suo tempore feliciter Rei literariae bono in publicum proferre non nequeam. Valete et favete porro Vestro consodali, Illustrissimae Societati Regiae devinctissimo J. Hevelio. Dabam Dantisci 1670 die 31 Octob. [N.S.]

TRANSLATION

J. Hevelius greets the illustrious Mr. Henry Oldenburg, Secretary of the Royal Society

I could not wait for your reply to my last letter of 27 August [N.S.][1] before writing to you a second time to inform you of certain recent phenomena and observations made successfully here by myself, particularly as I see that my celestial observations (such as they are) have hitherto proved not wholly unwelcome to our most illustrious Royal Society. Firstly, on 29 September [N.S.] in the morning, with a very clear sky, I observed the eclipse of the moon from beginning to end as well as one could wish; I here send you a sketch of this observation [*see figure, p. 210*]. You will see that the beginning occurred at 2 hours 2 minutes, although it was impossible to observe it with complete accuracy because of the Earth's very faint shadow. For throughout the eclipse the whole shadow was thin and faint, so that I could very well discern through it with my telescope of twenty feet (or even with shorter ones) all the chief markings. The greatest obscuration was at about 3 h. 50', the end at 5h. 21'. Thus the whole duration was 2h. 59', and the extent hardly exceeded nine digits. You shall judge to which tables the observation of this eclipse corresponded more closely. According to the Rudolphine Tables it should happen thus here at Danzig:

beginning	2h.	37′	5″
greatest obscuration	4h.	2	50
end	5h.	28	35
total duration	2h.	51	30
extent	9	4	0

or according to Riccioli's tables[2]

beginning	2h.	14′	47″
greatest obscuration	3h.	55	37
end	5h.	36	27
total duration	3h.	21	40
extent	11	43	0

About the middle of this eclipse (about 3h. 40′) I observed very clearly a certain unrecorded star, visible only in the telescope, which was covered by the moon near the Larger Black Lake;[3] I did not observe its reappearance. Then after the eclipse was over it was also observed with great pleasure that both luminaries were above the horizon at once, for the sun rose before the moon had set. You will note whatever else was worth observing about this eclipse in the figure of it [*see figure, p. 210*].

Secondly, there occurred here at Danzig on 11 October, N.S., in the morning after sunrise about eight o'clock, a conjunction of Venus and the moon which the Rudolphine computation predicted for about that time. According to that computation the moon was to conceal Venus for at least 23 seconds with its lower limb. I had made my twenty-foot tube ready for observing this very rare spectacle, and even though the air was not wholly pure, with very occasional clouds passing across here and there and the sun already risen, still we saw the moon and Venus very clearly up to ten o'clock and could have continued longer if necessary; but as the table of this occultation clearly shows, Venus was never concealed by the moon at that time, but was four or at least three minutes removed from conjunction with the moon's lower limb. So that there was no occultation at this time but a close transit only. This was a most agreeable day-time spectacle to contemplate indeed, for the sun was shining brilliantly and clearly, the moon was very slender and horned in her approach to conjunction, and Venus was practically full, much diminished in size. If the air had not been so full of vapors I would have taken more frequent and accurate measures of the distances of the moon and Venus from Jupiter or some fixed stars; now, in fact, it was only possible to observe those I send you.

On the same day at 7h. 46′ three parhelia appeared. What you learned of these matters I shall expect [to hear] at the first opportunity.

Thirdly, that new star under the head of Cygnus,[4] which at first appeared of the third magnitude, decreased surprisingly during the month of September so that by 14 October it could no longer be observed with the sextant although I made most diligent efforts. For it could hardly be perceived with the naked eye, if at all, so that I have not seen it since that day, although I have stared at it with all the power of my eyes on clear days. The other new star in the neck of Cetus[5] was up to the middle of October almost equal in magnitude to that in the jaw of Cetus[6] and almost surpassed it in brilliance, so that this year it appeared of the second magnitude and greater than in previous years except 1660, when I found it to be even greater than the star in the jaw. I do not recall that star exceeding the third magnitude at other times. It is certain, therefore, that it does not always show itself to be of the same magnitude and brightness, even at its time of greatest increase; for yesterday it had greatly decreased.

It has not yet been possible to test that seventy-foot lens of Mr. Burattini. He has also promised me another of 140 feet and as soon as I receive it I will explore the powers of both together and inform you about each and every one. The amber that takes impressions from a seal is justly regarded as among the greatest of the rarities ever found in these parts; indeed, all my life, apart from those two [pieces], I have seen not the least fragment of it, although I have inquired after it for many years. Nevertheless, in order to prove my readiness to serve the most illustrious Society, I will send it one of the two pieces that I have in my possession by some ship next spring, for I see no chance of sending it by land so as to retain an impressed image or symbol. Whether I can ever obtain a piece that is soft on one side and perfectly hard on the other I very much doubt, since it very rarely happens that one finds or obtains any.

Those treatises you mention of the celebrated Wallis, Barrow, and Boyle would be most welcome to me if I might have them all at the first opportunity, as also your *Transactions of the Learned* as I have advised you so many times. And so if it does not put you out too much, I beg you early next spring to buy all those books at once with the money you still have and send them to me; you will do something most agreeable to me especially if you will add that instrument for measuring small distances, and anything else relating to mathematics.

Mr. Christopher Cock lately begged me by letter to send £10 sterling more for the lenses, to whom I have replied in the attached letter (which I beg you to deliver to him)[7] almost in those words which I formerly addressed to yourself. Pay him another £5, therefore, and when that is done truly those lenses for a telescope of 50 feet will have been more dearly bought from him than if I had purchased them myself together with the tube from Mr. Reeve;[8] for he asked £45. The said Mr. Cock sent me the size of a lens for a tube of 100 feet; but I do not see what need I have of it, both because it does not seem sensible to me to buy more lenses so expensively and because I expect another lens for 140 feet soon. However, I would like to know how it proves in performance, if there is a chance of examining it.

There is a certain young man named Samuel Skütt[9] residing among you now, a Swede, whom I commend to you very warmly because he is modest and extremely devoted to astronomy. Perhaps I shall be able to employ his services later in preparing and computing the catalogue of fixed stars. Hence I have pretty well decided to summon him to Danzig, particularly if he has behaved himself laudably and performed the studies he had undertaken diligently. I go on constantly and eagerly with my *Machina coelestis* so far as my [other] business ever allows. May God Almighty grant your prayers that I may be able successfully to offer to the public all those things that I have in mind for the good of learning, in His good time. Farewell and continue to think well of your colleague in the Fellowship of the most illustrious Royal Society and its most obliged

J. Hevelius

Danzig, 31 October 1670 [N.S.]

NOTES

Despite the first sentence of this letter, it is obvious that its latter paragraphs are in reply to Letter 1520. The tables giving further details of the eclipse and the transit are printed in the *Philosophical Transactions* extract, pp. 2025, 2027.

1 Letter 1509.
2 In the *Almagestum novum* (Bologna, 1651).
3 This was Hevelius' name for the crater Plato, near the moon's southern pole.
4 See Letter 1474 and its note 2, and Letter 1509.
5 See Letter 1509, note 10.
6 ξ[1] Ceti.
7 This presumably went to Cock.
8 Compare Vol. IV, Letter 935a.
9 Presumably a member of the Skytte family (to use a more correct form), but we could not identify him.

1537
Huygens to Oldenburg

21 October 1670

From the original in Royal Society MS. H 1, no. 70
Printed in *Œuvres Complètes*, VII, 43–45

A la Haye ce dernier Octobr. 1670 [N.S.]

Monsieur

Je m'estois donnè l'honneur de vous escrire peu de jours auparavant que de recevoir la vostre qui m'a estè rendue par l'Estudiant Polonois avec le excellent livre de Mr. Wallis.[1] Mr. Morhovius estoit porteur de la mienne qui m'avoit prie de luy procurer vostre connoissance.[2] Je vous rends graces treshumbles de vostre conjouissance et bons souhaits en ce qui regarde l'heureux restablissement de ma santé, a la quelle Dieu mercy, il ne manque plus guere. La peur que j'ay de retomber apres un avertissement aussi fort qu'a estè ce dernier est cause que je n'oserois encore retourner aux speculations de Geometrie, et toutefois il m'a estè impossible de ne pas feuilleter ce nouveau traitè de Mr. Wallis, ou il y a des choses d'un subtilité merveilleuse, et qui font voir la force et l'universalité de sa methode. Je ne scay comment il ose se proposer des problemes aussi difficiles et desesperez qu'est celuy du centre de gravitè de la spirale, lequel cependant il semble avoir demeslè heureusement.[3] Je dis qu'il me le semble, parce que, a dire la verité, je n'entens pas encore clairement sa demonstration et le consulterois volontiers sur quelques passages obscurs que j'y ay trouvez, mais je le differe jusqu'a ce qu'il me soit permis d'estudier avec plus d'attention; et peut estre aussi qu'alors j'y verray plus clair, et me satisferay moy mesme.

Pour le livre de Mr. Barrow je l'ay veu a Paris et j'y ay remarquè un endroit ou il est parlè de moy a l'occasion de la dimension du cercle mais je n'avois garde alors d'examiner ce que cest qu'il pretend avoir adjoutè a ce que j'en ay trouvè.

En partant de Paris je ne scavois pas que Mr. Hevelius avoit observè la Nouvelle Estoile du Cigne, mais seulement qu'elle avoit estè decouverte par ce Chartreux de Dijon. Il n'y a rien de meilleur pour verifier des observations comme cella lá que d'en avoir de deux endroits differents. J'observay Saturne avec ma lunette de 22 pieds peu devant que partir de France, ayant trouvé moyen de m'en servir sans sortir de ma chambre, et remarquay sa figure tresconforme a ce qu'elle devoit estre suivant mon hypothese. C'est à dire les anses[4] fort estrecies, en sorte que leur ouverture ne paroissoit plus qu'obscurement. Je seray bien aise de voir dans vostre prochain Journal l'observation de Mr. Hook, et celle de Hevelius avec la lunette de 50 pieds, de la quelle pourtant je me souviens que vous m'avez mandè qu'elle n'estoit bonne que pour la Lune, et non pas pour Saturne.[5] Les experiences de Mr. Boile touchant la respiration sont tresbelles et je souhaite fort d'en voir la suite que vous promettez. Il me semble que cette matiere merite extremement d'estre examinée, et que surtout il faudroit faire des experiences pour trouver la qualité et la quantité de la partie de l'air qui sert a la nourriture des animaux et comment elle se communique au sang. Je n'ay pas veu ses autres petits traitez dont vous m'apprenez les sujects. Je les auray par le moyen de mon Pere, qui part demain avec Mr. le Pr. d'Orange.[6]

Je crois que vous aurez veu les Observations de Mr. Kercring[7] et le traitè de Insectis[8] de Mr. Swammerdam, qui est tout ce que j'ay icy trouvè de nouveau en Matiere de Physique. Je fus voir dernierement a Amsterdam ce Mr. Swammerdam[9] qui relevoit de Maladie, mais ne laissa pas de me montrer tout ce qu'il a amassè de curieux touchant les Insectes, ou il y a des choses estonnantes et qui n'ont jamais estè sceues auparavant.

Nous avons icy depuis quelques jours Mr. de Monceaux[10] gentilhomme de Condition et mon voisin à Paris, qui a voiagè au Levant ces dernieres annees, et a fait des remarques trescurieuses par tout ou il a estè, principale-ment en ce qui regarde les bastimens et ruines antiques, dont il a raportè une quantitè incroiable de desseins, qui meritent d'estre publiez, et le seront l'un de ces jours. Maintenant ayant envie de passer en Angleterre, il m'a priè que je luy enseignasse ou il pourroit faire tenir quelques lettres de consequence qu'il attend de chez luy, pour les trouver a Londres a son arrivée, sur quoy j'ay pris la libertè Monsieur de vous indiquer, ne doutant pas que vous ne fissiez volontiers ce plaisir a une personne de son merite. de sorte que je luy ay dit qu'il fit mettre sur le couvert des lettres qu'on luy envoiera, vostre adresse de Mr. Grubendol, et luy ay enseignè vostre demeure afin qu'aussi tost il pust les aller prendre. Si vous avez avec cela la bontè de le faire connoistre a Mr. Wren je ne doute pas que vous ne fassiez plaisir a l'un et a l'autre puis qu'ils se plaisent tous deux a l'architec-ture ou ce pelerin est fort scavant.

Vous m'aviez fait esperer des eschantillons de verre pour des lunettes qu'on fait chez vous, Je vous prieray lors que mon pere sera arrivè, de luy indiquer ou il en puisse avoir. Je vous baise les mains et suis a jamais Monsieur

Vostre treshumble et tresobeissant serviteur
Hugens de Zulichem

TRANSLATION

The Hague, the last day of October 1670 [N.S.]

Sir,

I gave myself the honor of writing to you a few days before receiving your letter, delivered by the Polish scholar with Mr. Wallis's excellent book.[1] Mr. Morhof was the bearer of my letter;[2] he had requested me to procure him an acquaintance with you. I thank you profoundly for your good wishes and your rejoicing in the fortunate re-establishment of my health, which is now, thanks be to God, fully restored. My fear of a relapse after so sharp a warning as this past one is the reason why I would not yet dare to return to geometrical speculations; yet I could not refrain from turning over the pages of this new treatise by Mr. Wallis, where there are matters of a marvelous subtlety which demonstrate the power and universality of his method. I do not know how he dares to consider problems as difficult and desperate as that of the center of gravity of a spiral; yet he seems to have extricated himself happily.[3] I say "seems," because, to speak truthfully, I do not yet clearly understand his demonstration, and I should like to consult him about several obscure passages which I have come across, but I defer this until I may be able to study it more attentively; perhaps then I shall even see more clearly into it and shall satisfy myself.

As for Mr. Barrow's book, I saw it in Paris and noted the place where I am mentioned in connection with the measure of the circle, but I did not then take care to examine what he claims to have added to what I had discovered about it.

Because of my departure from Paris I did not know that Mr. Hevelius had observed the new star in Cygnus, but only that it had been discovered by the Carthusian of Dijon. Nothing helps more to verify such observations than to have them observed in two different places. I observed Saturn with my twenty-two-foot telescope a little before leaving France, having found a means of using it without leaving my room, and found its shape very conformable to what it ought to be according to my hypothesis. That is to say, the anses[4] very contracted so that their opening only appeared obscurely. I shall be very glad to see in your next *Transactions* Mr. Hooke's observations and those of Hevelius with his fifty-foot telescope, though I recollect that you told me that it was only useful for the moon and not for Saturn.[5] Mr. Boyle's experiments on respiration are very fine and I very much hope to see the promised sequel. It seems to me a subject that very much deserves investigation, and especially that experiments ought to be made to determine the nature and quantity of that part of the air which serves to support animals, and the means by which it reaches the blood. I have not seen his other little tracts, whose subjects you described to me. I shall get them through my father who leaves tomorrow with the Prince of Orange.[6]

I suppose that you have already seen Mr. Kerckring's *Observations*[7] and Mr. Swammerdam's treatise on insects,[8] the only new works on science which I have found here. I recently went to see this Mr. Swammerdam in Amsterdam;[9] he was recovering from an illness but he did not fail to show me everything interesting which he had collected about insects, among which are some astonishing things, never known before now.

For some days we have had here Mr. de Monceaux,[10] a gentleman of rank and my neighbor in Paris, who has these last years traveled in the Levant and has made very interesting observations everywhere that he has been, especially concerning buildings and ancient ruins, of which he has brought back an incredible quantity of drawings which deserve to be published and will be one of these days. Now, as he wants to cross into England, he has begged me to instruct him about where he can have several letters of importance which he expects from home held for him so that he may find them at his arrival in London; on this matter I have taken the liberty, Sir, of naming you, not doubting but that you will willingly do this favor for a person of his worth. In fact, I have told him to have put on the envelopes of the letters to be sent to him your Grubendol address, and have instructed him about your residence, so that he may be able to go there to fetch them. If, further, you are so good as to make him acquainted with Mr. Wren, I am sure you will give pleasure to both, since they both delight in architecture, about which this traveler is very learned.

You gave me hope of some samples of optical glass as made among you. I beg you when my father arrives to tell him where he can get some. I kiss your hands and am always, Sir,

Your very humble and obedient servant,
Huygens of Zulichem

NOTES

Reply to Letter 1525.
1 See Letter 1531.
2 See Letter 1542.
3 Huygens refers to Props. 27 and 28 in the second part of *Mechanica, sive de motu* (London, 1670), entitled "De centro gravitatis ejusque calculo" (see *Opera mathematica*, Oxford, 1695, I, 878–903).
4 That is, the portions of Saturn's ring visible on either side of the planet; the term *anses* (literally, "handles") was customarily applied to these appendages.
5 Oldenburg's report on the second fifty-foot glass made by Cock and later sent to Hevelius is in Letter 1280 (Vol. VI, p. 222). It was Huygens himself who judged from this that the lens was a poor one; see his Letter 1307 (Vol. VI, p. 291).
6 See Letter 1531, note 3.
7 See Vol. VI, Letter 1451, note 2.
8 See Letter 1488, note 2.
9 Jan Swammerdam (1637–80), the son of an apothecary in Amsterdam, studied medicine at Leiden and became M.D. there in 1667. Meanwhile he had traveled in France where (along with Steno) he worked on comparative anatomy under the patronage of Thevenot, to whom he ultimately bequeathed all his own papers.
10 See Letter 1491, note.

1538
Winthrop to Oldenburg
26 October 1670
From the original in Royal Society MS. W. 3, no. 26

Boston in N England
Octob. 26: 1670

Sr

Since my former of Aug: last[1] I found out the fisherman who brought
that stellar fish from sea, I asked all the questions I could thinke needfull
concerning it: I understand from him, that he never saw, nor heard of any,
but those few, wch were taken by himselfe wch were not above six or 7 in
all, & those at severall tymes, not farr from the shoales of Nantuckett (wch
is an Iland upon the Coast of N: England) when he was fishing for codfish,
& such like merchantable fish: this stellar fish when it was alive, & first
puld out of the water, was like a baskett, had gathered it selfe round like a
round wicker basket, having taken fast hold of that bait upon the hooke,
wch he had put downe to the bottom to catch other fish, & having held
that wthin those surrounding brachia, would not lett it goe, though drawne
up into the vessell untill by lying a while on the deck, it felt the want of its
naturall element, & then voluntarily extended it selfe into that flatt round
forme, in wch it appeared, when presented to your veiw: what motion
it had in the water could not be knowne to him, for the water was deepe,
and they could not be seene in any other forme then so gethered up together
to hold fast the bait: The only use could be discerned of all that curious composure wth wch nature had adorned it, seemes to be to make it
as a pursnett to catch some other fish, or any other thing fitt for its food,
and as a basket or store to keepe some of it for future supply, or as a
receptacle to preserve & defend the young of the same kind from other
fish of pray, if not to feed on them also, (wch appeare probable the one,
or the other) for that somtymes were found peices of mackarell wthin that
concave, & he told me that once he catched one, wch had wthin that hollow of its Embracement a very small fish of the same kind together wth
some peice or peices of an other fishe, wch was Judged to be of a mackarell:
and that small one (it is like), was kept eyther for its preservation or for
food to the greater: but being alive it seems most likely it was there for

safety; except it were accidentally drawne wthin yt nett, wth yt peice of fish, upon wch it might be then feeding: He told me also that every one of those smallest parts had motion when it was alive, & a tenatious strength, but after it was dead & extended to a flatt round, it was so brittle yt it could not well be handled wthout breaking of some parts of it, but by carefull laijing of it to dry, it was therby somwhat hardned: he told me he had taken one the later end of this summer, but had left it wth a freind at an other port, where he had beene, but promised to procure it for me when he saileth thither againe, if it be not broken or defaced: I hope I shall ingage him for future to take better notice, of what may be observeable about it, if he hath oportunity: I have inquired of divers other fishermen, & seamen, but can meete wth none other by whome any of them have beene taken: He could not tell me any name it hath, & its likely it is yet namelesse, being not commonly knowne, as other fish are: but, untill a fitter English name be knowne, why may not it be called (in respect of what hath beene before mentioned) why may it not be called a basket fish, or a nett fish, or pursnet fish &c? I have put up in a box to be sent from Boston by Mr Fairwethers ship, as intended, some few of an other sort of shelfish, wch though very common in these parts probably are not knowne in England, nor other parts of Europe, they are found in the summer tyme in most (if not all) Harbours, coves, & creekes of the sea as farr as the salt water floweth: If they come to your hand safe, they wilbe seene to be (the body of them) like an horses foot and thence the English generally call this fish an Horsfoot,[2] from the likenesse to the foot of an horse, they have a long sharp taile, wch is of a strong horny or boney substance so tough, & sharp that the Indians have formerly (before they knew & could have brasse & iron) made arrow heads of them, & some doe use of them still, both in their hunting & other game, & in their warres. but what use that fish maketh of that taile doth not certainely appeare, as farre as I know, or can learne, possibly an helpe to steere in its motion in the water, or for some defence: they creepe up in shoale water in summer tyme very neere the shoare, so neere, yt they may easily be taken by hand, or throwne upon the shore wth a Gaffe or drawne upon the land by a staffe or pike wth an hooke upon the end of it, I know not whether they are good to be eaten yet have heard yt the Indians will sometymes eat of them roasted, but I never yet have heard that the English have eaten of them, they are of severall bignesses & of a slimy matter wthin, wch seemes very little, & not of substance fitt for food: but where planters have their ground neere the sea, they will fish their land (thats the terme for yt kind of manuring) wth them for their Indian corne, breaking them, & putting some of them wthin the little hillock where the corne is planted, & have greater crops thereby: If they be commonly found, and knowne in England, or other parts of Europe, its but to lay them aside, & to excuse my ignorance of it; yet please to compare them, whether any difference & to inquire what more is knowne of the nature & use of them, & whether they use to eat them, as other shelfish; For our knowledge of things of these parts is but, as of yesterday: There is also in the same box a small box wherin is a trifle yet rare to be had, even heere the place where its to be found: It is the nest of a bird (an Humming bird), so called from the humming noise it makes whiles it flieth) its an exceeding little bird, & only seene in summer & mostly in gardens, flying from flowre to flowre, sucking hony out of the flowres as a Bee doth, & as it flyeth not lighting on the flower, but hovering over it, sucking wth its long bill a sweet substance tasting like hony. If one of them was not sent last yeare amongst the other things, It miscarried at Boston by some accident, before it could be put up: and this yeare I had promise of an other, if it could be had, yet failed, but I hope next summer may supply some: there are also in the same Nest 2 of yt birds eggs, whether they use to have more at once I know not, I never saw but one of those nests before, and that was sent over formerly, as also those of those horsfoot fish, wth other collections but you had them not: an other very trifle is wth these in an other small box, wch because it seemed somwhat rare, is put wth the other (A fly wth feathers on the wings, or very like feathers) There is also a good quantity of the silkegrasse Downe according to Sr Robert Moray his Commands, as mentioned in your letter, it is put up in 2 linnin bags and those put into a sound tite caske; at the bottom of it are some of the pods wth the silken downe in them they are tied together in small bundles to keepe in the downe, wch otherwise would worke it selfe out: I intended to have sent it all in the pods, but being laid to dry in a chamber, the downe did worke out as it dried: except those few, wch are tied up, as before mentioned, some of the seeds remaine wth the downe, yt it might appeare to be of the right sort: there is in the same vessell, some pods of an other sort, wch grow only in very wett ground, the pods are smaller, & not so much of yt silke downe in them nor so splendid, these are sent to shew the difference & are in a paper in the same caske, the former sort grow in dry places, & higher lands then these. There are also Cranburies to be put up into a caske for yourselfe, and wilbe sent in the same ship wth the other things, wch are for presenting to the Royall Society. I am to returne to Hartford at Connecticut before these can be shipped, but my son stayeth heere and will take care for shipping of them: Please to excuse the repetition of the same things of former letters, and possibly the same againe after these, if oportunity. I have knowne so often miscarying of ships & letters especially in winter, yt I thought it might be convenient to write of the same matters by several postages, that by one or other, you may have such intelligence from

> your affectionate servant
> *John Winthrop*

ADDRESS

For Mr Henry
Oldenburge Secretary
to the Royall Society
in London

NOTES

This letter was received in June 1671; it was not read to the Society.
1 Letter 1514.
2 See Letter 1532, note 2. Most of what follows is a repetition.

1539
Wallis to Oldenburg
28 October 1670
From the original in Royal Society MS. W 1, no. 113

Oxford. Octob. 28. 1670.

Sr,

The inclosed is an answere to one from Mr Awbrey to mee,[1] in these Words

"Rev. Sr, I received a letter a little while since from a Jesuite of Paris, in answere to some Quaere's of mine concerning some Antiquities at Carnutes[2]
Chartres (the Metropolis of ye Druides) & withall he sent mee ye inclosed probleme, wch was sent to them from one of their order in ye Southern

part of France. If you please to honour mee wth ye Solution; I shal send it to Paris as done by you: which will be kindly taken by them, & you will much oblige, Sr, Yor most humble servant Jo: Awbrey. Broad-Chalke. Aug. 27. 1670."[3]

The Probleme you have recited in my Answere.[4] His letter (by reason of my absence from home) came not to my hand till Sunday last; which being not a day for business, I wrote ye inclosed on ye morrow, wch this Morning I send to you to transmit, since you are willing to see such transactions.

I was told, about 3 days since, from two several persons, that Dr Piers (our President of Magdalene College here)[5] had sent to Mr. Stubbe for his good service, a peice of Plate: &, yt it might be the more acceptable, by a Gentleman of quality. I was loth to take up such a report too hastily & therefore desired one of them that told it mee, to inform himself certainly & particularly about it; who assuring mee of ye truth of it, did withall promise to give me a particular account from the person who told him. And the next day brought mee this. That a Fellow of a College here (whom I could name if it were convenient) tells him; that about 7 or 8 weekes since (he knows not whether) on a Friday in August [wch must therefore by computation be Aug. 26][6] hee was at ye Angell in Oxford with a Gentleman of Warwickshire, Mr Thomas Wagstaffee[7] (sometime of Magdalene hall) heir to Sr Combe Wagstaf (a gentleman of a good estate;) & whilst he was there, Dr Piers's man came to Mr Wagstaf (then ready to goe out of town) from his master desiring him to go back to ye College (for hee had been there a little before, but had not found ye Dr then at lesure to be spoken with) for that his Mr had a great desire to speak wth him about some businesse. Hee did so. And when he returned back to this person at ye Inne, hee told him the businesse was, yt Dr Pierce had desired him to carry that piece of Plate (wch he shewcd this person, wrapped up in a paper, who took it in his hand & judged it by ye weight to bee about 5 or 6 lb price) to Mr Stubs for a present.

My relator tells mee further, that another Fellow of ye same house, (whom I could name allso,) tells him, that hee hath since mett Mr Stubs in the country, who told him, that hee had received a piece of Plate from [*word obliterated*] from Oxford; & that he expected another piece of Plate from London. These are ye particulars of matter [of] fact wch I meet with of certainty. I am told some others, but ye relators have not ye like evidence as of these. I am

                                                          Yours &c
                                                          Anonymus

ADDRESS

These
For Mr Henry Oldenburg
in the Palmal, near
St James's
London

NOTES

1 John Aubrey (1626–97)—see Vol. V, p. 457, note 9—was acquainted with Wallis through his own long connection with the University. He wrote no "Brief Life" of Wallis but did record some unflattering (and very probably untrue) stories concerning him. Aubrey believed that the long stone monuments at Stonehenge and elsewhere were works of the pre-Roman "Druids."

2 The *Carnutes* were inhabitants of the region of Chartres (*Carnutum*).

3 The parentheses were placed by Wallis. Broad Chalk, Wiltshire, was the home of Aubrey's cousins.

4 This seems to be lost, but compare Letter 1543.

5 Thomas Peirse; see Letter 1494, note 10.

6 The brackets are Wallis's.

7 Wallis presumably meant *John* Wagstaffe of Tachbrook, Warwickshire, who had matriculated at Magdalen Hall in July 1665; Sir Combe was also of Tachbrook. There was, however, a Thomas Wagstaffe (1645–1712) of New Inn Hall, from Stoke in Warwickshire, and a namesake still an undergraduate at St. Edmund Hall.

1540

Ludolf to Oldenburg

31 October 1670

From the original in Royal Society MS. L 5, no. 82

de Gota, ce 31. Octob. 1670.

Monsieur

La bonne occasion de voir Mons. Duré icy, et d'entendre de luy, qu'il est devenu vostre beau pere, et que vous vous trouvé en bon estat m'a tellement rejouy, et encouragé que je n'ay peu laisser passer l'occasion de renouveller la correspondance que jay eue cy devant avec vous.

Son Altesse Monseigneur le Duc Ernest[1] mesme a entendu volontiers, que vous avez lacharge de Secretaire de la Societé Royale; et comme elle approuve fort les desseins de cette honorable societé, ainsi elle a tesmoigné de vouloir communiquer de bon coeur ce qu'elle a de particulier en son pais. Quant a moy, je m'estimerois heureux si je pouvois contribuer quelque chose aux louables entreprises de la dite societé.

Le temps m'est a cette heur trop court de m'entretenir avec vous plus amplement, je le feray a l'avenir, si tost que je sauray que cette lettre vous a esté bien rendue, ou par qu'el moyen il faut addresser les lettres a vous le plus seurement. Je vous supplie en me daignant d'une response, de me faire savoir, si Mons. Edmund Castell[2] est encore en vie, et s'il se porte bien, Car il m'a envoyé la moitie de son grand Dictionaire Polyglotte, qui me sera inutile, s'il ne me favorise aussi de l'autre moitié. Outre cela nous avons un compatriote a Londres, qui s'appelle Lucas Leo natif de Salzungen, qui a cesse d'escrire en ce pais cy. Si vous le pouvez trouver et nous faire savoir son addresse ce nous sera chose aggreable. Je finis avec la fidelle asseurance, que je suis de tout mon coeur Monsieur

> Vostre treshumble tres obeissant
> et tres affectioneuse serviteur
> *J. Ludolf*

ADDRESS
      A Monsieur
Monsieur Henry Oldenburg
Secretaire de la Societé Royale
at his house in
the Old Palle male
in St. James fields
            a
          Londres

TRANSLATION
                                        Gotha, 31 October 1670
   Sir,

The happy event of seeing Mr. Dury here and or learning from him that he has become your father-in-law and that you are in a prosperous state so rejoiced and encouraged me that I could not overlook the opportunity of renewing the correspondence which I formerly maintained with you.

His Highness Duke Ernest[1] has also learned with pleasure that you have the office of Secretary of the Royal Society, and as he very much approves of the aims of that honorable society, he has given evidence of wishing to communicate freely whatever is peculiar to his country. As for myself, I should think myself happy if I could contribute something to the praiseworthy enterprises of the said society.

At the moment time is too short to converse with you more fully; I shall do this in the future as soon as I know that this letter has been safely delivered to you, or by what means I must address letters to you most surely. I beg you, in condescending to reply to me, to let me know if Mr. Edmund Castell[2] is still alive and if he is in good health, for he sent me half of his great polyglot dictionary which will be of no use unless he favors me also with the other half. Besides this, we have a compatriot in London, named Lucas Leo, a native of Salzungen, who has stopped writing to this country. If you can find him and let us know his address this will be gratifying to us. I close with the faithful assurance that I am, Sir, with all my heart,

Your very humble and affectionate servant,

J. Ludolf

ADDRESS

To Mr. Henry Oldenburg
Secretary of the Royal Society . . .

NOTES

For Job Ludolf (1624–1704), see Vol. I, p. 330.
1 See Vol. I, p. 184, note.
2 See Vol. II, p. 250, note 13.

1541
Oldenburg to Wallis
1 November 1670

This letter is known only from Wallis's acknowledgement of it in Letter 1543. It probably accompanied, or recorded the dispatch of, two books: Erasmus Bartholin's *Experimenta chrystalli Islandici dis-diaclastici* (Copenhagen, 1669) and Honoré Fabri's *Dialogi physici* (Lyons, 1669).

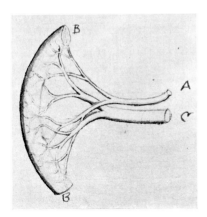

[Fig. 1]

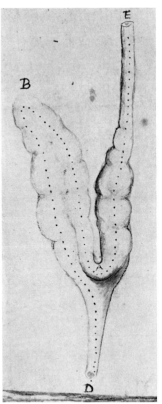

[Fig. 2]

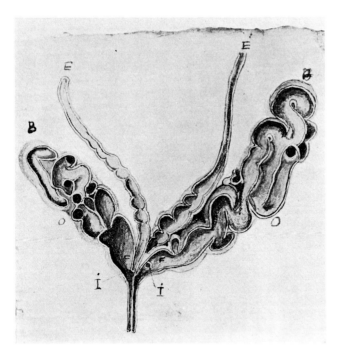

[Fig. 3]

PLATE I. Anatomical drawings
By De Graaf in Letter 1472

PLATE 11. Gottfried Wilhelm Leibniz
A copy after a German original
By courtesy of the Royal Society

PLATE III. Anatomical preparations

From Frederik Ruysch, *Thesaurus anatomicus* (Amsterdam, 1703), plate I. See Letter 1510

PLATE IV Hekla in Iceland

"Hekla, cursed with perpetual heat and snow vomits forth stones with a horrid groaning"
From Abraham Ortelius, *Theatrum orbis terrarum additimentum IV*
(Amsterdam, 1590). See Letter 1651
By courtesy of the Trustees of the British Museum

1542
Daniel Georg Morhof to Oldenburg
3 November 1670
From the original in Royal Society Boyle Letters VII, no. 27

Nobilissime Domine,

Cum nuper una essemus, et inter alias de rebus naturalibus dissertationes mentio a me fieret experimenti cujusdam circa vitrum clamore
intenso ruptum, cujus ego testis αὐτόπτης in Belgio fueram, efflagitaresque,
ut eius historiam consignarem, quo ad Regiam Societatem deferri ea res
possit et ulterius examinari;[1] parere nunc jussis tuis volui: praesertim cum
res dignissima sit quae coram Illustris vestri Senatus tribunali agitaretur.[2]
Narrabat mihi, cum Amstelodami essem, Iodocus Pluimer Bibliopola de
caupone quodam, qui clamore pocula vitrea etiam majora rumpere posset.
Res mihi primum ridicula visa. Is vero toties se vidisse experimentum
adseverabat, et inter testes plurimos Magnum quoque Etruriae Ducem,
priori anno apud Amstelodamenses hospitem laudabat, ad quem ipse hominem hunc adduxerit, non sine amplo munere, postquam successerat res
dimissum. Merebantur omnino fidem tam luculenta documenta: Ego vero
sciendi cupidine inductus rogare Bibliopolam non destiti, ut me ad illum
experimenti capiundi causa deduceret. Deduxit ad hominem, cuius nomen
mihi nunc excidit,[3] habitabat, si recte memini, non procul ab aede sacra
Lutheranorum. Promebat ille 4 vel 5 vitra ventricosa, cum nodulis in pede,
qualia sunt, quibus hic vinum Rhenanum bibitur, et Germanis Römer
dicuntur, pintae circiter Belgicae mensuram referentia, ut ex iis unum pro
experimento seligerem. Inspexi omnia sedulo, an quis forte subesset dolus.
Sed integra omnia inveni; et ex iis unum elegi, quod satis validum et
firmum. Filium ergo introvocabat, qui clamore rumperet, se enim aptum
ei rei negebat, quod ex catarrho vox sibi rauca esset et subobscura. Tene-
bam ego manu mea vitram paululum ab ore clamantis reclinatum, ut
inferiorem ventris partem vox feriret: ita enim praecipiebat. Primum
explorabat tonum vitri, quod si recte memini in ā sonabat. Eo tono cum
clamaret puer, leniter sonabat vitrum, caeteris nihil; nisi quod, cum in
sonos harmonicos incideret, lenem aliquem motum in vitro sentire mihi
viderer. Tandem cum puer octavo tono sonaret, fortissime ad stridorem
usque consonabat eodem tono vitrum, ut tremorem manus perciperet ex

motu. Cumque late diducto ore acuta et continua voce, ad sex vel septem circiter pulsuum Musicorum tempus clamare pergeret puer, ita ut nunquam sonare desineret vitrum, rumpebatur tandem, circa inferiorem ventris partem, qua cum pede committitur, obliquo circulo, ita ut ruptura per nodos priores pedis, ubi vitrum crassissimum est, iret, sono edito, qualem edere solet vitrum, cum ex intenso calore vel frigore rumpitur. Tentavi aliquoties an imitari possem, sed irrito conatu, quoniam obtusa mihi vox, et ob affectationem inconstans; donec tandem in vitro teniori successit. Circa hoc Experimentum ista praecipue consideratu digna mihi visa sunt. (1.) quod vitrum ventricosum fuerit; major enim est soni circulatio, et ideo violentior motus; (2.) quod ad inferiorem ventris partem os apposuerit; major enim impetus est soni oblique ascendentis, et in angustiore vitri circulo circa pedem contortior a sono motus. (3) quod os diduxerit: sic enim latior et diffusior aeris pulsus. (4) quod non nisi ad harmonicos tonos vitrum vel sonum ediderit, vel motum fuerit; cuius vera ratio hactenus me latet. Referre hic possum pene simile experimentum. Statuebam octo pocula vitrea, secundum ordinem octo tonorum sibi succedentium, quos infusa aqua facile moderabar. Aqua enim si ultra medietatem vitri talis ventricosi assurgit, exigua quantitate tonum deprimit, infra medietatem maiori etiam quantitate tonum vix variat. Digitum madefactum per oram superiorem vitri unius fortiter gyrabam, et intense sonabat, aqua crispabatur:[4] vitra caetera, quae tonum tertium vel quintum ad hoc exhibebant, leniter etiam aquam crispabant, ut vix deprehendi posset: vitrum quod octavum vel eundem tonum repraesentabat, fortius aquam commovebat, aliis licet vitris interpositis, quorum aqua quiescebat, quod diversum haberent sonum. Sic nuper cum hic Londini experimentum facere vellem, an tubae sonitu rumpi vitrum posset, cum tuba accurate vitri sonum referre non posset, aquam infudi vitro usque dum tonum haberet, quem assequi tubicen poterat, et accurate observavi ad sonos harmonicos tremere et sonare vitrum, ad eundem crispari satis sensibiliter aquam, ad octavum adeo vehementer commoveri, ut guttulas aqueas undequaque extra vitrum spargeret; nec dubito aliqua sui parte rumpi potuisse vitrum, si continuare tonum per aliquod tempus tubicen potuisset. Pertinere etiam huc videtur, quod saepe in conclavi, ubi multi alta voce colloquuntur, aut instrumenta Musica audiuntur, observaverim ad aliquorum voces et certos quosdam tonos lenem et tenuem motum, vel in sedili, vel in mensa, vel in pavimento, extra vero hos sonos vel tonos, nullum. quod fieri potuit, quoniam aliqua harmonia inter sonum vocis vel instrumenti, et ligni fuit, ex quo sedile vel mensa confecta: nam et hoc si exsiccatum, sonum aliquem habet, quamvis obtusum. (5) quod octavus tonus majorem vim ad frangendum vitrum habuerit: est enim pulsus aeris fortior et acutior. (6) quod ruptura vitri circularis fuerit, et ad terminum soni stringentis contigerit. Causa rupturae alia certi nulla est, quam quod vitrum, cuius minima omnis viscositatis expertia, per solam ignis violentiam compacta, ob fragilitatem illam tam vehementi aeris motui ex omni parte, resistere nequeat. Videmus enim idem accidere vitro ad dilatationem et constrictionem subitaneam aeris. Hinc iam plura experimenta fieri possent. (1.) an ad duorum vel trium voces citius rumpatur poculum vitreum. (2.) an cum aqua infusa rumpi possit: quod non facile crediderim, de inferiore parte vitri, qua aqua continetur: aqua enim motum vitri sua densitate impediret; nec afficeretur ea parte vitrum ob diversitatem soni, qui tantum inter spatium a superficie aquae ad summum vitri circulum agitatur. (3) an instrumentis Musicis, quae inflantur, idem effici possit: tuba ego tentare volui, sed non potui reperire vitrum, cuius tonum assequi potuerit tubicen; reliqua instrumenta Musica ad frangendum vitrum vix erunt apta. (4) an non si iusta sit harmonia 4 vocum citius frangatur vitrum. (5) an vasa fictilia eodem modo rumpi possint, et posse credo: quanquam hiatus major pororum vastiorem aliquem et magis fortem quam acutum et clarum sonum pro ruptura requirere videatur. Metalla ob eorum lentorem non rumpentur. (6) annon moles majores ex calce, lapidibus, arena, ita firmiter compactae, ut sonum aliquem habeant, sono, certa proportione intenso rumpi possint. Et fieri hoc nonnunquam observamus in fornicibus et muris, qui bombardarum majorum sono rumpuntur. et praecipue quidem fornicibus, qui ob cavitatem et compactionem firmam sensibiliorem sonum habent. Memini, in Patria mea collapsos aliquando fornices in templo, Organo Musico vicinos. Ac retulit mihi nuper Clarissimus Willisius cum experimenti huius mentionem facerem, hic Londini in aliqua domo Musica cvcrsum aliquoties fuisse pavimentum; quod ille efficaciae soni adscribere non dubitabat.

Habes hic, Nobilissime Domine, mea de hoc Experimento tam visa quam cogitata, quae tam tuo, quam Illustris Senatus iudicio lubens volensque submitto. Vale. Dabam Londini e Museo meo d. 3. Novembris Anno 1670.

Celeberrimi tui Nominis Cultor deditissimus
Daniel Georgius Morhofius D. Pr.[5]

TRANSLATION

Most noble Sir,

As we met recently and amid other conversation on matters of natural philoso-phy I mentioned some experiments about the breaking of glass by a very loud noise of which I was an eyewitness in Holland, and you earnestly begged me to consign an account of this [to paper] so that the matter might be laid before the Royal Society and examined further,[1] I am now eager to obey your commands, the more so because the matter is very worthy of being debated before the tribunal of your illustrious Council.[2] When I was at Amsterdam I was told by Jodocus Pluimer, a bookseller, of a certain tradesman who could shatter drinking glasses, even large ones, by singing. At first the thing seemed absurd to me. He asserted that he had seen it done many times, and among many witnesses named the Grand Duke of Tuscany, a visitor to Amsterdam last year, to whom he had himself brought this man, who was sent away with an ample reward after the thing had succeeded. Such copious evidence deserved all credence. Led on by desire for knowledge, I did not hesitate to ask the bookseller to take me to him to discern the reasons for this experiment. He took me to the man, whose name I now forget,[3] but he lived, if I remember rightly, near the Lutheran Church. He [the tradesman] brought out four or five round-bellied glasses with knobs on the foot of the kind used here for drinking Rhine wine, which the Germans call rummers, holding about a pint of the Dutch measure, so that I might choose one for the trial. I examined them all carefully to see if there was perchance any cheat. But all of them seemed sound, and I selected one of them that seemed solid. He then sum-moned his son, who was to break it, declaring that he was himself unfit for the task because catarrh had made his voice hoarse and indistinct. I held the glass in my hand, inclined a little away from the singer's mouth so that his voice should strike the lower part of the belly, for thus he directed me. First he tested the note of the glass, which, if I remember rightly, sounded in A. When the boy sang on this note the glass rang a little, but did not [respond] to other notes, except that when he happened upon harmonics I seemed to feel a slight motion in the glass. Finally when the boy sang with the note of the octave the glass rang very loudly at the same pitch, so much as to cause a rattle and vibration that I could feel in my hand. And when the boy went on singing with his mouth wide open on a high-pitched, continuous note for the period of six or seven musical beats, so that the glass never stopped ringing, it broke at last around the lower part of the belly where it joined the foot, in an oblique circle, the break passing through the fore-most of the knobs on the foot where the glass was thickest, after making just such a sound as glass always makes when intense heat or cold shatters it. I tried a few times to see if I could imitate him, but the attempt was vain for my voice was thick and unsteady with the strain, until in the end I succeeded with a thinner glass.

These are the points that seemed most noteworthy in this experiment: (1) That the glass was round-bellied, for thus the circulation of the sound is greater and the motion more violent. (2) That the mouth was placed opposite the lower part of the belly, for in ascending obliquely the impetus of the sound is greater and in the tight circle of the glass about the foot the motion created by the sound is more violent. (3) That the mouth was opened wide, for thus the aerial pulse was made wider and more diffuse. (4) That the glass only rang or was moved at the harmonic tones; the true reason for this is still hidden from me. Here I can allege an almost identical experiment. I set up eight drinking glasses each following the other in pitch like the notes of an octave, which I easily adjusted by pouring in water. For if water rises more than halfway up such a round-bellied glass a slight quantity lowers the pitch, but below the middle even a larger quantity hardly alters the pitch. I ran a damp finger round the mouth of one glass very forcibly, so that it rang strongly and the water became wrinkled;[4] the other glasses whose pitch was the third and the fifth of this also wrinkled the water in them slightly, but barely detectably; the glass representing the same tone, or the octave, disturbed its water more markedly, although there were other glasses between whose water remained still because their pitch was different. And so recently here in London when I wished to make trial whether a glass could be broken by the sound of a trumpet, as the trumpet could not be made to match the pitch of the glass exactly I poured water into the glass until it had a note that the trumpeter could attain, and I observed that the glass rang and vibrated accurately at the harmonics, the water wrinkling pretty plainly at the same sounds, being so violently disturbed at the octave that drops were scattered all about outside the glass. And I have no doubt that the glass would have broken at some point if the trumpeter could have maintained the note for some time. It also seems relevant here that I have often observed, in a chamber where many people speak in high voices or musical instruments are listened to, a slight and feeble motion in the seats, or in a table or in the floor, [associated] with the voices of particular individuals or certain particular tones and not otherwise. This could be produced by some harmony between the note of the voice or instrument and the wood of which the seat or table is made, for when it is dry this has a tone of its own, though a dull one. (5) That the octave had a greater force for breaking the glass, for the aerial pulse is stronger and sharper. (6) That the break in the glass was circular and occurred at the limit of the sound's impact Certainly the cause of the fracture is none other than this: that the glass, being wholly devoid of viscosity from its formation by the violence of fire alone, cannot because of this fragility resist such a violent movement in the air coming from every side. For we see that the same thing happens to glass when the air is suddenly dilated or compressed. Hence now several experiments can be made: (1) Is the drinking glass broken more quickly by two or three voices? (2) Can it be broken after water has been poured into it? This I find hard to believe as regards the lower part of the glass containing the water, for its density would obstruct the motion of the glass, nor would the glass be affected in that part because of the difference in the tone, which vibrates only in the space between the surface of the water and the rim of the glass. (3) Can the same thing be done with wind instruments? I wanted to try this with a trumpet but could find no glass whose pitch the trumpeter could attain; the other musical instruments seem less suitable for breaking glasses. (4) Whether if it were exact a harmony of four voices would fracture the glass more quickly? (5) Can earthenware vessels be broken in the same way, as I think they can? Though their greater porosity seems to require for breaking a sound that is full and strong, rather than sharp and clear. (6) Can greater masses composed of lime, sand, and stones so firmly compacted together that they have a certain tone be broken by a sound of a certain intensity? And particularly some vaults which because of their hollowness and close structure have a perceptible sound. I recall in my own country that vaults have collapsed in churches, close to the music of an organ. And the famous Mr. Willis told me lately, when I mentioned this experiment, that sometimes here in London the floor of a house where music [was played] was destroyed, and he did not hesitate to attribute this to the power of sound.

Here you have, most noble Sir, both my observation of this experiment and my reflections upon it, which I cheerfully and willingly submit to the judgment of yourself, and of your illustrious Council. Farewell.

London, from my study, 3 November 1670

> The most devoted adherent of your name,
> *Daniel Georg Morhof* D. Pr.[5]

NOTES

Daniel Georg Morhof (1639–91), born at Wismar, studied at Szczecin (Stettin), Rostock, and Oxford (1660). In 1660 he became Professor of Poetry at Rostock, moving to a similar chair at Kiel in 1665, where he became Professor of History in 1673. This was his second journey to the Netherlands and England. Morhof was an extremely prolific writer and translator, and a close friend of Vogel, who mentions him in Letter 1498. For a further note on Morhof's stay in England, see *Notes and Records*, XI (1954), 42–44.

1 In fact Morhof himself presented this account to the Society on the same day, 3 November. It was ordered that the experiment described should be attempted, but at the meeting of 17 November Hooke could report only that a man's voice had caused a glass to ring.

2 Some years later Morhof printed an account of this affair himself: *Epistolam ad J. D. Majorem de scypho vitreo per certum vocis humanae sonum . . . rupto* (Kiel, 1672).

3 It appears from Morhof's tract that his name was Nicolaas Petter.

4 Morhof means, of course, that (as we should say) standing waves formed on the water; but he seems to have had a very imprecise notion, if indeed any, of the relation between periodic vibration and audible sound.

5 "Doctor primarius" perhaps, although other interpretations are possible.

1543
Wallis to Oldenburg

3 November 1670

From the original in Royal Society MS. W 1, no. 114

Oxford. Novemb. 3. 1670.

Sir,

Yours of Nov. 1. I receive this morning. What concerns Mr Awbrey is answered allready.[1] The Probleme is either a pitiful one, or pitifully worded. 'Tis possible hee may mean yt ye 10 squares shall be all equal: & ye 4 cubes likewise: & perhaps that those & these should have ye same root. But there is no such thing in ye words of ye Probleme. And had it been so, I should scarce have meddled with it, as being a busynesse of more time than ye thing is worth. And those of France have sufficiently examined mee allready: 'tis time now that they give mee leave to mind my own busynesse. What concerns Mr Hugens, I do not much question but hee will satisfy himself.[2] But the thing is intricate, & will require attention: & will need to be read more then once. But the truth is, I have been detained abroad ye greatest part of ye summer by the sickness of friends:[3] & now at home by an ill companion, a severe quartan Ague, which seized me presently after I came home; (& I know not whether it wil give mee leave to make an end of this letter, for I expect a 7th visite by & bye) So that I have not had yet so much time as to read it over since it was printed,[4] to collect ye typographicall errors. The two books I have. That of Bartholine I have not so much as looked into.[5] That of Fabry,[6] I have part of (somewhat of what concerns Borelli:) but not all; onely some part of ye 2d dialogue: wherein I am not at all satisfyed with his objections agt Borelli, so far as I have read. But my Ague takes up so much time, & doth render me so indisposed for busynesse, that I can scarce either write or read an hour together with attention: so yt it will be ye longer ere I can give you a full account of it.[7] If you print yt of Mr Childrey, with my answere;[8] it will be expedient (where I refer to what I had written to you in a former letter, about ye Moones Perigaeum &c) to insert in ye Margin, somewhat to this purpose: [viz. in the Latine copy of ye letter of . . . (the English of wch is printed in Transact. . . .) in which are these words, . . .] for in the English they are not: & you will find them in a Marginal insertion of my Original

Latine.[9] You may if you have occasion present my humble service to Myn Heer Constantine Hugenius van Zulichem: who when hee was heretofore in Oxford,[10] gave mee a very civil visit with testimony of great respect upon ye account of my acquaintance with his son. Sir, I must break off when I have told you yt I am

Your most affectionate friend & servant
Joh. Wallis

When you se Mr Collins, desire that he would get ye Printers to make hast: For I would not willingly have it a Posthumous work; but see ye end of it. But possibly, if this ague continue, I must fain to crave his help to draw my schemes for mee; for it renders mee allready very indisposed for busynesse; & will do dayly more & more. I would write to him myself; but writing begins to grow troublesome.

ADDRESS
These
For Mr Henry Oldenburg in the
Palmal near St James's
London

POSTMARK NO 4

NOTES

Reply to Letter 1541.
1 See Letter 1539.
2 See Letter 1537, p. 217 above.
3 That is, close relatives, the word *family* at this time usually signifying one's household and servants.
4 Part II of *Mechanica*.
5 See Letter 1490 and its notes 3 and 4.
6 This volume of *Dialogi physici* was no doubt that sent from Paris by Vernon; see Letter 1484, p. 62. There is a notice of it in *Phil. Trans.*, no. 67 (16 January 1670/1), 2057–59.
7 See Letter 1559.
8 On Childrey's "Animadversions" (printed in *Phil. Trans.*, no. 64 (10 October 1670), 2061–68), see Vol. VI, Letter 1425. Wallis's reply is Letter 1429 (Vol. VI).
9 It seems that Wallis must refer to Letter 807 (Vol. IV), printed in *Phil. Trans.*, no. 33 (16 March 1667/8), 652–53. But in the Latin version of this letter (Royal Society MS. W 1, no. 41) there is no such insertion, nor anything very clear about the moon's apogee. The brackets were placed by Wallis.
10 Constantijn Huygens the elder (1596–1687) had first visited Oxford in 1618 (when

Wallis was two!) and again in 1622; he made another visit to Oxford in 1664, and referred to his meeting with Wallis then in a letter of 1 July 1668 [N.S.] (J. A. Worp, *Die Briefwisseling van Constantijn Huygens*, Vol. III, The Hague, 1917, p. 233 and note 3).

1544
Adam Martindale to Oldenburg
4 November 1670

From the original in Royal Society MS. M 1, no. 63
Partially printed in *Phil. Trans.*, no. 66 (12 December 1670), 2015–16

Rotherston in Cheshire November 12th 70[1]

Sr,

Though my genius leads me to spend my vacant hours rather in Mathematicall, then Mercuriall or Physicall studies; yet I am so great an honourer of the workes of Mr Boyle & others of your (truely called) Royall Society who have improved ordinary things to such high and unusuall advantages for Mankind, that I could not well refraine giving you this briefe hint following. A gentleman of good account and reputation assures me that in our County there is lately found out a very great raritie (as it is here accounted) viz a rocke of naturall salt from which issueth a vigorous sharpe brine, beyond any of the springs made use of in our saltworkes, And this not nigh unto any river or great brooke as all our saltsprings in this Countrey are: but in a wood farre distant from any such Running water.

I should scarcely have adventured to doe thus much had I not met with somethings in your Philosophicall transactions (and particularly the flaming well neare Wigan in Lancashire)[2] with which I was very well acquainted, but did not judge either so strange if a considering person had the weighing of the selfe evidencing causes, nor perhaps so usefull towards the filling up of some blank corner of a page in the History of nature as this poore discoverie may prove to be. However I expect that such ingenuitie as possesseth (I am assured) every member of that admirable societie cannot but pardon my boldnesse, arising from a zeale to serve such benefactours to humane nature; and if you desire to know any further concerning it a post letter directed to the post-master of Knutsfford for me shall command me to view the place to enquire out all knowable circumstances & to communicate the particularities to you. Or if it be the credibilitie of my reports that you stick at, because altogether unacquainted with me My Lord Delamer (Now at the Parliament)[3] or any of his servants can give you a character of me. The rest is onely that I am

Sr your humble servant though unknowne
Adam Martindale

ADDRESS

These
To the worthy Secretary
of the Royall Societie
at Gresham-Colledge
London

NOTES

Adam Martindale (1623–86) had been a preacher at Manchester and vicar of Rostherne until his ejection for nonconformity in 1662, after which he remained in the same village as an unlicensed preacher and teacher of mathematics at Warrington and Manchester. He had met John Wallis on a visit to Oxford in 1668.

1 The village is now known as Rostherne; it is three miles north of Knutsford, which is fifteen miles south-west of Manchester. The date on the letter has been altered (and appears in the same form in the *Philosophical Transactions*) but is clearly incorrect since Oldenburg received the letter on the tenth at Arundel House where he read it at the meeting on the same day. Birch gives the date from the minutes as 4 November.

2 See *Phil. Trans.*, no. 26 (3 June 1667), 482–84; the account was by Thomas Sherley, for whom see Vol. I, p. 98, note.

3 George Booth (1622–84), first Baron Delamer, an active royalist. Martindale, who had supported Booth's rising on behalf of the King in 1659, became his Chaplain in 1671.

1545
Oldenburg to Huygens

8 November 1670

From *Œuvres Complètes*, VII, 46–47
Copy in Royal Society MS. O 2, no. 35
Original in the Huygens Collection at Leiden

Monsieur

J'ay bien receu la faveur de vos deux lettres, l'une du 15. Octobre par la main de Monsieur Morhovius, amateur de la philosophie Experimentelle; l'autre, du dernier Octobre, un jour devant l'arrivee de Monsieur vostre Pere, que i'estois tres-aise de voir icy, et quantité d'autres personnes avec moy. J'ay mené ce professeur d'Holstein à nostre Assemblee,[1] où il raconta l'experience, qu'il avoit veue à Amsterdam, d'une certaine maniere de rompre un verre par la force de la voix humaine, surpassant d'une octave le ton du verre qui se doit rompre. On l'essayera icy à la premiere commodité, quoyque la chose nous vienne si bien attestée, qu'il n'y ait presque point de lieu de doubter de sa verité.

Vous avez tres bien fait de ne vous avoir pas hazardé a voyager dans cete saison, estant si ieune convalescant, quoyque nous eussions esté ravis de vous voir, si l'estat de vostre santé l'eut permis. Et ie croy, que vos Medecins vous blameront fort de ce que vous feuilletez des traitez, comme ceux de Monsieur Wallis et Monsieur Barrow, qui demandent une singuliere attention. le premier de ces deux personnes scavantes combat à present à Oxford avec une fievre quarte, qui le traite rudement, a ce que ie viens d'entendre par sa lettre.[2] Il vous salue tres affectueusement, et dit, qu'il ne doubte pas, que vous ne vous satisfassiez vous mesme touchant son probleme du Centre de gravité de la Spirale; adjoustant avec cela, que la chose est embarassante, et demande application, et la lecture reiterée.

On fait astheur imprimer icy les figures de Saturne comme elles ont apparues a Monsieur Hevelius, et à Monsieur Hook;[3] dont ie vous envoieray une copie, quand elles seront achevees d'inprimer. Il me souvient bien, que ie vous ay dit cy-devant, que nous ne pouvions rien affirmer precisement de la Lunette de 50 pieds pour Saturne, par ce que nous ne l'avions examinée sur ce planete que legerement et à la haste, et dans un meschant tube; mais non pas, que ie sache, qu'elle n'estoit bonne que pour la Lune.

Celle-cy viendra accompagnée de la seconde partie des Experiences de

Monsieur Boyle touchant la Respiration, qui ne vous desplairont pas, ie croy.[4] Je pense, que Monsieur vostre Pere aura soin de vous envoyer ses autres petits traitez, dont ie fis mention dans ma precedente,[5] comme aussi de quelques echantillons de verre pour des lunettes, qu'on fait icy à Lambeth avec approbation.

j'ay desia receu deux assez gros pacquets de lettres, pour Monsieur de Monceaux, mais non pas avec l'addresse de Monsieur Grubendol, comme vous la luy aviez donnée, et comme ie l'eusse souhaitée, mais avec celle de mon nom. Je ne manqueray pas de le servir icy à mon possible, et particulierement de le faire conoistre a Monsieur Wren, qui sera bien aise de l'entretenir sur le sujet de l'Architecture de la Perse etc.

Je ne scay pas, Monsieur, si vous conoissez un certain Docteur Leibnitzius à Mayence, qui est conseiller de cet Electeur, mais avec cela se mesle fort de la philosophie, principalement des speculations de la nature et des proprietez du mouvement. Il pretend d'avoir trouvé les principes mesmes des regles du mouvement, que les autres dit il, n'ont données que simplement, sans demonstrations a priori. Doubtant fort, si vous avez rien vû de luy sur ce sujet, ie vous feray part de ce qu'il m'a depuis peu envoyé dans une lettre sur cete matiere ce que ie vous donneray dans ses propres paroles;[6]

Je ne doubte nullement, Monsieur, que ie ne vous aye lassé aussi bien que moy mesme. Cependant, puisque le sujet est important a toute la physique, et mesme l'autheur semble avoir examiné tout ce qu'on a publié la dessus, i'ay crû, que vous seriez bien aise de voir ses meditations, vû principalement qu'elles divertissent l'esprit plustost que de le gener. Si vostre santé vous le permet de communiquer vos pensees sur le tout, ce pourra estre une occasion d'esclaircir la matiere d'avantage. Mais ie ne presse rien; ie vous assure seulement, que ie suis du meilleur de mon coeur Monsieur

Vostre tres humble et tres obeissant serviteur

H. Oldenburg

A Londres le 8 de Novembre 1670.

TRANSLATION

Sir,

I have indeed received the favor of your two letters, that of 15 October [N.S.] by the hand of Mr. Morhof, a lover of experimental philosophy, and the other, of the last of October [N.S.], a day before the arrival of your father, whom I with many other people was delighted to see here. I conducted the Holstein professor to our meeting,[1] where he described the experiment he had seen in Amsterdam of a certain way of breaking a glass by the force of the human voice one octave higher than the pitch of the glass to be broken. It will be tried here at the first convenient opportunity, although the thing reaches us so well attested that there is hardly room to question its truth.

You have acted very rightly in not risking travel at this season, being so recently convalescent, although we should have been overjoyed to see you if the state of your health had permitted it. And I think that your physicians will scold you severely for leafing through treatises like those of Mr. Wallis and Mr. Barrow, which require particular attention. The first of these learned men is at present in Oxford, struggling with a quartan fever which is treating him harshly, from what I have just learned from his letter.[2] He greets you very affectionately and says he has no doubt but that you will satisfy yourself about his problem of the center of gravity of a spiral, adding to this that the treatment is perplexing and requires application and repeated reading.

At the moment the drawings of Saturn as it appeared to Mr. Hevelius and to Mr. Hooke are being printed;[3] I shall send you a copy when they are printed off. I well remember that I formerly told you that we could not say anything exact about the fifty-foot lens for Saturn, because we had only examined it for that planet slightly and hastily and in a poor tube, but not, that I know, that it was only useful for the moon.

This letter will come accompanied by the second part of Mr. Boyle's "New Pneumatical Experiments about Respiration," which will not, I think, displease you.[4] I believe that your father will take care to send you his other little tracts which I mentioned in my preceding letter,[5] as also some samples of optical glass which is made here at Lambeth and well thought of.

I have already received two pretty big packets of letters for Mr. de Monceaux, but not with the Grubendol address which you gave to him and as I should have wished, but with my name. I shall not fail to be as useful to him as possible, and in particular to make him known to Mr. Wren, who will be very glad to discuss with him Persian architecture and so on.

I do not know, Sir, whether you are acquainted with a certain Dr. Leibniz of Mainz, who is a Councilor of the Elector there but with that concerns himself greatly with philosophy, principally with speculations on the nature and properties of motion. He claims to have found the very principles of the rules of motion which others (so he says) have only given simply without *a priori* demonstrations. Being very doubtful whether you have seen anything of his on this subject I shall let you share in what he recently sent me in a letter of this subject, which I shall give you in his very words:[6] [...]

I have no doubt, Sir, but that I have fatigued you as well as myself. However, as the subject is of importance for all natural philosophy and, besides, the author seems to have examined everything that has been published on the subject, I thought that you would be very pleased to see his thoughts, especially since they divert the mind rather than fatigue it. If your health permits you to communicate your reflections on the whole subject this will be an opportunity to clarify it advantageously. But I urge nothing; I simply assure you that I am, most heartfeltly, Sir,

Your very humble and obedient servant,
H. Oldenburg

London, 8 November 1670

NOTES

Reply to Letters 1531 and 1537.
1 See Letter 1542 and its note 2.
2 Letter 1543.
3 See the plate with *Phil. Trans.*, no. 65 (14 November 1670), figs. 2 and 3.
4 See Letter 1525, note 7.
5 See Letter 1525.
6 Oldenburg here inserted a slightly edited version of Letter 1524, beginning at the same point but ending with the words " ... tam vehementes exerceantur" (on p. 165). This version is printed in *Œuvres Complètes*, VII, 48–50.

1546
Oldenburg to Wallis

8 November 1670

This is the date of the reply to Letter 1543, as given by an endorsement on that letter and by Wallis's acknowledgement in Letter 1558. It announced the arrival of a Swiss visitor to Oxford, and the sending of the last *Transactions*, no. 64 of 10 October.

1547
Malpighi to Oldenburg
10 November 1670

From the original in Royal Society MS. Malpighi Letters I, no. 7
Printed in Pizzoli, pp. 56–57

Eruditissimo et Praeclarissimo Viro
Domino Henrico Olemburg Regiae Societatis Anglicanae Secretario
Marcellus Malpighius S.P.

Transmissis tandem meae historiae exemplaribus Domini Passerini ope
sum potitus,[1] et Regiae Societatis, tuique benevolentiae perpetuum
testimonium admiror. Bombycis enim historiam, licet inconcinnam, non
tantum luce donare voluistis, sed et eximiam vestrum omnium erga me
munificentiam testari publice non distulistis. Laetor testiculorum intestinula
ab Acuratissimo Domino Graaf transmissa, apud te extare:[2] In Locustis
absque ullo labore caecorum hujusmodi congeries, ablato exteriori involucro patet, et Pisis olim indicante Domino Claudio Uberio Lotharingio in
Apro saepius vidi, et publica etiam extat tabula, ut nil amplius haesitandum
videatur.[3]

Gaudeo, Praeclarissimi Mengoli librum de parallaxi ad vestras devenisse
manus,[4] in cujus confirmationem alia meditatur idem Auctor, et quamprimum luce fruentur. Audio, apud nos sub prelo Clarissimi Cassini Apologiam
in eundem librum extare una cum Domini Montanarij epistola circa idem
argumentum, quas quamprimum ad te dirigam.[5]

Elapso Maio librorum fasciculum ad Dominum Franciscum Teriesi
florentinum Mercatorem, Londini comorantem transmisi,[6] eorumque
indicem peculiari inclusum epistola publico Tabellario consignavi,[7] sicut
et librum Domini Mengoli de Musica,[8] nec adhuc tamen tibi redditum
fuisse persentio.[9] Libros a famigeratissimo Domino Boyle, et alijs postreme
editos avide exopto, et praecipue tractatum de Catharris Exercitatissimi
Domini Lowerij, quem meo nomine salutare ne dedigneris. Clarissimi
Suuamerdami librum etiam de insectis, cuius elegantissimas vidi figuras,
summopere desidero; et interim tanto Viro ob honorificam mei, quam
refers, mentionem non parum debeo. Nobilissimus Dominus Zanus[10] ex
Hispania redux paucis diebus domi conquiaevit, sed iterum caepto itinere

Germaniam petiit. Mei, ut tui mos est, amare perge, diuque incolumem literariae Reipublicae commodo te serva.
Dabam Bononiae die 20. Novem: 1670 [N.S.]

ADDRESS
 Eruditissimo et Praeclarissimo Viro Dno. Henrico
 Oldemburg Regiae Societatis Angli. Secretario
 Londini

TRANSLATION

Marcello Malpighi presents many greetings to the very learned and famous Mr. Henry Oldenburg, Secretary of the English Royal Society

Thanks to Mr. Passarini I have at last obtained the copies of my *History* that were sent [to me],[1] and I admire this everlasting testimony of the Royal Society's generosity, and your own. For you not only chose to publish the *History* of the silkworm, inelegant as it was, but did not refrain from making known the remarkable munificence of all of yourselves towards me. I am glad that you have the little internal tubes of the testes, sent by the very accurate Mr. De Graaf.[2] Without any effort a mass of hidden parts of this kind appears in locusts when the outer coating is removed, and formerly at Pisa, under the direction of Mr. Claude Aubry of Lorraine, I often saw [them] in the boar, and there is also a published picture extant, so that there seems no further reason for doubt.[3]

I am glad too that the very distinguished Mengoli's volume on parallax has come to your hands;[4] the same author is working on other things in order to substantiate that book, which will soon be brought to light. I hear that there is in press here the famous Cassini's *Apology* on behalf of the same work, together with Mr. Montanari's letter on the same subject, [both of] which I shall send you as soon as possible.[5]

At the end of May I sent a parcel of books to Mr. Francisco Teriesi, a Florentine merchant living in London,[6] and enclosed a list of them in a special letter which I entrusted to the public post,[7] as also Mr. Mengoli's book on music,[8] but I have as yet had no hint of their reaching you.[9] I eagerly long for the volumes published recently by the most renowned Mr. Boyle and others and especially the very experienced Mr. Lower's treatise *De origine catharri*; you will be so good as to greet him from me. I am also very anxious to have the famous Swammerdam's book on insects, whose very pretty illustrations I have seen, and in the meantime I am much indebted to so great a man for his flattering reference to myself, which you mention. The very noble Mr. Zani[10] has returned from Spain and is resting at his home for a few days, but he plans to begin another trip into Germany. Continue to love me as your custom is, and may you long enjoy good health for the good of learning.

Bologna, 20 November 1670 [N.S.]

ADDRESS

To the very learned and famous Mr. Henry
Oldenburg, Secretary of the English Royal Society
London

NOTES

Reply to Letter 1488.
1 See Vol. VI, Letters 1265, 1368, and 1450.
2 See Vol. VI, Letter 1244; this news must have been conveyed to Malpighi in Letter 1259, now lost.
3 Claude Aubry (or Aubery) had been brought from Padua to the University of Pisa in 1657 (see Adelmann, pp. 152 ff.), accompanied by his prosector, Tilman Trutwin (see Vol. II, p. 587, note 9), a man very highly regarded for his practical skill who remained long in Tuscany. Malpighi and Borelli agree in stating that it was at G. B. Borelli's house that Aubry first demonstrated the "tubular" structure of the testis, in 1658. It was accordingly he who published, under the anagrammatic name "Vauclius Dathirius Bonglarus," the "Florentine sheet" first mentioned by Timothy Clarke (see Vol. V, p. 270), which Oldenburg had reprinted in *Phil. Trans.*, no. 42 (14 December 1668), 843–44 (see Vol. V, p. 272, note 4). The original figure was reproduced in the accompanying plate. De Graaf's description was much superior to Aubry's.
4 See Letter 1470, note 2.
5 We could find out no more about these apologia.
6 Compare Letter 1470, where the same merchant is mentioned. The parcel had arrived by the beginning of November (see Vol. VI, Letter 1450, note 9).
7 Vol. VI, Letter 1450.
8 Both Letters 1450 (Vol. VI) and 1470 say, on the contrary, that this work (*Speculazioni di musica*) was not yet available. Possibly Malpighi was thinking of the same author's book on parallax, which did arrive separately.
9 Oldenburg did not write to Malpighi between 15 July and 20 December.
10 See Vol. VI, Letter 1372, note.

1548

Sluse to Oldenburg

12 November 1670

From the original in Royal Society MS. S 1, no. 66
Partially printed in *Phil. Trans.*, no. 97 (6 October 1673), 6119–22
Printed in Boncompagni, pp. 648–53

Nobilissimo et Clarissimo Viro
D. Henrico Oldenburgh Regiae Societatis Secretario,
Renatus Franciscus Slusius Salutem

Ut ad iucundissimas tuas respondeam quas nuper admodum accepi, cum variis de rebus agant, ab illa incipiam quae mihi statim in oculos incurrit: ab Alhazeni, nimirum Problemate, cuius constructionem a Viro Nobilissimo[1] ad vos transmissam ut vidi, protinus eandem esse cum mea suspicatus sum; sed inspectis Adversariis meis, non leve discrimen reperi ut mox videbis: et iam sane vidisses nisi me prolixitas antehac a scribendo deterruisset. Nequid tamen dissimulem, cum Nobilissimi Hugenii constructionem ad calculos revocarem, eandem omnino mecum analysim secutum esse deprehendi, sed cum ex illa duae nascantur effectiones, utraque per hyperbolam circa asymptotos, ille unam, ego alteram, uti faciliorem selegeram. Evidens est autem nihil aliud quaeri hoc Problemate (si illud ad terminos mere Geometricos revocemus) nisi in dato circulo, (cuius centrum *A*, radius *AP*) punctum aliquod ut *P*, a quo ductis ad puncta data *E B* inaequaliter a centro *A* distantia, rectis *PE PB*, recta *AP* producta bisecet angulum *EPB* [*Fig. 1*]. Quod quidem varios casus recipit. Vel enim

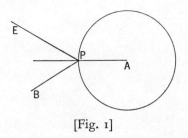

[Fig. 1]

normalis ex *A* in rectam *EB*, nimirum *AO*, cadit inter *E* et *B*, vel ultra

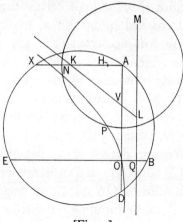

[Fig. 2]

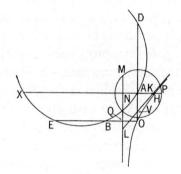

[Fig. 3]

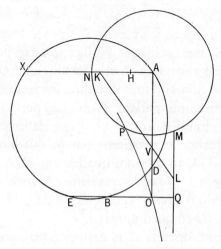

[Fig. 4]

B. Si ultra, vel rectangulum *EOB* aequale est quadrato *AO*, vel maius, vel minus. De casu aequalitatis videbimus infra: nunc vero tres alios casus eadem fere constructione complectemur. Per tria puncta *AEB* transeat circulus, ad cuius circumferentiam producatur *AO* in *D* [*Fig. 2*]. Ac siquidem punctum *O* cadat inter *E* et *B*, recta *AO* versus *O* producenda erit: sin autem ultra *B* [*Fig. 3*], sitque rectangulum *EOB* maius quadrato *AO*, producenda erit versus *A*: at si rectangulum quadrato minus fuerit, circulus in ipso puncto *D*, rectam *AO* secabit [*Fig. 4*]. Tum ducta *AX*, parallela *EB*, secante circulum datum in *N*, fiat ut rectangulum *DAO* ad quadratum *AN*, ita $\frac{1}{2}AX$ ad *AH*, quae sumenda erit versus *X* si *O* cadat inter *E* et *B*, aut rectangulum *EOB* minus sit quadrato *OA*, at ex parte contraria, si sit maius. Ponatur nunc *OQ* aequalis *AH* (in directum *EB* primo et secundo casu, tertio vero versus *E*) tum fiant proportionales *XA*, *NA*, *HK*, sumenda omni casu versus *X*: sectaque *AO* in *V*, ut sit eadem ratio *KA* ad *AV*, quae *AD* ad *AX*, iungatur *KV* ac producatur donec occurrat rectae *QM* parallelae *OA* indefinite productae in puncto *L*. Erunt omni casu *KL* et *QL* asymptoti hyperbolae, quae per punctum *O* descripta, proposito satisfaciet. Hoc tantum discrimine, quod primo et secundo casu hyperbola per *O*, Problema solvet in speculo convexo, sectio vero ei opposita in concavo. At 3° casu contra, hyperbola per *O* serviet concavo, eius opposita convexo. Atque id quidem cum punctum *V* cadit inter *A* et *O*; nam si ultra *O* caderet, unica hyperbola inter easdem *QL KL* descripta tam speculo convexo quam concavo satisfaceret. Caeterum si *V* caderet in ipsum punctum *O*, Problema tunc planum esset, et ipsae rectae *LQ LK* illud absolverent. Unde patet Problematis huius dari casus infinitos qui per locum planum[2] solvi possunt, quo magis venia digni videntur *ij*, qui illud per eundem locum universe solvi posse censuerunt, quod ipsis aliquoties calculus feliciter cecidisset. Nulla enim dari potest trium punctorum *AEB* positio (de casu aequalitatis rectanguli *EOB* et quadrati *OA* mox videbimus) quae non admittat circulum aliquem ex centro *A* describendum, ad cuius circumferentiam Problema per locum planum solvi queat. Huius autem circuli radius, si tanti est, ita invenietur. In primo et secundo casu superioris constructionis fiat ut quadratum *AX* una cum duplo rectangulo *OAD*, ad duplum quadratum *AD*, ita quadratum *AO* ad quadratum *AN*, erit *AN* radius quaesitus. At in 3° casu, faciendum est ut quadratum *AX* minus duplo rectangulo *OAD*, ad duplum quadratum *AD*, ita quadratum *AO* ad quadratum *AN*.

    Construendus nunc superest alius casus, aequalitatis nempe rectanguli *EOB* et quadrati *AO*, sive in quo circulus per puncta *A*, *B*, *E*, descriptus tangit rectam AO. Recte autem monuit Clarissimus Hugenius hoc casu describendam esse parabolam, quod tamen non ita intelligendum est quasi per hyperbolam solvi non possit, cum et Hyperbolam et Ellipsim, imo infinitas (si quis methodo mea uti velit) admittat: sed quod parabolam quoque recipiat, quam alii casus respuunt. Eadem ratione temperandum est quod ait constructionem suam omni casu quo Problema solidum est, locum habere: intelligit enim levi mutatione semper inveniri hyperbolam quae proposito serviat, quod casus a nobis superius constructos cum eius constructione comparanti planum fiet. Ut autem ad casum aequalitatis redeam, et ne quid temere asseruisse videar, ecce tibi non unam, sed duas parabolas, ac praeterea hyperbolas oppositas quae propositum absolvunt. Sint ut prius puncta data $E B$, circulus ex centro A, ac alius per tria puncta AEB, cuius tangens sit AO, centrum D [*Fig. 5*]. ducta diametro $NADX$

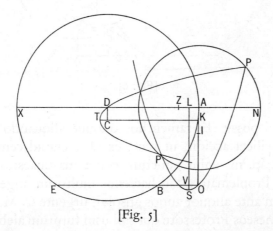

[Fig. 5]

fiant tres proportionales XA, NA, ZA, cuius dimidium sit AL. Fiant iterum tres proportionales $2OA$, NA, IA, cuius dimidium sit KA et perficiatur rectangulum $LAOV$, productaque LV in S, donec VS sit tertia proportionalis ipsarum AI, OV; axe SL, latere recto AI, vertice S, describatur parabola. haec enim circulum secabit in punctis PP quaesitis. Tantunden faciet alia, si perfecto rectangulo $DAKC$, et producta KC in T, ita ut CT sit tertia proportionalis ipsarum AZ, DC, describatur circa axem TK, vertice T latere recto ZA; occurret enim circulo in iisdem punctis PP.[3] Facilior adhuc est constructio per sectiones oppositas. factis enim, ut prius, tribus proportionalibus XA, NA, ZA, demittatur ZI normalis, tertia proportionalis duplae AO, et AN [*Fig. 6*]. erit itaque ZI maior ZA, cum dupla AO minor sit XA: Tum in puncto I, inclinentur utrinque

angulo semirecto ad lineam *IZ*, rectae *IQ*, *IM*, et ab utraque parte indefinite producantur: demum circa illas tanquam asymptotos describatur per
A hyperbola, et alia ipsi opposita: haec enim satisfaciet Problemati in
speculo convexo: illa in concavo. Cum vero, ut ostendimus, *ZI* semper
maior sit recta *ZA*, recta *IM* nunquam transibit per *A*. Non dabitur itaque
casus, quo ex hac constructione velut in praecedentibus, Problema per ipsas

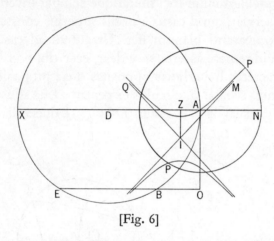

[Fig. 6]

asymptotos solvi possit. Et tamen hoc quoque aliquando locum planum
admittit: cum scilicet accidit, ut recta ex *O* ducta ad centrum *D* tangat
circulum *NPP*. ipsum enim punctum contactus quaestionem solvit. Et
hoc quidem de Problemate quod hactenus multorum ingenia exercuit, et
cuius solutionem ante aliquot annos absolvi, urgente C. M. V. Gutiscovio
Lovaniensi Matheseos Professore qui sibi usui futurum aiebat.⁴ moliebatur
enim nescio quid in Catoptricis: sed mors manum iniecit; neque enim (ut
hoc obiter addam) quidquam huiusmodi in schedis eius repertum esse
intellexi.

    Laudo eruditorum illorum consilium, qui lingua vernacula Opticam
tradere meditantur.⁵ Sed frustra a me petis quem potissimum autorem
vertere debeant, cum ex illis quos enumeras, nullum me videre contigerit
praeter Tacquetum, atque hunc valde leviter, cum eum non a multis diebus
acceperim. Crederem tamen ex omnibus conflandam novam synopsim,
selectis iis quae maxime ad rem faciunt, et vinculo Geometrico colligatis.
Prolixioris operae res esset, sed, meo iudicio, utilioris. In Tacqueto enim
ipso, quem prae aliis laudari audiveram, pleraque obiter animadverti quae
brevius explicari possent. Sed id viri illi ingeniosi omnium optime dispi-
cient, cum caeteris melius lectorum captum ac genium norint.

Occasione Tacqueti patere, quaeso, ut a te petam quid de propositione ipsius 39 libri primi Optices,[6] viris doctis videatur, in qua demonstrare satagit circulum oblique spectatum nunquam apparere ut circulum. Scio quidem ipsum addere, ut directe spectatum, et notare discrimen, quod in hoc non diametri modo sed etiam semidiametri aequales appareant, in illo nequaquam. Sed eodem argumento concludi posse videtur, lineam rectam oblique spectatam non apparere ut lineam rectam, nempe directe spectatam, cum si bifariam secta intelligatur, hoc casu partes eius aequales appareant, illo inaequales. Ac video quidem quid reponi possit, sed volo ἐπέχειν donec tuum ea de re iudicium intellexero.

Libri quibus me donatum Tu et Clarissimus Collinsius voluistis, nuper ad me pervenerunt, ac pro munere tam grato utriusque humanitati plurimum debere me profiteor. Illos hactenus legere mihi non licuit variis occupationibus distracto: imo Clarissimi Wallisii librum ne attigi quidem sed evolvendum per otium mihi seposui, quod temporis plusculum requirere existimem. At in Clarissimi Barrovii Lectionibus, quanquam ad finem nondum pervenerim, praeclara multa et auctore digna observavi, et non mediocriter in primis sum gavisus, eandem ipsi occurrisse ducendarum tangentium methodum, qua olim usus fueram. Verum in aliam mecum incidet longe faciliorem, et quae vix ullam calculi molestiam requirat, si paulo ulterius eadem via progressus fuerit. Ut verbo absolvam μοναχός tangens, maxima et minima, unum idemque sunt.[7] Gratulor interim Viro Clarissimo novae dignitatis accessionem quae aditum, ut spero, patefaciet ad maiora. Caeterum miseret me Geometriae, cuius fatum esse videtur, ut ab illa potissimum abstrahi soleant qui eam maxime promovere possent. Ad reliqua Epistolae tuae Problemata alia occasione mihi respondendum esse video, tum quod meditationem requirant, qualem nunc adhibere per occupationes non licet, tum etiam quod iam in scribendo modum excesserim, et vereor ne me ἀπεραντολογίας accuses. finem itaque faciam solenni formula testatus me semper virtutis tuae observatissimum esse. Vale. Dabam Leodii 22 Novembris 1670 [N.S.]

P.S.

Pene oblitus eram monere me P. Laloverae librum Amstelodamum misisse.[8] Distuleram per aliquot hebdomades, quod ex Nundinis Francofurtensibus vel ex Gallia interim aliquid me adepturum sperarem: sed frustra, nihil enim comparuit. quo magis indignor mihi inutilem fuisse hanc moram, quam tamen ut boni consulas, rogo, nec mihi imputes sed librariorum nostrorum ignorantiae dicam an τῃ ἀπειροκαλίᾳ, quod mandatis tuis tam male satisfaciam. Ne tamen Lalovera solus esset, libellum meum adiunxi, cui si aliquem in bibliotheca tua angulum concedere velis, omne punctum tulisse videbor. Expectantur hic brevi Caramueli Opera Mathematica⁹ Lugduni Galliae nuper simul edita, quae si cupias, verbulo indica, statim enim transmittam. Addo, literas tuas 24 Septembris 1669 datas cum adiuncta C. Wallisii epistola,¹⁰ quarum apographum ad me miseras, ab aliquot septimanis mihi redditas esse. Ubi tamdiu haeserint, coniectura assequi non possum.

Scire cuperem an vobis notus sit liber cui titulus Antoniana Margarita, auctor Gometius Pereira editus in Hispania ante centum et quod excurrit annos.¹¹ Is sane vel a Cartesio visus fuit, vel Cartesius saltem, in easdem cum illius auctore, de natura animalium et animae immortalitate cognitiones incidit. Sed jam plus satis. Iterum Vale.

ADDRESS

A Monsieur

Monsieur Grubendole
      Londres

Franc par Anvers

TRANSLATION

René François de Sluse greets the very noble and famous Mr. Henry Oldenburg, Secretary of the Royal Society

In order to reply to your very agreeable letter that I received quite recently, as it treats of a variety of topics, I will begin with that which struck my eyes at once, that is to say the problem of Alhazen, for as soon as I saw it I suspected that the construction sent to you by that very noble person¹ was completely identical with my own. But when I examined my notebooks I found no mean discrepancy, as you will soon see; and you surely would have seen it already if [my] prolixity had not deterred me from writing before this moment. Yet to conceal nothing from you, when I reduced the construction of the very noble Huygens to calculation I discovered that he had followed just the same line of analysis as myself; but, as two means of effecting [the solution] present themselves as a result, each by a hyperbola upon asymptotes, he chose one as the easier to use and I the other. It is obvious however that there is nothing sought for in this problem (if we reduce it to merely geometrical terms) other than a certain point P on a circle whose center is A, radius *AP*, from which two lines *PE*, *PB* are drawn to the points *B* and *E* at unequal distances from the center, such that the straight line *AP* produced may bisect the angle *EPB* [*see Fig. 1, p. 246*]. And this may be divided into a number of cases.

For the normal from *A* upon *EB*, *AO* that is, falls either between *E* and *B*, or beyond *B*. In the latter case the rectangle *EOB* is either equal to the square *AO*, or greater, or smaller. We shall see about the case of equality later; for the present we can embrace the other three cases within an almost identical construction. Let a circle pass through the three points *AEB*, to the circumference of which let *AO* be produced at *D* [*see Fig. 2, p. 247*]. Now if the point *O* falls between *E* and *B*, the straight line *AO* is to be produced in the direction of *O*; but if it falls on the far side of *B* [*see Fig. 3, p. 247*] and if the rectangle *EOB* is greater than the square *AO*, it must be produced in the direction of *A*. But if the rectangle is less than the square the circle will cut *AO* at the very point *D* [*see Fig. 4, p. 247*]. Then drawing *AX* parallel to *EB*, cutting the given circle at *N*, make

$$DA . AO : AN^2 = \tfrac{1}{2}AX : AH.$$

H must be placed towards *X* if *O* falls between *E* and *B* or the rectangle *EOB* is less than the square *OA*, and on the opposite side if the rectangle is greater. Now make *OQ* equal to *AH* (in the direction of *B* in the first and second case, but in the third case towards *E*) then set out the proportional lines *AX*, *AN*, *HK*, to be taken in each of the cases towards *X*; and dividing *AO* at *V* so that

$$AK : AV = AD : AX$$

join *KV* and produce it until it meets the straight line *QM* produced indefinitely and parallel to *OA*, in the point *L*. In each case *KL* and *QL* will be the asymptotes of a hyperbola which, when drawn through the point *O* will satisfy the proposition. Only make this distinction: in the first and second cases the hyperbola through *O* solves the problem for a convex mirror, and its opposite branch solves it for the concave mirror. But it is otherwise in the third case, where the hyperbola through *O* serves for the concave mirror and its opposite branch for the convex. And this is when the point *V* falls between *A* and *O*; for if it should fall beyond *O* a unique hyperbola described between the same asymptotes *QL*, *KL* would satisfy both the concave and the convex mirror. Moreover if *V* should coincide exactly with *O* the problem is a two-dimensional one solved by the lines *QL* and *KL* themselves.

Whence it appears that there are an infinite number of [special] cases of this problem which can be solved by plane loci,[2] which makes it easier to excuse those who thought that a universal solution by the same locus was possible, because sometimes such a calculation came out successfully for them. For there can be no position of the three points *A*, *E*, and *B* (we shall soon examine the case where *EO.OB* = *OA*^{2}) which does not allow of some circle's being drawn with center *A*, for whose circumference the problem can be solved by plane loci. The radius of this circle, if it is worthwhile, may be found thus: In the first and second cases of the construction above make

$$(AX^2 + 2OA.AD) : 2AD^2 = AO^2 : AN^2$$

and AN will be the radius required. But in the third case one must make

$$(AX^2 - 2OA.AD) : 2AD^2 = AO^2 : AN^2.$$

Now it remains for us to construct the remaining case, when $EO.OB = AO^2$, or that in which the circle described through the points A, B, and E is a tangent to the straight line AO. The very famous Huygens correctly proposes here that a parabola be described, but this is not to be taken as though a solution by a hyperbola is impossible, because [the problem] admits of [solution by] both hyperbola and ellipse, indeed infinite numbers of them, if one makes use of my method; but this case admits of the parabola too, which the others do not. For the same reason, when he says that his construction has a locus in every case where the problem is a three-dimensional one, he is to be understood as meaning that with a little alteration it is always possible to find a hyperbola which will satisfy the proposition, as will be clear when the cases constructed by myself above are compared with his construction.

But to return to the case of equality: so that I may not seem to have spoken rashly, here are not one but two hyperbolas for you, and opposite hyperbolas besides, which solve the proposition. As before, let the two given points be E and B, the circle with center A, and another with center D passing through the three points A, E, and B, to which AO is a tangent [*see Fig. 5, p. 249*]. Having drawn the diameter $NADX$ make three proportional lines AX, AN, AZ, half of the last being AL. Then make three more proportionals $2OA$, NA and IA, half of the last being KA; complete the rectangle $LAOV$ and produce LV to S until VS is a third proportional to AI and OV. With axis SL, latus rectum AI, vertex S describe a parabola, which will cut the circle at the points P, P, which are required. Another parabola will do just as much, if, after completing the rectangle $DAKC$ and producing KC to T so that CT may be a third proportional to AZ and DC, a parabola be drawn with axis TK, vertex T, and latus rectum ZA; for it will intersect the circle at the same points P, P.[3] But a construction by opposite branches of an hyperbola is still easier. As before, let three proportional lines be drawn AX, AN, and AZ and let ZI be erected as a perpendicular being a third proportional to $2OA$ and AN [*see Fig. 6, p. 250*]. So ZI will be greater than ZA, because $2OA$ is less than AX. Then at the point I let the straight lines IQ, IM be inclined at $45°$ on either side of IZ and produced indefinitely either way; finally, let a hyperbola be described through A having these lines as asymptotes, and the opposite branch also; for the one satisfies the problem for a convex mirror, the other for a concave. Since, as we have shown, ZI is always greater than ZA, the line IM never will pass through A. Accordingly the case will not arise in this construction where the problem can be solved by the asymptotes themselves as it could in earlier ones. And yet this does sometimes admit of a plane locus too, that is to say when it happens that the straight line drawn from O to the center D is a tangent to the circle NPP. For this point of contact itself solves the question. And so for this problem which has exercised the ingenuity of so many in the past, and whose solution I worked out a few years ago at the request of the famous Mr. Van Gutschoven, Professor of Mathematics at Louvain, who said it would be of use to him in the future.[4] For he was then working on something or other in catoptrics, until Death took a hand; and I have not heard (I may add by the by) of anything of this kind being found in his papers.

I approve of the opinion of those learned men, who think of putting optics into the common tongue.[5] But you ask of me in vain which author they should turn to by preference, for of those you list I have chanced to see none but Tacquet, and him very glancingly as I have not had the book many days. But I should imagine that a new synopsis ought to be made by conflating them all, choosing what is best for the purpose, and binding the whole together by geometry. It would be a longer task but to my mind more useful. For even in Tacquet himself, whom I have heard praised above others, I have noted many things here and there which could be explained more succinctly. But those ingenious men will have the best view of things, as among other things they are better acquainted with the knowledge and understanding of the readers.

Speaking of Tacquet, please tell me what your learned friends think of Proposition 39 in Book I of his *Optics*,[6] in which he strives to prove that the circle, seen obliquely, never appears as a circle. I know that he adds, as seen directly, and makes the distinction that in the latter case the radii as well as the diameters appear equal, whereas in the former [indirect] case they do not. But by the same argument it seems possible to conclude that a straight line seen obliquely does not appear as a straight line (seen directly), because if it is supposed to be bisected in the latter case [direct] the halves appear equal whereas in the former case [indirect] they do not. But I see too what reply can be made, though I prefer to pause until I have learned your opinion of the question.

The books of which you and the famous Mr. Collins wished to make me a present reached me recently, and I confess myself much indebted for so welcome a gift and for your kindness. Busied as I am in various affairs it has not yet been possible to read them; in particular I have not yet touched the celebrated Mr. Wallis's book but set it aside to peruse at my leisure, because I think it will need much time. But I have remarked many splendid things, worthy of their author, in the lectures of the famous Mr. Barrow, though I have not yet got to the end; I was expecially delighted that the same way of drawing tangents has occurred to him, which I have used in the past. He may indeed come upon another one, much easier and requiring scarcely any tedium of calculation, as I did, if he will continue a little further along the same track. To conclude with one word: *monachos*, tangent, maxima and minima, are one and the same thing.[7] Meanwhile I congratulate this distinguished person on a new accession of dignity which may, I hope, lead the way to greater ones. For the rest I lament the fate of geometry, which seems to be that those generally desert her who are best able to promote her interests. I see that I must reply to the rest of the problems in your letter on another occasion, both because they require reflection which my occupations prohibit my giving to them now, and because I have already written too much, so that I fear you will accuse me of an endless flow of words. So I make an end with the customary expression, testifying myself to be always a most devoted admirer of your merits. Farewell.

Liège, 22 November 1670 [N.S.]

P.S.   I almost forgot to give you notice that I had sent Fr. La Loubère's book to Amsterdam.[8] I delayed for some weeks because I hoped meanwhile to obtain something from the Frankfurt Fair or from France; but in vain, for nothing appeared. I am the more annoyed because this delay proved useless to me, which I beg you to forgive, and not to impute it to me but rather to the ignorance of our booksellers, I might almost say their philistinism, that I obeyed your wishes so ill. So that La Loubère should not be quite by itself I have added my little book; if you choose to grant it some corner in your library I shall be very satisfied. Caramuel's *Opera mathematica*,[9] recently printed in a collection at Lyons, are expected here shortly; if you wish for them, say the word and I will send them at once. I add that your letter of 24 September 1669, with one from Mr. Wallis attached,[10] of which you sent me copies, was delivered to me a few weeks ago. I cannot guess where they had so long stuck fast.

I would like to know whether you are acquainted with a book whose title is, *Antoniana margarita*, by Gomez Pereira, printed in Spain more than a century ago.[11] It was surely seen by Descartes, or at any rate Descartes hit upon the same notions of the nature of animals and of the soul's immortality as its author. But I have already said too much. Farewell again.

ADDRESS
>   To Mr. Grubendol
>   London

Postfree to Antwerp

NOTES

Reply to Letter 1528. A copy by Collins in Newton's possession is in CUL MS. Add. 3971.1, 13v–16r.

1   Huygens.
2   That is, by the intersection of a straight line and a circle; solid loci require the use of conics.
3   Actually each parabola intersects the circle in four points, but only two are useful solutions, one for the concave mirror and one for the convex.
4   Gérard van Gutschoven (1615–88) studied with Descartes, whose amanuensis he was, and then returned to his native Louvain to take a medical degree (1635). He suc-

ceeded Sturmius in the chair of mathematics (1640) but transferred to a medical "sofa" (anatomy, surgery, and botany) in 1659. He was also a Canon of Ghent Cathedral.

5 See Letter 1528, note 5.

6 For the work, see Letter 1528, note 7. Sluse actually refers to Prop. 34: "All the diameters of a circle seen from any oblique point *at a distance of one radius from its center* appear equal. Yet the circle in this case does not appear [the same] as a circle seen directly." Tacquet also states the corollary: "In no case can a circle seen obliquely appear like a circle seen directly," and otherwise as Sluse reports, but Sluse omitted the restriction italicized above in our translation.

7 Collins had seen this letter by December 1670 (Turnbull, *Gregory*, p. 146) and quoted this important passage to Gregory on 8 November 1672 (Turnbull, *Gregory*, p. 247). Sluse means, of course, that he has a general method of differentiation (to use anachronistic language).

8 See Letter 1507 *ad fin.*

9 A work of this title is not recorded, but Caramuel's *Mathesis biceps, vetus et nova* appeared at Lyons in 1670.

10 See Vol. VI, Letters 1284 and 1284a.

11 Gomez Pereyra (born at Medina del Campo, Spain, in 1500), who had qualified in medicine at Salamanca and was self-taught in philosophy, published *Antoniana margarita, opus nempe physicis, medicis ac theologis, non minus utile quam necessarium* at Medina del Campo in 1554. It anticipated Descartes in regarding animals as machines, without a "vital spirit." (See R. P. Miguel Sanchez Vega, "Estudio comparativo de la concepción mecánica del animal y sus fundamentos en Gomez Pereyra y Renato Descartes," *Revista de Filosofia*, Año XIII, 1954, pp. 15–68.)

1549
Oldenburg to Duhamel

12 November 1670

From the memorandum in Royal Society MS. H 1, no. 109

Rcc. le 22. May.
Promis. de luy envoier[1] ye late Tracts of M. Boyle, and N. 65.[2] and procure ye mony for his books [sent] to Collins or other Books.[3]

NOTES

Reply to Letter 1462. The date is derived from a further endorsement, but may be inexact as Oldenburg there says he received the letter on "May 31.70."

1 "Promised, to send him ... "

2 That is, *Phil. Trans.*, no 65 (14 November 1670), which contains an account of Duhamel's *De corporum affectionibus* (see Letter 1462, note 8).

3 In fact, Vernon paid Duhamel four livres five sous for the books, on Collins' behalf (see Rigaud, I, 139).

1550
Fermat to Oldenburg

15 November 1670

From the original in Royal Society MS. F 1, no. 49

A Tholose le 25me Novembre 1670 [N.S.]

Monsieur

Je n'ai pas voulu manquer d'avoir l'honneur de vous envoier un exemplaire du Diophante[1] desque l'impression en a esté achevée, Je voudrois bien qu'elle feut assès belle pour vous plaire, mais ie souhaitte encore plus, Monsieur, que les nouvelles observations que vous y trouverès plus considerables par le qualité que par la quantite et cet inventum novum Doctrinae Analyticae qui est au commencement aient vostre approbation qui ne peut que leur estre fort avantageuse, J'espere que vous aurès la bonté de m'apprendre quel est vostre sentiment ladessus et celui des sçavans de vostre illustre Academie,[2] J'attends cela avec impatience et ie ne doubte pas aussi que, si vous avès faict ou descouvert quelque chose de nouveau, vous ne soiès bienaise qu'on le scache en ce pais, Je vous coniure de croire qu'il n'y a personne qui aie pour vous plus d'estime que moi, et que je suis avec respect, Monsieur,

Vostre tres humble et tres obeissant serviteur
Fermat

ADDRESS
> A Monsieur
> Monsieur Oldenbourg Secre dela
> > Societè Royale
> > A Londres

TRANSLATION

Toulouse, 25 November 1670 [N.S.]

Sir,

I did not wish to lose the honor of sending you a copy of Diophantus,[1] as soon as the printing had been finished; I much wish that it may be handsome enough to please you, but I wish even more, Sir, that the new observations which you will find in it (and which are more notable for quality than quantity) and that new invention of an analytic doctrine which is at the beginning may receive your approval, which can only be to their advantage. I hope that you will be so good as to let me know your opinion of it and that of the learned members of your illustrious Society.[2] I await that impatiently, nor do I doubt that if you have done or discovered anything new you will be very glad to let us in this country know of it. I adjure you to believe that there is no one who esteems you more than I do, and that I am, with respect, Sir,

Your very humble and obedient servant,
Fermat

ADDRESS

Mr. Oldenburg
Secretary of the Royal Society
London

NOTES

1 The full title of the book is *Diophanti Alexandrini arithmeticorum libri sex, & de numeris multangelis liber unus; cum commentariis C. G. Bacheti, & observationibus D. P. de Fermat Senatoris Tholosani; cui accessit doctrinae analyticae inventum novum* (Toulouse, 1670). There is a brief note in *Phil. Trans.*, no 72 (19 June 1671), 2185.

2 It does not seem that Oldenburg presented the book to the Society; in fact, according to a letter from Collins to Gregory, "young Fermat sent one by the Lord Aylesburies man intended for Mr. Oldenburgh, but the fellow sold the Booke and spent the money" (Turnbull, *Gregory*, p. 179).

1551
Oldenburg to Martindale
15 November 1670

From the copy in Royal Society MS. O 2, no. 36

For Mr Adam Martyndale at Rotherton in Cheshire,
Recommended to ye postmaster at Knutsfort in Cheshire

London Nov. 15. 1670.

Sr

Your letter came to my hands Nov. 10. just at the houre of the meeting of the R. Society, to whom I communicated the contents there of, as soon as I had read it over. They gave mee order to returne you their hearty thanks, for your respect to them as well as for the accompt of the lately discovered rarity in those parts; as also to desire you, that if it may not too much divert or discommode you, you would please to gratify them in executing that offer, you have so obligingly made in your letter, wch is to view the place, and to inquire after, and observe the most remarkeable particulars at and about the salt rock, and to send us by caryer, or a freind, a peice of the same. Among those particulars, you will not omit to learne by whom, how long, and upon wt occasion it hath been found out? What kind of salt it is, wee shall easily know wn wee obtaine a specimen of ye Rock it selfe. It were worth while and to Philosophical purpose, to weigh a good lump of yt salt upon ye very place, as deepe as one can, and to weigh the same peice again at some distance, as also to observe whether it be colder in holes made in yt Rock of salt, than in the neighbouring Air? And one of our freinds wisheth, it might bee heeded here after, whether a part of this Rock being wasted, and a cavity made therein, it will in time bee filled up again.

you will also not omit to informe us, at wt depth this is underground? in whose possession it is? whether it be begun to be wrought, and if so wth wt successe?

And now, Sr, since you have declared your selfe to be so much a freind and well wisher to the Institution and designe of the R.S. let mee ask this further kindnesse of you, yt you would not think it a trouble to make constant Inquiryes into ye other curiousityes and Productions of Nature, wch yt countrey, wherein you reside, and the neighbourhood, may afford, and also to procure for us the practise of ye Cheshire Agriculture, Dairy,[1] brewing and the like, it being a great part of our designe to accumulate in our storehouse of Nature and art, wtsoever wee can meet wth, either in this or any other countrey yt may be referred to either, to ye end yt having obtained a faithfull History of both, yt may comprehend a competent stock of observations and Experiments, carefully made, there may here after by comparing and considering all together, be raised such a body of naturall Philosophy, as may give a rationall account of ye effects of nature, and enable men to inferr from confronted causes and effects, such deductions as may conduce to ye greater benefit, and better accommodations of human life.

Sr, your letters for mee, if hereafter they bee directed to mee at my house in ye Palmal, they will safely come to the hands of him, yt hath a great value for your franknesse and Ingenuity, and is Sr

your faithfull servant
H. Oldenburg

NOTES

Reply to Letter 1544.
1 Compare Vol. VI, Letter 1422 and its note 1.

1552
Oldenburg to E. Bartholin
15 November 1670
From the original in the Kgl. Bibliotek, Copenhagen, Boll. Brevs. U⁴, no. 730

Clarissimo et Doctissimo Viro
Domino Erasmio Bartolino, Mathematico Hafniensi
Henricus Oldenburg Salutem

Jam ante Tibi significavi, Vir Celeberrime, me munus tuum Islandicum juxta ac Philosophicum accepisse; eodemque tempore debitas pro eo gratias remisi. At cum Dominus Fogelius et Dominus Paisenius Hamburgo me nuper edocuerint, literas meas intercedisse[1] (quod valde me afficit) meum esse omnino duxi, mentis meae gratitudinem denuo Tibi contestari, simul et officiorum meorum reciprocationem offerre. Eximia illae esse agnoscimus, quae de lapido illo Islandiae Dis-diaclastico observasti, et commentationibus tuis locupletasti. Vestigatum nunc imus, Annon et alia quaedam corpora diaphana, eodem figurata modo, easdem apparentias sint editura?[2]

Domini Wallisii volumina duo, de Motu, et de Centro gravitatis etc; nec non Domini Barrovii Lectiones Opticas et Geometricas Hafniam pervenisse putem. Magni haec omnia fiunt ab omnibus subacti judicii viris, quibuscum hactenus de iis colloqui licuit. Eorum prior plurimam Tibi salutem remittit, et pro Experimentis tuis impressis maximas Tibi gratias reponit.[3] Cum febre quartana nunc graviter conflictatur, absque si esset, omni dubio procul, sua manu te salutasset, tuamque liberalitatem agnovisset. Interim laetantur Astronomi nostri, Te Operum Tychonis recensionem, Observationumque editionem, multo quam ante emendatiorem, curare; felicemque in operoso illo labore successum exoptant.[4]

Audio, Gallos quosdam Philosophos in eo laborare, ut nobis accuratam gradus coelestis in Terra quantitatem determinent: Fortasse et Angli nostri suam in ea re sagacitatem deproment.⁵ Dominus Boylius nuper insignia quaedam circa Respirationem Experimenta in No 62 et 63. Transactionum Philosophicarum edi curavit. Ea jam Hamburgum pervenisse credo; unde facile ad manus tuas incident. Haec sunt, quae per otium licet hac vice perscribere. Alias plura. Vale et Tui deditissimo favere perge. Dabam Londini d. 15. Nov. 1670.

Si me porro literis tuis honestare volueris, quaeso, eas tantummodo ad Dominum Paisenium cures, qui probe novit modum, eas porro ad me transmittendi.

ADDRESS
    Clarissimo et Doctissimo Viro
    Domino Erasmio Bartholino,
    Mathematico et Medico Hafniensi,
    Amico suo plurimum colendo.
            Hafniae

TRANSLATION

Henry Oldenburg greets the very famous and learned Mr. Erasmus Bartholin, Mathematician of Copenhagen

I have already informed you, famous Sir, that I have received your philosophical present from Iceland, and I returned you proper thanks for it at the same time. But as Messrs. Vogel and Paisen lately told me from Hamburg that my letter had got lost¹ (which annoys me very much), I thought it was altogether incumbent upon me to express my gratitude to you once more and at the same time offer an exchange of my services.

We confess that you have made some remarkable observations upon that double-refracting stone from Iceland, and enriched them with your commentary. We are now inquiring whether any other transparent substances of almost the same figure will yield the same phenomena.²

I think that Mr. Wallis's two volumes, on motion and the center of gravity, etc., will have reached Copenhagen, as also Mr. Barrow's *Lectiones opticae et geometricae*. All men of good judgment whom I have spoken to so far have a good opinion of them. The former [of these writers] sends you many greetings and repays you with his best thanks for your printed experiments.³ He is at present suffering from a severe quartan fever but for which he would, without doubt, have greeted you with his own pen and acknowledged your generosity. Meanwhile our astronomers are very happy that you are taking charge of an edition of Tycho's works and a publication of his observations which will be much more accurate than the earlier one; they wish you success in this heavy task.[4]

I hear that certain of the French are striving to determine more accurately for us the magnitude of a degree upon the Earth; perhaps our Englishmen may show some good sense in the same business.[5] Mr. Boyle has recently published in the *Philosophical Transactions*, nos. 62 and 63, some remarkable experiments on respiration. I believe that they have already reached Hamburg, whence they will easily come to your hands. This is as much as my leisure permits me to write at present. More another time. Farewell, and continue to think well of your most devoted. London, 15 November 1670

If you wish to honor me with a letter hereafter, please entrust it to Mr. Paisen, who knows very well how to send it on to me.

ADDRESS

> To the very famous and learned
> Mr. Erasmus Bartholin
> Mathematician and Physician at Copenhagen
> His very good friend
> > Copenhagen

NOTES

1 See Letter 1490 and its notes 4 and 5, and Letter 1498.
2 Although Hooke was asked to investigate the spar further, it does not appear that he (or anyone else) did so. On 29 September Collins had written to Gregory: "he [Bartholin] sent Mr Oldenburgh a small peece of it being a Parallel-ipipedon of an Inch square the base, and of an Inch height under which a Pin being laid, in one position it appeares two, in another foure, in a third Six, which strange unheard of Refractions, he [Bartholin] asserts he demonstrates" (Turnbull, *Gregory*, p. 107).
3 Compare Letter 1543.
4 See Vol. IV, p. 575, note 6.
5 It seems strange that Picard's work has not been mentioned earlier, since Oldenburg had known of it from the beginning of the year at least (see Vol. VI, Letter 1370 and its note 1). The English attempts amounted to nothing.

1553
Oldenburg to Vogel
15 November 1670

From the memorandum in Royal Society MS. F 1, no. 29

Resp. Nov. 15 1670. me inquisivisse in Toxicum.[1] me mittere No. 62 et 63. de respiratione,[2] et Basilum Valentinum Anglicum.[3] promisi Boyle de rarefactione Aeris.[4] petii ut de Historia Lynceorum me edoceat.[5] et me Transactiones vertere Latine.

TRANSLATION

I replied on 15 November 1670 that I had inquired after the arrow-poison;[1] that I was sending [*Transactions*] nos. 62 and 63 on respiration[2] and the English Basil Valentine.[3] I promised [him] Boyle on the rarefaction of air.[4] I asked him to tell me more about [his] history of the Lincei.[5] And that I am translating the *Transactions* into Latin.

NOTES

Reply to Letter 1498.

1 See Letter 1529.
2 That is, Boyle's experiments.
3 Recently there had appeared *The Last Will and Testament of Basil Valentine* . . . [etc.], translated by John Webster, containing also two other minor works; but some writings of this alchemist had been available in English since 1656.
4 The first tract in *Tractatus scripti a Roberto Boyle* . . . (London, 1670) was "Mira aeris (etiam citra Calorem) RAREFACTIO detecta." There were four short tracts in this volume, which appeared in English only in 1671.
5 See Vol. IV, p. 532, note 6. We should there have referred to a full study of Martin Vogel and his connection with the Lincei by Harcourt Brown, "Martin Fogel e l'Idea Accademica Lincea," *Reale Accademia Naz. dei Lincei, Rendiconti della Classe di Scienze morali, storiche e filologiche*, Ser. VI, Vol. XI, fasc. 11–12 (1935), pp. 814–33. Vogel's papers are now in the Leibniz Collection of the Lower Saxony Landesbibliothek, Hanover, whence we were courteously informed that no connected history of the Accademia dei Lincei appears extant among them now.

1553 bis
Oldenburg to Paisen
15 November 1670

This letter is mentioned in Letter 1633, Vogel's reply to Letter 1553, as accompanying a present of books to Paisen. Unfortunately it was sent after Paisen's death, which had occurred in October 1670.

1554
Flamsteed to Oldenburg
16 November 1670
From the original in Royal Society MS. F 1, no. 62

Derby No: 16: 1670

Mr Oldenburg:
Sir

I have now at lenght sent my praedictions of the next yeares appeareances into ye hands of my very good freind Mr Collins whom I have desir'd to commit them to yu with ye first occasion:[1] I beg your pardon that I have not put them immediately into yr hands, my freinds whom I trouble to convey them thought ye Pell mell too much out of theire way but no trouble to deliver them in Bloomsbury market.[2] else yu had had them first which I hope will scarce come the later to yu for passing through Mr Collins hands: They are done in such poore Latin as I have recovered lately wthout a tutor; which If yu find amisse expects as yu promised a castigation from yu: I had written an Epistle dedicatore to ye Royall Society to have been praefixed; but not haveing ye confidence to request such illustrious patronage to so poore tho troublesome a labor I praetermitted it. considereing that to appeare before them in yr hands would be a sufficient commendation. & my committeing them to so worthy a member a sufficient testimony of ye respect I beare & owe to that honorable corporation: Sr I request yu to receave them with yr usuall Candor, & desire yu would please to commend them to such of yr ingenuouse acquaintance as are studious of the heavens, to be more accurately observed then ye last,[3] in which I feare (praesiscini)[4] ye observators onely stood lookers on while ye appearances over slipt them: for I have not heard of any observation made except what came by yu & in those yu were pleased to communicate ye places of ye ingresse & emersion were not noted: If yu thinke I have beene long in produceing so poore a labor. I have for my excuse that, a 3 weekes sicknesse of ye common distemper & since an increase of businesse retarded my endeavours which else had seene yu long since. but yet I hope wil come in good time to yr hands. I leave them to be published or suppressed at yr discretion.

Sr I know not how I shall excuse my selfe for so long a silence as since I receaved so many favors from yu at London, and for deteining yr Hevelius all this time without yr further license.[5] truth is I intended not to write till I might put my calculations into yr hands, which being retarded by my sicknesse & otherwise, was put of till now. in the meane time I have had but little leasure to looke into Hevelius, except by intervalls & with lesse consideration. I intend now to reade him seriously thorow, & by Christmas I shall returne him with my sence upon him if yu can & shall permit me ye use of him till then. I cannot from that little I have seene in him, but esteeme him exceeding faulty. but because I may not judge at first sight I shall be silent concerneing him, till I made some second considerations. in the meanetime Sr with thanks for yr many civilities conferred extraordinaryly on all occasions with ye tender of my best services I rest

Yrs obliged to serve yu
John Flamsteed

Pray let me heare from yu on ye receipt of my papers.

NOTES

1 Flamsteed had completed his calculations by 1 October but could not tell whether to put them into English or Latin; the Letter with which he sent them to Collins is now missing (see Rigaud, II, 102–3). The predictions of lunar appulses for 1671 were published in *Phil. Trans.*, no. 66 (12 December 1670), 2029–34.
2 Where Collins lived.
3 "An Accompt of such of the more notable Celestial Phaenomena of the Year 1670, as will be conspicuous in the English Horizon" was published in *Phil. Trans.*, no. 55 (17 January 1669/70), 1099–1112.
4 Flamsteed confessed that his Latin was poor. Perhaps he meant to write *praesciscimini*, "you are forewarned."

5 On Flamsteed's visit to London, see Letter 1466, note 6. It would appear that he had borrowed Hevelius' *Selenographia* from Oldenburg during his visit; in a letter to Collins he declined a proposal that he might be presented with one of the copies that Oldenburg still had for sale, by the Royal Society (see Rigaud, II, 101).

1555
Oldenburg to Geminiano Montanari
19 November 1670
From the copy in Royal Society MS. O 2, no. 37

Clarissimo et Doctissimo Viro
Domino Geminiano Montanario Mathematico Bononiensi
H. Oldenburg Salutem

Munus geminum, tum manuscriptum, tum Tractatuum impressorum, quibus Societatem Regiam locupletare voluisti, nuper accepi, et in publico ejusdem consessu exhibui.[1] Non levi sane gaudio ipsa afficitur, dum Institutum suum, augendae solidae Philosophiae sacrum, tam cupide a Viro tam Docto collaudari sentit: mihique in mandatis omnino dedit, ut suo nomine debitas gratias tum pro libris impressis, tum pro docta circa stillatitium vitrum Dissertatione, nec non pro novis illis in coelo Observationibus, Claritati Tuae referrem, simul et de Uberrimo suo in Te et studia tua affectu certiorem Te redderem.[2] Commisit, more suo, dicta Societas scriptum illud, magno Hetruriae Duci consecratum, quibusdam e caetu suo philosophis perlegendum, qui summam ejus et animi sui de argumento illo sensa ipsi dehinc exponant. Praeterea mirandas illas de stellarum quarundam evanescentia observationes, Astrophilis quibusdam suis advertendas commendavit.[3] Cogitata vero tua Physico-Mathematica de liquorum in subtilioribus fistulis Adscensu,[4] caeteraque opuscula de septem Doctoris Rosetti Propositionibus,[5] typis evulgata cum sint, in omnium manibus nunc versantur, et doctorum ubivis sententias facile explorabunt. Convitia Rabulas, non Philosophos, decent, quaeque ijs scripta tumescunt, rationibus flaccescere solent. Talia nolimus mentem et studia tua a Firmamento illo tuo, quod moliris, adornando avocare. Communicavi, pace tua, quae de duabus stellis, non amplius apparentibus,

retulisti, Clarissimo Hevelio, Astronomo Dantiscano,[3] qui contemplandis
Astris magno sedulitate incumbit, inque machina sua caelesti, quam dudum
molitur, indefessa diligentia pergit. Asserit ille in literis nuper ad me scriptis[6] Novam illam stellam sub capite cygni, quae tertiae magnitudinis initio
videbatur, mirum in modum mense septembri decrevisse, nec. 14. Octobris
ulla ratione amplius sextante observari a se potuisse. De altera vero nova,
in collo ceti, notat, eam, ad medium usque mensis Octobris, magnitudine
propemodum aequalem extitisse Mandibulae Ceti, et claritate eam quasi
superasse, adeo ut hoc anno secundae magnitudinis extiterit, majorque
quam praecedentibus annis visa fuerit, excepto tamen Anno 1660, quo
majorem etiam ceti mandibula a se deprehensam fuisse affirmat, cum alijs
temporibus non meminerit, eam tertiae magnitudinis stellas superasse.

Adjicit idem 11. Oct. (st. n.) mane post solis ortum hora circiter octava
Dantisci apparuisse Conjunctionem Veneris et Lunae, quam calculus
Rudolphinus pariter eodem fere tempore indigitaverit, quo scilicet Luna
parte sui inferiore Venerem occultare ad 23″ minimum debebat: Ad quod
rarius spectaculum observandum, ait, se tubo 20. pedum se accinxisse,
atque aere licet non plane defaecato, nihilominus et Lunam et Venerem, sole
pariter jam orto, clarissime ad horam usque decimam conspexisse. Addit,
volupe omnino fuisse, jucundum illud Phaenomenon de die, soleque
splendente, adeo distincte ac dilucide contemplari; Lunam namque fuisse
tenuissam conjunctioni proximam, et valde corniculatam, Venerem vero
propemodum plenam, et corpore ad modum diminuto. Concludit, si Aer
non adeo extitisset vaporosus, se frequentius et accuratius Veneris et
Lunae a jove alijsque quibusdam fixis distantias capere potuisse; nunc vero
non nisi paucas observare sibi licuisse.

Num in Italia vestra idem Phaenomenon Observatum fuerit, scire
percuperemus. Intelligimus, Clarissimum Borellum suas de motu Animalium Meditationes;[7] Doctissimumque Milletum, Tabulas Geographicas
maris Mediterranei, nec non cursum Mathematicum in publicum edidisse:[8]
ad haec Michaelem Angelum Riccium, subacti judicij virum, multa sua
Italicis Ephemeridibus, Romae impressis, inseruisse:[9] Cum vero nulla
horum in oras nostras hactenus pervenerint, Bibliopolarum incuria,
rogatum Te velim, ut occasione commoda per navim aliquam Livornia huc
velificantem, dictos libellos mihi transmittere, meque vicissim ad similia
officia praestanda obligare digneris. Vale, Vir Eximie, et in virtutis ac
doctrinae tuae cultorum numero me semper habe. Dabam Londini die 19.
Novemb. 1670.

TRANSLATION

H. Oldenburg greets the very famous and learned Mr. Geminiano Montanari, Mathematician of Bologna

Your double gift of manuscript and printed books with which you have chosen to enrich the Royal Society I received of late and presented at the Society's regular meeting.[1] It felt no little joy on finding its object of advancing solid philosophy so eagerly commended by such a learned man, and gave me a firm direction to return your excellency in its name appropriate thanks not only for the printed books but also for the learned essay on glass drops, and for those new observations in the heavens, and that I should at the same time inform you of its great goodwill towards you and your work.[2] Following its normal practice the Society committed that paper which is dedicated to the Grand Duke of Tuscany to the perusal of certain among its philosophers, who will later convey to the Society a précis of it, and their opinion of its argument. Furthermore it commended those remarkable observations upon the vanishing of certain stars to some of its astronomers for their comment.[3] As your *Pensieri physico-mathematiche*[4] concerning the ascent of liquids in narrow pipes and the other work on the seven propositions of Dr. Rosetti[5] are now available in print and appear on every bookshelf, the opinion of the learned everywhere will easily be ascertained. Wrangling is for pettifogging attorneys, not for philosophers, and whenever a book is swollen with that, reason wastes away. We do not care for such things and would rather direct your studies to that "firmament" of yours, which you are striving to complete. By your leave, I have imparted what you have narrated about the two stars that appear no more to the famous Hevelius, the Danzig astronomer,[3] who is observing the stars with great persistence and continues with indefatigable diligence to press on with the *Machina coelestis* that now engages him. In a letter written to me recently[6] he says that that new star in the head of Cygnus, which at the beginning appeared of the third magnitude, decreased very strangely during the month of September, so that by 14 October he could no longer observe it at all with a sextant. Of the other nova, in the neck of Cetus, he notes that up to the middle of October it was nearly equal in magnitude to the star in the jaw of Cetus, and even surpassed it in brightness, so that this year it appeared as of the second magnitude, and as bigger than in previous years except 1660, when he says he discovered it to be even bigger than the star in the jaw, since he cannot recollect its surpassing third magnitude stars at other times.

He adds that on 11 October, N.S., in the morning after sunrise, about eight o'clock, there was seen at Danzig a conjunction of Venus and the moon, which the Rudolphine Tables had predicted for almost that time as giving an occultation of Venus by the lower part of the moon for at least twenty-three seconds; for the observation of this rare spectacle he had made ready, he says, his tube of twenty feet, and although the air was not absolutely clear, still he watched both the moon and Venus until ten o'clock, the sun also being above the horizon. He goes on to say that it was most agreeable to contemplate such a pretty spectacle in the daytime, with the sun shining, so clearly and distinctly. For the moon was very slender and horned, while Venus was practically full and much diminished in size. He concludes that if the air had not been so full of vapors he could have taken more frequent and accurate measures of the distances of the moon and Venus from Jupiter and some other fixed stars; now, in fact, he was able to observe only a few.

We are anxious to know whether the same phenomenon was observed in Italy. We have heard that the famous Borelli has given to the public his reflections on the motion of animals,[7] and the very learned Milliet de Challes some geographical tables of the Mediterranean Sea together with a *Cursus mathematicus*;[8] and further that Michelangelo Ricci, a man of most acute judgment, has inserted many of his things into the Italian journal published at Rome.[9] As none of these things has reached our part of the world as yet by the negligence of booksellers, I wish to ask you to send those books to me when there is a convenient opportunity of a ship sailing here from Leghorn, and to be so good as to demand similar services from me. Farewell, excellent Sir, and number me perpetually among the admirers of your merits and teaching.

London, 19 November 1670

NOTES

Geminiano Montanari (1632 or 1633–87), whose name and writings have been several times mentioned (see especially Vol. VI, Letter 1450 and notes, *passim*), had been since 1664 Professor of Mathematics at Bologna, where he was a close friend and associate of Malpighi's. He had previously studied law at Salzburg and Vienna, and been in the service of the Grand Duke of Tuscany and the Duke of Modena. He was a fairly prolific but not highly original author. In 1679 he left Bologna for a chair at Padua specially created for him.

1 See Vol. VI, Letter 1450; the books were presented to the Royal Society on 3 and 10 November, Oldenburg having mentioned them on 27 October.

2 For the letter and manuscript, see Vol. VI, Letter 1450, note 2. When Montanari's letter to the Royal Society of 20 April 1670 was read to the Society on 27 October, the manuscript on glass drops ("Prince Rupert's drops") was given to Sir Samuel Tuke and John Hoskins to peruse, translate, and report back. The translation was actually made by Thomas Henshaw, who presented it to the Society on 30 March 1671.

3 See Letter 1557 and notes. Montanari printed an account of his observations in *Prose de' Signori Accademici Gelati di Bologna* (Bologna, 1671), of which there is a long account, wholly devoted to this one topic, in *Phil. Trans.*, no. 89 (16 December 1672), 5125–28. Montanari apparently intended to publish a book called "The Inconstant Firmament" —hence the allusion to this word below.

4 See Vol. V, p. 240, note 9.

5 See Vol. VI, Letter 1450, note 14.

6 See Letter 1536.

7 This was a mistake; Borelli's *De motu animalium* appeared at Rome in 1680–81.
8 The book was Claude François Milliet de Chales, *Cursus seu mundus mathematicus* (3 vols.; Lyons, 1674). It does not seem that he published any separate maps.
9 The *Giornale de' Letterati* for 1670 does not, in fact, include anything from Ricci.

1556
Vernon to Oldenburg
19 November 1670
From the original in Royal Society MS. V, no. 15

Paris 9bre 29. 1670 [N.S.]

Sr

If you are not a little mercifull to mee in pardoning the slownesse of my returnes to your letters wch I extreamely value, I shall bee putt to a very great confusion for though nothing bee more in my desires then to bee punctuall in my correspondencies wth you.[1] Yet nothing is lesse in my power since as you know my imployment is rather worldly then Philosophicall. Yet if it should wholly deprive mee of some startes & stollen opportunities wch I make use of ever & anon, to returne to my old inclination & my most genuine delight Philosophy, I should hate it, more then I doe. those times then that I have of vacation from my businesse I spend in the conversation of those who are learned here & I spend them wth satisfaction: butt if I doe It not soe frequently as I would & if I am not able to answer your letters soe speedily & Regularly as you doe desire & as I could wish, since businesse is a necessary hinderance it must serve mee for a necessary excuse. Monsieur Picart (this Vacancy of the Royall Academie) hath beene in Picardie & hath finished those observations hee iudgeth necessary for his treatise of the measure of the Earth, wch is now pretty well advanced.[2] all his figures are cutt, wch was that part of it wch might most retard the edition, & by the beginning of next yeare it may bee published. It will bee a thinne folio of about some 50 leaves & I believe the world will bee well satisfied wth his exactnesse, for in nicitie and a most diligent examination of his measures certainly hee is to bee commended wch in the matter hee hath undertaken is the principall quality to bee desired.

I have a request to make to you in his name wch is the answer of this Quaestion, wch I desire you will procure from Mr Hooke or any other who is curious in Pendulums, wth what speed you can. for hee tells mee hee shall have need of it. these are his owne words.

"Longitudo Penduli simplicis, totidem secunda temporis medijs suis vibrationibus exhibentis, est iuxta mensuram Pedis Parisini pollicum 36 cum uncijs 8½, quaeritur quid conficiat, iuxta mensuram Anglicam."[3]

Soe that the whole of his question is only to know what the Length of a Pendulum is wch at every swing beates a second in English measure. the french measure hee hath putt downe in the quaestion. by his Pendulum simplex this hee meanes, pendulum simplex est quod componitur ex filo simplici, et sphaerula appensa.[4] that is a silken thread or some such like, for horse haire or stiff thread or lutestrings hee saith hath a spring wch something alters the time. the length of the thread, hee takes from the pin to wch It is fastned to the Center of the bowle[5] wch moves. his bowle is of brasse of an inch diameter. The Vibrations or swings hee would have little, not a great sweep. for those hee saith are more irregular. These explications are I believe superfluous to those who practise much wth pendulums, butt yet I venture to putt them downe to prevent all mistakes or ambiguities. Pray send the answer as soone as you can because hee telles mee hee shall stay for it. uncia (for I forgott that) is the 12th part of an inch.

Here I should give you an account of what new treatises are lately come forth. butt there are none of any very reputed Author. Here is a Capucine one Pere Cherubin who hath putt out a treatise of Dioptriques in folio.[6] there is enough of it & God knowes whether it bee good. There is another Fryar hath putt out a booke hee calles perspective affranchi I believe of the same stamp.[7] There is another volume of the Bizantine History putt out by Monsieur de Cange one very Learned in that kind, hee who writt is calld Cinnamus.[8] The same Monsieur de Cange is putting out a Lexicon of words des bas siecles, much like spelmans glossarium.[9] wch will bee Graeco & latino barbarum & I believe very ample & iudiciously written.[10] Monsieur Rohault is about putting out a body of Philosophy according to the Principalls of Monsieur Descartes wch is a worke of great expectation, because hee hath beene trained up in that Philosophy & is son in law to Monsieur de Clersilier who had Monsieur des Cartes his writings, soe that for that Philosophy hee hath the greatest meanes, if hee have equall partes to improve them.[11] I doe not specifie the new edition of Ferrarius Lexicon by Abbé Beaugrand much amplified & increased by about a third part, because I suppose there are many Copies of that sent into England by Muguet who printed it.[12] Nor Berniers Relation of the Indies for that I know you have.[13] Butt there is a piece lately come from Lions, written by one Gabriel Mouton, a secular Priest, de diametro Solis et Lunae, & the way of measuring by a Pendulum wch I believe will bee welcome in England.[14] as will Monsieur Claudes new Piece in answer to Arnaud, wch is printed & will shortly bee publique.[15] & Another Piece of Rabbinicall Learning wch Monsieur Ferrand is now about, wch is a history of Josephus Sacerdos, de Gestis francorum et Turcarum wch I am told will bee very curious in the kind.[16] Monsieur Nicoles booke the Jansenist del Education du Prince I believe you have & therefore will say nothing of it.[17] Out of Italy here are lately come to Paris of new Borellis treatise de vi Percussionis, wch you have long before had in England.[18] Marchetti a professor at Pisa de Resistentia solidorum.[19] Riccioli Chronologia reformata[20] a great Vast Bulke of Caramuel, Able to fill a Library. His Mathesis Biceps, speculative & Practicall 2 vol in Folio.[21] His Calamus 2 volumes more[22] & wch is worse hee is [not] contented wth the loade hee hath laid on the world already. but hee promiseth to Plague it wth I doe not know how many volumes more. Butt there is a Piece of more value, & lesse bulke preparing in Italy wch is the life of Galileo, & some letters of his wch will bee putt out by Sigre Viviani, but hee hath beene lately sick & that hath hindred ye edition.[23] Redi answer to Charras de Viperis I believe Monsieur Justell hath sent you.[24] butt what I hope will transcend all these new Pieces France I hope will furnish us wth, wch is the Diophantus of Monsieur Fermat wch is come out at Tholouse & I hope shortly wee shall have some Coppies of It here at Paris.

As concerning the Contents of what you demand of Monsieur Cassini, I should have answerd sooner butt that this Vacation hee hath beene out of Paris. However I spoke wth him two dayes agoe wch was the first opportunity I had of seeing, & as Concerning the Anse Saturni wch you writt mee word hee held were Round: Hee told mee hee had noe opinion concerning Saturne different from what Mr Huygens had published Concerning it, for hee found all his Hypothesis perfectly agree wth his observations.

As concerning Telescopes hee said that of 60 Palmes might have the Diameter of the Lens, some 5 inches, as the Charge.[25] hee said when there was one ocular glasse the Length of the Tube was 48. feet; when three glasses, 55. feet, & from thence you may gather the Charge. butt I understand from Monsieur Justel that Monsieur Auzout hath writt to him lately about Telescopes, wch hee I suppose will communicate to you, from whence you may have more full information. The Herball of the Royall Academie will come out next year, that is to say one volume.[26] in each volume they intend to have a 100 Plantes graven. 93 of these hundred are already finished, & the discourse quite made. Monsr Cassini tells mee his Ephemerides will bee out the beginning of the next yeare, they are begun to bee printed already.[27] the Kings observatoir wants butt two toyses that is 12 foot of the heigth it is to have. above the building they will rayse one tower 8 toyses high. they suppose[28]

ADDRESS

A Monsieur

Monsieur Grubendale

 a

  Londres

NOTES

1 The last written by Vernon was Letter 1513; we know nothing of Oldenburg's letters to him.
2 Compare Letter 1484 and its note 8.
3 "The length of the simple pendulum beating seconds with its mean vibrations is about 36 inches and 8½ lines, Paris measure; what is its length in English measure?" This was Huygens' measure also, and is equivalent to about 99½ cm.
4 "a simple pendulum is made up of a simple thread, with a little ball attached."
5 That is, ball.
6 P. Cherubin d'Orléans, *La Dioptrique Oculaire* (Paris, 1671) is reviewed at length in *Phil. Trans.*, no. 78 (18 December 1671), 3045–50.
7 There was published in Paris in this year *Optique de Portraiture & Peinture, contenant la Perspective Speculative & Pratique accomplie*, but the author was Gregoire Huret, Graveur du Roy.
8 Charles du Fresne, Sieur Ducange, had begun to publish in 1645 a *Corpus Byzantinae historiae*, of which the twenty-seventh and last volume appeared at Paris in 1702; in this series emerged in 1670 *Ioannis Cinnami historiarum libri sex seu de rebus gestis a Ioanne et Manuale Comnenis* . . . with a Latin translation and notes by Ducange. Cinnamus was a Greek historian of the twelfth century.
9 "Low Latin period"; see Sir Henry Spelman, *Glossarium archaiologicum: continens Latino-barbara, peregrina, obsoleta et novatae significationis vocabule* (London, 1664).
10 "on the Greek and Latin of the barbarians." The works were Ducange's *Glossarium ad scriptores mediae et infimae latinitatis* (Paris, 1678) and *Glossarium . . . graecitatis* (Lyons, 1688) which, revised, are still standard dictionaries.
11 See Jacques Rohault, *Traité de Physique* (Paris, 1671), the most successful textbook of Cartesian science, of which there is a long account in *Phil. Trans.*, no. 70 (17 April

1671), 2138–41. Rohault (1620–72) married Geneviève, second daughter of Claude Clerselier (1614–84), the leader of the Cartesian movement after the death of Descartes himself, and editor of his letters. It seems likely that Rohault (son of a wine merchant in Amiens) was "inducted" into Cartesian philosophy by Clerselier at an early age.

12 For Beaudrand's work, see Letter 1484, note 5 (this is the correct spelling).

13 See Letter 1484, note 11.

14 Gabriel Mouton, *Observationes diametrorum solis et lunae apparentium . . . Huic adjecta est brevis dissertatio de dierum naturalium inaequalitate* (Lyons, 1670).

15 Jean Claude, *Réponse au Livre de M. Arnaud intitulé, La Perpétuité de la Foy . . .* (Queuilly, 1670).

16 Louis Ferrand, *Conspectus seu synopsis libri hebraici qui inscribitur* [Hebrew] *Annales regum Franciae et regum domus Othomanicae* (Paris, 1670).

17 See Letter 1513, note 7.

18 It had been published at Bologna in 1667.

19 Alessandro Marchetti, *De resistentia solidorum* (Florence, 1669).

20 Published at Bologna in 1669.

21 See Letter 1548, note 9.

22 Juan Caramuel Lobkowitz, *Primus calamus ob oculos ponens metametricam . . .* (Rome, 1663); *Primus calamus, tomus II* (2nd ed.; Campania, 1668).

23 See Vol. V, p. 302, note 6.

24 *Lettera di Francesco Redi . . . sopra alcune opposizione fatte alle sue osservazione intorno alle vipere, scritta alli signori Abate Bourdelot . . . e A. Moro* (Florence, 1670) was reviewed in *Phil. Trans.*, no. 66 (12 December 1670), 2036–38, and was to be translated into English in 1673. For Charas' tract, see Vol. VI, Letter 1394, note 2.

25 The aperture.

26 See Vol. V, p. 22, note 3.

27 As already mentioned, we could not trace such a separate publication. However, Cassini did later communicate a score of immersions and one emersion of Jupiter's satellites for 1671, which were published in *Phil. Trans.*, no. 74 (14 August 1671), 2238.

28 The letter ends abrubtly at the foot of a page, the rest being lost.

1557
Oldenburg to Hevelius
21 November 1670

From the original in BN MS. N.a.L. 1641, ff. 16r–18r

Illustri et Perdocto Viro
Domino Johanni Hevelio Gedanensium Consuli dignissimo
Henricus Oldenburg Sal.

Ex novissimis tuis, Vir Celeberrime, ultimo Octobris ad me datis, colligo, Tibi meas, 8º Septembris[1] ad Te exaratas, et responsionemque ad binas tuas, 5. julij et 27. Augusti[2] mihi scriptas, ferentes, tum temporis nondum exhibetas fuisse. Complura ibi commemoraveram, quae ut scires tua interesse arbitrabar: inprimis quae spectant primam Observationem novae stellae infra Cygni caput, Variationem Magneticam, nuperam Impressionem librorum quorundam Physicorum et Mathematicorum. Nihil eorum in particulari hic repeto, cum de literarum mearum redditione vix dubitem. Maximas potius, Regiae nostrae Societatis nomine, gratias Tibi refero, quod tot Observationes insignes, tanta cura et ἀκρίβεια a Te institutas, una simul epistola Ipsi communicare voluisti. Eae in publico Consessu nuper praelectae, unanimem sociorum praesentium Applausam meruere; qui ut apud Te, literarum mearum beneficio, personaret, in mandatis protinus habui.[3]

Nobis non licuit esse, ob caelum nubibus obductum, adeo felicibus, ut vel Eclipsin Lunae, vel Conjunctionem Veneris et Lunae, observaremus. Tibi eo magis de Observationum tuarum felicitatae gratulamur; quodque reponamus, aliud non habemus, nisi mancam Deliquii istius Luneris Observationem, Romae habitam, et ab Amico mihi transmissam;[4] quae vult, Initium incidisse in h. 2.50′; durationem fuisse 2h 55′ vel 56′; quantitatem, 9¼ digitorum; Diametrum Umbrae apparuisse 90, minimum; Penumbram caepisse et finem habuisse plus quam ¼ horae, ante et post: Lunam conspectam fuisse sub caeruleam, quando vel 5. vel 6. digitorum Eclipsin patiebatur: Colorem Umbrae jugiter fuisse caesio-fuscum & nonnihil sub-rubentem: semper conspectos fuisse Lunae limbos clariores, et fere semper visas aliquot maculas. Dubito, an Domini Gottignes haec fuerit Observatio, cum quid accuratius a Viro tam celebri et perito sit exspectandum.

Dominus Hookius, ut ut observationi novae ad Cygni Rostrum stellae incubuerit mense Septembri, nihil ejus videre potuit. Fortasse alio tempore recurret in oculos; uti altera nova in Colli Ceti, singulis, ni fallor, annis occultare se et denuo comparere deprehenditur.

Nescio, an ad vos usque percrebuerint, quae in Italia de Caelo nova ab aliquot jam annis ibidem observata, perhibentur. Non-nulla earum nuper Societati nostrae significavit Clarissimus Geminianus Montanarius, Matheseos Professor Bononiensis, quae suis ipsius verbis Tibi perscribere non pigebit:[5]

"Multa possem" (ait ille) "nova, atque a seculis inaudita de Caelo vobis tradere, quae a multis annis observo, atque *Firmamento* meo *Instabili* exornando ac propediem evulgando materiam suppeditarunt; sed unum, quod [caeteris,] admirabilius est, proferam. Desunt in caelo duae stellae secundae Magnitudinis in Puppi Navis ejusque Transtris, Bayero β et γ;[6] prope Canem Majorem; a me et aliis, occasione praesertim [Cometae] Anni 1664. observatae et recognitae. Earum disparitionem, cui [subinde] anno debeam, non novi; hoc solum indubium, quod, inde a die 10 April. 1668, illarum ne vestigium quidem amplius adesse observo, caeteris circa eas, etiam quartae vel quintae Magnitudinis, immotis. Plura de aliarum stellarum mutationibus plusquam centenis, tametsi non tanti ponderis, annotavi: At una tantum Observatio, eaque caeteris omnibus praeponenda, si confirmetur, caeterarum Editionem procrastinat."

Hactenus Dn. Montanarius, qui his Observatis quamplurimos sine dubio ad diligentiorem, penitioremque Caelestium contemplationem pelliciet.

Clarissimus Hugenius, (quem omnes docti convaluisse gaudent) nuper mihi per literas,[7] Hagae scriptas, significavit, ante paucos menses se Parisiis Saturnum observasse, Telescopii 22. pedum beneficio, ac figuram ipsius Hypothesi suae perquam conformem deprehendisse: Ansas scilicet admodum esse strictas et coarctatas, adeo ut apertura earum non-nisi obscuriuscule nunc appareat. Communicavi ipsi, pace tua observationem tuam de hoc Planeta, nec non illam, quam Hookius noster mense Septembri instituit; cujus etiam figuram hic insertam ad Te transmitto; in qua umbrae non-nihil, quae in tua non cernitur, apparet.[8]

Bona tam venia, in Curiosorem gratiam, tuas de nova stella Cygni, deque praesenti phaenomeno Saturni figuras, imprimendus in Transactionibus meis curavi. Forte non adeo accuratus, fuit, Chalcographus in

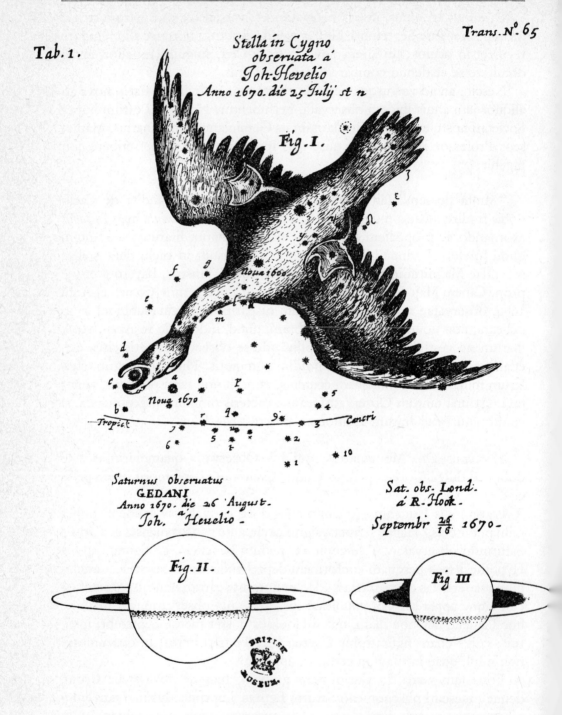

Tab. 1.

Stella in Cygno
obseruata á
Joh-Hevelio
Anno 1670. die 25 Iulÿ st n

Fig. I.

Saturnus Obseruatus
GEDANI
Anno 1670. die 26 August.
Joh. °Heuelio.

Fig. II.

Sat. obs. Lond.
á R. Hook.
Septembr $\frac{26}{16}$ 1670.

Fig III

officio suo imo fungendo. Vera proximo textum ipsum, una cum reliquis literis, ad Te curabo.

Quod superest, persuasum Tibi habeas velim, me proximo vere, prima novi, hinc Dantiscum velificatura, Tractatus illos omnes, quos cupis, lubenti animo transmissurum; operamque simul daturum, ut a Domino Hookio promissum Tibi Instrumentum extorqueam.[9]

Dominus Samuel Skütt, cujus in literis tuis mentionem fecisti, mihi hic adfuit, modestus satis, et Astronomiae amantissimus. Commendarerem illum Oxoniensibus, quantum potui, Regia Societate tunc temporis feriante. At brevi redux factus Oxonio, animum suum mihi exposuit in Belgium trajiciendi, ibique studia sua pro viribus promovendi. Id cum statutum fixumque ipsi esse perciperem, eum Lugduni et Amstelodami, nec non Hagae Comitis, amicis meis commendavi; ut ex quo profectus fuit, nil quicquam ab ipso inaudivi: quare literas tuas, ipsi inscriptas, ad Te remittere consultum duxi.

Frustrum illud rarissimi Succini, quando commode poterit transmitti ad Societatem regiam, grata mente excipiemus, operamque dabimus, ut Tuam in Nos egregiam voluntatem pari studio demereamur.

Vale diutissime, et ab Illustrissima nostra Societate atque a meipso plurimum Salve. Dabam Londini d. 21. Novemb. 1670.

P.S. Quae Dominum Cock scire voluisti, ipsi satis tum per literas tuas, tum ab ore meo innotuit. Condonanda est mentibus venalibus illiberalitas. Quinque illae librae, quas addidisti pro Telescopio, brevi a me exsolventur.

ADDRESS
    Per illustri Viro Domino
    Johanni Hevelio Gedanensium
    Consuli dignissimo etc.
        Dantisci

TRANSLATION

Henry Oldenburg greets the illustrious and very learned Mr. Johannes Hevelius, most worthy Senator of Danzig

I gather from your letter to me of the last day of October, famous Sir, that mine to you of 8 September,[1] answering your two letters to me of 5 July and 27 August,[2] had not been delivered at that time. I there recorded a good deal which I thought you would be interested to know about, especially what concerned the first observation of the new star below the head of Cygnus, the variation of the compass, and certain books recently printed treating physics and mathematics. I repeat nothing of all this in detail here, since I can hardly doubt that my letter will be delivered. I rather return you the Royal Society's best thanks for communicating to it in one and the same letter so many notable observations performed by you with such care and exactitude. When these were recently read aloud at a public meeting they won the unanimous applause of all the Fellows present, who at once ordered me to bring their cheers to your notice by my letter.[3]

By reason of cloudy skies we were not so happy as to observe either the eclipse of the moon or the conjunction of Venus and the moon. We congratulate you the more on the success of your observations; to which I can make no other return than the imperfect observation of that lunar eclipse made at Rome and sent me by a friend;[4] who says, that the beginning was at 2h. 50'; the duration was 2h. 55' or 56'; the extent was 9¼ digits; the diameter of the shadow appeared to be 90' at least; the penumbra began and ended more than a quarter of an hour before and after. The moon seemed bluish, when eclipsed to five or six digits; the color of the shadow was judged throughout to be dark blue-gray and with a reddish tinge. The limbs of the moon were always pretty clearly visible, and a few of the dark features could almost always be seen. I doubt that this observation came from Mr. Gottignies, for something more exact is to be expected from such a famous and skilful man.

Although Mr. Hooke applied himself to the observation of the new star in the beak of Cygnus in September, he could see nothing of it. Perhaps it will return to our eyes another time like that other new star in the neck of Cetus which, if I am not mistaken, is supposed to conceal itself in some years and then reveal itself again.

I do not know whether any rumor will have reached you of the novelties said to have been observed in the heavens a few years ago in Italy. The celebrated Geminiano Montanari lately informed our Society of some of them; you will not mind my transcribing the very words of this Professor of Mathematics at Bologna:[5]

"I can tell you of many novelties concerning the heavens," he writes, "unheard of through the centuries, which I have had under observation for many years and which will supply matter for my book on the *Inconstant Firmament*, which is now being perfected and soon to be published; but I present you with one more marvelous [than the rest]. Two second-magnitude stars in the poop and thwarts of the constellation Navis, Bayer's β and γ, near Canis Major, are missing from the heavens;[6] they were seen and recognized by myself and others, especially at the time [of the comet] of 1664. I do not know to what [subsequent] year I should attribute their disappearance; this only is beyond doubt, that since 10 April 1668 I have been able to observe no vestige of them at all, while the rest near by, even of the fourth and fifth magnitudes, remain motionless. I have recorded more than a hundred changes in other stars, though not of such importance. But one single observation, outweighing all the rest (if it is substantiated) delays the publication of the others."

So far Mr. Montanari, who will no doubt with these observations attract many people to a more diligent and profound contemplation of the heavens.

The celebrated Huygens, at whose recovery all the learned rejoice, informed me in a letter[7] from The Hague that he had observed Saturn at Paris, a few months ago, with a telescope of 22 feet, and found its figure to be pretty conformable to his hypothesis; that is to say, the anses were exceedingly narrow and constricted, so that the gap in them is now perceived only with difficulty. I hope you will forgive me for communicating to him your observation of this planet, and that made by Mr. Hooke in September. I send you here enclosed the appearance of the latter [*see figure, p. 278*], showing some shadowing not to be seen in yours.[8]

I have arranged for the printing in my *Transactions*, with your leave, of your sketches of the new star in Cygnus and of the present appearance of Saturn, in order to please the curious. Perhaps the engraver was not so accurate in doing his job as he might have been. Next spring I will take care to send you the actual text containing the other letters.

For the rest, please be assured that next spring I will be sure to send you all those treatises you wish for, most willingly, by the very first boat sailing from here to Danzig. And I will at the same time do my best to extract the promised instrument from Mr. Hooke for you.[9]

Mr. Samuel Skütt, whom you spoke of in your letter, called on me; he is pretty diffident but very keen on astronomy. I recommended him as warmly as I could to the people at Oxford, the Royal Society being then on vacation. But soon after he returned from Oxford and declared his intention to me of traveling to Holland in order to continue his studies there as hard as possible. When I saw that his mind was made up I recommended him to friends at Leiden, Amsterdam, and The Hague; what came of all that I have never heard from him. Hence I thought it best to return your letter addressed to him.

We shall most gratefully receive that piece of very rare amber when it can conveniently be sent to the Royal Society; and will do our best to deserve by similar zeal your goodwill towards us.

A long farewell, and with much prosperity is the wish of our illustrious Society and myself.
London, 21 November 1670

P.S.   What you wanted said to Mr. Cock has been told him often enough both in your letters and my words. Money-grubbers must be excused their meanness. Those five pounds which you have added for the telescope will soon be paid out by me.

ADDRESS

For the illustrious Mr.
Johannes Hevelius, most worthy
Senator of Danzig, etc.
Danzig

NOTES

Reply to Letter 1536.

1 Letter 1520.
2 Letters 1475 and 1509.
3 Hevelius' observations were read on 17 November.
4 We have not found this letter. Auzout and Francesco Serra observed this eclipse at Rome (*Giornale dei Letterati*, 26 October 1670, pp. 123–25). Although there are some slight discrepancies between this printed account—which obviously Oldenburg had not seen—and Oldenburg's summary, it is possible that they are the same.
5 The extract is from Montanari's letter to the Royal Society dated 20 April 1670 [N.S.], which is Royal Society MS. M 1, no. 60. It has been edited by Oldenburg. The words in square brackets are taken from the original, though omitted from Oldenburg's transcript. This passage was printed in *Phil. Trans.*, no 73 (17 July 1671), 2202, note.
6 The constellation Argo Navis is now divided into three: Vela, Puppis, and Carina. The star marked γ by Bayer is in Vela, not very far from Canis Major; that marked β is much farther south in Carina; both are of the second magnitude but neither is variable. It is difficult to understand Montanari's report. He had correctly perceived variability in Algol (1667) and was soon to discover another authentically variable star in Hydra. At the Royal Society meeting on 21 January 1713/4 Halley, in commenting on this report, declared that Montanari had simply made a mistake.
7 Letter 1537.
8 The page enclosed and reproduced here is the plate illustrating *Phil. Trans.*, no. 65 (14 November 1670), which also represents the nova in Cygnus next mentioned. The page is reproduced by courtesy of the British Museum.
9 A micrometer, spoken of long before.

1558
Wallis to Oldenburg
15 and 22 November 1670
From the original in Royal Society MS. W 1, no. 115

Oxford. Nov. 15. 1670.

Sr

I am sorry by yours of Nov. 8. to find my advertisement came too late.[1] But your Swiss Balleville is not yet come at mee, nor the Transaction you mention. (As neither those of April, nor August.) It may be inserted in your next, with a particular advertisement, of ye great mischief at Dover (on ye Kentish coast) at ye spring tides wch happened a few days before All-hollantide this year.[2] Of wch ye News letter (&, I think, ye Gazette) take notice.[3] Which I forgot to mind you of in my last. How it was then at London, I know not. I have read over again yt Proposition with ye Demonstration, wch Monr Hugens mentions;[4] but find nothing, wch upon a second reading will (probably) stick; if I know what it is, I shal be ready to satisfy him. The Peruvian bark (or Jesuits powder as it is called) hath putt by one fitt of my Ague; but it is supposed (as it is usual with it) yt it may in a weeks time return.[5] I am

Yours friend to serve you
John Wallis

Since I wrote this, I have yours with ye inclosed Transactions of October. But have not seen ye man; who I hear is not well.

Sr

This letter has been once at London allready but by reason of a mistake came back again. It now comes a second time with this Addition. I find between Fabri & Borelli a controversy about matter of Fact or Experiment.[6] Borelli supposeth (with many other) that a stone thrown or Bullet shot Horizontally, as in *HO*, doth by reason of its gravity sink downwards according to a curve line *HQ*, (& so far they agree;) but, sayth Borelli, it will in ye same time come at ye Horizontall plain *PQ*, at *Q*, as if (without ye motion of projection) it had fall directly down in ye perpendicular *HP*. This Fabri denies; (& allegeth an experiment of Mersennus to that pur-

pose;) & will have ye motion of descent retarded by ye additional Horizontall motion; supposing ye descent in ye curve to be, by ye obliquity of ye
motion, hindered, as in sloping Plains. I remember I have once formerly

[Figure supplied by the editors]

suggested the making of some Experiment by ye Society, for ye clearing
this matter: And I could be content now to renew ye same motion.[7] For
though I suppose most of us be rather of Borelli's than Fabri's opinion in
it: yet (especially since it is denyed) I think it might well deserve to be
experimented.

One thing more. I find in Transact. no. 46 (for Apr. 1669) Mr. Hugens's
laws of motion printed;[8] but not his Demonstration of them, which (as I
remember) came with them.[9] I desire you would favour mee with a Copy
thereof to peruse; & I shall (if you so desire) return it to you, from Sr

Your friend to serve you,

J. W.

I have (upon taking ye Peruvian Cortex) missed 3 or 4 fits of my Ague:
And could hope myself rid of it, were it not frequent (after yt Medicine)
to have it return again.

ADDRESS
   These for Mr Henry Oldenburgh
   at his house in the Palmal
      near St James's
         London
                                        POSTMARK NO 23

NOTES

   The second date is derived from the postmark.
 1 That is, about Wallis's tidal theory in Letter 1543 (p. 235), which was not inserted
   into *Phil. Trans.* no. 64.

2 This was not done.

3 That is, Henry Muddiman's *News-Letter* (see Vol. VI, Letter 1247, note 4) and the *London Gazette*, the official newspaper.

4 See Letter 1537, p. 219.

5 According to Collins (Turnbull, *Gregory*, p. 186), Wallis was still afflicted with malarial attacks in May 1671. He recovered to live another thirty years. The bark was, of course, cinchona.

6 The problem here is whether or not two separate motions can be compounded into one, without each modifying the other. Galileo had asserted that the perpendicular descent of a projectile is unaffected by its horizontal component of motion (see Stillman Drake, trans., *Galileo Galilei: Dialogue concerning the Two Chief World Systems*, Berkeley and Los Angeles, 1953, p. 155). Marin Mersenne examined the Galilean theory of projectiles in "Ballistica et Acontismologia" in *Cogitata physico-mathematica* (Paris, 1644). Times of flight and fall were tested by the Accademia del Cimento (see Richard Waller, *Essayes of Natural Experiments*, London, 1684, p. 143). Borelli's view was given as a statement of a "phenomenon" in *De vi percussionis* (Bologna, 1667), Cap. XXIII, p. 169; Fabri's in *Dialogi physici* (Lyons, 1669), p. 221 ff. The second and third dialogues are both directed against Borelli's book.

7 Attention was drawn to this proposal when the letter was read on 24 November, and on 8 December Hooke was asked to undertake the experiment. It was performed (inconclusively) on 26 January 1670/1 and several times repeated.

8 See *Phil. Trans.*, no. 46 (12 April 1669), 925–28: "A Summary Account of the Laws of Motion, communicated by Mr. Christian Hugens in a Letter to the R. Society . . . ," translated into Latin by Oldenburg from the *Journal des Sçavans* (cf. Vol. V, p. 357, note 5).

9 This was "De motu corporum ex mutuo impulsu hypothesis"—see Letter 1052 and its note 1 (Vol. V, p. 284).

1559
Wallis to Oldenburg
24 November 1670

From the original in Royal Society MS. W 1, no. 116

Oxford Nov 24. 1670.

Sir,

Since mine by ye last post,[1] I find (amongst my papers) a Copy of Mr. Hugens's demonstration (as it first came) of wch I sent to you for a copy:[2] that, in case hee added no more afterward, you may save yourself ye labour of sending ye Copy I desired. I find his propositions printed, to be somewhat different (in words, not in sense,) from those, with ye demonstrations, in my written paper: And that, in ye printed Copy (without demonstrations) there bee divers added. Whether you have any further demonstrations of those added, I know not. My paper begins with: De Motu Corporum ex mutuo impulsu Hypothesis. 1. Corpus quodlibet semel motum; &c. And ends with: Quod autem in navi contingit, idem in terra consistanti, uti diximus, evenire certum est. Igitur constat propositum. But I had, a little before, Quae celeritates cum sint in proportione reciproca ipsarum magnitudinum, necesse est ut corpora *AB* ejusdem spectatoris respectu resiliant a contactu ijsdem celeritatibus *CA*, *CB*; *Hoc enim postea demonstrabitur*.³ But of this promise, in my paper, there is no performance.⁴ Which makes mee suppose, there was some what to come after.

I have not yet read over all of Fabri against Borelli. That I have read gives mee no satisfaction. And hee doth manifestly cavil, very often, without any just cause. If you think fit to give any character of ye book:⁵ I think it best to bee some such purpose as this. That he doth therein (in six Dialogues) write against, Grimaldi, Alfonsus Borelli, & Montanarius: who in divers things differ from what Fabri hath written. Against ye first; *concerning Light*: Again ye second, About *Motion & Percussion*: Against ye third, About ye *Ascent of Liquors in Tubes*, (as in the Torricellian Experiment, &c:) But whether hee have ye better of those against whom hee writes; I shal not take upon mee to judge: but leave it to ye Reader to think as hee shall see cause. This is ye present thought of

Yours to serv you
John Wallis.

ADDRESS
    These
For Mr Henry Oldenburg,
  in the Palmal near
    St James's
      London

NOTES

1 Letter 1558.
2 See Letter 1558 and its note 9.
3 "An hypothesis concerning the motion of bodies from their mutual impact. 1. Any body once moved, etc. . . . . What happens upon a boat must happen on a motionless Earth, most certainly, just as we have said. And so the proposition stands . . . But as these velocities are inversely proportional to the sizes of the bodies, it is necessary

that the bodies *A, B,* rebound from impact with the same velocities *CA, CB,* as seen by the same observer; *for this will be demonstrated later.*"

4 In fact, this demonstration belonging to Huygens' *De motu corporum ex percussione* was only published posthumously as Prop. VIII in *Opera posthuma* (Leiden, 1703), II, 381; it is reprinted in *Œuvres Complètes,* XVI, 53. See Vol. V, Letter 1052.

5 In fact, though he used some of Wallis's phrases in the paragraph, Oldenburg prepared a fuller notice of Honoré Fabri's *Dialogi physici* for *Phil. Trans.,* no. 67 (16 January 1670/1), 2057–59.

1560
Bernard to Oldenburg
24 November 1670
From the original in Royal Society MS. B 2, no. 6

Worthy Sr.

I received yours by Mr Bazin,[1] & understand yt Mr Auzout intends to adorne Frontinus his booke de Aquaductibus wth his notes,[2] but I am very sorry yt our Libraryes will afford noe Mst of yt Excellent peice. For in Dr James's Catalogue of Mssts[3] I find noe more yn this:

J. Frontinus de Exemplis rei militaris.[4] Oxon. Lincoln Coll. 89. Cantabr. Publ. Biblioth. 217. & Petr. 18, ac 224.[5] Privat. L. 109.

If upon further search I happen upon ought worthy ye sight of yourselfe or Monsr. Auzout, I shall bee most ready to signifye my Esteeme of yt most Ingenious Mathematician & of yourselfe; in ye meane, & for ever believe mee

your most affectionate & humble servt.
Edw. Bernard

Nov. 24th 1670.

The Revd. & most learnd Dr Wallis is, I trust, quite rid of his Quartane haveing mist 5 fitts.

I entreate you upon ye next like occasion to advise mee whether Mr Mercator pursues what in ye Philosophicall Transacts hee seemd to designe the Consideration of Astronomie as it is most artificially delivered & freed from Ageometresy by ye Right Revd. Dr Ward &, as he intimates, by ye learned Cassini.[6]

My most humble service I pray you to take, & alsoe to commend to ye Right Worshipful ye Surveyor Generall.[7]

ADDRESS
   These
  For his worthy freind
  Henry Oldenburg Esq att the
    Pellmell
     London

NOTES

1 We have discovered nothing more about this letter, or of the French traveler who bore it to Oxford.

2 The *De aquis* [or, *De aquae ductibus*] *urbis Romae liber* of Sextus Julius Frontinus (A.D. 40–103) was first printed at Rome, 1484–92. It is the fundamental Roman treatise. Adrien Auzout, when at Rome, took much interest in studying and mapping the aqueducts; see R. F. Gaspari d'Urbin, *De aquis et aquaeductibus veteris Romae dissertationes* (Rome, 1680).

3 Thomas James, *Ecloga Oxonio-Cantabrigiensis . . . catalogum librorum manuscriptorum in bibliothecarum duarum academiarum . . .* (London, 1600).

4 More usually referred to as the *Strategemata* or *Strategematicon*, this work was first printed at Rome in 1487.

5 That is, Cambridge University Library and Peterhouse.

6 See Letter 1457, note 6, and Vol. VI, p. 449, note 2. "Ageometresy" presumably signifies "ignorance of geometrical principles."

7 Christopher Wren.

1561
Dodington to Oldenburg

25 November 1670

From the original in Royal Society MS. D 1, no. 17

Venice xber 5th 1670

Sr

When you shall have considered the short stay my ld Ambr. Faucon-berg[1] made heere, & shall withall understand that he gave a begin-ning to many troublesome & not yet perfected affaires, wherein my time was and yet is mostly taken up, I shall hope for an excuse of my tardinesse in performing you the services I had designed and you might justly re-quire from mee, But now that I think I beginn to have some relaxation, I will intend the observing yr directions wth more punctuality. Some few Collections and observations I have made in pursuance of yr Instructions as well as on other accompts, wch I shall ere long reduce to some series & transmitt to you.

The inclosed from Sigr Travagino is all I can yet obtayne from him, or he from his Lawsuits, wch take up all his thoughts.[2]

The last weeke I sent mr williamson one for you from Sgr Malpighi[3] who writes me word he will shortly send me a packett of Bookes for you, wch I shall convey forward, By sea, or some cheaper way then this, of postage. How beit I have adventured to send to mr Williamson for you the beginning of a Prodromus of Father Lanaos:[4] and will send ye rest by degrees, this being wch I now send above a third part of ye whole. I have this day sent 3 packetts of it, and hope you will approove of it, But for ye future I will wayt some cheaper conveyance, wch heere are not frequent. And this is al at present from Sr

Yr affectionate humble servant
John dodington

I send you a Catalogue to ye end you may comand me to serve you if you think fitt to comand any of them.

For mr Oldenburg

NOTES

1 Thomas Belasyse, Viscount Fauconberg (1627–1700); he had married Cromwell's daughter Mary but became a Privy Councilor to Charles II. See also Vol. VI, Letter 1364, note.
2 The latest extant is Letter 1519.
3 Presumably Letter 1547.
4 *Prodromo overo Saggio di alcune inventione nuove premesso all' Arte Maestra di P. Francisci Lana S. J.* (Brescia, 1670). What Dodington sent of this book was presented to the Royal Society on 26 January 1670/1; a notice appeared in *Phil. Trans.*, no. 69 (25 March 1671), 2114–16. Lana made the first proposal for a lighter-than-air flying machine.

1562

Martindale to Oldenburg

26 November 1670

From the original in Royal Society MS. M 1, no. 64
Printed in *Phil. Trans.*, no. 66 (12 December 1670), 2016–17

Worthy Sr

Iam just now returned from visiting & viewing the saltworke, and find things according to my friends relation, onely whereas I understood him that no running water came neare it I perceive he intended none of any consideration, or none to annoy it. There runneth neare to it (at least in the winter season) a small rindle[1] (or gutter rather) but it is wholly free from all feares of overflowing which threateneth all the salt-pits else in this county every great shower through the untoward vicinity of Rivers.

The rocke of salt (I understand by the workemen) is betweene 33 & 34 yards distant from the surface of the earth about 30 whereof they have digged alreadie and hope to be at the flagge[2] which covereth the salt-rocke about 3 weekes hence. But I feare it will be severall moneths before I can accomodate you with a parcell of it, that which the augar brought up being long since disposed of, so as not to be recovered, and the workeman not daring to remove the flag till the frame be finished and well setled for the securing of the worke from the circumjacent earth; Fully expecting from the experience they have had from an augars bore that when the flag of stone is removed, the brine will beat them out from parfecting any tedious worke within the pit. But the overseer thereof Mr Hawkins hath promised to furnish me with a piece of the rocke for your use, you[3] to signifie to me when they intend to uncover it that (if possible) we may make some experiments such as you hint at, but I feare the Churlish & brisk brine will not suffer us. That parcell of naturall salt which the instrument brought up, diverse that saw it assure me was as hard as allome and as pure, and when pulverized it became an excellent fine and sharpe salt. The first discoverer of it was one John Jackson of Hatton about Lady-day last as he was searching for coales on the behalfe of the Lord of the soile William Marbury of Marbury Esq, commonly stiled Mr Marbury of the Meire.[4] That is all I can at present serve you in, onely I am consulting diligent and experienced persons of both sexes as to what you desire touching husbandrie, dayries &c and shall ere long (God willing) give you such an account as I can; though I cannot hope to discover any thing worth the notice of the (worthily stiled) Royall societie. It will be enough to overlay my ambition if I may but be continued in your thoughts as well-willer to such noble persons & designes: In confidence whereof I subscribe my selfe Sr

> your very reall (though very
> inconsiderable) friend & servant
> *Adam Martindale*

Rotherston November 26° 70.

ADDRESS
      These
   To his highly honoured friend
      Mr Henrie Oldenburg
   Secretarie to the Royall-societie
   At his house in the Pal-mall
      in St James'es fields
         Westminster

                              POSTMARK NO 28

NOTES

Possibly a reply to Letter 1551.
1 Or runnel, a little watercourse.
2 A fissile rock.
3 Read "and."
4 This Marbury is a small place in N. Cheshire, near Northwich. There is a lake ("mere") in the grounds of the Hall, and another village named Mere nearby. William Marbury (1644–83) was the last member of this notable family, but the Hall still stands.

1563
Oldenburg to Bernard
1 December 1670

From the original in Bodleian Library MS. Smith 45, f. 71

Sir,

Since you have hitherto met wth nothing in yr University Libraries, yt may contribute to the designe of Mr Auzout, who would gladly make Frontinus de Aquae-ductibus more intelligible; I shall, after the returne of my hearty thanks for ye pains, you have been pleased to take in yt search, desire this other favour of you, yt you would see, whether you can find in yr libraries *Gometius Pereira* his *Margarita Antoniana*, printed in Spaine above 100. years agoe:[1] and if you doe, informe me, whether he does assert thesame, yt Des-Cartes doth, about the nature of Brutes, viz. yt they have no perception at all, and also about ye Humane Soul's Immortality: And what other particulars he delivers coincident wth those, left us by Des-Cartes.

Mr Mercator in ye Ph. Transact. doth not, if you consider his words well, speak any thing of his owne designe in Astronomicals, but wishes for ye execution of what Cassini had designed and promised: wch, I believe, sticketh, upon ye sight of what Mercator hath said touching Cassini's *Methodus Investigandi Apogea, Excentricitates et Anomalias Planetarum.*

I am very glad to hear of ye recovery of our worthy friend Dr Wallis, and am now going to congratulate wth him,[2] and to acquaint him wth some things, I have lately received from Slusius, and from Fermat; after I have assured you afresh, yt I am Sir

Yr very affectionate friend and servt
H. Oldenburg

London
Decemb. 1:70.

NOTES

Reply to Letter 1560.
1 See Letter 1548, note 11.
2 See Letter 1564.

1564
Oldenburg to Wallis
1 December 1670

From the memorandum in Royal Society MS. W 1, no. 116

Rec Nov. 25: 70. Answ. Dec. 1: 70. promised Diophantus and communication of Slusius letter,[1] when he comes to London.

NOTES

Reply to Letter 1559.
1 Presumably Letter 1548.

1565
Martindale to Oldenburg

2 December 1670

From the original in Royal Society MS. M 1, no. 65

Sr

Having lately given you (per post) such an account as I was able of Mr Marburies designed saltworkes (which I hope the next spring will set a going) and of the Rocke of salt there discovered,[1] I shall briefly satisfie your desires according to my poore skill and intelligence as to some other matters. viz.

1. For Agriculture

Cheshire being for the most part a valley watered with many fine Rivers & large brookes may be fitly divided into upland and waterland that is such as in flouds is ordinarily overflowne by water.

The former is most made use of for Corne and pasture, and (for want of waterland) for hay likewise; The latter is used most commonly for hay-grass sometimes for pasture, but very rarely for Corne.

Our upland againe is either Clay-land, blacke-land[2] or sand-land: (for that which some men make a distinct kind from all those viz Foxe-land is onely a browner and stiffer sort of sand-land) concerning all which I shall indeavour to show you 1 How we inrich them 2 to wt use we put them 3 How we order them to that purpose

1 For the enriching of our land, besides what it gets by rest, we have three great helpes; 1 Marle which is a fatt and fertill sort of Clay, though ordinarily distinguished from it. 2 Lime. 3 Muck or compost such as we cleanse out of our stables, cowhouses, and hog-sties the dung and litter throwne together on an heape and there Marinating till it be sufficiently rotten. The cleansings also of our houses of ease and the ashes which our fires yield us are also counted good muck for quality, but of these we have no considerable store. Concerning all which I suppose these uses will be found current

1 Lime and muck either single or conjoyned are a great enrichment to

any of the three sorts of land before mentioned yea indeed any other that needs

2 Marle is helpfull to all the three sorts but with great varietie. the sandland must have good store, and it will both yield exceeding freely & last long in Constant tillage, especially the foxland, but it may be over-marled and then it will not yield freely till loosened againe with mucke.

Blackeland will yet take more marle, and indeed can hardly have too much and yet for all that will not last long, but it will yield very freely especially in dry seasons, as the sand-land will in wetter. All the dispute is concerning clay land whether Marle be good for it, for we have a common proverb here.

> He that Marles sand may buy land
> He that marles Mosse, suffers no losse
> But He that Marles clay throwes all away,

But this is no irrefragable rule; for certaine experience makes it evident that a little marle that is very good will much advantage clay land & I could name diverse of my neighbours that have tried it. About 1000 loads of Marle of our largest sort of carts drawne by 3 horses will fit our ordinary sort of sand-land; Blackland and the loosist sort of sand land a great deale more, some 1500, some 1800, but clayland a great deale lesse. We usually set it upon the grasse in the summer season, spreading it with spades or shovels & so let it ly on at the least till after Christmasse before we breake it up.

2 For the use of our land thus inriched & the benefite we expect, take as follows.

1 Our clay-land will doe well for wheate and oates.

2 Our black-land (or Mosse-land) will give good oates barley and beanes especially the last to very great profite as I have experienced.

3 But above all our sand-land is the heart of the corne (as we say) for it will yield incredible profit in barley especially in dropping summers when other land misseth & consequently corne is deare. It will also give excellent oates or pease either white greene or gray (the last whereof sowne late & shorne high doe much refresh it) While it is stiffe it will yield good store of wheate, and when small it will give us as good store of rye.

Besides these sorts of graine our sand land or blackland that is not too wet being very small and ranke of muck, will yield good hemp; and our stiffe land at first breaking up as good flax.

3 As to the manner of ordering our land touching these graines,

(though I cannot give such universall rules as will fit every case without some exceptions through varietie of circumstances) I suppose these rules will come very neare to a just direction.

1 The better our land is the sooner we sow any graine respectively; for we hold that late sowing will make our corne upon good land overranke & apt to ly, but in poore land it will helpe it much.

2 For wheate we plow our land 3 times over the first furrow about midsummer, the second about st James tide[3] and the third (which is the sowing furrow) we give it about Michaelmasse having first sowen the wheat upon it & so plowing it under & ridging it up very high.

3 For barley also we plow three times, once soone after Christmasse (or before it if the ground be stiffe that the frost may breake and mellow it) The second time in the beginning of Aprill and the third time the beginning of May sowing it upon the third furrow and harrowing it in finely. but some ground that is very riche (especially near Chester-citie) is usuall sowed in March or Aprill.

4 We plow but once for rye, sowing it about the beginning of November, & make use of the harrow.

5 The like we do with our oates and pease, onely our sowing time for them is about the middle of March.

6 The ordering of beanes is much, that like barley onely I apprehend not the like necessity for so many furrows, though they will doe well.

7 Hempseed[4] is sowne at the same season & in the same manner as barley

8 Flaxseed is sowne at the same season but it hath but one furrow and the ground must be well harrowed both before and after the sowing that the seed may neither be buried in the cavities of the furrowes nor left uncovered.

9 Poore beaten land that is apt to bring weeds, needs much more seed there than that which is rich and not apt to produce them.

10 We sow rye and pease very thin & beanes very thicke in comparison of other graine.

11 We mow no corne almost here but cut it all with hookes & sickles binding it and setting it up carefully till the time of leading it home.

12 Our Hemp & flax are usually pulled, set up until sufficiently withered, and when the seed is got out (viz hemp-seed by beating, and the flaxbolls by rippling or putting through an Iron Combe) they are laid in water, then spread on the ground & when drie, bound up; dried on hurdles (or giggs) and so broken swingled & cleansed.

Thus much for land that we can enrich by the helpes aforesaid, but if it so ly that we have none of those advantages (as sometimes it comes to passe) we strive to get out of it what we can by other wayes though much inferiour.

1 We sowe sand-land with French-wheate two yeares together ordering it as for barley onely sowing it a fortnight later, and the third yeare with rye.

2 Clay land and some other will give a crop of oates without helpe

3 Other sorts of poore land we use to fleet[5] with a kind of Instrument called a push-plow which will cut a delicate thin turfe which being turned reared, dried and at last burned with gorse or furres the ashes are spread all over the ground and then fresh mold being plowed up it is sowne with barley for that yeare, and a yeare or two after and it will ordinarily bring abundance of corne, but usually very small. Or it will give very good flax or French wheat. This for our upland.

Our waterland or meadowland as it needs no enriching by Art, so we have noe wayes to reape the profite, but what are ordinary onely some gentlemen of this county and the Neighbouring Lancashire have hit upon a more compendious way then ordinarie (as to paines & cost) in making up their hay: And this is it; They suffer it when mowne to ly in the swath seven or eight dayes, till it bee withered. Then taking the benefite of a faire day, they turne it over and make it into great Cockes so large that three of them will load a cart, which they let alone for seven or eight dayes more; that the hay may sweat sufficiently, & then they load it and either stack it or lay it up in their buildings.

2 For brewing

I must referre you to my Lord Brereton a member of your owne societie whose Bread-ale was famous in this Countrey 2 or 3 yeares agoe.[6] What we have else worth communicating I know not. Sanbach[7] ale is indeed napping[8] liquor but I judge it is more beholden to the quantity & qualitie of the malt then any speciall art in the brewing of it.

3 For our dayries

I cannot but wonder that many counties both in the south and west of England are not rather above then below us as to dayries: for though its true that we have some very excellent land, yet (to say nothing that our richest meadows are bestowed upon our horses, the hay being not so proper for our kine, but apte to make them leane and weake) as to the generalitie of our pastures other places in the parts before mentioned do in mine opinion very much exceed us, and as to the practice, it is so plaine and ordinary a thing that I am ashamed to give you the trouble of reading it.

To omit the manner of gathering of butter which I suppose is the same all England over, Our huswives use this method in reference to their cheese

1 When veales are plentifull they furnish themselves from the butchers with the bagges of sucking calves which are usually called earning-bagges,[9] being like bladders, enclosing curdled milke. These they carefully pick and cleanse (if need be) and salt them soundly, then pricking them up with a skewer and covering them with paper they hang them up neare a fire, that they may drie and harden, and so they are fit for use.

2 These bagges thus prepared they lay in salt and water and thereby produce that which they call their steep (by some called rennet). But whereas formerly they were very curious to get such bagges as were fullest of curds and alwayes laid the whole bagge in the water: some of our best huswives have found by experience that the surest way to make cheese mild and least subject to putrefaction is to cast away the curd, and to make their steep onely of a piece of the skin of the bagge marinated in salt and water.

3 Their milke whether creame, new milke, or floten-milke[10] being put into the tub, a little steep put into it, and stirred well about (and ye lesse the better, provided it will doe the worke) makes it to coagulate and become like a custard (which they call coming) This they press downe gently with their open hands to the bottome of the tub and this separates (in some measure) the curdes from the whey.

4 Then setting their cheese-fat (or cheese-mold) over the tub upon a little frame called a throwe or cheeseladder they put their curdes into it breaking them somewhat and pressing out the whey with all their might: two of them ordinarily squeezing it at once, with their open hands & united strength, turning it over once or twice, and taking care that the cheesefat be not so capacious but that the cheese when they have squeezed it as well as they can with their hands may not onely fill it but stand on a heap about it.

5 Then taking a cleane linnen cloath they put one end of it under the cheese within the cheese-fat, and turne the other over it and so set it in ye

presse which is ordinarily a great hewen stone fetched up and let downe with a skrew or Leaver wherein it stands about 12 houres & then being taken out and salted it is set in againe for 12 houres more.

6 Some use not to salt it in the presse, but in stead there of to lay it either in naturall or artificiall brine. and this makes good sound & well-weighing cheese but somewhat harsher in taste.

7 The cheese being well pressed and salted as aforesaid is placed upon a little board (called a bredd) and set upon a shelfe to drie: both bread and cheese being usually turned over every day. Onely the creame-cheese is laid upon a dry upper floore amongst nettles which makes it very mellow and daintie for private use, especially if it be made thin; to which purpose they use to cut a thick cheese with threed or wire into 2 or 3.

8 Those cheeses which have the colour & tast of Rosemary, sage, mint, Marygolds Roses &c are made after the ordinary manner, onely mixing the juice of those hearbes with the milk.

9 There is a sort of cheese called broken-curd-cheese which is earned at twice the old curds being crumbled and mixt with the new. This is a cheese that some make when they cannot keep their milke long enough to make an handsome cheese at once, nor have the convenience of changing with neighbours: Others doe it out of thrift supposing that milke warme from the cow will yield a farr greater quantitie of curds then after it hath beene cooled & warmed againe. But this sort of cheese is somewhat more difficult to hit, both as to soundnesse and pleasantnesse then that which is made at once.

10 As to that delicate sort of cheese which they call slip-coate[11] I am not able to give you any punctuall account, but must referre you to some of our Cheshire Ladies now in London whose housekeepers can give you full satisfaction.

Sr I intreate a line from you signifying your reception hereof; withall craving pardon for my prolixitie and rudenesse, the language being such as sutes very harmoniously with plowes harrows and milk-pailes I shall not adde to your trouble save to say that I am Sr

> your humble servant
> *Ad: Martindale*

Rotherston Dec. 2d—70.

ADDRESS

These
For my worthy friend Mr Henrie Oldenburg
        secretarie of the Royall societie
At his house in the Palmal in st James'es
        fields   Westminster

                                        POSTMARK DE 5

NOTES

Further reply to Letter 1551.
1 See Letter 1562.
2 That is, peat.
3 25 July.
4 *Cannabis sativa*, a plant grown mainly for the sake of its fiber but also for the oil
  expressed from the seeds, thus resembling flax in its uses.
5 To skim (as milk), and so, to pare.
6 See Vol. III, p. 24, note, and p. 589, note 6.
7 Sandbach, north of Crewe.
8 Soporific, presumably.
9 The earning-bag is one stomach of the calf; to earn means to curdle (milk).
10 Skim milk.
11 A soft cream cheese.

1566
Helmfeld to Oldenburg

3 December 1670

From the original in Royal Society MS. H 3, no. 2

Parisijs $\frac{3}{13}$ Decembri anno 1670

Nobilissime Domine, Amice plurimum colende

Mensis ferme nunc agitur, e quo pronissime memor scribendo ad Te
debitum meum exsolvisse credidi: sed cum apices literarum ad
praescriptam Tuam formulam omisso scilicet genuino Tuo nomine et
substituo altero Domini Grubendol confecerim, probe est ut dubitem de
bene redditis illis.[1] Utcunque vero sit, nolui tamen deesse officio meo quin

paucis his certiorem Te reddam, missas tunc istas esse postis jamjam abeuntibus ad Dominum Leyonberg Residentem Sueticum apud vos,[2] in cujus manibus, si dudum Tibi redditae sunt spero eas usque requiescere. Tu interim amice suspiciendo noli haec male interpretari et cum non habeam hac vice quae de novis adjiciam, nec si haberem propter invaletudinem possim, vale hisce et fave

> Tui studiosissimo
> *Gustavo Helmfeld*

P.S. Si me responso dignaberis, quaeso fac reddatur a Mons. Nicolas Eosander[3] Secretaire pour le Roy de Suede a Paris.

ADDRESS
   A Monsieur
   Monsieur Grubendol
      a
     Londres

TRANSLATION

> Paris, 3/13 December 1670

Most noble Sir, very dear friend,

Almost a month has now elapsed since I believed myself to have discharged my obligation, being very fully mindful of writing to you. But as I wrote the address of my letter according to your previous formula, that is, omitting your real name and substituting that of Mr. Grubendol, the time has come when I may doubt of its safe delivery.[1] Whatever the case, I was reluctant to fail in my duty by not informing you in these few lines that that letter was sent by a post then traveling to Mr. Leijonberg, the Swedish Resident among you,[2] in whose hands it still rests, I hope, if [not] delivered to you previously. Meanwhile, since you will take all this as a friend, you will not put a bad interpretation upon it; and as I have no news to add at this time and could not on account of ill health if I had any, farewell now and cherish

> Your most zealous,
> *Gustavus Helmfeld*

P.S. If you honor me with an answer, please have it delivered to Mr. Nicolas Eosander,[3] Secretary to the King of Sweden, Paris.

NOTES

Reply to Letter 1517.

For the writer of this letter, see Letter 1508.

1 The sense is that the Grubendol address was inappropriate for a letter to be delivered by hand from the Swedish Embassy in London.

2 Johan Leijonberg (1625–91) had held diplomatic posts in Moscow and Spain before coming to England in 1653. He held the post of resident from 1661 to 1672 when he was appointed envoy.

3 Nils Eosander (1636–1705) was a diplomatic representative of the Swedish crown in Paris from 1669 to 1689; in 1674 he was to be ennobled under the name of Lillie-root.

1567

Flamsteed to Oldenburg

5 December 1670

From the original in Royal Society MS. F 1, no. 63

Clarissimo Henrico Oldenburg: Armigero
J. Flamsteedius: Faelicitatem:

Si nimis cuiquam libere in praefatis ad insequentis anni supputatas apparentias asseruisse videar.[1] id haud quaquam factim, subter de-scripta observatio potest evincere. quam ideo tibi unquamque caelorum studiosis ocyus communicatam velim; ut inde, quantum illorum referat calculatis phaenomenis indefesse invigilare, eaque accurate observare innotescat. Codnorae, quae septem circiter millaria a Derbia ad Septentrionem distat,[2] a sobrino Meo Mr Tho: Willson Anno 1670 Octobris 1° mane sesquihora saltem ante solis exortum, aut semihora post primam ortam lucem, Veneris sidus videbatur in paulo minore altitudine ac centrum lunae, & parte quarta diametri lunaris, vel summum 10 min a limbo suo occidentali distans. Codnorae meridianus distat a Londinensi ad occasum 5 min: et ejus est latitudo 53°–04′: Vult cognatus tempus observationis esse 5 hor: mane. Ego (ut infra videre est) ad 5h–02′–53″; angulum circuli verticalis, per centrum lunae transeuntis, acquisivi 29°–59′; Veneris-que locum Virginis 19°–11′–40″: & latitudinem 1°–23′–55″, unde locum lunae apparentem constituo in consequentia veneris 9 min: scilicet in Virginis 19°–21′, cum latitudine visibili 1° 44′ At emin id tempus juxta tabulas Carolinas[3]

			h ° ′ ″		h ° ′ ″
Anomalia media . . .	Veneris	6–03–32–14	lunae	11–08–25–55
locus verus	Virginis	19–11–40	Virginis	17–44–24
latitudo vera		1–23–55		2–14–56
Lunae semidiameter in horizonte				14–20
parallaxis horizontalis				53–03
Solis locus verus				18–04–16
Recta ascensio solis				196–39–32
Recta ascensio temporis				255–43–15
Recta ascensio Medij caeli				92–22–47
Medium Caeli			Cancri	2–10–57
declinatio ejusdem				23–29
altitudo ejus				60–24
Horoscopus			Librae	1–38
M Caeli ab Horoscopo				89–27
Luna ab Horoscopo in Ecliptica				13–54
in magno circulo				14–05
Angulus oriens lunae				69–41
Altitudo centri lunae				13–11
Azimuth ab horoscopo				4–59
Angulus parallacticus				60–01

Parallaxis lunae in ⎰	altitudine	51–50
	Longitudine	44–54
⎱	latitudine	25–54

sic luna visa	Virginis	18–29–18
cum latitudine boreali		1–49–02
in antecedentia a veneris		42–22
cum majora latitudine		25–22

Ast luna visa fuit a venere in consequentia 9 min: Error quamobrem tabularum est 51 min: Erroris utique hiatus, & quem nunquam, nisi de candore & peritia cognati probe mihi constaret, credidissem: Reflexio[4] a tabulis Carolinis id tempus est 32′ 57″: quam si ad salvandum phainomenon omittamus: non dum tamen observationi fiet satis, nisi porro aequatio minutorum circiter 18. addenda lunae motibus ab aliis causis petatur. Interim aliae observationes reflexionem omittere non sinent unde promp-

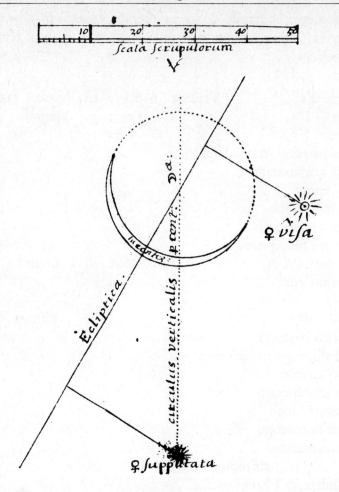

tum est arguere; Nondum penitus perspectum esse lunae systema; et ab
alijs causis secundas esse prosthaphareses[5] deducendas. Forsan ab alijs
tabulis minus aberratum credis: Attamen profecto paulo plus Brittanicas
Wingi[6] peccare tempori, quin et aliquantulum amplius Philolaicas.[7] Nec
minimum potest reperiri effugium ni serius factam observationem, supponamus, & in tempore notando observatorem errasse:[8] quod vix credo:
quippe eam esse lunae altitudinem conjecit, quae Solis est in meridie solstitij
brumalis: sed putemus illum in tempore assignando semihora aberrasse,
parum tamen hoc juvabit, cum luna tunc Apogea motu praetarda fuerit,
unde error in tabulis restabit major quam sit Reflexio. Utinam alibi non-
nemo hanc apparentiam, cujus jacturam admodum defleo, accuratius ani-
madvertit! plurimum certe debere fatebar ei, qui probam ejus observationem
dederit. Ipse Ephemeridibus & tabulis nimium fidens optimam, utilissi-

mamque observationem perdidi; ea etenim non nisi orta sole apparentiam promittunt. Curabis igitur vir amplissime, ut qui caelum observant admoveantur, ne nimium Astronomorum fidant numeris. Et ritius quam praescripsi, supputata a me phainomena praestolentur praeterea si ita videtur, ut haec etiamsi non accuratissime lucifera tamen observatio, cum chartis, quas tibi dedi, caeteris publici fiat juris, et una Illustrissimae Societati Regiae privatim ut a me offerantur.⁹ Cui nimirum eas deberi intelligo et in majores quam pro opere; patronos advocaturus viderer iis, quos omni debito cultu suspicio, publice dicassem. grata forsan ferantibus Astrosphorum ingenijs erit haec observatio nec non ad majorem in observando diligentiam adhibendam eos excitabat. Caeterum finem scribendi facere, non licet, nisi actis solenniter gratis pro benevola erga me mente & affectu, summisque quae in me extare voluisti quaeque semper agnoscere gestiam, beneficijs. Hisce valete jubeo, vir amplissime, qui sum

> Servus tui devinctissimus
> *Johannes Flamsteedius*

Derbia scribebam Decembris 5 1670.

By the Scale of Minutes in the former Scheme, all the figures of the next yeares appearances were delineated by ¹⁰

> *J F*

TRANSLATION

J. Flamsteed sends good wishes to the famous Henry Oldenburg, Gent.

If I seem to have spoken out with a certain excess of freedom in my preface to the computed appearances of the coming year,¹ the observation described below may show that I have not done so. Which I wanted to communicate without delay to you and at any time to students of the skies, so that from this they might gather how much it concerns them to watch out for the phenomena calculated, and observe them accurately.

At Codnor, which is about seven miles north of Derby,² Venus was seen by my cousin Mr. Thomas Wilson on the morning of 1 October 1670, at least half an hour before sunrise, or half an hour after the first rising of the moon, with an altitude a little less than that of the center of the moon and at a distance of a fourth part of the moon's diameter (or at most ten minutes) from its western limb. The meridian of Codnor is five minutes west of London's, and the latitude of the place is 53° 4′. He says that the time of the observation was 5 A.M. As may be seen below,

I took the angle of the vertical circle passing through the center of the moon at 5h 2' 53" [to be] 29° 59'; and Venus' place to be 19° 11' 40" of Virgo, latitude 1° 23' 55"; whence I put the apparent position of the moon nine minutes east of Venus, that is in 19° 21' of Virgo with a visible latitude of 1° 44' [*see figure p. 304*].

But at that time, according to the *Caroline Tables*[3]

		°	'	"
The true place of Venus	Virgo	19	11	40
With true latitude		1	23	55
The visible moon	Virgo	18	29	18
With north latitude		1	49	2
West of Venus			42	22
And with greater latitude			25	22

But the moon was seen nine minutes east; whence the error in the tables is 51 minutes; surely a wide margin of error, such as I would never have believed unless the honesty and skill of the observer were well known to me. By the *Caroline Tables* the reflection[4] at that time is 32' 57"; if we omit this in order to save the phenomenon, still it does not correspond to the observation unless an equation of about 18 minutes more be added to the lunar motions from other causes. Meanwhile, other observations do not tolerate the omission of reflection, whence one is prompted to argue, that the system of the moon has not yet been thoroughly examined, and that the second *prosthaphaereses*[5] are to be deduced from other causes. Perhaps you may believe other tables less erroneous: yet indeed the *Britannic Tables* of Wing[6] were a little more out as to the time, and the *Philolaic*[7] a little more still. And there is no way out of this to be found unless we suppose the observation to have been carelessly made, and the observer mistaken in noting the time;[8] which I can hardly believe, since he guessed the altitude of the moon to be that which the sun has at noon, at the winter solstice. But let us suppose him to have erred half an hour in assigning the time, it helps the case little, for the moon was then much retarded in her apogeal motion, so that the error in the tables remains greater than the reflection. Would that some other person elsewhere has observed this phenomenon, the loss of which I greatly lament! I should, I confess, be greatly indebted to anyone who would produce a sound observation of it. Trusting too much in ephemerides and tables, I was deprived of a most valuable observation; for they predicted the phenomenon only after sunrise. You will therefore, worthy Sir, see that watchers of the skies are warned not to rely too much on astronomers' figures. If it seems appropriate to publish this observation (which is informative if not highly accurate) together with the other papers I gave you, and to offer them privately to the Royal Society as from myself, the phenomena, as calculated more exactly by myself than when I wrote before, are ready besides, at hand.[9] For I understand them to be assignable to the Society, and for more reasons than the labor [?], and would be seen to pledge myself publicly to such patrons, whom I hold in all due respect. Perhaps this observation will be welcome to the minds of astronomers, and will excite them to greater diligence in observation. Moreover, I cannot lay down my pen without giving you solemn thanks for your kindness and goodwill towards me, and the many acts of generosity you have lavished on me, which I shall endeavor always to acknowledge. I wish you good health, worthy Sir, being

> Your most obliged servant,
> *John Flamsteed*

Derby, 5 December 1670

· · · · · · · · · · · · · · · · · ·

NOTES

It is likely that this document (it is more a paper than a letter) was enclosed by Flamsteed in a letter to Collins (Rigaud, II, 103–5) which seems to mention it, though that letter is printed with the date 1 December. The Latin here is extremely bad, so that it is not surprising that Oldenburg found it ambiguous. Flamsteed repeated some of the material, in English, in Letter 1573; nevertheless, it seemed worth while to offer a translation here.

1 This preface or introduction has been excised; see further, Letter 1554, note 1.
2 More exactly, about eight miles northeast of Derby.
3 That is, in Thomas Streete's *Astronomia Carolina* (London, 1661). We have simply extracted (in English) the important entries from Flamsteed's table. Note that there is an error in subtraction with regard to the latitudes: the last figures should be 25′ 7″.
4 Refraction, presumably (the same word occurs in Letter 1573).
5 Corrections for the anomalies in the motions of the moon or a planet.
6 Vincent Wing, *Astronomia Britannica* (London, 1669).
7 Ismael Boulliau, *Astronomia Philolaica* (Paris, 1645).
8 Since the difference in the velocities of the moon and Venus may amount to almost half a degree per hour, a fairly small error in the estimated time of the observation would greatly reduce its departure from the tables. Compare Hevelius' remarks in Letter 1536, p. 214.
9 Oldenburg apparently did not speak of this letter to the Society, nor did he publish further predictions; compare Letter 1554 and its note 1.
10 This sentence also appears at the close of the letter to Collins mentioned in note 1 above.

1568
Oldenburg to Leibniz

8 December 1670

From the original in Hannover MSS., ff. 3–4
Printed in Gerhardt, pp. 47–50

Consultissimo Doctissimoque Viro
Domino Gothofredo Guilielmo Leibnitio I.U.D. et Cons. Mogunt.
H. Oldenburg Soc. R. Secr. Salutem

Responsum ad locupletissimas tuas literas, 28. Septemb. ad me datas, invitus plane ad hoc usque tempus, ob varia impedimenta, distuli. Tu facile indolem provinciae meae dispicies, eoque pronius scripti hujus tarditatem excusabis. Dicere vix possum, quam gestiat animus, dum intelligit, Virum inter Leges et Aulam dispunctum, ista tam recenti aetate, magnorum in Philosophia Nominum, Baconi puta, Gassendi, Cartesii, similiumque, scripta, non dico perreptasse, sed tam subacto Judicio, ut a Te factum, excussisse. Quae de Jure constituendo brevi et dilucido, infinitis tamen casibus, sola paucarum ac pene simplicium Regularum Combinatione, suffecturo, moliris, totum ea sola hominem, quin totos homines quamplures, deposcunt. Rem arduam fateor, sed integritati, perspicaciae, solertiae, industriaeque, mea quidem sententia, nequaquam impossibilem. Felicem Tibi tuique geminis in conatu, non utili minus quam laudabili, successum ex animo comprecor, meque posse Tibi cordatos in tanto Opere Patronos et hyperaspistas conciliare, in votis quam maxime habeo. Re ferente cum nostris hic loci in Jure Civile Doctoribus de Instituto tuo forte disseram, eorumque opinionem exploratam suo tempore rescribam. Hac vice in reliqua hujus epistolae parte juvat philosophari, quaeque, literarum tuarum occasione, cogitata subnascuntur, enarrare.

Et primo quidem occurrit Hugenianum de Longitudinibus, Penduli ope inveniendis, conamen. Lutetia Parisiorum nuper accepi, Cordatos quosdam Viros, rerumque Mathematicorum peritos, sumptibus publicis, tum in Indiam Orientalem tum in Americam brevi navigaturos, Automatis aliquot, Hugeniano artificio fabrefactis, instructos;[1] eo plane consilio, ut memorati Penduli in agitatis maribus exactitudinem, summa cura explorent fidamque Regi suo de successu narrationem afferant.

Ille qui hic Londini incommodis illis, quae hac in re etiamnum superesse

censet, mederi satagit, est Doctissimus Mercator:[2] Promisit ille Automa-
tum, Longitudini deprehendendae idoneum, quod 1. habeat Duos Annulos
Cylindricos, qui id perpetuo in situ retineant perpendiculari, eidemque
Navis lateri obversum, quocunque demum fluctu ea feratur; unde, cum
motus fere tendat a Puppi ad Proram, certiores Penduli vibrationes evadant,
quam si in quamvis Navis plagam Machina digrediatur. 2. Quod Æquationem Temporis exhibeat perquam accurate, ipsi Automato applicandam.
3. Quod ab irregulari Aeris motu ingeritur incommodi (praecedentia, ipsius
quidem sententia, longe superantis) amoliatur. Tempus docebit eximii
hujus Inventi successum, eosque, qui authoritate et munificentia sua illud
juvent, Terrarum Principes excitabit.

Quid Machinae Aquaticae Memmingenses in fodinis Suacensibus, ab
Aquarum importunitate liberandis, praestiterint, scire perquam aveo.
Spes est, Serenissimum Bavariae Electorem, quem eo evocasse Machinas
scribis, rem pro merito examinaturum, Teque, ubi de exitu rei liquido
judicatum fuerit, pro humanitate tua perscripturum.

Ægerrime fero, Clarissimum Doctorem Mauritium tuas de Primis
Abstractisque Motus rationibus Meditationes nobis invidisse. Solatio
interim, quod generose adeo candideque aliud nobis Exemplum polliceris.
Eousque de Summa illa, mihi jam transmissa,[3] judicium suspendere nobis
fas fuerit, cum multo commodius rectiusque de re tota ex integro Scripto,
quam ex compendio pronuntiari possit. Interim, quae de natura Punctorum
eorumque Penetratione, inque partes antea non positas extra partes, seu in
partes antea se penetrantes Divisibilitate subtiliter disseris, majorem lucem,
firmiusque quo consistant talum postulare videntur.

Jungas, obsecro, Hypothesin integram, quae ex universali quodam
Motu, in Globo nostro supposito, plaerorumque in Corporibus Phaenomenum rationem reddit. Nec ea nos celes, quae ex ipsa de Abstractis Motus
rationibus Theoria duxisse Te in Mentium non Existentiam tandem, sed
et intimiorem a Corporea distinctam Naturam asseris. Gratissima haec
nobis futura sunt, et summo, mihi crede, candore excipienda.

Visa Tibi sine dubio fuere Elementa Physica Francisci Wilhelmi Baronis
de Nuland,[4] qui Cartesianorum Principiorum falsitatem se ostendisse,
ipsiusque errores ac paralogismos (sic vocat Author) ad oculum demon-
strasse arbitratur. In hoc libello cum *Motus* statuatur unicum productorum
Corporum Organon, ejusdem Natura et Leges investigantur; quas cum Te
vidisse et examinasse credam, hic commemorare supersedeo.

De Caetero, Societas Regia consectandis Experimentis pro viribus incumbit. Socii quidam ejus Tractatulos quosdam Physicos nuper edidere.

Nobilissimi Domini Boylii Origo Formarum et Qualitatum, juxta Philosophiam Corpuscularem Experimentis et Considerationibus illustrata, Latine
nunc extat, Oxoniae impressa, et propediem in Belgium magno Exempla-
rium numero transvehenda. Idem Author Anglice non ita dudum emisit
Dissertationes quasdam de Qualitatibus Cosmicis, deque Regionum Subterranearum et Submarinarum Temperie, nec non Maris Fundo; Adhaec,
Diatribas aliquas Experimentales de miranda Aeris, etiam citra Calorem
Expansione, deque Elasticitatis ejusdem Duratione: Quae omnia sine
dubio viris cordatis et sagacibus acceptissima erunt.

Quam cupis Josephi Glanvilli de Scientiarum et Artium incremento
Historiam,[5] lubens transmittam: sed Amicum expectem oportet, qui in
oras vestras commigret, sibique hujus aliorumque quorundam libellorum
fasciculum imponi sinat. Transactiones, quas vocamus, Philosophicas,
hinc a Te postulatas, forte non mittam, cum eas audiam Hamburgi sermone Latino nunc inprimi;[6] unde commodius Tibi eas comparare poteris.
Consilium edendae hoc loco Bibliothecae Philosophicae me latet: Si quid
tamen ea de re deinceps rescivero, perscribam; nec qui Catalogi librorum
recentiores apud nos extant, fasciculo dicto adjungere omittam.

Finem hic facerem, nisi ad Epistolae tuae calcem, de Motus perpetui
procurandi ratione perquam facili, a Te inventa, nonnulla innueres, quae
tantillum me remorantur. Ais, Te rei demonstrationem, stupentibus viris
magnis, expedivisse; animosque sumpsisse, specimen in machinula edendi,
atque ubi res successerit, vadum publicum tentandi, dummodo intelligas,
esse qui rem ex vero aestiment.

Facile, puto, credes, me in Anglia peregrinum, sine palpo et assenta-
tione Anglis pronunciaturum. Sunt inter eos viri complures, subacto in
rebus Mathematicis et Mechanicis Judicio praepollentes; quorum de Invento istoc tuo sententiam ut exquiras, priusquam id evulges, ejusve
Authorem te scribas, omnino et amice suaserim. Si consilium allubescat,
meque hac in re parario opus fuerit, provinciam non detrecto, omnemque
virum bonum decet candorem spondeo. Vale, Vir Egregie, et me Tibi
devinctissimum ama. Dabam Londini 8. Decembris 1670.

Si quo responso me digneris, literas tuas, quas tabellario committis,
hunc in modum inscribas, quaeso.

A Monsieur
Monsr Grubendol
à Londres.

Nihil praeterea; multo tutius literae sic inscriptae, et per tabellarium missae, ad manus meas perveniunt, quam si meum ipsius nomen adhibeatur. Interim si quis amico huc profecturo literas vel fasciculos pro me tradiderit, eo casu propio meo nomine utendum fuerit.

TRANSLATION

H. Oldenburg, Secretary of the Royal Society, greets the very wise and learned Mr. Gottfried Wilhelm Leibniz, LL.D. and Councilor at Mainz

I have reluctantly delayed my reply to your well-stocked letter to myself of 28 September [N.S.] until now, because of various hindrances. You will readily grasp the nature of my responsibilities and be the more ready to overlook this tardiness. I can hardly tell you how the spirit is rejoiced to find that a man balanced between the Court and the courts, and of such tender years, has examined with such practiced judgment—I do not say pored over—the writings of such great figures in philosophy as Bacon, Gassendi, Descartes, and the like, as you have done. What you are laboring at, to make Law more brief and clear, by substituting for its infinite cases a single complex of few and almost simple rules, is by itself a task that demands all the strength of one man, nay of many men. I confess it is a difficult thing, yet in my view not one that is impossible for integrity, clear vision, skill, and industry. From my heart I wish you and others like you success in an endeavor no less useful than praiseworthy, and I hope very much that I may be able to bring together some sensible patrons and champions of this important work. I may perhaps in making the matter known discuss your plan with our Doctors of Civil Laws here, and when I have sounded their opinion I will write to you in due course. For the present, it will be agreeable to devote the rest of this letter to philosophy and to relate some thoughts which occurred upon reading your letter.

First, something is to be said of Huygens' endeavor to discover longitudes by means of the pendulum [clock]. From Paris I have lately heard that certain shrewd men, skilled in mathematics, are to be sent on a sea voyage to the East Indies and America at the public expense, equipped with a few automata made according to Huygens' design,[1] with the obvious intention of investigating with the greatest care the accuracy of the forementioned pendulum [clocks] amid the tossing of the waves, and preparing a reliable report of the outcome for their King.

He who strives here at London to remedy those inconveniences which he thinks still remain in this business is the very learned Mercator;[2] he promises an automaton suitable for determining longitude: (i) Because he will have two cylindrical rings to keep it permanently in a perpendicular position and facing the same direction in the ship, however the latter may be moved by the waves; whence the oscillations of the pendulum are made more definite, since the motion is commonly a pitching from bow to stern, than if the machine swung about in any direction with the ship. (ii) Because he will show the equation of time very exactly by [a device] to be applied to the automaton itself. (iii) Because he removes the inconveniences introduced by the irregular movement of the air (exceeding the preceding [disturbances], in his own opinion, by far). Time will show us the outcome of this remarkable proposal, and will urge on those who by their authority and generosity can take advantage of it, the princes of the Earth.

I am very desirous of knowing what the Memmingen water engines will accomplish towards liberating the mines of Swabia from the annoyance of water. One hopes that the Elector of Bavaria, whom you say has ordered the machines to be brought there, will look into the business thoroughly and that you out of your kindness will write when the result of the test is clear.

I regret very much that the famous Dr. Mauritius should have grudged us your reflections on the basic and abstract principles of motion. Meanwhile, it is some consolation that you have so fairly and generously promised us another copy. As for that summary already sent me,[3] it was proper for us to suspend judgment since one can pronounce much more conveniently and properly upon the question from the whole paper than from an abstract. Meanwhile, your subtle disquisition on the nature of points and their interpenetration, and their divisibility into parts not previously placed outside the parts, or into parts previously interpenetrating, seems to require greater enlightenment and a firmer foundation on which to rest.

Please add the whole hypothesis giving the explanation of many physical phenomena by postulating a certain universal motion in our globe. And do not hide from us those things you say that you have deduced from that very theory of the abstract principles of motion bearing not on the existence of minds only, but on a more intimate nature distinct from the corporeal. These things will be most welcome to us and will, I believe, be examined with scrupulous fairness.

You have no doubt seen the *Elementa physica* of Franz Wilhelm, Freiherr von Nuland,[4] who believes that he has shown the falsity of Descartes's principles, and given an ocular demonstration (these are the author's own words) of Descartes's errors and paralogisms. In this little book as motion is taken to be the sole originator of compounded bodies, its nature and laws are investigated; since I believe you have seen and examined them, I omit to take notice of them here.

For the rest, the Royal Society is experimenting with all its resources. Certain of its Fellows have lately published some little treatises on physics. The noble Mr. Boyle's *Origine of Formes and Qualities, (According to the Corpuscular Philosophy) Illustrated by Considerations and Experiments* is now available in Latin, printed at Oxford, and soon a great number of copies is to be dispatched to Holland. The same author published not long ago some *Tracts . . . about the Cosmicall Qualities of Things*, and about the temperature of submarine and subterranean regions, and the bottom of the sea; and further, certain essays upon the wonderful expansion of the air, beyond that of heat, and the duration of this same elasticity; all which things will no doubt be very welcome to wise and sensible men. I will gladly send over what you wish for of Joseph Glanvill's *Plus Ultra, or the Progress and Advancement of Knowledge since the Dayes of Aristotle*;[5] but I must wait for some friend traveling in your direction, whom I can burden with a package containing this and other books.

Perhaps I will not send you the *Philosophical* (as we call them) *Transactions*, which you request from here, because I hear that they are now being printed at Hamburg in Latin;[6] whence you can more conveniently buy them. I do not know of a plan for publishing a *Library of Philosophy* here; but if I find out anything more about it, I will write; nor will I fail to add to that package catalogues of recent books that are available here.

I should come to a stop here, were it not for the close of your letter where you hint something about a very easy way of obtaining the perpetual motion, discovered by yourself, which holds me back a little. You say that you have prepared a demonstration astonishing some notables, and that you have it in mind to put out a specimen of it in a little machine, and when that has succeeded, to test the public reaction where you can discover that such things are properly valued.

You will readily believe, I think, that as I am a foreigner in England I shall speak out without flattering or wheedling the English. There are many men among them excelling in their experienced judgment upon questions of mathematics and mechanics. I would confidently and amicably urge you to seek their opinion of this discovery of yours, before you give it to the world and own yourself its inventor. If this advice commends itself and I could serve as a go-between in the business, I shall not refuse that responsibility and I promise all the straightforwardness proper to an honest man. Farewell, excellent Sir, and believe me most devotedly yours.

London, 8 December 1670

If you favor me with any reply, please address your letter by post in this way:

A Monsieur

Monsr Grubendol

à Londres

Nothing more; letters thus addressed and sent by post will come much more safely to my hands, than if they bore my own name. Meanwhile, if you entrust a letter or package for me to a friend journeying here, in that case my own name is to be used.

NOTES

Reply to Letter 1524.

1 See Vol. VI, Letter 1365, note 8. There is no record of such news coming recently from Paris, and of course Huygens had long been out of action through illness.

2 On 11 July 1667 Seth Ward "remarked, that Mr. Mercator had acquainted him with his theory of longitudes . . . and that it was to be performed with a pendulum-clock" (Birch, *History*, II, 187). He went on to specify the three features detailed here by

Oldenburg. It is said that such a clock was made for Mercator by Fromantil and presented to Charles II; this may have been the same as the "watch" displaying the equation of time which Mercator showed to the Royal Society at Moray's suggestion on 29 August and 12 September 1666.

3 See Letter 1524, p. 166 ff.

4 *Elementa physica, sive nova philosophiae principia . . . a Francisco Wilhelmo Libero Barone de Nuland* (The Hague, 1669) is noticed in *Phil. Trans.*, no. 65 (14 November 1670), 2007–9. The rest of Oldenburg's sentence is in the book's long title.

5 Published at London in 1668.

6 See below, Letter 1638. We have not found the source of Oldenburg's information, which he did not possess on 15 November.

1569
Brouncker to Oldenburg
?10 December 1670

From the copy in Royal Society Letter Book IV, 142

Sr

What my measure was of the second Pendulum, I do not certainly remember,[1] but think, that it was $39\frac{4}{10}$ inch, whereas the Parisian you will find to be but $39\frac{2}{10}$ or inconsiderably more.

The Paris foot is to the Engl. foot (according to Graves)[2] as 1068 to 1000.

Ergo 36 Paris inch $= 38\frac{448}{10000}$ Eng. inch. for,

$$1000:30003::36:38\frac{448}{10000}.$$

And $8\frac{1}{2}$ lines $= 0\frac{7565}{10000}.$

Therefore 36. paris. inches & $8\frac{1}{2}$ line $= 39\frac{2045}{10000}.$

Which difference though it seems to exceed on the wrong hand,[4] may be occasioned, if both were exactly made, from the different seasons of the yeare, theirs perhaps being made in winter or wet weather, and mine in summer and dry weather. Thus much in hast from Sr

Your Affect. freind and Servant
Brouncker

Dec. 16. 1670.

NOTES

The copy is headed "An Answer to M. Vernon's letter of Nov. 29. 1670. [N.S.] concerning the length of a second Pendulum," and Oldenburg has added "addressed to M. Oldenburg." Since the document must precede Letter 1570, we have guessed that "10" was miscopied as "16."

1 Brouncker had made pendulum experiments in 1661 (see Birch, *History*, I, 46, 70; cf. Vol. II, pp. 266–67).
2 John Greaves, *A Discourse of the Roman Foot and Denarius* (London, 1647); there is a table of comparison of the English foot, taken from the standard at the Guildhall, with the standard measures of lengths of other peoples; see Greaves's *Miscellaneous Works*, ed. Thomas Birch (London, 1737), I, 233.
3 Read: 1068.
4 Theoretically the second's pendulum *should* be slightly longer in London than in Paris, owing to the lesser effect of the Earth's rotation; but this was not yet understood (the variation in the pendulum's length was the subject of later researches by Huygens and Newton). The shortening of the pendulum beating seconds in southern latitudes was first observed by Richer in 1672.

1570

Oldenburg to Vernon

12 December 1670

From the memorandum in Royal Society MS. V, no. 15

Answ. Dec. 12:70. about ye length of 2d[1] pendulum of English measure, to be $39\frac{4}{10}$ inch. but yt 36 inch. and $\frac{8\frac{1}{2}}{12}$ of an inch of paris measure are equal to $39\frac{2}{10}$ or inconsiderably more.

Boyle de Form. et qual. orig. in Latin.[2] id. of ye adm[irable] rarefaction of Air etc. These I promised to send him. Miltons History,[3] Court of ye Gentils[4] Metallography Websters.[5] Hevel. and Flamsteed of ye conj-[unction] of Luna and Venus, in ye Transact. of Dec. wch will send.[6]

Promised to send him N. 64 and 65. of ye Transactions for Cassini.

The computation made by Ld Br[ouncker] about ye pendulum for Seconds is this,[7]

The Paris foot is to ye English foot (according to Graves) as 1068 to 1000.

Ergo 36. Paris. inch $= 38\dfrac{448}{10000}$ Engl. inches: For

$1000.3000::36. \ 38\dfrac{448}{10000}.$

And $8\frac{1}{2}$ lines $= 0\dfrac{7565}{10000}.$

Therefore 36. Par. inches and $8\frac{1}{2}$ lines $= 39\dfrac{2045}{10000}$

By wch it appears, yt ye measure for a second pendulum, assigned by ye Parisians is lesse yn yt assigned here, after ye measures are reduced and compared; whereas it should be more; wch difference though it seems to exceed on ye wrong hand (it being conceived, yt by reason of ye more gros air here, ye pendulum should be shorter yn where ye Air is thinner) may be occasioned, if both be exactly made, from ye different seasons of ye year, ye Parisian perhaps being made in winter or wet weather, and ye English in summer or dry weather.

NOTES

Reply to Letter 1556.
1 That is, "the second's."
2 Boyle's *Origo formarum et qualitatum* (Oxford, 1669) was possibly translated by Samuel Russell of Oxford.
3 John Milton, *The History of Britain* (London, 1670).
4 T[heophilus] G[ale], *The Court of the Gentiles; or, a Discourse touching the Original of Humane Literature, from the Scriptures and Jewish Church* (London, 1669).
5 John Webster, *Metallographia, or an History of Metals* (London, 1670).
6 See *Phil. Trans.*, no. 66 (12 December 1670), 2027–28. Flamsteed's account (Letter 1567) was not published.
7 What follows is from Letter 1569; the physical speculation at the end may well derive from Brouncker too.

1571
Oldenburg to Huygens
c. 12 December 1670

From *Œuvres Complètes*, VII, 51
Original in the Huygens Collection at Leiden

Monsieur

Le porteur de celle-cy me donne la commodité de vous faire mes baisemains et de vous prier d'accepter des papiers annexes,[1] où vous trouverez quelques observations des Anses de Saturne, qui vous donneront occassion de faire reflexion sur vostre systeme de ce planete. J'esperois de vous envoyer par le mesme, quelques nouveaux traités de Monsieur Boyle, touchant la merveilleuse rarefaction de l'Air, mesme sans chaleur, comme aussi touchant la duration de sa force elastique etc.[2] Mais l'inprimeur ayant tardé plus long temps que ie ne croyois, ie pourray vous faire tenir cela par les mains de Monsieur vostre pere, avec quelque bonne piece de verre pour un telescope.

Dans les Transactions de ce mois on fera inprimer l'observation de Monsieur Hevel de Transitu Lunae super Venerem l'11me d'Octobre 1670, ce qui a esté observé aussi par un Astronome Anglois, qui sera prié de nous la donner pareillement pour le faire inprimer le mois apres.[3] C'est tout ce que i'ay à vous dire à present, sinon que Monsieur Boyle et Monsieur Moray vous saluent tres affectueusement, et que ie suis Monsieur

Vostre treshumble & tresobeissant Serviteur
Oldenburg

ADDRESS
A Monsieur
Monsieur Christian Hugens de Zulichem
à la
Haye

TRANSLATION

Sir,

The bearer of this offers me the opportunity to send you my respects and to beg you to accept the attached papers,[1] in which you will find some observations of the anses of Saturn which will give you reason to reflect about your theory of this planet. I had hoped to send you by the same [hand] some new tracts of Mr. Boyle on the admirable rarefaction of the air, even without heat, and on the duration of its elastic force, etc.[2] But the printer having delayed longer than I hoped, I shall be able to let you have that by the hand of your father, together with a good piece of glass for a telescope.

In the *Transactions* of this month will be printed the observation of Mr. Hevelius on the transit of the moon across Venus of 11 October 1670 [N.S.], which was also observed by an English astronomer who will be requested to give [his observation] to us for similar printing in the month following.[3] This is all that I have to say to you at present, except that Mr. Boyle and Sir Robert Moray greet you very affectionately, and that I am, Sir,

Your very humble and obedient servant,
Oldenburg

ADDRESS
To Mr. Christiaan Huygens of Zulichem
at The Hague

NOTES

1   *Phil. Trans.*, no. 65 (14 November 1670).
2   See Letter 1553, note 4.
3   See Letter 1570, note 6.

1572
Oldenburg to Martindale
13 December 1670

Martindale's Letters 1562 and 1565 are endorsed as received on 29 November and 5 December and answered on 13 December 1670.

1573
Flamsteed to Oldenburg
13 December 1670

From the original in Royal Society MS. F 1, no. 64

Dec: 13 1670

Mr Oldenburge
Sr,

Yesterday I receaved a letter from my very good freind Mr Collins, importeing. yt hee had delivered ye paper with ye Moones transit by Venus to yu:[1] and also yr desire to have me describe ye observation, wth my thoughts thereon in English; lest saies hee, ye sense be mistaken, when[2] I rather feare my latine is too poore for a publick view, or the sight of such criticall censors as it may meet with: I confesse Sr, I am not happy in comiting my thoughts to paper, and rarely doe it, but, as I did those, with some difficulty; which makes mee feare, my English may prove as darke as my latine, & as little satisfactory.

Mr Collins informes me, yt yu have receaved an observation of the suns transit[3] made by Hevelius at Dantzick, & that you intend to publish it in yr transactions. I am infinitely pleasd with ye news, & to heare that this luciferous appearance which I esteemed as lost, hath beene, accurately no doubt, observed elsewhere. yu will much oblige such as with me are studious of Astronomy, by the communicateing of it. & yu have my thankes before hand: Mr Collins writes, yt you would publish my kinsmanes observation wth that of Hevelius, but, truely Sr I esteeme it not exact enough to appeare in publick especially since ye heavens have granted us one that is more accurate; which had it beene wanteing; his then might have served to excite ye ingenuous, & such as are carefull of the heavens to a greater vigilancy, & exactnesse in caelestiall observations; & further use I would have made none of it.

I had in an Ephemeris I compos'd for my owne use inserted a memoire of this appearance; but our Ephemerides & tables not permitting it till after sunrise, I noted yt, to us, it would not be observable; & therefore never waited for it: I shall be glad to see ye Dantzick observation by which I shall put our tables to triall; & it shall not be long after, ere I give you my iudgment what is to be learnt therefrom; & in what our tables doe not answer it. in the meane time that I may not faile my expectation, I shall describe my kinsmans observation, with my thoughts theron.[4]

At Codnor whose latitude is 53°–04′: & its meridian from London 1¼ gr. to ye West. October ye 1st in ye morne 1670: at five a clock as neare as could be ghest. or (in ye observers owne words) halfe an hour after ye first breake of day or 1½ hour before sunrise. Venus was seene in about 3 minutes lesse altitude then ye moons center. & about ¼ of her diameter or rather 10 min from her Westerne limbe to ye west: by the position of Venus, & ye Angle of ye verticall circle, passing over ye Moones Center with ye Ecliptick 29°–59′: I collect that ye Moone was 9 minutes in consequence of Venus, with 22 min: greater latitude; whereas by ye calculalation (of which yu have ye heads in ye latin paper & which, I suppose it needless to repeate) at 5h–03′ mane,[5] shee should be 42′–22″ in antecedence of her. so that ye numbers erre at least 51′ minutes. The Reflection in ye Caroline tables is 32′. 57″ which to helpe to salve ye appearance might be omitted, if other observed appulses would suffer it: but yet neither would the phainomenon be salved by 18 min: which will scarce be removd, should wee suppose yt ye observer erred 40 minutes, in stateing ye time. for ye Moone at Apogea fere,[6] & slow in motion, and being supposed higher at ye time of ye observation, the parallaxes of altitude, & longitude will necessarily be lesse, & the Moone still more removed from her observed place. but neither will my kinsman grant yt hee erred so much in stateing ye time of this appearance, neither will many other observed appulses permit us to reject ye Reflection, without which they cannot be salved, more especially yt of ye Moone to Jupiter seene & observed by Hevelius at Dantzick Anno 1646 December ye 14: & delineated in his Selenography page 476: at which tho ye distance of ye Sun from ye Moone first aequated was 4h–04°–37′–59″ & thence the Reflection 33′–24″ addend. yet ye appearance is represented by Streets tables with lesse then 2 minutes error. If the Dantzick observation dissent not wee may hence argue, yt ye observed irregularities in ye Moones motions are to be salved by other aequations then are yet excogitated. And in my opinion the physicall causes of them not being thorowly weighed & considered, doe cause that our tables, which I feare infringe reason, doe no better answer ye heavens. but till I may have considered some more observations of this I shall desire to be silent.[7]

I wish wee had Hevelius his observation of ye Eclipse of ye sun which happened on Octob. 25. 1668. if hee made any.[8] I doubt not but thence wee might better settle ye difference of our meridian from his. which as I hinted in a former letter I feare is stated to large: you may doe well Sr when yu write to him againe to enquire about it, or if yu know any thing allready to enforme mee by yr next.

I give yu many thankes for accomodateing me wth ye Selenography[9] & I shall returne it yu by ye carrier, ye first journey after Christmasse if in ye meane time yu desire it sooner, let me know yr mind I shall send it by the first opportunity: No more at present but that I am

Yr obliged servant
John Flamsteed

My service to Mr Collins. when yu see him, prey let him know yt my glasses I tried last weeke & find yt they will require a tube of 20 foot at least, but I feare they will prove but bad for in the triall they cast colours sadly.

ADDRESS
    To Henry Oldenburge Esq
       at his house in ye middle
         of ye pellmell in st James'es
           feilds Westminster
              these present

POSTMARK DE 16

NOTES

1 This letter does not seem to be in print; see further Letter 1567.
2 Read: whence.
3 Oldenburg altered this to read: "the moons transit by Venus"; see Letter 1536.
4 What follows is an English précis of Letter 1567.
5 "A.M."
6 "almost in apogee."
7 This passage (an expansion of that in Latin, p. 304) is of interest as being the first indication of Flamsteed's concern for the rectification of lunar theory, which was to occupy him greatly in future years and bring him into conflict with Newton.
8 See Vol. V, p. 185.
9 See Letter 1554, note 5.

1574
Vernon to Oldenburg
14 December 1670

From the original in Royal Society MS. V, no. 16
Partly printed in Brown, pp. 238–39

Paris Decembre 24. 1670 [N.S.]

Sr

There is an Italian here in towne, a native of Sicily, calld Sigre Paolo Boccone.[1] Hee was Herborist to the Duke of Florence. Hee is come to Paris to satisfie his Curiosity in the view of those Plantes wch this country produceth. Hee is Recommended From Florence by severall Letters as a Person very understanding In what hee professeth. Sigre Gornia the Grand dukes Physitian,[2] Vincenzo Viviani, Carlo Dati & severall others of the Vertuosos there have given a very handsome testimony Concerning him, & recommended him to severall Persons of Note here, as Monsieur Veillot,[3] Carcavi, Thevenot & others of Consideration in this place where they speake of him as one very deserving & knowing in Plantes. of wch hee hath brought a good Collection dryed & pasted in a booke, many of wch hee saith are rare, & undescribed by Authors, wch hee hath gott together in his travailles all Italy throughout & Sicily, wherein hee hath beene more then ordinarily exact. & indeed his whole Genius lies to Botaniques, wherein Indeed I thinke hee is very skilfull. Now that wch hee proposeth is: he saith hee hath spent most of his life in the search of Plants, to wch his inclination wholly carries him, & now hee is growing towards fourty, hee would bee glad to bee assisted in his expence: & if hee found any encouradgement hee would goe in to England where if hee had a Reasonable Provision made for him, he offers first to Present that Collection of Plantes hee hath made, wth the description & discourses hee hath annext to them, to the Royall Society to be printed, or disposed of as they Please; next if they are Curious to have a larger Collection of Forein Plantes then that hee hath yet made, hee proffers to goe into those Countries they shall designe for him, & procure & seeke them there. Provided hee have a Reasonable subsistence, & his expences defrayed; for hee saith hee hath noe other ambition butt only to spend his dayes in the Prosecution of this study. Now the Reason which hee would come into England &

leave Italy is because the Italians are not very Curious after Sciences, & are very penurious & loft[4] to make any expence for the encouradgeing of them, wch two defects hee hopes may bee remedied in England they having more dispositions to knowledge & more generosity to reward it. Sr John Finch hath given him a Letter to Dr Smith,[5] soe that you need not doubt butt that hee is sufficiently knowne, & Sr Bernard Gascon,[6] & all who have any Relation to the Court of Florence hee saith will give assurances for him that hee is noe deceiver. This is what hee intreated mee to write in his behalfe. & If you iudge him a Person usefull to your enterprises, or if the Royall society need him not, If any other of our nation stand disposed for a Person soe qualified, You may please to give mee advice of it, & you wil doe him a kindnesse, & oblidge

your most affecte servant
Francis Vernon

Diophantus of Fermats edition[7] is come to Paris & Monsr Justel will send you one by the first Convenience I can find for him. Monsr Claudes booke[8] is likewise Printed & come abroad.

NOTES

1 Paolo Boccone (1633–1704), born at Palermo, had taught botany to the Grand Duke Ferdinand of Tuscany, and was appointed professor at Padua. He traveled extensively and was author of many volumes. He did not, in fact, visit England until 1674.
2 See Vol. VI, Letter 1227.
3 Probably Antoine Vallot (1594–1671), a physician, appointed superintendent of the Jardin des Plantes in 1658, is intended.
4 loath.
5 It is not possible to identify this person with certainty: Hooke also knew a "Dr. Smith" (unidentified, but probably F.R.S.), no doubt the same person, but the only man of this name in the Royal Society was Edward Smith, not recorded as a "Dr" of any sort. Dr. John Smith, a physician of Bishopsgate, was not F.R.S.
6 For Sir Bernard Gascoigne (1614–87), see Vol. III, p. 594, note 7.
7 See Letter 1550, note 1.
8 See Letter 1556, note 15.

1575
Nelson to Oldenburg
15 December 1670
From the original in Royal Society MS. N 1, no. 32

Worthy Sr

It is now a good while since I designed to write to you, tho it were but only to assure you, that I have not any thing worth your acceptance to communicate;[1] wch you will not wonder at after I have told you that my quality and profession are such as doe prohibit me the advanges of stirring abroad in the world and doe engage me in a childish, rather than manly conversation: and therefore all you can expect from me, is my hearty wishes for the happiness of your illustrious company, and that you may goe on and prosper in that rationall and most likely way of advancing knowledge, wherein already you have made so faire a progress. Besides, this county so far as I know it, seems to afford either very few things extra-ordinary or very few heads disposed to observe them; the most remarkable that I can call to minde are the Salt Spring near this Towne,[2] and the Hell Kettles near Darlington of wch I thought once to have given you an Account, but then I remember'd that Mr. Cambden had long agoe said enough of them to spare me the labour.[3]

There are divers Cole Mines in this County as also near this Towne; and some workers there are who affirme yt. a Head of Garlick bruised in the bottome of a pit, has ye like stifling effect that the Damp has, or the Styth (as they call it,) but I have not met wth any that have try'd it.

Having heard some enquiry about, or some mention made of subter-raneall fumes, and vapours or steames issueing out of the Earth, it put me in minde of what I was told by a neighbour, (a man of a good understand-ing;) namely, that hee one evening having been a mile from home and returning about 9 of the clock (the time of the year was May and the Season faire, but somewhat a sharp thin Aire at that time of the evening) he, being on horse backe in a faire high way inclosed on each side wth hedges and Corne ground, was all on a sodaine surprized wth a strange heat as if hee had entered into some Stove or come near a very great fire, his horse shrunke under him, and his face was extremely sensible of the heat, wch lasted ye space of about 18 or 20 yards to his great astonishment, and then ceased. It was accompanied as he thought wth a kinde of earthly smell, wch made him looke about him, to see if there might not be some heape of pared Land or other thing on fire, but espying neither fire nor smoake within the compas of his Eyes, he condemned presently the folly of that enquiry, seeing he thought ye heat to have been as great as if a huge fire had been beside him; This if it signifie anything you may take for a certain truth.

There is one thing wch I have often observed and wondered at, bu never met wth any man that gave an Account of it, and that is a Noise heard about a fresh River as if it were a great fall or flowing of water; but it is most frequently heard when the Water is low and ye Aire calme, many times in summer evenings, and sometimes it is observed to have a Motion upwards, and sometimes downe the Channell. An ingenious friend of mine living in the edge of Yorkshire told me yt hee was one time at ye River side—The River of Tees near ye place where he lives—(fishing if I mistake not) when he heard the Noise below him, and after a while it drew near him and waxed lowder; he stept into the midst of the Chanell thinking there to discerne somewhat, and having staid till it came to him, he found himselfe surrounded wth a lowe murmur, wch past by him up the River and left him no otherwise informed then much amazed to thinke what it should be. The Country people that observe it use to foretell from thence the change of the weather.

Since first I read Dr Wallis his Hypothesis about ye fluxes and refluxes of the Sea,[4] I thought it so very rationall, that 'twas pitty any flaw should ever be found in it; yet there is one objection that haunts me, taken from a presumption (at least) that there are certaine seas in some parts of ye world that are perfectly Stagnant and without any fluctuation at all; And Heylin[5] takes it for granted that the Baltick Sea flows not & endeavours to give Reasons for it, wch how they agree, wth ye Dr's Hypothesis I understand not, neither can I apprehend how, if the Tides be derived from the Motions of the Earth, they should come, not to be universall, and why they should not flow equally and uniformly, agreeable to what hee supposes the Earth's motion to be, allowance being granted for the position of the Shoare, the winde and other accidents.

I know not what books M. Hevelius means of, (Numb. 64)[6] that he would have turned in Latine, but I suppose 'tis your monthly Tracts, and I am perswaded that if there were a Collection made out of them, of some of the more choise observations, and turned into such Latine as I have seen from your pen, it would be a most acceptable worke both abroad and at home. It were best indeed yt they went all together, if that were not too great an Addition to your burthen (sufficiently heavy already,) and too great a Volume to become vendible.

As to persons that seeme to be promoters of Ingenious Arts, I shall only mention 2 or 3 in these parts that I can thinke of at present; one is Sr Ralph Cole[7] a gentleman truly so called and a person no less obliging than ingenious; his fancy first lead him to the Art of Limming, in wch he is granted by all men to be Singular; and now he is growne a great Artificer in Iron, Wood & Silver as also in tempering of Steele: many gentlemen of his acquaintance are very proud of excellent Knives that they weare of his making. Hee has the best mechanicke head & is the only Virtuoso of any gentleman that I know in this Country.

Another is one Thomas Mossocke, his faculty lyes in making of Watches and graving in mettalls; in this latter he is equalled by few, scarce (I thinke) out done by any, and what makes him the more remarkable is, that hee was never taught any thing of those kindes of worke at all, but what he does, he has purely taken it up of himselfe, by wch yet he earnes abundance of money, tho' he lives in an obscure Country Towne. He tells me that he has contrived an Engine or Instrument for the speedy cutting downe of Watch wheels, by wch he can worke as much in an hour as wth files in twenty, and more exactly; The like Instrument I have heard that one of your Watch makers in London hath, but I am perswaded, that this man had his, from him, nor any other, but meerly from his owne Invention.

There is also one Ralph Coats[8] an excellent Bow maker living in Darlington a man of good understanding in mechanicke operations, and a good Artist at Gunns, of wch hee makes some to shoot divers times wth one charging.

The Physitians in this Towne that are of note are first Dr Wilson an ingenious man and a good Scholler, for the most part a Methodist, but yet not Juratus in verba Magistri;[9] he is a diligent peruser of your monthly Tracts.

The next is Mr Nicholson a Serious young man, and well educated, inclinable to Chymistry but no great Practitioner.

Next I reckon one Mr Selby who hath been as much beholding to fortune as Education; but a civill man and well spoken, has been borne under good thriving aspects, and is fallen into a notable way of practise; hee workes sometimes in the fire, and has a small Laboratory in wch hee makes some of the medicines he uses.[10]

There is one Mr Dancy, a man that is thought to have good skill &

hath done divers hansome cures, but hath not had the lucke to thrive and is not therefore so considerable as possibly he might have been.

I have given you these hints as to particular persons for your owne p[articular—*paper torn*] satisfaction, and with a desire yt you may (as much as possible) reall[*paper torn*] those imaginary people of the new Atlantis in having intelligence of a[ll] persons as well as things that may contribute to your designe; assuring my selfe in the meane time yt you will never have any occasion to make publick mention of these, or any other thing that I shall ever be able to acquaint you wth; and therefore I have taken ye larger Liberty of scribbling (for want of better things) almost Quicquid in buccam venit.[11] I can hardly hope yt my trifles should procure me any returne from you, tho you were pleased heretofore so much to honour me wth your Letters wch I treasure up, as a Rarity, and looke upon as a signall instance of the obliging Spirit of the Virtuosi: Yet when you can obtaine so much respit from worthier Imployments, I would beg a few lines from you, and wish to be thereby informed how the Honble Mr Boyle recovers his much desired health (in wch philosophy seems extremely concerned) and whether my friend Mr Oswell (from whom I have not heard this long time) be in his Service or no.[12]

I wish to hear whether any man be at worke to translate Bp. Wilkins's Caracter into Latine or no,[13] and whether Dr Spratt or any body else be engaged in defence of the R. Society and its' history against the vapouring cavills of the Hectoring Stubbs.[14] And now Sr were it not for fear of being yet more tedious I might make an Apologie for the length of my Letter, but having so great assurance of your patience and hopes of your pardon, I shall wth confidence & whilst there is roome subscribe my selfe (Honed Sr)

> Your most humble Servant
> *Peter Nelson*

Durham December 15th 1670.

Has the New Plough been tryed in England since you got it, and wth what success?[15]

ADDRESS

For my very much honoured friend
Henry Oldenburg Esqr at his house
in ye Pell-mell in St James's fields
　　　　These
　　　　　London

　　　　　　　　POSTMARK DE 19

NOTES

1 Nelson's last letter was written on 22 August 1668 (Vol. V, p. 23).
2 Durham.
3 Still so called; they are sulphurous pools. See Richard Gough (ed.), *Britannia, or a chorographical Description of the flourishing Kingdoms of England, Scotland and Ireland . . . by William Camden* (London, 1789), III, 104.
4 Printed in *Phil. Trans.*, no. 16 (6 August 1666), 263–81; see Vol. III.
5 Peter Heylyn, *Cosmographie* (London, 1652), p. 126. His "reasons" are the narrowness of the entrance and its being so far North!
6 This was published on 10 October 1670. Hevelius' remark will be found on p. 48 above.
7 Sir Ralph Cole (?1625–1704), the second baronet, of Brancepath Castle, Durham, a painter and patron of painters, later M.P. for his county.
8 In 1686 he was paid twelve pounds for a church clock; see W. H. D. Longstaffe, *The History and Antiquities of the Parish of Darlington* (London, 1909). It is perhaps worth noting that at this period "repeating" firearms employed either multiple barrels (or cylinders) rotated to a fixed lock, or a succession of charges—each with its own touch-hole—placed in the same barrel end-to-end, fired by a sliding lock.
9 "Sworn to the word of a master." We could not identify this physician, despite his title, nor any of the practitioners (apothecaries or quacks) mentioned below.
10 Robert Selbie appears below as the writer of Letter 1660, but is otherwise unknown.
11 "Whatever comes into my head."
12 The same person (presumably)wrote to Oldenburg from Utrecht in 1673. He is not mentioned in Boyle's will, or in Hooke's *Diary*, or indeed anywhere else.
13 See Vol. V, p. 281, note 7.
14 See Letter 1482, note 2. About the end of 1670 or early in 1671 were also published an anonymous *Letter to Mr. Hen. Stubbe in defence of the History of the Royal Society* (to which Stubbe rejoined) and Glanvill's *Further Discovery of Mr Stubbe* (whose "To the Reader" is dated 14 February 1670/1).
15 See *Phil. Trans.*, no. 60 (20 June 1670,) 1055–65, and Vol. VI, Letter 1402.

1576
Denis to Oldenburg
19 December 1670
From the original in Royal Society MS. D 1, no. 6

de paris ce 29 decembre [N.S.]

Monsieur

Je prend la liberté de vous écrire la presente a l'occasion d'un excellent
naturaliste nommé paolo Bocconi[1] herboriste du feu Duc de Toscane[2]
qui a apporté plusieurs semences et plantes incognues en ces payis des
pierres curieuses, des coraux, cristaux, sels, poissons, coquillages et choses
semblables sur les quelles il fait voir de tres belles observations qu'il a
faites pour en demonstrer physiquement et mechaniquement les premiers
commencemens, et la production jusqu'a la derniere perfection,[3] il a
outre cela une histoire des plantes de la sicile[4] enrichie de six vingt plantes
nouvelles dont il a apporté les feuilles et les semences, et m'a fait voir des
epreuves dun secret fort particulier quil a de tirer en un instant sur du
papier toutes sortes de feuilles, branches, et rameaux, en sorte qu'appli-
quant la plante mesme sur le papier il en demeure une image empreinte qui
represente avec la derniere perfection la figure les fibres et la couleur de la
plante ce qui seroit fort avantageux pour faire une histoire plus exacte des
plantes et pour en graver les figures, Je ne scais si l'on feroit cas de toutes
ces choses dans vostre illustre Academie, mais ie l'encourage fort dans le
dessein qu'il a de passer en Angleterre avec toutes ses raretés, et il ne s'est
point voulu mettre en chemin que ie ne sceusse auparavant de vous si
vous croyez que son voyage luy pourroit apporter quelque utilité. cest
le sujet pour le quel je vous importune vous priant de me faire un mot de
responce a vostre commodité et vous obligerez infiniment Monsieur

Vostre tres humble serviteur
Denis

n'a t'on point fait encore de traduction de vos transactions?[5]

ADDRESS
　A Monsieur
　Monsieur Oldenbourg
　Secretaire de l'academie
　Royalle d'Angleterre
　　　　　Londres

TRANSLATION

Paris, 29 December [N.S.]

　Sir,

Itake the liberty of writing this letter to you on behalf of an excellent naturalist named Paolo Boccone,[1] herbalist to the late Duke of Tuscany,[2] who has brought many seeds and plants unknown in this country, curious stones, corals, crystals, salts, fish and shellfish, and similar things with which he illustrates the many fine observations he has made, serving to reveal their physical and mechanical development from their first beginnings to the production of their final perfection.[3] Besides this he has a history of Sicilian plants,[4] enriched with twenty-six new plants whose leaves and seeds he has brought with him, and he showed me tests of a very special secret he has of tracing in an instant upon paper all sorts of leaves, branches, and boughs, in such a fashion that when the plant itself is applied to the paper an imprinted image remains behind, which represents with the utmost accuracy the shape, the fibers, and the color of the plant, which would be very helpful for making a more exact history of plants and for preparing engravings of their shapes. I do not know whether you value all these things in your illustrious Society, but I am encouraging him strongly in his plan to go to England with all his rarities; but he did not wish to set out unless I knew beforehand if you thought that his journey might be useful to him. This is the subject about which I intrude upon you, begging you to send me a word of reply at your convenience, and you will infinitely oblige, Sir,

Your very humble servant,
Denis

Has no one yet made a translation of your *Transactions*?[5]

ADDRESS
　Mr. Oldenburg
　Secretary of the Royal Society of England
　　　　London

NOTES

1 See Letter 1574 and its note 1.
2 Ferdinand II, who died in 1670.
3 We have rendered the French somewhat freely; it will be understood that "development" refers to the growth of the individual plant, not the evolution of a species.
4 Boccone had already published *Manifestum botanicum de plantis Siculis* (Catania, 1668); he was to print *Icones et descriptiones variarum plantarum Siciliae, Melitae, Galliae et Italiae* (Lyons and Oxford, 1674).
5 See Letter 1471 (and its note 7), and Letter 1553 *ad fin.*

1577

Oldenburg to Travagino

20 December 1670

From the memorandum in Royal Society MS. T, no. 12

Accepi d. 8. Dec. 1670. non retinui copiam.
Resp. d. 20. Dec. rogavi de Lanae Bresciani Jesuitae doctura et judicio.¹ S[ignifi]cavi libros hic editos, a Wallisio, Barrovio, Boylio, inprimis ejus Tractatulos et schedas de mira Aeris expansione, Websteri Metallographiam.²

TRANSLATION

Received 8 December 1670—did not keep a copy.
Replied 20 December: I asked about the learning and judgment of the Jesuit Lana, of Brescia.¹ I informed him of the books printed here, by Wallis, Barrow, Boyle, especially his tractates and notes on the wonderful expansion of the air; Webster's *Metallographia*.²

NOTES

Reply to Letter 1519.
1 See Letter 1519, note 4, and the similar inquiry in Letter 1578. Francisco Lana (1631–87), after being received in the Society of Jesus and beginning to teach literature, worked with Kircher at Rome for some time. He then taught at Terni, Brescia, Ferrara, and finally returned to Brescia, his native city. He was interested in mineralogy and the formation of crystals, but particularly in theoretical and practical mechanics. He invented (besides his aerostatic machine) a seed sower, clocks, lamps, fire engines and pumps, flying birds, etc. In Brescia he founded a short-lived philosophical society.
2 See Letter 1570, note 5.

1578
Oldenburg to Malpighi

20 December 1670

From the original in Bologna MS. 2085, VII, ff. 17–18
Printed in Pizzoli, pp. 57–58

Clarissimo atque Expertissimo Viro
Domino Marcello Malpighio, Philosopho et Medico Bononiensi,
H. Oldenburg Salutem

Perquam gaudeo, Te tandem Historiae tuae Bombycinae Exemplaribus hinc transmissis potitum. Oblata occasione commoda libellos quosdam a nostratibus pronuper editos expedire ad Te potero; Tractatulos puta Nobilissimi Boylii de Qualitatibus Cosmicis, deque mira Aeris, etiam citra Calorem, Expansione, nec non de ejusdem Elementi (sic vocare cum vulgo liceat) Elasticitatis Duratione; juncto Doctoris Lowerij de Catharris opusculo. Innuis, Doctissimum Mengolum plura de Parallaxibus moliri, Clarissimumque Borellum brevi secundum librum de vi percussionis evulgaturum; Cassinique Apologiam in cujusdam, quem non nominas, librum jam extare. Speramus, horum omnium copiam nobis suo tempore fore; nec dubitamus, quin Tu ipse plura acuminis et diligentiae tuae Anatomicae specimina sis editurus.

Est Brescianus quidam Philosophus, e Societate Jesu, qui Opus Physicum meditatur, ad vitae humanae usum, ut ait, comparatum. Institutum perquam laudabile, si oneri ferendo par sit Author. Tu sine dubio virum nosti, cui nomen *Lana*;[1] ejus doctrinam et Judicium abs Te edoceri cuperem. Jam quidem vulgavit Prodromi sui partem, quam Amicus quidam meus ex oris istis ad me transmisit;[2] sed ex tantillo vix quicquam possum de subacto viri judicio colligere.

Fuse nuper ad Celeberrimum Montanarium scripsi. Datae literae 19. Novembris.[3] Certiorem illum feci, tum Manuscriptum ejus, tum Tractatus impressos, Societati Regiae destinatos, hic appulisse, eidemque publice exhibitos fuisse. Necdum Socii illi, quibus dicta Societas scriptum Domini Montanarij, circa Vitra Stillatitia adornatum, commisit, sua de Argumento illo sensa exposuere.[4] Quamprimum id factum fuerit, sententiae summam perscribere non morabor. Speramus interim, Virum sagacem gnaviter in *Firmamento* suo *instabili*, ut vocat, concinnando laborare, idemque brevi expediturum. Utrumque vestrum plurimum salvere a Doctrinae et Virtutis vestrae Cultore devinctissimo velim. Vale. Dabam Londini die 20 Decemb. 1670.

ADDRESS

    Clarissimo et Doctissimo Viro
    Domino Marcello Malpighio
    Philosopho et Medico Bononensi
        meritissimo
           Bononiae

TRANSLATION

H. Oldenburg greets the very famous and skilful Mr. Marcello Malpighi, philosopher and physician of Bologna

I am very glad that you have at last obtained the copies of your silkworm history sent from here. When a convenient opportunity serves I shall furnish you with certain volumes recently published by us; that is to say the very noble Boyle's little tracts on cosmical qualities and upon the wonderful expansion of the air, exceeding that of heat, as well as upon the duration of the elasticity of that same element (if one may speak in ordinary terms), together with Dr. Lower's little monograph, *De catharris.* You indicate that the very learned Mengoli has done more on the subject of parallaxes, and that the famous Borelli will shortly publish the second volume of *De vi percussionis*; and that an *Apologia* by Cassini is already extant in some book that you do not name. We hope that in due course you will supply us with all of these, not doubting either that you will yourself be issuing more examples of your acuity and diligence in anatomy.

There is at Brescia a certain Jesuit philosopher who is planning some work in physics destined, as he says, to be of use to men. It is a most praiseworthy design, if the undertaker is equal to the responsibility. No doubt you know the man, whose name is Lana;[1] I would like to be informed by you of his learning and judgment. There is already in print part of his *Prodromus*, which a certain friend of mine sent me from that part of the world,[2] but from such a fragment I could gather scarcely anything of the man's disciplined judgment.

I recently wrote at length to the celebrated Montanari, the date of the letter being 19 November.[3] I informed him that both his manuscript and his printed books intended for the Royal Society had been delivered here, and publicly presented to it. Those Fellows to whom the Society entrusted Mr. Montanari's paper on glass drops have not yet disclosed their opinion of it.[4] As soon as they have I shall not delay in composing a summary of their views. Meanwhile, we

hope that that wise author is striving vigorously to compile his "Inconstant
Firmament" as he calls it, and will soon finish the book. As a most obliged admirer
of your learning and virtue, I offer you both all good wishes. Farewell.
London, 20 December 1670

ADDRESS

> To the very famous and learned
> Mr. Marcello Malpighi
> Most worthy philosopher and physician
> > at Bologna

NOTES

Reply to Letter 1547.
1 See Letter 1577, note 1.
2 See Letter 1561 and its note 4.
3 Letter 1555.
4 See Letter 1555, note 2.

1579
Oldenburg to Dodington

20 December 1670

From the copy in Royal Society MS. O 2, no. 38a

A letter to Mr Dodington at Venice, desiring certain Italian
communications from him.

Sr

You make so Obliging an Apology for yr unfrequency of writing, yt
you give us abundant satisfaction, and engage us to desire, yt you
would but continue after ye rate, you have done hitherto. I have received
ye beginning of Father Lanna's Prodromus, and do most cordially
acknowledge your liberality, desiring very much, wn you find conveniency,
to enrich us wth ye sequel of yt work, wch may be usefull to ye publick.
I wish only yt ye Authour would be sparing in the publication of such
Arguments, as seem to be above ye reach of human contrivance, as sayling
through ye Air, ye perpetual motion, the Philosopher's stone, and ye like;

such undertakings being rather like to prove a disadvantage to his writings and credit, yn otherwise.

If Borelli should have published any thing more de Vi Percussionis, or Mengolus of Parallaxes, or ye former something new de Motu Animalium, and the latter, de Sono et Musica, it would be worth having and further oblige us to you for your favour of transmitting such books unto us.[1]

I have wth much freedome enclosed here 2. letters, wch I am persuaded you will not faile to see delivered.[2] Therein I have acquainted those 2 worthy Gentlemen, wt Philosophicall books have been lately published here, wth a promise to send ym over wth the first conveniency by sea.

Sr my confidence in your readinesse of continuing this Philosophical commerce taketh still deeper root. I wish only you would give mee some occasion, wherby I might really manifest, wt I am, yt is Sr

Your humble servt
Oldenburg

London Dec. 20. 1670

As I thank you particularly for ye Venetian Catalogue of books so I should be glad to have ye Bombardiero Veneto mentioned therein.[3]

NOTES

Reply to Letter 1561.
1 This request relies on Malpighi's remarks in Letter 1547.
2 Presumably Letters 1577 and 1578.
3 From the time of Tartaglia in the mid-sixteenth century a succession of books on gunnery was printed at Venice, books by Capobianco, Collado, Colombino, Gentilini, Moretti, Rossetti, Sardi, etc. In the Earl of Anglesey's sale (1686)—which included Oldenburg's library—was Eugenio Gentilini da Este, *Instruttione de Bombardieri* (Venice, 1592). No book seems to be entitled *Il Bombardiero Veneto*.

1580

Oldenburg to Ludolf

20 December 1670

From the draft in Royal Society MS. O 2, no. 39

Amplissimo et Consultissimo Viro
Domino Jobo Ludolff Serenissimi Principis
de Gotha Consiliario Henricus Oldenburg Salutem

Gratulor mihi magnopere, Vir Amplissime, quod occasionem mihi praebuisti priscam nostram consuetudinem, per aliquod temporis spatium interruptam, redintegrandi. Significavi R. Societati benevolam Serenissimi Principis vestris in ejus institutum et studia voluntatem.[1] Mox illa, ut par erat, in mandatis mihi dedit, ut pro illo favore, junctaque gratiosa Serenitatis suae promptitudine, Regionum suarum Curiosa naturalia communicandi, summas gratias agerem. Tu, Vir Consultissime, fidum Te nobis pararium hac in re praebebis, nec de nostro in Te et merita tua affectione ullatenus dubitabis.

Cum Caetus hic Regius id unice propemodum agat, ut rerum naturalium Scientiam, Artesque Ingenuas, in majorem Cognitionis certitudinem, inque ampliora inprimis humanae vitae praesidia et commoda provehat, necessarium omnino credit, viros omnigena eruditionem et experientia illustres undequaque in institutum illud suum pertrahere, et ad colendum super his rebus commercium literarium sollicitare. Magnum quippe momentum ad veritatem indagandam afferre censent Ingeniorum et Laborum confarreationem; quae si per universum Orbem posset obtineri, eosque inter institui, qui mentem gerant exauthoratam, studioque partium superiorem, nec nisi veritati et hominum commodis litantem, in summum profecto culmen eluctaretur Philosophia.

Nos certe nulla in re magis, quam in locuplete Observationum et Experimentorum comparanda supellectile nunc occupamur, atque ad symbola sua huc conferenda quorumvis gentium viros sagaces solertesque invitamus. Operi igitur huic tam laudabili Principem vestrum aliosque magni Animi philosophos, in oris vestris delitescentes, haudquaquam defuturos arbitramur; quaeque proinde Patria vestra de Vegetabilium, Fossilorum, et Animantium familiis nec non circa Aerem, Aquas, Thermas, Meteora Etc. gignit exhibetque observata digna, candide nobis communicaturos omnino confidimus. Hocipsum omni officiorum genere provicibus demereri adnitemur. Submissam inprimis Observantiam meam Serenissimo Domino Ernesto deferre gestio, proque perenni ejus incolumitate Deum O.M. sollicitare precibus non desino. Vale, literarum decus, et Tui studiosissimum Oldenburgium porro ama. Dabam Londini d. 20. Dec. 1670.

TRANSLATION

Henry Oldenburg greets the very worthy and wise Mr. Job Ludolf, Councilor of His Serene Highness, the Duke of Gotha

I congratulate myself warmly, most worthy Sir, on your offering to me an opportunity for renewing our former intercourse, which had been interrupted for some time. I have informed the Royal Society of His Serene Highness's benevolent goodwill towards its objects and studies.[1] The Society at once instructed me, as was proper, to return you its best thanks for that favor and for His Highness's gracious readiness to communicate the natural curiosities of his region. You, learned Sir, will offer yourself as a trustworthy intermediary in this, and you will in no wise doubt of our concern for you and your merits.

As the Royal Society is almost solely concerned to advance the knowledge of natural things and the ingenious arts for the greater certainty of knowledge and especially for the greater protection and convenience of human life, it believes that it is necessary for it to attract to its purpose men from all quarters who are distinguished in every kind of learning and skill, and to invite them to maintain a correspondence upon these subjects. They think, indeed, that it is of great moment for the investigation of truth to bring about the marriage of brain and hand: if this could be extended over the whole globe, and embraced all whose intellects are free from the prejudice of authority and sect (endeavoring only to attain truth, and human well-being), then surely philosophy would attain to its highest perfection.

We, certainly, are now engaged on nothing more than the assembling of a rich store of observations and experiments, and we urge the wise and skilful of all peoples to add their own contributions. We do not imagine that your prince and the other philosophers of generous spirit who live in your neighborhood will be behindhand in this so laudable enterprise. And so we feel sure that you will openly communicate to us whatever your native land generates and displays in the vegetable, mineral, and animal kingdoms that is worthy of note, or what concerns the air, waters, hot baths, meteors, etc. This we will try to deserve by every kind of service in return. In particular I long to offer my humble duty to His Highness Duke Ernest, and I shall not cease my prayers to God Almighty for his long continuing good health. Farewell, thou ornament of learning, and continue to love your most zealous Oldenburg.

London, 20 December 1670

NOTES

Reply to Letter 1540.
1 There is no record of Oldenburg's having done so in the minutes.

1581
Oldenburg to Helmfeld
20 December 1670

Helmfeld's Letter 1566 was received by Oldenburg on 11 December; he replied on 20 December, according to his endorsement.

1582
Oldenburg to Flamsteed
22 December 1670
From the copy in Royal Society MS. O 2, no. 40

An Answer to Mr Flamsteads two letters of Nov. 20.
1670. and Dec. 13. 1670[1]

Good Mr Flamstead
Sir

Tis high time for mee to ask your pardon for my tardinesse to acknowledge ye receipt of your late letters to mee, and the present to ye R. Soc. I assure you, yt nothing but a throng of businesse wch I could not wind mee out of sooner, hath been so long a stop to my inclinations. Now I have got a few minutes leisure, I shall employ them to let you know, that your New Labors of predicting ye Appulse of the Moon to divers Fixed starrs and to Saturne; as also Mr Wilsons observation of the Moons Transit by Venus Oct. 1. 1670. were very acceptable to ye sd Soc. insomuch yt I received their expresse order to returne their hearty thanks to you both, and in their name to exhorte you to a steddy and sollicitous continuance of your industry and affection for the improvement of Astronomicall concerns.[2] Touching your owne manuscript it is thought fit, yt an extract of as much as is necessary for observation be printed in ye Transactions; wch will be done this month, and ready. I hope, before ye first occultation on January 4th next.[3] I wish, ye observers be but as careful on their part, as you have been in ye calculation. I shall not faile to mind and excite them. As to Mr Wilsons observation, I find yt to be so wide in point of time, from yt of M. Hevelius on ye same transit, yt I thought it safer to deferre ye publication of it, till you have seen and considered wt I am going to impart to you of ye Dantiscan observation, wch I shall do in the same language wherein I received it.[4] It will concerne you to consider, whether the difference of latitude, and of ye Meridians, and the Parallax of ye Moon; could make such a difference, as there is betweene the Hevelian and the Wilsonian observation. And I should be glad to know whether you will give mee leave to communicate to M. Hevelius (who is desirous to have somthing from hence upon yt Phaenomenon) ye observation of your kinsman.

Since you wish you had Hevelius's observation of ye Solar Eclipse on Oct. 25. 1668, for the better stating ye difference of your Meridian from his, I am glad, yt I can fulfill your wish, by giving you a copy of wt he was pleased to communicate to us concerning it, wch was this in his owne words.[5]

I am very sorry yt ye Glasses, wch you had from hence, prove bad. I will tell our friends, yt procured them for you, of it, as soon as I have an opportunity. Mean time, you are not to expect any Telescopicall Glasses of a Spherical figure, wthout casting colours. I remain Sir

yr. very affect. friend and servant
Henry Oldenburg

London Decemb. 22. 1670.

NOTES

1 Oldenburg seems to have misrecollected the dates of Flamsteed's letters; he here replies to Letters 1554 (16 November), 1567 (5 December), and 1573 (13 December).
2 Letter 1554 was presented to the Society on 24 November.
3 See *Phil. Trans.*, no. 66 (12 December 1670), 2029–34.
4 There is a note here in Oldenburg's hand: "Here was inserted an Extract of Hevelius Letter of Oct. 31. 1670. concerning this Transit." See Letter 1536.
5 Again, there is a note by Oldenburg: "See M. Hevelius his letter of this Eclipse N.2. of ye Letterbooks p. 336, 337, whence was extracted, what was sent to Mr. Flamstead." See Vol. V, p. 185.

1583
Lister to Oldenburg

23 December 1670

From the original in Royal Society MS. L 5, no. 21

Sr

I am glad to understand my Letter[1] came safe to your hands; You are, I am very sensible too well & usefully busied to be complimented & I should be too great a looser to interrupt you even in this private & agreable Diversion, ye composing of your monthly Tracts, much more should I be unwilling to disturbe you in yt publick & illustrious employment you are deservedly honoured wth. However yt I may not make this Letter a meer compliment, give me leave to entertain you now about ye subject of Insects, wch I see by your last Number, many persons are now curious in. & not to goe out of yt Tract; I take ye Forking of some thredds, (for ye Doctour excepts ye most) to be meerly accidental,[2] even as it is to our haire, neither doe I thinke, yt any such thing is designedly done by ye animal; &, for as much as I have observed, spiders thredds of ym selves are exceeding slick & smooth, & this was not unobserved by ye Ancients: Plinie in praise of a sort of Italian *linn* saies, Retovinis summa tenuitas, nulla lanugo, nervositas filo aequalior pene quam araneis.[3] There is, indeed, a dividing in ye projection of ye thredds of many sorts of spiders, & especially among those wch we distinguish by ye name of Lupi, wch Tribe is most frequent & particularly delighted in sailing, yet this dividing is much of an other nature than Forking. Those Lupi will dart a whole *Stamen* or Sheafe at once, consisting of many filaments yet all of one length, all divided each from ye other & distinct, untill some chance either snap ym off or entangle ym; but for ye most part, you may observe, yt ye longer they grow, the more they spread & appeare to a diligent observer like ye numerous rays in ye tail of a blazing starr. As for yt, wch carrys ym away into ye aire soe swift off hand, [it] is, as I formerly hinted, partly their suddain lep, & partly ye length, & number of ye thredds projected, ye stream of ye aire or wind beating more forcably upon ym & thus we see a rope yt unexpectedly slipps comes home wth a seeming violence & partly (& yt much too) ye posture & management of their feet, wch, at least by some sorts of ym, I have observed to have been used very like wings or Oares, ye several leggs (like our fingers) being sometimes clos joined & other times opened, again bent

or extended etc. according to ye several necessities & will of ye Sailer. To
fly they cannot strictly be said, they being carried into ye aire by external
force; but they can in case ye wind suffer ym to steer their course & perhapps mount & descend at pleasure: & to ye purpos of rowing ym selves
along in ye aire, 'tis observable, yt they ever take their flyght backwards,
yt is their head looking a contrary way, like a skuller on ye Thames. It is
scarce credible to what height they will mount, wch yet is precisely tru, &
a thing easily to be observed by one yt shall fixe his eye some time on any
one part of ye heavens ye white webbs at a vast distance very distinctly
appearing from ye Azure sky: but this is in Autumn only & yt in very
fair & calme weather, for in wind they delight as little (if possible) for ym
to mount, as for ye Indians in Pliny to fight a battle wth their reed Arrows.
Divers sorts have divers wayes & particularly in performing this surprising
phaenomenon. I am not willing to hasten a Historie wch further leisure
may improve, yet partly to excite ye curious & partly to satisfie ye promise
I made in my former printed Letter,[4] you may command from me, when
you please, a set of general Enquiries on this subject of spiders, most of ym
already answered by me & founded upon new discoveries. The account
given of ye Bees breeding in cases made of leaves exactly agrees with what
I have observed.[5] I add, yt they are not very scrupulous in ye choice of
those leaves, but will make use even of exotick plants, such as ye blew
pipe or syringe Tree.[6] There is a very strainge Oeconomie of nature yet
unsolved: ye further-most Bee, saies Mr Willoughby, makes her way out
along ye chanell through all ye intermediate Cartrages: and according as
these channells run upwards or downwards in ye body of ye Tree, ye
Maggots are either under their meat or above it, whence it is manifest, yt
ye Bee at ye farr or upper end of each channel is first laid & it should seem
both hatched & perfected first & must either wait untill ye rest be soe too;
or of necessity by working through their cases destroy ym. if it be soe, it
is very strange. but I take it otherwise, & perhapps it will be found by
diligent observers hereafter, yt yt Bee wch is neerest day, although it be
last laid, is yet ye first hatched; & I ground my conjecture(if we may give
reason) upon this, yt 'tis probable, yt ye eggs in ye mother are all fit for
laying or equally ripe & formed as we say at ye time yt ye first of ym was
laid, but are not therfore all laid by ye Damm, untill she has provided ym
of meat & housed each separately as is ye nature of Bees: & yet in recompense ye warmth of her body or rather ye daily encreasing heat of ye
summer season to wch ye mother Bee is continually exposed, whilst ye
first laid eggs are sheltered in their deep channells hastens their Vitalitie

soe much, yt they are hatched wormes & begin to feed before ye first laidd, & consequently are first perfected in to Bees. but this is conjecture only & not observation. And to this purpose, let me observe to you, yt we are not alwayes without our Viviparous flyes, although in a much colder region than Italie: ye first time I tooke notice of ym, was ye 2d yeare of ye sicknesse raging in Cambridge 1666.[7] I have of this sort some by me at present, wch you may command, for I doe not find ym cutt or described either in Aldrovandus or Mouffet,[8] though this sort of flye be very frequent wth us. And this was not ye only strange phenomenon, yt I observed amongst Insects, besides other things of nature, particularly yt yeare: for being in harvest time at Bassenburne[9] in Cambridge-shire, at ye house of Mr William Aylyffe, he invited me along wth him into ye Feilds, where, Cosen, saies he, I will shewe you a wonder; wch, indeed, was soe to me, for lifting up ye barley-Cockes with his Cane, there appeared millions of Maggotts on ye corne lands & in their barnes, too, ye Flooer would be covered wth ym yt fell from ye Carts. The maggotts were about halfe an intch long, noe thicker than a pidgeons feather, of a white colour somewhat shaded wth an Isabella[10] or faint yellowish stripes ye length of ye Worme, they had 14 feet after ye manner of many Catterpillars & I was almost confident would have produced some sort of Moath:[11] I tooke up about a score of ym & put ym into a box, but they immediately offended me wth an ungratefull & strong stinck wch yet is not usuall to ye catterpillar kinds, however I kept ym 2 dayes, but by reason of some apprehensions & feares ye Ladies had of ym where I sorjournd & upon their intreaties I rid myselfe of ym; I only observed, yt ye excrements wch they voided, were little hard pellets of pure white flower, like yt of barly. Those and other things might be arguments of ye power hot weather hath in ye hasty quickning ye births of Insects as well as producing ym; but I conceive it lesse usefull to Philosophy to dispute, then to deliver faithfully matters of Fact. I am Sr

> your most humble servant
> *Martin Lister*

From my house without Market-gate barr
        at Yorke
December 23d 1670

ADDRESS
    These
For Mr Henry Oldenburgh
to be left wth Mr Martin
Stationer at ye Bell in
Pauls church yard & a little
without Temple barr
         London

NOTES

1 Letter 1503, to which Oldenburg referred in *Phil. Trans.*, no. 65 (14 November 1670), 2104; clearly Lister had recently received this number.
2 See this same number, page 2103; for Dr. Hulse, see Letter 1479, note 1.
3 "[The linen thread] of Retovium is extremely fine, without any downiness, and in strength almost like spiders' thread." *Linn* (Latin *linum*, etc.) signifies linen, the thread made from flax. Lister has run two sentences together and omitted some words; see Pliny *Natural History* xix. c. I, *ad init.* Retovium was a town in Cisalpine Gaul at or near the modern Voghera.
4 See Letter 1479, note 2.
5 By Willughby; see Letters 1511 and 1518.
6 This is the common lilac, *Syringa vulgaris*, syringa meaning pipe. See John Parkinson, *Paradisi in sole* (1629; London, 1904), pp. 407–8, who says that the blue pipe tree was already a garden shrub although a fairly recent importation into Europe.,
7 The great plague of 1665 remained endemic in Cambridge into the following year, the University being closed.
8 Ulissi Aldrovandi, *De animalibus insectis liber VII* (Bologna, 1602, 1620, 1638); Thomas Mouffet, *Insectorum sive minimorum animalium theatrum* (London, 1634); there was an English edition of the latter book in 1658.
9 Bassingbourn.
10 Greyish yellow or light buff.
11 It is possible (if these really were Lepidopteran larvae) that they were those of the grass moth, *Crambus hortuellus*.

1584
Oldenburg to Denis
2 January 1670/1

Mentioned on the endorsement of Denis's Letter 1576.

1585

Flamsteed to Oldenburg

3 January 1670/1

From the original in Royal Society MS. F 1, no. 65

Derby January 3 1670

Worthy Mr Oldenburge
Sr

Yours of ye 22 last past I have reaceavd & hereby returne yu many thankes for yr communications: I am glad my papers came safe to yr hands, & were so kindly reaceavd by ye R. Society: I esteeme not [my] selfe to have merited theire thankes, it is more then enough that I have not their dislike when I rather feared theire censure for my bold assertaions then expected their approbation: I am obliged to them for theire good opinion & reception of my endeavors: & will not stick to shew my gratitude on all occasions. as for my Coz: Willsons observation[1] I thinke it not convenient to mention it to any one for I am confident since I reaceaved yrs, that hee is grossly mistaken in ye time tho not perhaps in ye manner of ye appearance. for ye difference of ye Meridians, latitudes, & parallaxes could never vary the time of ye appearance so much as is the difference of those observations. I am much pleased that yu sent me Hevelius his observation of ye Solar defect 1668 October 25[2] I could wish yt hee had observed ye beginning, for I am more confident yt I had ye exact time of it then of ye end, concerning which I much doubt, whether it was not sooner then my Instruments by chance misplaced gave it. for my assistants left me towards ye end of the Eclips & I can rather say I saw then observed it; I have not heard yt it was any where observed in England but by My selfe wch I wonder at & I can not thinke that all our Astronomers slept at Noone day that this Eclipse should passe unobserved: pray Sr if you have any English observations of it be pleasd to communicate them to me by yr next & I shall reaceave it as a great kindnesse. I wonder that Hevelius should then make ye suns semidiameter but 15′–15″, when by his observations made formerly, with ye consent of allmost all Astronomers, & I am sure of the heavens themselves, it could not be lesse then 16′–05″ or 06″: but of this when a further occasion shall be given, wch may be ere long,

I shall let yu know more of my mind. I thinke it might doe well to communicate my praedictions unto him, he may ghesse, from thence, what may be expected at Dantzick: I feare I shall not gaine time to transcribe what I have commented on his Mercury sub Sole.[3] I shall therefore ere long let yu know in some letter where hee hath erred, & what may be derived from some of his observations, that yu may informe him from me of them. Pray request ye observers who will waite for ye lunar observations to note ye times of the phases to ye seconds minutes where possibley & ye very points of ye ingresse, & emersion in corporall appulses. This wth respects thankes & services presented is from

Yr most obliged
John Flamsteed

I tanke yu for yr permitting me ye further use of Hevelius[4] whom by reason of severall occasions I have not had time to goe throug I shall restore him by ye day or before:

ADDRESS

> To Henry Oldenburge
> Esqe at his house in ye
> Middle of ye Pell mell in
> St James's feilds
> Westminster these

POSTMARK IA 13

NOTES

Reply to Letter 1582. The numerous faults are in the original.
1 Reported in Letter 1567.
2 See Vol. V, p. 185.
3 *Mercurius in sole visus* (Danzig, 1662)—many times mentioned before.
4 That is, the *Selenographia* borrowed from Oldenburg.

1586

Oldenburg to Lister

3 January 1670/1

From the original in Bodleian Library MS. Lister 34, f. 1

Sir

I think myself very much engaged to you for yr late obliging letter of Decemb. 23th. If our Society had not adjourn'd their meetings till after ye end of these H[oly] dayes, you would here receive their thoughts and esteem of yr uncommon enquiries and observations of Nature. I intend at their first meeting to communicate to ym ye contents of yr curious letter;[1] I could not delay so long the acknowledgement of having received it, nor my privat thanks for yr candid contributions to those collections, we make for a philosophical storehouse. If you countermand it not, I shall use ye freedome of inserting this last letter of yrs, as I have done another, in one of ye Transactions;[2] being well assured, yt it will be very acceptable to ye Curious. I am this very day making some Excerpta of it (by yr leave,) to send ym to Mr Willughby about ye forking of ye Threds of Spiders; and yr conjecture about ye worms yt are hatched and beginn to feed before the first laid, and consequently are first perfected into Bees; different from what he conceives of ye furthermost Bee's making her way out along ye Channel through all ye intermediate cartrages: Wch I doe purposely, to hear what he may have to say to yr conjecture, (wch appears very rational to me,) before I make it publick by ye Presse. Wch when I shall have received, I intend to impart to you likewise, before any thing be printed of it; yt so nothing may come abroad, yt may displease either of you, or appear contentious to the Reader.

I am much pleased wth yr relation of ye wonder you saw at Mr Aylef's house, concerning ye millions of maggots on ye corn-lands and in the barns; but am sorry, ye Lady's were so nice, as to cause you to throw those away, you had put in a boxe, before you saw what became of ym.

In ye place, wch you cite out of Pliny, there is a word, wch is unknown to me, and not having that Author about me, to guesse it by ye context, I must desire yr explication of yesame. You have written, *Retovinis summa tenuitas* etc.[3] Ye word, *Retovinis* is yt, wch I stick at; not knowing, whether I read it right, or whether I understand it not.

Sir, you will pardon this freedom to him, yt is Sir
Yr very humble and faithful servant
H. Oldenburg

London Januar. 3d. 16$\frac{70.}{71}$

I shall be very glad of ye favour of receiving yt set of general Enquiries, made by you on ye subject of Spiders, as also some of those viviparous flyes, wch you say, you have by you.

ADDRESS
> To his honored friend Martyn
> Lister Esquire, at his House
> wthout Mickel-gate barr at
> > Yorke

NOTES
Reply to Letter 1583.
1 The Royal Society next met on 12 January, when this letter was not, in fact, read.
2 Oldenburg had printed in *Phil. Trans.*, no. 50 (16 August 1669), 1011–16, Lister's letter to Ray concerning snail shells and the darting of spiders. He did not print Letter 1583.
3 See above, p. 340, and Lister's explanation, below p. 353.

1587
Oldenburg to Willughby

3 January 1670/1

From the memorandum in Royal Society MS. L 5, no. 21

rec. Dec. 29. 70.
Answ. jan. 3d. 70/71
At yesame time wrote to Willughby what concerns him out of this letter.

NOTE

This is the endorsement on Letter 1583 from Lister; as proposed in Letter 1586, Oldenburg sent extracts from it to Willughby.

1588

Martindale to Oldenburg

7 January 1670/1

From the original in Royal Society MS. M 1, no. 66

Worthy Sr:

Mr Marburies workemen have contrary to former resolution, broken up the flagge upon the salt-rocke, and laid bare the superficies of it alreadie, save that the brine and freshes render it oft invisible.[1] I have beene downe at it about 32 or 33 yards within ground, and caused a workeman to hew me up some lumps upon the place, some whereof I am sending up to you by one Thomas Chantler (a carrier) that lodgeth at the oxe in Aldermanbury and will be there (if God see good) about the 19th or 20th instant. If you judge it worth the while, you may be sending thither, know the particular time of his coming in and there receive it from his hands. I shall case it in some homely thing that will secure it; Paper being not so proper if the weather prove moist. I hope here after to accommodate you with that which is much more pure; for this being got off the very head is not without a mixture of red earth but I have seene some little that either by the Augar or some such device was fetched out of a deeper part, that is to see to just like sugar-candie, some perfectly white, but the most browne, & I have laid in with the overseer of the worke to befriend me with some of the purest so soone as it is to be had, and that he store himselfe (when opportunitie serves) with good quantities of it, that if it should hereafter prove usefull matter out which to extract spirit of salt, or for any other Chymicall operation, the R. societie may not faile of being sufficiently supplied. What quantitie there is of it cannot yet be guessed, but probably very great; for the Lord of it assures me they have bored into it 3 yards, & were forced to desist by the exceeding hardnesse of this most genuine

Sal petrae or petra salis.[2] Experiments concerning it I have had neither time nor skill to make any, but such as are obvious; As how fire makes it cracke and fly like bags of Kelp or sea-tang, Hote-water dissolves it speedily, & cold slowly. Pulverized it is a very sharpe salt, and the browne that is free from mixture full as sharpe (me thinks) as the whiter. The trialls you recommended to me were not feasible, for as for the first you may easily conjecture that having no way to touch upon the rocke save onely the surface, and that ever and anon overflowen; it must needs be impossible to trie whether the aire within were colder then elsewhere, And for the second, which was to weigh some quantitie of it deep within ground, and the same in the open aire at some distance I found that also cleare out of my power for though I was not wanting either in mine owne personall indeavours nor gratifying the workemen to assist me (which they cheerefully did) yet the running of the buckets which must be constantly plied, and the falling of water from the circumjacent earth above us caused (as it were) a continuall shower falling with that violence and plentie that my scales were almost quarter-filled at every essay: so that I could obtaine nothing but satisfaction that it is impossible to serve you in that kind. What I can in the things hinted in your last (for which I humbly thank you)[3] you may assure your selfe shall not be wanting. In particular the method of making slip-coat-cheese and some other particulars omitted in my last (though none worth your enquirie) I intend to communicate when I have first consulted a gentlewoman of mine acquaintance (a notable huswife) that lives in my way to a newfound petrifying well in Lancashire of which in my next you may expect some account.[4] In the interim I shall give you noe further trouble but to subscribe my selfe, Sr

your very loving friend & humble servt
Adam Martindale

Rotherston Jan. 7th–70.

ADDRESS

    These
  To his highly honoured friend
  Mr Henrie Oldenburg
  Secretary to the Royall-Societie
  at his house in the Pal-mal
  in St James's fields
      Westminster

POSTMARK JA 13

NOTES

1 Compare Letter 1562.
2 "Salt of rock or rock of salt."
3 Dated 13 December 1670, but now lost.
4 No more letters from Martindale survive, but see Letter 1610.

1589
Lister to Oldenburg
10 January 1670/1

From the original in Royal Society MS. L 5, no. 22
Printed in *Phil. Trans.*, no. 72 (19 June 1671), 2170–74

Sr,

I returne you thanks for your obliging Letter of ye 3d of January & have sent you ye Viviparous Flye & ye Sett of Enquiries you desire of me.[1] The flye is one, if not ye very biggest, of ye harmlesse Tribe yt I have met wth in England; I call ym harmlesse, because they are without yt hard Tongue or Stinge in ye mouth, wth wch all ye aestrum-kind, or Gad-flyes trouble & offend both man & beasts. This Fly is striped upon ye shoulders grey & black & as it were checkered on ye tail wth ye same two colours: the Female may be known by a rednesse on ye very point of ye tail.[2] ye very latter end of May 1666, I opened several of ym, & found two Baggs of live white wormes of a long & round shape, wth black heads;[3] they moved both in my hand and in ye unopened Vesicles, backwards & forwards, as being all disposed in ye Cells, length-wayes ye body of ye femal, like a Sheafe.

Some such thing is hinted by Aldrovandus lib. 1. de insect. pag. 57. edit. Bonon: "Tiro cum essem" (saies he) "e grandioribus muscis unam albis pictam lineis, specie illectus, cepi; ea, in vola manus aliquandiu retenta, plusculos edidit Vermiculos candidos, mobilitate propria insignes."[4]

This is ye only Fly I have observed wth live & moving Wormes in ye belly of it, yet I guesse, we may venture to suspect all of this Tribe to be in some measure Viviparous.

With these Flyes I have sent you a paper of those odd-turned Snails, mentioned in my former Letter,[5] wch perhaps you may thinke will deserve a Cutt, or at least a place in ye Repository amongst ye rarities of the R.S.[6]

Some general Enquiries concerning Spiders.

1. What sorts of Spiders to be found wth us in England, & what is ye best method to distinguish ym & to reduce ym to Classes.
2. Whether Spiders come not of Spiders, yt is, of creatures of their own kind: & whether of Spiders are bread grasshoppers, Cicadae, etc. as interpreters falsly make Aristotle to say, first Aldrovandus, & lately Kircher (V. Arist. Hist. Nat. lib. 1 cap. 19.[7] Confer Interpret.[8] Th. Gazae, Scaliger, Aldrov.)[9]
3. Whether Spiders are not Male & female; & whether Female Spiders growing bigger than ye Male, be sufficient to distinguish sexes.
4. Whether all kinds of Spiders be alike, as to ye place & number of Penes's; & whether all ye thread-yielding kinds, are not furnished wth a double penis or genital member, yt is, if ye Cornicula or certain knobbed Horns,[10] by wch all males are best distinguished, be not each a genital member & used in the Coit alternatively?
5. Whether the Eggs in Spiders be not formed, & very large before ye time of ye Coit?
6. What Spiders breed in Spring & what in Autumn? What Spiders are content wth one brood i'th yeare & to lay all their Eggs at a time? What seem to breed every Summer month, at least to have many subordinate broods? & whether ye Eggs be accordingly distinguishable in several Matrices or Cells in ye body of the Female?
7. Whether Spiders do not take their forme and perfection in ye egg, & are not thence hatched necessarily at a stated & set time, yt is, after a certain number of dayes, as 21. compleat Animals of its owne kind? & whether ye presence of ye Femal be necessary in order to ye hatching ye eggs, at least for 3 dayes, as ye Ancients seeme to affirme. V. Arist. Hist. Nat. lib. 1. cap. 27?[11]
8. Whether ye perfectly round eggs of Spiders ought to be called & esteemed Wormes, as Aristotle & Pliny will have ym,[12] yt is, in Swammerdam's phrase & doctrine, whether they be Puppetts[13] in ye egg & undergo all alterations accordingly, before they be thence hatched perfect Spiders?
9. What different colours observable in ye Eggs of Spiders, as well of pulpes as shell, as white, yellow, orange, purple, greenish? & what

respective tinctures they will give, or be made to strike wth ye several families of Salts?

10. Whether there be not Eggs of some sorts of Spiders, wch ye wormes of certain slender Wasps (ye kind in general being called by Mouffet Muscae tripiles)[14] delight to feed on: & whether ye Fable of Vespae Ichneumones, told us by ye Ancients,[15] be not to be made out by the same Observation, of these Wasp-wormes feeding on ye Eggs, & perfected into wasps in ye very webs of Spiders?

11. After what manner do Spiders feed, whether in sucking they devour not alsoe part of their prey? How long can they live without food, since they store up nothing against Winter?

12. Whether Spiders feed only of their owne kind of Creatures, as of Insects, yt is, of Flys, Beetles, Bees, Scolopendrae & even of one an other: or whether they kill Snakes too, as ye Ancients affirm,[16] for food or delight?

13. Whether some of ym choose not to feed on one sort of Flye or other Insect only, & what properties such have?

14. When, & how oft in the yeare they cast their skins, & ye manner of their casting it? What varietie of colours immediately after ye shifting ye Hackle in one & ye same species of Spider, yt may, if not well heeded, make ye history of them more confused?

15. What meane ye Ancients by Spiders casting their threads, wch Aristotle compares to a Porcupins darting her quills, or barke starting from a Tree, & Democritus to animals voiding of Excrements?[17]

16. Whether ye thread be formed in ye body of ye animal such as it comes from it; I meane, whether it be, as it were, unwound off of a stock or clew, as I may say, & wch indeed to me seemes to have been Aristotles meaning; or whether it be drawn off of a liquid Masse, as in spinning of Glasse or melted Wax, wch seemes to have been Democritus's sense, in saying, it was excrement corrupted or fluid at a certain time.

17. Whether ye Spiders thred being glutinous, every thing sticking to it upon ye lightest touch, be not so much ye reason of ye Spiders taking his prey, as ye Figure of ye Nett?

18. Whether a Webb be not uninflammable, & whether it can be dissolved & in what Menstruum?

19. What difference betwixt ye thread of Spiders & yt of ye silkworme or Catterpillars? what strength a Spiders thread is of, & what proportion it beares wth ye like twist of Silk? Whether there be not stronger thred from some sort of Spiders than from others, as there are threds from ym of very different colours, as white, greenish, blewish, dark hair-colourd, &c?

whether ye strength of ye Barmudo netts to hold a Thrush, mentioned in one of ye Transactions,[18] consist in ye thicknesse only, or much too in ye nature of ye thread?

20. Whether its being to be easily drawne out at any time & what length one pleases & many threads together in spight of ye animal, be not as advantageous to ye working of it up & twisting, etc, as ye unravelling ye Cods of Silkwormes?

21. Whether either ye Viscous substance of their bodies or Webbs be healing to green wounds etc. as ye ancients have taught us & we use vulgarly? & whether some kind of ym be not preferable for this purpos, before others?

22. What use may be made of those Animals, wch devour Spiders for their daily food, as Wrens, Red-breast, etc.? whether Spiders be a cure for sicke poultrey, as ye good Wives seem to experiment?

23. Whether ye reason why Spiders sail not in ye aire untill Autumn, be not because they are busily employed ye Summer months in breeding, or what other reasons may be assigned?

The first article of Enquiry I have in part answered, by sending you enclosed a Scheme,[19] wch, after some years observation, I have corrected & enlarged to what it is: yet I must acquaint you, yt such Draughts will be ever lyable to change & improvement, according to ye measure of knowledge a continued Observation may bring us to. However it is ye first, yt I know of, yt will be extant, on this subject, & it may be acceptable to ye curious. I am Sr

Your most humble servant
Martin Lister

Retovinis, is to be understood of a certain fine linnen thread made in yt part of Italie, for here Pliny praises ye several sorts of linnen manufacture of his owne countrey. H. Nat. lib. 19. c.l.[20]

You may expect to receive a small box directed to Mr Martin your stationer, by ye next returne of Loft, a Yorke & Tadcaster Carrier inning at ye white horse in Criple-gate.

I am engaged in one of ye Transactions for ye veracitie of an experiment I made ye last November but this, & communicated it to Mr Wray, concerning ye bleeding of a Sycamore yt month:[21] when it shall come further to be discussed, be pleased to acquaint your humble servant. I shall be glad to receive Mr Willoughbys thoughts about any subject of Natural Historie.

ADDRESS
    These
For my honoured Friend Mr Henry
        Oldenburg
To be left with Mr Martin Stationer
at ye Bell, in Pauls Churchyard
or without Temple barr
        London

NOTES

Reply to Letter 1586.
1 See Letter 1589a.
2 Probably one of the Scarphaginae or flesh flies, which have a striped grey and black thorax and a chequered grey and black abdomen; in several species the females do have a red area near the end of the abdomen.
3 These flies are viviparous and these worms are more likely to be larvae than para-sites.
4 Ulissi Aldrovandi, *De animalibus insectis libri VII* (Bologna, 1602). "When I was a beginner . . . I captured a fly of the larger sort marked with white lines, of an un-known species; holding it in the hollow of my hand for some time, it gave out several white worms which were remarkably active."
5 The letter to Ray printed in *Phil. Trans.*, no. 50 (16 August 1669), 1011–16.
6 None of the snail shells in Grew, *Musaeum*, seem to be identical with these, and none are said to have come from Lister.
7 *Sic*; but correctly, *Historia animalium*, Bk. V, ch. 19, where Aristotle in fact said, "And of insects some are derived from insect congeners, as the venom-spider and the common-spider, and so with the attelabus or locust, the acris or grasshopper, and the tettix or cicada." Translation by D'Arcy W. Thompson in Aristotle, *Works*, IV (Oxford, 1910).
8 "Compare the interpretation."
9 The translation of Aristotle's *Historia animalium* by Theodore Gaza was first publish-ed at Venice in 1476, and frequently thereafter; that by Julius Caesar Scaliger was printed posthumously at Lyons in 1584.
10 As Letter 1609 makes plain, Lister originally wrote "feelers," but Oldenburg cor-rected this to "horns" at Lister's request; the original word can no longer be read.
11 Actually Bk. V, ch. 27.
12 A marginal note here reads "Hist. Nat. lib. 1. cap. 27. lib. 3. cap. 9." The references would seem to be to *Historia animalium*, Bk. V, ch. 27, and *De generatione animalium*, Bk. III, ch. 9, where Aristotle refers to "the product of spiders as a kind of larva." Pliny discusses "Spiders and their reproduction" in Bk. XI, ch. 24, of his *Natural History*.
13 Pupae; the reference is to Swammerdam's *Historia insectorum generalis* (Utrecht, 1669). In his *Biblia naturae* (Leiden, 1737–38), Part I, ch. IV, Swammerdam in turn cited Lister's classification of spiders.
14 See Letter 1583, note 8.
15 A marginal note reads "Arist. Hist. nat. lib. 1. cap. 20." The correct reference is

Historia animalium, Bk. V, ch. 20: "ichneumon wasps," that is, those whose larvae feed on the larvae of other insects.

16 Aristotle (*Historia animalium*, Bk. IX, ch. 39) says that they will attack small lizards.

17 A marginal note reads "Arist. His. Nat. lib. 9. cap. 39." Aristotle here refers to the opinion of Democritus, as does Pliny in his account of spiders.

18 A marginal note reads "No. 50. p. 795." As usual, Lister's reference is erroneous; see *Phil. Trans.*, no. 40 (19 October 1668), 795, for Stafford's Letter 921 (Vol. V, p. 552).

19 Letter 1589a.

20 These three paragraphs are found on a separate sheet now pasted to Letter 1583. However, this information must have been supplied in answer to Letter 1586, so we place it here.

21 See Vol. VI, Letter 1420.

1589a

Table of English Spiders

Enclosure with Letter 1589
From the original in Royal Society MS. L 5, no. 22
Printed in *Phil. Trans.*, no. 72 (19 June 1671), 2175

Tabulae compendiariae Araneorum Angliae; quibus accedunt eorum Tituli, e notis maxime discriminantibus atque insignibus desumpti.

Aranei vel fila, mittunt, ut sunt qui
    aut praedandi causa texunt
        vel Reticula orbiculata, numero IX.
            1. Araneus subflavus, alvo paululum acuminata inflexaque.
            2. Araneus rufus, cruciger, cui utrinque ad Superiorem alvi partem velut singula tubercula eminent.
            3. Araneus cinereus, pictura clunium in 5 fere partes divulsa, ijsque plenis admodum.
            4. Araneus flavus, quatuor albis, praeter picturam foliaceam, in clune maculis insignitus.
            5. Araneus nigricans, clunibus ad similitudinem quernij folij pictis.
            6. Araneus ex viridi inauratus, alvo praetenui procerique.
            7. Araneus cinereus, sylvarum incola, alvo in mucronem fastigiata,[1] seu triquetra.

  8. Araneus viridis, cauda nigris punctis superne
   notata, ipso ano croceo.
  9. Araneus pullus, cruciger in alvo plena.

Plagas globatas, n. IV.

  10. Araneus variegatus, alvo orbiculata.
  11. Araneus rufus, clunium orbiculatorum fastigio
   in modum stella radiato.
  12. Araneus pullus, domesticus.
  13. Araneus cinereus macula nigra in summis clunibus insignitus, minimus.

Telas sive linteamina, n. VIII.

  14. Araneus subflavus, pilosus, praelongis pedibus,
   domesticus.
  15. Araneus nigricans, praegrandi macula in summis
   clunibus, caeterum ijsdem oblique virgatis, domesticus.
  16. Araneus fuligineus e Craven,[2] insigni candore
   distinctus cauda bifurca.
  17. Araneus subflavus, nigricantium macularum qua-
   dratarum catena in clunibus insignitus, item cui
   utrinque ad clunium latera singulae obliquae virgulae flavescentes.
  18. Araneus cinereus, maximus, cauda bifurca.
  19. Araneus niger aut castaneus, glaber, clunibus
   summo candore interstinctis.
  20. Araneus cinereus, mollis, cui in alvo, oblique
   virgata, macula latiuscula e nigro rubens.
  21. Araneus plerunque lividus, sine ulla pictura,
   alvo acuminata.

aut ideo nihil texunt (nisi filorum ejaculatio ac volatus illor-
sum spectet) cum tamen alias possint: nimirum Telas ad
tutandum faetum aut ad hyberna sed aperto Marto muscas
venantur; atque ij sunt vel Lupi dicti n.V. hi vero cum superioribus singulis octo habent oculos.

  22. Araneus subrufus, parvus, citissimo pede.
  23. Araneus cancriformis, oculis e viola purpurascen-
   tibus, tardipes.
  24. Araneus cinereus, alvo undulatim picta, insigni-
   ter procera, acuminata.

25. Araneus fuscus, alvo oblique virgata.
26. Araneus niger, sylvicola.
Phalangia, sive assultim ingredientes, n.III. Hi vero sex tantum oculos habent.
27. Araneus Cinereus, sive ex argento nigroque varius.
28. Araneus subflavus, oculis smaragdinis, item cui secundum clunes tres virgulae croceae.
29. Araneus subrufus e Craven, sive Ericetorum sive rupium.
vel omnino nulla fila mittunt, ut sunt qui plerique
Longissimis tenuissimisque pedibus donantur: atque hi duos tantum oculos habent, telaque sive brachia digitata, n.IV.
30. Araneus rufus, non cristatus, gregatum vivens.
31. Araneus cinereus, cristatus.
32. Araneus e candido nigroque varius, minima bestiola, sylvicola.
33. Araneus, ut puto, coccineus, vulgo dictus a Tant Anglice.[3]

TRANSLATION

Compendious Tables of the Spiders of England, to which are added their names, taken from their most noteworthy and peculiar characters.

Spiders either spin a thread, as these do
or make a net to catch prey [which is]
either a round net (nine types):
1. A buff spider, the belly rather pointed and bent.
2. A reddish, marked with a cross, and with bumps (as it were) on either side of the upper part of the belly.
3. An ash-colored spider, the coloring of the hinderparts being divided into almost five sections, and those very full.
4. A yellow spider, marked with four white spots at the rear, besides a leaf-like coloration on the rear.
5. A blackish spider, with the hinderparts colored like an oak leaf.
6. A gold-green spider, the belly thin and long.
7. An ash-colored spider, living in woods, the belly coming to a point,[1] or three-cornered.

8. A green spider, the tail marked with black dots on top, the rear saffron-colored.

9. A dusky spider, a full cross on the belly.

or a spherical trap (four types):

10. A variegated spider, with a round belly.

11. A reddish spider, the round hinderparts pointed like the rays of a star.

12. The dusky house-spider.

13. An ash-colored spider, very small, marked with a black spot at the top of its hinderparts.

or webs or fabrics (eight types):

14. A yellowish hairy house-spider with very long legs.

15. A blackish house-spider with a very large spot on top of its hinderparts, and oblique stripes.

16. A sooty spider from Craven,[2] notable for its unusual brilliance, with a forked tail.

17. A yellowish spider, distinguished by a row of square spots on the hinderparts, and with yellowish oblique stripes on either side of the rear.

18. A large ash-colored spider with a forked tail.

19. A black or chestnut spider, hairless, with brilliantly variegated hinderparts.

20. An ash-colored spider, soft, having on its obliquely striped belly, a reddish-black spot at the side.

21. A spider for the most part blue, without any coloration the belly pointed.

Or they weave nothing for that reason (unless the spinning of the threads also relates to their flying about) although otherwise capable of it; for they make webs to protect their young or against the winter, but at the beginning of March they hunt flies; and these are either called "wolves" (five types) and these have eight eyes like each of those above:

22. A little reddish spider, with very swift feet.

23. A crab-like spider, slow-footed, with violet-purple eyes.

24. An ash-colored spider, the belly colored in a wavy manner, pointed, notably high.

25. A dusky spider, the belly striped obliquely.

26. A black, woodland spider.

[or] "phalangia," moving by jumps (three types). These have only six eyes:

27. An ash-colored spider, or varying from silver to black.

28. A yellowish spider, with emerald eyes, with three gold-

en stripes near the hinderparts.
29. A reddish spider from Craven, out of the heather or crags.
Or else they spin no thread at all, as these very numerous ones;
they are provided with very long, thin legs, and only two eyes,
the stings [?] or arms being divided into "fingers" (four types).
30. A reddish, gregarious spider, not crested.
31. An ash-colored, crested spider.
32. A woodland spider, variegated black and white, the smallest of mites.
33. A spider that is, I think, of a scarlet color, commonly called in English a "tant."[3]

NOTES

1 As Letter 1613 states, "fastigiata" was a correction replacing "turbinata," but the original word is no longer visible.
2 Craven is a district in the West Riding of Yorkshire near Skipton, where Lister had settled after his marriage.
3 Or "taint." See Thomas Browne, *Pseudodoxia epidemica*, Bk. III, ch. XXVII, sect. 11, where Browne describes a supposedly very poisonous spider which he calls "tainct."

1590
Oldenburg to Sluse

12 January 1670/1

From the copy in Royal Society Letter Book IV, 164–74

Illustri et Reverendo admodum Viro
Domino Renato Francisco Slusio Canonico Leodiensi
H. Oldenburg Salutem

Quae in novissimis tuis literis, Vir Celeberrime, de Alhazeni Problemate, traditaque ejusdem a Domino Hugenio demonstratione, subtiliter commentatus es, singulari cum lubentia atque delectatione perlegimus. Si copiam mihi epistola proxima feceris, doctissima tua de illo argumento cogitata dicto Hugenio communicandi, accuratum scripti tui

apographum ipsi quantocyus transmittendum curabo.[1] Quod facilem tuam
ducendarum Tangentium methodum spectat, polliceri nobis non dubitamus, quin ea suo tempore Rempublicam literariam sis aucturus.[2] Nullus,
credo, Vir ingeniosus bonusque aegre feret, scientiae pomaeria longe
lateque proferri; neque adeo infrunitus quisquam fruerit [*read* fuerit] ut
sibi persuadeat, tot tantaque a se detecta fuisse, ut nullus aliorum spicile-
gijs locus supersit. Maxima profecto pars eorum quae scimus, minima est
eorum, quae ignoramus.

De Barrovij methodo Tangentium, Jacobus Gregorij, nunc St. An-
dreanus Mathematum in Scotia Professor, haec scribit:[3]

"Ex Domini Barrovij ducendarum Tangentium methodo, quibusdam
meis sociata, generalem detexi methodum Geometricam, citra calculum
Tangentes ad quasvas curvas ducendi, quae non modo dicti Barrovij
methodos particulares, sed et generalem ejus methodum Analyticam ad
Lectionis 10a calcem complectitur: Ac mea quidem methodus, non ultra
12 propositiones continet."

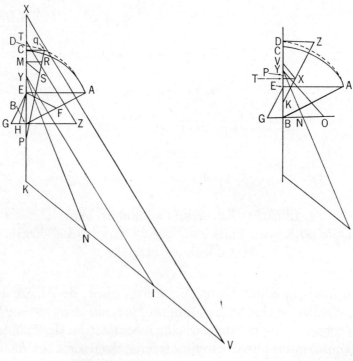

Fig. 1   Fig. 2

Hujus vero specimen ut exhiberet, Tangentem duxit ad spiralem arcuum rectificatricem (cujus mentionem antehac fecimus:)[4] Ejus copiam hic accipe:[5]

"Figura prima

"Sit circulus ABC, spiralis arcuum rectificatrix AD, quam oportet tangere in puncto D; in rectam BD sit perpendicularis AE, sitque $AF = FB$, jungaturque FE, et huic sit perpendicularis EG: porro fiat GB Perpendicularis ipsi CB, et $GH = BH$; sitque $CB : BE :: BE : CM$, et $BP = CM$. Ducantur Pq ipsi EH, et Cq, MR ipsi EA parallelae, et $RS = Rq$; jungaturque MS: fiat BT aequalis arcui $[AC]$ et $BC : BT :: BT : BX = $ 2 BZ, sitque BZ normalis ipsi BC, et $BY = XM$, item $BX = YK$: sint demum KV ipsi MS, et XV, YI ipsi TZ parallelae, et $IV = IN$, jungaturque YN.

"In Figura Secunda

"Sint rectae BA, BD, YN, EG, eaedem quae in priore figura, sitque BN perpendicularis ipsi BD, et $BN = NO$, et jungatur YO; fiant $PB = ED$; $TB = TD$; item $EK = KB = TV$, sitque KX parallela ipsi GE, et VX ipsi YO, jungaturque TX, et huic sit parallela DZ, quae spiralem tanget in Puncto D."

Idem Gregorius porro ait;[6]

"Optaverim, Barrovium inter Problemata sua unum inseruisse, Viz. fig. 156. suppositis ijs, quae in p.1. Lect. 12. et data figura $AKLD$; invenire curvam $ANMB$. Hoc equidem Problema resolvi si posset, Geometriae fines eximie proferret; at tantum in eo difficultatis mihi suboritur, ut a me saltem pro deplorato habeatur. Alium igitur cordatiorem hac provincia defungi pervelim."

Dominus Barrovius idem quoque secum expendit, sed et ipse desperare de eo videtur: Nihilominus praeter rem non fuerit, ipsius ea de re speculationes Tibi impertiri.[7]

"Ab Eruditissimo Domino Gregorio propositum Problema Solutionem hanc qualemcunque capit, an aliam meliorem ignoro.

"Theorema

"Sint tres lineae VMB, HNO, EZE,[8] communem habentes Axim AD, ac ita sese respicientes, ut arbitrarie ducta recta $NMGZ$, ad ipsam AD

perpendiculari, (quae lineas expositas secet, ut figura monstrat;) sit $GZq =$ $GMq+GNq$, ponaturque, rectas MP, NR, ZQ, curvis VMB, HNO, EZF Perpendiculares esse, erit $GQ = GP+GR$.

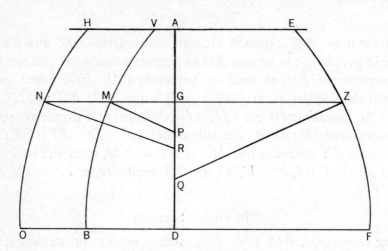

"Eatenus convertitur hoc Theorema, quatenus si $GP+GR = GQ$, sit GZq, vel aequale aggregato $GMq + GNq$, vel eo plus aut minus possit, eadem semper quantitate.

"Problema I

"Designare curvam DMM cujus Axis DQ, proprietate talem, ut si ad ipsam utcunque ducatur perpendicularis MP, et MG ad DQ Perpendicularis, sit $GM + GP$ aequalis datae Z *(see upper figure, p. 363)*.

"Const. Ad DO parem ipsi Z, ipsique DQ Perpendicularem, construatur quadratum $DOSR$, ac Asymptotis OD, OS per R describatur Hyperbola RYY, tum utcunque ducta recta $YEFM$ ad RD parallela, sit $Z \times EM$ aequale spatio FRY, erit punctum M ad curvam quaesitam. Subnotari possit, producta GMH, et ducta MT, curvam DMM contingente, fore $TH = ED$, vel $HM + HT = Z$.

"Problema II

"Esto linea quaepiam KXL (respiciens axem ad basin DL) designetur curva VMB talis, ut si ducatur utcunque recta MGX ad BDL parallela (lineas secans ut cernis) sitque MP curvae VMB Perpendicularis, sit $MG + GP = GX$ *(see lower figure, p. 363)*.

"Const. Sumatur $DO = GX$, et describatur Quadratum $DOSR$, et intra angulum DOS per R describatur Hyperbola RYY; tunc ita ducatur

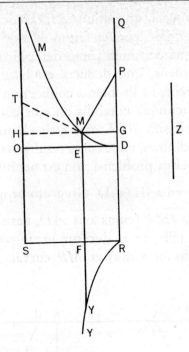

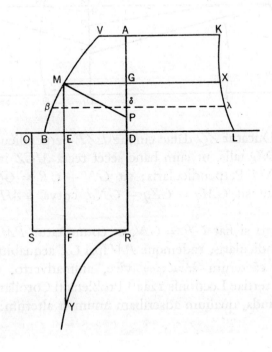

recta YF ad RD parallela, ut spatium RFY aequetur rectangulo ex OD, DG, et protractae YF, XG conveniant in M, erit M unum e curvae quaesitae punctis, et reliqua consimili pacto determinantur.

"Ratiocinium recolens, quo deducta est haec constructio, vereor ut sana sit, quinimo vereor, ut Problema confici non possit, a me saltem pro deplorato habetur, utcunque notabilis est ejus cum sequente connexio.

"Notetur autem, basim BDL arbitrarie desumi; potuisset enim alia quaevis (veluti βδλ) adhiberi, unde curva resultasset alia ac alia, eadem proprietate dotatae; quocirca problema non est penitus determinatum.

"Problema III (a. D. Gregorio propositum)

"Sit curva quaevis EZF (cujus axis AD, basis DF) curva designetur (puta VMB) natura talis, ut si ducatur utcunque recta MGZ ad BDF parallela (lineas secans ut vides) et MP curvae AMB⁹ perpendicularis sit $MP = GZ$.

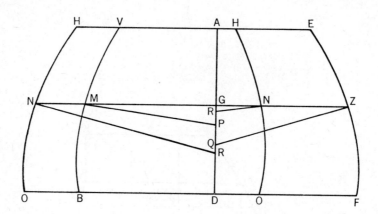

"Constr. Ducatur ZQ datae curvae EZF perpendicularis, tum reperiatur curva HNO talis, ut cum hanc secet recta MGZ in P,[10] ponaturque NR ipsi HNO Perpendicularis; sit $GN + GR = GQ$; tum sit curva VMB talis, ut sit $GMq = GZq - GNq$, curva VMB Proposito satisfaciet.

"Enim vero si fiat $GP = GN$, et connectatur PM, erit PM curvae VMB Perpendicularis, eademque PM ipsi GZ aequabitur. Ita quod istam rem attinet; caeterum ἐπιμέτρου vice, animadverto, potuisse secundo appendiculae tertiae Lectionis 12ae[11] Problemati Corollaria quaedam adponi non injucunda, qualium adscribam unum et alterum:

"Problema primum

"Detur linea quaepium AMB (cujus Axis AD, basis DB) curva ANE designetur talis, ut ducta libere recta MNG ad BD parallela, quae ipsam ANE secet in N, sit curva AN aequalis ipsi GM.

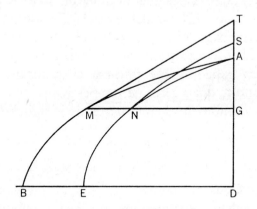

"Curva ANE talis sit, ut si MT curvam AMB, et NS curvam ANE tangant, sit $SG : GN :: TG : \sqrt{GMq - TGq}$; ipsa ANE proposito faciet satis.

"Problema 2dum

"Ijsdem quoad caetera suppositis et constitutis, curva ANE talis esse debeat, ut curva AN aequetur interceptae rectae NM. Curva ANE jam talis sit, ut sit $SG : GN :: 2TG \times GM : GMq - TGq$; erit ANE curva quae desideratur.

"Problema 3

"Datur curva quaepiam DXX, cujus Axis DA; reperiatur curva AMB proprietate talis, ut si libere ducatur recta GXM ad ipsam AD

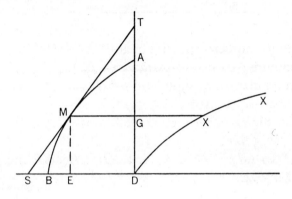

Perpendicularis, ponaturque *SMT* curvam *AM* tangere; sit *MS* aequalis ipsi *GX*.

"Liquet, rationem *TG* at *TM* (hoc est, rationem *GD* ad *MS* vel *GX*) dari: adeoque rationem *TG* ad *GM* quoque dari.

"Inservit hoc superficiebus designandis, quarum in promptu sit dimensio: etenim (ducta *ME* ad *AD* parallela) superficies solidi ex plani *BME* circa Axem *DB* rotatu progeniti adaequat Periph. Rad. *GDX*; ut habetur in 11a Lectionis 12. E tangentium porro contemplatione suborta est methodus, per quam expeditissime plurima circa maximas quantitates Theoremata deducuntur, quae certe, si tempestive se objecissent, digna censuissem, quae lectionibus insererentur; ex ijs indigitabo nonnulla

"Theoremata

"Sit curva quaepiam *ALB*, cujus Axis *AD*, basis *BD*, et huic parallelae *LG*, *λγ*; item *LT* curvam tangat.

1 Sit *m* numerus quicunque, potestates exponens; si ponatur $DG^{m-1} \times TG = GL^m$, erit $DG^m + GL^m$ maximum, seu majus quam $D\,\gamma^m + \gamma\lambda^m$.

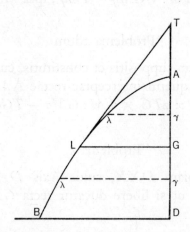

2 Itidem sumpto numero *m*, si ponatur $BL^{m-1} \times TL = GL^m$; erit $GL^m + BL^m$ maximum, seu majus quam $\gamma\lambda^m + B\lambda^m$.

3 Sint numeri quilibet *m*, *n*; si ponatur $m \times TG = n \times DG$, erit $DG^m \times GL^n$ maximum, seu majus quam $D\gamma^m \times \gamma\lambda^n$.

4 Quod si ponatur $m \times TL = n \times$ arc *BL*, erit $GL^n \times BL^m$ maximum, seu majus quam $\gamma\lambda^n \times B\lambda^m$.

5 Si fuerit $TG \times GL = DGLB$, erit $DGLB \times GL$ maximum seu majus quam $D\gamma\lambda B \times \gamma\lambda$.

6 Sin $TG \times GL = 2DGLB$, erit $GL \times \sqrt{DGLB}$ maximum, seu majus quam $\gamma\lambda \times \sqrt{D\gamma\lambda B}$.

"Haud difficili negotio, cum haec demonstrantur, tum ejusmodi complura deprehenduntur."

Hucusque Dn. Barrow. laudatus Dn. Gregorius Tractatum praelo parat, in quo novas quasdam methodos exspectamus:[12] nonnulla quoque circa argumentum illud, quod Michael Angelus Riccius antehac in sua de maximis et minimus Exercitatione[13] promiserat. Fieri interim poterit, ut inventa Riccij Gregorium antevertant, cum nuper a docto quodam viro, commercium literarium nobiscum colente,[14] Lugduno Galliarum acceperimus, Diarium Eruditorum singulis mensibus imprimi Romae, instar Transactionum Philosophicarum Angliae, et Diarij Eruditorum Galliae; in illo autem Romano multa haberi curiosa Mathematica, quae inserenda ei curet D. Michael Angelus Riccius.[15]

Idem Amicus Lugdunensis (ut hac occasione id adjiciam) perscribit nobis complurium librorum, nobis hactenus incognitiorum, titulos, quos hic indicare non gravabor, ut si forte de momento eorum quicquam Tibi constet, tuam de eo mentem nobis aperias.

Reinaldini Tom. 2us seu Geometra promotus cum Tractatu de Curvis Medicaeis.[16]

Barruelis Algebra Gallice.[17]

Billij duo Tomi Diophanti Redivivi.[18]

Fermati commentaria in Diophantum (hunc librum indies Parisijs exspecto.) Tanneur de Motu Locali accelerato.[19]

Antonij Laloverae Appendices polemicae contra Magnanum.[20] Et de quodam Moutono sic scribit: Dn. Mouton optat summopere, ut opera sua innotescant in Anglia, exactissimus observator: Habet Tractatum de Pendulis, et Methodum transmittendi ad posteros mensuras Corporum, et Tractatum de Logarithmis: Tabulas novas Declinationum Eclipticae in eo libro, quem modo edidit de mensura Diametri solis et lunae.[21]

Honoratus Fabri edidit hoc Anno Lugduni Galliarum quatuor Tomos Physicos, observationibus Physico-Mathematicis refertos.[22] Nunc Archimedem, ut accepimus, parat.[23] Edidit etiam Dialogos contra Grimaldum de Refractionibus; contra Borellum de Vi Percussionis, et contra Montanarium de Elevatione liquorum in Canaliculis:[24] Ad haec Synopsin Geometricam,[25] Tractatum de linea sinuum et Cycloide, una cum centuria de Maximis et Minimis.

Alexandri Marchetti Galilaeus promotus de Resistentia corporum[26]

Blondellus de Resistentia Corporum Ellipticorum.[27]

Rossetti Antignome, Tractatus Physico-Mathematicus.[28]

Thomas Cornelius Neapolitanus de Motu Liquorum in canaliculo.[29]

Caroli dati Historia Cycloideos.[30]

Euclides Gottignei.[31]

Euclides Claudij Milleti de Chales.[32] Parat idem cursum Mathematicum intra annum unum edendum, nec non Tabulas Hydrographicas novas maris Mediterranei.[33]

Iohannis Baptistae Baliani opuscula Posthuma.[34]

Theses Parisienses P. Harrovi contra Cartesium et Systema Copernicanum.[35]

Horum omnium copiam nobis brevi factum iri ex Gallia, speramus; Quod vero Caramuelis Lobkowitzij duo ampla volumina attinet, frigide ea laudari accepimus, unde nostrum videndi ea desiderium deferbuit:[36] nec ullam unquam procurandi libros molestiam Tibi facessemus, nisi forte prodierint aliqui, quorum copiam nonnisi favore tuo obtinere licuerit; Religioni quippe nobis omnino ducimus, tanti Amici benignitate abuti.

Quidam Butlerus Anglus Tractatulum quendam lingua vernacula edidit in quo probare contendit servatoris nostri Natalem in 25 Decembri incidere, et Christi Domini Annum juxta Æram Vulgarem recte computatum esse.[37] Seneschallum, quo nos donaveras, ipsi examinandum concesseramus.[38] Ei responsionem paravit, sermone Anglico, propediem imprimendam; deinceps vero ab Authore, postquam Grandamicum,[39] Ricciolum,[40] nonnullosque alios viderit, sermone Latine asserandam.

Operam dabimus, ut liberalitatem tuam in Laloverae, (jam ut putem, demortui) libro, nec non Mesolabo tuo transmittendo, ea qua par est gratitudine, pensemus: quibus si occasione commoda unum alterumve ex Tractatulis illis, quos antehac de Cycloide, sive circa Dettonvilij libellum edidisti, adjicere velis, rem sane pergratam Te nobis praestiturum credas.[41]

Hi dies festi Societatis Regiae conventus publicus interruperunt, nec commode potui cum viris ex illo caetu Mathematicis sermonem ea de re habere, quam Tu ex Tacqueto commemoras, circulum scilicet oblique spectatum nunquam ut circulum apparere.

Quidam vult, eum in oculi fundo Ellipsin formare: Alius, quem lubens de eo consuluissem, hinc abest; Hic ipse lineam duxit crescentem, Tangentium in aequi-differentibus Arcubus ad instar, apparentem vero (per pinnacidium certo modo applicatum si spectes) aequaliter divisam, sed de his alias plura.

Dominus Collins plurimam Tibi salutem scribit, et praeter caetera,

Tibi mittit modum construendi tabulam, in qua inveniri possint omnes Æquationes,[42] cui illa adaptatur.[43]

"Æquatio Cartesiana

$$x^4 - 4x^3 - 19x^2 + 106x = N$$

"Si conceperis N transpositam, eique praefixum signum negativum, tum quia hujus Æquationis signa ter mutata sunt habere illa potest tres Radices veras, et quia duo signa similia, vid. concurrunt, habere potest unam Radicem falsam vel negativam.

"Prop. Tabulam construere, in qua inveniri possint omnes Radices Æquationis, cui illa adaptatur.

"Assume seriem Radicum in progressione Arithmetica, et pro ea construe Tabulam N sive Homogeneorum.

"Hoc modo, si 9. sit Radix, tum 3060 est N.

"Nam si 9. $= x$, tum $x^4 = +6561$

$$+106x = + \ 954$$
$$\overline{7515}$$

$$-4x^3 = -2916 \Big\}$$
$$-19x^2 = -1539 \Big\} \ 4455$$
$$\overline{+3060}$$

x	N	Differentiae				
−10	+11240					
		−4056				
− 9	+ 6984		1152			
		−2904		−228		
− 8	+ 4080		924		24	
		−1980		−204		
− 7	+ 2100		720		24	
		−1260		−180		
− 6	+ 840		540		24	
		− 720		−156		
− 5	+ 120		384		24	
		− 336		−132		
− 4	− 216		252		24	
		− 84		−108		
− 3	− 300		144		24	
		+ 60		− 84		
− 2	− 240		60		24	
		+ 120		− 60		

−1	−120		0		24
	+120			−36	
±0	±0		−36		24
	+84			−12	
1	84		−48		24
	+36			+12	
2	120		−36		24
	0			+36	
3	120		0		24
	0			+60	
4	120		60		24
	60			84	
5	180		144		24
	204			108	
6	384		252		24
	456			132	
7	840		384		24
	840			156	
8	1680		540		24
	1380			180	
9	3060		720		
	2100				
10	5160				

"Sic pro Radicibus affirmativis vel veris; Pro radicibus negativis vel falsis (si quidem tales habuerit Æquatio) mutato signa potestatum parium, quando index par est, ut hic, nempe secundi et quarti termini &c. (sed muta signa potestatum imparium, si summa potestas Æquationis sit impar, nempe primi, tertij et quinti termini:) et erit talis Æquatio

$$x^4 + 4x^3 - 19x^2 - 106x = N,$$

atque excita Homogenea ad progressionem priorem (quae jam devenerunt Radices Negativae.) Sic si 5. sit Radix, Homogeneum erit 120

$$\begin{aligned}
\text{Nam} \quad +x^4 &= +\ 625 \\
+4x^3 &= +\ 500 \\
-19x^2 &= -\ 475 \\
-106x &= -\ 530 \\
\hline
&+\ 120
\end{aligned}$$

Tabula constructa si quod Homogeneum Æquationis, cui illud adaptatur, proponitur, quoties illud invenies in Tabula vel diserte, vel inter Homogenea affirmative relatum, tot Radices habebit Æquatio.

"Exemplum. si 120 sit $= N$, Æquatio talis est,

$$x^4 - 4x^3 - 19x^2 + 106x - 120.$$

Ac hujus Æquationis Radices sunt $+2, +3, +4, -5$.

Si $+ x^4 - 4x^3 - 19x^2 + 106x = 840$, Radices sunt $+7, -6$

"Æquatio jam amisit duas ex Radicibus suis, uti omnibus Æquationibus solenne est per paria. Ex superiori tabula observari est, ultimas differentias esse aequales, et easdem esse cum differentijs ultimis biquadratorum Progressionis Arithmeticae, unitate differentium.[44] Atque in Æquationibus falsas Radices habentibus aeque ac veras, omnes differentiae, exceptis primis, repetentur. Similiter, si 84 sit Homogeneum, non nisi bis inveniri potest inter Homogenea affirmativa; pro illo invenis Radicem affirmativam $+1$; et inter negativas habet Radicem inter 4 et 5 (unde series illa Homogeneorum affirmativorum intelligenda est incipere iterum a O) atque hoc arguit, Æquationem habere non nisi radices duas, posseque dividi in duas Æquationes Quadraticas, quarum altera est impossibilis, altera habet radicem Affirmativam et Negativam. Haec doctrina nos adigit ad Limites, ut ostendatur, quodnam esse oporteat Homogeneum, quod efficiat ut par aliquod radicum lucretur vel amittat possibilitatem suam; Atque ut statuantur isti limites pro omnibus Æquationibus, absque ejusmodi tabulae adminiculo, primarium est desideratum in Algebra, quod a Sagacissimo Slusio vel Riccio[45] expletum praestolamur, debetque praestari scandendo: primo praecise limitando Quadratica, tum Cubica, tum Biquadratica, quae omnia, ut Dn. Slusius in libri de Mesolab. innuit derivari possunt ab ipsius Capite de Maximis et Minimis, et jam tractata fuere ab Huddenio.[46]

"Constructio Geometrica

"Divide lineam rectam in partes aequales, incipiendo ab O, in medio excitando Homogenea ex partibus illis aequalibus, seu Perpendicularia,

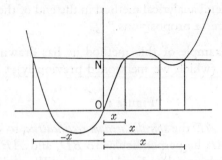

sive ordinatas super Radices suas respectivas; atque duc curvam per ordinatarum istarum summitate, eritque illa curva accommodata Æquationi, ita ut ad distantiam parallelam Basi, aequali cuivis Homogeneo dato, ducta linea secans hanc curvam, Tibi det Radices quaesitas.

Curva huc spectans, ita repraesentatur rudiori Minerva.

Atque hae curvae generantur ex diversis trilineis Parabolicis eorumve ordinatis congruis, positis a linea curvata, sursum vel deorsum, secundum Æquationis Affectiones." Vale. Dabam Londini die 12. jan. Anno 1671.

TRANSLATION

H. Oldenburg greets the illustrious and very reverend René François de Sluse, Canon of Liège

We have perused with singular pleasure and delight your subtle commentary in your most recent letter, famous Sir, upon the Problem of Alhazen and the demonstration of it offered by Mr. Huygens. If you will give me leave in your next letter to communicate to the said Huygens your very learned thoughts upon this subject, I will take care to send him an accurate copy of your paper as soon as possible.[1] As for your easy way of drawing tangents, we have no hesitation in anticipating that in good time you will adorn the world of letters with it.[2] I believe that no good and intelligent person will take it hard if the fruits of knowledge are spread far and wide; nor will any one be so foolish as to persuade himself that he has detected so many and such important things that no room remains for investigation by others. The bulk of what we know is but an infinitesimal part of what we do not know.

James Gregory, now Professor of Mathematics at St. Andrews in Scotland, writes thus concerning Barrow's method of tangents:[3]

"I have discovered from Barrow his method of drawing tangents together with some of my own, a general geometrical method, without calculation, of drawing tangents to all curves, and comphrehending not only Barrow's particular methods, but also his general analytical method in the end of the 10th lecture. My method contains not above 12 propositions."

In order to give an example of this method he has drawn a tangent to the *spiralis arcuum rectificatrix* (which we mentioned previously);[4] here is a copy of that:[5]

"Figure 1

"Let ABC be a circle, AD the *spiralis arcuum rectificatrix*, to which a tangent is to be drawn at D. Let AE be perpendicular to BD, and $AF = FB$; join FE, and make EG perpendicular to this. Further, make GB perpendicular to CB, and $GH = BH$; and let $\dfrac{CB}{BE} = \dfrac{BE}{CM}$, and $BP = CM$. Draw Pq parallel to EH, and Cq and MR parallel to EA, and $RS = Rq$. Join MS, and make BT equal to the arc $[AC]$, and $\dfrac{BC}{BT} = \dfrac{BT}{BX}$; $BX = 2BZ$, BZ being normal to BC, and $BY = XM$, also $BX = YK$. Lastly, KV is parallel to MS, and XV, YI are parallel to TZ, and $IV = IN$; join YN [*see Fig. 1, p. 360*].

"Figure 2

"Let the straight lines BA, BD, YN and EG be the same as in the former figure, and let BN be perpendicular to BD, and $BN = NO$; join YO. Make $PB = ED$, $TB = TD$; also $EK = KB = TV$, and let KX be parallel to GE, and VX parallel to YO. Join TX and let DZ be parallel to this, touching the spiral at D [*see Fig. 2, p. 360*]."

The same Gregory says further:[6]

"I could wish that among his problems he had imparted on[e] viz fig 156 [with the same things supposed as in the first page of Lecture XII and the given figure $AKLD$, to find the curve $ANMB$]. This problem (if it can be resolved) I imagine would advance geometrie beyond its present state, but I find so much difficulty into it, that I despair of it myself, and therefore I do humbly desire it of any else who can resolve it."

The same Mr. Barrow has also pondered on this, but he too seems to despair of it; nevertheless, it will not have been without value to impart his speculations on this point to you:[7]

"He takes the solution, such as it is, of the problem proposed by the very learned Mr. Gregory to be thus; I do not know if there is a better one:

"Theorem

"Let there be three lines VMB, HNO, EZE[8] having a common axis AD, and having such relations to each other that when the straight line $NMGZ$ is drawn at will perpendicular to AD (cutting the lines mentioned, as the figure shows) $GZ^2 = GM^2 + GN^2$; and postulating that the lines MP, NR, ZQ are normal to the curves VMB, HNO, EZF, $GQ = GP + GR$ [*see figure, p. 362*].

"This theorem may be so far modified that if $GP + GR = GQ$, GZ^2 may be either equal to the sum $GM^2 + GN^2$, or more or less than this sum by the same constant amount.

"Problem I

"To designate a curve DMM with axis DQ, having the property that if a normal MP is drawn to it at any point and MG perpendicular to DQ, $(MG + GP)$ will be equal to a given [length] Z [*see upper figure, p. 363*].

"Construction. Upon DO (equal to Z and normal to DQ) construct the square

DOSR and with asymptotes *OD*, *OS* describe the hyperbola *RYY* through *R*. Then having drawn any line *YFEM* parallel to *RD*, let $Z \times EM$ be equal to the area *FRY*; *M* will be a point on the curve sought for. It may be noted that with *GMH* produced and *MT* drawn, touching the curve *DMM*, *TH* will be equal to *ED*, or $HM + HT = Z$.

"Problem II

"Let there be any line whatever *KXL* (having an axis [*DA*] upon the base *DL*), and let the curve *VMB* be drawn such that when any straight line *MGX* is drawn parallel to *BDL* (meeting the lines [*KXL*, *VMB*] as you see), and *MP* is normal to the curve *VMB*, $MG + GP = GX$ [*see lower figure, p. 363*].

"Construction. Mark off $DO = GX$, and describe the square *DOSR*; describe an hyperbola through *R* in the angle *DOS*. Then draw *YF* parallel to *RD* so that the area *FRY* is equal to the rectangle *OD. DG. YF* and *XG* produced meet in *M*, and *M* is one point of the curve sought, whose other points may be determined in a similar fashion.

"Recalling to mind the reasoning upon which this construction is founded I do indeed doubt whether this problem can be resolved, which I at least regret because of its notable connection with the following one.

"However, it is to be observed that I have taken the base *BDL* arbitrarily; for any other base (such as *βδλ*) could be chosen, whence different curves would result endowed with the same property; for which reason the problem is not completely determined.

"Problem III (proposed by Mr. Gregory)

"Let *EZF* be any curve with axis *AD*, base *DF*, [and] the curve to be drawn (say *VMB*) of such a nature that if the straight line *MGZ* be drawn parallel to *BDF* (cutting the lines as you see), and *MP* normal to the curve *AMB*,[9] $MP = GZ$ [*see figure, p. 364*].

"Construction. Let *ZQ* be drawn normal to the given curve *EZF*, then a curve *HNO* may be found such that when cut by the line *MGZ* in *P*,[10] and *NR* drawn normal to *HNO*, $GN + GR = GQ$. Then if the curve *VMB* be such that $GM^2 = GZ^2 - GN^2$, this curve will satisfy the problem.

"For if $GP = GN$, and *PM* is joined, *PM* will be normal to the curve *VMB*, and the same *PM* will be equal to *GZ*. And thus it attains the same end; moreover, as a further bonus I notice that some not inelegant corollaries could have been added to the second problem of the third little appendix after Lecture XII,[11] of which I supply both:

"First Problem

"Given any line *AMB*, whose axis is *AD* and base *BD*, let the curve to be drawn *ANE* be such that when the line *MNG* is drawn arbitrarily parallel to *BD* cutting ANE at N, [the portion] AN of the curve may be equal to MG [*see upper figure, p. 365*].

"The curve ANE is to be such that if MT is a tangent to the curve AMB, and NS a tangent to ANE,

$$\frac{SG}{GN} = \frac{TG}{\sqrt{GM^2 - TG^2}};$$

this curve ANE satisfies the proposition.

"Second Problem

"With everything as above, the curve ANE is to be such that [the portion] AN is equal to the intercept NM. If the curve ANE be such that

$$\frac{SG}{GN} = \frac{2TG \cdot GM}{GM^2 - TG^2};$$

ANE will be the curve sought.

"Third Problem

"Any curve DXX is given whose axis is DA; a curve AMB is to be found having the property that if a straight line GXM is drawn arbitrarily perpendicular to AD and SMT is drawn to touch the curve AM, $MS = GX$ [*see lower figure, p. 365*].

"It is obvious that the ratio of TG to TM is given (that is, $GD:MS$ or GX); and so the ratio of TG to GM is also given.

"It is useful now to designate the areas whose dimensions are known, for (drawing ME parallel to AD) the surface of the solid generated by the plane BME rotating round the axis DB is equal to π. GDX; as may be seen from the eleventh [paragraph] of Lecture XII. From the study of tangents a method has been derived by which, with the greatest speed, many theorems concerning maximum quantities have been deduced which I would certainly have thought fit to insert in the lectures, if they had presented themselves in time. I will indicate some of them:

"Theorems

"Let ALB be any curve, whose axis is AD, and base BD and to this LG, $\lambda\gamma$, are parallel; also LT is a tangent to the curve [*see figure, p. 366*].

1. Let m be any number serving as an exponent; if it be postulated that DG^{m-1}. $TG = GL^m$, then $DG^m + GL^m$ is a maximum, that is exceeds $D\gamma^m + \gamma\lambda^m$.
2. With m as before, if $BL^{m-1} . TL = GL^m$, $GL^m + BL^m$ will be a maximum, that is exceeding $\gamma\lambda^m + B\lambda^m$.
3. Let m, n, be any numbers; if it be postulated that $m . TG = n.DG$, then $DG^m . GL^n$ is a maximum, or greater than $D\gamma^m . \gamma\lambda^n$.
4. That if it is postulated that $M . TL = n$. arc BL, $GL^n . BL^m$ will be a maximum, or greater than $\gamma\lambda^n . B\lambda^m$.

5. If $TG . GL = DGLB$, $DGLB . GL$ is a maximum, or greater than $D\gamma\lambda B . \gamma\lambda$.
6. If $TG . GL = 2DGLB$, $GL . \sqrt{DGLB}$ will be a maximum, or greater than $\gamma\lambda . \sqrt{D\gamma\lambda B}$.

"When these have been demonstrated it is easy enough to see one's way through many of the same sort."

So far Mr. Barrow. The worthy Mr. Gregory is preparing for the press a treatise in which we anticipate [finding] some new methods,[12] some of them devoted to that business which Michelangelo Ricci promised earlier in his essay concerning maxima and minima.[13] Yet it may be that Ricci's discoveries will precede Gregory's, for we learned recently from Lyons, from a certain learned person who corresponds with us,[14] that a learned journal is printed monthly at Rome (like the *Philosophical Transactions* of England and France's *Journal des Sçavans*) in which there are many curious mathematical notes inserted by Michelangelo Ricci.[15]

The same friend at Lyons (if I may take this opportunity to continue) writes us the titles of many books hitherto unknown to us; these I shall not scruple to set down now, so that if you know anything of their value you may disclose your opinion to us:

Renaldini's second tome, or *Geometra promotus* with a treatise on the Medician Curves.[16]

Barruel's *Algebra* in French.[17]

Billy's two volumes of *Diophantus redivivus*.[18]

Fermat's commentaries on *Diophantus*. This book I expect daily from Paris. Le Tenneur on accelerated local motion.[19]

Antoine de la Loubère's polemical appendices against Maignan.[20] And he writes thus of a man named Mouton: "Mr. Mouton very much desires to have his writings known in England. He is a most exact observer; he has a treatise on pendulums [or clocks] and a method of transmitting the measurements of things to posterity, and a treatise on logarithms; [he printed] new tables of the declination of the ecliptic in that book which he recently published on the measure of the lunar and solar diameters."[21]

Honoré Fabri has this year published at Lyons four tomes on physics, stuffed full of physico-mathematical matter.[22] Now we hear he is preparing an Archimedes.[23] He has also published dialogues against Grimaldi['s book] on refractions; against Borelli's *De vi percussionis*; and against Montanari on the rising of fluids in small pipes;[24] besides these, a synopsis of geometry,[25] a treatise on the line of sines and the cycloid, together with a century [of problems] concerning maxima and minima.

Alessandro Marchetti, *Galilaeus promotus* [*seu*] *de resistentia corporum*.[26]

Blondel, *De resistentia corporum ellipticorum*.[27]

Rosetti, *Antignome fisico-matematiche*.[28]

Tommaso Cornelio of Naples on the movement of fluids in little pipes.[29]

Carlo Dati, *Storia della cicloide*.[30]

Gottignies' *Euclid*.[31]

Milliet de Chales' *Euclid*.[32] He is preparing a *Course of Mathematics* for publication within a year, and new hydrographic charts of the Mediterranean Sea.[33]

The posthumous works of Giovanni Battista Baliani.[34]

The Parisian theses of Father de Harouis against Descartes and the Copernican System.[35]

We hope to be furnished with a supply of all these from France shortly. As for the two ample volumes of Caramuel Lobkowitz, we understand them to be damned with faint praise, which has cooled our desire to see them;[36] nor would we ever give you any trouble in obtaining books, unless some should be published of which copies are to be obtained only by your favor. We have too many scruples to abuse the kindness of so great a friend.

A certain Englishman named Butler has published a little vernacular tract in which he seeks to prove that the birth of our Saviour occurred on 25 December, and that the year of Our Lord is correctly computed in the common reckoning.[37] We have lent him Seneschall (which you presented to us) to study.[38] He has prepared a reply to him in English which is to be published soon; and then set out by the author in Latin after he has seen Grandami,[39] Riccioli,[40] and several others.

We shall strive to be properly grateful for your generosity in sending us La Loubère's book (the author, I think, is now dead) as well as your *Mesolabum*; if you please to add to these, should a convenient opportunity present itself, one or more of those little tracts which you published on the cycloid or about the pamphlet by Dettonville, you may be sure of doing something most welcome to us.[41]

During these holidays the Royal Society intermits its public meetings and I could not conveniently speak with its mathematical Fellows about that business you drew attention to in Tacquet, about the circle seen obliquely never appearing as a circle.

One man supposes that it forms an ellipse at the back of the eye; another, whom I would gladly have consulted about this, is away from here. He himself has drawn a line, increasing like the tangents to regularly increasing arcs, which seems to be evenly divided if you look through a peephole placed in a certain way. But more of this another time.

Mr. Collins sends you many greetings, and other things apart sends you a method for constructing a table in which all [roots of the][42] equation may be found, to which it is adapted:[43]

"The Cartesian Equation $x^4 - 4x^3 - 19x^2 + 106x = N$

"If you conceive N transposed and put with a Negative Signe, then because this Aequation hath its Signes thrice changed it may have 3 true rootes, and because two like Signes, viz. twice — come togeather (without change) it may have one false roote.

"Prop. [Any *N*, knowne Number (or Homogeneum Comparationis as Vieta calls it) being given,] to find all the rootes of the Aequation in a table made for that purpose.

"Assume a ranke of rootes to be in an Arithmeticall Progression and raise a table of *N* or Homogenea thereto

"Thus if +9 be a roote then 3060 = *N*

"For if $x = 9$ then $\quad +x^4 = +6561$

$$+106x \ = + \ 954$$
$$\overline{\quad\quad\quad +7515}$$

$$- \ 4x^3 = -2916$$
$$-19x^2 = -1539 \quad\quad -4455$$
$$\overline{\quad\quad\quad +3060}$$

[Here follows the table of differences, see p. 369]

"Thus for the affirmative or true rootes, for the Negative or false rootes (if the Aequation hath such) change the Signes of the even powers, when the degree of the first tearme, or highest power is even (as followeth) to wit of the 2d and 4th tearmes &c. (But of the odde powers if the highest power be odde, to wit of the first third and fifth tearmes) and the Aequation stands thus

$$x^4 + 4x^3 - 19x^2 - 106x = N$$

And raise Homogenea to the Progression againe and those belong to the negative rootes. Thus if $x = 5$, then [the Homogeneum will be 120. For] $+x^4 = +625$, $+4x^3 = +500$, $-19x^2 = -475$, $-106x = -530$. The table being thus prepared, if any Homogeneum [of the equation to which it is fitted] be given, as often as you find it either expressly in the table, or included amongst the affirmative Homogenea, so many rootes the Aequation hath.

"Example. If the Aequation be $x^4 - 4x^3 - 19x^2 + 106x = 120$, the rootes of this equation are $+2, +3, +4, -5$.

"If $x^4 - 4x^3 - 19x^2 + 106x = 840$, the rootes are $+7, -6$ the Aequation having now lost the possibliity of two of its rootes (as all Aequations doe by paires). You may observe [in the above table] that the last differences are equall and are the same as the last differences of the Biquadrates of an Arithmeticall Progression differing by Unit,[44] and in Aequations having false rootes as well as true, all but the first differences are repeated. [Similarly, if the *homogeneum* be 84, it can] be found but twice, amongst the affirmative Homogenea, [giving the positive root $+1$; and among the negative roots it has a root interpolated between 4 and 5 (whence that series of positive homogenea must be conceived to begin from zero). And this] argues that the Aequation hath but two rootes, and may be divided into two quadratick Aequations whereof one is impossible, the other has [both positive and negative roots]. This Doctrine casts you upon limits, to show what *N* must be to make a paire of roots gaine or loose their possibility, and to raise those limits for all Aequations without ayd is the grand desideratum in Algebra, to be expected from Slusius or Riccio,[45] and probably is to be performed by multiplication [in increasing order] first precisely limiting quadraticks, then Cubicks, then Biquadraticks all which Slusius hints may be derived from his chapter [on maxima and minima in his book *Mesolabum* and were previously treated by Hudde].[46]

"*Geometrick Construction*

"Divide a right line into equall parts commencing at *O*, in the middle, raising the Homogenea out of those equall parts as Perpendiculars or Ordinates upon their respective rootes, and draw a Curve through the tops of those Ordinates: it is a Curve suited to the Aequation, so that at a parallel distance, equall to any Homogeneum given drawing a line to cut those curves it gives you the rootes sought [*see figure, p. 371*]. The curve to this Aequation is thus shaped as we presume by a rude guesse and these curves are generated from the severall Trilinea Parabolica or their congruent Ordinates, being placed from the curved line upwards or downwards according to the affections of the Aequation."
Farewell. London, 12 January 1671

NOTES

Reply to Letter 1548. There is another (partial) copy in the Portsmouth Collection (CUL MS. Add. 3971, ff. 53–56).
1 See Vol. VIII, Letter 1752 (22 July 1671) for Oldenburg's quotation from Sluse's letter.
2 Oldenburg was to publish Sluse's letter of 7 January 1672/3 describing this method in *Phil. Trans.*, no. 90 (20 January 1672/3), 5143–47.
3 Oldenburg here quotes from Gregory's letter to Collins of 5 September 1670 (Turnbull, *Gregory*, p. 103). We have reverted to Gregory's English.
4 See Letter 1528, note 39.
5 What follows was enclosed by Gregory in his letter to Collins of 23 November 1670; see Turnbull, *Gregory*, pp. 134–35, printing the same Latin text, from which we have taken Figs. 1 and 2, not sketched in the Letter Book. For an explanation, see pp. 135–37 in the same book. In Fig. 2 the dimension $PB = DE$ is redundant.
6 Oldenburg now returns to the point in Gregory's letter where he broke off before (above note 3). The words in square brackets were written in Latin by Gregory. As Turnbull explains, Gregory seeks to find an unknown curve, given the length MP in Barrow's figure 156 of his *Lectiones geometricae*. What is required is a geometrical solution of the differential equation $y^2(1 + \left(\dfrac{dy}{dx}\right)^2) = X^2$, X being a known function of x.

7 Oldenburg now quotes from a paper or letter by Barrow lent him by Collins; strictly speaking the first sentence is Collins' voice, the "He" being Barrow. The same paper was sent to Gregory by Collins on 21 January 1670/1; it is printed by Turnbull with an ample discussion in *Gregory*, pp. 161–68.
8 Read: *EZF*.
9 Read: *VMB*.
10 Read: *N*.
11 Of *Lectiones geometricae*.

12 In fact Gregory published no more books on mathematical topics; his attention turned to astronomy, and he died in 1675.

13 See Letter 1489, note 10.

14 Père Jean Bertet (or Berthet), S.J. (1622–92), was a pupil of Honoré Fabri at Lyons; he moved to Paris in 1671. Collins became acquainted with him through one Mr. Hoote, an English traveler to France; he sent Bertet a parcel of books and asked for the like in return. Bertet's name first comes up in September 1670 (Turnbull, *Gregory*, p. 106).

15 Compare Letter 1555, note 9.

16 See Letter 1528, note 35. There is nothing on "Medician Curves" in this book.

17 We could find neither book nor author.

18 Jacques de Billy, S.J., *Diophanti redivivi pars prior . . . pars posterior* (Lyons, 1670).

19 Jacques Alexandre Tenneur (d. 1653) was author of *Traité des quantitez Incommensurables et le dixieme livre d'Euclide* (Paris, 1640). There is probably an error here.

20 See Letter 1507, note 8.

21 Gabriel Mouton, *Observationes diametrorum solis et lunae apparentium . . . Cum tabula declinatum solis . . .* (Lyons, 1670)—the only work attributed to this writer.

22 *Physica, id est scientia rerum corporearum* (Lyons, 1669–71).

23 This seems to be a false report.

24 These are all included in Fabri's *Dialogi physici* (see Letter 1471, note 2). Francesco Maria Grimaldi's *Physico-Mathesis de lumine, coloribus, et iride* appeared posthumously at Bologna in 1665.

25 *Synopsis geometrica, cui accessit tria opuscula, nimirum, de linea sinuum et cycloide, de maximis et minimis centuria, et synopsis trigonometriae planae* (Lyons, 1669).

26 See Letter 1556, note 19.

27 Possibly François Blondel's *Epistola ad* [Paulum Warzium] *in qua famosa Galilaei propositio discutitur . . .* (Paris, 1661).

28 Published at Livorno in 1667.

29 We could not discover what was meant.

30 Carlo Dati, *Lettera a Fileti . . ., della vera storia della cicloide e della famosissima esperienza dell'argento vivo* (Florence, 1663).

31 Probably his *Elementa geometriae planae* (Rome, 1669) is so described.

32 Claude François Milliet de Chales, S.J., *Euclidis elementorum libri* VIII (Lyons, 1660).

33 See Letter 1555, note 8.

34 Probably this is a mistake for G.B. Baliani, *Opere diverse* (Genoa, 1666), which were published a few months before the author's death.

35 Nicolas de Harouis, S.J. (Harouys, d'Arouis, etc.; 1622–98) was a teacher of mathematics and author of a *Traité de la Sphere* (Nantes, n.d.). Christiaan Huygens asked his father to send him a copy of these theses in a letter of 5 January 1664/5 (*Œuvres Complètes*, V, 197). They are not in the Bibliothèque Nationale. In 1665 de Harouis was in Paris.

36 See Letter 1556 and its note 22.

37 John Butler, χριστολογια (London, 1671). In 1675 this work was reissued as *God made Man: or an Account of Time. Stating the day, hour and minute of our Saviour's Nativity*, with a half-title "χριστολογια," and the date 1671.

38 See Vol. VI, Letter 1351, note 5.

39 Jacques Grandami, S.J., *Chronologia christiana de Christo nato et rebus gestis* (Paris, 1668).

40 See Letter 1484, note 14.

41 Sluse's letters to Pascal about the cycloid problems were not published; also, it is not clear which of Pascal's publications under the pseudonym of Dettonville is meant: perhaps the *Lettres de A. Dettonville* (Paris, 1659).

42 Read: "omnes radices Aequationis," as below.
43 This is another part of Collins' "Narrative on Equations." We have taken the English translation from the version sent to Gregory on 1 November 1670 (see Turnbull, *Gregory*, pp. 113–17). Our additions are in brackets.
44 That is, the series 1, 16, 81, 256, etc.
45 Ricci.
46 Johann Hudde's letters to Franz van Schooten were published in the latter's augmented edition of Descartes, *Geometria . . . anno 1637 Gallice edita . . .* (Amsterdam, 1659).

1591
Dodington to Oldenburg
13 January 1670/1
From the original in Royal Society MS. D 1, no. 18

Venice Janr. 23. 1671 [N.S.]

Sr

I am honoured wth yours of xbr. 20. wch should have binn acknowledg'd last post, but I was forced to deferr it until this. The inclosed to Sigr Malpighi is sent to Bologna,[1] That to Sigr Travagino is delivered,[2] from both, I hope to send you answeres by the next. Heerewith you have the Bombardiero Veneto, And ye rest of Padre Lanaes Booke.[3] His discourse on the perpetual Motion & Philosophers stone, are modest & not so vaynglorious as you imagine, when you have read it you will say so. There goe hence about the beginning of Febr. some vessels towards Engl. & some Gentlemen by land, in a months time, By the former or Latter I shall send you 2 Telescopes & 2 Microscopes of the SSri Eustachij Divini & Giuseppe Campani, wth such other Curiosities as Padre Kircherus will impart to me. You may also signify to me, if there be at present any other thing you desire from hence, in regard those opportunities come but once a yeare: and I pray make no difficulty in commanding me since I find a satisfaction in observing you. From Sigr Malpighj I expect some Bookes for you wch shall be sent forwards. And in case there be any thing of Bulk to come from you, you may direct it to Mr Humph. Sydney at Livorno, for me, by any shipp yt comes into the Straytes, or leave it wth

Mr Geo Ravenscroft a Merchant wellknown in Great St. Hellens, and he will convey it to me.[4]

Passing by Paris, I mett a Book newly printed, It was a Treatise of Vipers, I doubt not, but you have seen it;[5] I had the oportunity of being known to the Author. And have heere mett one Dr Tachenius[6] a learned man (as Dr Troutbeck[7] will tell you) who acquainted me wth 2 Accidents, in Re viperaria[8] Being a young Practitioner, & curious in drying of vipers, he used to chopp off their Heads wth 3 or 4 inches of the Body next adjoyning, fearing belike some noxious quality might remayn thereabouts, until at length he begann to perfect his Reading & observations. Having then Cutt off the Heads pro ut ante[9] & put even the Heads also, on a vessel, to dry them, wth the rest of the Body. He had ye Curiosity some 12 howers after they had binn so drying over a fire, to cutt of the Heads close to ye juncture of the neck, & so preserve the 2 or 3 Inches of the remayning Body, wth the rest of his Medicine, and so to cast away the Heads as uselesse; Accordingly striking away some of the Heads wth his Right hand, A tooth of one of the vipers, wch had binn drying some 12 howers, chance to hitt into his Thumb, in ye underskinn under his nayle. In Less then 3 Howers, it inflamed his hand & Arme, accompanyed wth a Fever: He applyed to it clothes wett in viper water. The next day, at ye previous hower, His fever returned, and the dr to his medicine, & drank it allso. The Third day the fevor returned periodically & more violent, wch invited ye dr to be more watchfull, he then took some Venice Treacle[10] wth a quantity of salt of vipers, and continued to use the Alcaly to his Thumb Hand & Arme, The 4th day it lessned & the 5 & 6 it Left him free from all remembrance of it The fever and ill symptomes returning no more.

The second Accident was two yeares after the former, when having cutt off the Heads of some vipers & given them to a servant to throw into a Howse of office, some 4 howers after a young full growne man, went to doe his Businesse there & had ye misfortune to sitt down upon one of the Heads wch it seemes, was not thrown in wth the rest, The man presently found him selfe prickd, but could not imagine wt hurt him, probably the said head fell in, upon his stirring for the man could see nothing. But though all the symptomes declared wt it was, and though ye dr did all he could the part gangrend and ye man dyed after 4 dayes. Sr I have at present no more to add Being in a hurry of Businesse, wch yet shall not hinder me from assuring you I am most heartily Sr

yr humble servant
John dodington

Mr Oldenburg

NOTES

Reply to Letter 1579.
1 Letter 1578.
2 Letter 1577.
3 See Letters 1561, note 4, and 1579, note 3.
4 It seems likely that this was the man soon to become famous as a maker of lead glass, rivaling Venice glass. Great St. Helens is north of Bishopsgate, near Liverpool Street Station, then full of fine houses. George Ravenscroft (1618–81) had been in the Venetian trade.
5 Presumably Moise Charas, *Nouvelles experiences sur la vipère* (Paris, 1669).
6 Otto Tachenius, originally German and educated as a pharmacist, went to Italy and took his M.D. at Padua in 1652, subsequently settling in Venice. He was still there in 1699.
7 John Troutbeck (d. 1684), originally from Yorkshire, may have been the man who received the M.D. from Cambridge in 1661, but he practised initially as a (highly successful) surgeon, and Pepys was very indignant when he was appointed Physician General of the Fleet in 1666, instead of Surgeon General. He was licensed to practise as a physician in London in March 1677/8.
8 "in viperine matters."
9 "as before".
10 A famous polypharmaceutical preparation.

1592
Willughby to Oldenburg

13 January 1670/1

From the original in Royal Society MS. W 3, no. 41

Middleton Jan: 13th 70/71

Sr

The account Mr Lister gives of How the first laid egges in the remotest cartrages may bee last Hatched, and the Nymphae come to perfection after all the incumbent are gone, and have made way For them, is very ingenious.[1] But dos not agree with the little experience I have had for these you sent mee had actually bored their way thorough severall placed above them. and having opened a great manie at Astrop purposely and upon a Wager about this very inquiry before my Ld. bisshop of Chester and Mr Wray I allwaies found the remotest from the entrance the most Forward and those that lay above them were still lesse and lesse and the least were allwaies those that were next the common entrance the other particulars in your letter I hope the enclosed from Mr Wray[2] will fully answer

your Faithfull servant
Francis W:

ADDRESS

    For Mr Henry
    Oldenburg Secretary
    to the royall Society:
    in the Palmall
          London

POSTMARK IA 16

NOTES

Reply to Letter 1587.
1 In Letter 1583.
2 Letter 1593.

1593
John Ray to Oldenburg

13 January 1670/1

From the original in Royal Society MS. R 1, no. 10
Printed in *Phil. Trans.*, no. 68 (20 February 1670/1), 2063–66

Sr

What I now send you concerning the juice of Pismires, I received not long since from Dr Hulse[1] & Mr Sam. Fisher;[2] & you may, if you think it worthy their notice, communicate to ye R. Society; & publish or suppresse as you see cause. Aug. 10. last past concerning this juice Dr Hulse sent me the following observations. Lately (saith he) consulting *Langhams garden of health*, I met with this passage.[3] Cast the flowers of Cichory amongst a heap of Ants, & they will soon become as red as blood. [N.B. Langham was not the first that made or published this observation: I find it delivered by Hieronymus Tragus Hist. Stirpium lib.

1. cap. 91. "Naturae miraculum in hoc flore observare licet: Siquidem cumulo formicarum abditus, caeruleum colorem in rubeum mutat, ac si terrore illarum erubesceret."[4] & before him by Otho Brunfelsius, as Johannes Bauhinus takes notice.][5] I presently got some Cichory flowers & made the experiment, & find it to be true that he saith; only he takes no notice of the manner how the flowers come to be so stain'd, wch therefore take as followes. Bare an Anthill with a stick, & then cast yr flowers upon it, & you shall see the Ants creep very thick over them. Now as they creep they let fall a drop of liquor from them, & where that chanceth to light there you shall have in a moment a large red stain. Sometimes they will be a pretty while before they discolour them, & at other times they will doe it suddainly. At the first I guessed that being vex't by stirring their hill, they might thrust their stings into the flowers, & through them convey that sharp liquor. But by bruising them, & rubbing the expressed juice agst the flowers I find they will be equally stained. It's a thing well known, that Ants, if they get into peoples clothes & so to their skin, will cause a smart & tingling as if they were netled, wch I conceive is done by letting fall the forementioned corrosive liquor, rather then by stinging. To what sort of liquor to referre this juice I know not. I drop't spirit of salt & oil of sulphur upon the flowers, but they would not at all discolour them. I likewise put salt of Tartar upon them, & dropt thereon a little spirit of salt; which caused a sufficient fermentation, but did not prevail to change the colour of ye flowers in the least. This Observation holds true not only in Cichory flowers, but also in Larkespurres, Borage flowers & I suppose all others that are of a blew colour.[6] It were worth the while to try, whether that sharp liquor, wch Mr Hook saith is in the stings of Bees,[7] if it may be got out by thrusting them into the leaves of flowers, will not cause a stain. So farre the Doctour. Upon reading these passages, I called to mind an experiment wch some years since Mr S. Fisher of Sheffield had made me acquainted with. viz. If with a staffe or other instrument you stirre a heap of Ants, (especially Horse-Ants) so as to anger them, they will let fall theron a liquor, wch if you presently smell to, will twinge your nose like newly-distilled spirit of Vitrioll. Considering this, & likewise that a few drops of the oil or spirit of Vitriol will soon turn the blewish syrup of violets into a bright red; & as I am credibly informed the juices & tinctures of any other flowers or fruits of that or the like colour, I was easily induced to think, that this juice of Pismires might be of the same nature with the oil of vitrioll & other acid spirits, (which have in the forementioned respects the same effects with that oil): And there upon I sent to enquire of

Mr Fisher What trialls he had made of it, who returned me the following account. A Weak spirit of Pismires will turn Borage flowers red in an instant; Vineger a little heated will doe the like.

Pismires distilled by themselves or with water yield a spirit like spirit of vineger or rather like the spirit of *Viride aeris.*[8]

Lead put into this spirit, or fair water with the Animals themselves being alive, makes a good *Saccharum Saturni*:[9] Iron put into the spirit affords an astringent tincture, & by repetition a *Crocus Martis.*[10]

Take *Saccharum Saturni* thus made, & distill it, & it will afford the same acid spirit again, which the *Sac. Sat.* made with Vineger will not doe, but returns an inflammable oil with water, & nothing that is acid. *Saccharum Saturni* made with Viride aeris doth the same in this respect with that made with Sp: of Pismires.

When you put the animals into water you must stirre them about to make them angry, and then they will spirt out their acid juice.

No animal that ever we destilled [he speaks of his brother and himself] except this yields an acid spirit, but constantly an urinous, and yet we have distilled many, both Flesh, Fish, & insects.

Hitherto Mr Fisher, who desires to be informed, whether any ingenious person conversant in these enquiries hath himself found out or heard of any other animal that by destillation or otherwise yields an acid spirit. For my part I know of none. But if any doe, probably the favificous[11] & gregarious kind, & generally such as are furnished with stings, of wch weapon Pismires are not unprovided. Indeed it seems very strange that Nature should prepare & separate in the body of this insect without any sensible heat, & that in good quantity considering the bulk of the animal, a liquor the same for kind with those acid spirits wch are by art extracted out of some minerals not without great force of fire.

I doubt not but this liquor may be of singular use in medicine. Mr Fisher hath assured me, that himself hath made triall thereof in some diseases with very good successe.

As for ye motion or passage of Spiders through the air, hanging on ye end of ye threads, they have darted out; though their progresse be wholly to be attributed to ye wind wafting of them, yet they seem to have a power to steer or direct their course upwards, downwards, & it may be laterally, as they please. For I have seen some mount up almost perpendicularly in the air to that height that I quite lost ye sight of them, others suddainly sink in their motion, & others proceed almost parallell to ye horizon. One or 2 observables in their flight I took notice of, not yet published. Viz. 1.

That a Spider hanging in ye air by a thread he draws after him (as there are few but have experienced some of them will doe, if shaken from ones hand or a stick) will, besides that, he hangs on, shoot out another before him to a great length: so that it seems he hath sundry holes, out of wch he can shoot threads, & can make use of some & not of others or of all together as he lists. *Blancanus* (as I find him quoted by F. *Redi*)[12] having observed this phaenomenon, but not understanding the projection of threads, imagined that the web that the Spider drew out & upon wch she hung did split in sunder, & part of it by the wind was driven before her, she hanging upon the other part. 2. Spiders thus hanging, when they have shot out such a thread as we mentioned seem to have power at their pleasure to snap insunder the thread they hang by, & sail away with the other.

NOTES

Oldenburg endorsed this letter as having been enclosed in Letter 1592. In both Letter Book IV (175) and *Phil. Trans.*, no. 68, the letter is attributed to Ray and the date of 13 January 1670/1 is given to it. The extract as printed (edited by Oldenburg as usual) does not include the last paragraph. The letter was printed in Ray, *Further Correspondence* (pp. 50–53) with the date 5 January.

For John Ray (1627–1705), England's most distinguished seventeenth-century naturalist, often mentioned in the correspondence since 1668, see Vol. V, p. 410, note 1.

1 See Letter 1479 and its note 1.
2 Samuel Fisher and his brother John, sons of James Fisher, formerly a vicar in Sheffield, both practised as physicians there, and were intimate friends of Ray.
3 William Langham, *The Garden of Health* (London, 1578; 2nd ed., 1633), p. 144.
4 Hieronymus Tragus (or Bock), *De stirpium historia* (Strasbourg, 1552), p. 271: "A miracle of nature may be observed in this flower: if one is hidden in a heap of ants, it changes its blue color into a red one, as if it grew red with fear of them."
5 One of the numerous works on botany by Jean Bauhin the younger (1541–1613) is doubtless referred to here, but the facts are erroneous. The statement that when these flowers are thrown into a "flock" of ants they turn red was made by Hieronymus Tragus in a letter addressed to Brunfels and published as part of an appendix to the 1630 Latin edition of Brunfels' herbal. See Otto Brunfels, *Herbarum vivae eicones . . .* (Strasbourg, 1630), p. 158.
6 Robert Boyle had recently established that acids turned all blue vegetable colors red. See *Experiments and Observations touching Colours* (London, 1664), Experiment 20ff.
7 See *Micrographia* (London, 1665), pp. 163–65.
8 Verdigris (copper acetate).
9 Sugar of lead (lead acetate).
10 Iron oxide.
11 "honeycomb making."
12 Francesco Redi, *Experiments on the Generation of Insects*, trans. Mab Bigelow from the 1688 edition (Chicago, 1909), p. 72. Josephus Blancanus or Giuseppe Biancani (1566–1624) was a Jesuit writer on cosmography, author of *Sphaera mundi* (Bologna, 1620 and 1635).

1594
Beale to Oldenburg
14 January 1670/1

Mentioned in Beale's Letter 1603 as probably "intercepted" in the post.

1595
Tonge to Oldenburg
c. 15 January 1670/1

From *Phil. Trans.*, no. 68 (20 February 1670/1), 2072–74

Sir,

Last night Sir R. Moray did me the favour to acquaint me in discourse with some particulars about the Gathering of Sap in Fruit-trees, and the Retarding the Ascent thereof; which he had received from an eminent Planter in Glocestershire: Concerning which, I thought it fit to communicate some Reflexions of mine; which you may dispose of, as you think good.

It was propounded to me by way of Quere; How to gather every drop of Sap that should rise in any Fruit-tree? This I said, I thought not feasible, by what I had experimented hitherto. My grounds were these; First, in those Trees, whose Sap seems to be of a Gummy nature when condensed, as Plums, Cherries &c. I knew no Experiment, by which any drop of Sap could be collected. And I suspect, some other Fruit-trees to be of that nature, whose Sap I could not draw out at any season, of hot or cold weather, though they have not been observed to yield any Gum. Perhaps there may also be some Fruit- and other Trees, whose Saps are viscous, though not Gummy; and these, I doubt, will not yield any Sap to be gather'd in any common or known way.

Secondly, it seem'd to me not feasible, to gather all the Sap of those Trees, whose Juyce is fluid and plentiful, and condenseth into a gelly, because it seems at most seasons of the Year to ascend imperceptibly; and that not only in the outward, but innermost parts and pores of the Tree; not only betwixt Bark and Wood, but betwixt every coat of the Wood, and even through the most solid parts of each Coat; as Mr. Willoughby's Observations have discover'd,[1] unless I mistake. The Experiment of the said Glocester shire Planter, by which he hoped to gather all the Rising Sap of Fruit-trees, was made, by binding the Trees round about very closely and strongly with cords, so as to intercept what riseth 'twixt Bark and Body; he being of opinion, that no considerable quantity riseth in any other part. To which I oppose, besides what was said just now, that some Trees will live though they be disbarked in some place quite round; especially if this be done in some season, when the blasting Winds stir not; which I have elsewhere discoursed of in my Letters to Sir R. M.

Mean time, though this Planter seem to me to mistake in the Rising of Sap, yet he maketh it up by discovering to us, that such Tying of Trees retards their Blossoming and Bearing; and so may in some years (as this present, in which the open weather hastening blossoms, is like to destroy the fruit) prevent a scarcity of forward fruit, usually nipped by the late Frosts.

Upon this discourse I shall take leave to suggest these following In-quiries:

1. Whether two Trees, running, when both are free and untied, equal quantities of Sap at like orifices of equal breadth and depth, will run unequally, when strongly tied; and if so, what will be the difference?

2. Whether the said Trees will run unequal quantities at equal orifices made in Roots?

3. Whether the delay of Sap, staying Fruit and Blossoms, as is sup-pos'd, by tying, will cure the *Phyllo-mania*,[2] as Cross-hacking?[3]

4. Whether a Tree kept wholly from bearing this year (its usual bearing year) will bear the next, and so to better advantage, when fruit is scarce?

5. Whether by this way, Trees may be brought to bear at other seasons, than yet hath been practised?

6. Whether tying of Trees, made before Mid summer, causeth the Bark to swell *under* the Ligature, and after Mid-summer, *above* it? and whether equally, or by what different proportion?

7. Whether it will direct Sap to inoculated Buds, if the contrary side only be stopp'd by strong binding?

8. Whether in paring the Bark quite round, or in part, covering the bare place with Lome, the same or like effects will follow?

9. Whether, in case the Bark above the Ligature swell most, it be to be

attributed to the Sap descending, or to the permeableness of all parts of Plants by their Sap (as resembling Bloud and other Humors in the Body,) which more readily descends than ascends to heal the wounded part, or to supply intercepted nourishment?

NOTES

This is inserted between some observations by Tonge "made in April, 1670" and some further, undated observations, all on the same subject, and following Lister's Letter 1627. Only this part of Tonge's communication is said to be a letter to Oldenburg in the printed heading. It is undated, but Sir Robert Moray was at a meeting of the Royal Society on 12 January, so we have assumed that he might have conversed with Tonge at about the same time.

1 These are printed in *Phil. Trans.*, no. 48 (21 June 1669), 963–65, under the title "Experiments Concerning the motion of the Sap in Trees, made this Spring by Mr. Willughby and Mr. Wray."
2 "abnormal development of the leaves."
3 "cutting across." (The nineteenth century introduced the term "cross-hatching.")

1596
Giuseppe Corcilli to Oldenburg

15 January 1670/1

From the original in Royal Society MSS. C 1, no. 104, and O 2, no. 72

Excellentissime et Doctissime Domine.

Ut tuam erga me benevolentiam, quam Leidini assequi,[1] et familiaritatem, quam tecum inire vehementer expectavi adipiscerem, me iam Parisios perventum esse, nulla intercedente mora tibi significandum putavi, eo magis, quia litteras tuas, antequam istinc gradum faciam expecto, quibus me de tua valetudine, et de disquisitionibus in vestra academia ultimo habitis non dubito quod certiorem facies. Me Literatorum duntaxat hominum colloquijs, et epistolis summopere delectavi, quod causis non ambigo. Idcirco ut excemplo ad me rescribas, te quam maxime rogo, et etiam atque etiam deprecor, ut me conscium facias de sale illo, quo istic ad arcendum capitij dolorem utuntur; persuasissimum enim habeo, salem volatilem vel cornu-cervi, vel cranij humani, similisve rei, cum hisce analogiam habentis.² Quum meo nomine perspicacissimo et eruditissimo nostro Boyli salutem dabis, ipsum petas velim, quid accidit in suo instrumento Pneumatico de Torricellae experimento, quando vas *ECD*;

est taliter conglutinatum cum fistula *ABC* ut aer intra vas *ED* clausus, sit cum externo prorsus incommunicabilis? certum enim habeo, fistulam *ABC* mercurio eximiri, quum vas *ECD* apertum est, attamen ignoro, an clauso vase idem eveniat. Ut etiam, an in breviori fistula, ita qua non sit vacuum *AB*, sed tota sit plena mercurio (supposito vase *ECD* aperto, ut est in vulgari experimento) cum fistula vacuatam, mercurius internus fistulae *ABC*; sit infra altitudinem *FD* externi mercurii, vasis *ECD*? an potius in eodem plano cum externo quiescat, discedente aere a Boyliano instrumento? Quoniam, quum hoc experimentum apud Boylem vidi; internus mercurius fistulae descendit infra planum externi mercurij; sed in fistula erat prius aliqua pars vacua, cum longior esset, quam mercurij altitudo requireret; quamobrem hoc experimentum in breviori fistula mallem Faciendum; ex his experimentis, non parvi momenti illationes inferam, si ut philosophatus sum eas se habebit. Scire denique a Boyle vellem, an ipse periculum fecit, si coepae, aliaeque bulbosae plantae in vitreis phiolis clausae, post aeris exanthlationem, temporis curriculo germinent, ut illis accidit, quum in aere suspenduntur. Tuas igitur litteras incredibli cupiditate expecto, quas ex assiduis meis, gratissimas mihi, et jucundissimas fore cognosces. Crastina die mittam tuam epistolam Domino *Justel*,³ et quum per tempus licebit eum petam. Interim dum ego quae ad tui nominis gloriam pertinere arbitrabor studiose, diligenterque curo, tu cura ut valeas. Parisijs VIII Kalendas Februarij 1671.

Dominationis tuae
Addictissimus servus
Joseph Corcilli

ADDRESS[4]

A Monsieur
Monsieur Oldenbergh Secretaire
de la Societe Royale
dans la rue Pelmel
    à Londra

TRANSLATION

Most excellent and learned Sir,

I thought I should without any lapse of time let you know of my arrival in Paris, in order to win what I eagerly look forward to, that your kindness will follow [me] to Leiden,[1] and that your friendship with me will begin; and this the rather because before I take a step from there I anticipate [receiving] your letters, by which no doubt you will tell me of the state of your health and the recent discussions in your Society. I only find real pleasure in the conversation and letters of learned men, because I do not argue about causation. On this topic, that you may reply to me in kind, I beseech you most humbly and implore you again and again to let me into the secret of that salt which is there used to relieve headache, for I am very sure it is sal volatile or the salt of hartshorn or of man's skull, or something of an analogous kind.[2] When you greet our most farsighted and learned Mr. Boyle for me, please ask him what happens, in making the Torricellian experiment in his pneumatic machine, when the vessel *ECD* is so luted to the tube *ABC* that the air shut up in the space *ED* is absolutely cut off from the external air [*see figure, p. 391*]? For I am confident that the tube *ABC* is emptied of mercury when the vessel *ED* is open, but I do not know whether this also happens with it closed. As also, whether with a shorter tube (so that *AB* is not a vacuous space, but the whole is filled with mercury, supposing the vessel *ECD* open as it is in the common experiment) when the tube is evacuated the mercury inside the pipe *ABC* is below the height *FD* of the mercury outside, in the vessel *ECD*? Or rather comes to rest at the same level as the external mercury when the air is withdrawn by the Boylian machine? For when I saw this experiment at Mr. Boyle's, the mercury inside the tube descended below the external level, yet the tube was in the first place partially empty, being longer than the height of the mercury requires. For which reason I prefer the experiment to be made in a shorter tube; from these experiments I draw inferences of no little moment, if things occur according to my philosophy. Lastly I wish to know from Mr. Boyle whether he has made an experiment [to see] if onions and other bulbous plants shut up in glass jars will germinate after exhaustion of the air and the passage of time, as do other [plants] hung up in the atmosphere.

Thus I look forward with incredible eagerness to your letters which, as you know from my enthusiasm, will be very welcome and agreeable to me. Tomorrow I send your letter to Mr. Justel,[3] and when time permits will seek him out. Meanwhile, while I zealously and diligently charge myself with whatever I judge to concern your reputation, do you take care of your health.

Paris, 27 January 1671 [N.S.]

Your lordship's
Most devoted servant
Joseph Corcilli

ADDRESS[4]

To Mr. Oldenburg
Secretary of the Royal Society
in the Pall Mall
London

NOTES

The writer of this letter is presumably the Neapolitan physician who watched Malpighi dissect the thorax of a puppy on 2 June 1671 (N.S.]. He had obviously just visited London but we have come across no other record of his visit.

1 The exact rendering of this sentence is obscure, though the sense is clear; presumably "Leidini" was written by mistake for *Lugdunum Batavorum*, unless Lyons were meant.

2 See Oldenburg's reply, Letter 1611.

3 This was presumably a letter of introduction, now lost.

4 This address is taken from O 2, no. 72, on which sheet Oldenburg drafted his reply.

1597
Oldenburg to Huet

16 January 1670/1

From the original in Laurenziana Huet MSS., Cassata 4, no. 1919 and the draft in Royal Society
MS. O 2, no. 41

A Londres le 16. janv 1671

Monsieur,

La vostre du 30me Octobre 1670. ne me fut rendue par Monsr dela
Faye que le 6me courant; sans cela ie n'eusse nullement manqué de vous
avoir fait raison de bonne heure. D'abord ie ne scaurois que vous feliciter
de l'employ honorable, que l'on a donné à vostre merite, et ie sens une
Joye interieure tout et quantefois que i'entends la vertue dignement recom-
pensée. Quoyque la presente occupation vous detasche de faire vous mesme des operations et Experiences pour advancer la belle Philosophie,
vous pourrez pourtant, dans la charge oú vous estez, animer d'autres, et
avec cela instiller aux occasions de bons sentimens aux Princes, pour les
induire a pousser l'accroissement des sciences utiles, et à encourager les
habiles gens par leur authorité et munificence. De faire cecy adroitement
et avec assiduité, vaut bien autant que de travailler soymesme; et ie me
veux persuader, que Monsr. Huet y est assez porté de son propre genie,
sans avoir aucunement besoin de luy en parler davantage.

J'ay communiqué vostre Experience faite pour la recherche du conduit
de l'Urine à quelques uns de nos Meilleurs Anatomistes,[1] desquels l'un[2] en
ayant fait une avec toute la precaution que luy fut possible, coupant mesme
les ureteres, et inserant des tubes solides d'argent dans la partie la plus
proche des Reins, et liant si bien cette partie tout autour des tubes afin que
rien ne put passer, ayant fait, dis-ie, tout cela avec grand soin, il ne trouva
pourtant point aucune liqueur dans la vessie du chien, auquel il avoit fait
boire auparavant une bonne quantité de lait, sans parler dela viande, qu'il
avoit aussi mangé avidement. D'autres de nos plus doctes Medicins sont
persuadez, qu'il n'y a point d'autre passage de l'urine à la vessie que par les
Ureteres, considerant toutes les recherches, qu'ils disent avoir faitez avec
la plus possible attention, pour en trouver. A quoy ils adjoustent, qu'apres
y avoir bien pensé, il n'est nullement besoin qu'il y en ait d'autre, vû la
merveilleusement prompte circulation du sang et des autres liqueurs par

le corps, et la subite fermentation et percolation des mesmes dans les parties où elles passent. C'est ce qu'i'avois à vous dire sur ce point là. Touchant la salubrité de l'eau dessalée par M. Hauton, elle est considerable; quoyque, si cette terre vierge, dont il parle, y est necessaire, et ne se trouve pas en abundance, l'invention ne pourroit pas estre generalement utile. Monsr Kufler[3] icy a fait la mesme chose, il y a plusieurs annees, par une jolie petite machine d'un artifice particulier, dans laquelle il a actuellement distillé avec peu de feu, soit de charbon ou de bois, une quantité fort considerable d'eau de mer dans peu de temps: Mais il est malaisé de persuader aux hommes de s'accommoder des nouveautez de cete nature là.

Je suis mary de ne vous pouvoir pas envoyer la mesure des spheres de l'oeil, les proportions desquelles Monsr Wren a faitez cy devant.[4] C'est que ce gentilhomme est tellement occupé dans la charge presente, qu'il sustient, qu'il n'y a pas moyen de l'arrester tont soit peu sur ces choses lá. S'il l'avoit donné par escrit, ie demanderois sa permission de vous en envoyer une copie: mais cela n'est pas. Et quant aux Balances qui examinent le magnetisme, cela n'est pas si bien adjusté, que ie l'ose debiter. Monsr Boyle a depuis peu donné au public quelques petits traitez de *Qualitatius Cosmicis,* et de *Temperie Regionum Subterran.* et *Submarinarum* &c. comme aussy un discours de la prodigieuse dilation de l'Air; qui seront bientost en Latin tous deux: j'ay seulement place pour vous assurer que je suis Monsieur

Vostre treshumble et tres-obeissant serviteur
Oldenburg

Je seray ravy d'entendre quelquefois de vos nouvelles; et quand vous me faitez l'honeur de m'escrire par la poste, vous n'avez que faire vostre addresse ainsi;

A Monsieur
Monsr Grubendol
à Londres

Tout me sera plus seurement livré par cete addresse qu'autrement.

ADDRESS

A Monsieur
Monsr Huet
chez Monsr Cramoisy Libraire
rue St Jacques
à
Paris

TRANSLATION

London, 16 January 1670/1

Sir,

Yours of 30 October 1670 [N.S.] was only delivered to me by Mr. de La Faye on the sixth of this month; otherwise I should not have failed to give you early satisfaction. And first, I cannot but congratulate you upon the honorable employment resulting from your ability, and I always feel an inward joy whenever I hear of virtue rightly rewarded. Although your present business prevents you from yourself making trials and experiments for the advancement of true philosophy, you can nevertheless in the position in which you find yourself stimulate others. At the same time you can on occasion instil right-mindedness in the princes to induce them to press for the development of the useful sciences and to encourage able men by their authority and munificence. It is as important to do this cleverly and assiduously as to work oneself; and I should like to believe that Mr. Huet has nearly enough reached this conclusion in his own mind so that there is no need to speak to him further about it.

I have communicated your experiment made to discover the passage of the urine to some of our best anatomists.[1] One of these,[2] having made one with all possible precaution, even cutting away the ureters and inserting solid silver rods into the part closest to the kidneys, and tying up that part so well all about the rods that nothing could pass through—having done all this, I say, with great care, he nevertheless found no liquid in the dog's bladder, although he had beforehand made [the dog] drink a good quantity of milk not to mention the meat which he had eaten greedily. Others of our most learned physicians are convinced that there is no passage of urine to the bladder except through the ureters in view of all the investigations which they say have been made with the greatest possible care to discover such a passage. To this they add that having thought it over carefully, they see no need of there being any other, considering the wonderfully rapid circulation of the blood and other liquids through the body and the swift fermentation and percolation of the same in the organs through which they pass. This is what I have to tell you on this matter.

The wholesomeness of the sea water distilled by Mr. Hauton is important;

however, if this pure earth of which he speaks is essential and is not commonly found, the discovery cannot be generally useful. Mr. Küffler[3] did the same thing here some years ago by means of a very pretty little machine specially contrived in which, with a small fire of either charcoal or wood, he actually distilled a very considerable quantity of sea water in a short time. But it is difficult to persuade men to accustom themselves to novelties of this sort.

I am disappointed in not being able to send you the measurement of the eyeballs, whose proportions Mr. Wren formerly determined here.[4] It is because this gentleman is so busy with his present office that he cannot stop even for an instant to deal with such matters. If he had given it in writing I should have asked his permission to send you a copy; but this is not the case. And as for the magnetic balances, that is not so well settled that I dare to give it out. Mr. Boyle has recently given the public some little tracts on *Cosmicall Qualities*, and on *The Temperature of the Subterraneall and Submarine Regions*, etc., and also a discourse on *The Admirable Rarefaction of the Air*. Both will soon be in Latin. I have only space to assure you, Sir, that I am

Your very humble and obedient servant,
Oldenburg

I shall be delighted to hear news of you sometimes, and when you do me the honor of writing to me by the post you have only to put my address thus:

A Monsieur
Monsr Grubendol
à Londres

Everything will reach me more safely with this address than otherwise.

ADDRESS

To Mr. Huet
care of Mr. Cramoisy, bookseller
rue St Jacques
Paris

NOTES

Reply to Letter 1535.
1 Huet's letter was read to the Royal Society on 12 January 1670/1.
2 Dr. King; see Birch, *History*, II, 463–64.
3 For J. S. Küffler, see Vol. I, p. 191, note 2.
4 See Vol. VI, Letter 1393 and its note 2, where the magnetic balances are also mentioned.

1598
Oldenburg to Lambecius

18 January 1670/1

This letter is mentioned in Lambecius' reply, Letter 1642, as containing an enclosure for a Mr. Donellan, probably from Edward Browne, who mentions this Irish gentleman as a companion of his in Hungary, where evidently he had remained (Browne, *Travels*, p. 15).

1599
Oldenburg to Hevelius

18 January 1670/1

From the original in BN MS. N.a.L. 1641, f. 19

Illustri et Perdocto Viro
Domino Johanni Hevelio, Gedani Consuli dignissimo
H. Oldenburg Sal. plur.

Ut verum fatear, Vir Amplissime, epistola inclusa hac vice me induxit, ut hac scriptiuncula molestias Tibi facesserem. Putem quippe, tutius posse per Dantiscum in Hungariam, quo hanc epistolam tendere vides, scribi, quam per Germaniae meditullium.[1] Ignoscas, quaeso, huic meae audaciae, et similia officia redhibendi occasionem praebeas. Nullus dubito, quin epistolam inclusam summa cura Eperias[2] sis transmissurus.

Caeterum, ternas ad Te dedi praeterita aestate literas, quarum novissimas 21. Novembris hinc ad Te per tabellarium expedivi.[3] Significabam in iis, me omnes tuas epistolas, 5 julij, 27. Aug. et 31. Octob. ad me datas recte accepisse;[4] pollicebarque me proximo vere, prima navi Dantiscum hinc veleficatura, tractatus illos omnes, a me desideratos, volente Deo, transmissurum. Plura inserebam, de Eclipsi Lunae a Te observata, nec non de Conjunctione Veneris et Lunae; ut et nonnulla de deperditis duabus stellis secundae magnitudinis in Puppi Navis, juxta Observationes Montanarij Bononiensis:[5] Adhaec, figuram Saturni, hic ab Hookio nostro spectati, adjeceram; quae omnia cum ad manus Tuas rite pervenisse sperem, hic repetere non lubet. Vale, et studiosissimi Cultoris Tui memor vive. Dab. Londini d. 18. januar. 1671.

P.S.

Praedixit Flamsteadius noster Lunae ad Fixas et Saturnum A. 1671. Appulsus observabiles, quorum copiam Tibi hic transmitto, impressam in Transactionibus.[6] Colliges inde, quid de eorum apparentis exspectandum Dantisci.

TRANSLATION

Henry Oldenburg sends many greetings to the illustrious and highly learned Mr. Hevelius, most worthy Senator of Danzig

To tell the truth, worthy Sir, it is the enclosed letter that has persuaded me to trouble you at the present moment with this scrap of paper. For I think that it may be safer to write to Hungary (whither, as you see, this letter is directed) through Danzig, than through the heart of Germany.[1] Please forgive this boldness of mine, and give me some opportunity of doing you a like service. I have no doubt but that you will transmit the letter enclosed with the greatest care to Eperjes.[2]

For the rest, I wrote you three letters last summer, of which the most recent was that I sent you hence by the post on 21 November.[3] In these I let you know that I had safely received all your letters to me of 5 July, 27 August, and 31 October;[4] and I promised that next spring (please God) I would dispatch to you by the first boat sailing hence for Danzig all those treatises that you wanted. I wrote a good deal about the lunar eclipse you had observed, and about the conjunction of Venus and the moon, as also about those two stars of the second magnitude missing from the poop of the [constellation] Navis according to the observations of Montanari of Bologna.[5] I further added the picture of Saturn, as observed here by our Mr. Hooke, all things which it is needless for me to repeat here as I hope they came safely to your hands. Farewell, and bear this zealous devotee in mind. London, 18 January 1671

P.S. Our Mr. Flamsteed has predicted the observable appulses of the moon with Saturn and the fixed stars for 1671; I send you the printed copy from the *Philosophical Transactions*.[6] From that you may gather which of those phenomena are to be expected at Danzig.

NOTES

1 It is likely that the letter was actually composed by someone else (for example, Edward Browne) making use of Oldenburg's good offices, and may have been another copy of the enclosure sent to Lambecius (Letter 1598). It would pass through Poland into Hungary.

2 Now Prešov, in Czechoslovakia.

3 Letters 1520 and 1557 are all we could trace for 1670.

4 Letters 1475, 1509, and 1536.

5 See Letters 1555, note 3, and 1557.

6 See *Phil. Trans.*, no. 66 (12 December 1660), 2029–34.

1600
Oldenburg to Edward Cotton

19 January 1670/1

From the copy in Royal Society MS. O 2, no. 42

To Dr Edward Cotton

Sr

The stone you sent by Dr Fulwood to ye Ld Bp of Sarum,[1] was by his Lordship's order by ye same Dr's hands presented to ye R.S.[2] who as they looked upon it as an uncommon variety, so they do herewith returne you their hearty thanks for your constancy in remembring their concerns, and in contributing wt you can to enlarge ye treasure of their Repository, in wch ye stone will be laid up as one of ye choicest things contained therein, together wth ye descriptions of ye observables about ye same, and ye name of ye Donor.[3] I find yt some of our Inquisitive Physitians have met wth ye like case, as to ye Urines forcing its passage another way, and ye like stones' being brought away by incision at yt passage, though none of them, yt I have met wth, hath ever seen so big a one come away after that manner. And since you are pleased to offer to ye Society, yt you will procure a Testimony under ye Patients own hand, they kindly accept of it, to be thereby ye better enabled to assure others of ye truth of ye thing, though they be sufficiently assured of it them selves by wt you have related thereof.[4]

The old age, wch Dr Fulwood affirmed ye Patient to be off, giveth mee occasion to let you know, yt I have begun to desire my Correspondents in all parts of England, to enquire diligently, and thereupon to informe mee wt persons of extraordinary old age are to be found now living in ye place where they reside and ye neighbourhood, together wth ye way of living they have used respectively, ye like I request of you, Sr, if it may consist wth your conveniency, to wch I would intreat you to adde ye names of all such persons, as are knowne in your countrey to, excell in any Ingenuity (wch I have likewise begun to sollicit of others) yt so wee may come to know ye men as well as ye things yt may contribute to ye designe of this Royall Institution. In ye doing of all wch you will, I am persuaded, do a very acceptable service to ye publick, and particularly oblige Sr

> your humble servant
> *Henry Oldenburg*

London jan. 19
$$\frac{1670}{71}$$

NOTES

Edward Cotton (*c.* 1616–75) entered Christ Church, Oxford, in 1632. He was D.D. 1660/1, Canon of Exeter Cathedral (Treasurer, 1672), and Archdeacon of Cornwall. He was an original Fellow of the Royal Society.

1 Cotton sent this stone (lodged for many years in a human urethra) to Seth Ward with an accompanying letter dated 7 January 1670/1 (Royal Society MS. C 1, no. 30). It weighed 355 grains. Dr. Fulwood is plausibly identified by Birch (*History*, II, 462) as Francis Fulwood (d. 1693) of Emmanuel College, Cambridge; he was B.A. 1647 and D.D. 1660. In 1660 he became Archdeacon of Totnes and in 1662 Prebendary of Exeter.

2 On 12 January 1670/1.

3 As it was; see Grew, *Musaeum*, pp. 9–10.

4 See Letter 1612a.

1601

Oldenburg to Lister

18 and 20 January 1670/1

From the original in Bodleian Library MS. Lister 34, f. 3

London Januar. 18. 70/71

Sir,

I gave you notice by my letter of januar. 3d,[1] that I had received ye favour of yr letter, and wthall communicated to Mr Willughby those particulars of it, wherein he was concern'd.[2] I have since received this returne from him,[3] yt ye Account is very ingenious, you give, How ye first laid eggs in ye remotest cartrages may be last hatched, and ye nymphae come to perfection after all the incumbent are gone, and make way for ym: But adds, yt this account does not agree wth ye Experience, he hath had; in regard that not only those, wch I (he means myself) sent him, had actually bored their way through severall placed above ym; but yt, having open'd a great many at Astrop purposely, and upon a wager about this very Inquiry, before ye Bp of Chester and Mr Wray, he always found ye remotest, from ye entrance ye most forward, and those yt lay above ym were still lesse and lesse, and ye least were always those yt were next ye common entrance.

As to what concerns ye darting of Spiders, Mr Wray Communicateth these Particulars:[4]

"Concerning ye Motion or passage of Spiders through ye Air, hanging on ye end of ye threads, they have darted out; though their progresse be wholly to be attributed to ye wind wafting of ym, yet they seem to have a power to steer or direct their course upwards, downwards, and, it may be, laterally, as they please. For I have seen some mount up almost perpendicularly in ye Air to yt hight, yt I quite lost ye sight of ym; others suddenly sink in their motion, and others proceed almost parallel to ye Horizon. One or two Observables in their flight I took notice of, not yet published; viz. 1. That a Spider hanging in ye Air by a thread, he draws after him (as there are few but have experienced some of ym will doe, if shaken from ones hand or a stick) will, besides yt, he hangs on, shoot out another before him to a great length; so yt it seems, he hath sundry holes out of wch he can shoot threads, and can make use of some & not of others, or of all together as he lists. *Blancanus* (as I find him quoted by *F. Redi*) having observ'd this Phaenomenon, but not understanding ye projection of threads, imagin'd, yt ye web wch the Spider drew out, and upon wch he hung, did split insunder, and part of it by ye wind was driven before her, she hanging upon ye other part. 2ly. Spiders thus hanging, when they have shot out such a thread as we mention'd, seem to have power at their pleasure to snap insunder the thread they hang by, and sail away wth ye other."

So far Mr Wray. To wch, for a conclusion, give me leave to add this Quere, Whether you have ever observ'd, yt ye Flowers of Cichory, cast among a heap of Ants, will soon become red; and if so, what yr thoughts are of ye manner, how those flowers (and some others too) come to be so stain'd?

I promise myself ye favor of a speedy Answer to these particulars, as also yr pardon for these importunities, comming from Sir

Yr faithful servt
Oldenburg

P.S.

jan. 20. 1670/71

After I had written this letter, I received yrs of januar. 10th, wch I communicated yesterday to ye R. Soc. at their publick meeting,[5] who received it with an uncommon applause, and commanded me to give you their most affectionate thanks, for such ingenious as well as industrious labors. They promise to ymselves, yt in time they shall see, upon so good a foundation, as you have already laid by yr Table and Inquiries about yt Insect, raised a proportionate superstructure vid. an excellent History of yt subject; wch exspectation if you shall please to comply wth, you will certainly oblige yt Illustrious Body, and all other Curious philosophical Men.

I would gladly insert both the Table and the Inquiries in the Transactions, to give a Pattern to others of ye manner how to consider and write on the like Arguments; but I must not doe so, before I have yr permission for it; wch I intreat you to signify to me by ye first conveniency.

One thing more I must add on this occasion; wch is, yt I consider yr vertue and merit to be such, as deserveth to make you a member of ye R. Society. If therefore you shall expresse to me yr desire to be received into yt Body (wch every one, ye highest as well as ye lowest hath done hitherto,) I shall propose you for a Candidat, and take care for yr Election.[6] I suppose, you know the requisits to be; 1. to contribute what one can, to ye end of yt Institution; 2. to give, for ye defraying of Experiments etc, one shill. per week, or 13 sh. a quarter; 3. and once 40. sh. admission-money, upon the Election.

Upon yr answer, I shall proceed, as becoms Sir

> Yr very humble and faithf servt
> *H. Oldenburg*

Q 1. What are yr thoughts about ye poysonousnes of Spiders?

2. Have you met wth or heard of men, yt durst eat Spiders on purpose, and did it innoxiously?7

To leave no vacuum of this paper, give me leave, Sir, to acquaint you, yt I have begun to desire my Correspondents in all parts of England, to inquire diligently, and accordingly to informe me, what persons of extraordinary old age are to be found now living in ye places, where they reside, and in their neighborhood, together wth ye way of living they have used respectively. The like I would request of you, Sir, if it may stand wth yr conveniency. To wch I would intreat you to add ye names of all such persons, as are known in yr Contry to excell in any ingenuity (wch I have like wise begun to sollicit of others,) yt so we may come to know ye Men as well as ye things, yt may contribute to ye designe of ye R. Society. Sr, I think, yt Experiment about ye bleeding of a Sycamore in Novemb. will now come to be further examin'd: I pray therefore, arme me wth what you can, to make good ye observation, and yt wth all possible speed.

ADDRESS
>   To his honored friend
>   Martin Lister Esquire,
>   At his house wthout Mickel-gate barr
> >   At
> >   Yorke

NOTES

Reply to Letters 1583 and 1589.
1 Letter 1586.
2 In Letter 1587.
3 Letter 1592.
4 In Letter 1593.

5 It was indeed read to the Society on 19 January 1670/1, but the minutes contain no comments upon it.
6 Lister was in fact elected F.R.S. on 2 November 1671, the first meeting of the Society since 30 June 1671. He had been proposed candidate by Oldenburg on 18 May 1671. See further, Letter 1622.
7 Compare Vol. III, pp. 316–19.

1602

Dodington to Oldenburg

20 January 1670/1

From the original in Royal Society MS. D 1, no. 19

Venice Janr. 30. 1671 [N.S.]

Sr

Since myne per last post[1] I have none from you, so as I was once endeavouring to finde out some reasons to excuse my not writing to you this weeke, when I received some leters from Rome, wch I will now impart to you. Padre Fabri hath lately putt forth a most accurate peece intituled Commentarij novi in Archimedem.[2] Padre Gottignes hath allmost finished a very Curious Booke concerning the admirable effects In dioptrica.[3] I will send you both these, as well as some of dr Malphighies tracts when they are finished & come to me.

Yr Instructions touching Prospectives & Microscopes I have perused & have this acct. Both Eustachij & Campana doe work them in Perfection; as well one as tother. But I can not send you any without particular direction, upon yr Consideration heereof.

There are 3 sorts of Prospective Glasses. one from 20 to 50 Palmes: These are for the Heavens, Planets &c some wth 2 Glasses others wth 4. These cost from 80 to 250 Crownes a peece, without the Case, wch is Generally made in the place where they are to be used.

For Terrestrial objects there are of 2 & 4 Glasses from 35 to 100 Crownes.

Those of 2 Glasses only, are little used, and serve only for small perspectives, and yet these are esteemed at about five & twenty shillings a peece.

Microscopes wth several Glasses, are from 18 to 50 Crownes. Now Sr If you direct me wt you would have, I will assuredly endeavour to serve you. And for ye expence, you may contrive some way how I may be reimbursed, And if you please to pay any sum to Mr George Ravenscroft in great St Hellens I will be accomptable for it. So not having else I rest

Sr yr humble servant
John Dodington

oblige me I pray by procuring Mr Allestree, Mr Bee,[4] & Mr Scott[5] to give you a Catalogue of Bookes Gr. & lat. worth buying here. They are very cheape, Learning being heere quite melted downe. I have bought heere Budaeus Epit. ling. Gr.[6] for 5s. Stephan. Thesaurus ling. Gr.[7] with ye Appendix 4 volumes 20s. Steph. ανθολογια[8] for 5s. I mention these to ye end you may ghesse ye at rest.

ADDRESS
For Mr Oldenburg these
     most humbly

NOTES

1 Letter 1591.
2 See Letter 1590, note 23.
3 Perhaps this is the work on telescopes which Bertet told Collins was on sale in Rome at the end of 1670. See Gregory, *Turnbull*, p. 140.
4 Cornelius Bee, a bookseller.
5 Possibly Robert Scott, another bookseller.
6 Guillaume Budé, *Graeci epistolae* (Paris, 1540).
7 Henri Estienne, *Thesaurus Graecae linguae* ([Geneva], 1572) and many later editions.
8 Henri Estienne, ανθολογια διαφορων ἐπιγραμματων παλαιων ("Anthology of excellent ancient epigrams") (Paris, 1566); there was a Latin edition in 1600 and a Latin and Greek edition in 1570.

1603
Beale to Oldenburg
21 January 1670/1
From the original in Royal Society MS. V, no. 27

Jan. 21. 70.

Deare Bror,

The 14th Instant I wrote to yu by Post, a full sheet, too large, being too much fretted at the Insolencyes of S,[1] & the intolerable Iniquityes of Oxf[ord], whom it did ill become to countenance Libells agst BB PPs.[2] I doubt it will rebound back to ye notorious Infamy of ye Abettors. But I heare of Post letters of late so frequently Intercepted, yt I am diffident, whether mine came safe.[3] And I doe almost dispaire of two letters, wch I sent to Mr. Eve;[4] The first I sent decemb. 24: The other sent Jan. 9th to enquire after ye former. Hitherto I have receiv'd no anwer to neyther of them. In ye later I complain'd of his late letter to mee lost on ye way.

Now I am to thank yu for yr Pacquet by Carrier; & to entreat yu to give my most humble acknowledgments to honourable Mr Boyle. Had I seen his Tracts,[5] before my last was sent, I should have added from thence an Argument; representing ye difficulty of determining positively ye height of ye Atmosphere of Air: But ye whole of mine is not *Operae pretium*,[6] since it only reflects upon those words *first started in Italy*. Mr Boyles *Tracts* doe seeme to mee to show how Agues & Feavors may so sadly afflict us (though for ye variety of ye Periodical Visits wee are yet in ye dark) & how ye Gout, Hypochondriacal, Hysterical, Spasmical, & Epileptical fitts, & ye toothach forsooth, may so much torment us & other Animals, as they doe. A Poet would say, yt in ye Pneumatical Engine thus managed, wee may clearly discern, how ye Prince of ye Air, if permitted to Lord it in his own Quarters, may afflict Mortalls more horribly than wee are yet apt to attribute to fascination & Magic.

Your last Num. 66 is richly full of Considerables.[7] If Mr. Flamsteads note could arrive time enough to ye hands of Hevelius, tis like he would take it into his Consideration. But wt hope can he have to manage Burattini's Tube of 140 foot long if he should get it, as he expects: Thence indeed, if manageable, wee may expect more wonderfull Discoveryes in ye faces of ye Planets. Sig. Donius may advise us for ye Salubrity of Cambridge, & of all our Fen-Countryes. And I wish ye RS had Oratory & influence strong enough, to perswade our Exchange of French-Sauce-makers, & Perriwig-makers for French Vine-dressers, Dutch Gardeners, Dutch Drayners, & ye Dutch Windmill, so often commended by Dr. Aglionby in ye *Present State of ye Netherlands*.[8] This would drayn our Luxury, & in one compre-hend our Salubrity & Agriculture; & be as proper for Ireland, as England. And tis time for us to learn of our masters, & chiefly to learn Industry & frugality. Our Hortulan affaires doe prosper already in many parts of England. Yet wee must not cease to drive it on in all parts. This & ye Fen-businesse if well undertaken, & constantly prosecuted, would satisfy fairely, & compensate sufficiently for all other poynts of Husbandry. & Lands freshly redeemed from ye Sea are most accomodable for Modern Improvements. I am more than halfe perswaded, yt if these hints were loudly whisper'd by Metalline & Sparkling spirits in ye Eares of yr weal-thiest Cittizens, & in your twelve Colleges of Lawes, as Cambden[9] hath taught mee to call them (& now I shall ye rather call them so, in some little revenge for ye Libelling Transgressions of ye envious sister) I say I am perswaded, yt the sedulous & frequent Negotiation of these Interests, would prove in a short time very effectuall, & successfull; And redound (indespight of Envy & Malice) to ye honour of ye RS. But without these joynt Ayds of welthy Citizens, & Potent Lawyers, & a constant Influence from ye RS, I can hardly expect it. And thus much for Salubrity, & for a Remedy agst ye Epidemical contagion of ye worse than French disease. Your encouraging applauses for *Websters Metallographia*[10] was in right sea-son for our English Occasion. Wee have good Mines, but we want Metall to search for them; & Minds to refine them. Now I wish these harmelesse Lines may escape Intercepting Villanyes. They might well permit affec-tions for ye public & innoxious Philosophy to passe freely, since wee doe not all Intermeddle wth their heats about aies & No'es.

Your very affectionate servant
Vinc. Ver.[11]

ADDRESS
   For my much honor'd Friend
      Henry Oldeburg Esqr
         At his house
           in Pell Mell
              Westminster.

NOTES

In spite of the signature, this is clearly a letter from Beale. The handwriting is identical with that of his usual letters written for him by a member of his family whose handwriting closely resembled his; and the style and content confirm that Beale was indeed the author.

1 Stubbe. It is not clear which of Stubbe's invectives is referred to here. In the latter part of 1670 he had published *Lord Bacons relation of the sweating-sickness examined* (London, 1671); his *Epistolary discourse concerning Phlebotomy* (London, 1671) is dated 14 February 1670/1 and cannot yet have appeared. "An Answer to the Letter of Dr Henry More" was dated 30 November 1670 and printed in *The Reply unto the Letter written to Mr Henry Stubbe in defence of the History of the Royal Society* (Oxford, 1671), written by Stubbe in Oxford, which was certainly on sale by early February and might have been available earlier.

2 Bishops?

3 It has not been preserved.

4 Evelyn.

5 Presumably *Tracts written by the Honourable Robert Boyle . . . of a Discovery of the Admirable Rarefaction of the Air*, etc. (London, 1671); see also Letter 1553, note 4.

6 "worthwhile."

7 *Phil. Trans.*, no. 66 (12 December 1670) contains Flamsteed's table of lunar appulses for 1671 (pp. 2029–34), Hevelius' Letter 1536, and (pp. 2017–19) "An Accompt given by a Florentin Patrician, call'd Jo. Battista Donius, concerning a way of restoring the Salubrity of the Country about Rome" from the *Giornale de' Letterati*.

8 William Aglionby, *The Present State of the United Provinces of the Low-Countries* (London, 1669).

9 William Camden (1551–1623), best known for his *Britannia* of 1568, was a prolific writer.

10 In *Phil. Trans.*, no. 66 (12 December 1670), 2034–36.

11 Perhaps "Vincet Verum," that is, "let truth prevail."

1604

Oldenburg to Willughby

21 January 1670/1

From the copy in Royal Society MS. O 2, no. 44

To Mr Willughby

Sr

Your last of jan. 13. wth ye inclosed of Mr. Wray I received jan. 18. and communicated both letters to ye Royall Soc. at their publick meeting yesterday,[1] who heard it read wth no ordinary satisfaction, and gave order to have all registred in their books; as also to returne to you and M. Wray their very affectionate thanks for such Ingenious communications. Wee had a numerous assembly, and ye whole company was much pleased wth those contents of your letters; and I herewth intreat you to let Mr Wray know so much, who will further oblige us, by continuing to impart upon occasion ye like Philosophicall observations, as you will do also by adding yours. The publication of such things will not only excite but prove a patterne to others, how to Inquire into ye nature of particular Bodyes, wch is ye thing yt will make Philosophy usefull, and therefore valuable; and wch requires also my particular thanks to you both, for as much as you do not forbid mee to insert them into ye Transactions. I perswade my selfe yt Dr Hulse and Mr Fisher (to both of whom ye Soc. gives also their hearty thanks, for their part in ye letter) will not scruple to let them know, in wt diseases they have successfully made triall of yt liquor therein mention'd of Ants, I am apt to think it to be very Diuretick, as yt distilled of Millepedes &c. is knowne to bee. As yt is a very curious Experiment, wch imports, yt lead put into ye Spirit of distilled pismires makes a good Saccharum Saturni, so it is to be considered, yt Spirit of Vitriol, as I am informed, will not make yt Saccharum: wch would inferre, yt though this Spirit of Pismires be an Acid, yet 'tis no vitriolate one.

I can meet wth no body yet, yt hath ever found or heard of any Animall, by distillation or otherwise yeilding an Acid Spirit. As it seems strange yt nature prepares and seperates in ye Body of ye Ant, wthout any sensible heat, an Acid Spirit, so it may as well, I think, be wondered, yt a Limon hath so great an acidity wthout any perceivable heat at all.

I am apt to beleive yt these observations will occasion in ye curious much inquiry, and that consideration makes mee redouble my thanks for making us sharers therein, who am Sr

your humble servant
Oldenburg

London
jan. 21. 1670
——
71

NOTES

Reply to Letters 1592 and 1593.
1 In fact the Society met on 19 January 1670/1.

1605

Cassini to Oldenburg

23 January 1670/1

From the original in Royal Society MS. C 1, no. 51

Clarissimo Nobilissimoque Viro D. Henrico Oldemburg
regiae Societatis Anglicae a secretis
Jo. Dominicus Cassinus S.P.D.

Commendatus mihi est a D. Gornio Serenissimi Magni Ducis Hetruriae Medico D. Paulus Boconius[1] Botanicus siculus, qui in re herbaria inserverit Serenissimo quondam Magno Duci Ferdinando, cuius acie iudicium in delectu virorum in artibus excellentium omnes novunt. Hic cum Parisijs nullam offenderit operae suae locandae occasionem, rogavit me ut eum tibi, Vir Clarissime, commendarem, ut si qua forte in Anglia eius adhibendi occurreret occasio, illam, te favente, posset amplecti.[2] Habet suae peritiae testimonia omnium fere quotquot sunt in Hetruria virorum eruditione illustrium, detulitque rara quaedam semina a se quaesita collataque.

Boni igitur consules, Vir Clarissime, si pro amore in viros bonis artibus addictos illum Tibi commendare audeo. Ego Tibi vicissim ad omnia officia me paratissimum exhibeo.

Parisijs die 2 februarij 1671 [N.S.]

Studium emendandi Theorias Jovialium Planetarum ex recentissimis observationibus, quarum annus hic opportunitatem obtulit, effecit ut illorum Ephemeridum editionem differem quo correctiores prodirent. Nunc hoc munere, Deo iuvante, functus tui antilij memor ero.[3]

TRANSLATION

Giovanni Domenico Cassini sends many greetings to the very famous and noble Mr. Henry Oldenburg, Secretary of the Royal Society of England

Mr. Gornia, physician to His Highness the Grand Duke of Tuscany, has recommended to me Mr. Paolo Boccone,[1] a Sicilian botanist, who has been in the service of the late Grand Duke Ferdinand for that science, whose keenness of judgment in choosing the outstanding practitioners of each art every one knows. Since he has come across no opportunity for employment of his services here at Paris, he has asked me to recommend him to you, famous Sir, so that if some chance of employing him in England should arise, he might with your assistance take it up.[2] He has testimonies to his skill from all the persons in Tuscany who are distinguished for their learning; and he has brought some rare seeds that he has sought and gathered together.

So, famous Sir, look kindly on my being so bold as to recommend him to you, because of my liking for all who are devoted to the worthy arts. I offer myself as very ready to do any service for you in return.
Paris, 2 February 1671 [N.S.]

My eager desire to correct the theories for Jupiter's satellites by the most recent observations, for which the year has provided an opportunity in this place, has caused me to postpone the publication of the satellites' ephemerides so that they may be issued in a more accurate form. Now by this favor, I shall with God's aid be mindful [to discharge my obligtion].[3]

NOTES

1 See Letter 1574, note 1.
2 Compare Letters 1574 and 1576.
3 We do not quite understand the words, but this is clearly the meaning.

1606
Oldenburg to Nelson
24 January 1670/1

This letter is only found mentioned in Nelson's reply, Letter 1661.

1607
Oldenburg to Beale
24 January 1670/1

According to his endorsement on the envelope, Oldenburg answered Beale's Letter 1603 on the twenty-fourth, the day after he received it; it is mentioned also in Beale's Letter 1624, as regretting the dispute between Beale and Glanvill.

1608
Newburgh to Oldenburg
25 January 1670/1

From the original in Royal Society MS. N 1, no. 6

Sr

Multiplicity of business hath fallen so heavily upon me ever since I saw my own house to wch I returnd but 2 days before Christmas, That I have not found leisure for one hours space to spend upon that Book Concerning Silkworms wch you courteously lent me.[1] However I do not forget my promise of returning it to yu this Term; wch according to my obligation I shall faithfully perform unlesse yu think fit to indulge me a longer time for ye perusall of it.

It is ye buisinesse of this Lre to beg such a favour at yr hands. If God send me life till Whitsuntide, I shall I hope be able to restore it wth a perfect acct of my own Experiments relating to yt Creature.

I have, as I guesse, many millions of those Insects in their seed, & am resolv'd to try ye utmost yt I can upon them in order to discours of their nature & profit the next spring, if it please God to lengthen out my life so long. Yr Book will hugely conduce to this End; but I must confesse I am asham'd to make so bold wth so generous a frd having already bin so long a miserable hoarder of this part of yr Treasure. I shall not therefore presse ye spade too far this way; but according to yr Resolution, wch I intreat you to vouchsafe me by your next Continuing, whether yu shall receive yr Treatise by ye term prefixt, or it shall be very carefully kept & used by

> Yr obliged frd & servt
> *John Newburgh*

Worth Francis
Jan 25 70/1

    I beg ye favor if yu please of hearing from yu whether any further discovery be made of ye salt Rocke wch was mentioned wn I had ye honor to mingle wth ye R.S.[2]

    My most humble service also I pray present to yr honorable neighbor Mr Boyl & vouchsafe a word to let me know how he does.

ADDRESS

    To my honored frd Henry
    Oldenburgh Esq
    At his hous in ye Pel-mel
    These present
            London

> Postpd 3d

NOTES

1 See Letters 1481, note 2, and 1495.
2 That is, 10 November 1670 when Martindale's letter about the salt deposit (Letter 1544) was read.

1609
Lister to Oldenburg

25 January 1670/1

From the original in Royal Society MS. L 5, no. 23
Printed in *Phil. Trans.*, no. 68 (20 February 1670/1), 2067–69

Yorke January 25th 70/71

Sr

Yours of ye 18th & 20th Instant I had & because you desire a speedy answer to ye many particulars therin contained, I shall returne you what thoughts come into my mind at present. I am glad to understand a refutation of my conjecture about ye hatching of those Bees by observation; Mr Willoughby has eased me of yt thought: & though it yet be unsolved, he hath made ye difficulty soe much ye more worthy our further enquiry, because he averrs it true & not imaginary. it is enough to have guessed once & we must wait an opportunity to find a Solution in observing more nicely ye thing it selfe. As to Spiders, there are many particularities in this surprising action of darting of threads & sailing of wch what I further have observed, I willingly keep for an other oppertunity & other Papers, as I doe likewise ye account of their poison: yet I am very glad to heare what others have observed. Concerning ye acid liquor of Pissmires, I have very lately received from Mr Wray ye Account (I suppose you have it alsoe by this time) yt was sent him from Mr Jessop & Mr Fisher:[1] wherin these two last gentlemen make this further enquiry, whether there be any other Insect or Animal Flesh or Fish, wch will afford an acid juice, they having wth great industrie tryed many Species amongst Insects & other Animals without lighting on ye like acid liquor. I am o'th mind there are: & a ready way to find such out may be, yt having observed, yt a pissmire bruised & smelt to emitts a strange fiery & peircing savour, like ye leafe of ye hearbe wch Botanists call *Flammula*[2] broken at ones nostrills, by this meanes I have, since Mr Wray put ye question to me found an Insect, wch I conceive will yield as acid liquor as well as a Pissmire, & yt is ye long- and round bodied-lead-coloured Julus,[3] the body of this Insect being bruised strikes ye Nostrills exceeding feircely; but I have not yet had an opportunity to furnish my selfe wth any quantity of ym for further Tryalls. The change of colours in Flowers etc is a subject I have a little considered,

& you shall have my thoughts & experiments about it more at leisure. To come to ye bleeding of ye Sycamore; ye last year I wintered at Nottingham, where I peirced a Sycamore about ye begining of November, ye turgescence of ye budds inviting me therto & some hopes of improving ye notion of winter-bleedings soe happily discovered by Mr Willoughby & Mr Wray: this succeeded soe well wth me, yt I did afterwards ingage my selfe in ye trouble of keeping a journal throughout ye whole Winter, from wch journal I thinke I may inferr 1. yt ye wounded Sycamores never bled, neither in November, nor December, nor January nor February nor March (wch yet they did above 40 several times, yt is totally ceasing & than begining anew) unlesse there proceeded a sensible & visible Frost, for I had noe other way of recording ye temper of ye Aire. 2. That ye Frosts did not ever set ableeding ye wounds it found made before they came, though sometimes they did; but upon ther breaking up, or very much relenting, ye wounds either made in yt instant of time, or made many months before, did never faile to bleed more or lesse. 3. yt particularly upon ye breaking up of ye two great & long frosts (ye first of wch happned yt year, in yt Countrey to be on ye 3d of January, ye 2d about ye 12 13 & 14 of February) all ye wounds ran most plentifully, soe yt such times may be looked upon, as ye most proper seasons of gathering great quantities of juice from this Tree. Removing into Craven ye latter end of March & thence to London my Journal was discontinued, I had yet upon my return into Craven some leisure to prosecute it. Those I there wounded ye latter end of May did not bleed, neither ye remaining part of yt month, nor ye following months of June & July, but ye orifice of ye wounds made wth a small auger, in a manner quite growne up & would scarce admitt of a pidgeons feather: wherfore ye 30th of July I cutt out a square peice about 2 intches of ye barke of a large & well grown Sycamore, about my height in ye body of it; this wound began to run ye next morning about 9 aclock soe as to drop & yt was all & dryed up by 11 aclocke; this it did constantly without intermission for 21 dayes, yt is, it let fall a teare or two betwixt 9 & 11 ith morning. The like cutt I made in a yong Sycamore, ye 8th of August, wch in like manner bled ye next morning but stopped before 9 aclock; it did soe for 2 or 3 dayes, but than totally drying. Afterwards removing to Yorke, the 1st of November I here peirced & otherwise wounded 2 sycamores & having observed ym my selfe at times, when, according to my former observations made in Nottinghamshire, I might well expect to have found ym bleeding yet they never stired, yt we could observe, to this day. since Mr Wray has assured me, yt those of Warwickshire bled ye 16th of November last past copiously & since ye Walnut Tree alsoe: & soe much for matter of Fact. To what cause wee may truly referr this anomolous bleeding, is not easy to say: for my part, I am not apt to thinke, yt there is a suddain & extempory ascent of Sap, at such times as these Trees are most disposed to bleed; but rather yt ye sap in all parts of ye Tree, is someways notably altered in its temper & consistence, & this bleeding by stresse of weather may in these Trees probably be looked upon as an injurie done to their natures from an unkind Climate, considering ye Walnut & Sycamore as strangers & not natives of England. 'Tis, indeed, tru, there are many sorts of English plants wch will bleed in Winter, but note alsoe, yt such plants never refuse to doe soe at any time of ye yeare, noe more than a man, who may break a veine when he pleases; but let ye Hypothesis be what it will, I am persuaded we shall have but very darke & imperfect notions of ye motion of ye juices of Vegetables, untill there tru Texture be better discovered. to conclude this subject, I put this Quaery. whether ye juice of Trees, whilst vegete & alive, can properly be said at any time of ye yeare to descend, or to be wanting in any part, or not to be therin in a much like quantitie.

I shall take care to inform my selfe about ye enquiry of very old Men. as for ye other particular, I am every way stranger in these parts of England. Sr I humbly thanke you for ye honour you would have conferred on me, & doe really thinke it more than I can deserve & shall gladly accept of it, but having thoughts & businesse, yt may happily call me up to London in Summer, I desire of you to wholly differ it till I have ye honour to kisse your hands in person. In ye meane time, I assure you, I desire nothing more than to contribute what I may to ye ends of yt illustrious assembly wth my weake endeavours.

The papers I shall send you from time to time may, if you thinke ym worthy, be disposed of as you please. I write but an ill hand & gave occasion in my former printed Letter to some mistakes, as for example *a Spring* is printed & I writ a *Syring Pipe*, yt is, a squirt or *jet d'eau*, by wch I meant what Mr Wray has explained by small holes or pipes.[4] be pleased to blot out in one of ye first Articles of Enquiry ye word *Feelers* & to write *Hornes*, alsoe to expunge *aliquot* in ye Title of ye Tables,[5] wch I inserted upon this, yt Mr Willoughby did judge yt there were as many more sorts of spiders as I had distinguished, but for my part I could never find one more in ye places where I have been, though I verily beleeve there are many more in England, yet it suffices, yt I can assure these to be all distinct species, as having much of their particular Histories & none other known to mee, & yt all may be adjusted (as they shall be discovered) to some one of those 6 Classes. Sr you will pardon my being sollicitous in this kind, from a particular humor I have, yt however I may be soe happy as to please others, I am still dissatisfied wth my owne doings & thinke ym never well enough. I am Sr

your most humble servant
Martin Lister

A small Box I gave to ye carrier John Loft inning at ye white horse without Criple gate ye last Saturday ye 21 of this instant directed as my Letters.

NOTES

Reply to Letter 1601.
1 See Letter 1593; "Mr. Jessop" (see Letter 1518, note 4) seems to be a mistake for "Dr. Hulse."
2 A kind of white-flowering clematis.
3 A millepede.
4 See Lister's letter to Ray, printed anonymously in *Phil. Trans.*, no. 50 (16 August 1669), p. 1014, the last line.
5 Both these alterations—in the title of the Table, and Article 4 of the Queries, in Letter 1589—were made by Oldenburg so as to obliterate the original text.

1610
Martindale to Oldenburg
25 January 1670/1

This is mentioned in Oldenburg's reply, Letter 1619; it contained an account of the petrifying well in Lancashire, mentioned in Letter 1588, and mentioned his having rules for solving problems about interest and annuities logarithmically.

1611
Oldenburg to Corcilli

28 January 1670/1

From the draft in Royal Society MS. O 2, no. 72

Excellentissime et Eruditissime Domine

Gratulor mihi, quod tuorum in Anglia Amicorum memoriam non deponas; quamvis male admodum me habeat, quod nomina et conditiones virorum, qui comitatum vestrum constituebant, nos latuerint, atque quo si fuisset, ampliorem certe, et magis philosophicam, prout omnino par erat, hospitalitatem, vobis exhibuissimus. Tu, Vir eximie, me apud caeteros juxta ac Teipsum pro singulari comitate tua excusare dignaberis. Salutavi tuo nomine Illustrissimum Boylium, qui Tibi maximas gratias et salutem officiossimas rescribit. Ad quaesita vero Tua sic ordine respondet: Ad 1. Se quandoque sale volatili cornu cervini, utplurium vero Spiritu Salis Ammoniaci contra Cephalalgiam uti. Ad 2. quod plantarum bulbosarum in phialis aere vacuatis germinationem spectat, ait, se plurima istius generis experimenta peregisse, ea tamen necdum in lucem emittere consuli tum putasse. Ad 3. quod Experimentum illud spectat, in quo nullum est Aeri interno cum ambiente commercium, patere ait, mercurium isto in casu non descensurum, cum Aer internus cum tota sua pressione, qua foras instructus erat intus concludatur, istiusque pressionis vi innitentem mercurium sustentet.[1]

In fistula vero 28. vel 29. pollicibus breviori, subsidebit quidem prope in eodem plano; prout scilicet ampliora vel strictiora erunt tuborum orificia, in quibus istiusmodi Experimenta fiunt.

TRANSLATION

Most excellent and learned Sir,

I congratulate myself because you have not forsaken the memory of your friends in England, although I take it very ill that we were ignorant of the names and ranks of the gentlemen in your party, for if we had known these things we would have shown you a richer and certainly a more philosophical hospitality, as would have been quite fitting. You will be so good, worthy Sir, as to make my excuses out of your exceptional courtesy, both to yourself and to the others. I have in your name greeted the illustrious Mr. Boyle, who returns you his best thanks and salutation. He replies thus in order to your questions: to the first, he has himself sometimes used the volatile salt of hartshorn, and often the spirit of sal ammoniac, against the headache. To the second, as regards the germination of bulbous plants in vessels evacuated of air, he says that he has performed many experiments of this sort, but has not yet thought it wise to publish them. As for the third, relating to that experiment in which there is no communication between the internal air and the atmosphere, he says that it is obvious that in that case the mercury will not descend, since the internal air is shut up inside with all that pressure with which it is endowed outside, and the force of that pressure sustains the compressing mercury.[1]

In a tube shorter than 28 or 29 inches it will subside almost to the same level, as the mouths of tubes are wider or narrower, in which experiments of this kind are made.

NOTES

Reply to Letter 1596, as is evident from the content. The date is given by an endorsement on the other side of this rough sheet, which was in fact the cover for Letter 1596: "Rec. le 24. janv. 1671. resp. le 28. jan 1671. Chez Justice Nelson in Martins Lane demeure le resident de venise."

1 At this point Oldenburg interpolates a query to himself, in English: "Q. so doth ye outward Air, and yet ye mercury falls down [*illegible*] a hight."

1612

Cotton to Oldenburg

28 January 1670/1

From the original in Royal Society MS. C 1, no. 31

Sr

Understanding by letter from Dr Fulwood yt the Society were desirous to have an account of some particulars (in his letter mentiond) from ye person who voided ye stone I sent for him to this Citty where I found him willing to give ye best account hee could but supposing his Childrens memory to bee better than his owne hee desir'd first to conferre wth them about it promising soon after to send mee a punctuall account wch you have here enclosed under his hand.[1] To this may bee added yt the Orifice opend by the violence of ye Urine is now closd up and ye Urine passes ye ordinary way. I would have examind his age by ye Church booke of Farindon[2] ye parish wherein hee was borne and where hee lives but ye old Register-booke is lost and yt wch is now there is not so old as this man. I remember hee told mee hee was eighteen yeares old when Queen Elizabeth died wch doth not much disagree wth ye enclos'd relation. As for the other particulars you mentiond when I meet wth any of them you shall have an account from

Your affectionate friend and servt
Edw. Cotton

Exon Jan 28
1670

ADDRESS

> For my honored friend
> Mr Henry Oldenburg
> at his house in the
> middle of Pel mel in
> St. James's fields,
>   Westminster

POSTMARK IA 30

NOTES

Reply to Letter 1600.
1 Letter 1612a.
2 Farringdon is $5\frac{1}{8}$ miles southeast of Exeter.

1612a

Thomas Westcott to Cotton

Late January 1670/1

From the original in Royal Society MS. C 1, no. 32

Sir

I have sent you an answer to yr desire concerning the stone. Ye time that ye stone was growing was about 18 yeares & was in ye yard about 14 yeares & grew alwaies biger & of the bignes it was now not long & I thinke my selfe to be about 88 yeares old: The first stopage of ye Urine was when the stone came into the yard. I voyded the stone about 3 yeares since.

The medicine was to boyle a quart of white wine: & in that boyle 2 or 3 burdocke Mocks[1] and boyle it very well Then put into that the bigness of a hazell nutt of black sope:[2] & drinke it morninge & noone & eveninge; anoynt the seat of your bodye very well wth black sope & take the skinne of a snake, and strike it wth venus tirpintine:[3] & put it round behind the members & come up over the yard clos to ye body this is the best account I can give you to doe you any service

Tho : Westcott

NOTES

1 Roots.
2 Common soft soap.
3 Venice turpentine.

1613
Lister to Oldenburg

28 January 1670/1

From the original in Royal Society MS. L 5, no. 24

Yorke
January 28th—70

Sr

I writ ye last post in great hast to you,[1] because you seemed to be very earnest wth me to doe soe. Give me leave therfore to trouble you wth a kind of Postscript to my last. I have sent out enquiries concerning two very old men, who to my knowledge ye last summer were both alive, of 120 yeares old a peice at least as it was told me they live wthin a mile one of an other in Craven. but I hope more of yt an other time.

You may be pleased to put this Quaerie alsoe concerning ye bleeding of ye Sycamore: what condition ye soile is of, where such Trees are planted yt shall either bleed or refuse to doe soe: whether sandy, as yt of Nottingham or a wett clay as that of ye 2 Trees I have observed here at Yorke.

In ye Title of ye 7th Spider be pleased to strike out ye word *turbinata* & put in *fastigiata*.[2]

I have thoughts of coming up to Town ye next Terme: but if I doe not, you will highly oblige me to signifie my desire to ye illustrious R. Society of standing Candidate provided ye thing can be downe wthout my appearance in person: otherwise we must remitt it till I can come up.

I shall be glad to heare you received ye small Box I sent you. excuse I pray that trouble; it is from ye affection I have to serve you. I am Sr

your most humble servant
Martin Lister

To ye Queries you put to me concerning ye poison of Spiders, I forbore to give you any particular Answer— for ye reasons I hinted: & yet to take off prejudice from such as may have a mind to search into this matter; I assure you, yt although I have handled wth my bare hands many 100 of most sorts yt I name, yet I never received ye least harme. but from other sorts of Insects I have & particularly I have had my flesh blistered wth a

very slight touch of certain *Cimices*[3] & yt much more feircely, than we
experience in our shopp cantharides.

ADDRESS
    These
For his honoured Friend Mr Oldenburg
    to be left wth Mr J. Martin
        stationer at ye Bell in
            Pauls Church-yard
                London

NOTES

Reply to Letter 1601.
1 Letter 1609.
2 See Letter 1589a, note 1.
3 The genus of bedbugs.

1614
Oldenburg to Newburgh

28 January 1670/1

Oldenburg's endorsement on Letter 1608 shows that he received it on 27 January
and answered it on the following day.

1615
Flamsteed to Oldenburg
28 January 1670/1
From the original in Royal Society MS. F 1, no. 66

Derby Jan: 28 1670

Worthy Sr:

Your last wth ye Transaction[1] included I have. In which I esteeme my selfe obliged, yt yu have beene pleased to insert ye product of my calculations; and all Astronomers amongst us will hold themselves engaged to yu for communicating ye observations of Hevelius:[2] as for ye Transit of ye Moone by Venus, haveing duely considered it I find it but a very slender observation; as it is related in ye table, & ye times there, except it be misprinted, are most inartificially stated for at 3h–47'–20" mane[3] his clock wants 6' 50", at ye end 9h–17'–39" it falls 1'–26" short of ye heavens. and yet in ye middle from after 5h–53' to 7h–45' by his clock, hee makes it to exceed them allways 5 minutes of time or 6: which except some reasons not laid downe induce him to doe, is done very unhandsomely; if wee suppose, which is most likely, yt his clock (which at 3h–47'–20" wanted 6'–50" of ye heavens, and 1'–25" at 9h–17'–39") moved so much faster then it ought as to absorbe the difference in 5h–24'–54" of time, which was included betwixt ye first & last caelestiall observation, & that ye same difference was absorbed gradually, then in my opinion the times corrected, supposeing they were truely noted, from his clock, ought to be as in ye margin: [*see table, pp. 426–27*][4] Nor yet supposing ye times thus truely converted will ye observation be of use: for first ye scheme of it, by which ye beareing of Venus from ye moone might be knowne, is wanteing; And tho at 7h–17'–00" juxta horologium; ye distance of Venus from ye Moones inferior limbe was judged 4 minutes, yet from what point of it tis not noted: So yt this note does no good: as for ye observed distances of ye moon & Venus from Jupiter they are little beneficiall except ye place of Jupiter or Venus had before beene explored by the observeing their distances from ye fixed stars. I suppose Sr Hevelius gave yu a figure of this transit which if yu have and can wthout trouble I would beg a copy of: And would further intreate you when yu write to him againe, on this occasion, to advise him to take more care to make his calculations accurate, & not to fastidiate the trouble of workeing them twice over when they are of greater tendency: when yu have occasion to write to mee, againe pray let me know what yu heare hee has done in his promised catalogue of ye fixed starrs whether it be publisht yet, & if not when it may be expected I will ere long (God willing) send you a Specimen of ye faults of his Mercury sub Sole. but my occasions & bussinesses prevent mee at present: pray when yu write exhort him to accuracy in his supputations which is much desired, I might say wanteing in most of his observations. for tis better wee have a few good observations made well & derived from exact calculations, then to [be] troubled with a many from dubious & rude ones:

I could wish yu had printed ye short synopsis, (which conteins the heads of ye calculations) with ye times of ye phasis; for ye Anomalys of ye moon not being knowne it will discourage ye observer if hee must be forced to calculate for them before hee can obteine them: but I must confesse yu have done enough for admonition, which is more then I could either desire or deserve: acknowledgeing yr favors I rest

Yrs to command
John Flamsteed.

ADDRESS
    To Henry Oldenburge Esqe
    at his house in ye middle of ye
    Pellmell in St Jamess
    feilds Westminster
        these present

tempus juxta horlogium ambulatorum Hevelii			Tempus verum ex altitudinibus convertum		
h	′	″	h	′	″
3	47	20	3	54	10
3	50	35	3	57	28
5	47	44	5	52	34
5	48	35	5	53	24
5	51	59	5	56	45
5	53	40	5	58	24
6	12	30	6	16	55
6	14	30	6	18	53
6	37	00	6	41	00
7	12	00	7	15	25

tempus juxta horlogium ambulatorum Hevelii			Tempus verum ex alti- tudinibus convertum		
h	'	"	h	'	"
7	17	00	7	20	20
7	35	00	7	38	02
7	45	00	7	47	52
9	11	00	9	12	26
9	15	48	9	17	20
9	17	39	9	19	04

NOTES

1 Presumably *Phil. Trans.*, no. 66 (12 December 1670); Flamsteed's predictions of lunar appulses are printed on pp. 2029–34.
2 From Letter 1536.
3 "in the morning."
4 The headings of the Table are "The time by Hevelius' clock"; "The true time converted from the altitudes."

1616
Beale to Oldenburg
28 January 1670/1

Mentioned in Beale's Letter 1624 as having probably miscarried in the post.

1617
Reed to Oldenburg
30 January 1670/1

From the original in Royal Society MS. R 1, no. 26

Worthy Sr

Yours I did receive, and in obedience thereto have sent you two fagotts of Redstreake grafts,[1] soe large as I presume will answer your desires for this season, however if you shall intimate your further intentions, I will send more, wch after I have notice from you may be return'd in good time. By Watts ye Heref[ord] Carrier at the white hors without Cripplegate you will receive them directed to you. I did not answer your last letter as to 2 Queries. 1. as to ye making of Cyder with Rotten apples, as to yt I could not out of experience but upon Enquiry, have learnt that we have palates wth us, that can distinguish if there be but one rotten apple in a hogshed; haud equidem invideo, miror magis:[2] but certeynly yt cannot be good, if most of ye Apples be rotten, for though ye Juice Corrupts not, yt cannot but pertake of ye Corruption of ye pulp. I made some afterward of Apples ye Frost had Corrupted, wch was not drinkeable; but that may be upon another reason. to your second, How much of Cyder I might estimate to have been made last yeare of wch indeed I was desired to give noe account when I began to make inquiry. We have a poore Country sorely burdened wth Taxes. our aunccient commodityes of Corne & Woole come to noething comparatively. And had not our accidentall [crop],[3] of Cyder & hopps beene favourable late yeares, we could not have p[ai]d rates wch They were Jealous least my intelligence (wch might be published) might occasionally inhance. And indeed my transmitting of grafts is some what muttered at by my narrow spirited neighbors, who thinke, yt it will have the same effect as the transporting of Cotshall[4] sheep to spayne, licenced in Ed. 4th time in that treaty wch they call Intercursus malus:[5] wch hath much decayed our owne native commodity. But I answer them, that though I transsmit grafts I doe not ye soyle; and indeed of all fruits I know none is more nice & humorsome as to ye soyle then is ye redstreak. if yt likes not ye soyle, yt will canker not only graft but ye stock whereon yt is set, come to noething. If yt likes (though at first yt was but a Crab) yt wilbe when fully ripe an Apple of good largnesse & of a brave goust to eate. Something I should have written concerning ye season of removing trees, & of pippin Cyder, of wch I had last yeare for Colour & tast beyond any I ever tasted of ye Redstreak, but I have exceeded, allmost to ye feare of ye losing of ye post. When I heare from you of yr receipt of ye grafts, You maybe troubled wth another paper from Sr

> Your very faythfull
> frend to serve you
> *Ric. Reed*

Jan. 30.70.

ADDRESS

For Henry Oldenburgh
Esqr at his house in the
Pall: Mall nere St
          Jameses by
                    Westminster

NOTES

1 These were distributed to various Fellows at a meeting of the Society on 16 February
  1670/1.
2 "For my part I do not envy it, but I am greatly surprised at it."
3 This word was inserted by Oldenburg.
4 Cotswold?
5 This is a most extraordinarily distorted notion. The *Intercursus magnus* was a commer-
  cial treaty made by Henry VII in 1496, which gave England very favorable terms of
  trade with Flanders. In 1506 he extorted an even better treaty, called for this reason
  by the Flemings *Intercursus malus* ("the evil exchange")—a term possibly also applied
  to the earlier treaty. As for Edward IV, his policy was to protect the English cloth
  trade by discouraging the export of raw wool; but one chronicler at least recorded a
  tale that Edward sent some English rams to the King of Aragon. Export of live
  sheep had been restricted by the statute 3 Henry VI, c. 2. The real development of
  Spanish sheep-farming occurred in the fourteenth century and was based on the
  merino breed, unknown in England at that time.

1618
Malpighi to Oldenburg
31 January 1670/1
From the original in Royal Society MS. Malpighi Letters I, no. 8

Eruditissimo et Praeclarissimo Viro
Dno. Henrico Olemburg Regiae Societatis Anglicanae Secretario
Marcellus Malpighius S.P.

Laetor librorum fasciculum a me transmissum redditum tandem tibi
fuisse, et quamplurimas tibi rependo gratias ob librorum munus,
quos ad me expedisse scribis.
  Praeclarissimi Montanarij epistolam olim transmissam, nunc vero

typis editam, et auctam, hic iniunctam habebis:¹ Tuas iam pridem epistolas Vir laudatus recepit, et Sociorum sensa de propriis scriptis, non tantum circa vitra stillaticia, quam circa controversias cum Dno. Rossetto avide expetat; reliquae Dni. Cassinij, et Mengoli exercitationes adhuc sub praelo typographi incuria laborant.²

Patrem Lanam e Societate Jesu non novi; Audio tamen ab eiusdem domesticis, ipsum non tanta iudicij acie pollere, quanta forte exigitur pro complendis iis, quae in Prodromo iactantur. Medendi importunae occupationes hisce praecipue temporibus, quibus morbi complicatissimi vagantur, inchoata olim observationum studia adeo perturbarunt, ut parum genio indulgere valeam. Diu te sospitum, incolumemque servent superi.

Dabam Bononiae die 10 Feb. 1671. [N.S.]

TRANSLATION

Marcello Malpighi sends greetings to the very famous and learned Mr. Henry Oldenburg, Secretary of the Royal Society of England

I am glad that the package of books I sent has at last been delivered to you, and I return you many thanks for the gift of books, which, you say, you have sent me. The letter of the distinguished Montanari formerly dispatched to you has now been printed and enlarged, and is enclosed here.¹ That praiseworthy gentleman received your letters some time ago, and he eagerly awaits the judgment of the Society upon his writings, not only the paper on glass drops but his controversies with Mr. Rosetti. The remaining essays by Messrs. Cassini and Mengoli are still lingering in the press, owing to the printer's negligence.²

I do not know Fr. Lana of the Society of Jesus, but I hear from his servants that he does not possess so acute a judgment as is required, perhaps, for accomplishing what is set out in his *Prodromus*. The pressing business of healing, especially at this season when very difficult diseases are prevalent, has so upset the formerly incomplete investigation of observations that I am little able to indulge my mind. May the Gods long keep you safe and well. Farewell.

Bologna, 10 February 1671 [N.S.]

NOTES

Reply to Letter 1578. Malpighi wrote the draft of this letter on 17 January (Bologna MS. 2085, VII, f. 3V).

1 See Letter 1450, note 2 (Vol. VI) and Letter 1555, note 2; the title was *Speculazioni fisiche . . . sopra gli effetti di que' vetri temprati, che rotti in una parte si risolvono tutti in polvere* (Bologna, 1671). On 20 April 1671 Oldenburg produced this volume, whereupon Henshaw agreed to translate the second part it contained, having completed the first that had previously been received in manuscript.

2 See Letter 1547, and its notes 5 and 8.

1619
Oldenburg to Martindale
2 February 1670/1

From the copy in Royal Society MS. O 2, no. 45

An Answer to Mr. Martindale's two letters

Sr

Both your Letters of jan. 7. and 25. are well come to my hands, together wth ye parcel of your Rock-salt, wch I produced before ye R. Society,[1] who, as they returne you their hearty thanks for your care and kindnesse in their concerns, so they have recommended some of this salt to the examination of an Ingenious member of theirs,[2] who is to report to them his tryalls thereon wth all convenient speed. And as to your dropping water, newly found in Lancashire, and being of a petrifying nature, you have done very well in placing sticks of severall sorts of wood therein, and we doubt not but you will give us notice of ye event, and if they turne into stone send us some specimina of it, together wth some of ye petrifyed masse, you say you have allready by you. I thank you also for those particulars concerning whey, and ye severall uses of its different preparations.

I am persuaded yt divers of our Society will be glad to see those particular rules of your owne invention, wch you intimate, for your Logarithmicall resolving divers questions touching interest and annuity: and if you please to communicate them, I believe I shall obtaine ye thoughts of some of our Mathematicall men upon them, wch is all I have now leisure to say to you, safe yt I am very affectionately yours

H. Oldenburg

London Feb. 2. 1670/71

P.S. I had almost forgot to desire you to observe, whether ye petrifying water doth only incrustate wood, or pervade it, as also to note the times wthin wch it effects petrifaction; and how far it is from ye place of yr abode. I shall also be glad to know, how farr the Salt-work is distant from any Salt-spring.[3]

NOTES

The heading and postscript are in Oldenburg's hand.
Reply to Letters 1588 and 1610.
1 On 26 January 1670/1.
2 Daniel Coxe.
3 This last question was put by an unnamed Fellow when the letter was read.

1620

Oldenburg to Sachs

2 February 1670/1

From the draft in Royal Society MS. O 2, no. 46
Partly printed in *Miscellanea curiosa*, II, 1671, sig. f. 3

Celeberrimo Viro
Dn. Philipo Jacobo Sachs à Lewenheimb, Phil. et Medico
Wratislaviensi, et Academico Germano Doctissimo
Henricus Oldenburg Sal. et Off.

Quas literas Cal. Octob. 1670. ad me dederas, Vir Clarissime, eas, una cum munere Philosophico. jan. 23. 1671. demum accepi. Quae scire ex iis Societatem Regiam voluisti, pronuper in publico ejus Consessu praelegi,[1] simul et Ephemerides Academiae vestrae Medico-physicas ibidem produxi. Impense equidem dicta Societas Vobis juxta ac Philosophiae de egregio caepto vestro gratulatur, quaeque opis suae fuerint in illius augmentum suppeditare, lubenti animo se collaturam pollicetur. In mandatis jam dedit Sociorum nonnullis,[2] ut Librum transmissum sedulo perlegant, ac de Observationum ibi Concinnatarum momentis publice referant. Nil sane magis ad proferenda verae philosophiae pomaeria conferre posse judicant, quam si omnium gentium Viri docti et solertes Ingenia et Studia sua, uti nunc faciunt, consociare pergant, inque Horreum philosophicum, locupletem Observationum et Experimentorum, candide et rite factorum, segetem certatim convehant. Excellentissima itaque Academia vestra, Vir Clarissime, de eo inprimis, sua sponte, erit sollicita, ne quicquam irrepat in Philosophicum hoc penum, quod sublestae sit fidei, Lydiumque experiundi Lapidem subire recuset. Genuinam omnino et castam esse oportere una nobiscum existimabitis illam Naturae Historiam, quam adornandae Physicae solidiori et feraciori substernere satagimus.

Regia Angliae Societas Institutum suum quantumpote consectatur, efflictimque gaudet, Italiam, Galliam et Germaniam ipsius vestigia premere, et longe lateque Experimentalem Philosophandi modum promovere.

Caeterum, Vir Doctissime, si quid penes me sigillatim fuerit, quo vestras possim Ephemerides annuas augere, officio pro tenuitate mea non deero, inque magna felicitatis meae parte posuero, si aliquo diligentiae et affectus mei specimine testatum facere queam, me tum donum vestrum quo me ornatis, magni pendere, tum Nobilissimam et Eruditissimam Academiam vestram demisso cultu venerari. Vale, Vir Spectabilis, et Tui studiosissimo favere perge. Dabam Londini die 2 Februarij A. 1670/71.

P.S.

Ut magis magisque pateat, nequaquam esse ex uno alterove Experimento quicquam certi in hanc vel illam partem concludendum, sinas me ad Observationem vestram 118[3] (quae discutiendam sibi sumit quaestionem illam, *Num Lien sit veneris Sedes*) hoc loco annotare, id quod Clarissimi Deckeri[4] vestri Experimento adversatur; Nobilissimum et judicij subactissimi verum[5] ex Societate Regia, ante aliquot annos hic Londini curasse, ut Cani faemellae Lien exscinderetur, quae sanata cum esset, et paulo post catulliret, admisso cane non semel sed bis terve concepit, et aliquot catulos enixa fuit. Est haec canis eadem est, in quam sanguis ovillus post Lienem exectum transfusus fuerat.

Non ita pridem per literas[6] nobis significavit doctissimus Dn. Johannes Rajus, e Societate Regia, Clarissimum Dn. Doctorem Hulsium comperisse, Flores Cichorij sive Intybi, Formicarum cumulo injectos vel abditos, colorem caeruleum in rubeum mutare. Adjicit, inductum eum fuisse ut Experimentum illud faceret, a quodam Langhamo Anglo, in libello suo Hortensi id asserente: atque idem traditum inveniri ab Hieronymo Trago Hist. Stirp. L.1.c.91. et ab Othone Brunsfelsio, dictum Tragum antegresso, Johanne Bauhino notante. Caeterum causam illius mutationis laudatus D. Hulsius arcessit a liquore quodam acido, quem insecta illa, flores dictos perreptantia, excernunt; quam aciditatem ait Experimentis aliquot Chymicis peritissimum Dominum Samuelem Fisherum jam diu ante comprobasse.

Quaeritur, an vobis in Germania de ullo alio Animali constet, quod distillatione aliove modo Spiritum acidum suppeditaverit?

TRANSLATION

Henry Oldenburg [presents] his greetings and services to Dr. Philipp Jacob Sachs, Philosopher and Physician of Breslau, and a most learned German Academician

I have at last received on 23 January 1671 the letter which you, famous Sir, addressed to me on 1 October 1670, together with a philosophical present. What you wished the Royal Society to hear from it I read aloud recently at its ordinary meeting,[1] and at the same time laid before the Society the *Miscellanea curiosa* of your Academy. The Royal Society earnestly congratulated you and Philosophy herself upon this distinguished beginning you have made, and promised to make over willingly whatever in its own stock might promote its advancement. The Society ordered several of its Fellows[2] to peruse carefully the volume you have sent and submit a public report on the importance of the observations there gathered together. They believe that nothing can better increase the stock of true philosophy than if the learned and skilful of all nations continue to unite their ingenuity and investigations, as now they do, and bring safely into the philosophical granary their rich harvest of observations and experiments properly and honestly performed. And so your most excellent Academy, famous Sir, will of its own volition be solicitous that nothing should be insinuated in this philosophical treasury of weak authenticity, or that refuses to be tested by the Lydian stone. That history of nature which we strive to make the foundation for perfecting a more solid and fruitful physics you will wish to see pure and genuine, as we do.

The Royal Society of England is pursuing its objective as well as may be, and heartily rejoices to see Italy, France, and Germany following the same path, so that far and wide the experimental way in philosophy is advancing.

For the rest, learned Sir, if there is anything locked up in my possession by which I might add to your annual periodical, I shall not fail in my duty (to the best of my abilities), and I shall count myself very happy if by any evidence of my diligence and goodwill I can prove how greatly I value the gift you honored me with, and how much I respect your noble and erudite Academy. Farewell, worthy Sir, and continue to cherish your most zealous friend.

London, 2 February 1670/1

P.S. To make it still more obvious that one can conclude nothing for certain (either in this sense or that) by making one or two trials, permit me to remark here on your Observation 118[3] (which takes under discussion that question, whether the spleen be the seat of venery?) what may be objected against the experiment of your celebrated Mr. Decker,[4] namely, that a certain nobleman[5] of very acute judgment in the Royal Society a few years ago had a bitch's spleen extirpated here in London, and when it was healed and a little afterwards came on heat, the bitch mated with a dog not once but two or three times and was delivered of several puppies. And this bitch was the same as that into which a sheep's blood was transfused after the removal of the spleen.

Not long ago the very learned Mr. John Ray, a Fellow of the Royal Society, informed us by letter[6] that the famous Dr. Hulse had discovered that the flowers of chicory or endive change their blue color to red when they are introduced or buried in an anthill. He adds that he was induced to make this experiment by what one Langham, an Englishman, says of it in his gardening book; and that the same is found reported by Hieronymus Tragus in *De stirpium historia*, Bk. I, chap. 91, and before him by Otto Brunfels as recorded by Jean Bauhin. The praiseworthy Dr. Hulse finds the cause of this change in a certain acid liquor which those insects excrete in crawling about on the flowers; this acidity he says was demonstrated by some chemical experiments made by the skilful Mr. Samuel Fisher long enough ago.

The question is raised, whether you in Germany know of any other animal that will yield an acid liquor by distillation or otherwise?

NOTES

Reply to Letter 1530.

1 On 26 January 1670/1.
2 Actually only Oldenburg, who was also instructed to write to Sachs.
3 Observation 118 of *Miscellanea curiosa* for 1670 (pp. 274–76) is by Joachim Georg Elsner, a physician of Breslau.
4 Frederick Decker, M.D., is said by Elsner to have recently published *Experimentum . . . in notis & observationibus editis ad Praxin Barbettianam.*
5 Boyle. Oldenburg had described the same case in *Phil. Trans.*, no. 28 (21 October 1667), 521, though there he said that the extirpation of the spleen took place after the transfusion.
6 Letter 1593.

1621

Dodington to Oldenburg

3 February 1670/1

From the original in Royal Society MS. D 1, no. 20

Venice Febr. 13th 1671 [N.S.]

Sr

The inclosed[1] came to me 2 dayes since, wch I would not detayn when you please to command me any thing in return to my Last of 30. Janr.[2] I shall readily obey you. In the mean time I shall place to yr accompt the small charges I have payed in the postage &c.

The sea heere ebbs & flowes 4 Foot, more or lesse, as the winds moove the waters. In ye Mediterranian sea, it eyther ebbs & flowes little or not at all But this realy strange though most certayne, The waters are allwayes higher heere in the somer then in the winter, And the ebbs much lower in Winter then somer, to my exact observation as well as of all men that live heere, Particularly they were so lowe on the 25. January That Boates could not pass, to & fro; yet the day was extreame calme.

It is so very cold this present time, that I can scarce write, yet I will adventure to give you an accompt of an accident occurred to my observation this morning. My servant had putt a glass of Fayre water in my windowe exposed to ye Ayre, I came to it in lesse then a quarter of an hower & washd my mouth wth it, after that I presently dipped a towell in it (pro more meo)[3] to wash my face, & returning in lesse then halfe a minute, to dipp the towell in it a second time, to wash my hands I found it all frozen very hard from topp to bottome. Sr I pray receive this, as all things wch I send you, for precise truths, since I profess to you, not to write any thing for ostentation, but for Information, and you may give intire Credit to wt I shall at any time send you. So I rest Sr

Yr most humble servant
John dodington

Mr Oldenburgh.

NOTES

1 Presumably Letter 1618.
2 Letter 1602.
3 "According to my habit."

1622
Oldenburg to Lister
4 February 1670/1

From the original in Bodleian Library MS. Lister 34, f. 5

Sir,

I did intend by my last[1] to desire you, yt you would please to direct yr letters to me immediately to my house in the Palmal, and not to Mr Martyn, because they may lye many days at his house before they come to my hands, and ye post coms as often into my quarters, as any where else about London. If yr two last had been thus directed to me in the Palmal, I might have imparted ye contents thereof, wch concern Philosophy, to ye R. Society at their last Assembly,[2] and now given you their sense and acknowledgement thereupon. I can at present only send you my particular thanks, and make it my request to you, to continue to us these so usefull and uncommon observations, and contributions, wch will very considerably enrich our philosophical Store-house. I have made the more haste to acknowledge the receipt of these last of yrs, (I mean of jan. 25. and 28.) because ye Carrier, whom you named for having received from you a boxe for me, positively denyeth it, though I have sent both yr letters, yt mention it expresly, to him, yt he might see it himself. I doubt not, but you will call him to an account for it, upon his return.

I am very much pleased (and so will doubtlesse ye Society, when they shall hear of it) that you have so successfully begun to prosecute ye inquiry, Whether there be any other Animal, besides ye Pismire, yt yields an acid Spirit. And yr Observations and Reflexions on ye Bleeding of Sycamores are so remarkable, that I am confident, it will excite many Observers of that and other particulars touching the Bleeding of Trees.

I am very glad also, you have begun to inquire after ye very old men in yr parts. The number of one of ym I cannot well discerne, whether it be 110 or 120, ye midle of ye numbers seeming to have a hook on ye top towards ye left hand.

I shall very carefully observe yr directions in altering those words, you have marked, in yr paper about Spiders. Pray, is not ye *Iulus*, you mention for its likeness to ye Ant in yielding an acid liquor, a kind of Scolopender, having many feet?³ And have not the Common people an English name for it?

Since you will have me stay, till the next Terme, in the matter of proposing you for a Candidate to the R. Society, I shall obey you; and in all things endeavor to demonstrate my readinesse to be in what I can Sir

Yr very humble and
faithful servant
Oldenburg

London Febr. 4. 1670.
        71.

ADDRESS

    To his honored friend
      Martyn Lister Esquire
      At his house wthout Mickel-gate-barr
            at
               Yorke

POSTMARK FE 4

NOTES

Reply to Letters 1609 and 1613.
1 Letter 1601.
2 On 2 February 1670/1.
3 See Letter 1609, note 3. "Scolopender" was a name applied to centipedes and millepedes.

1623
Oldenburg to Flamsteed

4 February 1670/1

Letter 1615 is endorsed to the effect that it was received on 2 February and answered on the fourth; the reply is further acknowledged in Letter 1636. It contained a request from Hooke for some further calculations of appulses.

1624
Beale to Oldenburg
4 February 1670/1

From the original in Royal Society MS. V, no. 28

Feb. 4 70.

Deare Bror,

I had not written to yu now, but yt I am in some feare, yt mine to yu of Jan. 28 sent by last Sat. post,[1] miscarried: And ye more I feare, because just now I received one from Mr. Eve[lyn] dated Feb. 1st, in wch he makes no mention at all, nor takes any notice of one I sent to him at ye very same time, wn I wrote to yu Jan. 28. If mine arriv'd not to yu, I have lost a great Designe towards ye Public, containing a full sheet of concernments for ye RS, some of such a Secret nature, yt I shall be much troubl'd, if They fell into other hands, yn such as are worthy to be of ye Councell to ye RS, as Honourable Charles Howard of Norfolk & Mr Hoskins, (to whom they are by yr favour & conduct addressed) frequently are. If they came safe to yu, I have somwt more to say, some other time, for ye Propagation of Mulberyes of all kinds all over England, then urged.

Now I will only answer to a more private note of yours of Jan. 24, wch I then omitted, because, (as I then said) all our private matters should give place to ye more public. Now I take speciall notice in yrs of these words: you say yu *cannot but deplore ye unhappinesse of ye difference still entertain'd betwixt mee & Mr G[lanvill]*.[2] Sr, I protest it, & can affirme it devoutly, I doe as sincerely apply myself to serve him, & to vindicate his reputation upon all occasions (ofttimes to ye utmost hazzard of my own) as at several public Meetings of Clergy. And this last weeke, to pacify a Clergyman, who hath ye spreading faculty, yt I could not adventure more, or wth more ardor, if it were for my own Father, or a Brother, if they were alive, or, as they are, in their Graves &c. Sr, This yu know may well stand wth ye free judgment wch I have sometimes given in yr eare, as to a Brother, in whome I doe absolutely confide. And I apprehend, yt Mr Eve[lyn] and others, who beare very hearty respects to Mr G, are of my Opinion; that it was not safe for Mr G to exasperate Marchamond,[3] since he, & Milton, wth their Junto, are able to doe us more mischiefe, than millions of S & C.[4]

In ye Front of my last, I told yu, yt I cannot by yrs understand, wt check is putt upon St[ubbe]. Mr E[velyn] sayes nothing of it. I shall take it for very good newes, If yr hint in that poynt be confirm'd. And I would gladly know, whether his Mouth be stopt by Legal processe, or how otherwise.

I have drawn up ye Alphabetical Table of 10 numbers;[5] As soon as I see ye 11th I shall have no more to doe, than to insert that number & to transcribe all faire for ye following Post; And then immediately I am ready for my other promises.

Sr, I beseech yu, wn yu chance to see Mr G, or write to him, doe not, whatever occurrs, take any notice of unkindnesse, or dissatisfaction betwixt us, of eyther side. For, as Salomon adviseth, he that repeateth a matter causeth strife,[6] wch you will abhor to doe, as I may well be confident. Possibly my last came to yu & yu were held close to yr businesse; Therefore, having Roome, I will now adde, yt as by Arguments I there offer'd to shew, yt ye season was now ripe, & in many respects, advantagious, to solicit ye propagation of Mulberryes of all sorts, at least by Nurseryes, all over ye Southern parts of England; so it would be largely & spreadingly oblieging, if Mr. Hoskins (to whom I present my very humble service) would engage my Ld Scudamore[7] in it. He resides in Petti-France. His example would be leading to all Herefordshire & much further: And also, if Mr. H & he would please to engage some other considerable persons constantly residing in yt County; acquainting them, where Seeds, Layers, or rooted Plants rather, (especially of ye best sort of White Mulberryes) may be had in London upon sure Trust, & at reasonable Rates: Other seeds proper for Nurseryes may under one be recommended. I wish ye Kings Gardiner John Rose, could offer all sorts of Mulberryes, as freely as he hath offer'd ye best sorts of Vines, at ye end of *English Vineyards*.[8] I have already taken much paines, in scribbles by letters, to set on this work afresh: And more effectuall I should be towards many, if yr solicitation (in junto wth ye assistance of Mr Howard, Mr Evelyn, Mr Hoskins &c) would enable mee to say expressly, yt this is ye present engagement of ye RS. For this is ye proper force of such a Society, yt it may prevaile more than a Royal Proclamation; as undoubtedly it would Doe, if every Member would heartily take ye hint, as from ye Councell, & communicate it as far as his Influence extends. Sr, I doe not spare you in this, because it can cost yu no more trouble, than a private conference

wth ye above named Gentlemen at yr public meetings; And may furnish
yu with a seasonable Line in yr other dispatches to Mr Willoughby, Mr
Wray, Dr Cotton &c.

Sr, Your very hearty servant
Vinc. Ver.

ADDRESS

> For my much honor'd Friend
> Henry Oldenburg Esqr
> At his house
> in Pell Mell
> Westminster

Postpaid 3d

NOTES

1 The letters mentioned in the text below are all lost.
2 No details of this are known, but Beale was certainly distrustful of Glanvill as the
 champion of the Royal Society; see also in Vol. VI. In 1667 Glanvill had preached
 and published a sermon entitled *A Loyal Tear dropt on the Vault of our late martyred
 Sovereign*, and from the allusions below it may be that Beale regretted too close an
 association of the Royal Society with Tory, royalist sentiment.
3 Presumably Marchamont Needham (1620–78) is meant, a journalist who at first
 supported the King in *Mercurius Pragmaticus*, then went over to the Commonwealth
 and Cromwell, under whom he edited the *Mercurius Politicus* newspaper. Although
 an opponent of the Restoration, he came to terms with the monarchy and lived
 by practising medicine without license.
4 Presumably Stubbe, who certainly expressed admiration of Milton's writings, and
 either Meric Casaubon (who had attacked Glanvill) or Robert Crosse, his first adversary.
5 Presumably Beale was indexing the *Philosophical Transactions* of 1670–71; he had indexed nos. 57–66 inclusive and awaited no. 67 (dated 16 January 1670/1). Oldenburg
 himself would index no. 68, the last issue for the year, in order to publish the index
 with that issue (dated 20 February 1670/1).
6 Prov. 17:9: "he that repeateth a matter separateth very friends."
7 See Vol. I, p. 480, note 6.
8 John Rose, *The English Vineyard vindicated* (London, 1666) was edited by Evelyn under
 the pseudonym "Philocepos."

1625

Oldenburg to Beale

7 February 1670/1

From the memorandum in Royal Society MS. V, no. 28

Rec. Feb. 6. 1670/71
Answ. Feb. 7.
To com[mend] index, dedication
Aged; and ingenious men.

NOTE

Reply to Letter 1624.

1626

Oldenburg to Reed

7 February 1670/1

From the endorsement on Royal Society MS. R 1, no. 26

Received Febr. 2. 1670/71
Answ. Febr. 7.

Of aged people, Mulberries, pipin-Cider, season of removing Trees

NOTE

Reply to Letter 1617.

1627
Lister to Oldenburg

8 February 1670/1

From the original in Royal Society MS. L 5, no. 25
Partially printed in *Phil. Trans.*, no. 68 (20 February 1670/1), 2069–70, and no. 70 (17 April 1671),
2120–21

Feb. 8. 70

Sr

I had yours of ye 4th Instant. I am sorry to hear my Box is in danger of being lost: it was delivered, but it seemes not to ye master, as I ordered, but to his man. if it shall be lost (wch I beleeve not, but mislaied) we will take care yt you have, as soone as may be, ye same things sent you again.

I have not yet received any answer to my Enquiries sent into Craven concerning ye old men, nor can I affirme for a certain truth ye just number of their yeares, but it was said to me they were 6 score yeares old; their names are————Montgomery living in Skipton & Thomas Wiggen of ye Parish of Carleton. but more, I hope, an other time.

The *Julus* I named to you for a likely Insect to afford an Acid juice is indeed a *Multipeda* or *Millepeda* as Pliny calls ym, but no *Scolopendra*: ours being a harmlesse Insect & those are armed wth dangerous *Forcipes*.[1] If I had had either Aldrovandus or Mouffet by me I should have spared my owne Title & sent you those Authors *synominas* [*synonymias*]. they have noe English name yt I know off: but besides ye Caracteristical notes of ye Title I gave ym, they may be well known from all other *Multipedas*, in yt their innumerable leggs are as small as haire & white & in going they are moved like Waves. they are not rare amongst dryer rubbish. their bodies are as round as whip-cords.

Concerning ye bleeding of ye Sycamore, be pleased yt [I] acquaint you wth ye following Experiment of very late date. The 1. instant it froze, ye wind at North; ye frost & wind continued (some little snow now & then falling) ye 2.3.4.5.6. untill ye 7th ith morning, when ye wind came about to ye South East & ye weather broake up a pace. ye sycamores bled not all this while, but ye 7th about noon all Trees of ye kind bledd very freely both at ye Twiggs & body & I strucke above a dozen.

at this same critical season I was willing to repeat ye experiment upon other Trees & to this end I forthwith strucke ye Hawthorn, Hazel, Wild-

Rose, Goose berry bush, Aple Tree, Cherry tree, Blather-nutt,[2] Apricock, Cherry-Laurel, Vine, Wall-nutt, yet none bled, but ye last named & yt but faintly in comparison of ye Sycamore. this is consonant to our former experiments & if it did happen, as I said in my former letter,[3] yt these Sycamores bled not all this Winger afore at ye wounds made at ye first of November, I doe now think yt if new wounds had been still made at every breatch of frost, some signes, at least of our Yorke trees bleeding, might have been discovered before now but I affirme noe more then I have seen & tryed.

In all ye Monuments of ye Ancients, soe happily collected by ye great industrie of Plinie, I find but few instances of this nature: amongst those few there is one yt is registered wth two or three remarkable circumstances to our purpos. He tell us, yt ye Phisitians of old, when they had a mind to draw ye juice of ye Mulberrie Tree, were wont to strike it skin-deep only & yt about two howers after sun rise: this experiment is twice mentioned by him & in both places as a strange phaenomenon. we might make our Comment upon ye places, but for this time are content only to transcribe ye Texts. lib. 16. cap. 38.

"Mirum hic (cortex) in Moro, medicis succum quaerentibus, fere hora diej secunda, lapide incussus manat, altius fractus siccus videtur." lib. 23.c.7. "Mora in Ægypto et Cypro suj generis, ut diximus, largo succo abundant, summo cortice desquammato: altiore plaga siccantur, mirabilj natura."[4]

I shall be glad to heare at your best leisure ye progresse of this Inquiry. Sr I am

Your most humble servant
Martin Lister

ADDRESS
 These
For his honoured Friend
  Mr. H. Oldenburgh att his
  house in ye Pallmall
   at
   London

POSTMARK FE 10

NOTES

Reply to Letter 1622. In *Phil. Trans.*, no. 68, it is wrongly attributed to Ray.
1 "Pincers."
2 *Staphylea pinnata*, bladdernut.
3 Letter 1609.
4 "It is remarkable that when this bark of the mulberry tree is struck with a stone by physicians seeking its juice, about the second hour of the day, it runs out; but when struck deeper it seems dry" . . . "The mulberry trees in Egypt and Cyprus pour out freely the juice of their kind, as we have said, when the upper bark is removed; but with a deeper wound they are dry, by a strange trick of nature."

1628
Ray to Oldenburg

8 February 1670/1

From the original in Royal Society MSS. R 1, nos. 11 and 12
Partly printed in Ray, *Further Correspondence*, p. 54

Sr,

Whereas in my former[1] there is a passage liable to exception & mistake viz. *Spirit of salt & oil of sulphur dropt upon Cichory flowers did not cause them to change colour*, for the clearing thereof, you may please to take notice, that it is to be understood of the flowers entire & unbruised: for any blew flowers being a little bruised, & then a drop of spirit of salt or any other acid spirit let fall thereon, will turn instantly red. The reason is obvious, for that the leaves of the flowers (as all the other parts of the plant) being invested with a skin or membrane, the liquor dropped thereon cannot easily penetrate it, & so commix it self with the interior juice or pulp. Hence it is that if those flowers be put into cold vineger, especially if the weather be cool, they will not change colour for a considerable time; but if you heat the vineger they will change immediately. Whether the Ants doe only drop this tinging liquor upon the surface of the flowers, or thrusting their stings into the body of the flower doe by them convey it immediately into the interiour included juice we cannot yet determine, but referre to future observation when the time of the year will afford us flowers. What diseases they are wherein Mr Fisher hath with successe exhibited this juice when I have consulted him I shall acquaint you.

Concerning the manner of Spiders projecting their threads I received the following account from Dr Hulse, from whom (to doe him right) I must acknowledge I had the first notice of this particular wch was not long after communicated to me by another ingenious friend, whose Lr I formerly sent you to be imparted to the Society.[2] Nor is it any great wonder that inquisitive persons applying themselves to observe & consider the same subjects should make the same discoveries.[3]

"I have" (saith he) "seen them shoot their webs 3 yds. long before they begin to sail, & then they will (as it were fly) away incredibly swift; wch *Phaenomenon* doth somewhat puzzle me, seeing oftentimes the air doth not [move] a quarter so fast as they seem to fly. Mostly they project their threads single without any dividing or forking at all to be seen in them; sometimes they will shoot the thread upward, & will mount up with it in a line almost perpendicular, & at other times they project it in line parallell to the plain of ye horizon, as you may often see by their threads that run from one tree to another, & likewise in chambers from one wall to another. I confesse this observation at first made me think that they could fly, because I could not conceive how a thread could be drawn so parallell to ye Horizon between two walls or trees as above said, unlesse the spider flew through ye air in a streight line. The way of forking their threads may be expressed by the following figure.

What reason should be given of this dividing I know not, except that their threads being thus winged become better able to sustein them in the air. They will often fasten their threads in severall places to the things they creep upon; the manner is by beating their tailes against them as they creep along wch may be understood by this line ─•─•─•─•─ By this frequent beating in of their thread among the asperities of the place where they creep they either secure it agst the wind, that it be not easily blown away, or else whilst they hang by it, if one stick breaks another holds fast, so that they doe not fall to the ground."

Midleton
Feb. 8.

ADDRESS
     For Mr Henry
        Oldenbergh

NOTES

Oldenburg has twice endorsed MS. R 1, no. 12, with the date 8 February 1670/1. This is a single sheet with the address at the back. MS. R 1, no. 11, contains the account of spiders; in Letter Book IV, 201–3, the two sheets are run together to make a continuous letter, as here.

1 Letter 1593.
2 Lister; see Letter 1479, note 2, and Letter 1503, note 1.
3 A sentence is here crossed out and rendered illegible.

1629
Oldenburg to Dodington

10 February 1670/1

From the memorandum in Royal Society MS. D 1, no. 18

Rec. Febr. 3. 1670/71
Answ. Febr. 10. Kept no copy

Desired to have Gottignies Dioptricks and Fabri in Archimedem; but to stay ye sending of Telesc. and Microscopes, till further order: To send bulky pacquets by sea.

Promised to send M. Boyles little Latin tract of ye admir. raref. of ye Air.

NOTES

Dodington's Letter 1602 is also endorsed as answered on this date.
Reply to Letters 1591 and 1602.

1630
Malpighi to Oldenburg

10 February 1670/1

From the original in Royal Society MS. Malpighi Letters I, no. 9
Printed in *Phil. Trans.*, no. 71 (22 May 1671), 2149–50

Eruditissimo et Praeclarissimo Viro
Domino Enrico Oldenburg Regiae Societatis Anglicanae Secretario
Marcellus Malpighius S.P.

Desideratissimus de respiratione Doctissimi Thrustoni libellus tandem
ad meas devenit manus,[1] ubi propugnatam vidi meam circa pulmonum substantiam sententiam; quapropter Te enixe rogo, ut ipsi meo
nomine officiosam dicas salutem, plurimasque eidem referas gratas pro
spontanea, et honorifica meorum dictorum tutela. Miratus sum valde,
animadversionum Auctori in testitudinum, lacertarum et ranarum sectioni-
bus non occurrisse commercium inter bronchia, et pulmones, quas vesiculas, a laxitate exterioris pulmonum membranae obortas, vocat:[2] cum
immissa in tracheam fistula, et simul insufflato aere, pulmones eidem tra-
cheae appensi hinc inde circa cor turgeant, quod et ad libitum animalis
frequenter etiam accidit: Hi etiam, dum aere turgent, si filo innodentur, ut
siccescant, secti, patenter oculis cellulas, et vesiculas, evidenter membraneas, exhibent. Et licet in ranis brevis sit bronchiorum processus, a laringe
tamen bini ductus, semicircularibus aliquot annulis constati, in membraneas vesiculas hiant, et ita succedit inspiratio, et expiratio; at in testitudine,
lacertis, et similibus oblonga trachea, in binos subdivisa ramos, aerem
pulmonaribus vesiculis subministrat. Scio in ranis prope os, hinc inde
binas interdum turgentes erumpere vesiculas (procul tamen a pulmonibus),
quae buccae sunt appendices, et aere interdum, a pulmonibus in oris
cavitatem expiratione propulso, foras exsilire.

Circa exaratos pulmones reticularem musculum locari scias, cuius
carneos plexus, sinus, et vesiculas ambientes alias ruditer delineavi.[3] Huius
mirabilis contextus patet in ranis, et lacertis praecipue, nam multiplices
carnei lacerti[4] per longum producuntur, et transversaliter elongatis fibris
invicem continuantur; intermediae vero areae reticularibus carneis plexi-
bus ulterius occupantur, non absmili ritu, ac in arborum foliis accidit:
Retis autem enarrata[5] haec minora spatia rectis postremo fibris, quasi

brevibus tendinibus pervaduntur. Mirabilis hic musculus non exteriorem tantum pulmonum ambit regionem, sed interiores quascunque vesiculas, et sinus circumdat, ita ut suo motu singulas pulmonis partes comprimendo expirationem sonumque promoveat. Haec eadem structura in pulmonibus perfectorum animalium proportionaliter observatur, et in agnorum extremis praecipue lobulis, aere turgidis, et adhuc mollibus, patet. Huius occasione communicandum tibi duxi. lienis fibras, quae tot ingenia torsere, nequaquam nerveas (quod et alias etiam autumavi) sed carneas esse, ita ut ex carneo exteriori involucro, et productis transversaliter fibris mirabilis fiat musculus, lienis cellulas comprimens, quo sanguis per splenicum ramum propellatur, non absimili structura, ac ritu, qualis in grandioribus cordis auriculis observatur. Carnei etenim lacerti,[4] transversum ducti, suarum fibrarum implicatione rete efformant, membraneas cellulas comprimens, suisque extremis finibus mirabiliter productis carneum involucrum constituunt.

Parum absimili structura equinos praecipue testes Natura ditavit: Interior etenim ipsorum tunica carneas fibras, seu extensum musculum in sui meditullio, una cum varicosis vasis continet, quae diversas inclinationes, ut in Liene, habentes per transversum productae, et reticulariter implicitae intestinulorum congeriem firmant, et comprimunt. Pauca haec et inordinata in mei amoris, et obsequij testimonium habeas deprecor. Vale. Dabam Bononiae Die 20 febr. 1671 [N.S.]

ADDRESS
   Eruditissimo et Praeclarissimo Viro Dno. Enrico
   Olenburg Regiae Societ. Anglicanae Secretario
   Londini

TRANSLATION

Marcello Malpighi sends many greetings to the very learned and famous Mr. Henry Oldenburg, Secretary of the English Royal Society

The greatly desired book on respiration of the very learned Thruston has at last come to my hands,[1] in which I see that he has propounded my opinion concerning the substance of the lungs; for which reason I earnestly beg you to return him most dutiful greetings on my behalf and to thank him many times for the spontaneous and honorific defense of my words. I am very much astonished that the author of the *Animadversions* should not, in dissecting tortoises, lizards, and frogs, have encountered the communication between the bronchi and the lungs, which he calls vesicles arising from the looseness of the lungs' external membrane.[2] For when a pipe is put into the trachea and air is blown in, the lungs attached to the trachea swell out on either side of the heart, which also happens frequently at the animal's volition. Again, if the lungs are tied with a thread when full of air, so that they dry out, and are cut through, they plainly display to the eye little cells and vesicles which are clearly membranous. And although the bronchial process is short in frogs, two ducts from the larynx made of a few semicircular rings open into the membranous vesicles, and thus it is that inspiration and expiration take place satisfactorily. But in tortoises, lizards, and similar creatures the rather long trachea is divided into two branches and so furnishes air to the pulmonary vesicles. I know that in frogs, near to and on either side of the mouth, two vesicles sometimes swell out, yet far from the lungs; these are appendages to the cheek and are sometimes distended by air which has been driven into the hollow of the mouth by expiration.

You know that there is a netlike muscle around the dissected lungs whose fleshy plexuses surrounding the sinuses and vesicles I have sketched crudely elsewhere.[3] The marvelous reticulation of this is evident in frogs and particularly in lizards, for multiple fleshy muscles[4] extend lengthwise and are interconnected by fibers running transversely. The intervening spaces are further occupied by fleshy reticular plexuses, in a manner similar to what happens in leaves. However, these lesser spaces[5] of the network are pervaded in the last place by straight fibers almost like short tendons. This wonderful muscle not only surrounds the external part of the lung but also certain internal vesicles and sinuses, so that its movement effects expiration and sound by compressing every part of the lung. The same structure is, to a degree, observed in the lungs of perfect animals and especially it is evident in the outermost lobes of lambs when these are filled with air and still soft.

It is to be imparted to you at this opportunity that I have found that the fibers of the spleen, which have so often tormented men's minds, are not at all sinewy (as I too once thought) but fleshy, so that a wonderful muscle is formed from the fleshy outer sheath and the transversely extended fibers; this compresses the cellules of the spleen, by which means the blood is driven through the splenic vein; in action and structure this muscle is not unlike that found in the larger auricles of the heart. For the fleshy muscles,[4] running transversely, form a network by the interlacing of their fibers, compressing the membranous cellules, and their extreme ends, marvelously extended, form a fleshy sheath.

Nature has enriched the testes (of the horse, particularly) with a rather similar structure. For their inner tunic contains fleshy fibers, or muscle extended into its very middle, together with varicose vessels; these fibers, running in different directions (as they do in the spleen), being extended transversely and interwoven like a net, strengthen the mass of intestinules and compress it.

I beg you to accept these few and disorganized remarks as a testimony to my love and respect.

Bologna, 20 February 1671 [N.S.]

ADDRESS

To the very learned and famous
Mr. Henry Oldenburg, Secretary
of the English Royal Society
                London

NOTES

1 Malachi Thruston's *De respirationis usu primario diatriba* (London, 1670) was mentioned to Malpighi in Letter 1368 (Vol. VI); no record of the dispatch of this book remains.
2 These were printed by Thruston, with his own answers to them, on Malpighi's behalf. The author of the criticisms was Sir George Ent, who did not maintain (as Malpighi seems to have supposed) that the frog has no lungs, but that the "vesicles" are not part of the structure of the lungs.
3 That is, in his *De pulmonibus observationes anatomicae* (Bologna, 1661), which has a single, rather poor, figure.
4 Literally, the word means "biceps," as it still does in modern Italian. Adelmann renders it by "bundles" (Vol. I, 364).
5 "These explained lesser spaces" does not make sense; perhaps Malpighi meant "just mentioned."

1631

Oldenburg to Sachs

10 February 1670/1

From the memorandum in Royal Society MS. O 2, no. 46

Sent a duplicate d. 10. Febr. 1670/71.

NOTE

This is written in the margin between the main body and the postscript of Letter 1620.

1632
Oldenburg to Lister

11 February 1670/1

From the original in Bodleian Library MS. Lister 34, ff. 7–8

Sir,

I am sorry I troubled you wth ye news of ye not-delivery of yr boxe, because it is come to hand since: but the viviparous flye was found altogether shaken into smal pieces, whilst the litle curious snailes were all very safe and entire. As I cannot but renew my humble thanks to you for yr continued favors and cares for our concerns, and particularly for yr late communications relating to Spiders, Pismires, Iulus's, as well as to ye Bleeding of Sycamores, and other Trees; so I must use this further freedom, to intreat you, yt, if you can spare any of yesd viviparous flyes, you would please to recruite yt loss, at yr conveniency. I have not stuck to send away to ye presse, among other things for the Transactions of February, yr contributions concerning ye Sycamores, and yr directions for finding more insects yt afford an acid liquor:[1] wch, I am persuaded, will be as welcome to others, as it was to ye R. Society at their last meeting;[2] who commanded me to assure you of their affectionate sense of yr ingenious observations. They were very copious at yt time in discoursing upon the motion of Sap in Trees, and amongst other particulars, upon the Question, Whether there be a circulation of their Juyce, as there is of ye Bloud in Animals; concerning wch it was propos'd, yt some Experiments should be made to decide it. A way was suggested, of making streight ligatures wth metallin rings about twiggs and branches, to see, whether there would be a turgescence on both sides of ye ligature, etc. I am confident, Sir, you have curiosity sufficient to make you devise some effectual way to try this experiment effectually; nor doe I doubt, but you will impart to us ye success of yr tryals, you shall have made of this nature.

'Tis yr ingenuity, yt makes me persist in these important sollicitations, knowing, yt a person of yr frame of spirit will easily pardon them to Sir

Yr humble and faithf. servt
Oldenburg

London Febr. 11. 1671.

When you have more certainty of those aged persons, I shall be glad to share in it, not doubting, but you will spread this inquiry as farr as you can in those parts. I was much pleased wth yr taking notice of what Pliny writes of Mulberries; but shall yet more, when you shall impart yr comment on it: And I hope, you will also make us participant of what you mention you have considered and experimented of ye change of Colors in Flowers. etc.

ADDRESS
    To his honour'd friend
        Martin Lister Esquire
        At his house wthout Mickel-
        gate barr
            in
                Yorke

POSTMARK FE 11

NOTES

    Reply to Letter 1627.
1   Letters 1609 and 1627.
2   On 9 February 1670/1, when Letter 1609 was read.

1633
Vogel to Oldenburg
February 1670/1
From the original in Royal Society MS. F 1, no. 30

Viro Nobilissimo & Doctissimo
HENRICO OLDENBURGIO
S.P.D.
Martinus Fogelius

Quo diutius Responsum tuum, Nobilissime Vir, expectavi, & quo magis de salute Morhofii[1] solicitus fui, eo gratiores mihi acciderunt literae Tuae, quas Clarissimus hic Vir una cum libellis Januario proximo reddidit.[2] Utinam Paisenius etiam suos libros & literas accipere potuisset!

Sed mors eheu immatura hunc praeclarissimae, summaeque spei Juvenem superiore Octobre, nobis nihil tale tum cito exspectantibus, sustulit, cum paucos tantum dies decubuisset ex Febre Intermittente. Cujus exemplo (mallem alio) & hoc docemus, quod Intermittentes Febres etiam Malignae sint, cum enim primus paroxysmus, qui Febrem indicabat, ingrueret, statim delirabat. rediit altero die iterum ad se, & sacra Synaxi usus fuit. 3º iterum deliravit. cum noctu illa ipsum accederem, epilepticos motus conjunctos observavi, nulla spe salutis relicta. nam tertium paroxysmum Mors anticipavit. Hic fuit exitus mihi unice cari Paisenii, quem studiorum philosophicorum solum hic habui socium, quemque unum Sapientiae solidioris praeceptis olim imbui, ut deinceps in Jungii scriptis edendis me adjuvaret.

Specimen laborum horum exhibere voluit, ad quod praecipue ferebatur, digerendis scilicet schedis philosophicis. Et si supervixisset, hac aestate forsan absolvisset. Interim Literae ad Erasmum Bartolinum recte curatae sunt.[3]

Vix dubito, quin & alia Corpora praebitura sint similia Phaenomena Selenitae Islandici. An non & Crystallus in eam figuram aptata eodem modo radios refringeret?

An Cervisiae Anglicae praeparandae modum nemo docuit?

proximis Nundinis pauci libri prodiere. Dissertatione de Croco videris.[4] de Pestis Veneno corrosivo Dissertatio non inelegans Amstelodi impressa forsan etiam jam ad vos delata est.[5]

Ephemerides Anglicae imprimi coeptae sunt Hafniae a Danielo Pauli; at interpreto Scoto, sed minime, ut mihi quidem videtur, idoneo.[6] Ut audio, jam favor remisit, forsan quod non omnia aeque intelligat. Mitto prima philyram. Ultra 4 nondum processerunt operae Typographicae. Voluerunt initium facere ab anno 1669. quia audiverunt, Te eundem laborem velle sumere. Si reliquas desideras, commoda occasione mittam.

Ubi de Hispanorum Toxico quidam ab amico tuo resciveris, fac ut quamprimum ea cognoscam. gratissimo animo agnoscum, per quos perfecerim.

Libellum Boilei de Qualitatibus Morhofius tolit, editionique jam paratum habet. pro Valentini[7] &c. libello gratias ago maximas.

Lynceorum Historiae Volumen 1 Editioni paratum habeo. Si Schulzium Bibliopolam velles ad ejus Editionem hortari, citius sine dubio prodiret, & ad eandem absolvendum, majus Calcar adderes. Continet autem hoc Historiam primo generalem hujus Societatis, deinde[8] Lynceographum Principis Caesii, in quo institutum, & leges ipsorum prolixe describuntur, hactenus a nemine editum.⁹ Subjungentur Acta, itidem hactenus non edita.¹⁰

Alterum Volumen cujuslibet Lyncei vitam exhibebit. quod erit variis Historiis Philosophicis gratum.¹¹ Obtulit Tevenotius Regios Typos. Sed ipse Editioni praeesse volo.¹²

Quae Amicus tuus Parisiensis de Pauliadae¹³ conatibus retulit, a me habeat, si ille est Nobilissimus Justellus.

Habeo penes me inepti cujusdam hominis, sed mire ambitiosi Tractatum de Motu manuscriptum, quem ut ad vos mitterem, per amicum rogavit. Quod si has ineptias desideras videre, submittam.

Quod Morhofium tibi commendatum habere volueris, gratias quas debeo ago referamque, quavis occasione. Vale, Nobilissime Vir, et me amare perge.

ADDRESS
   A Monsr
      Monsr Grubendal
            a
         Londres

TRANSLATION

Martin Vogel presents many greetings to the very noble and learned Henry Oldenburg

Your letter which the distinguished Mr. Morhof¹ delivered to me together with some little volumes at the end of January was the more welcome to me in that I had long awaited your reply,² noble Sir, and had been anxious about Mr. Morhof's well-being. Would that Paisen too might receive his letter and books! But alas, death prematurely robbed us of this exceedingly worthy and most hopeful young man last October, when we were without any fear of such a speedy loss, after he had been only a few days confined to bed by an intermittent fever. From this case (and I wish it were not so) we learn this also, that even intermittent fevers may be malignant, for when the first paroxysm giving signs of the fever came violently [upon him], he at once became delirious. On the second day he returned to his senses and took the Holy Sacraments. On the third day he was delirious again. When I went to visit him that night I observed that epileptic convulsions were now added, so that no hope of his recovery was left. For the third paroxysm preceded his death. This was the end of Paisen, who had been so uniquely dear to me, my sole companion in philosophical studies, whom I had brought up on the principles of solid scholarship in order that he might in the future assist me in editing the papers of Jungius.

He wished to furnish some specimen of those labors to which he was chiefly devoted, that is, the putting in order of the philosophical papers. And if he had lived longer he would perhaps have finished it this summer. Meanwhile, the letter to Erasmus Bartholin has been properly taken care of.[3]

I hardly doubt that all substances will yield phenomena similar to those of the Icelandic spar. Would not [another] crystal of the same configuration refract the rays in the same way?

Has no one explained the way of making English beer? At the last Fair few books appeared. You shall see the dissertation on saffron.[4] A not inelegant essay on the corrosive poison of plague has been printed at Amsterdam and perhaps has been conveyed to you too.[5]

The printing of the English *Transactions* has been begun at Copenhagen by Daniel Pauli, translated by a Scotsman who was, it seems to me, ill-suited [to the task].[6] As I hear, he has already resigned the employment, perhaps because he does not understand everything equally well. I send the first sheet. The printing has not yet proceeded beyond four sheets. They intend to make a start with the year 1669, because they have heard that you intend to take up the same task. If you want more, I will send it at a convenient opportunity.

When you have learned something about the Spanish poison from your friend, let me know as soon as may be. I shall cheerfully acknowledge from whom I have perfected [my account of it].

Morhof brought over Boyle's little book on [*Cosmic*] *Qualities*, and has already prepared it for publication. I give you many thanks for the little book of [Basil] Valentine,[7] etc. I have Volume I of the *History of the Lyncei* prepared for publication. If you would urge the bookseller Schulz to publish it, it would no doubt come out the sooner and give a great impetus towards its completion. This first [volume] contains, however, the general history of this Society, next[8] the *Linceographia* of Prince Cesi which has never yet been printed, in which their objects and laws are described at length.[9] To it are added their transactions, also unpublished hitherto.[10]

The second volume will set out the life of every one of the Lincei, which will be useful to various histories of philosophy.[11] Thevenot has obtained the King's Printer, but I wish to forestall his publication.[12] What your friend at Paris related of Pauli's[13] endeavors he may have had from me, if that friend is the noble Justel.

I have by me a manuscript treatise on motion by a certain incompetent person who is strangely ambitious and wishes me to send it to you by a friend. If you wish to look over his blundering I will agree.

I give you due thanks for being agreeable to Morhof, and will make a like return when an occasion arises. Farewell, noble Sir, and continue to love me.

ADDRESS

To Mr. Grubendol
London

NOTES

Reply to Letter 1553.

1 See Letter 1542.
2 See Letter 1498, of 28 July 1670.
3 Letter 1552.
4 *Crocologia*, by Johann Ferdinand Hertodt (Jena, 1671), was reviewed in *Phil. Trans.*, no. 74 (14 August 1671), 2236–38.
5 Charles de la Font, *Dissertationes duae medicae de veneno pestilenti* (Amsterdam, 1671) is noted in *Phil. Trans.*, no. 73 (17 July 1671), 2210–11.
6 See Letter 1638.
7 See Letter 1553, note 3.
8 In the letter, "d̄d̄" only.
9 The "Linceografo" of Prince Cesi, founder of the Accademia dei Lincei, was begun by him in its first years (1603–1609) and worked on during the rest of his life. It has never been published entire though it was used by Baldassare Odescalchi in compiling *Memorie istorico critiche dell'Accademia de'Lincei* (Rome, 1806). It was to have been a full and philosophical account of the constitution and objects of his Academy. (See G. Gabrieli, "Il Carteggio Linceo, Parte 2" in *Memoire della R. Accademia Nazionale dei Lincei* [Classe di scienze morali, etc.], Ser. 6, Vol. VIII [1939], pp. 133–34).
10 Johannes Eck (or Heck, born *c.* 1577), the first of the Lincei after Cesi himself, compiled "Gesta Lynceorum," which has also remained in manuscript.
11 Thirty-two Lincei were chosen—Galileo was the most distinguished of them—before the Academy collapsed in 1630.
12 We cannot explain this, as none of Melchisédec Thevenot's publications have any relation to the Lincei.
13 We have presumed that the allusion is to Daniel Pauli, the printer mentioned below in Letter 1638, note 1.

1634
Lister to Oldenburg
15 February 1670/1

From the original in Royal Society MS. L 5, no. 26, and the copy in Letter Book IV, 211–19
Printed in *Phil. Trans.*, no. 70 (17 April 1671), 2121–23 and 2132–36

Yorke, 15. Febr. 1670.

Sr

Yours of ye 11 instant I had. I am glad to heare ye little Box at length came safe to your hands; as for ye Viviparous Fly I sent you ye choice & most intire of my store, a Male & a Female; indeed they may well be dry & apt to be shaken to pieces I having had ym by me 4 yeares. I feare it will be April at soonest, before I can send you any of ym; yet being fresh caught they will be tougher and endure carriage better.

The Julus I named for a probable Insect, to afford an acid juice, will not like a Pismire change a blew flower red, at least soe farr as I have yet had meanes to make ye experiment: yet I dare say it will yield a smart & powerfull liquor, if my sleight way of examination deceive me not, for I have not mett wth any Insect more keen in ye Nose.

February 11th (to continue our experiments concerning ye motion of ye sap of Trees) all was here covered wth a white Frost, betwixt 9 & 11 ith morning ye weather changing I made ye experiments wch follow upon ye Sycamore, Walnut, Maple. A twigg cutt asunder would bleed very freely from yt part remaining to ye Tree, & for ye part separated it would be altogather dry & show noe signes of moisture, although we held it some pretty time wth ye cut end downwards; but if this separated twigg was never soe little tipped at ye other end wth a knife, it would forthwith shew moisture at both ends. The same day late ith after noone ye weather very open & warme; a twigg cutt off in like manner as in ye morning, would shew noe moisture at all from any part. These experiments we repeated very many times wth constant & like successe on all ye Trees above mentioned. I entered this Experiment wth those Quaeries for ye next opportunity. 1. Whether a twigg or ye small part of a root cutt asunder, will not bleed faster, upon ye breaking up of a Frost, from ye part remaining to ye Tree, than from ye part separated & whether ye part separated will bleed at all and shew no more signes of moisture than a twigg cutt from ye topp of ye Tree, unlesse yt small root be likewise cut off at ye other end alsoe. 2. Whether when it shall happen that a Sycamore shall be found to bleed upon ye setting in a great Frost ye topp twiggs & small roots will not both of ym bleed freelier from ye parts separated in proportion to their bignesse 3. And if it shall not Soe prove in ye Tryal, yt in cold weather ye sap moves inwards from root & branch to ye Trunk, & yt upon ye breaking of a Frost ye sap moves outward, from ye Trunk to ye extremities of both root & branch, I say if this prove not soe, whether there be any different motions of sap at a time in ye divers parts of one & ye same Tree; & where such motions of sap begin & whither they tend. 4. whether ye sap when it will run moves longer in ye branches than in ye roots, or whether it begin not to move in all parts of a Tree at a time & rest every where at a time. 5. when it rests whether it retires to ye body of ye Tree from ye roots & branches or sinkes down to ye root, or is any waye spent by insensible steames, or is quiet & lodged in every part of ye Tree in proportion.

I shall long to hear ye successe of your Experiments in ye Question of ye Circulation of Sap. I have many yeares been inclined to thinke yt there is some such motion in ye juices of Vegetables: ye reasons wch induced me are, 1. because I find yt all ye juice of a plant is not extravasate & loose & like water in a Spung, but yt there are apparent Vessells in plants, analogous to Veines in Animals, wch thing is most conspicuous & cleer in such plants whose juice, is either white or red or saffron-colored, for instance in each kind of juice we propose *Lactuca*,[1] *Atractilis*,[2] *Chelidonium majus*.[3] 2. because yt there are very many plants (& these last named are of ye number) whose juice seemes never to be at rest, but will spring at all times freely, as ye blood of Animals upon an incision. The way of Ligature by metalline Rings, is an expedient I have not used, but other Ligatures I have, upon a great number of our English Plants not without ye discovery of many curious phoenomena. The successe of an experiment of this nature upon *Cataputia minor Lob*.[4] was as follows. I tyed a silke thread upon one of ye branches of this plant, as hard as might be & not breake ye skin: there followed noe greater swelling, yt I could discern, on ye one side of ye silke than on ye other, although in often repeating ye experiment, some silkes were left howers & dayes unloosed, & yet ye dimple, ye thread had made in ye yielding branches, had a litle raised ye immediate sides, but both alike; ye plant in like manner would bleed very freely both above & under ye Ty: this was alsoe very remarkable, amongst other things, in this experiment, yt in drawing ye Rasour round about ye branch just above or below ye tye, ye milkie juice would suddainly spring out of infinite small holes besides ye made Orifice, for more than halfe an intch above & below ye tye. Wch seemes to argue, that though there was noe juice intercepted in appearance from any turgescence, as in ye like processe upon ye members of a sanguineous Animal, yet ye Veines were soe over thronged & full, yt a large Orifice, was not sufficient to discharge ye suddain impetus & pressure of a some-wayes streightned juice. I have endeavoured many wayes to discover ye configuration of ye Veines of Vegetables & ther other constituent parts & Texture, but enough of this in one Letter, I will tell you in ye next place my thoughts of Colours wch you desire.

Two things I conceive are cheifly aimed at in this Inquiry of Colours, ye one to encrease ye *Materia tinctoria*[5] & ye other, to fix, if possible those colours we either have already or shall herafter discover for Use. As to ye first, Animals & Vegetables, besides other parts of natural Historie, may abundantly furnish us. And in both these parts of N.H. some colours are *apparent*, as ye various colours of Flowers, & ye juices of Fruits etc. & ye *sanies*[6] of Animals. others are *latent* & discovered to us by ye effects ye several Families of salts & other things may have upon ym. Concerning ye Apparent colours of Vegetables & Animals, & ye various effects of different Salts in changing of ym from one colour to an other, we have many instances in Mr. Boile,[7] & if we might, with ye good leave of yt honourable & learned person range ym after our fashion, we should give you at least a new prospect of ym & observe to you ye conformity & agreement of ye effects of salts on ye divers parts of vegetables, viz. 1. yt acid salts advance ye colours of Flowers & Berries, yt is, according to ye experiments of Mr. Boile, they make ye infusions of Balaustiums[8] or pomegranate flowers and roses, clov-jillyflowers, mesereon,[9] pease-bloome, Violets, Cyanus-flowers,[10] of a fairer red; alsoe ye juices of ye berrie of Ligustrum,[11] of blackcherries, buckthorne berries, of a much fairer red; & to ye same purpose acid salts make noe great alterations upon ye white flowers of Jasmin & snowdroppes. 2. yt Urinous salts & Alcalys on ye contrary quite alter & change ye colours of ye same flowers now named, & ye juices of ye said berries alsoe from red to green, even Jasmin & snow dropps. 3. Again, yt in like manner Urinous spirits & Alcalys advance, at least do not quite spoyl ye colours of ye juices of leaves of Vegetables, of their wood & root. Thus mr Boile tells us, yt Urinous spirit & Alcalys makes ye yellow infusions of madder-roots red; of brazil wood, purplish, of Lignum nephriticum, blew; ye red infusion of Log-wood, purple; of ye leaves of Sena, red. 4. That on ye contrary, Acid salts quite alter & change ye said infusions from red or blew to a yellow. In ye next place we would note to you ye effects of salts upon Animals in ye production & change of colours; but ye instances are very few or none yt I meet wth in any authour. The Purple Fish[12] being quite out of use, & Cochineil & Kermes they are by most questioned, whether they are Animals or noe; but I thinke we may confidently beleeve ym both to be Insects yt is, wormes or Chrysalis of respective Flyes *in proxima faetura.*[13] We find yn & have tryed concerning Cochineil, wch of it selfe is red; yt upon ye affusion of oil of Vitriol, yt is an acid salt, it strikes ye most vivid crimson yt can be imagind: & wth Urinous Salts & Alcalys it will be again changed into an obscure colour 'twixt a Violet & a purple. Pliny some where tells us, yt ye Gaules in his time could dye wth Vegetables, what ye Romans wth soe much danger & pains sought for in ye bottome of ye sea. indeed, we find many Plants mentioned by ye same authour wch either are not known to us at this present or neglected.

To what we have breifly observed out of authours, we will subjoyne some
of our owne Considerations & Tryalls & first concerning ye *apparent*
colours in Flowers, we thinke we may inferr. 1. yt generally all red, blew
& white flowers are imediately upon ye affusion of an Alcaly changed into
a green colour & thence in processe of noe long time turned yellow. 2.
yt all ye parts of Vegetables wch are green, will in like manner strike a
yellow with an Alcaly. 3. yt what flowers are already yellow are not much
changed, if at all by an Alcaly or Urinous spirit. 4. ye blew seed-huskes of
Glastum sylvestre[14] old gathered & dry, diluted wth water staine a blew,
wch upon an affusion of Lye strikes a green, wch green or blew being
touched wth ye oil of Vitriol dyes a purple, all these 3 colours stand.[15] 5.
on ye topps of *Fungus tubulosus* soe called by Mr. Wray in his late Catalogue
of ye plants of England,[16] are certain red knotts, these upon ye affusion of
Lye will strike a purple & stand. As for ye *latent* colours in Vegetables &
Animals to be discovered to us by ye affusion of salts, they likewise noe
doubt are very many, we will sett downe only a few instances in both kinds,
wch have not been yt we know off, discovered or taken notice of by others.
Latent vegetable colours 1. ye milkie juice of *Lactuta sylvestris costa spinosa*[17]
& *sonchus asper & lavis*[18] upon ye affusion of Lye, will strike a vivid flame
colour or crimson, & after some time quite degenerate into a dirty yellow.
2. ye milke of *Cataputia minor* upon ye affusion of Lye, espeacially if it be
drawn wth a knife & have any time stood upon ye blade of it will strike a
purple or bloodred colour & by & by change into an ignoble yellow.
Latent animal Dyes 1. ye common haw-thorne Catterpillar will strike a
purple or carnation wth Lye & stands 2. ye heads of Beetles & Pismires
etc. will wth Lye strike ye same carnation colour & stand. 3. ye amber
coloured *Scolopendra* will give wth Lye a most beautiful & pleasant Azure
or Amesthestine & stand.

Lastly we might consider ye Fixing of colours for Use; but we are
willing to leave this to more experienced persons as alsoe ye philosophyz-
ing on ye particulars we have produced to better heads; some obvious inferences we may venture to take notice of. 1. yt in all ye instances above
mentioned, whether Vegetable or Animal, there is not one colour truly
fixed, however there may I conceive be some use made of ym, as they are
I say truly fixed, yt is proofe of salt & fire, for what seem to stand & be
Lye proofe, are either wholly destroyed by a different salt, or changed into
a much different colour, wch must needs prove a staine & blemish when it
shall happen in ye use of any of ym. 2 yt both ye apparent & latent colours
of Vegetables are fixable, an instance wherof we may observe in ye seed

huskes of *Glastum* & ye use dyers make of ye leaves after due praeparation. 3. it is probable from ye same instance yt we may learn from ye colour of some part of ye Fruit or seed, what colour ye leaves of any Vegetable & ye whole plant might be made to yield for our use. 4. yt ye latent colours of Vegetables are prae existant & not produced, from ye same instance of Woad & likewise from this yt ye milkie pure juice of *Lactuca sylvestris* does afford of it selfe a red *serum*. 5. yt ye change of colours in flowers is gradual and constant. 6. yt ye colours of flowers wch will not stand wth Lye, seem to be wholly destroyed by it & irrecoverable: thus it happens in ye experiment, yt one part of a Violet leafe upon ye affusion of Lye is changed very soon into a yellow & will never be revived into a red by an acid salt, but if an other part of ye same leafe be still given, it will be revived. 7. yt drynesse seemes to be a meanes, if not of fixing, yet bringing ye Vegetable colour into a condition of not wholly & suddainly perishing by ye otherwise destroying Alcaly. 8. yt those plants or animals wch will strike different & yet vivid colours upon ye affusion of different salts & stand, as ye Cochineil & Glastum, are probably of all others to be reckned ye best Materials.

It would have been much safer to have put these inferences in ye fashion of Quaeries, but, besides yt I affirme noe more than matter of Fact, it is lawfull for our encouragement (as my Lord Bacon advises) to set up Rests by ye way & refresh our selves wth looking backe, though perhapps we have not much advanced. You will be please to excuse ye little coherence I have used in these Notes & attribute it to ye readinesse & affection I have to answer such Inquiries as you put to me. I never did yet make this subject any thing of my businesse, but ye desire I have to search after & examine ye Medicinal qualities of things in Nature has by ye by presented me wth such phaenomena, as I was not willing to leave unnoted, nor to refuse ym you, though in a confused way, because you desire ym. To conclude however immethodical & barren these papers may seem, yet ye consideration of ym has led me to a way of fixing Colours, wch I willingly forbeare to relate, untill I may have an opportunity of shewing ye Experiment before ye R.S. I have found out a colour most exquisitely blacke & comparable to ye best Inke even for ye Use of ye pen & wch will not change either by fire or salts. This an English Vegetable yeilded me & for ought I know (for I have not repeated ye Tryal on any thing else) ye like method will succeed to good purpos. I am sr

your most humble servant
Martin Lister

ADDRESS
    These
    For his honoured Friend Mr Oldenburgh
        at his house in ye Palmal at
            London

NOTES

The edge of the paper is worn and torn in several places; the missing words have been restored from the Letter Book copy.
    Reply to Letter 1632.
 1 Lettuce.
 2 Oldenburg has written "wild safron," but in Parkinson it is given as a thistle.
 3 Greater celandine.
 4 Oldenburg has correctly identified this as spurge.
 5 Materials for dyeing.
 6 Any watery fluid of animal origin.
 7 In his *Experiments and Considerations touching Colours* (London, 1664).
 8 Pomegranate tree.
 9 Dwarf bay or flowering spurge olive.
10 Cornflowers, bluebottles, or bachelor's-buttons.
11 Privet.
12 Murex.
13 "about to come to birth."
14 Wild woad.
15 That is, are fast.
16 For the book see Letter 1525, note 8; but as Letter 1738 (Vol. VIII) makes plain, Ray described (p. 217) "*Muscus tubulosus*" or coralline-moss.
17 Wild lettuce with prickly ribs.
18 Prickly and smooth sow thistle.

1635
Oldenburg to Willughby
18 February 1670/1

From the memorandum in Royal Society MS. L 5, no. 26

Sent ye Experiments upon Sycamores[1] to Mr Willughby Feb. 18.

NOTE

This letter is acknowledged in Willughby's reply, Letter 1655.
 1 Lister's; see Letter 1634.

1636
Flamsteed to Oldenburg
18 February 1670/1

From the original in Royal Society MS. F 1, no. 67

Derby: Feb: 18 1670:

Worthy Sr

I had yrs of ye 4th instant some while since but delayd to give an answer because I hoped to gaine time to calculate some such appulses as Mr Hooke desires; I find a visible application of ye moon, to Venus on June ye 29 in ye morneing and to Jupiter on ye 20 of September before noone too, of both which if I had not beene hindred by a distemper, which seizd me riseing to observe ye appulse of tuesday morneing last I had intended to have given a good account: however I shall send yu ye praedictions of them time enough before ye appearance If providence concede mee health & leasure.

I find no appulses of ye moone to any of ye bigger fixed starrs save Spica this yeare: in all her applications to which I find none, save those in my papers which yu have allready, that will be observeable: but if Mr Hooke thinkes hee can by day observe her applications to ye Pleiades or starres of ye second or 3d magnitude[1] I shall bestow some houres paines to find him matter for ye experiment which if it succeed I hope wee may hereafter have more accurate observations for the restoreing of ye lunar numbers then as yet wee possesse: Sr if Mr Hooke esteeme not his invention as a secret to be concealed I would begg yt hee would bee pleasd to gratifie me with a communication of his method of observeing, & hee shall find mee alwaies readie to recompense with ye communication of such praedictions as may shew ye diurnall appulses, or any thinge else which may occur in ye course of my studies worth his knowledge, if hee can performe well in ye day, his way will be of singular use & great encouragement to such Astronomers as love ye science, yet like not ye practise; because it requires them to breake theire reste in makeing nocturnall observations: but however exceeding acceptable to my selfe because my weake body & frequent distempers permitte mee not to waite in ye colds of the night for observations: And further, by day, ye times & appearances may be more exactly observed with ye helpe of any vulgar assistant, when for night observations

tis necessary to have an expert & skillfull companion: pray therefore if
Mr Hooke be not nice of his method desire him to impart it to me; if hee
be pray urge him not much; aut ab alio discam, aut inveniam.[2] As for
Monsr: Hevelius I esteeme him a person of that candor and ingenuite, as
not to [grow] angry at any one, who shall civilly and without gall, informe
him of his errors: & hee cannot be so disintelligent as not [to] perceive, that
his freinds noteing them in a civil, may prevent his enemies from commen-
teing on them in a detracting way: but I resolve to acquiesce in what yu
say & submitte all waies my judgement to yours whilest I can be

> yr most obliged servant to command
> *John Flamsteed*

Pray when yu write againe let mee know if any of ye praedicted phaenomena have beene observed.

ADDRESS
> To Henry Oldenburge Esqr;
> at his house in the Middle
> of ye Pell mell in st Jameses
>   neare Westminster these present

NOTES

1 There is not much record of Hooke's astronomical activity at this period, but on 9
March 1670/1 he reported to the Society that he had observed "the congress of the
moon" with a third magnitude star, the middle one of three in the tail of Aries, and
found his observation "pretty near to that calculated by Mr. Flamsteed."
2 "I shall either learn it from another, or find it out [myself]."

1637
Hevelius to Oldenburg

22 February 1670/1

From the original in Royal Society MS. H 2, no. 24

Illustri Viro
Domino Henrico Oldenburg
Illustrissimae Regiae Societatis Secretario
J. Hevelius Salutem

Literae Tuae die 18 Januarij cum inclusis[1] optime mihi sunt redditae, quas per amicum Hungariam perferri animo lubentissimo curavi; quod Tibi significandum esse putavi; inprimis cum negotium pariter habeam, quod Londini expediri debeat, non dubito, quin hanc molestiam haud aegre in Te suscipias. Rogatus enim sum ab Illustrissimo Domino Mareschallo et Magno duci Exercitium Regni Poloniae[2] ut sibi fieri curarem Mycroscopium tale omnino, quale mihi anno praeterito transmisistis a domino Cock constructum. Qui cum Literis Literatisque propensi favet, volui quantocyus eius desiderio morem gerere. Quare, cum alia occasione id exequendi plane destituar, rogo quam humanissime, ut apud dominum Cock meo nomine tale expoliri atque construi cures; sed lentibus singulari diligentia elaboratis, imo meis si fieri potest melioribus; si tale forsitan ipsi obtingat elaborare, poteris me postmodum ea de re admonere, ut illud mihi reservare, meum vero eius loco transmittere dicto domino Mareschallo possem; sin minus meum retinebo, atque illud construendum transmittam. De pretio cum domino Cock meliori modo poteris convenire; quicquid promiseris statim per Mercatorem quandam Londini, quem brevi indicabo, numerari curabo; sed rogo ut primo quoque tempore id construetur, quo possit primis Navibus Dantiscum velificantibus tuto Mensi Majo transmitti. Haec sunt quae hac vice tantummodo perscribere debui ac volui; reliqua rem nostram Literariam concernentia in proximam occasionem rejiciens; praesertim quando exploravero vires Tubi Nostri 140. pedum,[3] cuius Machinam optime feliciterque iam penitus constructam habeo, facillimo negotio et peculiari ratione tractabilem: de quibus omnibus suo tempore fusius. De reliquo fac ut valens, et obsequiosissima nostra studia Illustrissimae Societati Regiae nostrae, praevia salutatione debita, decenter ut deferas etiam atque etiam rogo. Dabam Gedani Anno 1671 die 4 Martij S.n. raptim.

ADDRESS
      A Monsieur
  Monsieur Grubendol
            A
            Londres
  Franco Anvers

TRANSLATION

J. Hevelius greets the illustrious Mr. Henry Oldenburg, Secretary of the very illustrious Royal Society

Your letter of 18 January was delivered to me very safely with its enclosure,[1] which I very gladly took care of by means of an Hungarian friend. I thought I should let you know this, especially as I also have some business that ought to be discharged at London, and I have no doubt you will not mind taking this trouble on yourself. For I am asked by the most illustrious Lord Marshal and High General of the Armies of the Kingdom of Poland[2] to procure for him just such a microscope as was sent to me last year of Mr. Cock's making. As he is a patron of letters and learned men I wished to satisfy his desire as soon as possible. For which reason, since I obviously have no other resource for so doing, I beg you most kindly to have such a one made and polished for me at Mr. Cock's; but let the lenses be worked with the utmost care so that they may be even better than mine, if possible. If it should by any chance happen that he does work such [excellent ones], you can advise me to that effect, so that I may keep them for myself, and send mine in lieu to the Lord Marshal. But otherwise I will keep my own and send on those [just] constructed. As for price, you may come to the best agreement you can with Mr. Cock; I will take care to have whatever you shall have promised disbursed at once by some merchant at London whose name I will give you shortly. But I ask that just as soon as it is finished, it be sent in the propitious month of May by the first possible ships sailing for Danzig. This is all I wished and ought to write to you this time, leaving the rest of our learned correspondence for the next opportunity, especially after I have investigated the powers of our 140–foot telescope,[3] whose mounting I have already completely constructed in a new and very successful way which makes it easy to maneuver in a special manner. More about all those things in due time. For the rest, look after your health and, after a proper greeting, I beg you again and again to present my most humble services to our very illustrious Royal Society.

Danzig, 4 March 1671, N.S., in haste

ADDRESS
> To Mr. Grubendol
> > London
> Postfree to Antwerp

NOTES

Reply to Letter 1599.
1 From Letter 1642 it appears likely that this was a letter from Edward Browne to his friend Mr. Donellan; see also Letter 1598.
2 This was John Sobieski, who became King of Poland in 1674.
3 The objective was made by Burattini.

1638
John Sterpin to Oldenburg
24 February 1670/1

From the original in Royal Society MS. S 1, no. 114

Honoured Sir,

Knowing that every moment of your time is pretious, I had not presumed to disturb your more serious occasions with these lines, had not some advice from Hamborough imboldned mee unto it. This will then let you know that, to satisfye the desires of the knowing world of these, and other parts, who often complained that your Philosophicall Transactions were not intelligible to them, I have attempted to translate them into Latin, with what successe I cannot tell, onely I am something ill satisfied with the corrector, for haveing suffered some faults, though not very many, to enter in the impression:[1] but I will take care that it shall not happen so in the other parts. I expect daily the cutts from francfort, and as soone as I receive them I will make bold to send you that part which is printed, namely that of the yeare 1669. I was far from attributing the sd transactions to the Royall Society, for which I have all possible veneration, specially having perceived by some places of your book that it could not bee done without an errour, which I would have been loath to commit; Providence haveing so dispensed the time of my life that, being borne in france, that Contrey, England and Dennemark have almost been equall sharers in it, but oweing most of my education to England, I ought doubtlesse to interesse my selfe much in the glory of it, and specially of the Royall Society, as its chiefest ornament, to whom haveing such a relation, if you please to honour mee with your commands, I will endeavour, by their speedy execution, to shew how happy I would esteeme my selfe in receiving them. In the mean time, Sir, I humbly subscribe my selfe

Your most humble and obedient servant
John Sterpin

Coppenhaguen the 24th
febr stilo vet. 1671

P.S.   If I can do you any service in these parts, you may send your Letters to Mr. Robert finshams, at the signe of the Kings head and three Crowns over against St. Clements Church in the Strand,[2] directed to mee at the Lord High Chancellour of Dennemarkes house, at Coppenhaguen.

ADDRESS
    Monsieur
    Monsieur Oldenburg, secretaire
    de la Societé Royale, demeurant
        A Londres

NOTES

The writer of this letter, described as a "Doctor of Physick" on the title page of his translation into English of Lucas Debes' *Faeroae et Faeroa Reserta* (London, 1676), was also the author of *Trifolium medicum, seu universae medicinae synopsis* (Copenhagen, 1671).
  1 Oldenburg inserted in *Phil. Trans.*, no. 75 (18 September 1671), 2269–70, "An Advertisement necessary to be given to the Readers of the Latin Version, made by Mr. Sterpin at Copenhagen, of the Philosophical Transactions of A. 1669; printed at Frankfurt on the Main by Dan. Pauli, A. 1671." It contains a large number of corrections to this translation.
  2 Possibly this was the King's Head Inn in the Strand at the corner of Chancery Lane, mentioned twice by Pepys (26 June 1665; 2 April 1668).

1639
Huet to Oldenburg
24 February 1670/1

From the original in Royal Society MS. H 1, no. 99

A St. Germain le 6. Mar 1671 [N.S.]

Monsieur

Vostre derniere lettre apresque esté aussi long tems par les chemins que la mienne,[1] car elle ne m'a esté rendue que depuis deux jours, quoy qu'elle fust escrite du 16. Janv. Je me plains de ma mauvaise fortune qui me retient si long tems les tesmoignages de vostre souvenir. Dans la vie tumultueuse et agitée que je mene, et si peu convenable aux meditations, et aux observations philosophiques, ce m'est un tres sensible plaisir d'apprendre par vous Monsieur Le progrez que font les autres dans la Philosophie, et particulierement vos illustres Anglois, qui la cultivent avec tant d'application et tant de succez. Je vous rends de tres humbles graces du soin que vous avez pris de faire executer a vos savans Anatomistes l'operation que je vous avois proposée. Je ne doute pas qu'ils n'y ayent apporté toute la diligence possible, et ainsi je tiendray desormais pour constant qu'il n'y a point d'autre chemin pour l'Urine que les ureteres. Je voudrois pourtant bien savoir si vos doctes Medecins croyent assurement qu'il n'y ait point d'autre communication entre l'estomac, et les Reins que par les arteres emulgentes. Je vous avoue que j'ay de la peine a concevoir que l'odeur des asperges que l'on a mangées se conserve dans l'Urine, sans qu'elle paroisse aucunement dans le sang. Mr. Hauton croit qu'une certaine espece de terre vierge est plus propre a rendre salubre l'eau de mer distillé, que toute autre, & il ne m'a point appris qu'elle est cette terre. Mais il adjouste qu'au defaut de cette terre; toute autre terre vierge y peut servir. Je tiens impossible de donner une mesure certaine des spheres de l'oeil; parce qu elles changent de figure, de volume, et de consistence aprés la mort de l'animal, et elles en changent en proportion differente; car La cornée s'affaise sensiblement, n'estant soustenue que de l'humeur aqueuse qui est plus enflée par les esprits, lors que l'animal est plain de Vie, qu'aprés sa mort. Quand je dis la cornée, j'entens la partie diaphane qui couvre la prunelle; car cette partie est une portion d'un globe different du globe total de l'oeil. L'Humeur Crystallin qui est plus compacte et plus solide, souffre moins de changement, quoy qu'il en souffre aussi; car dans plusieurs dissections d'yeux que j'ay faites, j'ay observé que le Crystallin estant seché par sa superficie, la tunique crystalloide se vidoit; or ce dessechement est inevitable, quelque peu de tems que l'on mette a mesurer cette sphere, et tout au moins y arrive t'il une alteration assez grande pour en changer la mesure. De plus je suis persuadé que l'alteration des humeurs se faict très inegalément non seulement entre les animaux de different element, comme entre les animaux terrestres, et les aquatiques, mais aussi entre les animaux de differente espece, et mesme des animaux de mesme espece. Dans les poissons Le Crystallin est tres dur, particulierement vers le centre, et L'Humeur Vitrée est trés fluide; dans les chiens et presque tous les Quadrupedes le Crystallin est plus mollesse, et le Vitrée plus consistant; et j'ay souvent observé qu'un oeil d'un chien, estoit different en la consistence de ses humeurs, non seulement de l'oeil d'un autre chien, mais mesme de l'oeil du mesme chien. Je crois de plus que l'oeil d'un animal mort est different de luy mesme selon les dispositions de l'air et du tems, et que les humeurs s'affaissent davantage dans le froid que dans la chaleur. Jugez donc, s'il vous plaist Monsieur, avec quelle certitude on peut determiner la capacité et la mesure de ces Humeurs. Je vous avoue que je l'ay tenté quelquefois; mais i'y ay trouvé si peu d'assurance que j'ay abandonné cette recherche; je me suis contenté de comparer la conformation des yeux de certains animaux avec des yeux d'animaux differens, dont les uns ont la Veue trés aigue, & les autres trés foibles, et j'y ay remarqué des choses assez curieuses. Pour l'examen du magnetisme de la terre, il est vray que i'avois une trés grande curiosité pour savoir ce que l'on y a observé: car cette recherche pourroit apporter quelque esclaircissement a la cause de la gravitation, qui est si peu connue. Mr. Justel m'a appris qu'outre Les livres de Mr. Boyle *de qualitate cosmicis*, etc. et de la dilation de l'air, il a faict un Livre *de origine formarum*. Il m'a aussi mandé que l'on voit un 3e Livre *De motu* de Mr. Wallis. Je n'en connois que le premier, dont vous m'avez eu la bonté de me faire un present. Je vous supplie de m'apprendre si je pourrois esperer de vous la grace de m'envoyer les livres nouveaux qui s'impriment en vos quartiers, et j'en rendrois icy l'argent, soit a Mr. Justel, soit a telle autre personne que vous voudriez m'indiquer. Je vous serois très obligé de cette grace, dont pourtant je vous conjure de me refuser si elle vous fait le moindre embarras. Je suis de toute ma passion Monsieur

Vostre tres humble &
très obeissant serviteur
Huet

TRANSLATION

St. Germain, 6 March 1671 [N.S]

Sir,

Your last letter was nearly as long on its way as mine,[1] for it was only delivered to me two days ago, although it was written on 16 January. I lament the ill fortune which has kept from me for so long the testimony of your remembrance of me. In the tumultuous and restless life which I lead, so little suited to meditation or to philosophical observations, it is a very real pleasure to learn through you, Sir, of the progress made by others in philosophy, and especially by you illustrious English, who cultivate it so assiduously and successfully. I thank you very humbly for the care you have taken in having your anatomists perform the operation which I proposed to you. I do not doubt but that they bestowed all possible care on it, and so I shall take it as fixed that there is no path for the urine except the ureters. I should nevertheless very much like to know whether your learned physicians think that there is certainly no communication between the stomach and kidneys except through the emulgent arteries. I confess to you that I have difficulty in entertaining the idea that the odor of asparagus which one has eaten can be preserved in the urine without its at all appearing in the blood.

Mr. Hauton thinks that a certain kind of pure earth is fitter to make distilled sea water healthful than any other, and he has never told me what that earth is. But he adds that, in default of this earth, any other pure earth may be used.

I hold it impossible to give an accurate measurement of the eyeballs because they change their shape, size, and consistency after the death of the animal, and each in different proportions; for the cornea collapses noticeably, being supported only by the aqueous humor, which is more distended by the spirits when the animal is living than after its death. When I say the cornea, I understand the diaphanous part which covers the pupil, for this part is a portion of a different sphere from the total sphere of the eye. The crystalline humor, which is more compact and solid, suffers less change, although it experiences it also, for in several of the dissections of eyes which I have made I have observed that when the crystalline lens is dried out at the surface the crystalloid tunic empties; now this drying out is inevitable, however short the time taken to measure the sphere, and at the very least there occurs a large enough change to alter its measurement. Further, I am sure that the humors alter in a very uneven fashion, not only between animals of different elements, like terrestrial and aquatic animals, but also between animals of different species and even between animals of the same species. In fish the crystalline lens is very hard, particularly toward the center, and the vitreous humor is very fluid; in dogs and most quadrupeds the crystalline humor is softer and the vitreous firmer, and I have often observed that a dog's eye differed in the consistency of its humors not only from the eye of another dog, but even from the [other] eye of the same dog. Further, I believe that the eye of a dead animal itself differs according to the state of the air and the weather, and that the humors sub-side farther in cold than in heat. Judge then, if you please, Sir, with what certainty it is possible to determine the capacity and measurement of these humors. I confess that I have sometimes tried it, but I found it so uncertain that I have abandoned this investigation; I contented myself with comparing the structure of the eyes of certain animals with those of different animals—some with very sharp sight, and others with very weak sight—and I have noticed some pretty curious things.

As for the examination of terrestrial magnetism, it is true that I had a very great desire to know what had been observed about it, for this investigation could shed some light on the cause of gravity, so little understood.

Mr. Justel has told me that besides the books of Mr. Boyle *De qualitate cos-micis*, etc., and on the rarefaction of the air, he has written a book *De origine formarum*. He has also informed me that a third book of Mr. Wallis's *De motu* has appeared. I only know of the first which you kindly gave to me. I beg you to let me know whether I may hope for the favor from you of being sent the books newly printed in your parts, and I will deliver the money here either to Mr. Justel or to anyone else whom you wish to name. I should be very much obliged for this favor, which however I implore you to refuse if it causes you the slightest difficul-ty. I am, most forcefully, Sir,

Your very humble and obedient servant,
Huet

NOTES

Reply to Letter 1597.
1 Letter 1535 of 20 October 1670.

1640

Oldenburg to Lister

25 February 1670/1

From the original in Bodleian Library MS. Lister 34, f. 9

London Febr. 25. 1670
71

Sir,

O n Thursday last[1] I produced and read yr well-fraighted and excellent Letter before the R. Society, who were highly pleased wth all those curious observations, wch you have so generously communicated therein, especially those wch relate to Colours. They have commanded me to let you know not only, that they have a great sense of this respect of yrs to them and their philosophical engagements, but also, that they will take care to preserve these, and such other communications, as you shall further send to ym, in their Books among ye best Collections, they are making for an History of Nature. And when yr occasions shall permit you to come to London, and to visit their Assembly's, you may be sure of an hearty welcome; as may be also ye Experiment of Fixing Colors you intend to show before them yourself.

Some of ye Company, having taken particular notice of ye several colors, both vegetable and animal, mention'd by you for such as will *stand*, desired, yt I would inquire of you, whether you had seen any Tryals made thereof upon cloath or stuffe? And if you have, whether you would not gratify us wth communicating ye particular successes thereof?

What that English Vegetable is, wch hath yielded you an exquisit black colour, comparable to ye best Ink, and not changeable by fire or salt, we should also be very glad to be informed of, if you think fit.

The Society is now about ye employing of an Air-vessel, to try therein, what change the Rarefaction of ye Air will worke upon a Man, yt may sit in it, altogether shut up, and fortified against ye Ingresse of more Air, than is just requisite to his respiration.[2] Wch Contrivance is like to furnish us wth divers considerable phaenomena, to clear up the doctrine of Respiration, and to give light to other things: Of ye successe of wch trials you are like to be, as occasion shall serve, informed by Sir

Yr very humble servt
Henr. Oldenburg

ADDRESS
  To his honoured friend
  Martyn Lister Esquire,
  at his house wthout Mickel-
  gate barr at
              Yorke

NOTES

Reply to Letter 1634.
1 23 February 1670/1.
2 Hooke reported that this contrivance was ready for trying on 9 February 1670/1;
   there is a description of its design in Birch, *History*, II, 467–68. Hooke had first
   suggested it at a meeting on 12 January 1670/1. He tried sitting in it when the air was
   partially evacuated, and reported little inconvenience.

1641
Oldenburg to Reed
27 February 1670/1

Mentioned in Reed's reply, Letter 1652.

1642
Lambecius to Oldenburg
27 February 1670/1

From the original in Royal Society MS. L 5, no. 84

Praenobilis et Amplissime Domine,

Literas tuas humanissimas, d. 18. Januarij datas, recte accepi, et in-
clusas debita fide ac diligentia per ordinarium cursorem Hungaricum
direxi ad Generosum Dn. Donellanum, nec dubito, quin in ipsius manus
itidem recte pervenerint. Caeterum quod ad rem literarium attinet, signi-

fico, Librum tertium Commentariorum meorum de Augustissima Bibliotheca circa finem superioris anni prodijsse in publicum, ideoque nunc
Librum quartum sub praelo fervere, et, ut spero, non multo post festum
Pentecostei absolutum iri.[1] Quod superest, doctissimum Dn. Browne
officiosissime resaluto, et me constanti benevolentiae tuae obnixe commen-
dans, vicissim pari constantia permaneo

Praenobilis Amplitudinis Tuae observantissimus
Petrus Lambecius
S. Caes. Majest. Consiliarius, Historiographus
et Bibliothecarius

vindobonae sive Wiennae Austriae
d. 9 Martij A. 1671 [N.S.]

TRANSLATION

Most noble and worthy Sir,

I received your letter of 18 January safely, and I sent on the enclosure for the
honorable Mr. Donellan with due care and diligence by the ordinary courier
for Hungary, and I have no doubt that it came safely to his hands. As regards
literary matters, I can inform you that the third book of my *Commentaries* on the
Imperial Library was given to the public about the end of last year, and Book IV is
now in press, so that it will, I hope, be finished not long after Whitsuntide.[1] For
the rest, I salute the learned Mr. Browne very courteously once more, and earnestly commending myself to your unfailing goodwill again, remain with equal
constancy

Your very noble excellency's most humble
Petrus Lambecius
Councilor, Historian, and Librarian
to His Imperial Majesty

Vindobona or Vienna in Austria
9 March 1671 [N.S.]

NOTES

Reply to Letter 1598.
1 *P. Lambecii Commentariorum de Bibliotheca Caesarae Vincobonensi libri I-VIII* (Vienna,
1665–79).

1643

Sluse to Oldenburg

27 February 1670/1

From the original in Royal Society MS. S 1, no. 67
Printed in Boncompagni, pp. 653–55

Nobilissimo et Clarissimo Viro
D. Henrico Oldenburg Societatis Regiae Secretario
Renatus Franciscus Slusius Salutem

Ex literis tuis, Vir Clarissime quas ante tres septimanas accepi, libenter intellexi eximium D. Collinsium tabulis, quae aequationum resolutioni serviant, condendis operam impendere. erit enim res utilitatis non exiguae, et quae calculi laborem mirum in modum minuet. Caeterum quod a me petere videtur, ut aequationum limites[1] designandi methodum indicem, iam id obiter saltem, ac quasi aliud agens praestiti, Miscellaneorum meorum cap: 5 ac praesertim pag. 128, 129: ubi ostendi Conchoidicam meam certis casibus flecti et reflecti. Eo enim fine haec praecedenti de maximis et minimis capiti subiunxi, ut aliqualem saltem eius usum ostenderem. Sed iuvabit fortasse aliud exemplum addere, quo mentem meam uberius explicem. Proponatur itaque, Data recta indefinita *ZZ*, et ad illam normalibus *AB*, *GC*, ducere per *A*, rectam secantem *GC*. (productam si opus sit) in puncto *Q*, et rectam *ZZ* in *K*, ita ut rectangulum *GCQ* aequale sit rectangulo *QKC*. Ac problematis quidem solutio facilis est, divisa

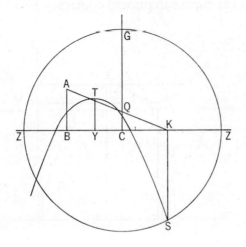

BC bifariam in *Y*, et erecta *YT* tertia proportionali ipsarum *AB*, *BY*, factaque vertice *T*, axe *TY*, latere recto *AB* parabola. Nam si centro *C*. intervallo *CG* describatur circulus secans parabolam in *S*, unde cadat in *ZZ* normalis *SK*, iuncta *KA*, satisfaciet proposito. Patet autem parabolam a circulo in pluribus punctis secari posse, et *K* inveniri vel in *BC* producta vel inter *B* et *C* (idque bis) vel ultra *B*. et si ad propositionem attendamus, cum illa in terminis maxime universalibus concepta sit, pari iure, omnes aequationis radices, nomen verarum sibi vindicabunt. Sed loquamur cum Analystis, et veras, exempli gratia, vocemus eas quae in *BC* producta reperiuntur. Sit igitur *AB* = *d*. *BC* = *q*. *CG* = *b*. *CK* = *y*. erit aequatio

pro veris radicibus $y^4 + 2qy^3 \begin{array}{c} + qqyy \\ + ddyy \end{array} = bbdd$. Ex qua satis constat unicam

tantum haberi posse, cum omnes quantitates in quibus *y* reperitur signum ha-

beant affirmativum. Pro falsis vero invenietur haec $y^4 - 2qy^3 \begin{array}{c} + ddyy \\ + qqyy \end{array} = bbdd$.

Supponamus itaque *bb* esse *xx*, nimirum quantitatem aliquam incognitam, et exploremus ad quem locum sit *x*, seu qua ratione flectatur curva quae huius aequationis proprietatem obtinet. ductis igitur tangentibus (prout in Conchoidica nostra fecimus) statim occurrit, primo lineam illam unicum habere flexum si $\frac{1}{2}$ *dd* aequale sit vel maius $\frac{1}{16}$ *qq*: ideoque, quaecumque tandem data sit *b*, aequationem hanc unicam tantum radicem habituram. At si $\frac{1}{2}$ *dd* supponatur esse minus $\frac{1}{16}$ *qq*, evidens quoque est curvam flecti et reflecti, ut in diagrammate hic adiecto. Inquirenda itaque sunt per tangentes puncta flexus *E* et *F*, et ex illis demittendae ad *BC* normales *EM*, *FR*, quae limites aequationis ostendunt. Si enim *CG* fuerit aequalis *FR* vel *EM*, aequatio duas radices habebit: ducta enim ex *G* parallela, occurret illa curvae in puncto contactus *E* vel *F*, et in alio rursus

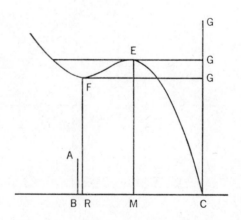

eandem secabit. At si *CG* fuerit vel minor *RF*, vel maior *ME*, palam est
ex eadem ratione unicam tantum radicem inventum iri. Cum vero longitudo
ipsius *CG* cadet inter duas *RF*, *ME*, tunc tres radices dari necesse erit,
quandoquidem parallela ex *G* ducta in tribus punctis curvae occursura
sit. quae vel ex sola diagrammatis consideratione, satis, ut existimo, elu-
cescunt. Geometrice autem facile invenitur punctum utrumque *E* et *F*.
Sumta enim $BX = \frac{1}{4} BC$, centro *X* intervallo *XC* describatur semicirculus *CPI*, et in *C* erigatur *CN*, quae possit dimidium quadratorum *AB*,

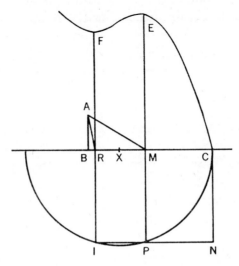

BC; tum ex *N* ducatur parallela *CB*, quae si vel circulo non occurrat, vel
occurrat in puncto supremo,[2] aequatio unicam tantum radicem habebit,
cuiuscumque magnitudinis *b* data fuerit. Nam eo casu $\frac{1}{2} qq + \frac{1}{2} dd$ aequale
erit vel maius $\frac{9}{16} qq$, ideoque $\frac{1}{2} dd$ aequale vel maius $\frac{1}{16} qq$, ut supra mo-
nuimus. Sin autem recta secet circulum in duobus punctis ut *P* et *I*,
demittantur normales *IR*, *PM* et producantur in *E* et *F*, ita ut iunctis
AR, *AM* rectangulum *AB*, *RF* aequale sit rectangulo *ARC*, et rectangulum *ABME* rectangulo *AMC* similiter aequale; erunt enim *RF*, *ME*
lineae quaesitae. Atque hac methodo aequatio quaelibet ac quomodolibet
affecta determinari potest, nisi quod aliquando loco circuli, locus solidus
abhibendus sit, ut in illa quam ad me misisti, quam idcirco Clarissimo
Collinsio me, ut existimo, minus occupato, hac methodo determinandam
propono. Ad curas Ecclesiasticas accedunt forenses et Politicae, quibus
me superesse oportet aut Τὰ καθήκοντα προδοῦναι. Quod tamen non addo,
ut te a literario hoc nostro commercio avocem; quemadmodum enim
illud maximo honori duco; ita me quoque mirum in modum delectat,

estque, ut ita dicam, παραμυθίας loco (quo etiam nomine plurimum semper tibi me debere profitebor): sed ut si quando indiligentem me experiaris, paratam apud te excusationem inveniam.

Recte autem observavit, Vir Clarissimus, in tabulis suis differentias ultimas et inter se aequales esse, et easdem cum differentijs ultimis biquadratorum progressionis Arithmeticae unitate differentis: Id enim omnibus omnino aequationibus, cuiuscumque gradus sint, accidit, ut ultimae homogeneorum ita inventorum differentiae, aequales sint differentijs ultimis potestatum eiusdem gradus, quarum radices ab unitate progressionem Arithmeticam servant. Cuius quidem demonstratio facilis est.

Quod ad Alhazenj Problema attinet, ut δεύτεραι φροντίδες esse solent ἀμείνονες duas alias eiusdem Analyses, priore quam ad te misi faciliores,[3] et constructione inter se et ab illa diversas, nuper inveni, quinimo praeparationem quandam generalem ex qua Problematum omnium, quae ad punctum reflexionis in speculis sphaericis concavis et convexis determinandum spectant, Analysis facile deduci potest. Sed haec et meliora acutissimo D. Hugenio iam occurrisse mihi persuadeo, qui me maiorem in hoc argumento operam posuit.[4] Si tamen nugas quoque nostras videre vellet, libenter cum ipso communicarem.

Ex libris, de quibus ad me scribis, nullus apud Bibliopolas nostros prostat praeter duos: Caramuelis nempe Opera Mathematica[5] et Marchetti de Resistentia Solidorum,[6] quem a me habebis si desideres. Hunc nondum examinare licuit, quod his diebus adhuc incompactum obtinuerim: Caramuelis vero farraginem pervolvi, et sane, ut lenissime dicam, par tantae moli respondere non videtur utilitas. Alii longe mihi gratiores huc allati sunt, Thruston scilicet De Respiratione, Responsio Clarissimi Willisii ad D. Higmori Epistolam,[7] cum duobus opusculis annexis, Brendelii quoque Chymia in artis formam redacta; brevis illa quidem sed non contemnenda.[8] Hac occasione scirem libenter a te an Chymici vestrates norint purissimum antimonii regulum, et ad argenti splendorem adductum, absque ulla additione sublimare; non in flores, quos tamen non paucos dare solet, eosque candidissimos, sed in verum sublimatum, vulgari vel potius argenteo simile: et si sciant cuinam usui illud adhibeant. Rem sane mihi gratissimam facies si id me docueris, et siquid aliud in rebus physicis, quibus plurimum delector, recenter observatum occurrat.

Novi Romae diarium Eruditorum edi, sed Clarissimum Riccium illa via inventa sua publico daturum non existimo.[9] Pergat itaque Clarissimus Gregorius et Geometriae pomoeria feliciter, ut solet, promoveat. Methodum ipsius tangentes ducendi eandem esse cum mea suspicor, saltem si Clarissimi Barrovii vestigiis institerit. An vero quemadmodum tangentibus ducendi servit, ita quoque curvis ex data tangentium proprietate inveniendis sit utilis (quod ipsius Problemata innuunt) hactenus non examinavi. Sed de his satis. Vale Vir Clarissime meque virtutis tuae observantissimum, quo soles affectu prosequi perge. Dabam Leodii IX Martii MDCLXXI [N.S.]

P.S.

Exciderat mihi te monere nullum a me de Cycloide tractatulum editum fuisse, sed ea de quibus fortasse audivisti et quae non magni sunt pretii, desumta esse ex editis ad Pascalium τὸν μακρίτην qui me humanissime compellarat.[10] Gomesii Pereirae de quo nuper ad te scripsi, quaeso memineris.[11]

ADDRESS
    A Monsieur
    Monsieur Grubendol
                Londre
    par Anvers

TRANSLATION

René François de Sluse greets the very noble and famous Mr. Henry Oldenburg, Secretary of the Royal Society

From your letter that I received more than three weeks ago, famous Sir, I learned with pleasure that the distinguished Mr. Collins has undertaken the task of preparing tables that may serve for resolving equations. This will be something of no little utility, which will wonderfully reduce the labor of calculation. Moreover, what you seem to ask of me, that I indicate my method of determining the limits of equations,[1] I did provide formerly (at least *en passant*, and while concerned with other things) in my *Miscellanies*, Chapter Five, and especially on pp. 128, 129, where I showed that in certain cases my conchoidic is inflected and inflected back. For I added this material to the preceding chapter on maxima and minima with the object of revealing at least a little of its usefulness. But perhaps it will help to give a further example by which I can explain my thoughts in greater detail. Let it be proposed thus: Given an indefinite straight line *ZZ* and the normals to it *AB*, *CG*, the problem is to draw a straight line through *A* cutting *CG* (produced if necessary) in the point Q, and the line *ZZ* in *K*, in such a way that the rectangle *GC* . *CQ* may be equal to the rectangle *QK* . *KC* [*see figure, p. 477*]. And indeed the problem is easy of solution, if *BC* is bisected at *Y*, and *YT* is erected as a third proportional to *AB*, *BY*, and then a parabola is drawn with vertex *T*, axis *TY* and latus rectum *AB*. For if a circle be drawn with center *C* and radius *CG* cutting the parabola at *S*, whence the normal *SK* falls upon *ZZ*, and *AK* be joined, this will satisfy the proposition.

However, it is obvious that the parabola may be intersected by the circle at several points, so that *K* may be found either in *BC* produced or at two points between *B* and *C* or beyond *B*. And if we examine the proposition, when it may be conceived in perfectly universal terms, by the same argument, all the roots of the equation will qualify as true. But we speak as the analysts do, and we call those roots *true*, for example, which occur along *BC* produced. So that if $AB = d$, $BC = q$, $CG = b$, and $CK = y$, the equation for the true roots will be

$$y^4 + 2qy^3 + q^2y^2 + d^2y^2 = b^2d^2.$$

From which it appears that there is a unique true root since all the terms in which *y* is found are positive. For the false roots this equation may be found

$$y^4 - 2qy^3 + q^2y^2 + d^2y^2 = b^2d^2.$$

Let us further suppose that $b^2 = x^2$, *x* being some unknown quantity, and let us discover where *x* may be, or in what proportion the curve must be inflected which has the property of this equation. Having drawn the tangents (just as we did with our conchoidic) it will at once be noticed in the first place that that line has a single inflection if

$$\tfrac{1}{2}d^2 \geq \tfrac{1}{16}q^2$$

and so whatever *b* may be given, this equation will have only a single root. But if

$$\tfrac{1}{2}d^2 < \tfrac{1}{16}q^2$$

it is also evident that the curve is inflected twice, as in the annexed diagram [*see figure, p. 478*].

Accordingly, the points of inflection *E* and *F* are to be sought for by the method of tangents, and dropping the normals *EM*, *FR* upon *BC*, these show the limits of the equation. For if $CG = FR$ or $CG = EM$ the equation will have two roots; since, drawing a parallel from *G*, it will meet the curve at the point of contact *E* or *F*, and will cut it again at another point. But if $CG < RF$ or $> ME$, from the same reasoning it is clear that only a single root can be found. And when the length of *CG* falls between the two lengths *RF*, *ME*, then necessarily there must be three roots, since the parallel from *G* meets the curve at three points, which is evident enough from a mere inspection of the figure [*p. 479*], I think. Either of the points *E* and *F* can easily be found geometrically, however. For taking $BX = \tfrac{1}{4}BC$, with center *X* and radius *CX* draw the semicircle *CPI*, and upon *C* erect *CN*, such that $CN^2 = \tfrac{1}{2}(AB^2 + BC^2)$. Then from *N* let a parallel to *CB* be drawn. If this does not meet the circle or meets it at the summit,[2] the equation will have one root only, whatever the magnitude of *b*. For in that case

$$\tfrac{1}{4}q^2 + \tfrac{1}{2}d^2 \geq \tfrac{9}{16}q^2,$$

and so $\tfrac{1}{2}d^2 \geq \tfrac{9}{16}q^2$, as we said before. But if the straight line cuts the circle at two points as *P* and *I*, let the two normals *IR*, *PM* be dropped and produced to *E* and

F, so that when *AR* and *AM* are joined the rectangle *AB* . *RF* shall be equal to the rectangle *AR* . *RC*, and the rectangle *AB* . *ME* to the rectangle *AM* . *MC*; then *RF*, *ME* will be the lines sought. And by this method any equation of whatever powers may be determined, except that sometimes a solid locus may be applied in lieu of a circle, as in that you sent me, which I propose for solution by this method to Mr. Collins, who is I suppose less busy than I am. To my ecclesiastical responsibilities legal and political ones have been added, with which I must continue to live, or be overwhelmed by my duty. I do not say this to cause you to withdraw from our literary correspondence, for it is a great honor to me; also I enjoy it very much and it is, so to speak, by way of a solace to me (for which reason I have many times professed myself indebted to you). But if you sometimes find me heedless, you will have received my apologies in advance.

The famous [Collins] has rightly noticed that in his tables the last differences are equal among themselves, and are the same as those of the squares of the arithmetical progression whose terms differ by unity. For this happens with all equations of any degree whatsoever, that the last differences of the *homogenea* thus found are equal to the last differences of the powers of the same degree, whose roots constitute an arithmetical progression from unity. Of this there is an easy proof.

As for Alhazen's Problem, second thoughts being often the best, I have recently discovered two other analyses of it, simpler than the one I sent you before[3] and differing in construction both from it and from each other; indeed, I have found a certain general treatment by which the analysis of all problems relating to the determination of the point of reflection on either convex or concave spherical mirrors can easily be deduced. But I am sure that these and better things have already occurred to the very acute Mr. Huygens, who has accomplished more than I in this business.[4] If he also wishes to see my trifles, however, I will gladly impart them to him.

No more than two of the books about which you write to me are to be found on sale at our booksellers', that is, Caramuel's *Opera mathematica*[5] and Marchetti's *De resistentia solidorum*,[6] the latter of which you may have from me if you choose. I have not examined it yet, because I obtained it only a day or two ago, unbound. I have looked through Caramuel's farrago, and indeed, to speak kindly, its utility does not seem proportionate to its bulk. Others far more welcome to me have been brought hither, that is to say Thruston on respiration, the famous Willis's reply to Highmore's letter, with two little pamphlets annexed,[7] as well as Brendel's *Chimia in artis formam redacta*—short, but not to be despised.[8] Speaking of this, I would gladly learn from you whether your chemists know that the purest regulus of antimony, brought to the brightness of silver, will sublimate without any addition, not as flowers of which nevertheless it usually yields a quantity and those very pure, but as a true sublimate like the common or silver sublimate, and if they know it, to what use do they put it? You will do me a most welcome service if you will instruct me on this point, and whether anything has recently been taken note of in physics, which interests me much.

I have heard that a learned journal is published at Rome but I do not think that the celebrated Ricci has published that method he invented.[9] So let the famous Gregory also go on with the successful extension of geometry, as is his wont. I suspect that his method of drawing tangents is the same as mine at least if he followed in the footsteps of the distinguished Barrow. Whether just as it serves for drawing tangents, so also it may be useful for discovering curves from a given property of the tangents (as his problems hint) I have not yet investigated. But enough of such things. Farewell, worthy Sir, and, as you are doing, continue to bestow your goodwill on me, who am most regardful of your merits.

Liège, 9 March 1671 [N.S.]

P.S.   It slipped my mind to advise you that I published no treatise on the cycloid, but those of which you have heard, perhaps, and which did not count for much, were taken from what was set out for the late Pascal, who had addressed me most courteously.[10] I beg you to remember Gomez Pereyra,[11] about whom I wrote to you recently.

ADDRESS

To Mr. Grubendol
London
via Antwerp

NOTES

Reply to Letter 1590.

1 Naturally Sluse does not use the word *limits* in the modern technical sense; he means here to define the conditions defining the occurrence of the various roots of an equation.
2 That is, when $CN = CX$ so that PN is a tangent to the semicircle.
3 See Letter 1548.
4 Compare Letter 1528.
5 Compare Letter 1548 and its note 9.
6 See Letter 1556, note 19.
7 Thomas Willis, *Affectionum quae dicuntur hystericae et hypochondriacae pathologia spasmodica, vindicata contra responsionem epistolarem Nath. Highmore M.D.* (London, 1670), published with two other tracts, *De sanguinis ascensione* and *De motu musculari.*
8 Zacharias Brendel, *Chimia in artis formam redacta* (Jena, 1630; Leiden, 1671).
9 See p. 376 and Letter 1555, note 9.
10 Compare Letter 1590, note 41.
11 See Letter 1548, note 11.

1644
Leibniz to Oldenburg

1 March 1670/1

From the copy in Royal Society Letter Book IV, 234-38
Printed in Gerhardt, pp. 50-53

Vir Amplissime,

Literas tuas responsorias humanissimas fructuosissimasque accepi dudum; sed cum replicationi meae addere Hypothesin, quam brevissime delineatam, consilium esset, adeoque typis excudendam dedissem, profectiunculis variis inopinatisque interrumpere operas coactus sum, expertus in absentia mea, praesertim in argumento ejusmodi, ubi vocibus ab usu communi remotis saepe utendum est, omnia innumerabilibus mendis foedari. Quare cum etiamnum interrumperer denuo, nec ante aliquot septimanarum exitum, finem sperarem, malui Tibi interim dimidiam, quam vides, partem mittere, quam totum differre.[1] Illud vero magnopere rogo, ut excuses audaciam meam inscribendi Schediasmation ejusmodi Societati tot magnis ingenio ac dignitate viris Illustri.[2] Solum, fateor, argumentum tantis lectoribus dignum est; caeteris si agnoscetur, satis rem ad votum cossisse putabo. Concise scripsi, quia intelligentibus. Hypothesin ipsam, credo, attendenti claram facilemque visum iri, fortasse et explicandis phaenomenis omnibus tanto magis suffecturam, quanto erit is, qui quandoque utitur, ingeniosior et in experimentis me versatior. Omnia vel naturae vel artis, ut sic dicam, horologia et machinamenta vel a Gravitate vel ab Elatere pendere, re expensa nemo diffitebitur: utramque, unicum quem explicui motum aetheris circularem, modo supponatur, consequuturum non est difficile cogitatu. Atqui hic est cardo totius contemplationis meae; hunc assecutus, quidquid susceperam obtinuero: Hypothesin scilicet breviorem clarioremque quam quae hactenus extat. Spero tamen, applicationi quoque specialiori aspersa nonnulla non omnino repudianda, ut in verticitate magnetis ab aetheris gyratione derivanda; in frigoris natura exemplo angiportuum declaranda, in Acidorum Alcaliumque, et omnino principiorum, quae vocant, Chymicorum reactionibus, fermentationibus, solutionibus; in restitutione balistae aut chordae tensae; in vibrationibus pendulorum, chordarumque, alijsque nonnullis explicandis. De magnete nonnulla adhuc inquirenda puto, antequam omnium rationem reddere sperem; ac potissimum, verumne sit experimentum Grandamici publicatum in libello, quem titulo demonstratae immobilitatis terrae edidit.[3] Quanquam enim Demonstratio, quam superstruit, infirma admodum videatur, experimentum tamen ipsum non negligendum est. Nimirum ait Grandamicus; si magnes sphaericus (vulgo terrellam vocant) raticulae e subere, vel alicui alteri vasculo innatanti imponatur, ea ratione ut polus ejus Borealis, id est, qui polum terrae borealem sibi relictus spectat, in raticula vergat deorsum, nadir versus, adeoque ad centrum terrae; Australis autem respiciat Zenith, atque ita constituto magnete, et librato, designatur in eo circulus, meridiano loci accurate reperto respondens, eum circulum fore meridianum universalem, ac toto orbe, magnete similiter constituto, meridianum loci, ac proinde plagas mundi sine ulla declinatione monstraturum. Scio, de hac narratione dubitari; ac proinde valde desidero severe examinari, cum plurimum referat ejus veritas falsitasve ad accuratam quandam de Phaenomenis Magneticis Hypothesin, cujus umbram animo concepi, construendam. Mihi accurate experimentum facere, hoc quidem statu negotiolorum meorum impossibile est, cum etiam magnetes satis validi, quales requiri aiunt, mihi desint, et terellam necesse sit satis exquisite tornari. Vos veritatem nullo negotio scieritis, praesertim si Petito (quem exquisitissimas terrellas, sed alio fine, ut scilicet gyrationem diurnam terrenae similem, quam Gilbertus magneti ascripserat, tentaret, fabricasse, ex ipsius ad vos literis, Transactionibus insertis, didici) negotium quoque rem examinandi demandetur.[4] Successum rei non contemnendae, si per Te intellexero, magno beneficio me accumulatum credam.

Instructionem de usu pendulorum Hugenianorum in particula Transactionum, ab amico mihi commodata, legi, sed constructio abfuit.[5] Ego vero nosse opto, ex quo principio procedant ista pendula novissimae constructionis, usui marino suffectura, an ex principio gravitatis, ut solent horologia majora, an ex principio Elateris, ut solent minora illa portabilia. Utrumque genus habet suum proprium incommodum primarium. Nam quae a naturali ponderum gravitate moventur, Non possunt de loco in locum sine Gravitationis mutatione transferri, ac proinde jactationi marinae non sunt accommodatae: contra, Elastica etsi transferri huc illuc tuto possint, rarissime tamen sunt accurata, ac vix unquam aequabili motu decurrunt; levissimis etiam ex causis, ut aeris, ut tensionis irregularis inaequalisque, maxime vero temporis tractu variantur; nam vis Elastica lassatur, gravitatio naturalis perseverat. Nihilne certi compertum est de ratione aquae dulcis habendae ex marinis, quam medicus quidam ex Britannia minore Regi Christianissimo proposuisse dicebatur.[6] Idem Keifferus quoque, ut audio, sola distillatione pollicetur.⁷ Ephemerides Collegii Naturae Curiosorum quod Medici aliquot Germani inierunt, uti nunc mediocri volumine in specimen anni primi prodiere,⁸ ad vos pervenisse non dubito, ac proinde de ijs plura scribere supersedeo. De Werneri Hydrotechnicis diu est, quod nihil fando inaudivi; expecto tamen successum, quisquis etiam futurus est, ex amico. Sunt quorum praejudicio non fit magni, sed ego has praedamnationes odi. Ingeniosissimi Gerickii Magdeburgenses Meditationes atque experimenta his nundinis in publico expectamus.⁹ Becherus promittit demonstrationem Chemicam, qua ferrum in notabili satis quantitate, ex terra, nihil ferri actualis continente, produci, ac metallorum genesis non parum illustrari possit.¹⁰ Quidam Helvetius eruditus rationem, ut intelligo, invenit, oppido facilem et regularem, lentes sectionum conicarum elaborandi, idque et specimine comprobatum aiunt. Expecto literis proximis de ejus instituto distinctiora. Francisci Wilhelmi liberi Baronis de Nuland Elementa nondum mihi visa sunt.¹¹ Delineationem brevem abstactae meae de Motu Theoriae adjicio postremis pagellis Hypotheseos vobis dedicatae; inde, opinor, apparebit, Paradoxa mea de motu, et Continuo non ita esse a ratione aliena, ut primo aspectu videntur:¹² Punctum non esse aliquid minimum, et omnium partium expers; esse tamen inextensum seu expers partium distantium; quin etiam punctum esse puncto majus, ut angulum angulo; Punctum non esse, cujus pars nulla est, nec cujus pars consideratur, sed quod quolibet extenso assignabili minus est; quod est fundamentum methodi Cavalerianae.¹³ Sed quid praeoccupo illic clarius dicenda? Credo tamen, vix aliter Labyrintho compositionis continui exiri posse. De Deo ac mente peculiares demonstrationes molior, in quibus nonnulla mirabilia, hactenus indicta, lucem tamen fortasse non vulgarem allatura, dicentur. Interim hic breviter innui, Omne corpus esse mentem momentaneam, ac proinde sine conscientia, sensu, recordatione. Si vero in uno corpore possent ultra momentum perseverare duo contrarij conatus simul, omne corpus foret mens vera. Ubicunque autem hoc effectum est, productae sunt mentes, eaeque naturaliter indestructibiles, quia, ut suo loco demonstrabo, duo contrarii conatus in eodem corporis puncto semel ultra momentum compatibiles, in aeternum nullo aliorum corporum allapsu, nulla vi adimi possunt. Haec prima specie exigua, vix credi potest quantum aperiant portam cogitationibus non contemnendis: Quae aliquando accuratius elaboratas demonstrationibus de jura naturali, (in quo argumento me pretium operae facturum spero, praesertim cum paucos extare arbitrer scriptores ingeniosiores in eo versatos, quos non contulerim, ac proinde rogo, ut si qui, quod non dubito, apud vos scientiam hanc, tanti ad omnem vitam momenti, excolunt, mihi Tuo beneficio innotescant) cujus magna pars demonstrationibus de DEO ac mente innititur, jungere consilium est. Hypotheseos meae non nisi unum Tibi, ut vides, exemplum, ob locorum distantiam, mittere possum; cum[14] vero Illustri Societati inscripserim, cum egregios viros, qui in ea sunt, censores, sed placidos, optem; fortasse, nisi Tibi aliter videtur, potest totum Schediasma meum, quippe nonnisi quatuor plagellarum, vel totum simul, vel particulatim Transactionibus inseri, eruditorumque judicia candida placidaque explorari: materiam certe multis fortasse novis cogitationibus praebere poterit.[15] Judicia si per Te resciero, plurimum accedet tot beneficiis, quibus Tibi me obstrictum sentio.

Si excusabis audaciam apud magnos viros, collegas Tuos; si praeparabis animos eorum homini ignoto et obscuro; si censuris eorum doceri me, perfici cogitata mea feceris, faxo ut intelligas, incidisse Te in hominem beneficii agnoscentem. Reliqua Hypotheseos mox sequentur; sed finiendi tempus est. Vale, faveque Vir Amplissime

Cultori Tuo,
Gottfredo Guilielmo Leibnitio J.U.D.

Mogunt. 11. Martii. st. n. 1671.

TRANSLATION

Most worthy Sir,

I received your very kind and fruitful letter of reply some time ago. As it seemed wise to add to my answer a brief sketch of my hypothesis, I sent it to be printed, but I was compelled to interrupt the work with various unexpected little trips and I found that during my absence the whole thing was ruined by innumerable [printer's] errors, especially in that type of argument where words must often be used out of their ordinary meanings. For which reason, as I am even now interrupted again and until several weeks have elapsed cannot hope for a conclusion, I preferred in the meantime to send you the half part, rather than defer the whole.[1] But this I ask very earnestly, that you will excuse my boldness in dedicating the sketch of it to a Society [made] illustrious by so many men notable for intellect and rank.[2] The subject alone is, I confess, worthy of such distinguished readers; if it may be admitted by others, I shall think that the outcome corresponded to the intention. I have written succinctly, for informed readers. I believe that the hypothesis itself will seem clear and straightforward enough to the attentive mind, and perhaps it will seem the more adequate for explaining all phenomena, in proportion as he who uses it at any time shall be more ingenious than I am, and better versed in experiments. That all the clockwork and machinery (if I may so put it) of nature or artifice depend either on gravity or on elasticity no one will deny who has considered the matter; and it is not difficult to reason that both follow in the manner postulated from the single circular motion of the ether that I have explained. And this is the core of all my thought; if I have gained this point, then I shall have gained all I aimed at, that is to say an hypothesis more concise and clear than any known hitherto. Yet I hope also that in the particular applications there are some scattered topics that are not to be dismissed outright, as in the derivation of the verticity of the magnet from the spinning of the ether; in the explanation of the nature of cold by analogy with narrow passages; in the reactions, fermentations, and solutions of acids, alkalis, and chemical principles, so-called, in general; in the springing back of catapults and stretched cords; in explaining the oscillations of pendulums and the vibration of strings, and many other things. As regards the magnet there are, I think, several things to be looked into before I could hope to account for everything, and particularly whether the experiment of Grandami published in his little book bearing the title *Nova demonstratio immobilitatis terrae* is really true.[3] For although the demonstration he has based upon it seems quite fallacious, the experiment itself is not a negligible one. Grandami says that if a spherical lodestone (commonly called a terrella) is placed in a little raft of cork or any other floating vessel in such a way that its north pole (that is, the pole pointing towards the North Pole of the Earth when it is left to itself) is turned downwards in the raft, towards the nadir, which is towards the center of the Earth, while its south pole points to the zenith; and if with the lodestone arranged and poised in this manner [after it has come to rest] a circle is marked round it corresponding to the meridian of the place, accurately measured, this circle will be a universal meridian, and when the lodestone is similarly arranged at any place on the globe it will show the meridian of that place without any declination, and thus the points of the compass. I know that this tale has been doubted and so I greatly desire to have it strictly tested, since its truth or falsity is very relevant to the construction of a certain hypothesis about magnetic phenomena of which I have an outline in my head. It is impossible for me to make exact experiments at the present state of my little affairs, while I also lack the powerful lodestones said to be necessary, and the terrella must be precisely turned [on a lathe]. You will be able to learn the truth without any bother, especially if Petit also is asked to investigate the matter, he having had very precise terrellas made for another purpose, that he might put to the test that daily rotation like that of the Earth which Gilbert assigned to the lodestone, as I have gathered from his letter to you printed in the *Transactions*.[4] I shall judge myself overwhelmed with great goodness if I shall learn from you of the result of such a notable thing.

I read the instructions for the use of Huygens' pendulum clocks in a number of the *Transactions* lent me by a friend, but the construction was lacking.[5] I really desire to be told on what principles these clocks of the new construction proceed when they are intended for use at sea; do they go by weights, as big clocks normally do, or by springs, as small portable clocks generally do? Either kind has its own chief disadvantage. For those driven by the gravitational principle cannot be moved from place to place without varying the gravitation and so are not well adapted for tossing about at sea; and although spring clocks can safely be shifted hither and thither they are very rarely accurate and scarcely ever run with a uniform movement, for they vary with the least of causes, with the atmosphere, with the irregular and non-uniform tension of the spring, and most of all with the lapse of time. For elastic force relaxes, while natural gravitation stays constant. Has anything certain been ascertained about the way of making salt water sweet, which a certain physician of Brittany was said to have proposed to the Most Christian King?[6] Küffler too, as I hear, promised to do it by distillation alone.[7] I do not doubt that the journal of the Collegium Naturae Curiosorum, which a few German physicians have founded, now produced as a specimen of the first year in a middling-sized volume,[8] will have reached you and so I refrain from saying more about this. For a long time I have heard nothing spoken of Werner's hydraulic machines, yet I expect [to hear] the result from a friend, whatever it shall be. Some out of prejudice belittle them, but I loathe such prejudgments. We expect the thoughts and experiments of the very ingenious Guericke of Magdeburg to be published at the next Fair.[9] Becher promises a chemical demonstration in which iron is to be produced in fair quantity from an earth containing no actual iron, and [affirms] that the genesis of metals can be illustrated to no slight extent.[10] A certain learned Swiss has, as I understand it, found out a very easy and regular way of working lenses to a conic section, and they say he has proved this with a sample. In the next letter I expect clearer details of his design. I have not yet seen the *Elementa physica* of Franz Wilhelm, Freiherr von Nuland.[11] I add to the last pages of the *Hypothesis* dedicated to you [the Royal Society] a brief sketch of my abstract theory of motion whence, I think, it will appear that my paradoxes concerning motion and the continuum are not so irrational as they seem at first sight:[12] a point is not something minimal and utterly devoid of parts, yet it is unextended or devoid of separated parts, so that one point cannot be greater than another point, as an angle may be greater than an angle. There is no point whose part is nothing, nor whose part can be measured, but it is less than any assignable extended quantity: this is the foundation of Cavalieri's method.[13] But who do I concern myself in advance with what is to be said more clearly in another place? Yet I believe I can hardly escape in any other way from the maze of continued composition. I am struggling with some particular demonstrations on God and mind, in which some marvelous things may be expressed, never uttered before, and yet perhaps conferring no ordinary illumination. Meanwhile I have given this brief hint, that every body is a momentary mind, and hence without consciousness, sensation, or memory. If two endeavors can actually persist together for more than an instant in a single body, any body will be a true mind. And whenever this comes about minds are formed and these are by nature indestructible because, as I shall show in its proper place, two contrary endeavors compatible one with another for more than a single moment in the same point of a body can be removed by no force nor by the impact of other bodies, throughout eternity. From this first trifling glance one can hardly guess how these [ideas] open a door to some admirable speculations. Sometime, when they have been more accurately worked out, it will be advisable to combine them with demonstrations concerning natural law (a field in which I hope I shall do something worthwhile, especially as there are, to my mind, few clever writers skilled in it whom I have not studied, and so I ask that if there are some among you who cultivate this subject—as I do not doubt, being so important for every human life—you will be so kind as to bring them to my notice), for the greater part of natural law rests upon demonstrations concerning God and mind. As you see I can only send you one copy of my *Hypothesis* because of the distance between us. I had dedicated it[14] to the illustrious Society because I choose the outstanding men who compose it as my critics, though lenient ones. Unless you think otherwise, perhaps you can insert the whole of my sketch in the *Transactions* (either all at once, or split into parts) as it only fills four pages, and so test the fair and kindly judgment of the learned, since it can certainly provide matter for many reflections, possibly novel ones.[15] If I receive their opinion from you you will add greatly to the kindnesses for which I feel myself obliged to you.

If you will make apology for my boldness to those great men, your colleagues; if you will make way in their minds for so unknown and obscure a man; if you will inform me of their opinion for the purpose of improving my reflections, I shall make you understand that you have become acquainted with a man who acknowledges kindness. The remainder of the *Hypothesis* will soon follow, but it is time to conclude. Farewell, and think well, worthy Sir, of your devoted

Gottfried Wilhelm Leibniz
Doctor of both Laws

Mainz, 11 March 1671, N.S.

NOTES

Reply to Letter 1568.

1 This was Part I of his *Hypothesis physica nova* (Mainz, 1671), separately entitled *Theoria motus concreti seu hypothesis de rationibus phaenomenorum nostri orbis*, which was presented to the Royal Society (together with this letter) on 23 March 1670/1.

2 The dedication to the Royal Society appears on sig. A2 of *Hypothesis*, and mentions Oldenburg ("vir eximius") as encouraging Leibniz to lay his conjectures about the explanation of natural phenomena before the Society.,

3 This book by Jacques Grandami was published at La Flèche in 1645; Henry Power refutes it in his *Experimental Philosophy* (London, 1664).

4 See Letter 626 (Vol. III, p. 380), printed in *Phil. Trans.*, no. 28 (21 October 1667), 527 ff., in English.

5 See *Phil. Trans.*, no. 47 (10 May 1669), 937–53.

6 Mr. Hauton of Caen, many times mentioned. See Vol. VI, pp. 486–88.
7 Compare Letter 1597. J. S. Küffler's name was commonly thus misspelled.
8 That is, _Miscellanea curiosa_; see Letter 1530.
9 See _Ottonis de Guericke, Experimenta nova (ut vocantur) Magdeburgica de vacuo spatio_ (Amsterdam, 1672).
10 See J. J. Becher's "first supplement" to his _Physica subterranea_ (Frankfurt, 1667), entitled _Experimentum chymicum novum, quo artificialis & instantanea mettallorum generatio & transmutatio ad oculorum demonstratur_ (Frankfurt, 1671).
11 See Letter 1568, note 4.
12 The _Theoria motus abstracti seu rationes motuum universales_ forms (with a separate title page) Part II of the _Hypothesis physica nova_. It was dedicated to the Académie Royale des Sciences. Leibniz sent the _Theoria motus abstracti_ to Oldenburg on 29 April 1671.
13 The method of Bonaventura Cavalieri's _Geometria indivisibilibus continuorum nova quadam ratione promota_ (Bologna, 1635).
14 So the text, but _eam_ was probably written in the original.
15 In fact Oldenburg had both parts of the _Hypothesis_ reprinted in London by John Martin, printer to the Royal Society. His notice of this publication appeared in _Phil. Trans._, no. 73 (17 July 1671), 2213–14. See also Oldenburg's reply, Letter 1676.

1645
Lister to Oldenburg

4 March 1670/1

From the original in Royal Society MS. L 5, no. 27

Yorke, March 4th ——70

Sr

It is a great satisfaction to me to understand, yt my Papers are soe fortunate as in some measure to please ye R. Society wch noble institution I truly honour & admire. I sent you indeed, a hudle of abbreviated Notes about Colours.[1] I engage my credit for ye truth of matter of Fact as farr as I understand, but for ye philosophical part, they are such notions as please me for ye present. As to ye particular of English-black, I say although I am exceeding cautious not to impose upon my selfe & others, yet you will oblige mee wth a singular favour to further ye Expt by exposing it to ye most rigid Tryalls of practised men in yt Art. to this purpos I shall as soon as ye season of ye yeare will afford fit leaves send you a quantitie of ye Colour & likewise some parcells of all yt I said would stand wth Lye.

I am glad to heare ye businesse of Respiration will be accurately examined.

Mr. Wray latly enquired of me, whether I had imparted to you my Expts
about ye bleeding of ye Sycamore & desired me to doe it, if I had not yet
done it. I presume this was to second ym wth their[2] owne, wch I shall be
glad to know are come to your hands, they having I dare say prosecuted
this matter, wth great diligence this Winter.

I have not received any satisfactory answer of ye Enquiries I sent into
Craven about ye very old men; but I hope to make a journey shortly thither & than I will be mindfull of your commands. Sr pardon this trouble
'tis from ye passion I have to serve you. I am

> Your most humble & devoted servant
> *Martin Lister*

I will tell you (yt this Letter may have something worth your notice in
it) concerning Kermes, what came into my memory since my last to you,
yt I was credibly informed when I was in Languedoc,[3] yt some of ye
Gatherers of ye reputed-Berries, doe not wait untill ye worme hath made it
selfe up within a round husk or Chrysalis, affixed to ye branches of ye
scrub-Oake, but doe take ye wormes ym selves & exposing ym to ye
scorching sun in a sheet, suspended by ye 4 corners, beating still upon it as
ye wormes cropp up, to make ym perish by heat, & thus dryed they
praepare ym for furhter use either medical or Ornamental. Again yt they
use in yt Country to set fire of ye Ilex or scrub-oake (as we in England
burn up our Ling (i.e. Erica)[4] in ye moores) when it is grown old & dry
barked, to ye end it may put up again wth more tender & succulent
shootes, fitter for ye nourishment of ye Kermes Insect.

ADDRESS

These
For his honoured Friend
    Mr Oldenburg
at his house in ye Palmal
    London

POSTMARK MR 6

NOTES

Reply to Letter 1640.
1 In Letter 1634.
2 That is, the experiments of Ray and Willughby.
3 Lister was in and about Montpellier in the autumn of 1665. For a discussion of the alkermes gathered near there, see John Ray, *Observations . . . Made in a Journey through part of the Low-Countries, Germany, Italy, and France* (London, 1673), p. 457.
4 Heather.

1646
Thomas Tenison to Oldenburg

4 March 1670/1

From the original in Royal Society MS. T, no. 36

Honoured Sr.

With this you will receive a Copy of that Pamphlet, wch, with honest intention, I wrote against Mr. Hobbes; & wch hath receiv'd ye honour of being mentiond in your Transactions.[1] Such an acknowledgment I ow'd you long since, but was unwilling to pay it by a Present of ye first Edition, wherein ye Presse, so notoriously, injur'd me, in my absence. Though I am a stranger to your Person, yet I have allwaies had thoughts of reverence for yr Society, & for that generous & communicative temper wch appeareth in your self: & (I assure you) I am somwhat concernd that my present circumstances will not permit me to contribute any thing wch is considerable towards that design wch is of such advantage to humane nature. I have sometimes thought I might a little serve you in an account of a minerall water, together wth ye stones of curious figure digged up about the spring, in a Town, nigh Huntingdon, where I sometimes dwell;[2] & of wch nothing yet has bin publicly said, though ye neighbourhood, for many years, have bin acquainted with it.

If such an Account as I am able to give, may seem to you, worth your perusall, you may, be ye least line, command it from

your much obliged Friend
T. Tenison

From ye house of Dr. Stoyt,[3]
  Dr. of Physic in Cambridg
    March. 4. 1670.

NOTES

Thomas Tenison (1636–1715), a Fellow of Corpus Christi College, Cambridge, and formerly a vicar of a Cambridge church, was at this time in a Huntingdonshire rectory presented by his patron, the Earl of Manchester. He became active in politics after his move to London in 1680, was rewarded for his support by William III, and became Archbishop of Canterbury in 1694.

1 *The Creed of M. Hobbes, Examined by M. Tenison* (London, 1670) was briefly reviewed in *Phil. Trans.*, no. 64 (10 October 1670), 2080–81.
2 Holywell cum Needingworth (1½ miles east-southeast of St. Ives), where Tenison was Rector; see below, pp. 552–58.
3 Edward Stoyte (? 1619–1702) was a Cambridge M.A. (1644) and M.D. (1651) and a Fellow of St. John's College.

1647
Oldenburg to Vogel

6 March 1670/1

From the memorandum in Royal Society MS. F 1, no. 30

Acc. d. 3 Martis 1670/71. Resp. d. 6 Mart. remisi Acta philosophica.[1]

TRANSLATION

Received 3 March 1670/1. Replied 6 March. Sent off the *Philosophical Transactions.*[1]

NOTES

Reply to Letter 1633.
1 Presumably *Phil. Trans.*, no. 68 (20 February 1670/1).

1648
Vernon to Oldenburg
8 March 1670/1
From the original in Royal Society MS. V, no. 17

Paris, March 18 1671 [N.S.]

Sr

I must desire your pardon for my slow returnes,[1] really I have beene very intent upon a businesse wch dispenct not wth any intermissions. Soe I must intreate you to accept of what time I have in my owne dispose & not bee severe to account wth me for that wch necessary diversions engrosse to themselves. Yet one thing I may pleade in my excuse that there is noe[2] little of new here that It makes my not writing extreamely veniall. Those Pieces wch are soe much expected of Monsieur Cassinis ephemerides, & Monsieur Picarts measure of the earth, lye ready for the presse & want nothing butt the stamps to fall upon them. & yet they hang still yet Monsieur Picart tells mee that immediately after Easter, they will goe to worke upon his, the Coppy of wch is faire written & the plates all graven. It seemes they weight till Monsr Colbert gives the word, who as I believe intends to have more treatises then one come a broad that soe they may make some show when they appeare in the world together Soe that wth those two pieces I beleeve there will come forth a volume of Anatom-icall experiments, wth observations wch have beene made in the dissec-tion of severall Creatures, in the same nature that they had done already in Sixe[:] the dromidarie the Gazelle &c.[3] And then the first volume of the herball a hundred of whose plates are already graven, (al eau forte)[4] & to wch there will bee added a discourse of the vertues wth the Chymicall analysis of each plant into its oyles salts & spirits, wch will render it the most compleat & usefull worke wch hath yet beene seene in that kind.[5]

Monsieur Picart desires your favour in one particular wch is to send him what is the exact length of pendulum wch wth one vibration measures a second.[6] hee finds it in Paris measure of the length of 36 pounces $8\frac{1}{2}$ lignes. wherein hee hath beene very nice for

in summer hee finds the Length.	36 Pounces	$8\frac{3}{5}$ ligne
at the equinoxes	36	$8\frac{1}{2}$
in winter	36	$8\frac{2}{5}$

Soe the measure hee hath pitcht on as you see is the meane measure, & hee supposeth if the experiment bee exactly made there will bee little difference in the Climate for Monsr Huygens writes him out of holland,[7] that hee finds the length there 38 pounces ½ ligne du Pie de Rhin[8] or Leyden measure, wch comes to much the same wth his observation.

Pray if you please let the observation bee exactly made, & the length of the line stated & send it him. hee desires likewise to know who it was that marked that brasse scale for a halfe foot wch hee sent into england, & whether hee may securely depend upon it as the exact english measure, for hee intends to make use of it in his booke.[9] according to his computation, the difference betweene the english & Parisian foot is butt 7. lignes butt according to the measure you send there should bee 9 hee still very much doubts whether the length of a Pendulum should bee 39 inches 4/10 english measure, soe that hee feares there is a mistake either in the observation or the scale. ease him if you can.

Hee is likewise in great uncertainty concerning the multiplication of sounds, wch wee heare here Mr Moreland hath attained by the help of an Instrument like a trumpett wch hee that speakes is to make use of, whereas hee rather supposed it was to help him wch heard.[10] The invention is of that Consequence that it deserves a distinct explication there fore if it bee not troublesome to you pray oblidge him & mee soe farre as to give a particular description of it, & at what distance one can heare & wth what circumstances it is effected & how hee came to light on it.

He hath not observed any thing of late in the heavens, that is new. the starre in Cygnus is disappeared butt next year hee expects to see it againe. There is butt little hope of finding the longitude by a pendulum since Monsr Richers coming home,[11] for the motion of the ship doth soe alter the regularity of the pendulum that they can conclude nothing from it, butt when they are come on shore they intend to observe wth Instruments & there is a most delicate Sextant made now, of some 5 foot semidiameter wch is to serve for that purpose & to observe starres in different meridians, to the end to make their Chartes more exact. Monsr Huygens is expected back againe here this spring after Easter it is supposed hee will begin his iourney.[12] The Royall Academie is not about any great matters, they are more imployed upon the examination of Plantes in order to the new treattise, & reviewing their old experiments, about Gravity & Motion.[13] Monsr Blondel one of their members is gone into Italy wth the Marquis de Seignelay.[14] Monsr Auzout when hee comes back, I believe will bee received in againe. Monsr Herbelott[15] Is some time since returned from Florence, hee hath brought a very Curious Collection of Oriental pieces neere 200 volumes, besides a Choyce extract of his owne of all the morality, & the medicinall knowne of the Arabs & other Levantines wth their notions of divinity. besides this hee hath severall pieces of History Mircon in the Persian Language,[16] & many others. Steno is still at Florence hee is about his treatise de Coquilles[17] Bellini hath written a small piece de organo gustus.[18] Sigre Magalotti writes mee word that Francesco Redi is about publishing a discourse concerning the Indian drugges & the Vertues wch have been observed in them,[19] wch hee hath conceived in the forme of a letter wch hee sends to Father Kircher in Rome. The same Redi hath found out a new powder wch when it is melted wthout smoake or flame gives a report in the open aire as big as gunpowder doth out of a musquet. Sigre Carlo Dati is about a treatise hee calles noctes Florentinae in Immitation of Gellius his noctes atticae.[20] Borelli will shortly publish the treatise hee hath made concerning this late eruption of Mount Aetna, & Thomaso Cornelio his observations and reflexions on the grotto de Cane out by Naples.[21] Le Pere Bertet told mee hee had coming out of Italy some of the posthumous workes of Baliani the genoese.[22] & some experiments of Guastaferri.[23] I sent Mr Collins Monsr Regnaults reflexions de descensu gravium wch I believe hee will communicate to the Royall Society.[24]

There is little new here le Pere de Billy hath putt out a booke of algebra.[25] Monsr Berniers Cashmir a Country In India like that in Spaine[,] wch was discovered in the Duke of Alvas time, will bee shortly to be sould.[26] there is another volume of the Bizantyne history finisht[27] here was last weeke a tryall before the premier premier[28] who was the Author of that booke de imitatione Christi, whether Thomas a Kempis a Canon Regular in the Monasteries of St Agnes nere Zwöll in Overyssel. or else one Joan Gersenne a benedictine Abbot of Venelles.[29] the Pere Alemand a Canon regular Chancelour of the Universitie pleaded for Kempis le Pere quatremer a Benedictine of the abby of St Germaines for Gersenne.[30] severall arguments & manuscripts were produced the question was doubtfull & remaines yet undecided there beeing much to say for both sides I delivered your letter to Doctor Denis.[31] Pray lett mee heare what novelties you have. I rest

your most obedient servt
Francis Vernon

NOTES

1 Vernon's last letter was written on 14 December (Letter 1574); there is no record of the date of Oldenburg's reply.

2 *Sic*, for soe.

3 [Charles Perrault], *Mémoires pour servir à l'histoire naturelle des animaux* was indeed published in 1671; the earlier work, *Description anatomique d'un Cameleon, d'un Castor, d'un Dromidaire, d'un Ours et d'une Gazelle* (Paris, 1669), in fact contains a description of only five animals.

4 "by etching."

5 This is the herbal often referred to in Vols. IV and V, with plates engraved by Abraham Bosse and others; see Letter 1484. It was not in fact published in 1671. The chemical analyses were by Samuel Duclos and Claude Bourdelin.

6 See Letters 1569 and 1570.

7 There is no record of this exchange in *Œuvres Complètes*.

8 "Rhineland foot."

9 See Vol. VI, Letter 1398. In the *Mesure de la Terre*, Article XI, Picard published equivalent lengths of the Paris, Rhineland, and English foot as 100: 96.66: 93.75. Here the difference between the French and English measure is 9 lines (F).

10 Oldenburg published an account of Samuel Morland's *Tuba Stentor-ophonica* (London, 1671), in *Phil. Trans.*, no. 79 (22 January 1671/2), 3056–58.

11 Compare Vol. VI, Letter 1365, note 8. Richer left for Acadia on the *Saint-Sébastien* with Huygens' chronometers in May 1670; almost at once a severe storm caused damage to both clocks, and neither could be used during the voyage. The expedition returned to La Rochelle on 17 September 1670, and Richer presented a report to the Académie des Sciences in January 1671. (See Olmsted, pp. 625, 632.)

12 Huygens in fact returned to Paris at the end of June 1671.

13 See Letter 1484.

14 This is not the physician mentioned in Vol. VI, Letter 1395, but François Blondel (1617–86), now known as the writer on ballistics and as an architect; at this time he was best known as a diplomat. The Marquis de Seignelay was the younger Jean-Baptiste Colbert, Secretary of the French Navy (d. 1690).

15 Barthélemy D'Herbelot (or Dherbelot, 1625–95), a notable orientalist, had been at the Tuscan court, but was ordered home by Colbert. His collection of oriental manuscripts was largely the gift of Ferdinand II of Tuscany.

16 Mirkhwand or Mirkhond (Mohammed ibn Khwandshah ibn Mahmud, 1433–98) lived at Herat, Afghanistan, and was the author of a general history of Persia down to his own time, much used by later European scholars.

17 It seems that Vernon was confused, though indeed Steno may well have been working at conchology, fossil or recent; but the only *book* produced by Steno that could be alluded to here was *De solido intra solidum naturaliter contento dissertationis Prodromus* (Florence, 1669), of which Oldenburg was about to publish a translation under the title *The Prodromus of a Dissertation* ... (London, 1671; see *Phil. Trans.*, no. 72 (19 June 1671), 2186–90).

18 Lorenzo Bellini, *Gustus organum ... novissime deprehensum* (Bologna, 1665); here too Vernon's news was a little musty.

19 Francesco Redi, *Esperienze intorno a diverse cose naturali, e particolarmente a quelle che si son portata dall'Indie* was published in Florence in 1671.

20 We could not find such a work published at this time by Carlo Dati, though a work entitled *Lepidezze di spiriti bizzarri e curiosi avvenimenti* was published at Florence in 1829. Aulus Gellius was a Roman scholar of the second century A.D.; his *Attic*

Nights is a compendium of miscellaneous information culled from other books, many now lost.

21 Again, we failed to trace this; on the Grotto, see Vol. V, p. 479, note 3.

22 See Letter 1590, note 34.

23 Fabritio Guastaferri published a series of *Lettere al Sig. Gio. Francesco Saliti* (Rome, 1663, 1666, 1665, 1667); see also Vol. VI, p. 206, note 2.

24 Probably André de Regnauld (d. ?1702), a Jesuit at Lyons and an acquaintance of Bertet. Collins, who described him as "one of the best mathematicians in France," knew of him at least as early as January 1670/1 (Rigaud, I, 157; II, 222). We could find no publications of his, but he wrote to Huygens (who had presented him with a copy of *Horologium oscillatorium*) on some points in mechanics (*Œuvres Complètes*, VII, 374). No "reflections of the descent of heavy bodies" by Regnauld were offered to the Royal Society.

25 See Letter 1590, note 18.

26 Vernon refers to the *Suite des mémoires du Sieur Bernier sur l'Empire du Grand Mogol* (Paris, 1671). Ferdinand Alvarez de Toledo, Duke of Alva, the notorious Spanish general in the Dutch war of independence, lived from 1508 to 1582; was Vernon perhaps aware that Kashmir passed under Mogul rule in 1586?

27 See Letter 1556, note 8.

28 Read "premier president" (of the Parlement de Paris).

29 The *Imitatio Christi* is now definitely attributed to Thomas à Kempis (*c.* 1380–1471) of Zwolle in Overijssel, on the opposite side of the Zuider Zee from Amsterdam. Jean de Gerson (1363–1429) was a French theologian; Venelles is a little north of Aix-en-Provence.

30 Pierre Lallemant (1622–73), a religious writer, became chancellor of the University of Paris in 1662. The Benedictine was Jean Robert de Quatremaire (1611–71), best known as a participant in this controversy; in 1649–50 he had published *Jo. Gersen Librorum De imatatione Christi auctor assertus*. His chief adversary previously had been Jean Fronteau (1614–62).

31 Letter 1584.

1649
Collins to Oldenburg
c. 10 March 1670/1

From the original in Royal Society Classified Papers XXIV, no. 25

[*See note, page 504, on this "model" letter.*]

Venerande Slusius,

Yours dated the [27th February] was very welcome and I likewise returne you the thankes of Mr Collins for your inclosed method of Determinations, and those other methods of yours about the Opticall Problemes which you most candidly offer to communicate, and doubtlesse anything else that you shall please to impart will meete with ye same Reception, though not with a Returne Proportionall thereto, as to the Lalover togeather with one of your owne Treatises de Mesolabo, which you sent to Amsterdam to be transmitted hither we have not yet heard of the same, though doubt not of the carefull conveyance after it shall come to Mr Daems to whom if you likewise send the Booke of Marchetti you mention intituled Galilaeus promotus seu de resistentia Corporum, or any good Booke you approve of, we shall not doubt of his care in sending, nor be negligent in desiring him to pay Mr Elziveer or whome you appoint for the same, whereby you will much oblige us for to say the truth Bookes that are published in Italy, or the remote parts of Germany, are very slow in arriving here, if at all, we are informed that in Italy there is lately come foorth Gottignies Dioptricks,[1] and Mengolus Body of Musick[2] both which we cannot but desire as presuming they represent the Idea of their Authors, from hence we could send you in English sorrily printed Butlers Tract of the time of our Savoiurs Nativity and Passion[3] wherein he clasheth against your most learned Seneschall[4] and to say the truth our Authors Booke by reason of his Astrologicall Vanities is prohibited, such as it is we hope ere long to send accompanied with a better booke to wit Dr Wallis his 3d and last Part on Mechanicks

These Physick Bookes are preparing

Dr Willis De anima et morbis Capitis[5]

Dr Needham de Saliva[6]

　　　De animalibus sub-terram vel aquam degentibus

And lately here came foorth translated into Latin

    Mr Boyles Booke de Origine formarum[7]

        Et Experimenta de Respiratione[8]

Gulielmi Hoelli Epitome historiae universalis[9]

    Mr Oldenburg you may promise to send such of the Bookes here mentioned as you thinke fitt

    The Paper of Mr Barrowes concerning Mr Gregories Probleme (wch I formerly sent you)[10] hath had some observations made thereon by the said Mr Gregory which we think fitt to impart to you as followeth[11]

"In primo Praeclarissimi D. Barrow Problemate $HMDO = \dfrac{DE^2}{2}$,[12]

etiam posito rectam *THO* eandem esse cum curva *KXL* in 2do Problemate: Nescio an ex hoc Capite ulla possit dari 2di Problematis solutio, Vereor plenam tertij Problematis Solutionem a secundo non dependere: si enim *EZF* fuerit recta, rectae *AD* parallela; ex secundo Problemate (quod in hoc Casu idem est cum 1°) integre soluto, datur tantummodo sicut ego percipio una tertij Problematis solutio, nempe *VADB* rectangulum, cuius Latus $VA = AE$ vel *DF*: si vero infinitae non dentur sicut dubito in omnibus hisce, datur saltem altera nimirum *VADB* semicirculus, cuius radius est aequalis ipsi *AE* vel *DF*:[13] subtilissima sunt et acerrimi Ingenij Specimina, quae subiungit vir doctissimus. existimo Theoremata illa non solum maximas quantitates sed etiam minimas quandoque determinare ex gratia (in primo Theoremate) si Cycloformis potestatis *m*,[14] Centro *D*, Diametro *DA* (si ita loqui liceat) descripta per Punctum *L*, tota intra curvam *BLA* cadat; erit $DG^m + GL^m$ absolute minimum, si vero dicta Cycloformis alibi occurrat curvae *BLA*, dantur plura minima. Si Cycloformis tota extra curvam *BLA* cadat; erit $DG^m + GL^m$ absolute maximum, si alibi occurrat dantur plura maxima.

    Idem etiam dicimus in 2do Theoremate; si supponatur *BLA* extendi in rectam et super eadem in Punctis suis respectivis ordinatas *LG* perpendicula[riter] erigi; item Centro *B*, Diametro *BLA*, per Punctum *G* Cycloformem describi: quae hic censemus, tertio et quarto Theoremati applicamus, ponendo hyperboliformem Potestatibus debitam Loco Cycloformis, in hoc solo est discrimen quod (cum Hyperboliformis sit figura interminabilis) in figura terminata *BDA* non detur absolute minimum, si fuerit *TG* semper ad *GL* sicut determinata *R*, ad aliam ex Puncto *G*, ipsi *AD* perpendiculariter erectam, et ex hisce alijs descripta figura vel illi analoga ponatur loco Cycloformis, eandem adhuc quinto applicando; Denique si super AD ex Punctis G erigantur Perpendiculares quarum quadrata aequentur Spatij semper respectivi $ADGL$ duplo, et figura ex his conflata ponatur vice Cycloformis dicta quoque sexto applicantur"

TRANSLATION

. . . .

"In the first of the very famous Mr. Barrow's problems $HMDO = \dfrac{DE^2}{2},$[12] even supposing that the straight line THO is the same as the curve KXL in Problem 2, I do not know whether a solution of Problem 2 may be found under this head. I fear that a full solution of Problem 3 does not depend upon the second; for if EZF were a straight line parallel to AD, when Problem 2 (which in this case is identical with the first) has been solved, only a single solution of Problem 3 is given so far as I can see, namely when $VADB$ is a rectangle, whose side $VA = AE = DF$; if indeed there is not an infinite number of solutions (of which I am doubtful) for all of these, still there is at least one other, when $VADB$ is a semicircle, whose radius is $AE = DF$.[13] The specimens of his thought that this learned man has brought forth are extremely acute and subtle. I believe that those theorems determine not only maximum quantities but also, sometimes, minima; for example (in the first theorem) if a cycloform of degree m,[14] with center D and diameter DA (if one may so speak) is described through the point L, the whole of it falls within the curve BLA, [and] $DG^m + GL^m$ is an absolute minimum; if the said cycloform meets the curve BLA anywhere else, there are several minima. If the cycloform falls wholly without the curve BLA, $DG^m + GL^m$ will be an absolute maximum; if it meets it anywhere else there are several maxima. The same may be said of Theorem 2, if BLA be supposed to be extended as a straight line and ordinates LG erected normally upon it at their respective points, and also a cycloform described with center B, diameter BLA, through the point G. What we take notice of here we apply to the third and fourth theorems by taking a hyperboliform of appropriate degrees in place of the cycloform. Only this distinction is to be made: as the hyperboliform is an unlimited figure no absolute minimum is given in the limited figure BDA, if TG were always to GL as the determinate [line] R to another erected normally upon AD at G, and the figure described by these other [lines] or some other analogous to it is to be taken in place of the cycloform, in applying the same to the fifth theorem. Lastly, if perpendiculars be erected upon AD from the points G whose squares are equal to twice the respective area $ADGL$ in each case, and the figure composed of these is taken in place of the cycloform, what has been said may also be applied to the sixth theorem."

NOTES

This is Collins' "model" (in his own hand) for Oldenburg's reply to Letter 1643; Oldenburg wrote this reply, using Collins' model, on 28 April 1671. The date can only be guessed at.

1 See Letter 1602, note 3.
2 See Letter 1470, note 2.
3 See Letter 1590, note 37.
4 See Vol. VI, Letter 1351, note 5.
5 Thomas Willis, *De anima brutorum quae hominis vitalis ac sensitiva est, exercitationes duae* (London, 1672). Reviewed in *Phil. Trans.*, no. 83 (20 May 1672), 4071–73.
6 "On saliva ... on the animals living under the air or water." Neither of these exists in print.
7 See Letter 1570, note 2.
8 See Letter 1525, note 7.
9 [William Howell], *G. Hoeli ... Elementa historiae ab orbe condito usque ad monarchiam Constanti Magni*, etc. (London, 1671), first published in English in 1611 as *An Institution of General History ...*
10 In Letter 1590, pp. 373–76.
11 All that follows (written on the back of the sheet) is copied from James Gregory's letter to Collins of 15 February 1670/1 (Turnbull, *Gregory*, pp. 171–72, with commentary, pp. 173–76). In brief, Gregory comments on Barrow's solution of the differential equation given in Letter 1590, note 6, considering two special cases, and showing that there is another type of solution besides that considered by Barrow. According to Turnbull the basis of Gregory's reasoning here is uncertain, but "these exchanges show the greatest acuity of thought in both Barrow and Gregory."
12 See figure, p. 363.
13 See figure, p. 364.
14 That is, a curve of the form $x^m + y^m = $ a constant.

1650
Oldenburg to Lister
11 March 1670/1

From the original in Bodleian Library MS. Lister 34, f. 11

London March 11. 1670/71.

Sir,

The R. Society was very well pleased, when I acquainted them[1] from yr last letter wth the confirmation, you therein gave of ye English black, as also wth ye promise you made of sending in due time some of ye colour and some parcels of all you said would stand wth Lixivium's. Since you have not thought fit to name to us the plant, wch yields the unchangeable Black, we must not urge you to doe so; though it would be very obliging to the Company.

Mr Willughby and Mr Wray have not yet sent us any thing relating to ye bleeding of ye Sycamore. When they doe, you shall quickly know, though I doubt not, but you will have ym as soon as we.

What you adde in yr last letter concerning kermes, is very curious and remarquable; of wch something was formerly brought in by Dr Croon (printed also in Number 20. of ye Transactions) but more darkly, than in yr account.[2] I know not, whether I intimated to you in my former letter, what I intended to doe concerning an Observation related in the German Transactions (lately begun in that nation under the Title of *Ephemerides Medico-physicae*) viz. That ye grains of Polygonum Cocciferum being exposed to the Sun, are turned into live Worms, wch when dried, and so moisten'd, tinge wth a Crimson-colour.[3]

Sr, I thank you particularly for yr remembring the very Old men, and remaine Sir

> Yr very humble and faithful servt
> *Oldenburg*

NOTES

Reply to Letter 1645.
1 At the meeting on 9 March 1670/1.
2 See *Phil. Trans.*, no 20 (17 December 1666), for Croone's "Accompt of the Use of the Grain of Kermes," written by an apothecary at Montpellier, which he had produced at the Royal Society's meeting on 17 October 1666; this was translated into English by Oldenburg.
3 In the *Miscellanea curiosa* (Vol. I, 1670), Observation 8 (p. 27) is on "Polygonum polonicum cocciferum seu chermesianum polonicum"; it was written by Georg Seger, physician to the King of Poland and practitioner at Thorn.

1651

Oldenburg to Páll Björnsson

11 March 1670/1

From the copy in Royal Society Letter Book IV, 239–41

Reverendo admodum et Doctissimo Viro
Domino Paulo Biornonio
Episcopo In Islandia dignissimo
H. Oldenburg S.R. Secret. Sal.

Cum intellexerit Regia Societas a generoso Viro Domino Martino,[1] Reverendam Tuam observandis atque indagandis rebus naturalibus haud vulgari solertia incumbere, ejusque instituti sit undequaque ea conquirere, quae ad augendam et ornandam Naturae Historiam conducere possunt, Te etiam inter complures alios, multarum gentium viros doctos et sagaces, invitare hac epistola voluere, ut quae Tibi de Insulae vestrae statu naturali constant, vel diligenti Vestigatione innotescere poterunt, ipsis communicare ne graveris.

Et primo circa Aerem et Tempestates; quaenam sit usitata, salubritas vel insalubritas Aeris? Quibus morbis praecipue Regio sit obnoxia, quaeque ijs praesto sint remedia? Quaenam sint Caeli mutationes pro diversis Tempestatibus Anni? Quinam liquores intensissimo Regionis illius frigore sub dio incongelati maneant? Num argentum vivum ibi unquam congeletur? Quousque Gelu Terram penetret? Quaenam nivis figura? Sitne sexangularis? Qua magnitudine Grando cadat, quaque figura? Quaenam corpora praeservari possint beneficio Nivis, quae non? Utrum congelata corpora tumescant, an vero constringantur? Mutenturne colore vel sapore? Quae meteororum genera potissimum ibi gignantur? Speciatimque qui venti inprimis flare soleant? Num eorum ulli sint stati, et ordinarij &c. Ferrumne ibi cito ferruginem contrahat?

Secundo, circa Aquam; Quaenam sit profunditas Maris circa Islandiam; quis Salsedinis gradus; quantumque Salis largiatur Agua marina excocta? Num Aqua maris tenebrosa nocte hyemali luceat? Quaenam ibi sint fluenta, sive currentes ut vocant? Quae Æstuum marinorum ratio; quodnam scilicet praecise sit tempus Accessus et Recessus Maris in Fluminibus et Promontorijs? Quam plagam versus mare in aestibus volvatur? Quaenam sit distantia perpendicularis inter Tumores summos et imas detumescentias? Quinam sint gradus Affluxus et Refluxus Aquarum in aequalibus temporis spatijs, quaeque motus earum velocitas in diversis altitudinibus? Quo die aetatis lunae; quibus temporibus Anni, Summi Æstus et infimae subsidentiae contingant?

Quoad Flumina, quaenam sit eorum latitudo, longitudo, qui cursus, quae inundationes, quae salubritas &c?

Quoad Lacus et Fontes, Aquas minerales, Thermas, quaenam eorum qualitates et Virtutes; Speciatim vero, denturne ibi fontes adeo fervidi, ut, dimidio horae spatio, caro bovina satis in ijs decoquatur? Praeterea, quinam pisces gignantur in Aquis Islandicis, qua copia, magnitudine, bonitate &c.

Tertio, circa Terram; quaenam sit montium celsissimorum Altitudo? Num montes jaceant sparsim, an jugatim? Num Juga montium disposita sint versus Boream et Austrum? An vero Eurum et Zephyrum versus? Quinam dentur Montes ignivomi praeter Heclam?[2] Quaenam saxa, quas glebas fuliginesquae Hecla eructet? Qua praecise die novissimum Heclae Incendium caeperit, et quam diu duraverit, quaeque notatu digna tota incendij tempus occurrerint?

Quaenam sit Magnetis declinatio in diversis partibus Islandiae, quaeque declinationis variatio in eodem loco?

Quaenam sit natura Soli, num Argillosa, Arenosa, Sabulosa, Cretacea, Levis, ullorumque granorum, aliorumve vegitabilium ferax, quaeque Agriculturae ratio?

Quibus Animalibus Regio abundet, sive feris, sive domesticis? Quo pastu eadem utantur, inprimis hyeme?

Et quoad incolas homines, tum viros, tum faeminas, quaenam eorum Indoles, statura, Forma, Fortitudo, Agilitas, vivendi ratio, quibus studijs et exercitijs maxime incumbant?

Quaenam fossilia ibi reperiantur? Quae fodinae lapideae?

Quales glebas largiatur Insula, ut sunt Margae, Terrae fictiles, Terrae Fulloniae, Boli aliaeque terrae medicatae?

Quaenam alia fossilia Regio suppeditet, puta Carbones fossiles, salinas, Alumen, Chalcanthum, stibium, Sulphur? Quaenam metalla?

Haec sunt, quae hac vice mentem subierunt, quibus si responsiones parare Reverendae Tuae libuerit, rem pergratam Regiae huic Societate praestiteris, quam nullo non officiorum genere demereri enitemur. Vale, Vir admodum Reverende, et Tui observantissimo fave. Dabam Londini die 11. Martis 1671.

TRANSLATION

Henry Oldenburg, Secretary of the Royal Society, greets the very reverend and learned Mr. Páll Björnsson, the very worthy Bishop in Iceland

When the Royal Society learned from the worthy Mr. Martin[1] that your reverence is engaged in observing and investigating natural phenomena with unusual keenness, and as its purpose is to bring all those things together from any part of the globe that may contribute to enlarging and perfecting the history of nature, it resolved to invite you by this letter (along with many other wise and learned men of many nations) to be so good as to communicate to it whatever you may know of the natural condition of your island, or what may be learned by diligent inquiry.

And firstly, concerning the air and climate: is the air ordinarily healthful, or not? To what diseases is the region specially liable, and what remedy against them is available? What are the changes in the heavens at the different seasons of the year? What fluids remain unfrozen in the open exposed to the hardest frost of that region? Does quicksilver ever freeze there? How far does the frost penetrate into the ground? What is the shape of the snow? Is it hexagonal? At what size does hail fall, and of what shape? What bodies can be preserved with the aid of snow, and what not? Do frozen bodies swell, or contract? Do they change in color or taste? What sorts of meteors chiefly occur there? And especially which winds generally blow there? Are there any fixed and customary ones, etc. Does iron quickly grow rusty?

Secondly, as to water: what is the depth of the sea round the island, what is its saltness, how much salt does boiled sea water yield? Does the sea water shine on a dark winter night? Are there any flowing streams, or currents as they are called, in the sea? What is the manner of the tides, that is to say, what precisely is the time of ebb and flow at rivers and promontories? Toward what direction is the sea moved by the tides? What is the perpendicular distance between the highest full tide and the lowest ebb? What amount do the waters ebb and flow in equal intervals of time, and what is the velocity of their motion at different states of the tide? At what day of the moon, and at what times of the year, do the highest tides and lowest ebbs occur?

As to rivers, what is their breadth, length, flow, floods, healthiness, etc?

As to springs and lakes, mineral waters, hot springs, what are their qualities and virtues; and particularly are there in that place springs so hot that beef can be fully cooked in them in half an hour? Moreover, what fishes live in the Icelandic waters, of what plenty, size, and edibility?

Thirdly, concerning earth: what is the height of the highest mountains? Are the mountains separated or joined in a massif? Are their summits arranged towards the north and south? Or east and west? What volcanoes are there besides Hekla?[2]

What are the rocks and lumps of soot that Hekla has thrown out? On what day exactly did the recent eruption of Hekla begin, and how long did it last, and what things worthy of note occurred during the whole course of the eruption? What is the magnetic declination in various parts of Iceland, and what is the variation of the declination in the same place?

What is the nature of the soil, is it clayey, sandy, gravelly, chalky, or light, what grain or other crop does it bear, and what is the practice of agriculture?

What animals abound in the region, either wild or domestic? What pasture do they have, especially in winter?

And as for the human inhabitants, both male and female, what are their characteristics, stature, form, strength, agility, way of life, and what studies and exercises do they chiefly adopt?

What minerals are found there? What quarries of stone?

What earths does the island yield, such as marl, potter's clay, fuller's earth, bole, and other medical earths?

What other minerals does the region furnish, such as coal, salt springs, alum, copperas, stibnite, sulphur? What metals?

These are the things that came to mind on the present occasion. If your reverence pleases to prepare answers to them, you will furnish something very welcome to the Royal Society which we will try to deserve by every kind of service. Farewell, very reverend Sir, and think well of your most humble servant. London, 11 March 1671

NOTES

The recipient of this letter was not a bishop in Iceland, but had been parish priest at Selardu in that country and rural dean of Bastaðrud. Páll Björnsson (1621–1706) was a native of Iceland, and went from grammar school there to the University of Copenhagen (B.A., 1644). He was a considerable scholar in Greek and Hebrew as well as other languages. The answers to these queries were printed in the *Philosophical Transactions* in 1675, and thence copied into the *Journal des Sçavans*.

1 Presumably this was John Martyn, printer to the Royal Society, and if so it may be that Páll Björnsson had come across the *Transactions* and so wrote to him. But an earlier letter from him to a certain Robert Flint had been read to the Society on 23 November 1664 (see Vol. II, p. 325, note 9, and Birch, *History*, I, 492–94).

2 There are 107 volcanoes in Iceland, the largest being Askja, with a crater area of 34 square miles. There had been half a dozen especially notable eruptions of Hekla (see Plate IV) since 1104, the most recent having been that of 1599; it has continued active in recent times.

1652

Reed to Oldenburg

14 March 1670/1

From the original in Royal Society MS. R 1, no. 27
Partly printed in *Phil. Trans.*, no. 70 (17 April 1671), 2128–32

Worthy Sr.

Your letters both came to me in due time from the dates thereon but have beene interrupted in my intended answere by a Violent Ischia[1] wch seised me, after a double Quartan wch held me good part of ye last winter, & I haveing gotten a little of respitt from my Fitts doe hasten to undeceive you concerning ye miscarriage of them.

As to that you Inquire of concerning white Mulberyes I doe not remember I ever saw the Fruits or Tree, therefore can passe noe Judgment whether they may thrive wth us (Red ones wth us doe very well & grow of Slipps.) only in generall I believe there is noe sort of tree that will thrive in England, but will find a fitt soyle in our County. for I never came into a Country (though many far Richer in soyle) wherein all sorts of trees to grow more kindly, & smoothly than in ours.

To the inquiry you desire mee to make into the age of our Countrimen my weaknesse hath been such as as yet I can render you noe account. but at Easter sessions if God give me health I intend to sett yt on foot, where I shall have opportunity to meet wth some of every part of our Country, in the meane time I desire to know of you whether I may not have a Retrospect for the last 30 or 40 yeares; for I do not observe that Longaevity among us as formerly when I was a Lad I doe remember to be[,] the late warrs I thinke affrighting many aged men wch might have lived yet into the other world. But if you would receive an account of a man aged to a Miracle (though not of our Country) I commend you to inquire the name of him yet or late alive from an honorable person now at Parliament & of the house of Peers, the Lord Evers,[2] who in August last att Astropp Wells in Northamptonshire told me of a man 3 yeares since in one of ye Rideings of Yorkshire examined in Fanshawes office[3] whose age was then 173 (The name of ye person & Towne I have forgott.) 21 years older than old Parr.[4] It is very fit his age shuld be taken notice of & recorded. It being a speciall argument of Gods providence asserted by Dr Hackwell,[5] that the world as to yts vigour does not senescere,[6] & that our lives might be as long as at any time since the flood they were did not distemperate liveing cutt us of. If you attend upon the L. Evers for satisfaction herin I intreat you to carry my service to him also. Being upon miracles let this go along.

On Thursday last, ye 9th Instant, there was at the next house to mine a swarme of bees: It was a very fayre day to intice them, but we never have them till the middle of May. I had yt from the owner one Parry now in my worke, & inquired of him, whether they did not all leave the hive as sometimes they doe unseasonably either for want of food or out of distast. he told me No, but there are as many left behind as came forth, but I (who have sometime studyed the Regiment of that little industrious wise creature) doe conceive that poverty drew them abroad to seeke their fortunes; the infinite and divine wisdome haveing imparted such a providence to that little Commonwealth as to send part of theyr Company abroad to shift, before theyr whole stock of food should be consumed to the destruction of them all, (Deus maximus in minimis.)[7]

And now Sr to that I promised. I have read that Excellent booke of Mr Evelins sent unto me by your worthy friend & mine Dr. Beale. Especially his Pomona,[8] & have learned many things out of yt, wch I before had not observed; Especially the new way of planting therin mentioned out of the papers of my auncient and worthy Friend Mr John Buckland[9] whom I do never remember but wth very great respects. And the new way of making Pipin Cyder in the Aphorismes of Sr Paull Neale. To whom (unknowne) I doe & our whole Country ought to returne very many thankes. for certaynly the reasons rendred by him of ye harshnesse & ye cure of yt in Pipin Cyder are very sound, & may be used to ye advancement of all our Cyders.[10] I have ye last yeare Two parcells of pipin Cyder. of the one but few bottles and that was ye droppings of the Cheese (for soe we call the Apples when ground & prest) after we had wrung yt as far as we could, & that come away wthout any mixture at all of ye pulp of ye Apple, being that flying-lee mentioned in his Aphorisme; The other a Vessell contayning two hogsheads and that (following the reason of the directions he gives but not having vessells to draw yt of that flying Lee when setled, & to pursue those directions exactly) I strayned through a Coarse Cloth into the vessell & by that meanes eased yt of much of that Lee. Both were Excellent good both for Colour and taste, but the bottles best, being ye most delicious & Luxuriant Cyder & most pleaseing both for Colour and tast that ever I knew, yet I have had as good Redstrake as ever I dranke in any place. I doe commend for the advancing of Cyder in richnesse both for tast and

Colour, a New Cask. provided yt be made of Timber very well seasoned. other wise it may spoyle yt utterly. The vessell I mentioned wherin I had my pipin Cyder, was such. & I have often tryed yt, & found that sort of Caske to improve Cyder. The next best Cyder I ever had was Redstreake grafted upon a Gennet Moyle Stock: for as those kinds doe best agree, & the trees soe grafted seldome Canker as doe the Redstreak upon a Crab-stock, soe the fruite is far more ingenuous and milder & being ripe both rich & large & good to eate, & the Cyder is more smooth, & abates in strength & harshnesse of yt on ye Crabb & needs lesse of melloweing before making. The stock in degree altering & reclayming ye nature of the fruit. For, as an Apple does best grafted on a Crabb wch gives quickness & acrimony to the fruit; soe a Crab (& ye Redstreak is noe other) grafted on an Apple from whence yt receives gentlenesse & softnesse & largenesse. And an excellent Alloy to ye sharpnesse, & as Mr Evelin calls yt the wickednesse of ye fruit. Wch (being but a discourse of the intercourse betweene the sapps both of stock & graft) puts me in mind to beg from you the Judgment of those gentlemen of your Royall Society that bend their thoughts to this way of knowledge concerning the descent of the sapp, in winter; wch is now generally denyed. though I as yet cannot assent to yt for I thinke yt a heresy in husbandry obstinately to deny ye descent of ye Sap. Besides many other experiments to prove the descent, This I have observed, wch I never heard any did besides. that the graft hath influence to Corrupt or to heale the stock, nay further to alter & change the very nature & way of growing of the Root in the Earth. wch I cannot see how yt should [be] but by sending downe yts sap thither. I have by Certeyn observation found, that Crab stocks grafted wth some sort of fruit wch the soyle likes not, they not the Soyle[,] will (not one or two but all of that sort) Canker not only in ye graft, but the stock allso. wch if you graft agayne upon the former graft, wth a fruit likeing to the soyle will all heale & become Trees. And further, certeyne yt is by my observation that 20 peare stockes being wild grafted yong wth ye same sort of peare, and 20 of another. The roots of each of them of one sort will grow alike, & soe of the other. generally those that naturally grow high, as your barland peare, root deep, and all doe soe. Those whose heades are bushy & thick as ye Summer Bone Christien theyr roots run wide & are mattered below.[11] all are soe. This alteration of the way of groweing of the Roots must be by grafting, & could not be but by inter-course of Sap wch yt receives from the grafte. for Omne agens agit per Contactum.[12] & that cannot be but by the returne of the Sapp. But in this

I desire rather the judgement of others then give mine owne, because yt is of a Constant use to me to be well assured herein, for if the Sap returnes not then may I prune or Lop my trees in anytime of yeare wthout losse of sap wch I take to be their blood and wherein theyr life consists.

Your last of the 27th of Febr atteyned me the 1⁰ instant. as I was busye in beginning to plant a new Orchard wch I intended to name St Davids Orchard [not] in honor or jeere of our Welsh saint,[13] but for my distinction sake because I have more then one. The cold day brought me into a Relapse soe that I reserve the finishing till that day next yeare, if God repreives me soe long. By what I doe you may easily gather what I thinke concerning the season of transplanting. wch Mr Evelin directs to be in October. Soe I did thinke & used to doe, but for these later yeares never doe begin to plant till at Valentines day though I have a mild & good winter as this was: And I approve late planting before earlier, and as yet however the spring or summer after prove, loose fewer by miscarriages. The Cold in the winter kills more then the drought in summer however yt prouves (as the last was the worst I have knowne;) only the cold does the worke & we put yt upon the drought because they languish untill summer upon the fatall blow they receive by the Cold in ye winter and then dye. For either we take our stockes out of woods or out of Nurseryes in either place they lye warme if you then in October transplant them you expose them on a sudden to an open ayre & adventure them being warme to a Long & perhapps cold winter wch they cannot beare noe more then our men unused to a Voyage beyond the Line can the heate, you endanger them. Add hereunto that I can relieve them against the drought by watering & covering the ground to keep yt coole. but there is noe fence agst the frost. wch many times getts into ye rootes & kills soe that they never spring, or if they doe yet pulingly & dye in ye spring. Or if they survive as many doe yet come on very slowly and pitifully, for the barke does cleave to the wood by reason of the cold wch dryes & Clings them togeather that like a hidebound horse they will not admitt the sap the root would send up. And other suckers grow out at the earth, & the tree growes drye, & turnes red, all wch discovers the obstruction in the receiveing the sap wch the root would send up. & then we are forced to score & loosen the barke as we can. Now on the other side if the summer prove moyst the danger & feare of late setting is over & they will thrive and come forward amayne; if otherwise, I seldome see but they alwayes keep greene & fresh, being maynteyned in Lyfe and verdure by ye sap they receive in ye beginning of the spring before they be transplanted: & the next following yeare they florish exceedingly. This therefore I doe, wch I submit to better Judgments and experience: In the dead of winter I prune & cut the tree I intend to transplant, as I would have yt be, to ye end to loose nothing of yt strength when I transplant; when I suffer yt to abide untoucht by ye spade till after St. Valentine, & then remove yt after yt hath taken in somewhat of the spring. This I thinke will make yt take better & grow better: Nicetyes in grafting or planting I will not trouble you wth, nor care I for; but this I thought good to offer to experience of others, (haveing found yt for best in mine) because It is that wch is of dayly & generall use, & if this season be found best yt will be that wch will be of great advantage to this kind of husbandry. In transplanting I am very carefull to preserve & sett the roots as Large as I may, supposing the Larger the root, ye more of strength & sapp yt conteynes & will advance the growth of ye tree since every thing growes in proportion to the root beneath but I am doubtfull in this whether I doe well or ill and desire the Judgment of others, for I have heard first from some planters, & afterward from Sr Symon Degge[14] who had experience therein, that roots cut short doe best, for they send forth new roots wch draw sap & nourishment best: And we see that our Moyles sett on slippe that have noe roots come to a tree sooner: & have observed often times that a Moyle transplanted after yt hath taken Roote doe not live soe certaynly or thrive soe well as a slip newly sett. The full of the moone (though we often observe yt not) I suppose if yt be in our choyce is the rather to be chosen, for then all moyst sublunary things have most of strength. I have heard from a wise & active person now in place, & a planter neere London That yt was an observation of our husbandmen that they respected not the Moone in Cutting theyr grafts: for then yt will not shrink soe much as when cut in the wane. My late planting being most in Arable Land I (after my intended orchard finished) haveing noe more place for Orcharde doe rather make choyce of planting in peaseland, for that grayne will, if yt thrive, keep the ground moyst and coole all the summer.

Worthy Sr: I have deteyned you wth an impertinent scribble to give you satisfaction in what I can in that thing wch I make my Recreation & take some delight in. I have gotten beyond the bounds of a letter, & truly beyond my strength wch now I find & am forced abruptly to subscripe my self.

Your faythfull frend to serve & honor you
Ric Reed

Lugwardine,
March 14.70.

ADDRESS
To his worthy Frend
Henrye Oldenburgh Esqr
Secretary to the Royall Society
at his house in the
	Pall Mall nere
Westminster these.

POSTMARK M 17

NOTES

Reply to Letters 1626 and 1641.
1 Sciatica, probably.
2 George, Baron Eure (the more usual orthography) or Evers (d. 1672), a Member of Parliament during the Commonwealth; he had succeeded to the title in 1652.
3 The Fanshawes had held the office of King's Remembrancer of the Exchequer since the mid-sixteenth century. The incumbent at this time was Thomas, second Viscount Fanshawe (1632–74).
4 Thomas Parr (1483?–1635), always denominated "old Parr," who acquired notoriety when brought to London in 1635 by Thomas Howard, second Earl of Arundel. At his death William Harvey performed an autopsy, John Taylor wrote his biography in a pamphlet entitled *Old, Old, Very Old Man,* and he was buried in Westminster Abbey.
5 George Hakewill (1578–1649), divine and author, had published *An Apologie of the Power and Providence of God in the Government of the World* in 1627.
6 "grow old."
7 "God is greatest in least things."
8 Presumably the second edition of *Sylva* (London, 1670), containing *Pomona* and the other pieces mentioned.
9 See Vol. II, p. 25, note.
10 Compare Vol. II, p. 20, note 6.
11 The Barland pear is especially used in making perry; the Bon Chrétien is similar to the William or Bartlett pear.
12 "Every agent works by contact."
13 1 March is St. David's Day.
14 Sir Simon Degge (1612–1704) was at this time one of the justices of the Welsh Marches.

1653
Oldenburg to Dodington

15 March 1670/1

From the memorandum in Royal Society MS. D 1, no. 20

Answ. March 15. 1670/71
Sent Boyle de Aere for Travagino.

NOTE

Reply to Letter 1621. For the book, see Letter 1553, note 4.

1654
Oldenburg to Malpighi

15 March 1670/1

From the original in Bologna MS. 2085, VII, ff. 19–20

Celeberrimo et Doctissimo Viro
Domino Marcello Malpighio,
Philosopho et Medico Bononiensi
Henricus Oldenburg Salutem

Avide hanc occasionem arripio Te salutande, Vir Prae-clarissime, quam mihi suppeditat Nobilissimus Marchio Bartholomei, hinc Florentiam reversurus.[1] Quidam ex ejus comitatu Medicus promisit, se hanc ad Te summa cura expediturum.[2] Mitto Tibi et Eximio Domino Montanario Tractatulum quendam, a Domino Boylio de Mira Aeris Rare-factione nuper editum, de quo ut sententiam vestram nobis aperiatis, percupimus. Domini Montanarii De vitris stillatitiis Scriptum egregia doctrina et solertia adornatum existimamus; num vero de Phaenomenum, circa eadem deprehensorum, causa rem acu tetigerit, lubet etiamnum ἐπέχειν: Nec de controversiis, inter eundem Virum et Doctum et Dominum Rosettum agitatis, pronunciare quicquam festinamus.

Speramus, Domini Cassini et Domini Mengoli Exercitationes praelo jam emancipatos esse, commodaque occasione nobis aliquo navigio transmissum iri.

Praelo nuper commissi fuerunt Tractatus Latini de Qualitatibus et Suspicionibus Cosmicis, deque Regionum Subterranearum et Submarinarum Temperie;[3] non ita dudum a Domino Boylio sermone vernaculo in lucem emissi; quos etiam suo tempore ad Vos expediemus. Idem plura molitur ad augendam scientiam Physicam adornata, nequiquam obstante valetudinis et oculorum debilitate.

Accepi nuper, Philosophos Parisienses brevi edituros varia experimenta Anatomica, de diversis Animalibus habita, nec non Plantarum, jam aeri incisarum, Centuriam unam alteramve, multis de singularum virtute observationibus sociatam.[4]

Mathesin et Physicam hoc ipso tempore ubivis vigere et incrementa sumere palam est. Ut ardor iste jugiter perennet, in votis quam maxime habet Tibi Addictissimus Oldenburgius. Vale et me favore tuo prosequi perge.

Dabam Londini d.15 Martii 1671.

Clarissimum Dominum Montanarium plurimum ex me salvere velim, eique gratias maximas ago pro Epistola de vitro stillatitio typis edita; quam recte accepi, favore Domini Doddingtoni, Venetiis nomine Regis Angliae agentis.

Rogo peramanter, ut fasciculus hic inclusus prima quaque occasione commoda et tuta, Venetias ad Dominum Doddingtonum transmittatur.[5]

TRANSLATION

Henry Oldenburg greets the very celebrated and learned Mr. Marcello Malpighi, philosopher and physician of Bologna

I eagerly seize this opportunity of greeting you, most famous Sir, provided me by the return hence to Florence of the very noble Marchese Bartolommei;[1] a certain physician in his retinue has promised that he will take great care to send this on to you.[2] I send you and the distinguished Mr. Montanari a certain little treatise lately published by Mr. Boyle concerning the *Admirable Rarefaction of the Air,* and we very much urge you both to reveal your opinion of it. We think that Mr. Montanari's piece on Prince Rupert's drops is graced by remarkable learning and assiduity; it is still preferable to say nothing as to whether he has got to the bottom of the cause of the phenomena involved. Nor do we hasten to pronounce on the controversies between him and the learned Mr. Rosetti.

We hope that the essays of Mr. Cassini and Mr. Mengoli are now released from the press and that at a convenient opportunity they will be sent us by some ship.

The Latin treatises on *Cosmicall Qualities and Suspitions, and the Temperature of the Subterraneall and Submarine Regions*, published in English by Mr. Boyle not long since, have recently gone to press;[3] these too we will send you in due course. The same person strives to complete many things for the advancement of natural knowledge, notwithstanding the weakness of his health and eyes.

I heard lately that the Parisian philosophers are soon to publish a variety of anatomical experiments performed on different animals, and also a hundred or two of plants, already engraved on copper, together with numerous observations on the virtue of each.[4]

It is clear that mathematics and natural science are everywhere flourishing and developing at this present time. Your very devoted Oldenburg very much wishes that this eagerness may long continue. Farewell, and continue to favor me with your goodwill.

London, 15 March 1671

I beg you to salute the famous Montanari from me many times, and I return him my best thanks for the printed letter on Prince Rupert's drops, which I received safely by the favor of Mr. Dodington, His Majesty's resident at Venice.

I beg you most affectionately to send the enclosed package by the first safe and convenient opportunity to Mr. Dodington at Venice.[5]

NOTES

Reply to Letter 1618.

1 Not identified; the Bartolommei were an old and noble Florentine family. The marquis, and Count Bardi, visited the Royal Society to witness experiments on 9 March 1670/1.
2 According to Malpighi's draft reply (of 24 May 1671) his name was Pecorini.
3 At Amsterdam and Hamburg; see Letter 1553, note 4.
4 See Letter 1648 and its notes 3 through 5.
5 Probably Letter 1653.

1655
Willughby to Oldenburg
16 March 1670/1

From the original in Royal Society MS. W 3, no. 42
Printed in *Phil. Trans.*, no. 70 (17 April 1671), 2125–26

Middleton March 16. 1670/1

Sr

my businesse and want of time to prosecute experiments I hope will plead my excuse For not answering yours of Feb 18 sooner. since that wee have reviewed our old notes and made some Few experiments, and Find that Branches of Willow, Birch and Sycamore cut of and held perpendicularly will bleed without tipping and that the cutting of of [*sic*] their tops dos not sensibly promote their bleeding. Wee have not yet made tryall in Maple and Wallnut, the Weather having been such, that those trees have not run Freely since the receit of your letter: We doubt not of Mr Listers diligence and Veracitie and wonder our Experiments should differ. The Tryalls wee have made this yeare confirme those wee communicated to you Formerly Viz: the sycamore bleeds upon the first considerable Frost after ye leafe is Fallen, as it did plentifully ye 16 of november last; and both that, Wallnut and Maple all Winter long after Frosts, when the weather relents or the sun shines out: but Wallnut and Maple begin not so soone as the Sycamore the Birch will not bleed till towards the spring, this year it began somthing sooner then ordinary about the beginning of February.

Wee cut of pretty big branches of Birch and having tipped the ends inverted them, and fastened a limbus[1] or ring of soft waxe to the great ends which wee held upwards, making with the plane of the end a vessel of about an Inch deep, where into wee powred water, which in a few minutes sunke into the pores of the wood and running quite through the lenght of the branch dropped out of the ends considerably fast, continuing so to doe as long as wee poured on water. The like experiment wee make by fastening such rings of Waxe to ye lesser ends, and pouring in Water which run thorough ye Wood, and dropped out of the greater ends as fast or faster. This wee tried once upon a sycamore without successe. manie thankes for both your letters

I am Sr

your Faithfull servant
F. Willughby

The double refracting stone described in the 67th transaction is found near St Ithes[2] in Huntingtoneshire and in other places. Mr Wray desires the favour of you to know what Mr Boiles opinion is of Van Helmont who is now or was lately in England.[3]

ADDRESS

For Mr Henry
Oldenburg Secritery
to the Royall Society
   in the pellmell
        London

POSTMARK MR 20

NOTES

1   A circular lip or rim.
2   St. Ives; the allusion is to Oldenburg's summary of Bartholin's experiments—see Vol. VI, Letter 1405.
3   Francis Mercury van Helmont (1614–99), son of the more famous Johann Baptist, like his father combined medicine and chemistry. However, his life was wilder and more mysterious: he was imprisoned by the Inquisition from 1661 to 1663, yet familiar with all the intellectual world of Europe. In addition he seems to have exerted a strange fascination upon various prominent and eminent people. Upon his arrival in England in the autumn of 1670 he was admitted to the Royal Household at Newmarket, visited Henry More at Cambridge, and examined Lady Anne Conway (Sir John Finch's sister, a great sufferer from migraine) at her home in Warwickshire (also Willughby's county). He remained in her household for nine years.

1656
Lister to Oldenburg

17 March 1670/1

From the original in Royal Society MS. L 5, no. 28
Partly printed in *Phil. Trans.*, no. 70 (17 April 1671), 2123–25

Sr

Since my last to you[1] I have been in Craven, when I was not unmindfull of your commands, but, indeed, I find it a very hard & troublesome businesse to verify precisely ye ages of such persons as either affirme ym selves or are beleeved very old: ye best information & reports I could get, I send you.

Robert Montgomery now living in Skipton, but borne in Scotland, tells me yt he is 126 yeares of age: ye oldest persons in Skipton say that they never knew him other than an old man: he is exceedingly decayed of late, but yet goes about a begging; to wch his debauchery (as is said) has brought him.

Mary Allison of Thorlby in ye parish of Skipton died 1668, aged about 108: she spun a webb of linnen cloath a yeare or two afore she died, wch as they say ye Countesse of Pembroke[2] keepes by her as a raritie.

J. Sagar of Burnley in Lancashire about 10 miles of Skipton died about ye yeare 1668 & was of ye age (as is reported) of 112.

Th. Wiggen of Carleton in Craven died 1670 of ye age of 108 & odd months: he went about till within few weekes of his last & was a very faire *corps*. The register of Maladale[3] was looked over upon wager & this account (as is said) found true.

Francis Woodworth of Carleton, died 1662 of ye age of 102 odd months: ye mother of 7 children alwayes a very lean woman, yet to her very last went about as streight & upright as a yong Girle & of perfect memory: her sight & hearing decayed, though not wholly deprived of either. This by information from ye sonn Robert Woodworth now living in Carleton of ye age of 69, as able a man to ditch & plough as any in ye Towne.

Will. Garthorp & Will. Baxter of Carleton informes me yt they two being upon ye jury at Yorke 1664, they saw & spoake wth in ye Assisse Hall, two men, Father & Son, sommoned as witnesses in some cause or other out of Dent, a small vally in Craven 8 miles beyond *Settle*. The Father told ym, yt he & his sonn made twelve score betwixt ym, yt his sonn was above 100 & yt hee wanted not half a yeare of 140; he told ym further yt he could & did make Fish-hookes as small as would take a Trout wth a single haire. They observed yt ye sonn looked much ye older & had ye white haire this sonn he had by a 2d wife. They could not remember the names of these persons.

I add, yt is to be observed, yt ye food of all this Mountanous Countrey is exceeding course as salted & dryed beefe & sower-leavened Oate bread.

I am confident many scores of persons might be found of ye age of 100 yeares among these northern Mountains but its troublesome to veryfy & you must not take these reports as authentick & exact, but yet credible enough, to make ye matter worth ye examination.

To ye end yt I might satisfy my selfe in some measure about some of ye doubts I sent you,[4] I have been most concerned according to former thoughts & inclinations in examining ye truth of these Queries viz. whether Saps are not be found at all seasons of ye yeare in a much like Consistence & quantitie in ye respective parts of a Vegetable & what communication one part of a plant may have wth an other in relation to ye Ascent & Descent of Sap.

now because Sap is than said to ascend from ye root, when it is found to move in Tapping, I lopped off certain branches of a Sycamore ye morning betimes of a hard Frost (Feb. 21) before they would bleed or show any signe of moisture. this I did to vary ye efficient, not wishing to wait ye change of ye weather & ye Suns heat, but brought ym within ye aire of ye Fire & by & by as I expected they bled apace, without being sensibly ye warmer.

This experiment repeated afforded me divers *phaenomena*, wch follow; & proved almost an Universal way of bleeding all sorts of Trees, even those wch of ym selves would not shew any signes of moisture.

1. poles of Maple, Sycamore & walnut cut downe in open weather & brought within ye warmth of ye Fire did bleed in an instant. Alsoe Willow, Hazel, Cherry, Wood-bine, Blathernutt,[5] Vine, Elder, Barberry, Aple Tree, Ivy etc. Whicking & Egg-berry Tree (1. Padus Theophrasti)[6] tryed in ye same manner in Craven.

2. Briar and Rasberrie rodds were more obstinate, Ash utterly refused, even heated hot.

3. Branches, yt is, poles with their topps intire & uncut bleed alsoe, when brought to ye Fire side, but seem not soe freely to drinke up their sap again when inverted, as when made poles

4. ye same Willow poles left all night in ye grasse Spott & returned ye next day to ye Fireside bleed afresh.

5. Maple & Willow poles bleed & cease at pleasure again & again, if quickly withdrawn & balanced in ye hand & often inverted to hinder ye Falling & Expence of Sap: yet being often heated they will at length quite cease, though no Sap was at any time sensibly lost. And when they have given over bleeding, yt is, showing any moisture by being brought within ye warmth of ye Fire, ye bark will be yet found very full of juice

6. A hard ligature made within a quarter of an intch of ye end of a wood-bine rod, did not hinder its bleeding at all, when brought within ye warmth of ye Fire.

7. Maple & Willow poles etc quite bared of bark & brought to ye Fire, will shew noe moisture at all in any part

8. One barberry or pipridge[7] pole bared of its barke & brought to ye Fire, did shew moisture from within ye more inwards Circles, though not any from ye outwards.

9. Maple & Willow poles etc. halfe bared of barke, would bleed by ye Fire from ye halfe only of those Circles, wch lay under ye barke.

10. Maple & Willow poles split in two & planed, would not shew any moisture on ye planed sides, but at ye ends only.

11. a pole of Ivy did of it selfe exudate & shew a liquid & yellowish resin from ye barke & neer ye pith: but when brought to ye Fire side, it bleed a dilute thin & colourlesse sap from ye intermediate wood-Circles.

12. A pole of willow for example bent like a bow will ouse its sap freely, as in bleeding either Spontaneous or by ye Fire.

I thanke you for ye expt about polygonum cocciferum, yet I doe not remember I have seen such a plant & desire of you to know whether ye Title be imposed by ye Experimenters *pro re nata*,[8] or ye name wch some Botanick author hath formerly given it.

I find in my Notes yt some yeares agoe I gathered off our English-Oake round-Worme huskes very like Kermes-berries but I than made no tryal of ym.

Again yt I have often observed on plumb Trees & Cherrie Trees Alsoe on ye Vine & Cherry-Laurel certain *Patellae* or flat Huskes containing wormes wch (or at least ye huskes, for them only I had ye opportunity of making ye Expt on) will strike a carnation wth ly, & stand. I am Sr

Your most humble servant
Martin Lister

Yorke
March 17 1670

Fabius Columna[9] reports some where, as I remember (for I have not now ye booke by me,) yt he observed certain blewish *patellae* on ye Mirtle; these alsoe, I guesse, were Worme-huskes Kermes like.

NOTES

Reply to Letter 1650.
1　Letter 1645.
2　Presumably Anne Clifford, Countess of Dorset, Pembroke, and Montgomery, widow of the fourth Earl of Pembroke.
3　Since there is no parish of this name, Lister was probably thinking of Malham, a parish including the source of the Aire river. Malhamdale, often spelled "Malghdale," was a bailiwick of the honor of Skipton.
4　In Letter 1609 (p. 417).
5　Bladdernut, *Staphylea pinnata*.
6　It is difficult to explain this; the whicken or quicken tree is either the ash, the mountain ash (rowan), or juniper; *Padus Theophrasti* is identified by Parkinson as a wild cherry, probably the bird-cherry, dialectically called egg-berry (*Prunus padus* L.).
7　Pipperidge is a local name for barberry (*Berberis*).
8　"for this present occasion."
9　Fabio Colonna (*c*. 1567–1650) was an Italian botanist and prolific author, much studied by Ray as well as by Lister.

1657

Sachs to Oldenburg

20 March 1670/1

From the original in Royal Society MS. S 1, no. 34

Praenobili et Amplissimo et Excellentissimo
Viro
Domino Henrico OLDENBURGIO
Illustrissimae Societatis Regiae Anglicae Secretario
Philippus Jacobus Sachs a Lewenheimb. Ph. et Med.D. et Acad. Cur.
Salutem et Officia paratissima

Illuxit tandem faustissima dies; Vir Excellentissime, tot desiderijs a me expectata, quae mihi Amplitudinis Tui Litteras per tot maris terrarumque intervalla feliciter exhibuit. Non dubito praecessisse alias, quas ab Amplitudine Tuo aliquot ab annis avide expectaveram; omnes tamen naufragio etiam terrestri perijsse certum est praeter illas quas Anno 1668 mense Septembri Amplitudinis Tui Londini Dn Kretschman obtulerat,[1] quamvis etiam illae varia fortuna hinc inde jactatae, a maligniore Sorte tamdiu denegatae, nec prius oblatae nisi Duorum Annorum spatium cum binis mensibus elapsum fuisset: finiente enim Anno LXXmo praedictae Litterae serius equidem, non tamen ingratae Museum intrarunt. Quae sane si citius appulis[2] sint Academiae Nostrae institutum in edendis Ephemeridibus perfectiore methodo informare potuissent: unde si forte non omnia futura sint ad Eruditorum Palatum excusationem aliquam et veniam mereri posse credimus quod privato paucorum Medicorum consilio Primus proruperit Annus, indies et annuatim nitidior proditurus labor, si eruditae et candidae censurae limam Eruditissimi Viri apportaverint. Unde etiam maxima cum gratiarum actione excepimus Amplitudinis Tui admonitionem, ut cautiores simus in adducendis experimentis saepe fallacibus, aut relationibus incertis: quod si interdum praeter spem ac voluntatem nostram quosdam a recta veritatis semita aberrasse probatum fuerit, ut in posterioribus laboribus hac de re fiat admonitio curabimus. Nec dubitamus quaedam in Primo Nostro Anno inveniri posse quae Censuram mereantur non minus, quam Typographi incuria poenam ob tot commissa sphalmata: cautiores tamen erimus et magis providi in sequentibus; ne ratis nostra ijsdem rursus impingat scopulis. Hoc pro Summae Felicitatis et Authoritatis argumento aestimamus Illustrissimae Societatis Regiae non ingratam fuisse visam nostri Instituti rationem: nec molestum fore speramus, si auderemus quaedam ex Anglicorum Transactionibus Ephemeridibus nostris passim inspergere, ut cum Lingua Anglica Germanis ignotior sit, Eruditi isti et Curiosi Discursus eo citius Germaniae dissitos transirent angulos: non silebimus vastae Eruditionis Mare, ex quo tam limpidi exhausti fontes. Me non monente videbit Amplitudo Tua Collegas Curiosos tanquam fere omnes medicos potius Medicis et Physicis inhaerere quam reliquis Philosophiae et Matheseos studijs, quamvis nec haec velimus esse exclusa, licet priorum tractatio primarius noster scopus sit. De formicarum vi acida mutante colores caeruleos in rubros experimenta faciemus: sed forte non omnes formicae id praestabunt nisi majorum species; quare etiam mulierculae formicas venantes ad balnea formicarum acervos baculis fodiunt, et odoratu explorant an acidum sentiant, quod illae acidae etiam in Usu Medico praevaleant.[3] Narratum mihi Dn. D. Marcum Marci Mathematicum et Medicum insignem in Anglia maximopere aestimari: inter posthuma ejus scripta detinetur Tractatus de Impulsu cujus capita si recenseantur non ingratum fore Iudico.[4]

Denique si Amplitudo Tua pro privato in meam Tenuitatem affectu oblata occasione per Dn. Godefr. Scholzium Bibliopolam Hamburgensem continuationem Transactionum Anglicarum quam usque ad Num LXI possidemus 18. Jul. 1670. habitam ex Illustris Societatis liberalitate imposterum gratiose Hamburgo Vratislaviam dirigerit (solet etenim praeditus Scholzius Libros e Londino Hamburgum transportare) pro summo merito et beneficio agnosceram et oblatione nostrorum laborum redhostire tentarem. Vale interim Vir Amplissime quam diutissime in totius Reipublicae Litterariae Emolumentum, et Illustris Societatis Regiae Ornamentum. Vratislaviae Silesiae 1671. 20. Martis.

Elenchus Opusculi D. Marci Marci Medici Pragensis
De Impulsu

Pars Prima de Natura Impulsus

De motu voluntario, et an Musculorum motus sit naturalis.

Impulsum non nisi per accidens differre ab alio impulsu.

Cujusmodi differentias habeat impulsus et a quo desumatur.

Qua ratione Impulsus terminetur.

De principio Motus non voluntarij.

An motus necessario fiat per Impulsum.

An accidentia habeant Impulsum et qua ratione moveantur.

De modo producendi Impulsum, et an rationem habeat substantiae

An motus fiat mediante spiritu, et quae sit differentia inter Motum Animalium et reliquorum corporum motum.

Unde proveniat Differentia Motus in Animalibus, et an sufficiat Voluntas seu appetitus ad hujus determinationem

Motus impedimenta non a principio interno, seu ab Anima, sed ab organis varie affectis provenire.

Qua ratione Anima in corpore moveatur.

Impulsum esse qualitatem, et a principio interno mobilis nasci.

Gravitatem esse causam exemplarem, non vero efficientem motus.

An Idea Motus Elementi sit ejusdem speciei cum Idea motus voluntarij.

Rebus etiam inanimatis inesse quandam notitiam ab ejusmodi Ideis, quam naturalem vocant et de causa illarum efficiente.

Qua ratione et a quo fiat motus ad vacuum prohibendum.

Qua ratione motus gravium a violentia excisetur.[5]

An Spiritus mediante Impulsu moveant obsessos.

Qua ratione impulsus ad partes ejusdem mobilis se extendet.

Eadem sequi sive a motore externo, sive a principio interno proveniat impulsus.

Pars Secunda
De Gravitate ad Mundi Centrum relata.

An inaequalia pondera motu aequali deorsum ferantur.

An Motus gravium in descensu augeatur.

Unde oriatur tarditas motus in diversis medijs.

Quae sit ratio gravitatis in mobili ad medium relata.

ADDRESS

    VIRO

Praenobili, Amplissimo, et Excellentissimo

Dn. HENRICO OLDENBURG illustrissimae

Societatis Regiae in Anglia Secretario Meritissimo,

    Patrono Summo

        Londinum

TRANSLATION

Philipp Jacob Sachs von Lewenheimb, Ph.D., M.D., of the Academia Curiosorum, presents his greetings and ready services to the most noble, worthy, and excellent Mr. Henry Oldenburg, Secretary of the very illustrious English Royal Society

At last the longed-for happy day has dawned that has successfully presented me with your worhip's letter, excellent Sir, after so lengthy a passage o'er lands and seas. I have no doubt that it was preceded by the others that I have eagerly awaited from your worship during the last few years, but these have certainly perished in some shipwreck (on sea or land), apart from that which Mr. Kretschmann brought back from your worship from London, in September 1668.[1] Yet even this, tossed hither and yon by caprice, was so long denied me by an evil fate that it was only delivered after the lapse of two years and two months, for that letter came tardily (though no less welcome) to my study at the end of 1670. If it had been brought[2] more quickly it could have influenced our Academy's design towards publishing its *Miscellanies* by a more perfect method; whence we believe we may deserve some condonation and forgiveness if everything is not to the taste of the learned, in that this first year they were dashed off in accord with the personal views of a few physicians; daily and yearly our labors will be brought to greater perfection if the learned will give them the polish of honest and learned criticism. Accordingly we have received with great thankfulness your worship's warning that we should be more cautious in alleging experiments that are often fallacious, and reports that are unreliable, because if it shall be proved that sometimes certain things have (contrary to our will and intent) erred from the strict line of truth we shall take care to give notice of the fact in our subsequent labors. And we must believe that certain matters may be found in our first year which merit censure no less than the negligence of the printer in making so many errors. But we shall be more cautious and vigilant in future years lest our bark strike upon the same rocks. Hence we esteem it an argument for great success and authority that the manner of our design did not seem unwelcome to the most illustrious Royal Society, and we hope it will not be disagreeable if we dare to scatter some things out of the *Transactions* of the English here and there among our *Miscellanies*, so that (the English tongue being pretty unknown among Germans) those learned and curious papers may the more rapidly penetrate to the remote corners of Germany. We shall not be silent concerning that sea of vast erudition from which such pure springs are fed. Without direction from me your worship will see that our Academicians, being almost all medical men, interest themselves in medicine and physic rather than other philosophical studies or mathematics, although we had no wish to exclude these even if the former [medicine] was the object of our first treatise. We have made the experiment on the acidic power of ants turning blue colors into red, but perhaps only the larger kinds of ants, not all of them, will do this. For which reason too, girls catching ants for the bath-houses dig up antheaps with sticks, and try by smell whether they can sense an acidity, because the acid ants are best for medical purposes.[3] I am told that the distinguished mathematician and physician Marcus Marci is greatly esteemed in England; among his posthumous writings there remains a treatise on impulse, whose chief headings, I believe, you will be glad to see rehearsed [*see below, p. 529*].[4]

Lastly, if your worship out of your personal indulgence towards my feeble capacities will kindly address the continuation of the English *Transactions* (which we have up to No. 61, dated 18 July 1670) by means of Mr. Gottfried Schulz, bookseller at Hamburg, via Hamburg to Breslau, when opportunity serves and by the generosity of the illustrious Society, I shall acknowledge your great kindness and attempt some return by presenting our labors. The aforesaid Schulz is accustomed to importing books from London to Hamburg. Meanwhile, farewell most worthy Sir, and may you long remain an ornament of the illustrious Royal Society and a benefactor of the whole republic of letters.
Breslau in Silesia, 20 March 1671

The contents of the little tract *De impulsu* by
Mr. Marcus Marci, physician of Prague

Part I: The nature of impulse

On voluntary motion, and whether the motion of the muscles is natural.
One impulse differs from any other only accidentally.
What kind of distinctions an impulse may have, and their origins.
Why an impulse comes to an end.
On the commencement of motion not effected by will.
Whether motion is necessarily brought about by impulse.
Whether accidents have impulse, and in what way they are moved.
On the manner of producing impulse, and whether it is proportionate to substance.
Whether motion is effected by means of a spirit, and on the difference between the movements of animals and the motion of other bodies.
Whence the difference in the movement of animals arises, and whether will or desire suffices to determine it.
The hindrances to motion arise from no internal principle nor from the soul but from the variously affected organs.
How the soul may be moved in the body.
Impulse is a quality arising from a principle internal to the moving body.
Gravity is an example of a cause of motion, not a truly efficient cause.
Whether the idea of the motion of an element is of the same kind as the idea of voluntary motion.
That there is even in inanimate things a type of notion [arising] from ideas of the same kind, which they call natural, and on their efficient cause.
How and whence arises the motion preventing a vacuum.
How the motion of heavy bodies may be destroyed by violence.
Whether spirits may by means of impulse move victims of possession.
How impulse extends itself into the parts of the same moving body.
That the same things follow whether the impulse comes from an external mover, or from an internal principle.

Part II: On gravity referred to the center of the world

Whether unequal weights are carried downwards at equal speeds.
Whether the motion of heavy bodies increases in descent.
Whence the sluggishness of the motion in various media arises.
What is the reason for the gravity in the moving body referred to the medium.

ADDRESS

To the very noble, worthy, and excellent
Mr. Henry Oldenburg, very worthy Secretary
of the most illustrious Royal Society in England
My chief patron

London

NOTES

Reply to Letter 1620 (or 1631).

1 There is no other record of this letter, breaking the long silence between Sachs and Oldenburg since 1665, but compare the latter's directions to Halticks of February 1668 (Vol. IV, p. 164), proving that Sachs was by no means forgotten at that time. It is not possible to identify the Mr. Kretschmann who visited London.

2 So, apparently, the MS.; read, "appulsae."

3 A water distilled from ants was common in pharmacy but we cannot specify their use in bathing; possibly they were employed as counter-irritants.

4 Compare Vol. IV, pp. 164–65, indicating Oldenburg's previous hearsay knowledge of this very treatise. Johannes Marcus Marci (Jan Marek, 1595–1667) left several posthumous works. This one was published by J. J. W. Dobrzensky under the title *Ortho-Sophia seu philosophia impulsus universalis* (Prague, 1682; 2nd ed., 1683). These "headings" are in fact the titles of the chapters of the printed book.

5 *Sic*; the printed text reads "excusetur," which is also an incorrect form, but the meaning seems clear.

1658
Wallis to Oldenburg
23 March 1670/1

From the original in Royal Society MS. W 1, no. 118

Oxford March 23. 1670/71

Sir,

If I had so well considered the trouble of transcribing, & that it had not been into a Book, I should have saved ye scribe that trouble. As it is, if your Nephew[1] stay but so long as yt there be time so to do; if you send mee ye Copy that your man hath done, I will by it cause another to be transcribed here & sent you for France, & you may keep my original; I have no copy of it here at all; that wch I sent you being the onely one yt I had written. If your Nephew stay not so long, you may send the transcript you have (provided it bee well compared;) & let me have my original back so long as to copy it. But I would have those words in ye preamble (beginning, as I remember, with *praesertim,*) which concern a person there not named (but a blank left for it) to bee blotted out: For Monsr Carcavi is ye person there meant (who, amongst a great deal more of uncivil language had in expresse terms given me ye Ly; *il menti:*) but so far as is general; (*quod in materia de Cycloide expertus sum,*[2] or to that purpose,) may stand. But if you send it, let it be as from yourself, & as ye copy of a thing you have had some time in your hand, and ye Demonstrations much longer in my Lo. Brounckers hand, but wch I did not til lately consent to have sent over; till now learning of Fermat's works ready to come abroad (of wch wee have yet seen none in England,) I was content it be sent, that I might not bee supposed to have taken any hint from thence. No more (ye post being going) but that I am

Yours to serve you
John Wallis

If you publish ye other thing of ye numbers, let it be as in a Letter from that Monsr Pelshofer[3] to yourself, & in latin; & in terms modest & not too extravagant.

ADDRESS

> For Mr Henry Oldenburg,
> in the Palmal near St
>   James's
>   London

NOTES

The context of this letter is obscure. Apparently the document to be copied was a letter from Wallis to Brouncker; this is now lost, but Brouncker's reply dated 15 February 1670/1 is in Royal Society MS. B 2, no. 9 (see Letter 1665). It seems likely that Wallis's letter was a defense against something which, he had been informed, had appeared in Fermat's "works" (presumably the *Diophantus*), possibly insisting on William Neile's priority in the rectification of a curve (1657) against a claim by Fermat to have done this first.

1 Heinrich Coccejus; see Vol. IV, p. 222, note, and Letter 1663, below. He was to take the copy to Vernon in Paris—see Letter 1662.

2 "what I have discovered with regard to the cycloid."

3 Several scholars have borne the name Pelzhover, but none seemed clearly to fit here; no such correspondence survives.

1659

Oldenburg to Huygens

Late March 1671

This letter, now lost, is mentioned in Letter 1663 as having accompanied a copy of *Phil. Trans.*, no 67 (16 January 1670/1). It was to be delivered by Martin von Kempen (1642–83), a poet from Königsberg who, after his travels, became official historian to the Elector of Brandenburg.

1660

Robert Selbie to Oldenburg

Late March 1671

From the original in Royal Society MS. S 1, no. 109

Honored Sr.

Thoe unacquainted yett meeting with a Letter from my good Freinde Mr. Nelson wherein you are pleased to mention and Take Cognizance of me a favor highly beyond my deserts,[1] Could doe noe less then assume the boldness to gratifie your desires by Giving you a generall Accompt of some more then ordinarie Success in my practice. As alsoe the medicines I most frequently use. The maladies I have observed (of those most feral and trucullent) are your dropsies, Convulsions, and Convulsive motions: As your Emprostotonos & opistotonos[2] wch are much more strainge and terrible then a Compleat Convulsion. A Diabetes, and lately a younge man in 20 dayes time of a scorbutick palsey. Consumptions as alsoe the Ricketts: But Especially an old Gentlewoman of this Towen past 80 yeares of a Confirmed dropsie, & if I may farther speake without ostentation equally Successfull in what ever Distemper occurrs wth my fellowe practitioners: nowe if this seeme Hyperbolicall to any I cann mention upon Certificate severall persons cured of all the Diseases specified through the Concurrance of the good hand of God: As to medicines that I have used for this 6 or 7 yeares are these principally vizd, dissoluble Magistery of Corrall prepared with your Acetum philosophorum:[3] your Elixer proprietatis[4] after severall other menstruums, made wth Spiritum Vini Subtilissimum et Spiritum salis[5] well Incorporated by often drawing over, wch I should commend to younge Tyroes in Chymistrie as the only proper menstrum till they Cann meett wth the Liquor Alcahest[,] Ens Veneris[6] in wch Sublimation I alwaies Receive a Spiritt first of good use: Spiritum Cornus Cervj[,][7] Antimonium Diaphoreticum[,][8] Salem Antimonium:[9] Alsoe a pleasant Tinctura Antimonii[10] Imbodied wth Tarter wch I use upon all occasions where Vomits are Required, Volatile Salt of Tartar Converted into a Liquor wth wch I prepare severall Catharticks cum multis Alijs:[11] My Furnaces being for the most part Constantly Imployed: Butt the Cheife Champions I most Eagerly desire to Anatomize, is your Antimonie[,] Coral and your Spiritum Salis Tartarij[12] I must Confess I could never yett discover a right Menstruum for Coral except that of Zwelfers,[13] wch doth Excellently well for its Magisterie yett for its Tincture a better must bee found out which if itt Could soe as to Convert it into a Rubie Spermatique Juice, I should nott doubt of a Cure for the Scurvey wch is a distemper wee are much at a loss in and very Epidemicall in our parts and I presume all England over. Now Sr being in a probable way to bee Crowned wth the felicity of youre Acquaintance, and such of your noble Virtuosi as you shall Judge Requisite, I shall begg pardon in Supplicatinge a Request from you wch is to give mee your Sentiments of a worthy patient now under my hands whose distemper I have here Inclosed[14] beseeching perusall and how farr you and the venerable Esquire Boyle doe approve of the Kinges Bath this Summer In such a Case he being Inclineable to make Tryall soe humblely Craveing Excuse for this Boldness and Trouble beeing bigg wth Expectation of a Line from you at your most Leisur & opportunity, I subscribe Sr

Yours most faithfully to serve you in what possibly I can
Ro : Selbie

NOTES

1 The writer of this letter is known only by Nelson's allusion to him in Letter 1575. Nelson probably sent it with his own Letter 1661. Presumably Oldenburg referred to Selbie in Letter 1606, now lost.

2 Tetanic convulsions and spasms of the torso.

3 "Vinegar of the philosophers"; the magistery was prepared by dissolving coral in distilled vinegar (acetic acid) and precipitating with oil of tartar.

4 "The elixer of property," devised by Paracelsus, was basically aloes, myrrh, and

saffron extracted with alcohol. An acid was often added, as here. This was a favorite remedy.

5 "Very subtle spirit of wine, and spirit of salt."

6 Alkahest was the universal solvent of Paracelsus; *ens veneris* (literally, "that made of Venus [copper]"), a universal remedy of J. P. van Helmont's.

7 "Spirit of hartshorn"—dissolved ammonia.

8 "Sweating antimony"; the nitrate of antimony, in fact.

9 "Salt of antimony."

10 "Tincture of antimony" (possibly prepared with vinegar as the solvent).

11 "with many others"; the salt of tartar is reflux distilled with alcohol.

12 "Spirit of salt of tartar."

13 Johann Zwelfer (?1618–68), born at Pfalz, was for many years an apothecary; then (having graduated M.D. at Padua) practised medicine at Vienna. His many writings on pharmacology were frequently reprinted. All notable pharmacists of this period devised recipes for dissolving coral into a harmless fluid without loss of color, however Zwelfer in his *Pharmacopoeia Augustana et eius mantissa* (Gouda, 1653), p. 790, expressly states that the calcination of coral followed by solution in acid destroys its virtue.

14 This is not now with the letter.

1661

Nelson to Oldenburg

25 March 1671

From the original in Royal Society MS. S 1, no. 110

Worthy Sir

Your Letter dated Jan: 24th I received within 3 dayes after; yet had not againe troubled you wth these, (untill I had gathered up some more particulars in answer,) but that Mr Selby upon the Account of his Patient, rather wisht that his,[1] might visitt you a little sooner, wth whom I prevailed as you see to write himselfe, tho' wth some reluctancy.

You will apprehend Sr (I have) by this partiall reply as well my willingness as want of ability to doe you service. I have communicated your Letter to Sr Ralph Cole[2] in hopes to procure you a correspondence from him, and of other things I am not forgetfull nor shall be hereafter as occasion shall serve.

Sr. I thinke it not improper to insert here two words concerning Mr. John Webster,[3] Authour of a late Book called Metallographia, of wch also you gave an Account.[4] Hee was of my acquaintance when I lived in Lancashire, about 7 or 8 yeares agoe, and tho' hee may have heretofore writ somewhat that may not possibly relish so well wth some of the Virtuosi, nor perhaps wth himselfe now, yet I reckon him a man of more than ordinary acuteness and very fit for your Correspondence, he has practised Chymistry now a great while, is a smart and ready man in discourse and not unacquainted wth books. If that part of the Country where he lives (being Clitheroe in Lancashire) should afford any thing worth your notice, I know no man so fit to give you an Account of it.

There is a Gentleman in this Towne of my acquaintance sadly afflicted wth a distemper in his eyes, that would gladly have your Judgement, how far he may confide in that booke (or in the Author there of) mentioned Number 64. Pag. 2081,[5] he intreats to know where the Author lives & where the booke is to be had.

I suppose you will thinke it no strange thing to heare of a Calfe wth 2 heads (or rather a double heade) they being united towards the backe parts, have 3 ears, 4 eyes, 2 mouths, and the Noses somewhat widely distant the one from the other; and of a great bigness; This if worth the mentioning was brought forth yesterday at a place adjoyning to this Towne, but wth such difficulty that (beyond what is fabled of the Viper) it was the destruction both of it selfe & ye damme. — — —I thanke you for the satisfaction you have given me as to my objection about the Tides. I have not yet heard from Mr. Oswell[6] and therefore doubt much of his health. But Sr it is time to conclude, seeing most of this is but trouble, wch I hope you will pardon because you have done the like heretofore to

> Your very humble Servant
> *P. Nelson*

Durham, March 25th 1671

ADDRESS
> For
> His honored frd Henry Oldenburg
> Esq at his house in the pell mell
> in St. Jamess feilds
> these present
> London

POSTMARK MR 29

NOTES

1 Letter 1660.
2 For Sir Ralph Cole, see Letter 1575, note 7. No trace of a separate letter from Oldenburg to him, nor of subsequent correspondence, has survived.
3 John Webster (1610–82) was both puritan divine, chemist, and surgeon. At this time he was practising medicine at Clitheroe, thirty-five miles north of Manchester. In Cromwell's time he had composed a severe critique of the traditional University education in *Academiarum examen, or the examination of Academies* (London, 1654), arguing for the teaching of such new and practical subjects as chemistry; this was answered by Seth Ward in *Vindiciae academiarum* (Oxford, 1654). Webster also wrote on religious topics and was to write against the belief in witchcraft. *Metallographia* (London, 1670) is his only scientific book.
4 In *Phil. Trans.*, no. 66 (12 December 1670), 2034–36.
5 Giuseppe Francesco Borri, *Epistolae duae ad Thomam Bartholinum* (Copenhagen, 1669), includes some extravagant claims for the author's success in surgical treatment of the eye.
6 See Letter 1575 and its note 12.

1662

Oldenburg to Vernon

25 March 1671

From the memorandum in Royal Society MS. W 1, no. 118

Observed these directions in my letter to Vernon, to whom I sent Dr Wallis's Latin letter to Ld Brouncker, assuring him, we had [not] seen any thing yet of Fermat's works; omitted those lines of Dr Wallis wch are included in [   ] By my neveu March 25, 1671.

NOTE

This is written on Letter 1658, to which it relates.

1663
Oldenburg to Huygens

28 March 1671

From *Œuvres Complètes*, VII, 55–56
Original in the Huygens Collection at Leiden

A londres le 28 Mars 1671

Monsieur,

Il n'y a que peu de iours, que ie baillay à un certain Monsieur Kempe, de Koningsberg, un petit pacquet pour vous, ou il y avoit le Nomb. 67. des Transactions.[1] Dans ma lettre, qui l'accompagnoit, ie vous promis de vous envoyer, par une autre commodité, un petit discours de Monsieur Boyle touchant l'admirable Rarefaction de l'Air; de la quelle promesse ie m'acquitte presentement, avec les baisemains de son Autheur. La personne, qui vous porte cecy, est de Bremen,[2] dont le principal estude est le Droit civil, mais qui avec cela aime fort la moderne maniere de philosopher, quoy qu'il n'y ait fait que des petits commencements. Il a passe son hyver icy, apprenant l'Anglois, et s'informant de l'Estat du pais, et faisant estat de passer de la Hollande (où il avoit estudié au Droit l'espace de 3. ou 4. ans) en France, pour s'y rendre maistre de cette langue là, et pour voir le beau monde. C'est un tres honeste homme et de grande industrie, fidelle au dernier point en des choses, dont on le charge. S'il vous peut servir dans son chemin, ou à Paris, vous n'avez qu'à le luy commander franchement; il s'en acquitera, au possible, à vostre satisfaction.

Au reste; il faut que ie vous fasse scavoir, que i'ay receu depuis peu de Mayence la moitié d'un petit traité, fait par Monsieur Leibnitz, Conseiller de cet Electeur là, qui porte le titre; "Hypothesis Physica Nova; qua Phaenomen[or]um Naturae plaerorumque Causae ab unico quodam Universali motu, in Globo nostro supposito, neque Tychonicis neque Copernicanis aspernando, repetuntur."[3]

Il a dedié ce discours à la Societe Royale, qui le fera examiner par quelques uns de ses membres. Il ne semble pas un Esprit du commun, mais qui ait esplusché ce que les grands hommes, anciens et modernes ont commenté sur la Nature, et trouvant bien de difficultez qui restent, travaillé d'y satisfaire. Je ne vous scaurois pas dire comment il y ait reussi; i'oseray pourtant affirmer, que ses pensees meritent d'estre considerées. Entre autres choses il fait des Reflexions sur les Regles du mouvement, comme elles ont esté posées par vous et Monsieur Wren; dont ie vous donneray cet eschantillon;

"Supersunt nonnulla etiam in motibus vulgaribus phaenomena, prima specie contemnenda, at solutu difficilia, si acutius introspicias. E.g. Cur Dura duris impacta resiliant; cur quaedam Flexa se tanta vi restituant; cur, si Ingeniosissimorum virorum Hugenij Wrennique Experimenta universalia sunt, corpus impactum quiescenti, quasi permutatione facta, ipsum in ejus loco consistat, motum vero suum in alterum transferat: Talia enim, et multa alia id genus, abstractis motuum rationibus (nisi Globi nostri Oeconomia accedit) consentanea non sunt."

Et dans une autre place:

"Hugenii Wrennique Phaenomena, si comperta sunt, causam eorum ex Hypothesi mea reddere, difficile non est."

Car il semble de juger que ny vous ny Monsieur Wren ayez assigné les causes de ces Phaenomenes, que vous avez considerez en establissant vos regles. C'est à vous astheur, d'en juger, et de bien examiner les meditations de ce nouveau Philosophe. Il vous sera facile d'en faire venir de Mayence, si vostre santé le permet de vous appliquer à ces estudes là, dont ie souhaite fort l'entier accomplissement, comme Monsieur

Vostre tres humble et tres obeissant serviteur
H. Oldenburg

ADDRESS

A Monsieur
Monsieur Christian Hugens de Zulichem á la Haye.

TRANSLATION

London, 28 March 1671

Sir,

Only a few days ago I gave a little packet for you (containing Number 67 of the *Philosophical Transactions*) to a certain Mr. von Kempen of Königsberg.[1] In my accompanying letter I promised to send you at another opportunity a little tract by Mr. Boyle concerning the admirable rarefaction of the air; this promise I am now fulfilling, with its author's compliments. The person who brings you this is from Bremen;[2] his principal study is civil law but at the same time he is fond of the modern method of philosophizing, although he has so far only made a small start at it. He spent the winter here, learning English and investigating the state of the country; and preparing himself to remove from Holland (where he studied law for three or four years) to France, in order to master the language and observe good society. He is a very cultivated and industrious man, and absolutely trustworthy in every situation. If he can serve you on his way or at Paris you have only to command him freely; he will acquit himself to your satisfaction to the best of his ability.

For the rest, I must tell you that I recently received from Mainz half a little work written by Mr. Leibniz, Councilor to the Elector there, bearing the title *Hypothesis physica nova* (*A new physical hypothesis, by which the causes of the phenomena of Nature and of many other things are deduced from a single universal motion postulated in this globe of ours, which is not to be rejected by either Tychonians of Copernicans*).[3]

He has dedicated this treatise to the Royal Society, which will have it examined by some of its Fellows. He seems no ordinary intelligence, but is one who has examined minutely what great men, both ancient and modern, have had to say about Nature, and finding that plenty of difficulties remain, has set to work to resolve them. I cannot tell you how far he has succeeded, but I dare affirm that his ideas deserve consideration. Among other matters he has made some reflections upon the rules of motion as laid down by you and Mr. Wren, of which I shall give you the following sample:

"Even in the phenomena of ordinary motions there are still several points remaining that are pretty hard to resolve, if you examine them carefully, though to a superficial eye they seem trivial. For example, why hard bodies dashed together spring apart; why some elastic bodies spring back so strongly; why (if the experiments of the most ingenious Huygens and Wren are universally valid) a body striking another at rest by (as it were) a permutation remains at rest in the latter's place, transferring its own motion to the other body. Such things and many others of the same kind are not consonant with the abstract concepts of motions, except it happens by the disposition of our globe."

And in another place:

"It is not difficult to deduce the cause of the phenomena of Huygens and Wren from my hypothesis, if they are found to be true."

For he seems to judge that neither you nor Mr. Wren has assigned causes to the phenomena which you considered in establishing your rules. It is now up to you to judge this matter and to examine carefully the thoughts of this new philosopher. It would be easy for you to obtain a copy from Mainz, if your health permits you to apply yourself to these studies, the complete accomplishment of which is, Sir, the wish of

Your very humble and obedient servant,
H. Oldenburg

ADDRESS

To Mr. Christiaan Huygens of Zulichem
       The Hague

NOTES

1 See Letter 1659.
2 This was obviously Oldenburg's nephew, Heinrich Coccejus; see Letter 1658, note 1.
3 See Letter 1644.

1664
Christopher Kirkby to Oldenburg

29 March 1671

From the original in Royal Society MS. K, no. 7
Partly printed in *Phil. Trans.*, no 71 (22 May 1671), 2158–59

Dantzigk 8th Aprill 71. st.n.

Sr

Monsieur Hevelius desireing me to order you moneys to satisfie for paijment of the Microscope he hath desired you to provide for him, I herewith send you an inclosed upon sight whereof my friend will pay you what moneys you desire for Monsr Hevelius account. And now Sr upon this occasion I laij holde to quit my selfe in part of the promise made you when I was last in England; to Comunicate what I might meete with worth the troubleing you with; The followeing observations were comunicated to mee by an ingenious Doctor my acquaintance which to mee doe seeme strange and are concerneing petrification in humane Bodies, and although you may have perhaps others of the like nature yet I Doubt not but these may have their use, at least to Delucidate & Confirme the former—

A virgin of 56 yeares whose whole course of life had beene extremely sedentarij was troubled some yeares before her Death with greate paines in her Back, espetially towards the right side, a continuall inclination to, & effective Vomitting, whose urine for some time before was troubled and as mingled with Blood; yett that left her about a yeare before her Death so that her urine was almost totally void of Salsuginous[1] matter; shee was under the cure of the best Doctors in this place who adiudged that Symptome of Bloudy water to have proceeded from the Earelij loss of her naturall flowers (which left her in the 40th yeare of her age) thereby perhaps deceived because there was never either stone or gravell voided by her, But her last Doctor from whom I have this relation did adjudge it to proceed ab affectu Nephritico & quidam gravissimo.[2] This person Dijeing troubled with these distempers was opened by her last phisitian, and amongst many other but common phaenomena's he found The left Kidneij filled with large stones, but the right wholly petrifijed as hee might justly judge that stone to bee which was exactly formed like the kidney covered with the ordinary skin laxae,[3] without anij flesh; the halfe of which (the other being broken by uncurious Dissection) representing still the Kidney I have seene, it beeing both massy & ponderous as effected by the closer conjunction of minute Sand, which may bee rubbed of it with your finger—

The other a boy about 19 yeares old who from his cradle was disposed to a consumption: with continuall cougheing, greate emuceration[4] & continuall heate so that [he] was reduced to a Skeleton and under this distemper Lubaureing,[5] Died, beeing opened a great quantety of watry matter run out of the abdomen, chili consistentiam emula.[6] The most yea almost all the glanduls of the Mesenterij through which pass the Vena lactae were extraordinarij greate and ultra scirrosam Duritiem[7] hardned; The brest being opened the Lungs were found growne to it round about almost inseperable; full of matterij ulcers, but more espetiallij the left side obstructed & filled with much gravell and small stones yea whole pieces espetiallij the extremeties, the thicknes of a finger and more were hardned into a stonij matter:—

Your candor will pardon the meaneness of these two faithfull relations, which your kinde acceptance maij not onelij encrease into more but forme into better [wi]th more accurate observations & raticionations god spareing life

[I mu]st now Beg of you to lett mee have a line from you, more espetiallij [to l]et mee know how the truely Honorable Mr Boyle does;[8] wee have beene [her]e alaramed with reports of his death, which I hope are false, I entreate the favour [fro]m you to present him with my humble Service, and assure him I have [no]t beene unmindefull of obseveing the Barometer nor forgettfull to make experiments about colde, but the milde weather wee have had this winter hath frustrated my endeavours so that as yett I have nothing worth the writeing—

This part of the world Longs for his second part of the usefulnes of Experimentall philosophy if come out in print or any thing else from him pray let mee know it: one favour more That when you walke to white hall you will bee pleased to enquire at the footegard in tiltyard for Colonel Kirkbij[9] and present to him my due & true respects, and then shall onelij crave your pardon & Remaine

Yours at comand
Chri Kirkbij

The truely Learned Consuls Hevelius & Behme[10] present you with their best respects wishing all encrease to the Royall Society & that the philosophicall transactions might bee printed in Latine that so might bee rendred more communicable.

ADDRESS

> For
> Henry Oldenburgh Esqr
> Secretarij to The Royall
> Societaij: at his house
> in Pallmall
> London

NOTES

The writer of this letter is mentioned in Vol. IV, pp. 581–82; he had been in Danzig since the spring of 1668. He was obviously engaged in trade, and previously acquainted with Oldenburg.

1 salty.
2 "a kidney disease, and indeed a very serious one."
3 "loose."
4 production of mucous.
5 laboring.
6 "resembling the consistency of chyle."
7 "made harder than a scirrhus [morbid growth]."
8 Boyle wrote Kirkby a note about the Act of Henry VI against alchemists in 1689 (Birch, *Boyle*, VI, 60).
9 There were several branches of the Kirkby family in Lancashire, one of whom is addressed as "Col." in *C.S.P.D.* 1665. More probably the man (to whom the writer was presumably related) was Col. Richard Kirkby, appointed captain in the Duke of Albemarle's regiment in 1666, a commissioner for prizes in both the Second and Third Dutch Wars.
10 For Michael Behm (d. 1677), see Vol. III, pp. 562–77.

1665

Oldenburg to Wallis

30 March 1671

From the memorandum in Royal Society MS. W 1, no. 118

Rec. March 25. 71. Answ. March. 30. sent his owne Copy of letter to Ld Brouncker by Oxford Coach recommended to Geffreys. And Leibniz's book to examine.[1]

NOTES

Reply to Letter 1658.
1 When Leibniz's *Hypothesis physica nova* (see Letter 1644, note 1) was shown to the Society on 23 March 1670/1, Wallis was one of those ordered to report upon it.

1666

Borelli to Oldenburg

31 March 1671

From the original in Royal Society MS. B 1, no. 114

Illustrissimo et Doctissimo Viro
Domino Henrico Oldenburgh Soc. R. Secretario
Joan. Alphonsus Borellus S.P.

Doleo vir praestantissime, Me serius Historiam et Meteorologiam incendii aetnaei quam clarissimae vestrae Regiae societati pollicitus fueram transmittere potuisse.[1] Scis, nos neque valetudinem adversam, neque negotia et sollicitudines pro lubitu removere, nec incuriam ministrorum, aut artificium perfidiam quorum opera utimur corrigere posse. Sed licet tarde, accipe tamen opusculum, quod Doctissimae Regiae Societati meo nomine offeres,[2] cuius insignem Doctrinam summopere admiror et exosculor.

In arcula, quam ad te mitto, reperies duo exemplaria operis a me postremo editi De Motionibus naturalibus a gravitate pendentibus,[3] quae recipere digneris opto; et sexdecim exemplaria opusculi de Ætnaeo incendio Doctissimis Sociis tribuenda. Obsecro praeterea Domino Joan. Collins tradere velis reliquos libellos in eadem arca inclusos,[4] nempe 14. exemplaria de incendio Ætnaeo, Grimaldi opus postumum de lumine,[5] Fr. Redi epistolae 2. de viperae veneni sede,[6] et ridiculum opusculum de eodem Aetnae incendio.[7] Vale vir praeclarissime et me amare perge. Messanae 10 Aprilis 1671 [N.S.].

ADDRESS

    Illustri et Doctissimo Viro D. Henrico
    Oldenburgh Regiae Societatis Angliae Secretario
          Londini

TRANSLATION

Giovanni Alphonso Borelli sends many greetings to the very illustrious and learned Mr. Henry Oldenburg, Secretary of the Royal Society

I regret very much, excellent Sir, that I could only send my *Historia et meteorologia incendii Aetnaei anni 1669* later than I had promised your celebrated Society.[1] You know that we cannot at will relieve ourselves of ill health, or business, or other cares, nor can we make good the carelessness of assistants or the bad faith of workmen whose labors we employ. But receive this little work at last, though tardily, and present it in my name to the most learned Royal Society,[2] whose remarkable teachings I admire and embrace before all others.

In the little box I send you, you will find two copies of my recently published *De motionibus naturalibus a gravitate pendentibus*,[3] which I beg you to accept kindly, and sixteen copies of the little work on the eruption of Etna for distribution to the learned Fellows. Moreover I beg you to deliver to Mr. John Collins the remaining books packed in the same box,[4] that is to say fourteen copies of the *Etna*, Grimaldi's posthumous work on light,[5] Francisco Redi's two letters on the seat of the viper's venom,[6] and a ridiculous little piece on the same eruption of Etna.[7] Farewell, famous Sir, and continue to love me.
Messina, 10 April 1671 [N.S.]

ADDRESS

    To the illustrious and very learned
    Mr. Henry Oldenburg, Secretary of
    the Royal Society of England
          London

NOTES

1 See Vol. VI, p. 116.
2 This letter was received on 9 August; it was read, and the presentations made, to the Society on 2 November.
3 See Letter 1470, note 3.
4 Borelli also wrote to Collins about this on the same date; see Rigaud, I, 165–66.
5 See Letter 1590, note 24.
6 See Letter 1556, note 24.
7 We do not know what this was; this too is recorded in the letter to Collins.

1667
Oldenburg to Willughby
4 April 1671

From the memorandum in Royal Society MS. W 3, no. 42

Rec. March 20. 1670/71.
Answ. April 4. 1671 communicating part of Mr Listers of March 17. 71.[1]

NOTES

This memorandum is on the envelope of Willughby's Letter 1655; as Willughby's subsequent Letter 1684 shows, it was lost in the post.
1 Letter 1656.

1668
Vogel to Oldenburg
4 April 1671

From the original in Royal Society MS. F 1, no 31

Nobilissimo Viro
HENRICO OLDENBURGIO
S.P.D.
Martinus Fogelius

Videram equidem, Sterpinum ineptum esse Interpretem.[1] Sed tam enormia Errata ipsius non exspectaveram. Simul ac tuas accepi literas, significandum Pauliadae Bibliopolae,[2] curavi tuum super hac Versione judicium. et jam ante monui ipsum, ut ab opere isto desisteret. impressae sunt omnes Anni 1669 Ephemerides, sed non continuabit, spero, reliquas.

Alius quidam Germanus doctus Schulzio operam suam obtulit, easdem Latine vertendi sed tibi ante censendam mittet Versionem, quam imprimatur, siquidem conditionem accipiet.

Morhofius Boilei libro de Qualitatibus Cosmicis, subterraneis &c. a se verso & jam impresso, me auctore addidit alterum ejusdem Nobilissimi Viri librum de negata Corporum Quiete. quo additamento spero emtores magis alliciet, quam ille qui sub vestro praelo sudat.[3]

pro Boilei libello de Aeris mira rarefactione promisso gratias quam maximas ago. Videbo ut munus hoc pari compensem.

Schulzius, se quamprimum aliquid de Historiae Lynceae impressione statuturum, spopondit. interea, quia in Speciali Historia, sola Galilei vita admodum imperfecta est, & Viviani de ea promissum me hactenus fefellit, ex te, Vir Nobilissime, scire aveo, an Galilei operibus Anglice versis[?], Vita ipsius praemissa fuerit, & an non separatum haberi possit.[4]

Siferum a Phoranomica satis diu avocavit Cathedralis Bibliothecae, cui praefectus est, Catalogus conficiendus, & spes nondum plane frustrata Professionis Mathematum apud Lyneburgenses consequendae. hac aestate tamen eam resumet curam. Est hic apud amicum insignis Selenitis Islandicus, qualem Bartolinus nuper descripsit. venibit 12 Imperialibus. longitudine est fere dimidii cubiti, latitude circiter quadrantis cubiti, forma prismatis obliquanguli. Quod significandum duxi, ut, si forsan Societati illum emere placeat, quamprimum certiorem me facias. Vale, & me amare perge. Scribam Hamburgi d. 4 Aprilis 1671. Quod de Cervisia nostra per Paisenium communicavi tecum, noli publici juris facere ante quam me monueris.5 iterum vale.

ADDRESS
  A Monsr
    Mons Grubendal
      a
    Londres

TRANSLATION

Martin Vogel presents many greetings to the very noble Henry Oldenburg

I had indeed seen that Sterpin was an incompetent translator.1 But I had not expected such enormous errors from him. As soon as I received your letter I took care to let Pauli, the publisher,2 know your opinion of this translation. And I had already warned him previously to leave off the work. The *Transactions* for 1669 are all printed, but I hope he will not go on with the rest.

A certain other learned German has offered his services to Schulz in turning them into Latin; he will send them to you for approval before they are printed, if the bargain is made.

Morhof, at my instigation, has added to Boyle's book on cosmic qualities, subterranean things, etc. (by him translated and printed already), another by the same noble author on the *Absolute Rest in Bodies*. With which addition it will, I hope, be a better enticement to purchasers than that which is in your own press.3

I return you my best thanks for Boyle's promised book on the wonderful rarefaction of air. I shall see to it that I recompense this gift with a like one.

Schulz has promised that he will at the first opportunity take a decision about printing the history of the Lyncei. Meanwhile, noble Sir, I long to know from you whether a *Life* of Galileo was prefaced to the English translation of his works, and whether it may be obtained separately or not, because within the detailed history only the biography of Galileo is very imperfect, and Viviani has so far failed me with respect to that which he promised me.4

Sivers has been a pretty long time away from the *Phoranomica*, compiling a catalogue of the Cathedral Library, which is in his charge, and he has not yet quite given up hope of a post teaching mathematics at Lüneburg. Yet he may this summer return to his work on it. A friend here has a remarkable [piece of that] Iceland spar described recently by Bartholin. He will sell it for twelve Imperial crowns. It is almost half a cubit long, its breadth is about a fortieth of a cubit, and its shape is that of an irregular prism. I am induced to tell you this so that if by chance the Society wishes to buy it, you may let me know as soon as may be. Farewell, and continue to love me.

Written at Hamburg, 4 April 1671

What I communicated to you about our brewing methods through Paisen I do not wish to have made public without prior notice.[5] Farewell again.

ADDRESS

To Mr. Grubendol
London

NOTES

Reply to Letter 1647.

1 See Letter 1638.
2 See Letters 1633, note 13, and 1638, note 1.
3 Compare the allusion in Letter 1633, p. 456. The later issues of *Tractatus de cosmicis rerum qualitatibus* (Amsterdam and Hamburg, 1671) include *Tractatus de absoluta quiete in corporibus*. The Latin version of *Cosmicall Qualities* issued at London dated 1672 has as its additions, however, three tracts not previously issued in English: *De salsedine maris*; *De motu intestino particularum*; *Nova experimenta pneumatica*.
4 The *Life* of Galileo, in five books, was written by Thomas Salusbury to appear in Tome II, Part II, of his *Mathematical Collections and Translations*, containing largely the writings of Galileo. Tome I of this work had been published at London in 1661, and Tome II, Part I, in 1665. A unique copy of Tome II, Part II, is known to have existed in a private library down to recent times; this copy is the source of the quotations from Salusbury's *Life* that survive in print. (See the introduction by Stillman Drake to the facsimile reprint of Salusbury's work published at London and Los Angeles, 1967.) Vogel had known Viviani when he was in Florence in 1664; see Brown, *Fogel*, p. 5.
5 See Vol. VI, p. 345.

1669
Oldenburg to Lister

4 April 1671

From the original in Bodleian Library MS. Lister 34, f. 21

London April 4. 1671.

Sir,

The R. Society was so well pleased wth the contents of yr last of March 17. (wch was read before them on Thursday last) that they gave me fresh orders, to return to you most affectionate thanks, and to assure you anew of ye great sense they have of yr so important communications; wch they promise themselves the continuance of. I doe persuade myself, yt you will not be displeased at my publishing in the Transactions what you have imparted in relation to ye Ascent and Descent of Sap:[1] a discourse yt is likely very much to excite inquisitive men to further observations and tryals.

The last, I received from Mr Willughby of March. 16.,[2] contains some particulars, wch I cannot hide from you. He saith, that upon reviewing their old notes and making some new Expts, they find, yt branches of Willow, Birch and Sycamore, cutt off and held perpendicularly, will bleed wthout tipping, and yt ye cutting off of their tops doth not sensibly promote the bleeding. That as yet they have made no tryal in Maple and Walnut, ye weather having been such, yt those trees have not run freely since the receit of my last letter to him. He adds these words;

"We doubt not of Mr Listers diligence and veracity, and wonder, our Expermts should differ. The tryals we have made this year" (*so he goes on*) "confirme those communicated to you formerly, viz. the Sycamore bleeds upon the first considerable frost after ye leaf is fallen; as it did plentifully Nov. 16. last, and both yt, and Walnut and Maple all winter long after frosts when the weather relents or the Sun shines out: But Walnut and Maple begin not so soon as the Sycamore. The Birch will not bleed till towards Spring: This year it began somewhat sooner than ordinary, about ye beginning of February. We cutt off pretty big branches of birch, and having tipp'd ye ends, inverted ym, and fasten'd a limbus or ring of soft waxe to ye great ends wch we held upwards, making wth ye plane of ye end a vessel of about an inch deep; where into we powred water, wch in a few minuts sank into ye pores of ye wood, and running quite through ye length of ye branch dropp'd out of ye ends considerably fast, continuing so to doe as long as we powred on water. The like Expt we made by fastning such wax-rings to ye lesser ends, and powring in water, wch ran thorough ye wood, and dropp'd out of ye greater ends as fast or faster. This we tried once upon a Sycamore wthout successe."

So far He.

This I thought fit to transcribe for yr perusal, and for comparing it wth some of yr observations, formerly sent, supposing it to be acceptable to ingenious and candid men, to heare what is taken notice of in several parts, to enable ymselves the better to make wary deductions from what is thus severally observed.

Hoping, Sir, yt you poursue yr researches after colours and their fixation, I conclude wth assuring you, yt I am

Sir, Yr faithfull servt
H. Old.

P.S.

I supposed, ye title of polygonum coniferum was imposed by ye Expts pro re nata.[3]

ADDRESS

> To his honour'd friend
> Martin Lister Esq
> at his house wthout
> Mickel-gate barre at
>   York

NOTES

Reply to Letter 1656, which was read to the Society on 30 March.

1 In *Phil. Trans.*, no. 70 (17 April 1671), Oldenburg made up an article on this subject by Lister consisting of extracts from Letters 1613, 1627, 1634, and 1656.
2 Letter 1655.
3 "for this present occasion."

1670
Dodington to Oldenburg
4 April 1671

From the original in Royal Society MS. D 1, no. 21

Venice Apr. 14th 1671 [N.S.]

Sr

I hope you will pardon my tardy answering yrs of the 10th Febr. the truth is I cannot yet answere it so as this is only to acknowledg the Receipt of it. But I have written to Rome for a solution of yr QQ.[1] & when they come to me, I will transmitt them towards you. Heerafter I will hope to serve you according to yr desires, but sending such things as come out heere, upon vessels or by Friends who pass this way towards England, As I now doe, the three inclosed Jornales of the Literati heere:[2] I finde it is very Lately they have begunn this work & possibly yr monthly Experiments gave them the Model. But I feare twil not hold long heere, not only in regard there are very few who pursue solid enquiries heere, but that a small pittance of Learning sufficeth to acquire the repute of being a Vertuoso, the Achme of their Ambition, But I doe not heereby conclude All. Another thing is Their Religion will not permitt them to pursue even Philosophical truths too Far.

When Padre Lanaes promised peece is extant, as well as Fabri on Archimedes & Gottignies in Re dioptrica I will convey them onwards, as I will disperse yrs that come to me eyther, for Bologna, Rome or Naples. I have now a Corrispondent in this last place too,[3] and have sent thither to procure a true history of all the effects of ye Tarantula &c as ye Instructions yr last yeare directed me.

I will goe on collecting these Jornals heere, and so send them, if you desire it. I rest most affectionately

Sr yr faythful humble servant
John Dodington

Mr Oldenburg.

NOTES

Reply to Letter 1629.
1 Queries or questions; these were not noted in the memorandum but probably related to the work of Fabri and Gottignies.
2 The *Giornale de' Letterati.*
3 Tommaso Cornelio.

1671
Oldenburg to Sachs
4 April 1671

Letter 1657 bears an endorsement showing that it was received on 24 March 1670/1 and answered on 4 April 1671. No copy of this answer survives.

1672
Tenison to Oldenburg
6 April 1671
From the original in Royal Society MS. T, no. 37

Holywell Aprill ye 6t 1671

Sr.

I can deny nothing to you who are so generously communicative to all ye Learned world:[1] & therefore, for your first Request concerning ye way of Agriculture in ye Countie of Huntingdon; I here promise to return Answer to the Queries, if, upon sufficient discours with those who best understand such affaires, I find any thing worth ye writing down. & for your next Request, concerning ye waters of Holywell in ye same Countie, I will, now, give you such satisfaction, as, at present, I am able. Within ye precincts of That Parish there are two Wells of note. The first, & most considerable, is that wch ye People call ye Bath-Well. This issues southward on ye brow of a very high hill: The Hill is part of a mountainous Heath, known formerly by ye name of Mallwood, & distant, on ye north & East, about two miles from part of ye great Levell of ye Fenns.[2] That this well has bin anciently known, & esteem'd as I learn from an old Licence wherein we have a fine story of a Shephard, at ye Command of St. Ivo's Ghost, digging, & finding ye Body of St. Ivo, &, thereby, occasioning this common benefit of a Medicinall water springing out of his Grave.[3] This ancient well has bin, more or less, frequented, according to ye varietie of Weather in ye severall summers, or (wch seemeth of as great inconstancie) ye humours of People. In ye very drie seasons of 54, 55, 56, the Concours was great: since that time 'till these two last years, the number of ye water-Drinkers has decreas'd. I wonder that neither Mr. Camden,[4] nor Dr. Fuller,[5] take any notice of this water, whilst they mention Those wch are much less considerable, ye Fontilets at Hail-Weston nigh St. Neots in this Countie: For one of Them seems a Common clear spring-water; & ye other, (call'd ye Salt-bath) has so few degrees of saltness in it, that it scarce invites ye Pigeons: I was told by one of those who made ye Experiment, that ye Extraction of one poor ounce of salt from thence, cost them three shillings in firing. Now, concerning Our Bath-well, by them inobserved, there are three things especially to be taken notice of. The Rock out of wch it issues. The stones, of curious figure, wch are digg'd up, by it. The mineral water it self. For ye Rock; I never heard, or saw, anything of it, 'till ye last August, 'though, in former years, I have visited ye Well, &, inquir'd concerning it. Whilst ye Shephard, who serv'd ye water, was digging further for ye clearing of ye Passage, I was surpriz'd by ye glittering of a Part of it, wch his spade had broken of. In searching further, I perceiv'd yt ye water issued betwixt a double mass of ye like rockie substance about a foot distance from one another. This Rock abounds wth a Glassie matter of irregular figure, unlike to that of ye transparent stones wch, by & by, I shall speak of more largelie. With this matter are mixed, earths of divers colours, & particularly a certain friable substance not much unlike to that of rotten Oystershells. Wth this Paper, you will receive a peice of this Rock, wch may be better examin'd by ye Curious.

The Stones digg'd up about ye Well, at unequal depths, are distinguish'd into two sorts, though they differ only in ye Figure of their surface. The first sort, ye People have called, Sea-glass; ye second, Diamonds. The figure of ye first is a kind of Parallelogram, extending, in some there found, to four Inches in length, & one, in breadth. The figure of ye other is not, that of ye diamond-cutt, in any by me observ'd; but, in some, an exact Lozenge; in more, a Rhomboides. I, sometimes, conceiv'd that these latter were peices obliquely broken of, at each end, from ye former; but, since that, I have seen them taken, single, out of good Quantities of a stiff-clay. Both sorts are transparent; both look, & cut, & scrape, alike, & both are us'd without distinction. In some especially of ye former sort, in ye middle part of them, there appears a blackish substance, of remarkable fashion. Some compare ye Figure of it to that of an Ear of Corn or of ye Stalk of a dwarfish herb: But ye Countriemen have more happily resembled it to ye shape of that Feather wch makes their Cart-horses so proud.

In Cutting of ye stone (wch is done with difficulty cross-wise, but, from pole to pole, with more ease then any wood wch is cleav'd according to ye grain) this Feather appears to be nothing but curiously-disposed durt: yet there have bin found many hundreds of Them, in wch that dark substance keeps ye same shape. This Curiositie reminds me of somthing wch I have read in ye Travells of Peter Della Valle.[6] he had passed ye Cape wch they call in Persian Com barick, & ye Peak of Giasck: & sailing on in ye main sea, &, as he conceiv'd, at a good distance from Macran, he saw, in ye water, abundance of certain things, wch he took to be snakes, or fishes in ye form of them. they had (he saies) exactly ye shape of large Eeles, & according to ye motion of ye water they seemed crooked as they floated along ye Sea. & yet he understood, after due inquiry, that they were only a kind of durtie excrement of ye Sea in that form. I have now sent you as good a sort as I can, readily, procure of these stones they call Diamonds; as also of the Seaglass, both with, & without, ye enclosed dusky earth for ye fairest of wch (& ye best, in all respects, that I have seen) I am beholding to Mr. Willis of St. Ives. Some (who are easily refuted by both by ye Ey & tast) have resembled these stones to Borax. Others come nigher ye business, who think yem a sort of Talcum; not ye Venetian, but a whiter sort wch is said to come from some parts of Scotland.

Concerning ye Origin of these stones, there is little doubt but water is ye mother of them, wch is also fruitfull in infinite productions of firmer consistence. Brunus (remembered in ye Life of ye noble Peiresc)[7] took from a child, three stones, ye first of wch was perfectly hard; Ye next, yeilding; & ye third, almost as fluid as a substance of Gelly. It is easie to say, that Every body must have some figure, & yt a divers contexture of parts begettes a divers surface; but to explain ye particular manner of such contexture as produceth such a shape, is a difficulty with wch I will not here encounter. yet in the Figure of these stones, ye wonder is not greater, then, in Nitre wch shoots it self into ye shape of needles; or in many salts wch are square or of other curious form; or in Fairy-stones, & many other found under our feet in ye shape of Scalops & Cockles. It would require yet greater skill to explain ye generation of yt stone wch is calld ye Achates of ye King of Epirus. for (it seems) it represented Apollo with his Harp, in ye Chorus of ye Muses, if Plinie do's not Romance.[8] Pancirollus outgoes him, telling of one wch represents ye Priest at Mass, & ye Host in elevation.[9] This (said he) Paul the third did cutt, supposing it painted, but found it naturall. Whither it be so or not, I resolve not to journey to Ravenna, to prove. for those I discours of, though they are not miraculous, I think they are rare. And (if I well remember) Des-Cartes (in one of his Epistles)[10] seems much pleased with a Stone, five-cornerd, wch a Friend had sent him.

For ye use of these stones, we are more at certainty. Those of ye neighbourhood scrape them into a green wound, to good effect. A moneth has not passed since a poor man, who, by a stoke, had bloud settled in his Ey, found good releif by ye very fine, dust of them putt into it. They afford when calcind, a very excellent Fucus, wch Schroder[11] also saies of Talc, which he cheifly commends as it is Cosmetic. I have bin assur'd from yt very person in whose house ye Experiment was made above twentie years agoe, yt ye substance of them grossly pulveris'd & taken inwards without any vehicle, has drawn up ye Fundament, after other Recipes in vain prescrib'd.

Last of all, for ye water it self, it is of great strength, & as farr as I can discern by ye descriptions we have from Monsieur Gherinx[12] & Dr Wittie,[13] not very unlike, & not inferiour, to ye Spaws of Sauvenir or Scarborough. ye nice disgust it, & express their dislike by comparing it to ye Water of Blac-Smiths: & doubtless it is a Chalybeate-water in no mean degree. a Quantity of Sal Martis[14] dissolv'd in common water has deceiv'd ye Palates of some who have bin us'd to this Spaw. The Chalybeate spirit of it will fume into ye nose; & from ye stomac, in some, it flyes into ye head, & yet so farr as we can judg from Tast, it retains much virtue when remov'd from ye Spring-head: It works very well with those who send for it eight or tenn miles, & keep it some small space by them. The water so kept precipitates an ochre. It tingeth with ye wither'd leaves of Oak, or with a few dusts or slices of Gall. It tingeth immediatelie, &, soon after, precipitates a blac sediment, wch looks to ye Ey like an irony substance: yet seperated & dried, it hath not hitherto appear'd to be mov'd by ye Loadstone. The Earth, nigh ye fountain, & ye Grass, in ye channell wch conveighs ye water from ye well, is rusty-coloured. At ye end of the Channell, where ye water is receiv'd into a little Pitt, there stands a Scumm, as on a water where steel is quench'd, & it hath ye exact tast of such steely saltness. It is certain, from our sense of Tast, that there is a great astringencie in these waters; & yet they are of such weight as to become highly laxative. Two Quarts have moved some, more then a dozen times by Chambres, wch are perfectly blac; & very often by urine, wch is clear as from white-wine. If the waters find not a convenient passage, they discharge themselves upwards. If they be drunk with discretion, they comfort ye stomac, & help to remouve hydropic, scorbutic, & leprous, distempers. Applyed outwardly, they help Rheumatic Eys, & cleane old soars; & they are, therefore, not unfrequently, or unsuccessfully, used to such purposes. There are many stories setting forth their virtue wch I will forbear to write down, seeing they would as much choak your Fayth as ye Miracles & hard words in ye Bill of a Mountebank. Perhaps, if Baths were made for ye whole bodie with such astringent Waters, they would be more effectuall towards ye Prolonging of mens daies then ye Oils of ye Ancients, & ye delicate devices of ye Modern, by opposing ye air, & imprisoning ye spirit of life.

After all these Remarks (wch begin to grow tedious to my very self) I will not enter into a controversie concerning ye Ingredients of this minerall water. I have hopes that, in time, it may be chymically anatomiz'd by a person of more agreable employment, & greater acuteness. Let others dispute concerning five minerals, of vitriol, & iron (wch yet, as most know, are but as mother & daughter) of Alume, nitre, & Salt, wch other Spaws are said to have imbibed & wch may, perhaps, as aptly be ascrib'd to this: For ye Sediments, upon Evaporation, are such as those wch we find de-scrib'd in ye thirteenth, fourteenth & fifteenth pages of ye book entituled Scarborough Spaw. It sufficeth me that it is impregnated with vitriolate salt. I will only add, that it may seem yt Chymists doe not make, but rather find, their salts in many waters & other bodies spagyrically dealt with. I will not say this of such parts in bodies as are separable by filtration, & such other easie operations wch doe no violence to nature: neither am I so absurd as to deny that there is in one substance a greater disposition to their Ternarie[15] of productions, then in an other. but it seems not yet proved yt all such supposed Principles as, by extreme torture of fires or menstruum's, are produced, were actually there, before such operation. All salts they speak of, are made up of portions wch are not salts, as all agree who anatomize beyond ye perceptible parts of matter, who consider that no figure can appertain to a mere indivisible, & who favour not Anaxagoras in his Dogma of Homoeomerie. The motion by fire or other vehement means doth seem to me to create such figur'd matter as some pretend to be formerly extant, but conceald: Of many of their Extracts it may be said (as some men conceit of Spirits) that they are then created when they appear. The Swedish stone describ'd by Sr Gilbert Talbot[16] (an Excellent member of your Societie) is prepared after such manner, by wetting, mattocking, breaking, milling, exposing two years to ye Sun & air, firing, infusing, mixing with urin & ye Lees of wood-ashes &c. that it may be thought rather to be turn'd into, then afford from it salt, Sulphur, Vitriol, Allum, & Minium. Philosophers beleive not at this day, (neither did many of them, before ye deposing of Aristotle from his Popedome) that Fire is actually in a Flint, but only in ye potentiall atoms of it, wch receive great change by vehement Collision: & ye effect seemeth to depend more upon ye floating of ye Earthy parts in affus'd matter, procured by yt Action, then upon ye parts themselves. It is so commonly said by Chymists that I am come to know it, yt Acids & Alkalys, by mutuall operation, do, at length so loose their particular Forms, as to pass into a third, distinct from either: How ye Furnace, through motion, wch causeth all varietie, may produce a conflict of ye Parts, to ye abating of their proper activitie, & ye resulting of a new texture, & there bring forth such salt of sulphur as it has created, or as it found only in ye praedisposition of parts apt to be so wrought upon, is not hard to be beleivd. But in these matters I love not to dogmatize; neither is it fitting that I proceed in them. for I have so enlarged alreadie as if I were talking with a man of superfluous leisure, & not writing a Letter to a Philosopher who has no hour hanging idly upon his hands. I will therefore releive you, after I have said a very few things concerning ye second Fountain of Note wch is in Holywell.[17]

This issues southward of ye Foot of an high hill, of gravell, on wch ye Parish Church is situate. From this ye Town is suppos'd to have taken its name. It is call'd St. John's Well, & it is said to have bin much frequented &, for its virtue, extolled, before ye Reformation, by ye Brotherhood of st. Ives. why it is sacred to st. John, I am not able to understand: For ye Apostle of ye Town (as appears by ye Wake, or Feast of ye Churches ded-ication) is St. James: & the Priory of st Ivo was under ye Protection of St. Peter: And, for St. John he is suppos'd (by That sort of men who oftner suppose then prove such things) ye Healer of ye Falling-sickness, to ye Cure of which this Water has no pretence. They might have rather calld it ye Well of st. Clare who (they say) Protects or heals ye Eys; for it contains, like other such common springs, a water not unagreable to them: Touch-ing other virtues for wch it was fam'd in ye daies of Monkerie, I am not so happy as to find them out. The Neighbourhood like it enough, being served by it, in ye greatest droughts, for their common uses. I have bin, often, at a fountain of greater Fame, in Bawburgh[18] nigh Norwch; ye Well of St. Walstan. I found it to be a good abstersive[19] water, but for its miracles, they are ceased. yet I have seen an ancient Legend, wch tells of so many Cures done by it as require a Fayth more miraculous then ye Stories themselves.

And thus, Sr, you have my thoughts upon yt matter of wch you, latelie, desir'd some account: How very much undigested they are, I am enough conscious to my self. however, I am the less displeased at them, because they are some testimonie of my readiness to serve you in such an imperfect manner as my circumstances admitt of, & a kind of new descant upon the old complement of

yr humble servt
Tho : Tenison

Please to pardon, & correct, what you find amiss in this paper wch ye Carryer permits me not to review consideratelie.

NOTES

1 We have not discovered the date of Oldenburg's reply to Tenison's Letter 1646.

2 The Great or Bedford Level (so named after the fourth Earl of Bedford, the chief "undertaker") is the great area of the East Anglian fenland (between the river Nene and the uplands of Norfolk) drained and reclaimed by works effected by Cornelis Vermuyden, completed in 1653. The fenland extends close to St. Ives and Huntingdon.

3 A genuine St. Ivo (or Yves) of Chartres died in 1116. St. Ives in Huntingdonshire was said to be named after a Persian bishop, St. Ive, whose grave was found there in 1101, having formerly been known as "Slepe."

4 See Letter 1603, note 9.

5 Thomas Fuller (1608–61) was a divine, prebendary of Salisbury and holder of various livings, who became vigorous in the royalist cause; of his many, once well-read books the most familiar now is his *Worthies of England* (London, 1662).

6 Pietro della Valle (1586–1652) left Naples in 1614 for a journey through Turkey, Syria, Persia, and India before his return in 1626. Tenison here refers to G. Havers, *The Travels of Sig. Pietro della Valle . . . into East-India* (London, 1665), pp. 3–4. Valle had passed between the island of Ormuz and the Arabian coast in January 1623 on an English ship bound for Surat; "Macran" was "upon the Sea Coast between the States of the Persian and those of the Moghol," and he observed this phenomenon in the "middle" of the Persian Gulf.

7 By Pierre Gassendi, in Book IV; in *The Mirrour of True Nobility & Gentility. Being the Life of the Renowned Nicolaus Claudius Fabricius Lord of Peiresk* (London, 1657), p. 48, he is called "John Brown the Chirurgion" (*Lat.* "Ioannes Brunus chirurgus").

8 Pliny *Natural History* xxxvii, Ch. 3. "the jewel of King Pyrrhus"; it was "an agate, upon which were to be seen the Nine Muses and Apollo holding a lyre; not a work of art, but the spontaneous produce of Nature."

9 It was of marble, and is described in Ch. XVI of Guido Panciroli, *Rerum memorabilium jam olim deperditarum : & contra recens atque ingeniose inventarum : libri duo* (Amberg, 1599), which also contains a reference to Pliny.

10 *Lettres de Mr Descartes* [ed. Claude Clerselier], 3 vols., (Paris, 1657–67).

11 See Vol. VI, p. 614, note 6.

12 Philippe Gherincx, *Description des fontaines acides de Spa et de la fontaine de fer de Tungre* (Liège, 1583). Sauvenière lies between Brussels and Namur in Belgium.

13 See Vol. VI, pp. 613–14, note.

14 Salt of iron.

15 Three-fold or trinity; a reference to the *tria prima* (alt, sulphur, and mercury) of the Paracelsans.

16 See Vol. III, p. 154 and p. 156, note 6. Sir Gilbert Talbot (*c.* 1607–95), nominated a member of the Council of the Royal Society in the second charter (1663), had been the King's agent in Venice.

17 Just east of St. Ives. The well still exists, and Tenison's statement that the town is named from the well is still accepted.

18 It is 5 miles west of Norwich on the River Yare; the well still exists under the same name.

19 purging.

1673
Wallis to Oldenburg
7 April 1671

From the original in Royal Society MS. W 1, no. 119
Printed in *Phil. Trans.*, no. 74 (14 August 1671) 2227–30

Oxoniae Aprilis 7. 1671.

Clarissime Vir,

Legi ego semel atque iterum, quam impertijsti D. Leibnitzii Hypothesim novam; de qua opinionem meam petis. Authorem quod spectat, utut de nomine (quod memini) mihi ignotum prius, aestimare tamen debeo, ut qui, in loco magno inter magna negotia positus, vacare tamen potest liberae Philosophiae, et rerum causis investigandis, quique ad multa respexisse videtur.

Opus quod attinet, multa inibi reperio summa cum ratione dicta, et quibus ego plane assentior, ut quae sint sensis meis consona. Talia sunt,

Debere Physicum ad Mechanicas rationes, quam fieri potest, omnia accommodare,
§ 15, *Nihil seipsum, ex abstractis motus rationibus, in lineam priorem restituere,
etiam sublato impedimento nisi accedat nova vis.* § 22. *Omnia corpora sensibilia,
saltem dura, esse Elastica*; Atque, *Ab Elatere oriri Reflexionem,* § 21. (Quae
meis de Motu hypothesibus, Transactionibus Philosophicis jam antehac a
te insertis omnino congruunt;[1] quaeque in Mechanicis seu de Motu
tractatu fusius prosequor Cap. 11. et 13.) Item, *Attolli gravia non metu
Vacui, sed propter Atmosphaerae aequilibrium,* § 25. *Levitatem vero per accidens
tantum sequi ex Gravitate* (gravioribus minus gravia sursum pellentibus) § 24.
*Irruptionem aeris (sed et aquae &c) in vas exhaustum, ob aeris Gravitatem et
Elaterem fieri*; § 26. Item, *Exhausti atque Distenti* (ut loquitur) *effectus, (unde
fermentationes, deflagrationes, et displosionum omne genus,) nempe, displodente
altero quod alterum absorbet,* (seu admittit potius,) § 27, 39, 40. Nam et haec
etiam ab Elatere fiunt; vel in Contento vel in Continente, vel utroque;
illic, se explicante quod nimis fuerat, compressum; hic, se contrahente
quod nimis distentum fuerat; quippe utrovis modo, nedum utroque fiet
irruptio vel explosio, dummodo locus sit quo, sine impedimento, recipi
possit quod projiciendum erit. Suntque haec plane consona traditis nostris,
Mechan. cap. 14. Sed et illud, *Gravitatem in inferioribus oriri ex motu* (vel
pressu) *superioris aetheris,* § 13, 16. magna saltem verisimilitudine dicitur:
quanquam enim Gravitatis causa (ut et Elateris) tam sit in abscondito ut
mihi nondum usque quoque satisfactum sit quid ea in re statuam, naturae
tamen phaenomena pulsione quam tractione felicius ut plurimum explican-
tur. Aliaque multa sunt, quae repetitu non est opus, quae magna verisimilitudine, si non et certitudine, dicta judico; quaeque per se satis consis-
tunt independenter ab alijs: neque enim ita inter se sunt connexa omnia,
ut uno vacillante caetera simul ruent. De tota vero hypothesi nequid statim
pronuntiem, id saltem facit, quod non sim pronus ego (in rebus saltem pure
Physicis, non Mathematicis) assensum novis traditis adhibere, donec vel
eruditorum sententijs in utramque partem ventilatis quid statuendum sit
rectius constet, vel ipsa sui evidentia (quod in veris hypothesibus non raro
fit) veritas eluceat. Fundamentum Hypotheseos novae repetit ex *Abstracta
sua motus theorica,* (quam non vidi, ut nec hujus tractatus posteriora, quae
passim citantur,) nempe, *Quod nulla sit cohaesio quiescentis, sed omnis consistentia
seu cohaesio oriatur a motu,* § 7, 12, 34. (Quod cum Guilielmi Neilij nostri
placitis coincidit.) Contra vero, Honoratissimus Boylius *Consistentiam in
particularum quiete, et Fluiditate in earundem continuo motu,* collocat.[2] Alij *ad
varias Atomorum figuras, hamatas et varie implicitas,* rem referunt. Neque ego
is sum qui in tanta sententiarum variete me velim arbitrum interponere.

Sed tempori res permittenda est, et doctorum in utramque partem rationibus. Quippe idem fere obtinet in novis Hypothesibus atque in Pendulorum oscillationibus; ubi, post crebras hinc inde reciprocationes factas, tandem in perpendiculo fit quies. Id vidimus in Hypothesi Copernicana, quae utut fuerit Veteribus cognita, tamdiu tamen jacuit sepulta ut pro nova haberetur: Et quamvis erat optima ratione suffulta, non tamen statim obtinuit, sed a varijs fuit varijs modis impetita, et acriter disputata, donec tandem rationibus authoritati praevalentibus ita jam universim admittitur, ut vix quispiam harum rerum gnarus de ea dubitet nisi quibus Cardinalium decretum praejudicio est: Et quanquam Tycho novam illius loco substituerit quae illi aequipolleret, ea tamen tot incommodis onerata est ut existimandus videatur potius ad frangendam invidiam id fecisse (quoniam Telluris motus ita vulgi opinionibus horribilis videbatur) quam quod Copernici Hypothesin ex animo repudiaverit. Idem dicendum est de Circulatione Sanguinis Harvaeana; quae utut optime stabilita fuerit et oculorum αὐτοψια comprobata, disceptata tamen fuit inter Londinenses Medicos viginti plus minus annis antequam in publicum prodiret; et ab alijs postea: Quae tamen post maturam rei pensitationem (quod tempori dandum erat) ab omnibus ut indubitata recipitur. Sic Galilaei hypothesis (ob antlias aquam non ultra certam altitudinem attrahentes primum excogitata) quam Torricellius in graviori liquido adeoque magis tractabili promovit, Aequilibrium Atmosphaerae pro Veterum fuga vacui substituens, non nisi post diutinas hinc inde disputationes eum apud viros doctos locum obtinuit quem jam habet. Idem dicendum de Jolivij nostri vasis Lymphaticis,[3] ante multos annos Medicis Londinensibus ab illo indicatis atque ab eis admissis et approbatis, dicendum erit; Quae tamen ita rationi consona reperta sunt et oculari inspectioni manifesta ut tandem longo post tempore inter alios aliquot acriter disputatum est quis eorum primus inventor fuerit.

Similiter Whartoni nostri ductus salivales,[4] quos libro edito indicaverat, quo libro quasi dissimulato, tandem inter Stenonem et Bartholinum disputatum est, uter horum prior invenerit. Item Infusio liquorum in venas animalium jam ante viginti fere annos a Wrennio nostro excogitata Oxoniae, ibique postmodum crebro administrata; et sanguinis Transfusio ab animali uno in alterum, a Lowero nostro feliciter aliquoties administrata Oxoniae, atque Londini postea coram Societate Regia, ab exteris interim, et quidem Parisiensibus, non credita sed pro impossibili habita et tantum non irrisa; tandem tamen ita illis placuit (post totum processus tenorem illis indicatum) ut illius authores haberi cupiant, atque apud illos nescio quem jam ante aliquid obiter dixisse quod eo jam trahant.[5] Idemque in hoc

negotio, alijsque novis hypothesibus, expectandum erit, quae nec oculi
inspectione nec certa demonstratione probari possunt, ut, si veris rationibus fundatae sint, tandem, sed non nisi post velitationes utrinque factas, in
libere philosophantium animis locum obtinebunt; interea pendulae man-
surae. Clarissimo interim Viro habendae gratiae, qui eam de Societate
nostra opinionem concepit, ut dignatus fuerit sensa sua cum illis communicare, novamque suam Hypothesin exhibere, quibus certe res erit non
ingrata. Tu vero vale.

Tuus,
Johannes Wallis

ADDRESS
    These
For Mr Henry Oldenburg,
  at his house in the Palmal
    near St James's
      London

TRANSLATION

Oxford, 7 April 1671

Famous Sir,

The new hypothesis of Mr. Leibniz, which you imparted to me with a request
for my opinion of it, I have perused and re-perused. As for the author,
although his name has been hitherto unknown to me (so far as I can recall), yet
I must esteem him as one who, when situated in a great place and surrounded with
great business, can still find leisure for liberal philosophy and investigation of the
causes of things, and look into many of them carefully.

As for the work itself, I find many things expressed in it with very good reason,
and to which I can fully assent since my own views are the same. Such are:
"Everything in physics ought to be accommodated, so far as is possible, to mechanical reasoning" (§ 15); "By the abstract theory of motion, no body can of itself
return again in the same line as before, even with resistance removed, unless a new
force is applied" (§ 22); "All perceptible bodies, hard ones at any rate, are elastic,"
and "Resilience arises from elasticity" (§ 21). These are in complete agreement
with my hypotheses concerning motion which you formerly inserted in the
Philosophical Transactions,[1] which I have developed more fully in Chs. 11 and 13 of
my *Mechanica sive de motu*. Further, "Heavy bodies are borne along not by the
horror vacui but because of the air's equilibrium" (§ 25); "Levity is in fact an accidental consequence of gravity" (the heavier bodies driving the less heavy upwards,

§24); "The inrush of air, water, etc., into an exhausted vessel is caused by the weight and elasticity of the air" (§ 26); also, "the effecting of expansion and contraction," as he puts it, "whence [follow] fermentations, deflagrations, and explosions of all kinds, namely, by one thing expanding what another absorbs," or rather admits (§§ 27, 39, 40). For these things are also effected by the elasticity either of the container or the thing contained, or both; the one expanding because it was too much compressed, the other contracting because it was too much expanded; indeed, irruption or expansion may be effected by either method, not to say by both, so long as there is a place into which that which is to be thrust out may be received without hindrance. These things are clearly agreeable to our treatment in *Mechanica*, Chapter 14. And again it is said at least with great plausibility: "Gravity in things at lower levels arises from the motion," or pressure, "of the aether above" (§§13, 16). For although the cause of gravity (and elasticity too) is so very obscure that I also have never yet been satisfied as to what conclusion I should reach concerning it, still the phenomena of nature are for the most part better explained by pressures than by attractions. There are many other things it is needless to recite here which in my opinion are said with great probability if not with certainty, each of them standing pretty independently of the rest, for each point is not so integrally bound up with everything else that if one point fails all the rest falls to the ground as well. I shall say nothing immediately about the hypothesis as a whole, for the reason at least that I am not apt to give my assent to a thing newly proposed (at any rate in physics, if not mathematics), either until it appears more directly through the arguments of the learned on both sides of the question what is to be thought of it, or until the truth emerges through the very clearness of the thing, as happens not rarely with true hypotheses. He repeats the foundation of the new hypothesis from "his abstract theory of motion" (which I have not seen, any more than I have the treatises subsequent to this one which are quoted here and there), that is to say: "That there is no cohesion of rest, but that all firmness or cohesion arises from motion" (§§ 7, 12, 34), which coincides with the opinions of our William Neile. On the other hand the very honorable Boyle ascribes "firmness to the rest of particles, and fluidity to their continual motion."[2] Others relate it "to the different shapes of the atoms, hooked and linked together in various ways." And I am not one to rush in as umpire where there is so great diversity of opinion. The question must be left to time and the arguments of the learned on either side. Indeed, almost the same things happen with new hypotheses as with the swings of pendulums; after many oscillations either side, at last they come to rest perpendicular. We have seen this with the Copernican hypothesis which, though known to the ancients, lay buried so long that it was regarded as new; and although it had the strongest possible support it did not at once prevail but was attacked by different persons in different ways and bitterly disputed, until in the end through the ascendancy of reason over authority it was so universally acknowledged that virtually no one with any knowledge of the matter has any doubt about it, except those swayed by the Cardinals' decree. And though Tycho replaced it by a new and equivalent hypothesis, his is burdened with so many inconveniencies that, it may seem, he is to be regarded rather as having framed it in order to deflect prejudice (since the motion of the Earth seemed so dreadful to minds of the multitude) than as having rejected the hypothesis of Copernicus in his soul. The same may be said of Harvey's circulation of the blood; which although extremely well founded and proved by the evidence of the eyes was debated among the London physicians for twenty years, more or less, before he produced it in public, and by others after that. And yet this theory, after a mature consideration (for which time must be allowed), is accepted by all as indubitable. So the hypothesis of Galileo substituting the equilibrium of the atmosphere for the *horror vacui* of the ancients (first devised because suction pumps do not raise water above a certain height, and which Torricelli developed with a heavier and so more convenient fluid) only gained that esteem with the learned that it still has after protracted disputes this way and that. The same thing is to be said of the lympathic vessels of our countryman Joyliffe,[3] which he displayed to the physicians of London many years ago, and which they acknowledged and confirmed; which have been found so agreeable to reason and so obvious to the eye that at length, long after, it was bitterly disputed between some other men, who among them was the first discoverer.

Similarly with the salivary ducts of our Wharton, indicated in his printed book;[4] with that book as it were passed over in silence at length Steno and Bartholin fall to wrangling, which of them was the first discoverer. Further, the injection of fluids into the veins of animals was thought of by our Wren at Oxford almost twenty years ago, and by him frequently practised there; and the transfusion of blood from one animal into another was several times performed with success by our Lower at Oxford, and later at London before the Royal Society, while foreigners and even the Parisians did not believe it, declaring it impossible and practically a joke; however, in time they liked it so much that (after the whole way of proceeding has been disclosed to them) they wish to be thought inventors of it, and claim that I know not whom of their countrymen said something formerly which they now drag into it.[5] And the same is to be expected in this affair, and in the case of other new hypotheses that can be proved neither by ocular inspection nor by certain demonstration, so that if they are founded on true reasoning they will at last (but not without wrangles on both sides) find a place in the minds of those who philosophize freely; meanwhile they remain in suspense. In the interim the distinguished author deserves thanks, having formed such an opinion of our Society that he was good enough to share his ideas with us and to present his new hypothesis to the Society, to whom certainly it will not be unwelcome. For yourself, fare you well.

Yours,
John Wallis

NOTES

Reply to Letter 1665. The printed version shows some trivial variations from the MS., and omits several lines towards the end. This letter was read to the Society on 20 April.

1 See Vol. V, pp. 164–70.
2 Compare Boyle's "History of Fluidity and Firmness" in *Certain Physiological Essays* (London, 1661), especially the opening of Part II.
3 See Vol. IV, p. 368, note 4.
4 Thomas Wharton described the duct of the submaxillary gland and postulated that all glands secreted through such ducts in *Adenographia* (London, 1656; compare Vol. V, p. 272, note 6). Steno made a fuller study of the salivary glands, discovering the parotid and lachrymal ducts (1660). Wallis is confused here: Thomas Bartholin was a teacher and patron of Steno, and it was Gerard Blaes (Blasius; d. 1692) who disputed offensively his right to prior discovery of the parotid duct.
5 See Vol. IV, *passim*.

1674
Lister to Oldenburg

8 April 1671

From the original in Royal Society MS. L 5, no. 29
Printed in *Phil. Trans.*, no. 70 (17 April 1671), 2126–28

Yorks April. 8th 1671

Sr

Yours of ye 4th instant came safe to my hands. This last month has been a busie time wth mee in my private conserns soe yt I have but a few things to returne you to what you have been pleased to communicate to me in relation to ye further discovery of ye motion of juices in Vegetables. And I must acquaint you, yt these notes are above 14 dayes old, for I have scarce busied my head or put my hand to any Expt of latter date.

One or both ends of ye pith of a Willow pole sealed up wth hard wax, will yet freely bleed by the warmth of ye Fire: this was tryed when ye last experiments I sent you were[,] & I thinke, omitted.

March 23d was ye greatest frost & snow we have had this winter in these parts about Yorke. Some twiggs & branches of ye very same Willow Tree as formerly and likewise of many other Willow Trees taken off this morning March 23d when brought within ye aire of ye Fire would shew noe moisture at all; noe not when heated warme & often & long turned.

March 24th ye same willow branches wch yesterday would not bleed & were thrown upon ye Grasse spott all night did, both they & all others now cutt downe by ye Fire side freely shew moisture & bleed this morning upon ye breaking up of ye frost.

Ash poles & branches this day, nor yesterday would by ye fire be noe more moist, than when I formerly tryed ym.

The same morning March 23d, a Twigg of Maple, wch had had ye top cut off ye 7 of February last past, & wch than bledd, this day being quite taken off from ye Tree, & brought within ye aire of Fire, & held wth ye formerly-cut-end downewards, did not run at all at yt end, but held-on in yt posture it did run apace at ye other non-cutt end uppermost soe as to spring & trickle downe.

Note, yt this doth well agree wth my Experiments made ye last yeare at Nottingham, where I observed wounds of some months standing to bleed apace at ye breaking up of any hard Frost. For first in these parts there hath been noe hard frost this yeare, not comparable to ye last yeare: Again those Nottingham Trees I wounded in ye Trunke & they stood against a brick wall & ye wounds were on yt side next it, & besides had horse-dung stopped in all of ym for some reasons, wch things did undoubtedly deffend ym much from ye aire & winds & keep ye wounds still green & open. Wheras ye topps of these Maple-twiggs spoake of in ye last expt, were exposed in an open hadge to ye aire & winds: as alsoe ye 2. Sycamores here at Yorke, mentioned in my former Letters, to have been wounded in November last & not to have shewed any signes of moisture for yt very cause, yt they were not fresh struck at bleeding times.

Concerning ye bleeding of poles & entire branches held perpendicular, Mr. Willoughby is ith right & some expts in my last to you of 17th of March[1] confirme it. Yet is it very true what I observed though ye cause I did not than well take notice of, when I first made ye expt & sent you an account of it. For I held ye twiggs, wch I had cutt off a-slop, joining & holding up ye cutts togathar in my left hand yt I might ye better observe wch part or cut would bleed or not bleed or bleed ye faster; & because I found yt ye cut of ye separated Twigg did not in yt posture (holding it upwards, as I said, for ye advantage of my eye) did not bleed at all, when as ye cut of ye branch remaining to ye Tree did freely bleed, I therefore inverted ye separated Twigg & held it perpendicular wth ye cut end downward & found yt yt little they were exposed to ye aire in an upright posture had soe very much checked ye motion of ye Sap, yt I concluded they would not bleed at all, & yet striking of their topps & making poles of ym, I found some of ym, if not all yt I chanced to try, as I remember, would shew moisture; but I am convinced since, yt it was rather some unheeded accident, as violently bending ym or perhapps ye warmth of my hand & person or place, wch caused this new motion of Sap, than meerly ye striking off their topps.

I have sent you enclosed a *Pastillus* of some few grains of *English black*, as I call it, wch was all what ye season would yet well afford me;[2] ye Expt I made long since upon an other occasion & purpos, but upon ye question of ye usefulnesse of it as to its dye, in this late repeating of it, I found, yt ye plant does not afford a mealy Substance such as Indigo is & ye *feculas*[3] of Bryonie & some other plants, but a substance altogathar & purly resinous; for it will burne wth a very quiet & lasting flame. The Expt is accompanied wth circumstances of good light in order to ye further discovery of ye natures of Vegetable juices, wch is ye only reason, yt I am backward to name ye plant to you at present, but soe farr as ye businesse of colours may be improved by it I shall willingly impart & shew upon ye first opportunity to ye R.S. I doubt not but by ye few grains I send you, there may be persons of your acquaintance, yt may tell me more of it, yn I understand at least undeceive me if I be in an errour. Whilst liquid it is a most exquisite black & staines accordingly any thing it touches; & neither Fire nor a strong Lye of pot-ashes does in ye least, yt I can discerne, alter it.

There is a mistake of ye presse in ye Transactions of February, wch I desire you would be pleased to put into ye *Errata* of some of your next Transact, if you have an opportunity. my 2d. Letter in yt Transact. beares Mr. Wrays name, wch is some confusion, if ye reader shall not well heed it.[4] I am Sr

> Your most humble servant
> *Martin Lister*

ADDRESS
   These
For his honoured friend
Mr Oldenburgh
at his house in ye .
    Palmal
     London

NOTES

Reply to Letter 1669.
1 Letter 1556.
2 It was conveyed to Boyle for examination when Oldenburg produced it and this letter at a meeting of the Society on 20 April 1671.
3 "dregs" or "remains."
4 Letter 1627. No correction was made, but the letter was reprinted (with Lister's name) in *Phil. Trans.*, no. 70, along with several of Lister's letters.

1675
Oldenburg to Winthrop
11 April 1671

From the original in the Winthrop Papers XVI, 39
Printed in MHS (1878), pp. 250–51

London April 11. 1671.

Sir,

Yr letter of Octob. 11. 1670. to me, and yr present to the R. Society, together with that to Sr R. Moray, I have well received from the hands of Mr Fairwather, who deserveth to be commended for his care of the particulars, you had entrusted him wth. I soon deliver'd to yesd Society their parcell, viz. the Shell-fish (call'd Horse-foot,) ye Humming bird-nest wth ye two Eggs in it, being yet whole; ye feather'd Fly; and ye shells, bullets, and clays taken out of ye overturn'd Hill. For all wch, that Noble Company returns you their hearty thanks, and very much desires the continuance of such curious communications, for the enlargement of their repository, and consequently of ye intended History of Nature. These curiosities being view'd at one of our publick meetings, some of ye Company conceived, yt what you call ye sharp taile of ye Horse-foot is rather the fore part and nose of ye fish; yesame persons having also found, yt two of the knobbs on the shell, now dry'd up, had been the places of the Eyes, and did still by ye manner of their ductus's expresse, yt they had looked towards yesd nose, when the animal was alive.[1] The Humbird-nest was also shew'd to his Majty, who was as much pl[ea]sed with it, as ye Society.

And I doubt not, but Sr Rob. Moray will tell you the same, and wthall acknowledge ye receipt of those silke pods, yt were directed to him.

Concerning ye overturned Hill, it is wished, that a more certain and punctual relation might be procured of all the circumstances of yt accident. It seems strange, yt no Earth-quake was perceived, and yet that ye Hill is said to have been carried over the Tops of ye Trees into ye River, as also, yt people living near it should not certainly know the day, when this happened. I doubt not, Sir, but yr owne curiosity will have carried you, since you wrote this, to view ye place, and to examine all the particulars remarkable in this matter. I hope, MyLord Brereton, to whom you communicated the story at length,[2] will also write to you by this returne, and joyne wth me in the request of giving us a fuller account of this wonder.

I cannot yet desist from recommending to you the Composure of a good History of New England, from the beginning of ye English arrival there, to this very time, containing ye Geography, Natural Productions, and Civill Administration thereof, together wth the Notable progresse of yt Plantation, and the remarkable occurences in thesame. An undertaking worthy of Mr Winthrop, and a member of ye Royal Society!

I herewith send you a few philosophical Books, lately printed here; viz.

1. Mr Boyl's new Tracts about ye wonderful rarefaction and Condensation of the Air etc.

2. Monsr Charas's New Experiments upon Vipers.

3. The Transactions of 1670.

To these I adde a small Discourse, originally written in French against yt great Sorbonist, Monsr Arnaud, touching ye Perpetuity of ye Romish Faith about the Eucharist.[3] And so wishing you much health and happinesse, I remain Sir

yr faithful servant,
Henry Oldenburg

Sr, when you send any thing more for the R. Society, or for me, I pray, add my dwelling place (in *ye Palmal*) to the superscription. I must not forget to give you very many thanks for ye Cranberies: they tasted of ye Cask, or else they would have been very good.

P.S. I just now received Sr R. Moray's letter, as you find it here unsealed. MyLd Brereton hath not yet sent his, and I dare stay no longer from doing up this packet, the master of ye Ship having appointed this morning for the delivering of it.

ADDRESS
   To his honord friend
   John Winthrop Esquire
   Governor of Conecticut
   In New England

NOTES

   Reply to Letter 1532, which had been read to the Royal Society on 23 March 1670/1.
1 This criticism is not recorded in the minutes of the meeting.
2 Winthrop's letter to Brereton is printed in Birch, *History*, II, 473–74.
3 See Letter 1556, note 15. No seventeenth-century edition in English is recorded;
   possibly Oldenburg was merely apologizing for sending the work in French.

1676
Oldenburg to Leibniz
14 April 1671

From the original in Hanover MSS., f. 6
Printed in Gerhardt, p. 54

Amplissimo et Consultissimo Viro
Domino Gothofredo Guilielmo Leibnitzio J.U.D. et
Consilio Moguntino dignissimo
H. Oldenburg Salutem

Recte accepi, Vir Nobilissime, Hypothesin tuam Physicam, typis Moguntinis editam, et mox prima ferente occasione coram Soc. Regia produxi. Praelecta ipsi fuit honorifica Dedicatio, protinusque nonnullis ejus sociis in mandatis datum, ut libellum istum evolverent et expenderent, suamque de eo sententiam, quam primum fieri commode posset, in caetu publico referrent.[1] Id dum agitur, suadere velim, Vir optime, ut partem alteram quantocyus ad me, tuta occasione, expedire ne graveris, cum intelligam Ego, viros illos, quibus examinis hujus provincia est demandata, vix quicquam de re tota pronunciaturos esse, nisi et tuam de Abstracta Motus theoria doctrinam, saepe a Te citatam et pluribus positionibus substratam, cognoverint.[2] Interim, quantum colligo, non displicet opera tua iis qui inspexere, certe mihi perplacet, qui ad multa Te respexisse percipio. Cum posteriora videro scripti hujus, mox Hypothesi tota Transactiones Philosophicas exornare satagam.[3]

Quamprimum de Machinae Wernerianae successu certi quid acceperis, nobis quoque impertiri ne graveris. Rationem dulcificandi aquam Marinam invenies impressam No. 67 Transactionum philosophicarum, quantum quidem ejus retegere Inventori visum fuit.[4]

Famigeratum illud Grandamici de Terella Magnetica Experimentum successu carere, satis liquet ex iis, quae ex Domini Petiti epistola in Transactionibus philosophicis no. 28. inserta habentur.[5]

Operam dabo, ut cura Martini nostri libros a Te hinc desideratos accipias: Vale et porro Tui studiosissimo fave. Raptim Londini d. 14. April. 1671.

P.S. Ne, quaeso, invideas mihi peculiares illas, quas dicis, de Deo ac mente demonstrationes; circa quas nonulla innuis, quae me perquam attonitum habent, adeoque stimulant, ut tanto importunius eorum communicationem expetam.

Literae tuae mihi destinatae per tabellionem semper, quaeso, inscribantur

  A Monsieur
   Monsr Grubendol
    A Londres
Franc à Anvers
  ou Amsterdam.

ADDRESS

  Nobillissimo et Consultissimo Viro
  Domino Gothofredo Guilielmo Leibnitzio
  J.U.D. et Consolario Moguntino etc.
    Mogunt.

TRANSLATION

H. Oldenburg greets the very worthy and wise Mr. Gottfried Wilhelm Leibniz, LL.D. and most worthy Councilor at Mainz

I received safely your *Physical Hypothesis*, published from the press at Mainz, most noble Sir, and produced it before the Royal Society at the first opportunity. The honorific Dedication was read to it and at once several of the Fellows were ordered to read and weigh your little book, relating their judgments as soon as convenient at an ordinary meeting.[1] While this is going forward I wish to urge you, excellent Sir, to be so good as to hasten the remaining part to me by the first safe opportunity, for I understand that those persons charged with this examination will hardly pronounce upon the whole unless they are also acquainted with your teaching concerning the abstract theory of motion, often quoted by yourself and adopted as a postulate in many instances.[2] Meanwhile, so far as I can discover, your work is not displeasing to those who have looked into it, and certainly it is very agreeable to myself, who observe that you have inquired into many things. When I have seen the latter part of this piece, I shall strive without delay to make the whole hypothesis an ornament of the *Philosophical Transactions*.[3]

As soon as you hear anything of the outcome of Werner's machine, be so good as to impart the news to us. You will find the way of making sea water sweet printed in no. 67 of the *Philosophical Transactions*, in so far as the inventor thought fit to reveal it.[4]

From what was inserted in no. 28 of the *Philosophical Transactions* out of Mr. Petit's letter it is obvious enough that that rumored experiment of Grandami on the magnetic terrella failed.[5]

I will make it my business to have you receive from our Mr. Martin the books you desire. Farewell, and continue to cherish your most zealous [Oldenburg]. In haste, London, 14 April 1671

P.S. Please do not grudge me those particular demonstrations, of which you speak, concerning God and mind, about which your several hints fill me with great amazement, and so excite me that I look forward to their communication the more impatiently.

Always, please, address your letters to me intended for the post as follows:
> A Monsieur
>   Monsr Grubendol
>   A Londres
Post free to Antwerp or Amsterdam

ADDRESS
> To the very noble and wise
> Mr. Gottfried Wilhelm Leibniz
> LL.D. and Councilor of Mainz, etc.
>   Mainz

NOTES

Reply to Letter 1644.
1 At the meeting of the Society on 23 March Boyle, Hooke, Wallis, and Wren "were desired to peruse and consider" Leibniz's work, and report.
2 Compare Wallis's remarks in Letter 1673.
3 See Letter 1644, note 15.
4 See Letter 1644, note 6; the extract was printed in *Phil. Trans.*, no. 67 (16 January 1670/1), 2048.
5 See Letter 1644, note 4.

1677
Oldenburg to Sterpin
17 April 1671

Sterpin's Letter 1638 is endorsed as received on 8 April and answered on 17 April. The answer forbade Sterpin to continue with his edition of the Latin *Philosophical Transactions*.

1678
Oldenburg to Vogel
17 April 1671

From the memorandum in Royal Society MS. F 1, no. 31

Acc. d. 8 Apr. 1671. resp. d. 17 Apr. Dixi, hic imprimi Tractatum de quiete cum Exp[erimentis] de respiratione.[1] Oportet, ut imposterum praesciat Boyleus, versionem librorum ejus parari, ut possit suggerere monita. Transmittam Boylei de rarefactione. Galilaei vita hic impressa Anglice.[2] sit satis bene, quibus cum digressionibus in locos communes Designatus a duce Flor. Vivianus, quondam ejus Amanuensis, et omnium consiliorum et actorum conscius.[3] Scripsi Sterpino, et prohibui versionem Transact. Latinarum.

TRANSLATION

Received 8 April 1671, answered 17 April. I said that the treatise on rest was being printed here with the experiments on respiration;[1] that in the future Boyle ought to know in advance when a translation of his books is to appear, so that he can offer comments. I shall send Boyle on rarefraction. The life of Galileo is printed here in English.[2] It is pretty fair, with some digressions into common-places. Viviani was appointed [to write it?] by the Duke of Tuscany, Viviani having formerly been Galileo's amanuensis, and acquainted with all his opinions and deeds.[3] I have written to Sterpin and forbidden his translation of the *Transactions* into Latin.

NOTES

Reply to Letter 1668. As usual with Oldenburg, the memoranda are very hasty and cryptic; but the general sense seems clear enough.

1   See Letter 1668, note 3.
2   See Letter 1668, note 4. It is likely that Salusbury had few facts about Galileo's life at his disposal.
3   For Vincenzo Viviani (1622–1703), see Vol. I, p. 444, note. He had written his short sketch of Galileo's life for Leopold de'Medici in 1654, but never completed a full biography. His *Racconto istorico della vita del Sig. Galileo Galilei* was first published by S. Salvini at Florence in 1717.

1679
Oldenburg to Nelson
18 April 1671

The endorsement on Letter 1661 indicates that it was received on 29 March and answered on 18 April.

1680
Oldenburg to Hevelius
18 April 1671
From the original in Observatoire X, no. 80

Per-illustri Viro
Domino Johanni Hevelio, Consuli Dantiscano dignissimo
Henr. Oldenburg S.P.D.

Spero, Vir Celeberrime, Te accepisse meam ad tuas, 31. Octob. 1670 ad me datas literas, responsionem.[1] Ex eo tempore traditum mihi fuit Epistolium tuum, 4 Martis 1671. ad me exaratum.[2] Mox parui mandatis inibi perscriptis, et Dn. Cock ad optimum, quoad fieri ab ipso potest, construendum Microscopicum adstrinxi. Solemniter promisit, se rem bona fide curaturum, atque intra septimanam unam alteramve, Microscopium, quale optas, decem librarum sterlinganarum precio confecturum. Ait, sperare se, praestantius id fore, quam quod antehac Tibi transmisit. Fidere tamen ipsi nolim, quin, quando constructum fuerit, rigido peritorum examini subjicere decrevi. Nec suaserim, ut tuum illud, quod penes Te habes, in Poloniam mittas, priusquam cum novo idipsum comparaveris. Non dubito, quin copia mihi sit futura, proximo mense Majo, navis cujusdam Anglicanae beneficio, illud ad Te transmittendi, junctis illis libris, quos a me epistola superiori petieras.[3]

Supersunt adhuc Exemplaria Cometographiae tuae bene multa: Si vendi ea possent, haud opus foret pecuniam pro Microscopio novo suppeditare. At quia id valde dubium, mandata tua ad mercatorem quendam Londinensem, dicti precii solutionem injungentia Artificem eo magis animabunt ad operam hanc tuto citius et melius expediendam.

Avide exspectamus, quid Tubus vester 140. pedum praestiterit. Cockius noster, inter alia, conficiendis speculis Ustoriis, 6. pedum diametri nunc occupatur qualia singula dummodo ex voto res cedat centum libris Anglicanis se venditurum sperat. De successu dubitamus; de quo tamen, qualiuscunque fuerit, suo tempore a me edoceberis. Vale, et ab Amicis tuis Anglis quos non paucos habes, plurimum salve. Dabam Londini raptissime, d. 18. April. 1671

P.S. Ex quo haec scripsi, commodum mihi redditae sunt literae Domini

Kirkby,[4] inque iis epistola ad mercatorem, qui solvere debet pecuniam pro Microscopio. Tempus nunc non patitur, ut Domino Kirkbaeo manu propria gratis agam; quod tamen propediem fiet, quamprimum scilicet ea expedivero, quae in dicta epistola ad me exspectat. Interim plurimum salvere eum velim nec non Illustrem Collegum tuum, Amplissimum Dominum Behmium, quem, una tecum, omnes docti et boni colunt.

TRANSLATION

Henry Oldenburg sends many greetings to the very illustrious Mr. Johannes Hevelius, most worthy Senator of Danzig

I hope that you have received my reply, excellent Sir, to your letter to myself dated 31 October 1670.[1] Since that time your note of 4 March 1671 was delivered to me.[2] I thereupon obeyed the instructions contained in it, and contracted with Mr. Cock for making as fine a microscope as he can. He solemnly promised that he would take most particular care of it, and that in a week or two such a microscope as you desire will be finished, for the price of ten pounds sterling. He says that he hopes to make it even more excellent than the one he sent you previously. However, I do not trust him so much but that I am resolved, when it is finished, to have the microscope tested by skilful persons. Nor am I confident that you should send the one you now possess into Poland before you have compared it with this new one. I have no doubt that there will be an opportunity, next May, for me to send it to you by some English vessel, together with those books you desired of me in your earlier letter.[3]

There still remain over a good many copies of your *Cometographia*; if these can be sold, it will hardly be necessary to supply money for the new microscope. But as that is extremely doubtful, your order to some London merchant for the payment of the sum above mentioned will the more encourage the craftsman to the safe, speedy, and successful completion of this task.

We eagerly anticipate [news of] what your 140-foot tube will furnish. Our Mr. Cock is, among other things, engaged now in completing burning mirrors six feet in diameter, each of which he hopes to sell for one hundred English pounds, if they succeed as he desires. We are doubtful of the outcome of which however you will learn from me in due course, whatever it prove. Farewell, with many wishes of goodwill from your numerous friends in England.
In great haste, London, 18 April 1671

P.S.   Since I wrote this, the letter from Mr. Kirkby[4] has been opportunely delivered to me, and in it the letter to a merchant who is to pay out the money for the microscope. Time does not now permit me to thank Mr. Kirkby with my own pen, though this shall be done as soon as possible, that is to say when I have been able to perform what he expects of me in that letter. Meanwhile, I bid him many farewells, as well as your illustrious colleague the very worthy Mr. Behm, whom (along with yourself) all good and learned men admire.

NOTES

A memorandum on Letter 1637 (received on 29 March), to which this is a reply, gives the date of this letter as 17 April.
1 Letter 1557 was a reply to Letter 1536.
2 Letter 1637.
3 See Letter 1536, p. 215.
4 Letter 1664.

1681
Oldenburg to Willughby
18 April 1671

From the memorandum in Royal Society MS. W 3, no. 42

Apr. 18. desired him to resolve a doubt in this letter.[1]

NOTES

This is written on the envelope of Willughby's Letter 1655, obviously added at a later date than the memorandum for Letter 1667.
1 Lister's Letter 1656.

1682
Justel to Oldenburg
19 April 1671

This letter accompanied a manuscript on leveling by Mariotte, and expressed Mariotte's wish that "it be communicated to the Royal Society" (Birch, *History*, II, 479). It was mentioned on 4 May when Mariotte's manuscript was produced; the manuscript was subsequently given to Wren for his judgment, which was that it deserved publication. Mariotte's *Traité du Nivellement* was published at Paris in 1672.

Index

Boldface figures indicate Letter numbers. Both originals and translations have been indexed.

ADDENDUM TO
THE CORRESPONDENCE OF
HENRY OLDENBURG, VOLUME VI

The following index entries were inadvertently
omitted from the end of the letter *V:*